John Sutter

John Sutter

A Life on the North American Frontier

Albert L. Hurtado

University of Oklahoma Press : Norman

ALSO BY ALBERT L. HURTADO

Indian Survival on the California Frontier (New Haven, 1988)

(ed., with Peter Iverson) *Major Problems in American Indian History: Documents and Essays* (Lexington, 1994)

Intimate Frontiers: Sex, Gender, and Culture in Old California (Albuquerque, 1999)

Library of Congress Cataloging-in-Publication Data

Hurtado, Albert L., 1946–
    John Sutter : a life on the North American frontier / Albert L. Hurtado.
        p. cm.
    Includes bibliographical references and index.
    ISBN 0-8061-3772-X (alk. paper)
        1. Sutter, John Augustus, 1803–1880. 2. Pioneers—California—
Biography. 3. Frontier and pioneer life—California. 4. Sutter's Fort
(Sacramento, Calif.) 5. California—History—19th century. 6. California—
Biography. 7. Frontier and pioneer life—West (U.S.) 8. West (U.S.)—
History—19th century. I. Title.

F865.S93H87 2006
979.4′03092—dc22
[B]   2006040435

The paper in this book meets the guidelines for permanence and durability of
the Committee on Production Guidelines for Book Longevity of the Council
on Library Resources, Inc. ∞

1 2 3 4 5 6 7 8 9 10

For Kenneth N. Owens,
teacher, friend, fellow traveler on Sutter's Trail

Contents

Illustrations

MAPS

TABLES

Preface

There is no denying the historical importance of John A. Sutter. Conqueror of the Sacramento Valley, builder of Sutter's Fort, savior of overland immigrants, pioneer ranchman and farmer, agent of the gold discovery, Sutter was the very embodiment of early California. Without knowing his story, we simply cannot understand the last years of Mexican California, the American conquest, the gold rush, and its aftermath. His life reveals the main currents of imperial ambition on the Pacific Coast and sheds light on the nature of the North American frontier in the mid-nineteenth century. Sutter's story is international in scope and continental in dimension, embracing as it does the United States, Russian Alaska, Hawaii, northern Mexico, and even Central America. Famous in his own time, Sutter is now a lightning rod for controversies concerning the moral dimensions of the conquest of the American West.

Sutter was too important to be ignored by his contemporaries and those who wrote California history. Indeed, his story served a needful purpose for Californians and historians of the nineteenth century, connecting the Mexican and Anglo phases of California history. Sutter was the pivot around which that transformation materialized. Moreover, elements of the Sutter story justified the conquest by portraying him as the protector of American immigrants against Indians and Mexicans alike. These oversimplified and inaccurate inter-pretations played well with Anglos who wished to portray themselves in the best possible light. More recent interpreters of California history reject the notion that Sutter was a manifestation of America's destiny to expand across the continent and the implication that Indians and Mexicans had it coming. Popular opinion about him has always been divided. When Sutter lived in

California, he had passionate friends and implacable enemies. Now popular feeling against Sutter in some circles is so strong that attempts to name public streets for him raise an outcry from opponents who condemn him as a racist killer, while his supporters denounce them as politically correct, revisionist historians. Such strongly held divergent views argue for a full-length biography of the man who inspires them.

Eight writers published biographies of Sutter in the twentieth century, a testament to the public's enduring interest in him. The first was written by T. J. Schoonover (1895, rev. ed. 1907), a Sacramento enthusiast who relied on locally available sources. Blaise Cendrars, a French author, published a novelized biography in 1926. It is almost pure fiction, although many accepted it as history when it first appeared. In 1934 Julian Dana offered a better account of Sutter's life but included fictional conversations and factual errors. Erwin Gudde, professor of German at the University of California, tried to set the record straight by quoting extensively from Sutter's writings. Gudde published first a German-language edition in Leipzig (1934) and then the English-language version, *Sutter's Own Story* (1936). He improved on Sutter's language, however, in order to make the book more readable. Many an unwary student has mistaken Gudde's words for Sutter's.

The first reliable full-length biography was by the German historian James Peter Zollinger, entitled *Sutter: The Man and His Empire* (1939). Using original sources, Zollinger produced a critical work that was somewhat Freudian in its outlook. Still, it was a great improvement over everything that had gone before. While Zollinger's work is still useful, especially for Sutter's European career, he included only cursory endnotes citing his sources. Zollinger paid little attention to the thirty years between the gold rush and Sutter's death. In a bid to make Sutter seem more exciting and heroic, Marguerite Eyer Wilbur wrote another biography with fictional dialog in 1949, just in time for the gold rush centennial celebration. Oscar Lewis's undocumented study of Sutter's Fort (1966) is also a life of Sutter, based primarily on secondary sources. In 1967 Richard Dillon published *Fool's Gold: The Decline and Fall of Captain John Sutter of California*, which has remained for nearly forty years the most thorough analysis of Sutter's life in California. Dillon bases his work on archival sources that can almost always be easily identified, but he did not include footnotes. Like Zollinger, Dillon pays insufficient attention to Sutter's post-1848 life in California; nor does he sort out Sutter's complicated financial and family affairs.

Surprisingly, there is no thoroughly documented, full-length biography of Sutter. New sources have come to light that make such a treatment possible. Local records reveal aspects of Sutter's life in Missouri. Papers of the California state militia clarify his connection with filibusters in Central America in the

1850s. The recently opened Sutter/Link Family Papers at the Bancroft Library offer new insights into the Sutter family. The Lancaster County Historical Society and the Lititz Historical Museum provide information about his last years in Pennsylvania. Sources in the Hawaiian State Archives reveal details concerning Sutter's six-month stay there.

This book is not a hero's tale. I have tried to sketch a fair and accurate account of Sutter's life that portrays his strengths and failings. He sometimes skirted the law and acted unethically. He was one of the poorest businessmen in the history of capitalism. The exploitation and killing of California Indians was an inexcusable part of his daily routine as lord of the Sacramento Valley. Sutter abandoned his family to a life of dependency in Switzerland and did not reunite with them for sixteen years. He stretched the truth when it suited his purposes and lied when he thought it was necessary. His accounts must be used cautiously, but they are essential sources for the period as well as for his life. I have used critical Mexican accounts of Sutter to discern just what his presence in California meant to them. Likewise I recognize the importance of Sutter's role in the dispossession and destruction of California Indians, a subject that I treat at length in *Indian Survival on the California Frontier* (1988). I emphasize his alcoholism because I think some of his actions are understandable only in that context. There is no way to "balance" his flaws against the virtues that often reinforced his defects. Sutter has to be swallowed whole: hook, line, bait, and sinker. Remove a part of him, and you have a different person who could not have done what he did.

Sutter had an impressive array of positive qualities that served him well throughout his life. He was by all accounts a handsome, gregarious, and altogether lovable man. Almost everyone he met liked him at once. Only hard experience caused them to reevaluate the affable Swiss gentleman who seemed so plausible at first meeting. Sutter was able to seduce people because they instinctively believed that he liked them. His attitude was not feigned. He really did like people, to a fault. Will Rogers said that he never met a man he didn't like. Sutter lived this aphorism. He also lived to regret it by trusting people who were untrustworthy. Sutter was meticulously well-mannered, an especially striking trait in the rough society of the American frontier. Ladies, gentlemen, and vagabonds alike responded to Sutter's polite demeanor, which was at once commanding and deferential. He was proud that he spoke four languages, although his broken English reveals that he was not equally fluent in all of them. Enthusiasm and optimism marked everything that Sutter did. Generosity was perhaps his most endearing trait. He helped everyone he could, and there is no doubt that his generosity saved the lives of many an overland immigrant. True, as the historian Hubert Howe Bancroft said, it was in Sutter's interest to help people so that he could cultivate them as clients and workers; but that ungenerous assessment fails to recognize an essential part of Sutter's personality. He wanted to be liked. More than that, he craved respect. His careful manners and his love of military rank and uniforms all spoke to that need. His entire life was a struggle to achieve status and respect.

Those who have judged Sutter a failure because he did not succeed in business have missed the point. If Sutter had cared about money, he would have paid more attention to it. No, he only cared for what money could buy: land, clothes, oil portraits of himself, the ability to entertain in the grand style—the status symbols that declared him to be a gentleman of substance, someone to be respected and reckoned with. To the extent that he could keep up his bold front, Sutter regarded himself as a success. Close Yankee reasoning judged him otherwise.

Popular psychology says that anyone who is that status conscious must be fundamentally insecure. I suppose so. I have looked for the roots of Sutter's insecurity and tentatively locate it in his identity as an outsider. German-born Swiss, outlander in Switzerland, immigrant in Missouri, foreigner in Santa Fe and California, Sutter was never at home. He was a native of nowhere. It is no wonder that international borders enticed him when he got into trouble. I suspect that a detailed knowledge of Sutter's childhood and his parents would tell more about the formation of his essential personality, but little information is available. It is perhaps revealing that Sutter says almost nothing about his parents and childhood. His relationship with his in-laws was troubled, but he established a lifelong and affectionate bond that he kept up in letters. Similar letters to his blood relations have not surfaced.

Sutter's writings are frequently ungrammatical and filled with misspellings. I have retained his original language without editorial comment wherever possible. To do otherwise would force the reader to negotiate dense thickets of bracketed "[sic]"s. More importantly, Sutter's unedited language provides a sense of him that is not obtainable in any other way. His colorful, sometimes awkward, but always descriptive prose was as characteristic of him as his pressed uniforms and elegant manners—part of Captain Sutter's distinctive panoply of personal attributes that must be swallowed whole in order to understand him.

Although Sutter's strong and vibrant personality is easy to parody, I have tried to avoid doing that. In his own era the most important people on the North American frontier took him very seriously. There is no reason why we should not do likewise. Telling Sutter's story as honestly as possible is the best way I know to give him the respect that he sought, even though it is likely that he would be dissatisfied with the result. I hope that my telling of Sutter's life helps to sort out the multiple and contested meanings embedded in the history of the American West and his central place in it.

Acknowledgments

I began doing serious research on Sutter in 1974, when Kenneth N. Owens, my graduate advisor at California State University, Sacramento, recommended that I should look into Sutter documents at the California State Library if I wanted to learn something about Native American history in central California. That was the beginning of this book. In following his suggestion I found that there were English translations of Sutter's letters in French that Richard Dillon (a Sutter biographer) thought should be used with care. Being young and thinking myself a scrupulous researcher, I asked my friend William Walker to photocopy the originals (I had already decamped for Santa Barbara to enroll in the doctoral program) and gave them to another friend, Jane Callaghy, who was a French major. I had no idea how much work I was asking her to do, but she cheerfully provided her own translations. I thank Janie now (thirty years late) for her work and her concern for my career.

Everything about this project has been delayed for one reason or another. I was one of the first to sign with the University of Oklahoma Press Western Biography series, edited by Richard Etulain. Dick was forbearing when I failed to deliver a manuscript in 1995, as the original contract required (well, strongly suggested). He was forgiving when I decided that I could not write the short, undocumented book intended for the series. John Drayton, director of the press, approved a new contract that permitted me to write this larger, fully documented book. For five years my wife, Jean Hurtado, was my editor at the press. I hoped to complete the project while she was on the staff; but alas, she decided to retire. Charles Rankin then took up the thankless task of waiting for me to finish the manuscript and has seen it through the editorial process. My editors' consistent support has helped sustain my enthusiasm as the Sutter story grew in length and complexity.

I am grateful for the generous support provided by the Travis Chair in Modern American History (which I occupy) that made it possible for me to travel without the added burden of seeking research grants. The University of Oklahoma history department assigned research assistants, including Richard Adkins, Willy Bauer, Linda English, Brian Frehner, Sunu Kodumthara, Nicky Michael, Jeri Reed, and Mandy Taylor-Montoya. They have eased many a burden from my shoulders. May their lives and careers flourish!

The work of translators deserves special mention. Sutter spoke and wrote four languages: German, French, Spanish, and English. While I have modest abilities in Spanish and German, I am entirely innocent of French: hence my appreciation of Jane Callaghy. Dirk Voss, a graduate student at Oklahoma and native German speaker, translated some of Sutter's German letters for me. In Spanish I was aided by scholars who deposited their translations at the Bancroft Library and California Room in the State Library. Nellie Vandergrift Sánchez's reliable translations of the Spanish sources are well known to California scholars. A second good translation of many relevant Spanish-language documents may be found in the Clarence DuFour Papers in the Bancroft Library.

Librarian and historian Walter Brem, my old friend from graduate school days, immeasurably aided my research in the Bancroft. I regard his retirement as a great loss, for I have not only relied on him for my own work but sent many of my graduate students to him for help. Gary F. Kurutz, who is the most knowledgeable bibliographer of Californiana, has helped me with the collections in the state library's California Room.

I am certain that the dozens of other people who have assisted me at the Bancroft, California Room, California State Archives, and Huntington Library will regard my heartfelt thanks to "staff" as short rations. I would say more, space permitting. Likewise I wish to acknowledge the help of librarians, archivists, and docents from Lititz, Pennsylvania, to Honolulu, Hawaii.

I have been fortunate to travel in the company of many fine scholars who have been generous with their time, advice, and ideas. My friend Donald J. Pisani, who holds the Merrick Chair in the University of Oklahoma history department, has been especially helpful and simpatico in every way. Don was preparing his own magisterial study of California land while I was working on Sutter. What luck to have the leading authority on this knotty subject available when I was sorting the Sutter land grant questions! David J. Weber, dean of the borderland historians, helped me immeasurably by assuring me that he had *not* seen Sutter's name in the Mexican records of New Mexico when he researched *Taos Trappers.* James Rawls read the manuscript and made helpful suggestions.

I have dedicated this volume to Ken Owens, who initiated my training in the honorable craft guild that we call the historical profession. During the process we became friends. For more than thirty years we have shared adventures in Sierra Nevada backpacking, fishing, public history, plain history, family history, storytelling, and general tomfoolery. From him I learned that history was important, interesting, fun, and intellectually demanding. When I have a question about history, I ask him first, because he is one of the most knowledgeable people I have ever known. He also has been splendidly generous with his time in helping me with this project. Ken was working on *Gold Rush Saints,* his fine book on Mormons in the gold rush, when I was writing this volume. Needless to say, I have made use of his deep knowledge of the gold rush, California Mormons, and the Russian-American Company on more occasions than I can rightly remember. He read, marked, and improved the entire manuscript. With grateful thanks for everything, Ken, this book is for you.

John Sutter

CHAPTER 1

A Man and His Time

One could not see it by looking at the land or testing the wind, but 1803 was a season of change in the American West. Events of that year would close old doors and open new ones as European empires, the young American republic, and scores of Indian nations realigned their fortunes according to new circumstances. Gradually old, familiar pasts receded in the background as new, uncertain futures emerged. From the Mississippi River to the Pacific Rim, history's tectonic forces were at work; but in 1803 no one could foresee the new landscape that would ultimately materialize.

In January President Thomas Jefferson asked Congress for $2,500 to send a party of explorers up the Missouri River to its source in the Rocky Mountains. From there Jefferson directed the men to descend a convenient river to the Pacific Coast. Jefferson's geographical instructions were vague, because there were no published maps of the great, unknown West. The president thought of this expedition as a corps of discovery that would reveal geographical and scientific knowledge, but it was more than that. None of this territory belonged to the United States. France claimed the lands whose waters flowed into the Mississippi River, including the country drained by the Missouri River. Spain, England, Russia, and the United States made conflicting claims to the Pacific Northwest, which included the present states of Oregon, Washington, and Idaho and modern British Columbia. West of Louisiana and south of Oregon, Spain claimed everything from Texas to California.[1]

The European and American claims to these lands were imperial in dimension and intent, but Indian nations actually held the bulk of the continental mass from the Mississippi to the western sea. Sioux, Cheyennes, Arapahos,

Kiowas, Comanches, and other mounted tribes patrolled the Great Plains from Texas to the Dakotas. Mandan and Hidatsa farming villages on the bluffs above the upper Missouri River dominated much of the surrounding plains area. Pueblo communities in the desert Southwest lived in their fortified stone towns and farmed the thin soils of the Rio Grande Valley. The Pueblos had lived in close association with Spanish colonists since 1542. Many had adopted the Roman Catholic religion and adapted to Spanish frontier society. Apaches, Navahos, and Utes found another way to adjust to the Spanish presence. They traded with and sometimes raided the Spanish and Pueblo settlements in New Mexico, taking horses and other livestock as booty.[2]

Many small tribes populated the rich microclimates of the coast and interior valleys of California. There may have been three hundred thousand or more Native peoples in California before the Spaniards arrived in 1769, but the Franciscan missionaries who spearheaded the Spanish invasion brought devastating Old World diseases as well as the Roman Catholic catechism. Indians had little resistance to these newly introduced maladies, and their populations sharply declined even as missionaries directed the construction of a string of missions along the California coast from San Diego to San Francisco Bay. The Yokuts, Miwoks, Nisenans, Konkows, and other tribes in the Great Central Valley and Sierra Nevada maintained their independence from Spanish military, civil, and religious authorities. The deadly diseases, trade goods, livestock, and other innovations that eventually affected all Native peoples in North America had yet to affect these California Indians.[3]

In the Oregon country Nez Perce, Palouse, Coeur d'Alene, and Walla Walla Indians occupied the reaches of the upper Snake River, while Cayuse, Yakima, Umatilla, Klickitat, and Chinook Indians lived along the Columbia. The vast arid expanse of the Great Basin was the home of the Shoshone and Paiute bands, who extracted a living from this demanding environment. Dozens of other tribes large and small occupied and exploited virtually all of the lands that are now known as the American West.[4]

At first glance, many of these people seemed to live an independent existence, far removed from the influences of European capitals and the designs of the inquisitive President Jefferson and his ambitious compatriots. But in truth Indian sovereignty became more precarious with each passing decade. Neither Native peoples nor newcomers fully understood the complex web of relationships that progressively altered the balance of forces among them. The trade in beaver and other pelts and hides had long shaped the social and economic relations of Europeans and Indians. For more than a century French woodsmen from Canada and English representatives of the Hudson's Bay Company had trapped and traded among the tribes of Canada and along the tributaries of the Mississippi and Missouri Rivers. Traders working for American companies and independent trappers—the so-called mountain men of western lore—followed Meriwether Lewis and William Clark to the headwaters of the Missouri River and beyond. Whatever the national origins of the participants, they set powerful forces in motion. These outlanders brought potent new diseases that killed many Indians. The trade in furs reoriented Indian economies so that they funneled pelts and hides into traders' stores in exchange for manufactured goods that replaced locally produced handmade items. Native peoples adopted rifles in place of bows and arrows, used steel needles instead of bone awls, and wrapped themselves in wool blankets instead of fur robes and hides. As diseases eroded Indian communities and the trade became all important, tribes fought for the richest fur-trapping grounds. Thus the fur trade was accompanied by cycles of death and violence that disrupted Indian societies even as the trade enriched some tribes and the white entrepreneurs who supplied them.[5]

Yet the world of the fur trade was neither entirely chaotic nor without redeeming features. Everywhere traders and trappers married Indian women and raised children. The men and women who founded these families did so for many reasons. Love and mutual companionship figured in many of these relationships, as did calculating self-interest. Traders and their spouses saw marriage as an economic alliance that benefited both parties as well as the trader's company and the wife's Indian family. Marriage to an Indian woman gave the trader a tribal affiliation that protected him and his privilege to trade with the tribe. Indian wives provided invaluable service in cooking and household care, the preparation of hides and pelts, translation, and most of all goodwill among Native tribes.[6]

Not all fur-trade marriages were founded on the participants' free will. The demand for Indian women as spouses for fur-trade men was so great that Indian women (usually prisoners who were taken in war) became articles of trade among tribesmen and men in the fur trade. Sacagawea, the famous Shoshone woman who accompanied the Lewis and Clark expedition, had become the wife of a French Canadian trapper in just this way. The conquest of the American West caused disharmony and strife among Indian nations, and Indian women suffered as a result of these disjunctures. Whether based on free will or on force, these interracial social relationships were a foundation stone of a "middle ground," as historian Richard White has called it, that was not wholly Indian or European but a mixture of both. The society of the middle ground was not a permanent basis for racial and cultural relations; it was a way station en route to another destination. When Lewis and Clark were poised to ascend the Missouri River, few realized how quickly that they would arrive at this new place. In Anglo-American culture there would be little room for mixed marriages, their progeny, or unambiguous tribal sovereignty.[7]

In January 1803 Jefferson contemplated a reconnaissance of foreign territory; but unbeknownst to him the political map of North America was already on the verge of dramatic change. The exact location of the new nation's western border had been in dispute since the Peace of Paris ended the Revolutionary War in 1783. The treaty had provided for a Mississippi River boundary, but Spain (which controlled Louisiana until 1803) threatened to stop Americans from navigating the river. Worse, Spain had undisputed control of New Orleans and the mouth of the Mississippi River, so Americans who lived in the Ohio River Valley and wished to use the river to transport their goods were at the mercy of Spain or any of its successors. In 1801 Emperor Napoleon Bonaparte entered into a secret arrangement with Spain that provided for the Spanish cession of Louisiana to France. President Jefferson learned of this clandestine arrangement and resolved to do something about it. He sent three representatives to negotiate with Napoleon's government for the purchase of New Orleans. If Napoleon would not sell, the commission should secure a permanent agreement with France that would allow U.S. citizens to deposit their goods in New Orleans while awaiting transhipment to other ports. Jefferson was prepared to pay 10 million dollars for New Orleans. To the surprise of the commission and Jefferson, Napoleon (who needed money to finance his contemplated war with England) offered to sell all of Louisiana to the Americans for about 15 million dollars. Although there was no precedent or clear constitutional authority for such a purchase of new territory, Jefferson and the Congress quickly assented: the United States purchased a vast, little-known western empire for a few cents per acre.

So in 1803 everything in the region that we now call the American West was about to change. Indian, European, and American boundaries on the political map moved as the balance of power in North America shifted and future expansion became possible for the United States. But the outlines of the future had not congealed into reality; nor were historical outcomes predetermined. Much was left to chance in the far reaches of North America. In 1803 the future—what we now call history—was hostage to a million unforeseen acts by thousands of individuals who would look at the West and wonder what it held for them.

While Napoleon, Jefferson, and Lewis and Clark took center stage in the unfolding drama of western North America, an unlikely new actor emerged far offstage. On February 15, 1803, a baby was born to Johann Jakob Sutter and his wife, Christine Wilhemine, at five o'clock in the morning in Kandern, a small village in the Margravate of Baden (now part of Germany). The father of the new babe was a papermaker who lived above the mill that he ran for his Swiss employers. They called their first child Johann August Sutter. Johann Jakob Sutter (originally spelled with one *t*) was Swiss but had moved to Kandern at the behest of the mill owners. Johann August was thus a German-born Swiss citizen.[8]

Not much is known of young Sutter's childhood in Kandern, but some things may be surmised from the circumstances of his birth. He grew up in a household with middle-class aspirations. His father was scarcely a generation away from peasantry. Some of his forebears were ribbon weavers, but Johann Jakob's father had taken up paper-making and doubtless taught the craft to his son, who became a master and foreman of the small Kandern mill. Sutter's family conferred on him some extraordinary advantages. His mother was the daughter of a German pastor. There is no evidence that young Sutter was seriously devoted to any religious doctrine, but his mother was literate and passed on her love of reading to Johann August; he continued to read and educate himself throughout his life. We do not know what Sutter read as a boy, but books doubtless acquainted him with a wider world beyond the majestic Alps.

One event in Sutter's childhood undoubtedly affected his life. When he was six years old his mother gave birth to another son, Jakob Friedrich. Johann August was no longer the baby of the family but the eldest son, with the usual rights and responsibilities that the eldest child inherits in even the most democratic families. If Johann August was a role model for his younger sibling, the results were mixed, as Jakob Friedrich's life course dramatically illustrated—but more of that later.[9]

Because the adult Sutter was a remarkable personality, one might reasonably suspect that he developed his character traits as a child living in the Kandern paper mill. While his formative years are little known, it is possible to surmise the sort of childhood that Sutter enjoyed. He was the firstborn son, after all, and his parents probably doted on him, perhaps to the point of spoiling him. We may suppose that Sutter's mother at least temporarily transferred her affection and attention from Johann August to his infant sibling. Perhaps six-year-old Johann August's effort to regain his paramount place in the affection of his parents was his first struggle to achieve a status that he believed was rightfully his. Throughout his life, the way Sutter dressed and comported himself said, "Look at me." He probably began to develop his social style when he was a child. The adult Sutter was a persuasive man who always tried to escape trouble by talking his way out of it. He was a skilled prevaricator when he had to be, a bald-faced liar when he thought he could get away with it. Perhaps he told fancy tales in order to remain in his parents' good graces. Sutter's doting parents may or may not have believed all of their son's stories. Maybe it was enough for them that he was affable, clever, and resourceful. We may surmise that they forgave his juvenile transgressions perhaps a little too often and that young Sutter learned that a mouthful of promises was as good as a wagonload of accomplishments.

Still, Sutter was not an amoral criminal. As the firstborn son he believed in the established order of things, so he always sought approval from authority figures. Visualize the child Johann August marching around the paper mill, giving mock orders to the bemused men who worked for his father. Later in life he preferred to present himself as the defender of established authority and strove to be identified with the elite class wherever he was. He believed in lawful power and wanted to wield as much authority as his betters would confer on him. His purpose was not to overthrow them but to join them as their equal and, better yet, to become their superior.

When Johann August looked at his father, what did he see? Johann Jakob managed a substantial mill and (judging from pictures) commanded the labor of perhaps a dozen men. His father was the master of the mill and the master of the Sutter household domiciled above the working floor. Even though Johann Jakob was not native to Kandern, he was an important person in that small world. Herr Sutter derived his managerial authority from afar, however—from the Häussler family in Basel. This circumstance, too, may have influenced young Sutter's notions about the order of things. His father was an outsider with powerful foreign protectors.

In the early nineteenth century it would have been natural for the father to plan that his son would succeed him as mill manager, but Johann August's father had bigger things in mind for his son. At age fifteen young Sutter enrolled for a year of school at Neuchâtel, Switzerland. The Sutters' registration of their firstborn son in a Swiss school suggests that at the very least young Sutter was meant for the managerial classes, or perhaps even something better. Moreover, his future lay in Switzerland, not in some German border town. Neuchâtel had strong French influences that marked young Sutter as a lifelong Francophile. For a time he even frenchified his name to "J. Auguste Souter," but this youthful affectation did not last long.

If his experience at Neuchâtel expanded Sutter's horizons, they soon narrowed again. After his year of education, he moved to Basel, where he apprenticed with the firm of Emanuel Thurneysen, printers, publishers, and booksellers. Thurneysen had just acquired the paper mill at Kandern, so Sutter doubtless used his father's business connection to obtain his position. Basel was a stodgy, conservative city, owing much to the religious legacy of Calvinism. Sutter could observe wealth and display in Basel, but they were not for a poor, immigrant apprentice like him to enjoy. Fine things like the books that Sutter sold were for the wealthy burghers of Basel. If he stayed there, Sutter's destiny was foretold: he would remain a disfranchised outlander who worked for the natives of the place as a mere clerk.

Sutter had been a foreigner in Kandern too, a citizen of the Swiss town of Rünenberg by virtue of his father's citizenship in that tiny Swiss village. His alien status in Kandern might not have chafed too harshly on Sutter's childhood ego, although we may imagine that his playmates noticed his Swiss ethnicity. Whatever ethnic jibes he may have endured from his juvenile companions, young Sutter grew up secure in the knowledge that his father ran the paper mill and supervised the other men who worked there. Switzerland was Sutter's home country; but if he expected to be warmly received when he left Kandern and relocated in his homeland, he was soon disappointed. Switzerland was so parochial at the time that he could enjoy the rights of citizenship only in his *Heimatdorf* (hometown), the tiny village of Rünenberg. To the natives of Neuchâtel, Basel, and the other Swiss cities and towns, he would always be a foreigner who could never enjoy political rights or substantial social status. Sutter was born an outsider and would always be an outsider. He would never escape this fate, even in America.

Sutter was a mere clerk selling books in Basel in 1819, but he had access to reading material even though he did not have the means to purchase the books that he sold. After his term of apprenticeship was up, the house of Thurneysen dismissed him, although it retained his fellow apprentice, Johann Jakob Weber. If the Thurneysen firm had only the means to employ one of the apprentices permanently, the managers made an excellent choice. Weber became one of the leading publishers in Europe, while Sutter went on to another kind of fame. On the strength of his apprenticeship, Sutter landed a clerk's job in a draper's shop in Aarberg, a village about fifteen miles from Neuchâtel. He probably worked there from 1822 until sometime before 1826, when he was in Burgdorf, working as a grocery clerk.

Sutter moved to Burgdorf in order to court Anna Dübeld, whom he had met in Aarberg.[10] Perhaps he waited on her in the drapery shop. However he may have met Anna, he was smitten and resolved to move to Burgdorf, where she lived with her mother, a well-to-do widow. Anna was tall, slender, and aristocratic-looking, physical features that no doubt appealed to her short, social-climbing suitor. It is reasonable to suppose that Anna's personal attractions were enhanced in Sutter's mind by her mother's fiscal situation. Sutter did not move to Burgdorf merely to be rebuffed. Early in 1826 the ambitious grocery clerk impregnated Anna. Sutter asked for his lover's hand in marriage, but it was not hers to give without the permission of her mother and the town fathers of their respective hometowns. These high personages were slow to grant permission to unite an unpromising foreign-born grocery clerk with a highly eligible young woman of good family, who would inherit a small fortune from her mother.

Frau Rosina Dübeld, who was not pleased with having a Sutter for a prospective son-in-law, may have withheld permission until Anna was forced to reveal her condition or until her swelling belly offered the best and final argument in favor of the marriage. Sutter applied to the burghers of Rünenberg for permission to marry in June 1826, when Anna was about five months along. The good Rünenbergers deliberately considered the matter and in due course agreed to the union in September. Then the happy couple had to plan a wedding that did not look too hasty, although at eight months Anna must have been the object of some attention from nosy Burgdorf gossips. We can only imagine the psychological atmosphere in the Dübeld home as the wedding and birth dates approached. Which would come first? The couple married on October 24, 1826, and Johann A. Sutter, Jr., was born the next day.

The calendar saved Johann Junior (or August, as his parents called him) from bastardy, but the circumstances of his birth were remarkable nonetheless. Prenuptial pregnancies were not unusual in Switzerland in the early nineteenth century. In Neuchâtel, where Sutter received his education, more than 50 percent of brides were pregnant at the time of their marriages. Among the propertied classes, however, the rate of prenuptial marriages was only about 25 percent.[11] Anna's pregnancy was not so much a badge of unusual moral turpitude as it was a symbol of her déclassé behavior, a fitting advertisement of her marriage to a penniless social climber. It is also worth noting that she coupled with Sutter at a time when personal choice in marriage was overcoming the influence of economic considerations, parental control, and religious authority that had dominated matchmaking in earlier times. Burgdorfers no doubt sniggered behind their hands when Anna and Sutter exchanged vows, but they were a modern couple by the standards of the day.

Anna's display of modern independence could not have pleased Frau Dübeld, who must have found her daughter's pregnancy hard to bear while facing customers in her shop. After all, Burgdorf was a very small town. While a man like Sutter thought of her as wealthy, her fortune was hard-earned. She was the proprietor of her late husband's prosperous bakery and restaurant, with debt-free assets of twenty thousand Swiss francs—a substantial sum that, if properly managed, guaranteed her and her daughters a good life. Marriage to a foreign grocery clerk could not have been the future that she had in mind for Anna.

Sutter's biographers have generally characterized the Sutter-Dübeld marriage in unflattering terms. The first child was obviously unwanted, they say, and the marriage was a trap for a man with the expansive dreams and ambitions of young Sutter. They portray Anna as a complaining, embittered woman, although they base this assessment on observations of her in the 1850s and later. By then she had reasons to be bitter. Richard Dillon in his otherwise even-handed biography admits that Anna was a "handsome young woman" but says that her photographs "show her with a mouth like a cicatrice above a square-set jaw worthy of a Marine sergeant."[12] Perhaps, but there is no direct testimony that Anna was a shrew as a newlywed or that the marriage was loveless. Indeed, the circumstances warrant an equally plausible argument that the Sutters were glad to be married, at least at first.

Sutter, after all, had abandoned his job in Aarberg to pursue Anna in Burgdorf. Unless he was a complete fool in such matters, she must have given him some sign that she was willing to entertain his advances. And why not? Sutter was a handsome young man with a sense of style and military bearing. He dressed well, danced well, spoke persuasively, and impressed the ladies in America in the 1830s. Anna probably swooned for him in Aarberg and Burgdorf in the 1820s. Assuming that Anna's pregnancy was not the result of sexual assault, their sexual intimacy speaks of an ardent courtship that Anna perhaps too readily accepted. Maybe she loved him. It is even possible that she wanted to get pregnant so that she could marry Johann and escape her overbearing mother. She would not have been the first young woman to plan her escape from parental control in just this way. She would not be the last to discover that her seeming freedom was short-lived and came at a heavy price.

Whatever Anna was thinking about when she had sex with good-looking Johann, he was likely thanking his lucky star that an attractive woman was willing to bed him—and she was rich, too! Maybe he loved her. It is possible that he hoped to get her with child in order to force a marriage into a family with substantial means that he would share. He would not have been the first young man who married for money. He would not be the last to discover that his newfound wealth came at a heavy price.

Were the newlyweds happy with an instant family and a cross mother-in-law? Why not? Youth, love, and optimism are powerful aphrodisiacs. If they were poor, they shared that condition with most young couples of their era. If in time Sutter's financial troubles caused strains on their marriage, this too was a common situation that many young married people endured. Between 1826 and 1834 the Sutters had five children. The production of children is not necessarily a sign of a happy household; but if the Sutters were unhappy, their anxiety had not led to sexual estrangement.

Frau Dübeld made the best of a bad situation. She probably helped with Johann August's purchase of a large house and shop in Burgdorf, where he established Sutter and Company (a dry-goods store) in 1828. Perhaps she hoped that her flamboyant son-in-law would make good after all, but it was not to be. Johann August displayed some business acumen, but he had a large talent for creating debt that he paid with promises while he lived beyond his means and made grandiose plans for the future. He showed particularly poor judgment in his choice of business associates. Chief among them were his younger brother Jakob Friedrich, who followed him to Burgdorf, and a dishonest consumptive, Benedikt Seelhofer. When times were good Sutter and Company gave the outward appearance of prosperity, but flush times would not last.

In 1828 Sutter, who admired the martial life, volunteered for the reserve corps of the Swiss Canton of Berne.[13] He took a training course and received an appointment as a second underlieutenant in the first Center Company of the Third Battalion of the infantry reserve. Three years later he was promoted to first underlieutenant in the same battalion. How could it be that Lieutenant Sutter, who was so often reckless and irresponsible in his personal and business affairs, accepted the straitjacket of military discipline? For one thing a government had conferred official authority on Sutter. As a junior officer Sutter enjoyed the privileges of rank. He commanded enlisted men and cultivated his taste for military dress and ritual. All of his life Sutter—the outlander—hungered for recognition, respectability, and status. A uniform gave him all of these things. His service in the Swiss militia probably convinced him that he was born to command other men and that a great future awaited him, if only he had the opportunity. Sutter may have hoped that his military acquaintances would help his business too.

Sutter's martial connections would not be enough to make his commercial venture a success. The arrival of Jakob Friedrich considerably complicated Sutter-Dübeld family relations. In addition to the business connection with his older brother, Jakob Friedrich formed a new family link by marrying Anna's sister, Marie Sophie, a double alliance that must have horrified Frau Dübeld. At about the time of the second Sutter-Dübeld marriage the business climate began to decline, and Johann August could not pay his debts. In 1832 Seelhofer ran off with much of Sutter and Company's inventory and sold it. When Sutter became aware of Seelhofer's embezzlement, he neglected to sever his partnership with him formally, an oversight that foreshadowed his long history of inattention to legal details. Consequently, when Seelhofer died a short time later, Sutter and Company was liable for the dead man's debts. In 1832 Johann August arranged to pay his creditors at a steep discount. He also sold his house to his mother-in-law for eleven thousand francs so that he could meet his most urgent financial obligations. Still, his debts threatened to overwhelm him, and the future looked grim. His mother-in-law was now his landlord, a reversal of fortune that gave her the whip hand in his family and financial arrangements.

While Johann August's commercial dreams were disintegrating, his brother's marriage to Marie Sophie was rapidly deteriorating. Jakob Friedrich was an even less reliable breadwinner than his older brother. Their marriage was so unsatisfactory that Marie Sophie successfully sued for divorce and sent him packing in 1833, a turn of events that must have pleased Frau Dübeld and in which she may have had a hand. The divorce set Jakob Friedrich on a downward path. He moved to Geneva but soon proved unable to support himself and was deported to Rünenberg, where he lived as a public charge. There he died at age thirty-five, "a physical and moral wreck," according to historian James Peter Zollinger.[14] The divorce and deportation of his younger brother must have saddened and alarmed Johann August. Even in democratic Switzerland bankrupts and derelicts paid stiff penalties. Financial failure would mean the irrecoverable loss of everything that he had worked to gain.

If Frau Dübeld plotted revenge against the Sutters for ruining her daughters and staining her good name, the time was at hand. In the spring of 1834, without warning, she sold the home in which Johann August lived with his family and conducted the business of Sutter and Company. Now there was nothing standing between him and debtor's prison—and imprisonment was not an acceptable option for Johann August Sutter. To finance his flight from Switzerland, he secretly sold some of his remaining goods. After obtaining a passport, with Anna's help he absconded in May, leaving a huge debt as his only estate to Anna and their five children, who remained in Burgdorf. He took a sizable wardrobe of fine clothes, the remaining inventory of goods, and at least some of his books. Two weeks later he wrote to say that he would never return. He was going to America.

If Frau Dübeld gaily raised a glass of sweet German wine upon receipt of that letter, few Burgdorfers would have blamed her. She had reclaimed the lives of her two daughters from two fortune hunters. Now she could convince Anna, like Marie Sophie, to divorce her ne'er-do-well absentee husband. In time, perhaps, the scandal would fade and a suitable man would marry Anna, perhaps with one eye on the damaged goods and her five children and the other on the Dübeld estate and his self-interest. All would yet be well.

Frau Dübeld oversaw the path to Anna's future for only a short time. Within six months she was dead. Anna inherited a share of the estate of twenty-five thousand francs that her mother left; but she was still married to Johann August, who owed over fifty thousand in bad debts and had only fifteen thousand in assets. The court withheld Anna's portion of her mother's estate against her husband's obligations, so she could not inherit until Sutter's debts were settled. She and the children moved into an old farmhouse on the out-skirts of town that had been owned by her grandparents and relied on the charity of her three sisters.

Anna endured this shameful existence for sixteen years. Why not divorce the husband who deserted her? Perhaps she hoped to be reunited with him. Despite the letter that said he would not return to Burgdorf, Sutter may have given her private assurances of his loyalty to her and his intentions to recon-stitute their family in America as soon as conditions permitted. It was in character for Sutter to make large promises about what he would do when his bright future finally arrived. In 1834 the future was a long time off, and promises were thin gruel on which to feed a family. While Anna waited for Sutter to rescue her, she lived a desolate life in a small town where everyone knew her past and believed that they knew her future too. Of all Sutter's creditors, Anna, his four sons, and his daughter were the ones who suffered most. The time, place, and circumstances of the redemption of those debts were impossible to imagine in Burgdorf in 1834.

But for now Sutter was on the road to a prosperous future in a new land where all would be made right—or so he hoped. While sailing to New York, he had plenty of time to think about his wife and family and to consider the causes for his failure. What had the eternal optimist learned from his dismal slide into bankruptcy and family disunion? Sutter never mentioned it; but if his documented life is any guide, we may suppose that above all he convinced himself that he was not at fault. Others had caused his downfall. Creditors who would not wait for Sutter to pay as he had promised to do were blameworthy. Seelhofer, his dishonest business partner, and his feckless brother were to blame. Business conditions were to blame. The narrow-mindedness and clan-nishness of Swiss society were to blame. His scheming mother-in-law was to blame. Family relations that were supposed to be a bulwark against financial disaster had failed him utterly. Sutter's main fault was that he was too trusting. He meant no harm; others, including close friends and relatives, had done him dirt. While Sutter exonerated himself from the Burgdorf disaster, he also un-derstood that in adversity he could rely only on himself.

There were positive lessons too. Sutter had founded a company that oper-ated successfully for several years, even in the stultifying atmosphere of Burg-dorf. In Switzerland Sutter learned that he had a knack for persuading bankers and businessmen to extend him credit. True, he was unable to pay all his debts; but he paid some of them and he had intended to pay the rest until Frau Dübeld dispossessed him. Amazingly, Sutter believed that credit was his friend. He had done great things with other people's money. If only there had been more of it! He had been an officer in the reserve infantry and loved military ritual, heraldry, and dress. Above all Sutter loved to command. He would use his military training and experience (suitably inflated to impress his new audience) to advantage in America. Sutter also learned that he could run away from problems if the going got tough. The habit of flight from financial difficulties was a well-established trait by the time he reached California.

Sutter—the lover of fine clothes and dress uniforms—believed that appearances were all important. An officer's uniform proclaimed rank and status and set him apart from the ordinary soldiers. Fancy civilian dress announced that Sutter had money to spend, that he was a man of means. People in Burgdorf knew that Sutter's wardrobe falsely proclaimed his status, but in America who would know? Clothes would be his mask at the ball; finery and manners would be his key to gain admission to the inner offices of society—such as it was on the American frontier.

Clothing was only a part of the capital that Sutter transported to the New World and not the main part at that. His principal asset was himself. First and foremost, Sutter sold himself to his would-be creditors. He was his own stock in trade, his own inventory of resplendent goods. And he was his own best customer in buying pretty stories about the future. He could not resist his own incessant come-ons, proclaiming the big things that he would soon accomplish. Of course, he was not his only customer. He convinced many a cold-eyed businessman of the truth in his promises, which is perhaps the best evidence that he believed in his own pledges. In America, he promised himself, his ambition and talent would overcome the petty obstacles that small men had thrown in his way. In America there were no boundaries for a man of enterprise such as Sutter. For him, the hasty journey to North America was not about flight and hiding from the law but about display and performance.

CHAPTER 2

Opportunity on the American Frontier

Sutter disembarked on the New York docks in July 1834, an immigrant in what was fast becoming a city of immigrants. Sutter was one of tens of thousands of newcomers who thronged New York City every year in the 1830s. Two and a half million Europeans migrated to the United States between 1830 and 1850. Many decided to stay in New York City, which grew from two hundred thousand to three hundred thousand and became the largest city in the country during the 1830s. About one-third of the émigrés were from the Germanies. A slightly higher proportion came from Ireland, and the rest hailed from other European nations.[1]

The high number of German immigrants in New York must have suited the German-speaking Sutter. He would have had no trouble finding lodging, meals, companionship, and perhaps even a temporary job. There were successful German American role models too. The richest man in the United States was John Jacob Astor, a native of Waldorf, Germany, who had arrived in 1784. Astor, like Sutter, had carried a small stock of goods with him to America (musical instruments in Astor's case), hoping to turn a profit with them. Astor chanced to meet a man in the fur business who advised him to invest his profits in furs and locate in New York. Unlike Sutter, Astor was an excellent businessman who recognized good advice when he heard it. He immersed himself in the fur business, worked aggressively to dominate the fur trade in the western territories, and became the preeminent businessman of his age. His fur business spanned the continent, with seaborne connections around the globe. Astor's success story, which was well known in Sutter's time, must have been encouraging to Sutter, who arrived in New York in about the same circumstances in which Astor had arrived half a century earlier. Like Astor, Sutter believed that his fortune lay in the West, but there the similarities ended.[2]

New York was not in all respects attractive to newcomers, especially to an ambitious climber like Sutter. The poor immigrant's life was not an easy one. Native-born Americans tended to look down on them (although the thrifty Germans enjoyed a better reputation than the Irish). Immigrant communities emerged in tenement neighborhoods, where apartments without windows or toilet facilities were all too common. Growing, bustling New York offered plenty of work, but unskilled immigrants of all nationalities were most likely to find undesirable jobs in construction and menial occupations. Many of the Germans moved to rural communities, where they could take up farming.[3]

The squalid immigrant's life and the ferment of New York were not for Sutter. He and four traveling companions (two Germans and two Frenchmen) journeyed toward the Old Northwest. They stayed for a while in Cincinnati, where Sutter separated from his friends. Then he moved on to Indiana and finally to St. Louis, Missouri.[4] The German colony in Missouri had probably been Sutter's destination from the beginning. A German writer by the name of Gottfried Duden had publicized the rich farmlands of Missouri in glowing terms.[5] Since Duden's book was well known in Switzerland, it is likely that Sutter was familiar with it. "My object in coming to America," Sutter later explained, "was to become a farmer."[6] Perhaps, but he could not have meant that he intended to become a forty-acres-and-a-mule, dirt-under-the-fingernails sort of a farmer. He did not share Jefferson's image of the independent yeoman farmer scratching a living from the American soil and enjoying the riches of Republican virtue along with the certain knowledge that nobody was better than him. Sutter had grander visions than that, especially after he got a close look at Missouri's agricultural riches, who obtained them, and how.

Sutter moved into a German hotel on Front Street, a place where he could consort with his compatriots while he considered the opportunities that then presented themselves to greenhorns like himself. Here he fell in with another new arrival, John A. Laufkotter, a German from Wunnenburg. Laufkotter was only twenty-two and—like so many others—was favorably impressed with Sutter.[7] They were friends and roommates until Laufkotter moved on to St. Charles, about fifteen miles northwest of St. Louis on the north side of the Missouri River. Laufkotter took a partner and opened a grocery store.[8] Shortly thereafter Sutter also moved to St. Charles.

In late 1834 Sutter surveyed the prospects in eastern Missouri. French settlers had founded St. Louis in 1763 as well as several smaller communities.

Many of them were farmers, but the most influential French families, like the Chouteaus, were rich from the fur trade and from land grants received from Spain and France. The French had been involved in the trade in beaver, otter, and other skins since they had colonized the St. Lawrence River in the sixteenth century. Few became as wealthy as the Chouteau family, yet one could strike it rich in the fur trade.[9] John Jacob Astor certainly proved that. Missouri was part of the Louisiana Purchase and became a state in 1820, but the wealthy French fur-trading families were still conspicuous in Missouri society. Located on the banks of the Missouri River, St. Louis and St. Charles were important entrepôts for the upriver fur trade. The prospect of quick riches in the fur trade must have attracted Sutter's attention, but he had no experience, no connections, and little capital except the bundles of clothing and other goods that he had taken from his bankrupt store.

There was money in farming, but the agrarian paradise that Duden had described to his avid German and Swiss readers had a troubling side. Missouri was a slave state. Large landholders with gangs of African American slaves made a great deal of money and lavishly displayed it in their homes, clothing, and showy carriages. Slavery dominated even little St. Charles, where nearly one thousand slaves outnumbered eligible voters by more than two hundred.[10] Hard-working small farmers without slaves, like the Swiss and German émigrés with whom Sutter consorted, could make a comfortable living; but Sutter had no experience at it and would never master the habits of thrifty management that were required of small farmers. Besides, he was seeking more than middle-class comfort. He wanted to hit it big—and quickly too, if he had any hope for reuniting his broken family.

A third opportunity was available to entrepreneurs on the Missouri frontier—the Santa Fe trade in New Mexico. Spain had tightly controlled trade with its American colonies and prohibited foreigners from entering the frontier outposts in Texas, New Mexico, and California. All this changed in 1821, when the newly independent Mexican nation jettisoned the old trade policies of Spain and opened its borders to foreign trade and settlers. The people of New Mexico were especially anxious to welcome American traders from the Missouri frontier. While under Spain's rule, New Mexico was an isolated economic backwater at the very end of a long road that began in Spain. Now New Mexico would be part of a burgeoning international trade that connected the U.S. and Mexican frontiers. Horses, mules, sheep, wool, textiles, and other New Mexican products moved up the trail, passing wagonloads of U.S. goods bound for Santa Fe. Profits for Mexican and American merchants could be substantial, but there were risks too. American entrepreneurs never knew the state of the market in Santa Fe when they left the Missouri settlements. They might drive their oxen a thousand miles across plains and deserts only to find that the New Mexican markets were saturated with the merchandise that they had transported. Trade was legal; but taxes could eat up profits, and local officials demanded bribes. Missouri merchants on both ends of the trail soon learned that shrewd New Mexican customers who were accustomed to hard bargaining in a harsh desert land were not easy marks. The long trail itself also took its toll, especially in the Cimarron Desert. The Santa Fe trade demanded much of the hardy souls who prodded their oxen along the trail.[11] It was not a game for greenhorns, but it attracted Sutter's attention almost immediately.

In the winter of 1834–35 Sutter considered his options over glasses of beer and wine in the German saloons of St. Louis and St. Charles. He made many friends in these haunts, especially among the German population. Some of them invited the newcomer to join the German Club, a social organization that met twice a week in St. Louis.

Among the socializers was a man who represented himself as a colonel in the Prussian army and a former adjutant to the crown prince of Prussia. Although he had lately resided in the town of Prairie du Chien in Wisconsin Territory, he was (according to his own word) a man of great wealth. Indeed, the colonel's steamboat stuffed with merchandise and money would arrive presently— or so he said. In the meantime he ran up big bills entertaining his new friends (who evidently included most of the German men in St. Louis). He threw parties, rented carriages and sleighs for the revelers, and provided them with plenty to drink. The colonel's manners were impeccable, and his German acquaintances had no doubt that he was the genuine article. They were glad to loan him small sums from time to time, just to tide him over until his steamer arrived. The colonel told stories about his exploits and encouraged his listeners to form a trading caravan to Santa Fe. The Prussian "pretended to have been there, and gave the most fabulous accounts of the wealth of the surrounding country," Laufkotter recalled.[12] Sutter heard these stories too.

The high living continued in St. Louis until merchants tired of accepting the Prussian's IOUs. Then he went to St. Charles, where he reacquainted himself with Sutter and Laufkotter and repeated his St. Louis performance, always settling his tabs with the confidential words: "I will pay as soon as the steamer arrives."[13] When his creditors eventually demanded payment, the Prussian colonel was revealed as a fraud. At least one of his creditors felt some sympathy: Sutter told Laufkotter that "he felt very sorry about our Adjutant's misfortunes, considering him a man above the ordinary sphere"; but the penurious Sutter felt worse about fifty dollars that he had recklessly loaned to the great prevaricator.[14]

It was an expensive lesson, but one that Sutter may have felt was worth the price. With nothing but good manners, nice clothes, and a glib tongue, the "colonel" had impressed the German community. The man had precisely the same resources that Sutter already possessed. If one German newcomer could live well by spinning stories out of thin air, then why not Sutter? He had been an underlieutenant in the Bernese reserve corps. It would be easy enough to inflate his exploits by promoting himself to a higher rank and associating himself with a more prestigious military unit and heroic exploits. This he began to do with his bragging in St. Louis beer halls. Throughout his life Sutter would claim to have been a member of the elite Swiss Guards and to have participated in various European military exploits. The German farmers with whom he drank thought he was a "capital fellow," according to Laufkotter, and began to call him Captain Sutter.[15]

Captain Sutter's fictional military reputation would not pay the rent or put bread on the table, although his tales probably earned him more than a few steins full of beer. In the spring of 1835 "[o]ur winter's extravagance had entirely exhausted my friend's treasury," Laufkotter recalled, "and his situation became quite critical." Captain Sutter, the toast of the German saloons, now had to find some way to earn a living in America, but he was "dissatisfied with every branch of business," as Laufkotter delicately put it.[16] Indeed Sutter did not even have enough money to pay taxes in St. Charles.[17] Then he fortuitously met several "French gentlemen," who were bound for New Mexico on a trading expedition.[18] They took Sutter with them and headed down the Santa Fe trail when the spring weather freshened.

Laufkotter (our only firsthand source for this period of Sutter's career) did not name or describe the Frenchmen with whom Sutter joined company, but it is doubtful that they wore lace at their sleeves. It is more likely that they were from the French and Indian community that had grown out of the fur trade on the Missouri River. When Mexico opened its borders to foreign trade, some of these fellows tried their hands at the Santa Fe trade and found that New Mexico was to their liking. They married Mexican women and settled in Taos, Santa Fe, and other New Mexican hamlets. As the Missouri beaver populations diminished before the relentless assault of trappers and traders, some of them used New Mexico as a base for new trapping operations south and west of New Mexico, going as far afield as California. These "French gentlemen," rough and restless, owed as much of their heritage to their Osage, Mandan, and Shoshone mothers as to their French fathers.[19] But they spoke French, and they proved willing to take another man with them to Santa Fe. That was good enough for Sutter, who took some of his stock of Swiss clothing to barter in New Mexico. Perhaps the Prussian colonel's advice and his flattering descriptions of New Mexico rang in Sutter's ears as he marched across the Mexican border.

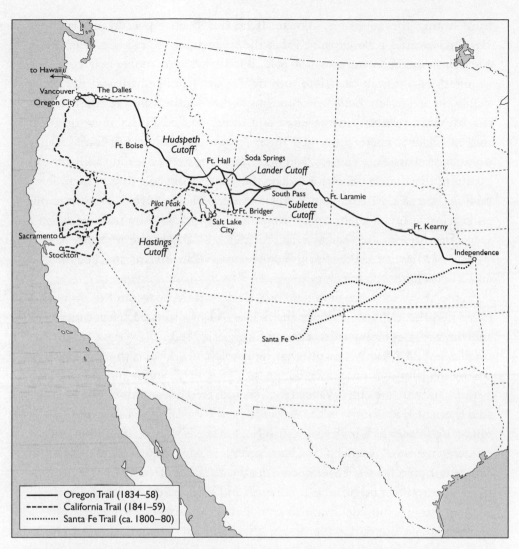

Western trails in Sutter's era. Based on map 32 in Warren A. Beck and Ynez D. Haase, *Historical Atlas of the American West* (Norman: University of Oklahoma Press, 1989).

Little is known of Sutter's first venture to Santa Fe. He was ill and bedridden while he was there, but he turned a good profit nonetheless.[20] Sutter also met well-traveled and knowledgeable trappers and traders, including the Taos *alcalde* (mayor) Carlos Beaubien, a French American trapper and naturalized Mexican citizen. Beaubien, Sutter later recalled, "was an educated Canadian, who had studied for the clergy but had never taken the orders."[21] Beaubien had journeyed to California in the 1830s like many other Taos trappers and gave Sutter "much information about this country."[22]

Sutter did not explain just what Beaubien told him about California, aside from noting the salubrious climate. If he had been especially informative, Beaubien would have explained that the main item of trade between New Mexico and California was not pelts but horses and mules that could be acquired legally from the californios or illegally from Indians and mountain men who had stolen them.[23] The Indians of the Central Valley regularly raided the Mexican ranchos on the coast and drove rustled horses into the great interior valley, where they used them for transportation and food. Angry californios chased the rustlers, and occasionally mounted serious military expeditions that attacked interior Indians, but never were able to stop them from raiding the coast. Miwoks and Yokuts were especially active in this dangerous enterprise. Some of them were former mission Indians who no longer had a secure livelihood after Mexican authorities secularized the missions. Other Indians had never accepted Spanish or Mexican authority and attacked mission and rancho herds as a means of resistance.[24]

In the 1830s scores of mountain men dealt with Miwok and Yokuts raiders or rustled the californios' herds themselves. Horse rustling by outsiders and Indians was a constant irritant to californios. In 1833 California authorities caught several New Mexicans who had stolen nearly one thousand horses. Two years later mountain men Thomas L. "Peg-leg" Smith and James Beckwourth and the Ute chief Walkara took six hundred horses from California and sold them at Bent's Fort on the Arkansas River. In 1837 Jean Baptiste Chalifoux (also known as Charlevoix, Chalifon, Charlefoux, and other phonetically rendered names), a French Canadian from New Mexico, made off with about fifteen hundred horses.[25] Some of the raids on California were of epic proportions, as the 1839 raid of "Peg-leg" Smith and Walkara dramatically illustrates. They and their comrades rounded up nearly six thousand animals in southern California and bolted for the desert. The californios organized a substantial posse and gave chase. With so many animals the rustlers' trail was not hard to follow; the dust cloud from their hooves was visible for nearly twenty miles. The californios did not capture the thieves, but they got some of the horses back. In later years Smith reminisced that he got away with "only about 3,000; the rascals got half of what we started with away from us, damn them."[26]

Walkara and the Utes were not the only non-California Indians to take horses from the californios. Delawares and Shawnees came from the Indian territory (now Kansas and Oklahoma) and took their share too. The Shawnees were so adept at this game that the californios called foreign horse thieves *chaguanosos,* a Spanish corruption of "Shawnees." Truly, as the rancheros said, the men who pillaged the horse and mule herds were "adventurers of all nations," including their own.[27]

The demand for horses on the American frontier was nearly insatiable. They were a necessity for farmers and ranchers of all nationalities. Native peoples had come to rely on them as well, and in Indian societies the horse had become a source of wealth, pride, and power. Tribesmen from Canada to Mexico raided other Indians who might have stolen their stock from Anglo, French, and Hispanic owners. New Mexicans who purchased stolen California horses in the evening might well wake up the next morning to find that Apaches had taken them away to sell to some other needy frontiersmen. The Apaches might just as easily lose their new mounts to Comanches or to vengeful New Mexicans. People of every nationality purchased horses from Indians without inquiring too closely about the origins of the merchandise. The Santa Fe Trail was one link in this vast, transcontinental illicit horse and mule market.[28]

In the fall of 1835 Sutter came riding back from New Mexico in triumph with a barrel of Santa Fe wine, seven mules, and probably some money to boot. He joined Laufkotter in St. Charles, where his friend had opened a grocery store with another German.[29] Sutter spent his profits freely and lubricated eager German listeners with liberal doses of New Mexican wine. He pastured the mules on the land of a widow "where pasturage was good, charges low"— and, Laufkotter snidely added, where there were "many other opportunities."[30] Laufkotter would not be the last observer to remark on Sutter's reputation as a womanizer. Sutter's initial trading success, and his habit of entertaining everyone with plenty of liquor, strengthened his reputation among German farmers with whom he did business. As in Switzerland, he often gave his personal note in lieu of cash. Laufkotter, his friend and sometime business associate, explained that Sutter punctually redeemed these notes, after borrowing the money from another of his friends.

In the German beer halls and saloons of Missouri, Sutter (relying on his old habit of using other people's money) created an American persona—the visionary frontier entrepreneur. He spoke well, looked the part in his fine clothes, and painted a rosy picture of future success in which his friends would share if they had the courage to invest. Sutter had a business scheme that he assured his drinking companions would not fail. He proposed to assemble a caravan for the next trading season in Santa Fe. As he expatiated on his dreamy business plans during his drinking bouts, some of his German companions were convinced that men like Sutter would transform the frontier from an isolated, rural, and primitive place into a bustling and prosperous community. And some of them were even willing to place their money in Captain Sutter's hands, believing that under his bold management their capital would increase. Hard experience would teach them that Sutter's magnetic personality, grand imaginings, enthusiasm, and confidence would not pay the bills when they came due. In the meantime trusting innocents and ruthless speculators alike were willing to invest in Sutter's plan to take a caravan to Santa Fe.

Seventeen men joined up and pooled their money after electing Sutter as captain. All but Sutter put their money in a common fund. He bought $14,000 worth of goods on his own, paying half in cash (probably with the profits from his first Santa Fe venture) and the other half by a note against the company to be paid upon their return. This was a very good arrangement for Sutter, who owned the goods without financial encumbrance after paying half their worth. The company spent several thousand dollars on oxen and wagons. There was great enthusiasm for this venture among the Germans, who deemed it an honor to be included. According to Laufkotter, a German from New Orleans heard about the caravan and gave Sutter $1,300 to invest in goods for the trip. With it Sutter purchased toys, although this proved to be singularly poor judgment on his part; these trifles realized less than $20 in New Mexico. Sutter also decided that it was important to buy plenty of liquor for the trip; he and his companions consumed much of it in Missouri. By the time the caravan was ready to leave, the company treasury was empty, so Sutter found another man willing to invest $100 in return for a share of the profits—and off they went.

Laufkotter, who was a member of this promising concern, described the scene: "The train was accompanied with its seventeen owners, who were composed of bankers, doctors, colonels, captains, merchants, mechanics and farmers, single and married men, all equipped with a good sized canteen, which was filled [with liquor] every morning by the provision master."[31] The first of many well-documented drinking sprees, Sutter's second Santa Fe trip foreshadowed a life of heavy drinking. His earliest manifestation of alcoholic behavior—hard drinking among convivial companions—was scarcely remarkable in antebellum America. Still, among a group of enthusiastic drinkers, Sutter led the way, Laufkotter recalled two decades later. They were a company of drunken greenhorns, led by Sutter and headed for the promised riches of Santa Fe.

It was not long before dreary reality interrupted their march to glory and handsome profits. In Marthasville, scarcely twenty miles from St. Charles, Sutter announced that the treasury was again empty. He was able to obtain another $200 from a new investor, however, and the train pushed on, "after greasing the wheels, and thoroughly wetting our throats," Laufkotter recalled.[32] The ox train lumbered on to Independence, Missouri, where there was a new surprise waiting for the well-lubricated travelers. Sutter had ordered goods to be sent there by steamer, and the company received a storage bill that had to be paid by assessing each member. Then Sutter announced that the caravan had no flour, which was indispensable for the long journey to Santa Fe. Once more he prevailed on a friend (no doubt on credit or for a share in the company). With the new flour, the wagons were overloaded; so the company had to hire teams, thus adding one more expense that the investors had not foreseen. After these demonstrations of Sutter's poor planning, fecklessness, and questionable business acumen, a few of his fellow travelers began to lose faith in the enterprise. At Council Grove some of them sold their shares to Sutter—who purchased them on credit, of course.

Other caravans bound for Santa Fe met at Council Grove and formed one grand train that pushed down the trail in a mile-long column. The journey took them from the Big Bend of the Arkansas River out on the open plains, where the blue sky arched into a vast canopy that covered the greening spring plains. Numberless grazing buffalo and antelope scattered at the approach of creaking wagons and straining oxen. The Great Plains could seem like an endless ocean of gently rolling grass, a place where a compass seemed as fitting a tool for navigation as on the sea. Trees grew only in the river bottoms and creek beds, which became scarce as the army of traders marched beneath this heaven-bound space. South of the Arkansas they crossed the Cimarron Desert, a sere sixty-mile stretch of desolation without water. Thirst-maddened oxen used their last reserves of energy to run across the final stretch of desert and plunge headlong into the Cimarron River. The oxen drank their fill at the river before crossing the Oklahoma panhandle and heading into New Mexico.[33]

The desert was fearsome, but greenhorns and old hands alike worried most about Indians who might attack the train. Pawnees, Kiowas, and Comanches called these parts of the plains home, but Santa Fe traders encountered southward-roaming Sioux, Cheyennes, and other Plains tribes too. Indian alarms were more common than actual attacks on these large and well-armed ox trains. Sometimes the trains traveled in four parallel columns so that they could quickly draw into a defensive hollow square. Laufkotter, the only member of the Sutter party who left a recollection of the trip, did not report any Indian scares.

Once refreshed by the waters of the Cimarron, several ambitious traders (including Sutter) sprinted ahead to Santa Fe to rent sales and storage space. Sutter rejoined the plodding train at San Miguel, about forty miles southeast of Santa Fe. He brought with him several Mexican riders and a risky new scheme for those who were brave or foolhardy enough. He told Laufkotter that they could make "a pile" by "trading with the Apache Indians who were in possession of a great many horses, mules and proved jacks."[34] This stock was undoubtedly stolen, and dealings with the Apaches were against Mexican law;

violators risked prison or worse. Still, Laufkotter sold his share in the caravan to Sutter and joined the scheme on the condition that he could choose a third partner, an unnamed man with a $1,300 stake in the caravan. Sutter agreed, and the third partner bought into the enterprise; his share was financed by company goods, "delivered up with such promptness, that the other members of the company . . . never discovered it."[35] Sutter took a fourth partner into the secret company, an unnamed man described as a French guide—probably one of the many mountain men who drifted through New Mexico in the 1830s. Now Sutter and his secret partners embarked on parallel trading enterprises: the original Santa Fe trade in partnership with the Missouri greenhorns and the illegal horse trade with the Apaches.

Sutter conducted the legal trade with his usual gusto and dramatic flair. He hired a clerk, spent money, and entertained lavishly. When he was accused of smuggling, Sutter paid off a Mexican official with a few baskets of champagne. Nevertheless, trade was slow except in fancy articles, which "diminished rapidly on account of the gallantry of the members [of the company] who vied with one another in winning the esteem of the ladies," Laufkotter recalled. "Mr. Sutter even competed for the prize," he added.[36] Law limited the trading season in Santa Fe to four weeks. At the end of this period some of the Missourians wanted to take their unsold goods farther south to Chihuahua, but Sutter was opposed. Finally the company sold the remaining stock to a New Mexican official for $2,000, for which they received forty mules and a note for $1,000.[37] The dispirited partners returned to Missouri, but Sutter and his secret partners in the Apache scheme remained behind, claiming that one of them was ill.

Free of the partners whom they had misled and swindled, Sutter, Laufkotter, and their two partners turned to the Apache horse business. Now it was their turn to be fleeced. Sutter had imprudently turned over the partners' trade goods for the scheme to their French confederate, who said he would procure horses, mules, and provisions for the Apache venture. When the animals and other stuff did not appear, the Frenchman made excuses. Finally the Frenchman's brother warned Sutter and the others that they should reclaim the goods "that were still left." When confronted, the French partner confessed: "I've got into bad luck in gambling, and lost the whole."[38]

This turn of events enraged Laufkotter's $1,300 partner, who packed up and left Santa Fe with another French guide of dubious reputation. The party headed back to Missouri by way of Bent's Fort on the Arkansas River. Somewhere along the way the Frenchman (perhaps with the help of an American who joined them at Bent's Fort) murdered their star-crossed companion and buried him in a creek bottom near the trail. The following year Laufkotter discovered the body (which had been dug up by wolves) and identified it by the clothes. In 1877 Benjamin D. Wilson, an old-timer who was at Santa Fe in 1836, hinted that Sutter may have taken a hand in the killing.[39] But even Laufkotter, who in later years developed a bitter enmity against Sutter, did not accuse him of murder. Laufkotter merely blamed Sutter for his former partner's death, because the deal had turned sour and caused the murdered man to leave Santa Fe rashly with a dangerous companion. Sutter had many flaws, but cold-blooded murder seems out of character for the genial Swiss.

While their partner advanced up the trail toward his doom, Sutter and Laufkotter were marooned in Santa Fe with no money. They scraped by as best they could, one of them taking work as a cook and the other (probably Sutter) finding employment as a store clerk. Their prosaic routine was interrupted when someone arrived from the South Platte River with a gold nugget. That inspired Laufkotter to try his hand at mining, and he left for the nearby diggings.

Sutter stayed behind and evidently tended to business well enough to gain sufficient capital to buy Indian trade goods. Or perhaps he had secreted some of the company stock that Laufkotter knew nothing about. Whether by thrift or by craft, Sutter managed to get into the illicit horse business that he had first described to Laufkotter in San Miguel earlier in the year. Wilson testified that Sutter had a stock of "galvanized jewlry [sic] that he peddled around to the Indians, and other portions that he exchanged for mules."[40] He obtained a hundred horses from Apaches, who had probably stolen them in Sonora, perhaps three hundred miles south of Santa Fe. Now furnished with a sizable herd, Sutter returned to the Missouri frontier in the fall of 1836. He drove his horses and mules back over the Santa Fe Trail with the help of Pablo Gutiérrez, a Mexican man he had hired in Santa Fe. Little is known about Gutiérrez except that he worked for Sutter until he died. Gutiérrez's knowledge of Hispanic culture and the Spanish language as well as his skills as a vaquero were of great value to Sutter.

Some of the herd was lost along the way, but Sutter arrived in Missouri with enough animals to go into business in Westport, a Missouri River town where Kansas City now stands. Many years later John G. McCoy, the town's founder, described Sutter's arrival with "a retinue of Mexican greasers as servants and herdsmen, a wagon or two, and forty or fifty mules." Sutter was a "soldierly-looking man with a great deal of dash and restless energy, wore high-topped boots, a splendid blue cloth cloak, the capes reaching nearly to the ground, and altogether was well calculated to create a profound impression upon us simple backwoods men."[41]

The flamboyant Sutter disposed of his herd and invested the proceeds in

Westport real estate. In 1837 he purchased two town lots from McCoy.[42] In the spring he paid $3,000 for 320 acres of farm and grazing land, where he evidently pastured his livestock.[43] Sutter built a stable and corral on one of his lots so that he could carry on his horse and mule business and built a hotel too. He bought out a store, formerly known as Lucas and Cavanaugh, and set up a shop, where he catered to the Santa Fe traders. He was moving fast, building a small empire on credit extended by his neighbors.[44]

Westport was a likely-looking new frontier town on the make, just the sort of place for an operator like Sutter. It had a good steamboat landing on the Missouri River, which made it a strong competitor with Independence merchants. The Indian trade beckoned too. The reserved lands of the relocated Delawares and Shawnees were just across the river, and the United States paid these tribes annual annuities. The Delawares alone received more than $7,400 per year in silver, plus more for individual chiefs. White traders eventually got the bulk of these payments.[45]

Westport recommended itself to Sutter for another reason. It was on the west side of Missouri, more than two hundred miles away from angry St. Louis creditors. The greenhorns who had returned to their homes in eastern Missouri soon learned that their meager gains from the trip did not cover their debts. Creditors quickly took charge of the mules and other goods that the German traders had salvaged from their venture. One man lost his farm, and his family was "thrown upon the charity of the world," as Laufkotter put it.[46] Others went to jail, back to Germany, or south to Texas.

As Laufkotter rode up the Santa Fe Trail in the summer of 1837, he heard stories that Sutter owned the whole town. Laufkotter could not believe that his former partner had done so well for himself; he had to see for himself. The truth was more prosaic. In Westport he found Sutter keeping store, trading horses, and building the Far West Hotel with Shawnee labor. Sutter wanted his hostelry to boast the best accommodation on the western frontier. He ordered an expensive gilt sign from a St. Louis artisan to advertise the hotel's high-class qualities.

Despite Sutter's pretensions, the Far West was a hand-hewn log structure. His Shawnee workmen received seventy-five cents per day for ordinary labor and one dollar if they were cornermen (skilled laborers who could notch and lay in the corner logs so that they were square and plumb). Sutter paid his men at the end of the day. Laufkotter reported that when Sutter asked each Shawnee man what part of the work he was doing, "he always said 'cornerman,' and consequently received his dollar without hesitation."[47]

Faced with a payroll every night, Sutter had to find a ready source of cash. Laufkotter suspected that he obtained it by smuggling liquor to the Indians across the river, contrary to federal law. Sutter's dealings with the Indians were not confined to employment and the illicit liquor trade. Laufkotter also accused him of dallying with Shawnee women to such an extent that he scandalized the white women of Westport.

When Laufkotter left Westport three weeks later for another trip to California via New Mexico, Sutter's finances were in shaky condition. Indeed his small empire crumbled almost as quickly as it had arisen. By the time Laufkotter departed, Sutter owed at least $3,160.50 to creditors and had not made much progress in paying them off.[48] He began to sell his property, probably at a loss, although this is difficult to determine from the property records.[49] Desperate for cash, Sutter sold one piece of property twice and gave warranty deeds to buyers who purchased property that he had not yet paid for. These illicit sales were not enough to pay his debts immediately, so lenders began to sue him. Sutter held them off for as long as he could, but the end of his Westport enterprise was clearly in sight.

Perhaps that is why Sutter agreed to meet Laufkotter in Santa Fe in the spring of 1838. Laufkotter did not write in detail about his plans or Sutter's. Sutter's first two trips to Santa Fe had turned into adventures in horse trading, however, so perhaps Laufkotter and Sutter were scheming about a California horse-rustling project like the ones that Peg-leg Smith and Jean Baptiste Chalifoux commanded. In the winter of 1837, while Laufkotter was in California, Chalifoux and forty Shawnee Indians stole a herd of fifteen hundred horses and wintered them in the San Joaquin Valley before driving them to New Mexico.[50] There is no evidence that Laufkotter was involved with Chalifoux, but this suggestive chain of events demonstrates the possibilities for transcontinental rustling operations.

The general outlines of Sutter's life in Missouri and New Mexico in the 1830s are in keeping with his much better documented shenanigans in California in the 1840s. The Swiss émigré was a man who looked good, spoke with confidence, promised much, and delivered little. Sutter was a confidence man who at first favorably impressed nearly all who met him. He attracted people with his brilliant personality and convinced them that his schemes were excellent business propositions. He plied them with liquor, fleeced them with sleight of hand, and paid them with promises that might be redeemed later on steeply discounted terms. In Switzerland these tactics had nearly landed Sutter in jail, but the North American frontier was not so well policed as little Burgdorf. The fluid circumstances and transnational character of the region favored someone like Sutter, at least in the short term. If creditors became too demanding and belligerent, he had plenty of space in which to disappear. Whole new countries beckoned across the wide Missouri.

CHAPTER 3

A Tour of Western Enterprises

On March 9, 1838, John King, sheriff of Jackson County, Missouri, read a summons to Sutter that commanded him to appear in circuit court on April 2 to answer the charges of one of his creditors.[1] With no means to pay, Sutter stood to lose everything. This turn of events seriously depressed him. The failure of his business plans meant another postponement of his family reunion. Four years had passed since his hasty flight from Switzerland. Letters between Sutter and his wife have not survived, but it is likely that he wrote and made promises to Anna. One can imagine him explaining that as soon as he returned from his Santa Fe trip, or as soon as his hotel was finished, or as soon as some person paid him, he would send enough money to settle his Swiss debts and transport the family to America. The realization of these dreams would be many years in coming. For now, Sutter looked for fast ways to make money. Doing things on credit always seemed to him the best solution to his financial problems; but his fiscal house of cards collapsed in Westport, just as it had in Burgdorf and Santa Fe.

Sutter's latest setback was a hard blow. Ordinarily his boundless enthusiasm, unrealistic and reckless though it often was, carried him from one defeat to the next glimmering project; but in the late winter of 1838 his high hopes were temporarily exhausted. If Sutter was drinking as much as Laufkotter claimed, alcohol may have contributed to his depression. Not knowing what else to do, Sutter despairingly confessed to his friend and creditor John G. McCoy that he planned to blow out his brains. McCoy would not hear of it and offered to help him financially. McCoy's generosity restored Sutter's self-confidence. The revived Sutter got a grubstake to take him to the Mexican province of California.

McCoy, Westport's founder, leading merchant, and major property owner, had the resources to provide a loan. But his assistance may have been more than a straight business proposition. It may have been prompted by Sutter's generosity to his father, Isaac McCoy, the well-known Baptist missionary to the Shawnees. Sutter had aided the elder McCoy when he was in straitened circumstances. Often in need himself, Sutter was always willing to help the down-and-out if he could.[2]

What attracted Sutter to California? His own words on the subject, uttered in old age, are few and vague. Sutter explained that he had first heard of California from Carlos Beaubien at Taos, which seems plausible. Beaubien gave Sutter "much information" about California, which had "a beautiful perpetual summer and a fine climate"—a sunny advertisement worthy of a Golden State real estate promoter.[3] It is too bad that Sutter did not say more about the "information" that Beaubien provided, but he probably talked about more than the weather. The French Canadian fur trader, New Mexican *poblador,* and now Mexican citizen and alcalde at Taos had visited California and was well informed about the trade in furs and horses that flowed across the Gila River route and Spanish Trail.[4] Beaubien was not Sutter's only California informant. Laufkotter, it is safe to assume, shared information about California with his sometime friend and business partner. Sutter spent much time in New Mexico and Missouri with other trappers and traders, who were probably well informed about California. In Missouri and Kansas he was in close contact with the Delaware and Shawnee Indians, whom the californios accused of raiding their horse herds. In this varied crowd Sutter apparently learned enough about California so that he was willing to make a 2,000-mile journey on horseback to get there.

McCoy gave the forlorn Swiss a horse. In return Sutter left "a lot of fashionable toggery" with his benefactor, probably the last of the fine clothing that he had brought with him from Switzerland. It was an odd lot of clothing, including "a long, black silk velvet circular coat, satin-lined; some knee-breeches, a silk vest or two," McCoy recalled.[5] Knee-breeches could not have been a lively item in local stores in 1838. Perhaps gentlemen in Switzerland wore such things, but it is difficult to imagine that anyone in western Missouri would wear such a get-up. No doubt Sutter gave these articles to McCoy as a heartfelt gift, but they were useless for trade in any case and would only have weighed him down. Benjamin Wilson, a Californian who had known Sutter in New Mexico, later claimed that Sutter provided additional financing for his overland trek by forging several drafts.[6] According to Wilson, when the victims of these drafts learned of Sutter's apparent success in California, Sutter quietly paid them off to avoid scandal. If Wilson's story is true (he was usually a reliable witness), it seems that Sutter outfitted himself for his California expedition with a combination of charity, legitimate loans, and forgeries.

Sutter left Westport on April 1, 1838, just one day before he was scheduled to appear in circuit court. He rode out "on a pretty good plug and leading another packed horse with provisions and camp equipment," McCoy recalled, "and I was the happy owner of very fine cloth, a few pictures and a gold watch chain."[7] At least two friends accompanied Sutter: Pablo Gutiérrez (unmentioned by McCoy) and a German known only as Wetler who had bought some property from Sutter. As Sutter said, they were headed for California but by way of the fur traders' Rocky Mountain rendezvous, an annual gathering of white traders, trappers, and Native peoples involved in the fur trade. They stayed for a couple of weeks among the Delawares and Shawnees while waiting for a fur-trade caravan to arrive. This was another opportunity to learn something about California from the chaguanosos who so nettled the californios.

Sutter stayed on the Delaware reservation until April 22, when the American Fur Company wagon train forded the Kansas River and creaked into view. Dust from the line of carts and pack animals rising over the plains advertised the arrival of representatives of one of the major companies then operating on the western frontier. John Jacob Astor had founded the American Fur Company in 1808. In the ensuing decades he built his multifaceted fur business into a vast enterprise that was continental in scope and became a wealthy man in the process. The German-born magnate recognized the opportunities that the western fur trade presented—and (shrewd businessman that he was) he knew when to cash in his chips. In 1834 Astor deduced that the fur business was on the wane, so he sold his western interests to Pratte, Chouteau, and Company of St. Louis. By the time Sutter joined the slow-moving procession, Pierre Chouteau, Jr., and Company controlled Astor's old western outfit.[8]

Andrew Drips (called captain, the customary honorific title given to such leaders) led the collection of about sixty men, with two hundred horses and mules and seventeen wagons and two-wheeled Red River carts loaded with trade goods for the rendezvous.[9] Sutter and his companions fell in and marched along the Kansas River trail. On April 28 nine riders caught up with them, a company of Protestant missionaries who would travel with the traders to the rendezvous before continuing to Oregon.[10]

William Gray had recruited this missionary contingent, which included four newlywed couples. All of the brides were from the East. Gray had gone to Oregon in 1836 with the first Protestant mission but had returned to the United States for reinforcements in 1837.[11] This distinctly pious group must have stood out among the profane bull-whackers, fur traders, and coarse frontiersmen and the well-dressed Swiss entrepreneur with whom they traveled. So devout (and impractical) were these missionary sojourners that they fretted over the question of traveling on the Sabbath. When they joined the caravan in Westport, they were dismayed to learn that Drips would leave on Sunday, April 22 (come hell or high water, so to speak). Instead of accompanying the carts, they decided to keep the Sabbath and catch up with the caravan later.[12] It would be their last sabbatical observance for some time.

Observing the Sabbath in Westport must have lifted the spirits of Asa Bowen Smith, who described the country as he rode out of Westport. "Little spots of woodland now to be seen here & there, but most of the land was entirely destitute of trees—some covered with small shrubs, but most of it seemed like a meadow covered with grass. Often as far as the eye could reach nothing was to be seen but the beautiful grass land, rising in gentle undulations."[13] Smith's smiling description of the plains belied the hardships that lay ahead, especially for the women. Only two white women had made the overland trip before: Narcissa Whitman and Eliza Spalding, married to Methodist missionaries Marcus Whitman and Henry Spalding, did it in 1836. Two years later four additional Christian women were on their way. Like their predecessors, they made the entire journey riding sidesaddle, each woman perched on her mount with one leg in a stirrup and the other hooked over a special pommel, in the serene conviction that this precarious pose kept her dignity intact. Plains Indian women customarily rode astride; their reaction to these sidesaddle Christian sisters was not recorded, but it is doubtful that they envied them. If this was the vanguard of civilization, its benefits for Indian women were not readily apparent.

Insofar as there was envy on either side, it may have been the missionary women who envied the Indians. Sarah Smith described in elegant detail the riding tack of the Indian wives of Captain Drips: Macompemay (an Oto) and his second wife, whose tribal affiliation was not identified. They were "trimmed off in high style, I assure you." Macompemay was riding a beautiful white horse, with a saddle decorated with "beads and many little gingles [sic]. A handsome white sheepskin covering for the horse, cut in fringes ½ a yard deep, ornamented with collars and a great number of thimbles pierced in the top and hung to the fringe like little bells, making a fine gingle as she rides along." Then came the second wife, "with her scarlet blanket, painted face & handkerchief on her head, sitting astride," Smith added. "This is the fashion of the country."[14]

On the second day out of Westport, Mary Walker was so sore and tired that she could hardly sit up in camp, yet she found the energy to write to her parents. "We are traveling on the dry sea. For days and weeks we shall see nothing but the big buffalow [*sic*] pasture."[15] This was a far cry from the gently undulating meadow described by Asa Smith, who snored loudly in the same tent with the Walkers. It was going to be a long trip for Mary Walker.

Sutter found more convivial companionship than the missionary contingent, in the person of Sir William Drummond Stewart, formerly of Murthley Castle in Scotland. Sir William was some of the things that Sutter pretended to be: an officer who had fought in the Napoleonic Wars, was decorated for gallantry at Waterloo, and was rich. There was something impulsive in the handsome Scot's character too. Stewart had impregnated a servant, but he had the decency to marry her and legitimize his child. Married life was not for Sir William, however, so he sought excitement in North America, where he hunted buffalo and the lesser creatures that abounded on the western plains. He hired several mountain men to escort him on his 1838 expedition. Sir William loved the frontier life, but he traveled in a style that befitted his wealth and station. The epicurean Scot stuffed his wagon with liquors and delicacies that were beyond the ken of the average fur trapper. The bibulous Sutter would have treasured a wee dram of fine Scotch or a snifter of well-aged brandy after a hard day in the saddle. Sutter knew that whiskey improved his disposition, if not his character.[16]

Stewart was more than just a traveling bartender for itinerant merchants who were down on their luck. He was a font of knowledge about the West. Many years later, when Sutter told his story to the California historian Hubert Howe Bancroft, he claimed that he originally planned to go to California "through Sonora, but was advised by Sir William Drummond Stewart . . . to go by way of Fort Hall by the Oregon route."[17] Sutter's recollection is puzzling. If he intended to take the Sonoran route to California, why did he bother to connect with the American Fur Company caravan that was headed in the wrong direction? He knew the way to Santa Fe. Perhaps he had told his friends in Westport that he was taking the southwestern route to California to mislead his creditors. Maybe he invented the change of route in order to respond to Laufkotter's claim (published nine years before Sutter dictated his reminiscence to Bancroft) that the two were supposed to meet in Santa Fe. Sutter was an inveterate name dropper and perhaps merely wanted to use Stewart's name in order to bolster his own reputation with Bancroft by associating himself with the Scot. Whatever the case, Sutter was off on a roundabout tour of far western enterprises that would delay his arrival in California by many months.

During the day the travelers fell into a predictable routine. The wagons and carts led the procession in single file, followed by pack animals and cattle. "Sometimes we ladies ride behind the whole, sometimes behind the hindermost wagon and the mules," Myra Eells recounted. "It is not safe for any to be far in the rear," she continued, "because they are always exposed to be robbed of their horses and, if not killed by wild Indians, themselves left to wander on foot."[18] The parade of mountain men, merchants, missionaries, and their livestock stretched to half a mile. But the women sometimes fell behind and found themselves in the company of the well-dressed (but not so well-mounted) Swiss adventurer. One day he (or perhaps Stewart) regaled Mrs. Eells with stories about "Swiss dogs digging men out who are buried in snow."[19] On another occasion Mary Walker lagged behind after a sleepless night caused by a toothache. "Capt. Sutor happened to be with me," she recorded in her diary, "and not having on his spurs was unable to keep up. So he & I were left alone without guide."[20] The laggards made it into camp without mishap.

The route to the rendezvous followed the path that would soon be known as the Oregon Trail. They skirted the Kansas River until they struck north along the Big Blue River, which took them to the Platte River in today's Nebraska. As they headed west along the Platte, the country rose up before the caravan. The higher country was drier too, a blessing after rains had soaked the sojourners in early May. The climatic change transfigured the environment. Grass and trees became scarce, and the land took on a barren aspect unlike anything east of the 100th meridian. Sutter had seen this magical change occur on the Santa Fe Trail, but it must have come as a surprise to the missionaries.

Impressive red rock formations began to mark the trail. Asa Smith described one of these huge monoliths (perhaps Courthouse Rock) as having "the appearance of the work of art rather than of nature." It was "nearly perpendicular . . . & seemed nearly square." On May 26 Smith marveled at Chimney Rock, one the Oregon Trail's great landmarks: "Its form is pyramidal, & at the top it shoots up perpendicularly to the height of several [hundred] feet." "How the earth around [it] should have washed away," he wondered, "is very singular."[21] His wife thought the massive bluffs along this part of the route looked like "statuary, forts, temples, etc. As if nature[,] tired of waiting the advances of civilization[,] had erected her own temples."[22] Thus, sidesaddles and all, they rode on through a landscape that turned strange and romantic before their eyes.

Four days' march from Chimney Rock brought the caravan to Fort Laramie at the junction of the North Platte and Laramie Rivers. Two enterprising fur traders, William Sublette and Robert Campbell, originally built and operated the post in 1836, but the American Fur Company bought them out. When Sutter passed through its gates, the Chouteau brothers owned the company and the fort. Hand-hewn cottonwood pickets formed the palisade that enclosed the fort. Like most fur-trading establishments the post had two bastions situated at diagonal corners. Within the fort's walls were storage rooms and a store where Indians and traders exchanged goods.

Even though the beaver trade was in decline, Fort Laramie was a going concern when Sutter saw it. The post produced an annual average of a thousand packs of buffalo robes as well as substantial quantities of other skins and small furs. In 1840 the post was still profitable enough to justify rebuilding it in adobe instead of wood. After a month on the plains, Sutter must have savored the bustle and prosperity of this important frontier enterprise. If he had his eye out for model establishments, he would have done well to pay close attention to Fort Laramie and the other fur-trade posts that he encountered on his way to California. Indeed, the physical layout of the fort that he built in the Sacramento Valley was much like the design of the places that he saw on his way to Oregon.[23]

Mary Walker noted the presence of children of mixed racial parentage within the fort, and it seemed not to please her. "The half breed children look as likely as any," she dryly observed.[24] This free and easy life must have seemed barbarous to the missionaries. In the East racially mixed marriages placed spouses and their children beyond the pale of polite society; in the Far West such unions between fur traders and Indian women were common and acceptable. Miscegenation was a commonplace fact of life at Fort Laramie, just as it would be at Sutter's California fort in a few years.[25]

On June 2, after two days' rest, the caravan moved up the trail toward the Popo Agie River, site of the 1838 rendezvous. Captain Drips sent a courier to the Green River, where the previous year's rendezvous had occurred, to alert anyone there to the change in locations. The messenger erected a sign that gave the geographical particulars of the new gathering place and the two main attractions to be found there: "Plenty of whiskey and white women."[26] How the mountain men interpreted this pithy advertisement is an open question. Likewise, one can only wonder what the pious Christian women would have thought about their presence at the Popo Agie being associated with liquor.

The trail was becoming steeper and more rugged. Occasional rain made the going uncomfortable, as did the diarrhea that was apparently caused by the constant diet of buffalo meat. On June 12 Sutter and his companions caught sight of the snow-clad Wind River Range, their first glimpse of the Rocky Mountains, a sight that must have reminded Sutter of Switzerland and his family. Two days later they reached Independence Rock, another of the overland trail's great landmarks. As migration along this trail swelled in the 1840s, hundreds of Oregon- and California-bound overlanders carved their names in its rock surface. The caravan then creaked up into the sublime Sweetwater River country, where mountains rose on either side of the clear and fresh stream. The rigors of travel became more pronounced, but inspiring mountain vistas distracted the attention of weary mountaineers, missionaries, and private adventurers alike.

On June 23 the caravan crossed the Popo Agie and heaved into the rendezvous grounds. Company trappers, free (independent) trappers, traders, Nez Perces, Flatheads, and Indians from a medley of other tribes were already there. Now-famous trappers like Jim Bridger, Joseph Meek, and Joseph R. Walker mingled with the unheralded buckskin-clad men and women who were the shock troops of the fur business. The rendezvous was a month-long, brawling trade fair. Free trappers lived in the mountains during the trapping season and sold their furs to the highest bidder at one of the trading posts or at the annual rendezvous. Company men took their cache of cured furs to their firm's representative for payment. Trappers who had purchased their provisions and equipment on credit from merchants the year before showed up to pay off their debts and have a spree. Freed from the isolation of mountain camps and the social constraints of life in Indian communities, mountain men raced horses, gambled, consorted with Indian prostitutes, wrestled, sang at the tops of their lungs, danced, gambled some more, fought promiscuously, shot targets, shot each other, drank continuously, and slept it off. They thought they were having a grand time.

Business at the rendezvous floated on a sea of whiskey, the worst kind of cheap, adulterated liquor that was custom blended for the fur trade. Mountain men and Indians alike drank their fill with predictable results: a diminished sense of responsibility, blurred judgment, and violence. Not a few of these people left the rendezvous poorer than when they had arrived. Sharp traders drove their best bargains with men who were stinking drunk, blind drunk, roaring drunk, mean drunk, and just plain drunk. Captain Drips had included a goodly portion of liquor with the wares he transported from Missouri. Some American Fur Company mules packed a pair of oddly configured barrels that were concave on one side in order to fit the conformation of the animals who carried them. Thus some of the fur-bearing animals of the Rocky Mountains were exchanged for alcohol that was consumed in a few weeks' time. The profits from this exchange trickled down the mountain streams to the Platte, to the Missouri, and eventually into the pockets of hard-fisted businessmen like Pierre Chouteau, Jr., in St. Louis and John Jacob Astor in New York City.[27] This conspicuous liquor trade was contrary to the U.S. trade and intercourse act that prohibited the importation of alcohol to Indian country, but federal officials were nowhere to be seen.

Mountain men were more than colorful drunks. Their numbers were not huge, but their impact was large. Free trappers, company men, and Indian trappers alike transformed the ecology of the American Far West. Furs had been a high-profit item on the North American frontier since the beginning of colonial times, but in the first half of the nineteenth century the demand for broad-brimmed, high-crowned beaver felt hats drove the American fur trade. Manufacturers in the United States and Europe made the highest-quality hats from beaver fur felt, so trappers scoured the continent and trapped beaver to near extinction in first one watershed then another.

In Sutter's time trappers killed about a hundred thousand beavers per year. The destruction of the beaver population had an impact throughout the environment. Most beavers are dam builders. Their log, mud, and brush constructions created reservoirs that flooded lowlands and sustained a wetter, nutrient-rich environment. Marshes and meadows extended from the margins of beaver ponds. Succulent grasses, a stable water source, and fish attracted large and small animals, followed by predators and scavengers, including bears, mountain lions, wolves, coyotes, and humans. When the trappers destroyed the beavers, the dams disintegrated, ponds emptied, meadows dried up, and the animals moved on or starved. The mountain men moved on too, leaving the Indians with an environment that was measurably less productive and less able to support a hunting and gathering economy, much less the fur trade.[28] It was as though the fur traders had dropped poison pellets into the clear mountain streams of the West. By 1838 the fur trade was in a permanent state of decline. The roistering mountain men at the rendezvous would soon be unemployed and would need someplace to go. While some returned to the East, and others went to New Mexico and Oregon, Sutter would provide them with new prospects in California.

Indians were left with hard choices. For a generation or more they had based their economies in part on the fur trade. They relied on traders for metal ware, blankets, textiles, guns, ammunition, and—sadly—alcohol. Without beaver they had to move on to new hunting grounds, emphasize raiding their neighbors (Indian and white alike), join other tribes with reliable resources, or take up some entirely new kind of life—perhaps the settled agricultural existence that U.S. Indian agents recommended. The choices that they made were forced on them in part by the devastating aftermath of the fur trade.

John Sutter did not consider the implications of fur trapping at the rendezvous. He came to the Popo Agie to do business, and he probably did it in the customary way among the mountain men and traders. Liquor was likely a part of Sutter's small inventory, if his emphasis on alcohol in the Santa Fe trade and other business dealings provides any guide. In one of his deals Sutter took an order for a hundred dollars' worth of beaver payable by the Hudson's Bay Company. He figured that the order was worth $130 at the rendezvous and decided to turn it to account there. He bought an Indian boy from Bill Burroughs, who had acquired him from Kit Carson. "This was a large price," Sutter recalled, "but the boy could speak English," presumably an Indian language, and perhaps Spanish too.[29]

The origins of the Indian boy are a mystery. Carson and Burroughs had traveled and trapped widely in the West, from the northern Rockies to New Mexico and California. The boy could have come from any of these places. New Mexicans and the Apaches, Navahos, and Utes had been stealing each other's women and children for centuries. This vengeful practice had resulted in a trade in slaves that stretched from old Mexico to Canada.[30] The purchase of the anonymous Indian boy was Sutter's first foray into the Indian slave-trading game. It would not be his last.

Not all the business opportunities at the rendezvous appealed to Sutter. Several men offered to join his California expedition, "to go as a band of robbers" to steal livestock from the missions and ranchos.[31] Sutter rejected these offers but found two new companions who were more to his liking: mountain men Niklaus Allgeier, a German, and the Austrian Sebastian Keyser. The terms of their engagement with Sutter are not known, but the two men worked for him in California for several years. Other mountain men from the rendezvous may merely have decided to travel with Sutter without any formal obligations to him. Perhaps others invested in Sutter's enterprise or agreed to work for him in return for future considerations. Three weeks of besotted trading, carousing, and convivial conversation gave Sutter ample opportunities to convince his inebriated listeners that the road to California was the way to riches.

A few days after a raucous Fourth of July celebration, Francis Ermatinger, a Hudson's Bay Company trader, arrived with a party of Cayuses and other Indians to guide the missionaries to Oregon. On July 12 Ermatinger, missionaries, the Sutter entourage, and the Oregon Indians headed up the trail. The mountainous terrain was rugged, and the missionary women suffered greatly. On June 15 the party crossed South Pass and the Great Divide and entered the Oregon Country—that vast territory extending west of the Great Divide to the Pacific Ocean and bounded by latitudes 54° 40′ on the north and 42° on the south. The United States and Great Britain disputed ownership of Oregon but in 1819 had agreed to joint occupation. Neither the United States nor England established formal government control in any part of Oregon. Because it was large and well-organized, the Hudson's Bay Company exercised quasi-governmental authority over everyone, including the Americans who settled in the Willamette Valley.

For all practical purposes, the "Honorable Company" controlled the fur trade in all of the Oregon Country, and its managers wanted to keep it that way.

The royal monopoly on the fur trade gave the Hudson's Bay Company the luxury of conserving the fur-bearing animal population that it trapped so that it could sustain the yield of pelts in the country it controlled. When faced with U.S. competition, however, the company's practical-minded British businessmen decided to obliterate fur-bearing animals on Oregon's southern flank. As early as 1824 Governor George Simpson of the Hudson's Bay Company wrote that "if the country becomes exhausted in Fur bearing animals [Americans] can have no inducement to proceed thither."[32] Simpson ordered the creation of what he called a "fur desert" that would deter Americans from encroaching on the Honorable Company's domain. In 1827 the American fur trapper Jedediah Smith drove a herd of California horses into southern Oregon, thus demonstrating that the Hudson's Bay Company domain was vulnerable from that direction. Dr. John McLoughlin, the alarmed Hudson's Bay Company chief factor at Fort Vancouver, therefore sent an annual company brigade into California in order to scour the country from the Snake River into northern Mexico.[33] Michel Laframboise led a company brigade into the Sacramento Valley while Sutter marched across the continent as a guest of the Hudson's Bay Company.[34]

In late July Sutter and his companions reached Fort Hall, on the Snake River near the site of modern Pocatello. The Hudson's Bay Company factor, Thomas McKay (stepson of the redoubtable Dr. McLoughlin), entertained the tired emigrants. McKay gave the travelers good advice about the hard road that lay ahead of them, and three days later they pushed on.[35] They followed the Snake River for a while and then veered northwest to the Boise River. On August 15 they reached Fort Boise, another Hudson's Bay Company post, where Francis Payette entertained them. Payette set a sumptuous table, filled with wild game, fish, and vegetables from the post's garden, a far cry from the simple fare that McKay had provided. Payette perhaps furnished a model for Sutter's famed hospitality in California.[36]

Five days later Sutter and what remained of the party (some of the missionaries had gone ahead of him) left Fort Boise and headed for Waiilatpu, the Methodist mission run by Marcus and Narcissa Whitman on the Columbia River. On August 29 Sutter and his companions caught sight of the mission. It was a primitive place, thought Myra Eells: "The bedsteads are boards nailed to the side of the house, sink fashion, then some blankets and husks make the bed"; but she allowed that such beds were "good compared with traveling accommodations." There were signs of prosperity too. Wheat, corn, and potato fields surrounded the mission house. Just as everyone sat down to a noon meal of melons, pumpkin pies, and milk, "the house became thronged with

Indians & we were obliged to suspend eating & shake hands with some 30, 40, or 50 of them."[37] They were probably Cayuses, Walla Wallas, and Nez Perces.

Sutter permanently parted company with the missionaries at the Whitman mission. He gave his French and English dictionary to the Walkers, a sentimental present that they kept for many years.[38] Sutter's objective was now to reach Fort Vancouver by way of Fort Walla Walla (another Hudson's Bay Company post), and the Dalles, the rapids of the Columbia River. Then, he thought, he would turn south to California. The route was not as direct as he believed it might be. He reached the Dalles without incident and agreed to go with Daniel Lee, a missionary who was driving a herd of horses to the Willamette Valley. The way through the Cascade Mountains was circuitous because of the ruggedness of the terrain. Sutter's mountain men companions, probably Allgeier and Keyser, became impatient and convinced him to take a direct route through the mountains. Sutter complied, made his excuses to Lee, and soon learned why the missionary's route seemed so roundabout. The country was the most rugged that Sutter had ever seen. He later claimed that they had to fashion rope slings to lower their horses over cliffs. Nevertheless, the famished men reached the Willamette eight days ahead of Lee.[39] The arduous journey through the Cascades tells a great deal about Sutter's ruggedness when he was in his early thirties. He probably recalled this experience years later when he sent relief to immigrants in the California mountains.

Sutter rested in the Willamette Valley settlements until early October. The Oregon settlers thought well of Sutter and hoped he would stay, but he would not be persuaded. He canoed downstream to Fort Vancouver, where the chief trader, James Douglas, welcomed him in late October.[40] Sutter presented a letter of introduction from Sir William Drummond Stewart to Douglas, who was suitably impressed with the letter and with Sutter too. He judged the Swiss to be a likely man, which is not too surprising considering the sanitized biography that he heard. Sutter claimed that he held a captaincy in the French army and that he had left Europe with substantial capital. He had invested in businesses, but the panic of 1837 had caused a reversal in his fortunes. The canny Scot reported that "the object of his visit is not exactly known," but he was relieved to know that Sutter had "no connection whatever with the U.S. government. At present, he proposes to drive cattle from California to the Willamette."[41] Following Stewart's example, Douglas then wrote a letter of introduction for Sutter, who added it to his collection of similar documents. He would have an impressive sheaf of letters from some of the most-respected men in the American West by the time he reached California.

Sutter intended to go overland to California from Oregon. Many years later he claimed that several former Hudson's Bay Company employees had "wanted to go with me to buy cattle for their farms on the Columbia River."[42] But with winter closing in, a cattle drive would have to wait until spring. Sutter was anxious to get to California, so Douglas convinced him to take the Hudson's Bay Company bark *Columbia* to the Sandwich (Hawaiian) Islands, where he could find another ship for the voyage to California. If a California-bound ship was available, Sutter could probably make it to California faster than by crossing the mountains. So he sold his horses and mules (some of which he evidently acquired at the rendezvous) and bought cabin passage for himself and steerage for his Indian boy and Wetler. The other men, including Allgeier and Keyser, were supposed to complete the journey to California by land and rendezvous with Sutter.[43]

By the end of 1838 Sutter had seen most of the important frontier enterprises in the North American West—the Santa Fe trade in the Southwest and the American and British fur trade in Oregon and the Rocky Mountains. He had also seen something of the illicit trade in stolen horses and Indians. Sutter formed friendships with many of the important figures who dominated the scene at the time. He apparently made good use of the trade goods that he brought with him, but the journey had given him something even more valuable than money—knowledge of how frontier business was conducted. The information and acquaintances that Sutter made on the Oregon Trail would be invaluable in California. He boarded the *Columbia* bound for Hawaii, hoping that this roundabout route would quickly get him to his destination, but the islands held surprises and unexpected opportunities.

CHAPTER 4

Crossroads of the Pacific

The *Columbia* sailed for the Sandwich Islands on November 11. Twenty-eight days later Sutter disembarked at Honolulu. Unfortunately for him, the *Bolívar Libertador* had just sailed for California; there would not be another ship bound for the Mexican province for many months.[1] Of course, Sutter had no idea that he would be marooned in the islands for that long. We might imagine that he greatly enjoyed his first weeks in the balmy Pacific climate after months of enduring the rain and damp of the Pacific Northwest.

Sutter quickly became acquainted with Honolulu's leading merchants. George Pelly (the local Hudson's Bay Company agent) and William French met him on shipboard. French struck up an especially close relationship with the plausible and well-dressed Swiss. The day after Sutter debarked French entered a credit on Sutter's new account: "Labour .50."[2] It is unlikely that Sutter "laboured" for French for such a paltry sum, but he may have employed his Indian servant on some small task for the Honolulu merchant. Sutter wisely placed the sum on his account as a credit. Over the next few weeks he purchased clothing, pipes, cigars, and other items amounting to $104. Then on January 24 he paid his account in full, an event that would be unremarkable except for his track record with payment of debts.[3] Sutter, however, was not finished with running up the debit side of his ledger.

Sutter had scarcely reached shore before the merchant class noted his presence. Faxon Dean Atherton, already an experienced trader in California and Hawaii at twenty-three, met "a Swiss gent called Shuiter" on the day of Sutter's arrival. He informed Atherton that "he was going to California for the purpose of taking a look at the country. [He] has been travelling in the Rocky

Mountains these last two years, has a farm in Missouri, [and] is looking for a place suitable for settlers which he hopes to bring from Switzerland."[4] On Christmas day Sutter dined with sea captains, merchants, and the American consul, John Coffin Jones.[5] Many of these figures had sailed to California several times and doubtless told Sutter a good deal about it.

Although he was impatient to leave, Sutter soon settled into the social life of Honolulu, where he made many useful contacts. The members of foreign community of Hawaii were glad to know Sutter. After they read his letters of recommendation, they were happy to provide him with more of the same. In addition to American consul Jones, Sutter met consular officials of England and France. Through Jones, he made the acquaintance of his stepson, William Heath Davis, who knew the Hawaii-California trade and who would eventually help Sutter get established in California. He also met plenty of merchants, some of whom did business with the California coast. William French succumbed to Sutter's charm and sold him hundreds of dollars' worth of clothing and other goods on credit. Merchant sea captains Eliab Grimes, his nephew Hiram Grimes, and their partner John Sinclair found Sutter to be a compatible spirit. Sutter chafed at being marooned in Hawaii, but the months he spent there were instrumental in assuring that he would later gain a financial foothold in California.[6]

In Sutter's time the Kingdom of Hawaii was still in Native Hawaiian hands, but there was a small and influential foreign community of British, French, and American merchants and missionaries. The Hawaiian chiefs, called Alii, supposedly had divine origins. Commoners, known as Kanakas (now a term applied to all Native Hawaiians), were required to prostrate themselves before the Alii lest their shadows pollute the power of their superiors. Death was the penalty for violating this and other strictly enforced customs. A collection of independent chieftaincies ruled the islands before Captain James Cook arrived in 1778. Cook's discovery, however, led to swift and dramatic changes in Hawaiian society. As with American Indians, the acquisition of guns and metal weapons transformed the war-making capability of Native Hawaiians, while exotic diseases sharply reduced the Hawaiian population. Kamehameha I seized the advantages that European weapons provided, eventually consolidating his power as the first king of Hawaii. In due course Protestant missionaries from the United States established themselves, along with Yankee merchants and entrepreneurs from other nations. In general Hawaiians treated the newcomers (except for common sailors and such) as an elite class who were permitted to mingle with the Alii. Meanwhile Christian religion and other new ideas broke down adherence to time-honored customs and eroded the hierarchical structure of Hawaiian society.[7]

The advent of seaborne trade also provided an escape for some Kanaka commoners who shipped as crew aboard whalers and merchantmen, although they were not entirely free to decide how to sell their own labor. The Alii often acted as labor contractors, arranging three-year contracts with Europeans who needed workers. The Alii received a percentage of the Kanakas' wages as part of the bargain. Working under these coercive contracts, hundreds of Kanakas scattered across the Pacific and around the world. Some Hawaiians worked at Fort Vancouver and other Hudson's Bay Company posts. Other islanders worked under contract to the Russian-American Company in Alaska. Marcus and Narcissa Whitman employed a Kanaka at their Oregon mission. In the 1830s Hawaiians were a common sight in the Pacific Northwest and California, where they worked as able-bodied seamen, fur trappers, agricultural labor, herders, and domestics.[8]

King Kamehameha III ruled Hawaii when Sutter got there, although the local Alii had much to say in the islands' governance. In 1838 Hawaiians and foreigners alike recognized that the island kingdom was ripe for the plucking, but who would take it: Russia, England, France, the United States? The king made powerful friends where he could find them and affected the sartorial splendor of European nobility: dress uniform, epaulettes, sword, sash, medal, and gold brocade; but the image of power was not in accord with the military and political reality of the Pacific. Any man-of-war could quickly reduce Honolulu's fortifications to rubble and drive its army from the field. Kamehameha III, therefore, walked a decidedly narrow path in the politics of the Pacific frontier. Sutter would soon play a small role in these matters.[9]

Sutter's brilliant personality and splendid clothes impressed high-ranking Hawaiians as well as foreigners. He later claimed that King Kamehameha III was so taken with his pretended military experience that he offered him the command of the Hawaiian army, but Sutter turned down the offer.[10] When he insisted on continuing his voyage to California, "the King gave me eight men . . . for three years."[11] Sutter was supposed to pay them ten dollars a month for three years and send them back to Hawaii, the usual labor contract arrangement. According to one historian, Sutter's contract was not with Kamehameha but with the Alii Mataio Kekuanoa, governor of Honolulu.[12] Whether Sutter acquired the services of the Hawaiians because of the king's generosity or the governor's calculation of profit on Hawaii's human capital, the Kanakas proved helpful to Sutter in California. Two of the men brought their wives, who were "very useful in teaching the Indian girls to wash, sew, &c. . . . I could not have settled the country without the aid of these Kanakas." "The men were very glad to go with me, and at the expiration of their time, they would not leave me."[13] So now Sutter had a band of thirteen followers: Wetler (who had passed the time in Hawaii as a cabinet-maker), a second unnamed German artisan who joined Sutter in Honolulu, the Indian boy, and ten Native Hawaiians. Pablo Gutiérrez, Niklaus Allgeier, and others would join him in California. But no ship appeared on the horizon to take Sutter and his retinue to California.

Help was at hand. The 88-ton bark *Clementine* was for sale, but no one was interested in purchasing it. William French chartered the vessel for inter-island trade and made one voyage to Maui while Sutter was in Honolulu.[14] French approached the owner, Jules Dudoit, with a scheme that might make some money out of the ship and provide Sutter with passage to California. He proposed to charter the *Clementine* for a trading voyage to California via New Archangel, the Russian-American Company post in Alaska, with Sutter as supercargo (the person in charge of selling the goods). Dudoit agreed to this arrangement. The bulk of the cargo belonged to French and Dudoit.[15] Sutter had some goods of his own. He served as supercargo without pay but purchased merchandise to sell on his own account, running up his bill with French to almost three thousand dollars before sailing.[16] He later claimed that he purchased the *Clementine* with the proceeds of his voyage to Alaska, but that was not true.[17]

While French, Dudoit, and Sutter were packing goods aboard the *Clementine,* the Reverend Hiram Bingham published a letter in the *Hawaiian Spectator.* Bingham, who was from Vermont, was among the first contingent of Protestant missionaries sent by the American Board of Commissioners for Foreign Missions—the same outfit that sponsored the Oregon missionaries. He also advised Kamehameha III on matters of domestic and foreign relations. Bingham's letter reported that a party of Indians "headed by a FRENCHMAN" had attacked, wounded, and robbed William Gray, one of the Oregon missionaries with whom Sutter traveled. This report was old news and referred to an event that had taken place in 1837 when Gray was on his way back to the United States from Oregon Territory to recruit reinforcements for the mission.[18]

Bingham's misleading report was part of a long-standing religious quarrel between Protestant missionaries and Roman Catholic priests and an international dispute involving the Hawaiian Kingdom, France, and England. The *Clementine* bobbed in the middle of these roiled waters. The trouble began in 1831 when the Hawaiian chiefs (at the urging of Bingham and other Protestant missionaries) expelled Catholic priests from the islands. In 1836 a Catholic priest belonging to a French missionary order attempted to break the Alii's ban, only to have the Hawaiians order him out of the kingdom. Now the matter became embroiled in national and imperial ambitions. While the priest waited for the order to be carried out, the coincidental arrival of French and

British warships forestalled his expulsion. The Hawaiians' religious restrictions were an affront to France, which was then maneuvering to obtain the Marquesa Islands and perhaps Hawaii too. The priest happened to be a British subject, so the British consul in Honolulu (backed by British naval strength) and the captain of the French man-of-war cooperated in maintaining the right of the missionary to remain in Hawaii. The Alii agreed, but only under the condition that the missionary would not preach or teach the Catholic faith.[19]

Perhaps encouraged by the willingness of British and French authorities to compel the admission of priests to the islands, if not to preach, two priests disembarked at Honolulu in 1837. One was French and the other British, an unlikely but winning combination in this case. Both had been expelled in 1831, and now the Hawaiians again ordered them out. They had come aboard the brig *Clementine,* which was owned by Dudoit, a British citizen of French extraction. When the *Clementine* was scheduled to sail, Hawaiian constables forcibly placed the priests aboard over the objections of Dudoit, who claimed that by compelling him to carry the unwilling priests the Hawaiian authorities had seized his ship. He struck the British flag from the masthead and took his crew ashore, leaving the priests to fend for themselves on the unmanned vessel. The British consul promptly met Dudoit in the street and burned the British colors, which was evidently a dramatic protest against the Hawaiians' actions.[20]

Once again British and French men-of-war appeared on the horizon at about the same time. The two commanders first tried diplomacy to get the priests back onto Hawaiian soil, but to no avail. Without further ado, they jointly blockaded the harbor. The British officer boarded the *Clementine* and hoisted the Union Jack, while his French counterpart landed three hundred sailors and marines to protect the priests as they made the short walk from the harbor to the mission buildings. The Hawaiians had no answer for this show of force except to permit the priests to stay until a ship arrived to take them to some "civilized" part of the world. The Alii saved face by forbidding the priests to preach or teach their religion while they remained in Hawaii. While events transpired, Dudoit offered his services to the French captain, who immediately appointed him a French consular agent.[21]

All of this explains why Bingham's letter was so inflammatory. Moreover, Sutter read it as he was preparing to sail to California on the *Clementine.* Bingham's story seemed calculated to raise anti-French feelings and to drive a wedge into French-British cooperation in the ongoing controversy over Catholic missionaries. Dudoit may have encouraged Sutter to respond to Bingham's assertions; but Sutter, a dedicated Francophile, did not need much encouragement. On March 28, 1839, the *Sandwich Island Gazette* published his response, correcting "a little error" in Bingham's account. The editor prefaced Sutter's letter with his regret that "the Sandwich Island Missionaries should seize with such avidity on every circumstance, which may by them be considered calculated to reflect dishonor on the French people, particularly at a time when a French ship of war is expected here, to demand satisfaction for the insults offered to that nation by this government."[22]

Characteristically, Sutter combined fabrication with fact in order to save French honor. "As I was formerly an officer of the Swiss guard in the French service," he lied, "I consider it my duty to defend the honour of the French nation" against Bingham's assertion that a Frenchman had led Sioux warriors against Gray's party. After explaining the basic facts surrounding the incident, Sutter got to the heart of the matter. "The Sioux war party was not commanded by a Frenchman, but by a three fourth[s] Indian," the son of "a Sioux woman and du Chene," an interpreter for the Sioux.[23] Thus Sutter countered Bingham's religious and national bigotry with his own racial bigotry.

It is difficult to tell what effect Sutter's newspaper letter may have had on Hawaiian and foreigners' feelings about the French. Ten weeks after Sutter left Hawaii, Captain C. P. T. Laplace, commander of a French frigate, forced the Hawaiian government to recognize religious freedom for Catholics and required a $20,000 bond from the chiefs to guarantee it. Had they refused, the French ship would have bombarded Honolulu and the Native Hawaiian population who lived there. Laplace offered sanctuary on his ship for foreigners, except for Bingham and the other American missionaries, whom he regarded as the true instigators of these unfortunate events. In the end, the chiefs posted bond and bombardment was not necessary. The Protestant monopoly on Christian proselyting was broken, and Bingham sailed for the United States.[24]

The *Clementine* sailed for the Russian-American Company outpost of New Archangel on Sitka Sound on April 20. Sutter's main memory of his one-month visit to New Archangel concerned the lively social life at this isolated post and the exotic dances that he shared with the Russian ladies. The community was isolated, but its inhabitants attempted to re-create the class distinctions, social life, and comforts of Russia. The orderly, hierarchical society that included Sutter among the elite was much to his liking. More importantly, he found in New Archangel another variation on the basic strategy of exploiting Native peoples' labor for the benefit of Europeans.[25]

Like the Hudson's Bay Company, the Russian-American Company, founded in 1799, was a royal fur-trade monopoly with quasi-governmental powers. The chief objects of the Russians, however, were the fur seal and especially the sea otter, since its thick pelt was highly prized in China. Beginning in the Aleutian Islands, Russian sea-otter hunting eventually extended to Kodiak Island, the southeast Alaskan mainland, and down the coast to California—much to the consternation of Spanish and Mexican authorities, who regarded the Russians as poachers. Sea-otter hunting was a seagoing venture. The hunters, principally Aleuts and Koniags from the territory claimed by the Russians, went out in small skin-covered kayaks (called *baidarka*s by the Russians) and killed the otters with darts or arrows attached to a line. The hunters were so effective that they managed to destroy sea-otter populations in Alaska, a situation that had brought Russians into California's coastal waters by 1803.[26]

The success of the sea-otter trade rested on the availability of skilled hunters, principally Native Alaskans who worked on shares under the supervision of company officials, their wages depending on the success of the hunt. The Russian-American Company recruited Russian and Siberian men for seal hunting and for supervising the Native sea-otter hunters as well as for general labor. By Sutter's time, these fur hunters—still called *promyshlenniki* in the fur trade—worked for wages under contract for a term of several years. Because insufficient numbers of men were willing to immigrate even temporarily to Alaska, the company had increasingly come to rely on Native workers and the Creole offspring of Russian men and their Native American wives. These employees too customarily worked on a contract basis before the formation of the Russian-American Company, although in the early period of fur exploitation in Alaska the Russians sometimes had used brutal means to force Aleut and Koniag hunters to do their bidding. The company also drafted Native Alaskans to defend their posts, a practice that Sutter must have noticed during his visit.[27]

As always, epidemic diseases accompanied the European invasion of Alaska; so the Aleut and Koniag population had sharply declined. Russians tried to replace them with Tlingits, whose powerful clans dominated southeastern Alaska. But the Tlingits, armed by Yankee and British seagoing traders, at first resisted Russian advances and the attempted Russian invasion of their hunting territories. Ultimately, the most reliable source of labor turned out to be the offspring of Russian men and Aleut, Koniag, and even Tlingit women. As in the case of the British, French, and American fur business, children turned out to be an unforeseen but important by-product of the Russian-American Company's errand in the wilderness. And as in other parts of North America the Creole population became indispensable to the trade and to the work demands of the company's isolated American colony.[28]

First Yankee ships under contract and then Russian vessels carried the hunters and their baidarkas into California waters. The company eventually occupied California land too. The fur posts in Alaska could not produce enough food to be self-sufficient, and Russian sources could not supply the shortfall. Consequently, the hungry Russians, lacking grain, flour, beef, and vegetables, looked to California for relief. In 1812 the company established a small port facility at Bodega Bay, about twenty miles north of the Spanish settlements around San Francisco Bay, and a fortified post at Ross, twenty miles farther north. Spain (and Mexico after 1821) claimed this territory. Neither nation had occupied it or had the military power to evict the Russians. In the face of ineffective Spanish and Mexican protests the Russian-American Company built a palisaded fort and developed farms and livestock ranchos at Bodega Bay and along the lower Slavianka (Russian) River.[29] Ross was supposed to be an agricultural colony that would furnish provender for the northern company posts. Native Alaskans, Kanakas, and local Pomo Indians farmed and herded cattle, but Ross never succeeded in fulfilling the Russian-American Company's expectations. By the time Sutter visited Sitka, company officials were thinking about abandoning the place.[30] The Russian headquarters at Sitka was the penultimate stop on Sutter's tour of western enterprises. Here, too, he learned about California and broadened his knowledge of frontier business and labor practices.

What did Sutter learn on his journey? Most importantly, he could see that access to and control over Native peoples' labor was indispensable to most frontier enterprises where fortunes were to be made. In some cases direct control—as with contract laborers and wage employees—was best. Circumstances sometimes permitted the outright enslavement of Native peoples. Indirect access to a seemingly independent Native labor force could be serviceable too, as in the case of Indians who participated in the American fur trade or transcontinental horse rustling. In all cases, mastery over economic exchange through the manipulation of prices for goods sold and received was helpful. By extending credit to workers, traders converted Native peoples into a debtor class who were obligated to bring in furs or to work directly for the traders. Caught up in debt, free workers became peons who owed their labor to their creditors.

Sutter's second lesson was that frontier enterprise was not about competition and free markets but about control and monopoly if one could achieve it. The Hudson's Bay Company and the Russian-American Company held extensive government privileges and political power within their respective territories. The owners of the American Fur Company and similar firms would have cherished such governmental arrangements if they could have been obtained. Instead men like Astor tried to drive out competitors with sharp business practices.

Third, Sutter relearned an old lesson that he knew from his life in Switzerland: connections counted. At the various stops on his grand tour of frontier enterprises, he gathered letters of recommendation from respected westerners.

Some of Sutter's biographers have portrayed this exercise as a kind of con game where he induced important men to write letters that repeated his suave prevarications about a fine military career and business experience.[31] Certainly there was some of that, but the men who endorsed Sutter did not do so because they had been fooled. They recommended him to the attention of their frontier peers precisely because they were *not* fooled. They did not see him as green and untried, a visionary with utopian ideas. They recognized in him a man who was as calculating and ruthless as they were. They understood that Sutter was a man of energy and nerve, someone who had already crossed continents and oceans in pursuit of his goal. They saw him as a practical man—someone who was quite capable of replicating their own accomplishments. And that is precisely what Sutter intended to do in California.

CHAPTER 5

Into the Valley

The passage from Sitka to California was not an easy voyage. Early summer gales buffeted the *Clementine* as it sailed down the Northwest Coast. By the time the brig reached San Francisco Bay on July 1 or 2, 1839, everyone on board was "starving," Sutter recalled, and he was probably in no condition to savor the realization of his long-sought goal: California, at last.[1]

The diminutive bayside Mexican settlements did not match the splendor of the vast protected bay and its estuaries. In 1839 the ungarrisoned presidio with its few inoperable cannons guarded the bay's entrance, later named the Golden Gate. On the sheltered side of the peninsula the village of Yerba Buena consisted of a few adobe buildings near the anchorage. There were no wharves at the hamlet that in a few years would be renamed San Francisco. A short distance south lay the remnants of the Mission San Francisco de Asís. The *Clementine* may have kept company with a few of the old launches that the merchant William Richardson used to collect produce from around the great, nearly empty bay. Indians sailed Richardson's boats and maintained a small *temescal* (sweat lodge) at the foot of modern-day Sacramento Street, probably within sight of the *Clementine*.[2] The hills around the bay were cloaked in redwood forest, a natural wonder that would be gone in a heartbeat once the gold rush got underway.[3] But the gold discovery was nine years in the future, and much would happen in the meantime. As the battered hull of the *Clementine* rose on the tidal currents that scoured San Francisco Bay, no one could have predicted that Sutter would become a central character in the history of Mexican California.

The Mexican commander of the presidio certainly did not recognize Sutter's arrival as a watershed in Pacific Coast history. He sent an officer and fifteen men to order Sutter to get out. The lawful port of entry was Monterey, the provincial capital, eighty miles to the south. Sutter presented his collection of letters of introduction and pleaded that he and his crew could not venture out again to the pitiless Pacific Ocean without obtaining provisions and repairing the *Clementine*. He got forty-eight hours' grace before sailing to Monterey.[4]

Sutter was in Monterey in time for the Fourth of July.[5] He promptly introduced himself to Monterey's leading merchants, including David Spence, a Scot who had married a *californiana* (a Mexican woman from California). Like many other merchants from the United States and the British Isles, Spence became a Mexican citizen and married into a prominent California family—a move that gained him social, political, and economic connections.[6] Sutter also met Thomas O. Larkin, an American merchant who had been in California for about seven years. Unlike many of his merchant friends, Larkin retained his U.S. citizenship and married a woman from New England. Mexican Californians respected Larkin, and his business acumen ultimately made him a substantial fortune.[7]

Larkin threw a party to celebrate the Fourth of July and invited Sutter to attend.[8] The celebrants represented the elite class of Mexican California: government officials, landholders, and foreign merchants. The guests included Larkin's neighbor, Governor Juan Bautista Alvarado. On Larkin's patio Americans, Scots, Englishmen, one Swiss, and many Mexicans celebrated the independence of the nation that in seven years would wrest California from Mexico. Governor Alvarado no doubt raised a glass to toast the United States on July 4, 1839; a few years later he would be sorry.

Monterey was much like Honolulu, where the Hawaiian king and Alii ostensibly ruled but warily watched the horizon for foreign warships. The navies of the United States, England, Russia, and France routinely patrolled the Pacific Coast and stopped at California ports. Each of these nations had sent exploring expeditions into this region or would soon do so. Californios wondered if these naval and scientific probes were harbingers of political change. England, France, and the United States were the leading contenders to replace Mexico as California's ruler. In the meantime californios professed loyalty to Mexico, while complaining of the government's inefficiency.[9]

California politics were more complicated than Sutter may have gauged from the obvious national and economic interests of the Monterey crowd. Larkin's half brother, John R. Cooper, was married to Governor Alvarado's niece. Larkin had strengthened his relationship with the governor by supporting the revolution through which Alvarado seized power in 1836.[10] Alvarado and other elite, liberal-minded californios—opposed to the conservative, centralist government in Mexico—threw out the lawfully appointed governor and other supporters of centralism with the aid of thirty American riflemen who were willing to fight for Mexican liberalism in return for a fee. Isaac Graham, a Tennesseean, led this motley frontier militia, formed of mountain men, foreign seamen who had jumped ship, and others who loafed around Graham's saw pit and whiskey still in the Santa Cruz Mountains. Governor Alvarado would regret taking help from these rough, impertinent frontiersmen. The Mexican government, with the Texas Revolution and internal politics on its hands, chose to legitimize the revolt by recognizing Alvarado as governor. Larkin quietly supported Alvarado and hoped that his in-law's regime would foster stability and commerce.[11]

The success and quick legitimation of the California coup did not breed unity among the californios. Support for the new regime came mostly from rancheros in the northern part of California, including Governor Alvarado's uncle, Mariano Guadalupe Vallejo, an army officer and landholder who under Alvarado became the comandante general of Mexican forces in California. The central government validated Vallejo's promotion when it recognized Alvarado as California's governor, but Alvarado's troubles had just begun. Southern Californians, feeling that now they did not have enough influence in governmental affairs, opposed the new government. Despite their kinship, Vallejo grew disenchanted with his nephew (both men were in their late twenties in 1836) and became his rival. These details and the nuances of family relationships and rivalries were all lost on the newcomer Sutter, but he was glad to meet the governor and other important people at Larkin's Monterey adobe home.[12]

And, as always, they were glad to meet Sutter. His ambitions—inchoate as they were—matched California's unrealized potential. He used his sheaf of letters of introduction from the leading men on the western frontier like a talisman to gain the trust of Mexicans and foreigners alike. David Spence, Sutter's host in Monterey, said that he had never seen so many letters. Still young (Sutter was thirty-six when he first stood on Larkin's patio), handsome, well-mannered (even in broken Spanish and imperfect English), tanned and fit from more than a year of outdoor life, the well-dressed Swiss gentleman rehearsed anew the well-practiced stories that had served him well for the past several years. He spoke of his military rank and experience—Captain Sutter, formerly of the Swiss Guards in the service of France. He had business experience in Switzerland, Missouri, Santa Fe, and Hawaii. And now here he was, with his brig the *Clementine* (or so he claimed) and his Kanaka and European employees. Sutter was prepared to invest his capital, energy, and imagination in California. At his best, when there were no annoying matters like unpaid debts to disturb the confidence of his listeners, he was irresistible.

On July 5 Sutter formally called on Governor Alvarado in order to elaborate on his plan to settle in California. By this time he had decided to locate in the interior, on the Sacramento River. Precisely when he came to this decision is not known; but from the time of his first visit to Santa Fe Sutter had met mountain men, Indians, and New Mexicans who had been to the Sacramento Valley. It is likely that his scheme matured slowly in the months that he spent on the trail and at sea. He told the governor that he wanted to be an *empresario de colonización,* after the manner of Moses and Stephen Austin, who had obtained permission from the Mexican government to settle Anglo-American families in Texas. This bold project was too grand for Alvarado to accept. An empresario was obligated to settle many families, and Sutter had only his Kanakas and a few white men. Besides, the governor explained, under Mexican law at the end of ten years the empresario would be required to distribute the land among his followers, a revelation that made Sutter "thoughtful for a little while," Alvarado recalled.[13] Still, Alvarado liked the idea of a permanent inland settlement, and he encouraged Sutter. If Sutter became a Mexican citizen, which he could do after residing in California for twelve months, he would be eligible to receive a grant of land. In the meantime he could go to the Sacramento Valley and select the land that he wanted.

Alvarado's proposition appealed to Sutter, even though the governor warned him about the Indians who lived there. "The Indians," Sutter recalled, "was very hostile, and stole horses from the inhabitants, near San José."[14] These Miwok and Yokuts Indians were often in cahoots with New Mexicans, chaguanosos, and "adventurers of all nations," as the californios called these horse thieves who drove thousands of horses out of California each year. This serious problem had prompted Alvarado in 1838 (the year of Peg-leg Smith's great horse raid on southern California) to take the extreme measure of asking Michel Laframboise, leader of the Hudson's Bay Company Sacramento River fur brigade, to "chastise" the chaguanosos.[15] The prospect of turning his trappers into a posse to pursue these formidable rustlers scared Laframboise, who promptly left California. Horse rustling remained a major problem, and Alvarado expected Sutter to do everything he could to stop the traffic in stolen horses in his district. He even cloaked Sutter with an official title to carry out these responsibilities: "Representante del Govierno en las fronteras del Norte, y Encargado de la Justicia," which translated roughly as representative of the government and agent of the law on the northern frontier.[16] He also warned Sutter to steer clear of Comandante General Vallejo, who governed the Sonoma district as his fiefdom.

Now Sutter had what he wanted: official permission and a title that he could expand into grand claims of governmental power. Out of this veneer of authority he wove the fantasy that on the banks of the Sacramento he had absolute authority over all matters civil, judicial, and military. This was true only insofar as his isolation from Mexican authorities and his armed force made it so. Nevertheless, Alvarado granted Sutter (who was, after all, still a foreigner) extraordinary authority, and Sutter's mere existence east of Vallejo's domain would soon prove nettlesome to the comandante. These troubles were in the future. For the time being, Sutter wanted to meet Vallejo and see his great rancho.

After striking his deal with Governor Alvarado, Sutter returned to Yerba Buena and settled his accounts with the Russians and French. The *Clementine* sailed back to Hawaii—to be sold, Sutter claimed. The ship went back to its actual owners, of course, but it took something even more valuable: Sutter's payment for the debt that he had run up with French. The Swiss supercargo had done well enough to leave a small credit to his account.[17] As far as William French was concerned, Sutter was in the black, so his credit was good with one of the most important merchants in the Hawaii-California trade.

Before venturing up the Sacramento River, Sutter went to Sonoma to pay his respects to Vallejo and become better informed about the country. Near the end of July Captain John Wilson provided a rowboat and crew that transported Sutter across the bay to the mouth of Sonoma slough and then up to Vallejo's Sonoma embarcadero. Captain William Richardson, harbor master of the nascent port of San Francisco, went along for the ride.[18] The comandante's Rancho Petaluma was impressive. Thousands of cattle roamed over tens of thousands of acres granted to him under Mexican law. During the 1830s and 1840s Vallejo acquired more land, including the Suisun, Yulupa, and Agua Caliente grants. Vallejo was also the government's *comisionado* (administrator), who oversaw the secularization of the Mission San Francisco de Solano, with its inventory of 6,000 cattle, 6,000 sheep, and 3,000 orchard trees. Vallejo disposed of the mission property, using half for the benefit of the Sonoma pueblo and half for the Indians. By the end of the Mexican era Vallejo owned 175,000 acres of land outright and controlled much more of the country, including parts of the now-famous Sonoma and Napa wine-producing regions.[19] The merchant William Heath Davis reckoned that Vallejo owned more than fifty thousand cattle and took in $96,000 annually in trade for hides and tallow alone: "This made the general the largest cattle owner in early California."[20] Davis may have exaggerated Vallejo's holdings, but his recollections are indicative of Vallejo's wealth and power. Vallejo governed the domain from Carquinez Strait to Mendocino like a petty duke.

Hundreds of Indian workers tilled Vallejo's fields and herded his livestock. He preferred peace to war with the surrounding Indians, but raw force backed

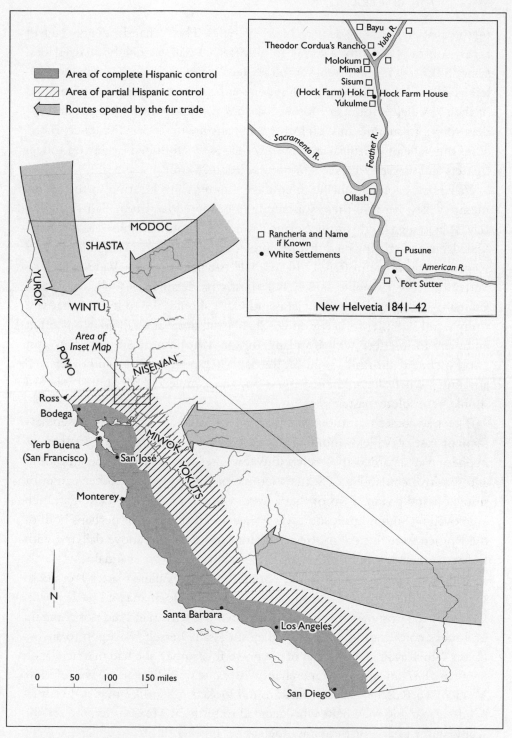

Legend

- Area of complete Hispanic control
- Area of partial Hispanic control
- Routes opened by the fur trade

New Helvetia 1841–42

- Bayu
- Theodor Cordua's Rancho
- *Yuba R.*
- Molokum
- Mimal
- Sisum
- (Hock Farm) Hok — Hock Farm House
- Yukulme
- *Sacramento R.*
- *Feather R.*
- Ollash
- Pusune
- *American R.*
- Fort Sutter

☐ Ranchería and Name if Known
● White Settlements

Main map labels

- MODOC
- SHASTA
- YUROK
- WINTU
- POMO
- *Area of Inset Map*
- NISENAN
- Ross
- Bodega
- Yerb Buena (San Francisco)
- San José
- MIWOK
- YOKUTS
- Monterey
- Santa Barbara
- Los Angeles
- San Diego

N

0   50   100   150 miles

Hispanic and fur-trade influences on California's interior Indians, 1821–41. Based on map in Albert L. Hurtado, *Indian Survival on the California Frontier* (New Haven: Yale University Press, 1988), p. 33.

up the treaties that he made with Native peoples. The comandante general had a garrison of about fifty soldiers to enforce his will on neighboring tribes. Chief Solano, who reportedly stood six feet, seven inches tall, rallied to Vallejo's cause some of his Patwin tribesmen (perhaps as many as fourteen hundred of them). Vallejo's younger brother Salvador ruthlessly used Mexican and Indian forces to subdue and exploit the Indians north of San Francisco Bay.[21] Thus the Vallejos' financial and military success was founded largely on Indian fighters and workers. This lesson was not lost on Sutter.

Vallejo was cordial, but he discouraged Sutter from locating in the Sacramento Valley, because there was ample unoccupied land near San Francisco Bay. Vallejo suggested Suisun (Solano's country), Mount Diablo, and the Napa Valley, but Sutter explained that he "preferred to settle by a navigable river."[22] Captain Wilson even offered his own well-stocked Sonoma Valley ranch to Sutter on very favorable terms, but the Swiss declined. "Well, my God," Captain Wilson exclaimed in exasperation, "I should like to know what you really want!"[23] Sutter's real reason was that he did not want Vallejo or any other authority to interfere with his plans. In Sonoma, he noticed, "the hat must come off before the military guard, the flag staff, and the church and I preferred a country where I could keep mine on, and I preferred a country where I should be absolute master."[24]

The newcomer's attitude was irksome to Vallejo. Sutter's proposed settlement east of Vallejo's holdings as well as the official recognition that his nephew had accorded the pretentious foreigner also bothered the ambitious and sensitive comandante. Sutter's retinue of Kanakas was another cause for suspicion and gossip. Two of them were women, married to Hawaiian men employed by Sutter, but it soon was noised about that one or perhaps both of the women were Sutter's mistresses. Californios were not above dallying with Indian women, but public revelations of such liaisons were scandalous.

Still, Sutter's charm was potent enough to cause Vallejo's sister Rosalía to suggest that the Swiss gentleman should marry a californiana and settle down. Evidently the existence of a wife and children in Switzerland did not come up in Sutter's conversation with the Vallejos. Rosalía herself was open to such a union. Much against the wishes of her powerful brother, she had married Jacob Leese in 1837, an American merchant who came to California by way of New Mexico. To Rosalía, Sutter's background looked much like that of her husband—a roaming merchant who decided to settle in Mexico. Eventually she would come to despise Sutter as much as her brother did.[25]

After surveying the Vallejo property, Sutter and one of the comandante general's vaqueros rode to the Russian establishment at Ross. Baron Alexander Rotchev governed the Russian outpost. "Rotcheff's lady was a Princess Ga-

garin," Sutter recalled. "He eloped with her, otherwise he could not have married her," he added, perhaps recalling the difficult circumstances of his own marriage.[26] Again he employed one of his letters of introduction, this one from the governor of Sitka—Rotchev's superior in the Russian-American Company. Situated about fifty miles northwest of Vallejo's property, the main Russian establishment was a palisaded fort situated on the headlands north of Bodega Bay. Russians were in charge of a large labor force of Aleut, Pomo, and Kanaka workers. Hunters took sea otters whenever they could, but food production and trade in foodstuffs with Mexicans were the primary purposes of the Ross settlement. Wheat, barley, and vegetables grew on the Russian farms, which also kept livestock. Sutter claimed that the residents of Russian Alaska were so dependent on the produce of their California post that the New Archangel governor's milk cows munched hay shipped from Ross. Whatever the governor's cows may have eaten, the Ross settlement was a disappointment to the Russians, for it never produced enough food to justify the expense. Illicit trade with the missions provided vital provender for Alaska, however, until secularization ruined this arrangement.

Still, Ross was an impressive establishment, much like other places that Sutter had seen on his westward journey: a fortified frontier outpost that depended on Indian labor. He noticed the array of artisans that Fort Ross housed, including "laborers and mechanics of the colonial service, blacksmiths, tailors, shoemakers, etc. There was a tannery also." These small-scale industries helped to support the post and also produced goods for trade with Mexican Californians, whom Governor Rotchev "supplied . . . only as a special mark of favor."[27] This was the sort of settlement that Sutter was interested in founding in the Sacramento Valley. He wanted an enterprise where he could set the terms of trade with Indians and californios alike, much as Rotchev did at Ross. Of course, Rotchev had the power and prestige of the Russian-American Company and, if need be, the Russian Imperial Navy to back him up. Sutter would never have that kind of economic or military backing, but he had the next best things—pure gall and boundless self-confidence. The very existence of Ross palpably demonstrated Mexican military inability—or at least reluctance—to remove the Russians from Mexican territory. If the californios quietly accepted the Russians, indeed traded with them against the laws of Mexico, then what might Sutter be able to get away with in the way of personal empire-building? He began to test these uncertain waters almost immediately.

Upon his return to San Francisco Bay, Sutter used his newly established credit with California merchants to lay in supplies. He also acquired a small flotilla for his expedition to the Sacramento Valley. His largest vessel was a

22-ton schooner, the *Isabel,* which he chartered from Nathan Spear and William Hinckley, merchants with Hawaiian connections.[28] Hinckley also sold Sutter another small schooner, the *Nicholas,* "formerly a pleasure boat of the Sandwich Islands King," Sutter said.[29] He bought a third craft from Captain Wilson, a pinnace (a small boat from a larger ship), to round out his fleet. "Agricultural implements, blacksmith tools, and carpenter tools" found their way into the holds of his vessels, as well as "arms and ammunition, three cannon, muskets & rifles."[30] Sutter was prepared to use all the customary tools of frontier conquest and trade—axe and plow, powder and ball. He manned his small navy with the eight or so Kanakas and four white men who had accompanied him from Honolulu, plus five sailors that he engaged at Yerba Buena.

One of the newcomers was William Heath Davis, the seventeen-year-old adopted son of John Coffin Jones, U.S. consul in Honolulu. Davis, who was the son of Jones's Hawaiian wife and her first husband, was known as "Kanaka Bill." Despite his youth, he was an excellent sailor and merchant due to experience gained at the side of Jones on his many trading voyages. By early August the patchwork fleet was ready to sail.[31]

Suitable ritual marked the eve before Sutter's embarkation. The captain of the *Monsoon,* an American merchantman riding at anchor in San Francisco Bay, invited Sutter, "the commanding officers of all vessels in port," and "the principal men on shore" to a farewell dinner aboard his ship. "All were there to bid me goodbye," Sutter remembered many years later, "as to one they never expected to see again."[32] When the festivities were over, he boarded his pinnace and set his face toward a very uncertain future.

The first leg of the journey was the easiest. The fleet sailed across the bay to Carquinez Strait, which opened into another large bay named Suisun. Here he stopped to greet Don Ygnacio Martínez, proprietor of a large rancho on the bay's south shore. Sutter purchased cattle and horses that would be delivered once he decided on a location for his settlement. This crucial business completed, the inland voyagers began to search for the elusive mouth of the Sacramento River. Finding the river was no mean feat. The inland waters of California were uncharted. Not only did the Sacramento and San Joaquin Rivers empty into Suisun Bay; so too did many sloughs that extended back into the seemingly endless tule marshes bordering the waterways. There were many false starts. Davis directed the flotilla into the San Joaquin River, thinking that it was the Sacramento. His error cost two days. Once back in Suisun Bay, Sutter took the pinnace with his Kanaka oarsmen into myriad bays, inlets, and sloughs, hoping to discover the Sacramento, a frustrating process that he recalled as consuming eight days.[33]

Sutter finally found the river by accident. One evening at sundown he saw what he thought was a small bay where they could camp for the night. Once inside, he saw the Sacramento spread out before him.[34] Now the final leg of the journey could begin, though the river's course was a maze of islands and sloughs. The Mokelumne and Cosumnes Rivers joined it from the east, adding to the jigsaw puzzle that Sutter and Davis had to solve. In its natural state the Sacramento River delta was a unique landscape. The spring flooding of the rivers deposited loads of silt at the margins of the delta islands, forming natural levees a few feet higher than the level of the river. The growth upon the levees resembled a tangled jungle. Wild grape and clematis vines draped from cotton-wood, elder, and other deciduous trees. The understory was an uninviting snarl of berry vines, wild rose, and poison oak. The nearly impenetrable levees gave way to more open ground studded with majestic oak trees. On the larger islands elk, deer, and antelope browsed while wolves and coyotes lurked, waiting to seize unwary prey. Grizzly bears also prowled the dense riparian environment and woe betide the thoughtless traveler who ambled across the path of one of these creatures. Overhead and in the water numberless birds took advantage of this wet, prolific world, haunting the ear with their cries and darkening the sun when they rose in great flocks above the mossy green islands and muddy waterways.[35]

There were dense clouds of insects too, especially mosquitoes, "exceeding anything we ever experienced before," Davis said.[36] The mosquitoes made it impossible for the voyagers to rest at night. Perhaps it was during one of these sleepless, mosquito-infested evenings that Sutter confided his plans to young Davis. He intended to build a fort to defend against the Indians, "and also against government of the department of California in case any hostility should be manifested in that quarter," Davis recalled.[37] Once it was established, Sutter intended to build a colony for his Swiss compatriots, who would develop the rich agricultural potential of the Sacramento Valley. Such were the waking dreams of John Sutter on a hot August night in the Sacramento River delta. As expressed to Davis, Sutter's plan displayed a frank lack of loyalty and trust in the Mexican government. This loose evening talk said something about his character, and it also said something about recent events in the global West. Mexico could not hold Texas. Hawaii was up for grabs. The United States and Great Britain shared Oregon for the time being, but American settlements there were growing. If California became an object of foreign intrigue, Mexican authorities might take a dim view of resident aliens such as Sutter. Suspicion, self-interest, and healthy circumspection motivated his plans to fortify his inland settlement.

Worries about Indians increased the nightly unease of Sutter and his men. He believed that the Indians were watching him as his boats moved upstream, but none appeared. Sutter saw bunches of white feathers tied to the trees, "prayers to gods and devils for fish and food," he thought, but the supplicants remained out of sight. So Sutter moved slowly upriver, taking the lead in the pinnace as the schooners followed. Finally, two days out of Suisun Bay and about ten miles south of the present site of Sacramento, Sutter saw Indians on the eastern bank of the river. The moment made a lasting impression on him. "Suddenly I saw in an open space two hundred warriors painted yellow, black, and red, armed and keen for fight."[38]

These men were probably Miwoks from the Gualacomne ranchería and the nearby Ochejamne communities, which included some former mission Indians too.[39] It was a critical moment. Some of his men wanted to open fire at once, but Sutter restrained them. Although his oarsmen were armed, the Miwoks outnumbered them by at least twenty to one, and the schooners were still downriver. Even if he repelled an attack, Sutter knew that the success of his enterprise depended on establishing a good working relationship with at least some of the valley's Indian residents. He did not want a fight with the first Indians he encountered. Sutter told his men to conceal their weapons while he went ashore.

Covered by the discreetly hidden muskets of his men, Sutter nudged the pinnace into the riverbank and jumped ashore, unarmed and alone. In the hope that there were some Indians who spoke Spanish among them, perhaps runaways from the missions and ranchos, he shouted a strange salutation, "Á Dios, amigos!"[40] To his relief, two men stepped up and addressed him in Spanish. It is likely that one of these men was Anashe, a well-known Gualacomne leader, who was at this first meeting.[41] Narciso, an Ochejamne headman who soon formed an alliance with Sutter, may also have been there.[42] Sutter explained that he came to their country not to make war or to send them back to the missions but to live among them and to be their friends. Somehow his explanation in broken Spanish got through to his listeners. One of them agreed to take a letter to the schooners in a tule canoe, and the other man agreed to guide Sutter upriver. The mission Indians spoke to the crowd, after which they "appeared satisfied," or so Sutter thought.[43] Through the interpreter he told the assembled Indian men to come to his camp so that he could give them presents. Then he sailed upriver to find a suitable spot for his post.

Sutter's initial exploration may have extended as far north as the lower reaches of the Feather River before he returned to the mouth of the American River. His account conflicts with that of Davis, who wrote that the flotilla anchored in the lower American River on the first night after meeting the Indians. Davis claimed that once the sailors had delivered Sutter and his cargo

to the confluence of the Sacramento and American Rivers their job was done.
He and the other sailors then took the schooners back to Yerba Buena.[44] Sutter
told a more dramatic story of a mutinous crew that did not wish to stay in the
dangerous Sacramento Valley wilderness. As he retired to the cabin of one of
his schooners anchored at the mouth of the Feather River, the crew demanded
to know how much longer he "intended to travell [sic] with them in such a
Wilderness. I saw plain that it was a mutiny."[45] Sutter replied that he would tell
them in the morning. After a fitful night he ordered the ships back to the
American River and anchored about a mile upstream, where the men un-
loaded Sutter's goods, pitched tents, and mounted the cannons. Then he told
them that anyone who was not content with his leadership could return on the
Isabella. Six of the nine white men decided to return, and Sutter paid them
with drafts on Nathan Spear, who was to pay them in goods. (In effect this was
another loan that Spear applied to Sutter's already large line of credit.) Sutter
did not accuse these men of cowardice in the midst of so many Indians but said
that they "were not willing to stand the discomforts of the wilderness."[46]
Perhaps the droning mosquitoes had gotten to them.

Whether Davis and the others left as semi-mutineers, as Sutter claimed, or
merely took their leave as the logical culmination of their employment with
him remains a matter of conjecture. However it may have been, in his old age
Davis recalled the scene of his departure with Technicolor vividness. As the
schooner moved away, the teenaged Davis watched from the deck as Sutter
gave the departing men a nine-gun salute with the cannons. "A large number
of deer, elk and other animals on the plains were startled, running to and fro,
stopping to listen, their heads raised, full of curiosity and wonder," Davis
remembered. "From the interior of the adjacent wood the howls of wolves and
coyotes filled the air," he continued, "and immense flocks of waterfowl flew
wildly over the camp."[47]

Hundreds of Indians came to Sutter's encampment to receive the presents
that he had promised them. It was a good opportunity to demonstrate the
power of his cannons by firing at a target. "They didn't care to have them tried
on them."[48] Artillery instantly made him a big man in the Sacramento Valley.

Soon Sutter moved his provisions and guns to higher ground, where his
men began to erect more substantial shelter. He called the place New Helvetia
(New Switzerland), a name that embodied his hope to attract Swiss and German immigrants (and that insulted Mexican Californians).

The fulfillment of Sutter's dreams of a personal empire depended on his
dealing with pressing practical concerns. He needed provisions. "Please send
me the Horses and Cattle so quick as possible," Sutter wrote Martínez, also
asking for oxen, saddles, beans, dried meat, and Indian corn for seed.[49] Sutter

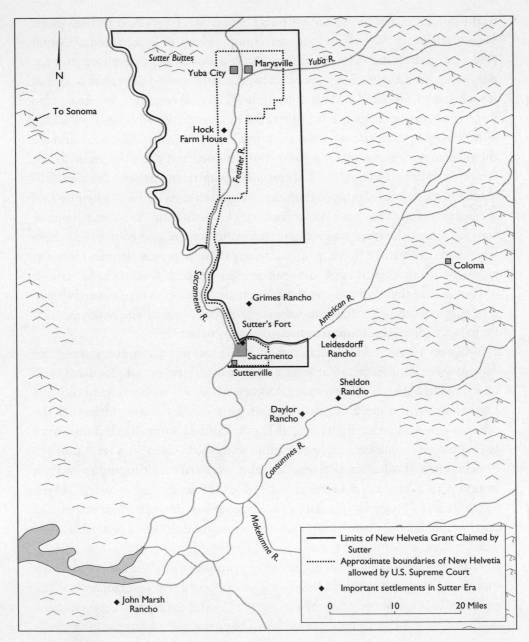

New Helvetia and other settlements. Based on map in Albert L. Hurtado, *Indian Survival on the California Frontier* (New Haven: Yale University Press, 1988), p. 33.

had to work quickly to erect shelter for himself and his employees before the rainy season set in. The Kanakas put up frames for two houses roofed with tule grass in the Hawaiian fashion. Then they built a more permanent structure, a forty-foot-long, one-story adobe building also thatched with tules. It had three rooms, a blacksmith shop, a kitchen, and living quarters for Sutter. This was the crude nucleus of Sutter's Fort.[50]

Martínez sent the livestock and other goods that Sutter requested, but he kept Clemente and Julián, two Indians that Sutter had sent with his message. They were probably Ochejamne Indians who had formerly lived in the Mission San José.[51] Martínez made them work for him while sending the cattle and other goods to Sutter under the control of other Indian vaqueros. For some reason Martínez's men frightened the Indians at Sutter's place, who fled. "This interferes very much with my work," Sutter complained. To make matters worse, the Sacramento Valley Indians believed that Clemente and Julián were prisoners, and they refused to return to work until they were released. Evidently Martínez was short of Indian hands, because he asked Sutter to send him more Indian workers. Once Julián and Clemente were released, Sutter assured him, "I will be able to serve you with all of the Indians that you may need."[52] Martínez eventually returned the two Indian men, but this was not the end of it. They told Sutter that they had not been paid, so he compensated them and subtracted the amount from his debt to Martínez.[53] This was the beginning of a long-running feud that colored Mexican opinions about Sutter, but he had little time to worry about that now.

A handful of Kanakas, three white men, several cannons, a few Indian friends, and a line of credit were the modest foundations on which Sutter hoped to build a wilderness establishment patterned after the great American, British, and Russian enterprises in the American West. He would create his own version of the militarized and fortified outposts of capitalism that he had studied from Missouri to the Pacific. Anyone who knew Sutter's history would have given him little chance to succeed. His string of business failures and his tendency to flee from creditors when the bills came due did not forecast success in his new frontier business venture. Almost everything stood against him. He had little money and depended on credit for everything. He was a poor businessman. He had no experience as a cattleman, the principal business of the country. He knew nothing of the hide and tallow trade. He had only a few men to help him, and they might leave at any time. Even the Kanaka men and women could have abandoned their Swiss master to his fate. Who would have stopped them?

The region had natural resources aplenty for Sutter to exploit. He planned to trap the beaver and sell their pelts, but he had no experience as a fur trapper and only scant knowledge of the fur trade that he had gained by observation. His chief competitor would be the Hudson's Bay Company, the world's largest fur-trading company, backed by the most powerful nation on the planet. Vallejo, commander of the only military force in the neighborhood, was suspicious of Sutter, a hunch that would harden into hatred as the Mexican comandante gained more knowledge of his Swiss neighbor and competitor. The sheer isolation of New Helvetia militated against its success as a center of colonization. Finally, the Native peoples who surrounded Sutter were numerous and antagonistic to Mexican authority. There was no reason to believe that the Nisenans and Miwoks would be favorably disposed to permanent military and civilian settlements in their midst.

But Sutter had a few things in his favor. Governor Alvarado supported him and hoped to offset his uncle's ambitions with Sutter's inland settlement. Several influential merchants believed in Sutter's prospects and advanced him goods and credit to prove it. As always, his most important asset was himself. Sheer energy and optimistic enthusiasm suffused all of his plans, no matter how grandiose or improbable of realization. Sutter was convinced that if he dreamed enough large dreams eventually he would succeed—if only he could hold off narrow-minded and unreasonable men who demanded payment when notes fell due. He had an uncanny ability to stall his creditors. As John Laufkotter had observed of Sutter's Westport venture, "All that was necessary for Mr Sutter was to keep up a brilliant front and prosperous appearance as long as possible."[54] Sutter already had plenty of practice at keeping up his brilliant front; he would gain even more experience in California.

Sutter never revealed how he weighed his Swiss family in the balance as he cast his lot in the Sacramento Valley. He wrote to his family and friends in Switzerland, but none of the family letters have come to light. It is easy to imagine that he sent Anna hopeful missives that were full of promises of future prosperity and family reunion. Sutter was good at making promises and probably meant to keep most of them; but for the time being his family would have to wait in Switzerland. As time passed for Anna in Burgdorf, the value of Sutter's promises must have declined sharply. She probably retained some faith in her wayward husband; otherwise, it is reasonable to suspect, she would have divorced him just as her sister had divorced his worthless brother. Five years had passed since he had absconded with the last of his inventory and abandoned his family. One of their sons had died, and the broken family lived on the charity of Anna's sisters. Though neither Anna nor John knew it, another decade would pass before the Sutter family would be together again. In the meantime the name of Sutter, the feckless dreamer, would become known around the world, but not for any reason that he could have imagined in August 1839.

CHAPTER 6

An Entrepreneur in Indian Country

In August 1839 Sutter perched tenuously in the Sacramento Valley. He was not the first intruder in the valley, but he would be the first to live permanently among the Indians. The presence of a substantial Indian population was an integral part of Sutter's scheme. All of the large-scale fur trading and agrarian enterprises in North America depended on Indian labor, and it would have been inconceivable to contemplate a settlement in the Sacramento Valley without it. Indians were the ubiquitous toilers at Fort Vancouver, Sitka, Ross, and every California mission and rancho. They would be the indispensable builders of New Helvetia.

Sutter put his convincing personality and knowledge of the Indian trade to work among the Miwoks and Nisenans who surrounded him, but he would need more than confidence and a winning smile to persevere in the Sacramento Valley. In 1839 the valley was a dangerous place, and Sutter's success among the Indians was no certain thing. Isolation enhanced his independence from the Mexican government, but it also meant that there would be little chance of getting help if the Miwok and Nisenan Indians decided to drive him out. His nearest non-Indian neighbor was John Marsh, ill-tempered and miserly, who hailed from Massachusetts. A graduate of Andover and Harvard, Marsh decided to take his education to the frontier. He tutored officers' children at Fort Snelling in Minnesota Territory before accepting an appointment as an Indian subagent to the Sioux and Sac and Fox tribes in Wisconsin. He compiled a Sioux dictionary and grammar and lived with a Sioux woman whose father was French Canadian. In the minds of some whites Marsh identified too closely with the Sioux. Consequently, he lost his position as Indian agent and eventually faced charges for selling guns to the enemy during the Black Hawk War. He fled to the Rockies and then to western Missouri.[1]

In 1833 Marsh opened a store in Independence, where he catered to traders bound for Santa Fe and the Rocky Mountains. This is where he first met Sutter, perhaps doing business with him in the spring of 1835, the year that Marsh's business failed. To make matters worse, Marsh learned that the military was aware of his residence in Missouri. Bankrupt and fearing prosecution on the old gun-running charge, Marsh fled to Mexican territory, where neither prosecutors nor creditors could follow. In mid-June Marsh took the trail to Santa Fe, where he lingered a few weeks. There he likely bumped into Sutter again, but there is no record of it. He then took the well-trodden Gila River route, used by horse thieves and mountain men, to the Colorado River crossing and thence to Los Angeles. In California he claimed to be a physician, hanging his Harvard diploma (which proclaimed his bachelor's degree in Latin) on the wall to prove it. He took cattle and hides as payment for medical services and with the proceeds in 1837 purchased the Los Meganos grant on the eastern slope of Mount Diablo, some fifty miles from New Helvetia.[2]

Their past acquaintance, common interests, proximity (they were close neighbors by California standards), and similar situations in Mexican California should have made Marsh and Sutter fast friends, but their personalities were entirely different. Marsh was penny-pinching and mean-spirited; Sutter was voluble, friendly, and generous. Perhaps they knew too much about each other. Marsh talked about Sutter's shady business dealings in Missouri, while Sutter revealed to californios that "Doctor" Marsh had not been a physician in Missouri and was a wanted man in the States.[3] Help from Marsh was unlikely.

Don Ygnacio Martínez, whose ranch was about fifteen miles west of Los Meganos, was Sutter's other "near" neighbor. Martínez was also Sutter's creditor, and their relationship soured quickly, as we shall see. If need arose, Sutter could call on Mariano Vallejo for military assistance; but the comandante general's mistrust grew steadily as the newcomer encroached on his prerogatives. Vallejo was unlikely to send his scant troops to assist a man he thought to be a charlatan. Sutter was on his own in Indian country.

Without realistic prospects for help from his Mexican neighbors, Sutter depended on the goodwill and assistance of Indians to maintain his enterprise. He required a large seasonal workforce for the extensive pastoral and agricultural pursuits that he envisioned. Before he could attract the white craftsmen to build and operate the small shops and manufactories at New Helvetia, Sutter had to guarantee the safety of the place. Labor and security for New Helvetia would come from the surrounding Indian communities, which represented the overwhelming majority of the valley population until the gold rush.[4] The success of New Helvetia depended on Sutter's ability to mold at least some of his Miwok and Nisenan neighbors to his own purposes. If he failed in this, he failed in all.

By good luck or shrewd judgment Sutter had chosen to erect his settlement in a region where the Indian population, though still large, was already sharply reduced. The country along the Cosumnes River, immediately south of New Helvetia, was the northernmost territory of the Miwok Indians. Like most California Indians, the Miwoks were hunters, fishers, and wild food collectors. They caught and dried the innumerable salmon that seasonally ran in the rivers. Deer, elk, and antelope added fresh meat for the Miwok diet. Women probably supplied the bulk of Miwok nutrition with plant foods, seeds, and especially acorns, which they ground into a protein-rich meal.[5] Franciscans began recruiting Miwoks into the missions in 1811. The neophyte Miwoks were restive in the missions, and some of them became notorious fugitives after returning to their homelands with stolen mission livestock.

North of the Cosumnes River lay Nisenan country. The Nisenans were hunters and food collectors who lived much as the Miwoks did, but they had less direct contact with Hispanic intruders from the coast.[6] Spanish missionaries had not incorporated Nisenans in the missions, so they remained relatively independent of Spanish and then Mexican authority. That is not to say that they were unaffected by Hispanic society. During the 1830s, when Franciscan missionaries heavily recruited the Miwoks, some Miwok refugees sought safety among the Nisenans.[7] Spanish and Mexican forces occasionally trooped through Nisenan country in order to explore and recover fleeing neophytes and stolen livestock.[8]

In the late 1820s Miwoks began consorting with American mountain men and chaguanosos who were interested in relieving California ranchos of their horses. In 1827 the American trapper Jedediah Smith with his men traversed Miwok country, where he met the feared horse thieves who plundered the missions. Then he traveled into Nisenan territory and killed several Indians to set an example when they appeared threatening. Initially Smith sought beaver, but horses finally captured the attention of his trader's eye. He bought a herd from californios and drove them to Oregon, hoping to sell them at the rendezvous. Umpqua Indians attacked Smith, killed most of his men, and stole the horses; but his foray alerted other mountain men to the possibility of getting California horses by fair means or foul and driving them east, where there was a ready market.[9] In the years that followed other North American trappers, traders, and horse thieves from the east camped in Miwok and Nisenan territory, as did Hudson's Bay Company brigades from Oregon. Miwok raiders now had a market for the stolen mission horses that men like Ute chief Walkara and the mountain men Jim Beckwourth and "Peg-leg" Smith drove out of California.[10]

These raids seriously threatened the economic foundations of Mexican California. Without horses—especially the well-trained horses that Indians and mountain men preferred to steal—rancheros could not tend their vast herds of wild cattle. Governor José Figueroa knew who was to blame. "British and Americans," he wrote in 1833, "make frequent incursions into this country on the pretext of trapping beaver." These foreigners identified "themselves with the wild natives, following the same kind of life." "Influenced by these adventurers," the governor continued, "the natives have dedicated themselves with the greatest determination to the stealing of horses from all the missions and towns of this territory."[11] Figueroa and other governors issued orders and decrees to put a stop to these depredations, but to no avail.[12]

Occasionally mountain men, who usually avoided Mexican authority, joined forces with californios to punish suspected horse thieves. In 1830 the Ochejamne Miwok community a few miles south of the site of Sutter's future encampment, together with a few other northern Miwok rancherías, had harbored fugitives from the missions and refused to turn them over to Mexican authorities. Mexican forces and several hundred Indian auxiliaries under José Berreyessa's command invaded Ochejamne country to capture the neophyte truants. Instead, the Ochejamnes defied Berreyessa, wounded eleven of his men, and forced the Mexican troops to withdraw. Berreyessa prevailed on Ewing Young, leader of a nearby band of trappers, to join him against the Ochejamne Miwoks. The mountain men (including young Kit Carson) combined with the Mexican force, defeated the Ochejamnes, and burned their houses.[13] The following year nearly four hundred Ochejamnes under the leadership of Narciso entered the Mission San José. During the 1830s some unhappy Miwok neophytes evidently slipped back to their homelands, a migration that was hastened by the secularization (conversion to a parish church) of the Mission San José in 1834 and a smallpox epidemic in 1838.[14]

The year 1833 brought perhaps the most deadly newcomer to the Sacramento Valley: malaria, a disease caused by a parasite in the blood that destroys red cells. The infection is transmitted by *Anopheles* mosquitoes that ingest the parasite with blood when they bite infected humans and then deposit the parasite in a new victim when they take their next blood. Intermittent chills and fever characterize the disease, which in extreme cases causes death. The virulent strain of malaria that attacked California in 1833 was truly a world traveler. It arrived in Oregon aboard Hudson's Bay Company ships from Hawaii. Infected members of a Hudson's Bay Company brigade unwittingly carried the disease from Oregon to the wetlands of central California, which happened to be prime habitat for the *Anopheles* mosquitoes that transmitted the disease. A virgin population in epidemiological terms, Indians in the Sacramento Valley died by the thousands. Unable to cope with the frightening new malady, Indians fled to higher ground, where the disease did not become established (because the *Anopheles* did not live there, although no one then understood the direct relationship between the mosquito and the disease). An unknown number of Miwoks and Nisenans lost their lives. The most careful student of the event has estimated that twenty thousand Indians died in the Sacramento and San Joaquin Valleys in the summer of 1833.[15]

From then on malaria was a permanent resident of central California, much to the dismay of Indians and whites alike. The irritating mosquitoes that pestered Davis and Sutter in 1839 carried the microscopic parasites that prepared the way for Sutter's settlement. The Indians that Sutter met were survivors of the first, most deadly wave of the disease. Many of them probably suffered intermittently from malaria's debilitating fevers and chills. Thus, by the time of Sutter's arrival, the Indians in the Sacramento Valley were a reduced and weakened population, less able to resist intruders than they otherwise might have been.

Malaria temporarily slowed the livestock raiders but did not stop them. Miwoks continued to devastate the Mexican herds, much to the dismay of californios. In 1837 Comandante General Vallejo made a treaty with the Ochejamnes (formerly of the Mission San José and probably led by Narciso). Under this agreement the Ochejamnes agreed to help Vallejo recover stolen horses from the Muquelemne Miwoks, who had taken the animals from Sonoma. Accordingly the Ochejamnes raided the Muquelemnes, who retaliated, thus initiating an intratribal conflict in the northern San Joaquin Valley.[16]

The California Indian world was a complicated place in 1839. Sutter was only the most recent intruder in Nisenan and Miwok country. In the preceding twenty-five years missionaries, soldiers, horse thieves, fur traders, malaria, and smallpox had all swept through the valley. Each of these new developments had weakened Indian communities and eased the way for Sutter. While the Native population numbered in the tens of thousands, they were by no means united. Divided by ethnicity, language, and historical experiences, some of them wished to drive out newcomers such as Sutter. Others welcomed Sutter, who promised to provide trade goods to them on an unprecedented scale—for a price.

When they arrived in 1839, Sutter and his men were well-armed; but he relied on more than brute force to gain his first tenuous foothold in the Sacramento Valley. As he had promised, Sutter distributed presents to the assembled Indians. "The beads, blankets and shirts I gave them left them well satisfied," he concluded.[17] Hawaiian sugar also had great attractive power among the Indians.[18] Sutter hoped that these first offerings would demonstrate his good faith, but he did not intend to dole out gifts forever. The gifts were meant to demonstrate his value as a trading partner and employer, and they had the desired effect.

Sutter's first encounter with Indians on the Sacramento River was with Gualacomne and Ochejamne Miwoks who lived about ten miles south of the mouth of the American River. The leaders of these two groups (Anashe and Narciso respectively) quickly associated themselves with Sutter. The Ochejamnes under Narciso shifted their loyalty from Vallejo to Sutter, perhaps thinking that nearby allies would be of greater assistance than distant ones. The Ochejamnes moved their community to Sutter's settlement, where they added muscle to his military force as well as supplying him with agricultural labor.[19] Narciso's defection to Sutter must have rankled Vallejo, who already had reasons to distrust the cheeky Swiss interloper. Anashe, the Ochejamne chief, who likewise befriended Sutter, "was inclined to be in favor of peace," Sutter recalled, "and always proved to be a great friend."[20] Maximo, another Miwok headman, also cooperated with Sutter in the beginning.[21]

The Pusune Nisenan community was located on the north bank of the American River, across from Sutter's encampment. The Nisenans were not so quick to embrace Sutter. His relocation of Miwoks to their very doorstep—indeed in territory that had formerly belonged to the Nisenans—was an alarming development. In Sutter's initial exploration of the Sacramento and Feather Rivers, Nisenans hid or fled, but eventually his combined use of diplomacy and naked force brought them under his control.[22]

Sutter's store of goods proved a powerful magnet among Native peoples of the valley, but not always in the ways that he intended. Many years later Sutter recalled a night when the cry of "Oh, Señor!" interrupted his conversation with Octave Custot, his French-Canadian clerk. The clerk ran out to investigate and found "an Indian pinned to the ground and being worried by a fine large bull-dog which I had brought over from the Sandwich Islands," Sutter said. Custot took the man to Sutter for interrogation, but soon another yell came from a second Indian pinned by the dog. Now Sutter had two injured men in his quarters. The captives explained that they had "come to kill us all and take the place."[23] Sutter dealt shrewdly with his would-be assailants. He sewed up their wounds with silk thread and pardoned them but "warned them in the same sentence that any further overt act would meet with swift punishment."[24]

Diplomacy only temporarily discouraged Sutter's Indian opponents. During the winter of 1839–40 more Indians came to his camp with weapons concealed beneath the blankets that he had given them. Sutter's men seized the armed Indians, and he "angrily asked why they wished to kill" him. "I had been good to them," he claimed.[25] They admitted that they simply wanted his goods. Sutter did not report whether he meted out any punishment to these foiled attackers, but he continued to see signs of Indian dissatisfaction.

In the spring of 1840 Sutter directed his white and Indian laborers to make adobes for a wall to surround the first buildings. The wall was not complete until 1844, but it was an impressive structure in the California wilderness even while under construction.[26] Sutter located the fort on a low rise immediately south of a small slough from the American River, which was about one mile away. In its finished state the walls would stand eighteen feet high and two and a half feet thick, with bastions for cannon on the southeast and northwest corners.[27] Sutter enlarged the central building and added a second story. Eventually shops and living quarters lined the inside of walls approximately 500 feet long on the north and south sides and 150 feet long on the east and west sides.[28] Sutter purchased lumber from California merchants to make the fort's doors and windows. "The white men taught the Indians in the use of the rip saw and other implements," he recalled.[29] Such were the beginnings of Sutter's Fort, a structure designed much like the fur trade posts that he had seen in 1838.

In the early days of his settlement Sutter did not have thick walls to protect him. When William Wiggins (at twenty-three) saw Sutter at New Helvetia in 1840, he was impressed with the nerve of the proprietor in his nascent trading house. "His house was a one story adobe with three rooms," Wiggins recalled.[30] "He kept upon his table a brace of pistols, and he would allow the wild Indians to come into his room by scores, oftentimes being, as it were, entirely alone."[31] He described Sutter as "the best Indian tamer & civilizer that I know of, or ever heard of." Wiggins was not the only white man to marvel at Sutter's seeming skill in dealing with the Indians, but he also pointed out that the Indians knew that any transgressions "would be punished by death."[32] The pistols on Sutter's table reminded them of that.

Sutter's two-gun bravado did not awe all the valley Indians. Many saw no advantage in maintaining a permanent white settlement in their midst. The alliance of Pusune Nisenans and Ochejamne and Gaualcomne Miwoks with Sutter created discord among other Miwoks and Nisenans. Given the Indians' historic animosity against Mexicans and occasional conflicts with mountain men, it is not surprising that some Indians resisted Sutter too.

Indians were especially threatening in the spring of 1840, when they killed cattle and stole horses from Sutter. Two hundred to three hundred Indians (probably Miwoks) collected on the Cosumnes River, where they prepared to attack Sutter's rude settlement. He decided to make a preemptive strike. With

"Canons and other Arms loaded . . . 6 brave men and 2 Baqueros," Sutter marched to the Cosumnes at night.[33] At dawn he opened fire without warning, killing about thirty Indians. Sutter's men suffered no casualties. The surprise attack, firearms, and especially artillery fired at the sleeping village brought a quick end to hostilities. "After this lecon [*sic*]," Sutter reminisced, "they behaved very well, and became my best friends and Soldiers, with which I has been assisted to conquer the whole Sacramento and a part of the San Joaquin Valley."[34]

Sutter preferred to use diplomacy and trade in securing the loyalty and labor of the surrounding Indians; but when these methods failed he unhesitatingly used violence. The cannons that he had so deliberately and laboriously transported to the Sacramento Valley were not merely for parades and target practice, as the Cosumnes learned to their horror in 1840. Nor would they be the last Indians to wake at dawn to the sound of Sutter's guns.

Although Sutter had demonstrated that he could bludgeon Indians who opposed him, he also had to prove that he could protect Indians who worked for him. In 1840 a murderous incident gave him an opportunity to use military force to protect his Indian workers, but it also caused a collision with Mexican authorities and the Vallejo brothers. In early October Accacio and several other Indians from the Mission San José arrived at New Helvetia bearing passports from General Vallejo's brother, José de Jesús, the secular administrator of the mission. Accacio and his friends told Sutter that they wanted to visit their friends and relatives in the valley; but there was more to it than that. Julián, one of the men whom Martínez had dragooned the previous year, asked to accompany the neophytes to trade for feathers and baskets. Julián also told Sutter that the San José men wanted to trade for women at the Sakayakumne Miwok ranchería on the Mokelumne River. It is likely that the men were Miwoks, perhaps associated with the Ochejamne ranchería on the Sacramento River. Sutter assented but ordered the Indians to refrain from fighting and told them that the Sakayakumne women must "go with them free voluntary . . . and not by force which is against the laws of the country."[35] The neophytes and Julián blandly assured Sutter that they meant no harm and left the fort.

The outcome of this visit turned out to be a disaster for the Yalisumni Nisenans, whose able-bodied men were working for Sutter. Instead of going to Sakayakumne, the Miwoks went to the vulnerable Yalisumni ranchería, a few miles from New Helvetia, killed the elderly people and infants too young to travel, and kidnapped the women and older children.[36] They intended to sell their captives to rancheros on the coast, which was "common in those days," Sutter later admitted. An old man who escaped brought the horrifying news to the fort. The Yalisumni men nearly turned on Sutter because they thought that he had conspired with the murderers. He assured them that he had not known of the plan to steal the Yalisumni women and promised to avenge the attack. The next morning Sutter rode out of the fort with "twenty men, and a lot of Indians," catching the raiders near a lake about thirty miles south of New Helvetia.[37] After a brief fight, most of the San José men surrendered. Gerato, one of the mission Indians, took four women and plunged into the lake in a vain attempt to escape. Sutter called out to him; but when Gerato ignored him, Sutter ordered him shot. Several other kidnappers assumed that they would be killed by Sutter or by the angry Indians who accompanied him, and they made good their escape. Sutter marched back to his settlement and interrogated the Indians that he managed to catch. After identifying ten men as "great Rascals," he "sh[oo]t them here, for [to] show the others an exemple [sic] more, to see what bad acting get for recompense."[38] When Sutter wrote to José de Jesús Vallejo explaining his actions, he took the opportunity to tell him that he wanted no more mission Indians in his territory.

In refusing to honor the passports of mission Indians from Vallejo, Sutter asserted his authority over the valley and all its resources, including the Indians. The Vallejo brothers had repeatedly sent armed forces and Indians into the Sacramento Valley in order to retrieve stolen livestock, apprehend runaway mission Indians, and capture "gentile" (nonmission) Indians to work on Mexican ranchos.[39] Now Sutter intended to do all of those things without interference from other Mexican authorities. He had strong reasons for controlling access to Indians. First, he required enough men to defend and run New Helvetia. Second, Sutter could use Indian workers as a resource to balance his books, especially in his dealings with other labor-hungry rancheros, as we shall see.

Indian labor was indispensable to Sutter's enterprise. He was proud that his settlement soon attracted white laborers and mechanics; but without the hundreds of Indians who cooperated with him, he could not have succeeded. No one understood this better than Sutter. He spent a great deal of his time making sure that he had sufficient trade goods and presents on hand to pay his Indian workers. Eventually he contrived a currency of sorts for them. His blacksmith fabricated a metal disk that Indians wore on a necklace. Sutter punched a star-shaped hole in the disk to signify the amount of labor that the wearer had done. "With this money they could buy at my store blankets, or anything they required," he explained. Sutter claimed that when whites tried to cheat an Indian out of a disk he "refused to take it from them and so confined the arrangement to Indians."[40] Indians could redeem the disks for goods only at Sutter's store, where two weeks of work earned a cotton shirt or a pair of blue drill pantaloons.[41] This arrangement gave Sutter extraordinary control over the terms of the Indian trade and his labor costs. Through the use of tin money and his trade store, Indians became his workers and his customers too.

Sutter also created a small Indian army that protected his interests and made him a man to be reckoned with in Mexican California. This force consisted of about a hundred and fifty infantrymen and fifty cavalry. Most of the officers and sergeants were whites, but a few were Indians. Ensign Homobono, a literate ex-mission Indian, impressed Sutter the most. "The Spaniards [Mexicans] were much surprised when they saw my Indian soldiers," Sutter recalled, especially Homobono, "who could read and write which many of them could not do."[42] It was no wonder that the Mexicans were astonished. In 1841 Sutter's army wore green and blue uniforms with red trim that he had acquired from the Russians, and they marched to cadence called in German by a white officer—an exotic parade in the California wilderness. Sutter kept military discipline with a guard of twelve or fifteen Indian soldiers. At night sentinels kept watch and marked time with an hour glass, striking a bell and calling, "All is well" every half hour.[43] Eventually Sutter added a cadet corps of Indian boys, who wore "blue drill pantaloons, white cotton shirts & red handkerchiefs tied around their heads."[44] He claimed that the soldiers and cadets were proud of the uniforms that marked them as his men. These well-disciplined Indian soldiers were the defensive bulwark for New Helvetia, and they also symbolized the personal power of John A. Sutter in California. It was his private army: armed, trained, and paid by Sutter, not by the Mexican government. Only his word could command them to attack or stand them at ease. Without this force, New Helvetia could not have existed.

Sutter made other business arrangements with local Indians that raised the suspicions of Mexican rancheros. Soon after his arrival, Indians (probably Miwoks) "brought some sore-backed horses to me that they had stolen from some settlers" and offered them for sale, he recalled. "I bought them at a very low price, pastured them until they were well, and then returned them to the owners, who paid me back what I had paid."[45] Sutter remembered these matters as a kind of public service, but Mexicans saw it differently. From their point of view, Sutter appeared to be in league with Indian horse thieves and was selling them their own stolen horses.[46]

Was Sutter in cahoots with the various horse thieves who plagued the Mexican ranchos in the 1830s and 1840s? There is a circumstantial case for it. He had been involved with the illicit horse trade from the time of his first sojourn in New Mexico. In Missouri and Kansas Sutter had lived among the Shawnees and Delawares, the so-called chaquanosos that the Mexicans hated so much. He knew and employed mountain men, who doubtless had been involved in rustling California horses. Sutter's Fort was perfectly located to deal with Miwok horse raiders. And from time to time Sutter returned stolen livestock to their rightful owners (for a fee).[47] Mexicans had every reason to be suspicious. He may not have been a horse thief himself, but he lived among them, consorted with them, and acquired livestock from them. As Mexicans counted the losses from their dwindling herds, who could blame them for accusing Sutter of being what he appeared to be?

For his part, Sutter always claimed that he strove to eliminate horse stealing and punish the rustlers.[48] He was never fully successful, but some Anglo-American admirers gave him great credit for his efforts. William Wiggins claimed that Sutter "put a stop to horse-stealing by Indians in that section" but added: "when they were stealing horses by the hundred in all other parts of California."[49] Without meaning to imply it, Wiggins may have struck the nail on the head. Indians who did not steal horses from New Helvetia stole them elsewhere, which was hardly a consolation to hard-pressed californios.

Sutter, who was no doubt aware of the suspicions of his Mexican neighbors, turned the tables and charged californios with stealing livestock. In his reminiscences he claimed that the people who lived in Vallejo's vicinity "had a way of marking other people's calves that I did not like."[50] This unattractive trait, he claimed, was one of the reasons why he preferred to settle in the Sacramento Valley, although some might have thought that in going to the interior to avoid livestock thieves he was jumping from the frying pan into the fire.

Perhaps Governor Alvarado came closest to the truth. He defended Sutter against the californios' accusations in the early 1840s, but in his reminiscences he characterized Sutter as self-serving and disloyal. Alvarado stopped short of tarring the Swiss frontiersman with a brush made from the tail hair of stolen horses, although he noted Sutter's close association with rustlers. "In a short time Captain Sutter succeeded in bringing to New Helvetia a large number of strangers," Alvarado declared, "the greatest part of them lazy fellows, horse thieves, and deserters from merchant ships." He described the men who joined Sutter as "a throng of depraved creatures"; Sutter needed them to protect his herds from the Indian horse thieves. Without the assistance of "the most depraved men," Sutter "would not have been able to build the fort of New Helvetia," Alvarado believed.[51] In other words, Sutter needed horse thieves (white and Indian alike) to protect himself from other horse thieves. Sutter's making a business out of restoring stolen livestock to their rightful owners merely convinced rancheros that he was a horse thief too.

Alvarado was certainly correct in believing that Sutter needed all of the help that he could get, and the lord of New Helvetia was not choosy about his employees' backgrounds. Octave Custot, for example, was indispensable as Sutter's clerk and major-domo from 1839 to the early 1840s, but he had a shady background. A Frenchman, Custot arrived in California in 1837 claiming to have been a professor of agriculture in Nancy. In 1838 he convinced Vallejo that he could manufacture sugar from beets and made a fair trial of it in the employ of the comandante general. Occasionally Custot produced a small quantity of refined sugar to demonstrate his progress. The sweet stuff proved to be phony. Custot had stolen the sugar from Vallejo's own kitchen. When Vallejo discovered the domestic secret of sugar refining, the Frenchman sought less demanding employment elsewhere and joined Sutter soon after his arrival.[52] Alvarado drolly described Custot as "a man of unknown antecedents" who "spoke the patois of the [French] Canadians in the service of the Hudson's Bay Company."[53] By means of flattery, Alvarado explained, Custot induced several Hudson's Bay men to transfer their employment to Sutter.

In 1840 Niklaus Allgeier and Sebastian Keyser, the former Hudson's Bay men whom Sutter had met at the rendezvous in 1838, arrived at Sutter's Fort.[54] John Sinclair also came to Sutter's door in 1840. Sinclair, a Scot, had worked for the Hudson's Bay Company and later edited a newspaper in Honolulu, where Sutter may have known him. In partnership with Eliab Grimes, another Hawaiian merchant who did business with Sutter, Sinclair eventually established a rancho near Sutter.[55] John Smith, a Nova Scotia carpenter, showed up in 1842 and obtained land from Sutter near present-day Marysville and a few years later secured a Mexican land grant east of the Sacramento River.[56] Theodore Sicard, a French carpenter who had resided in California since 1833, gravitated to New Helvetia, worked for Sutter, obtained a land grant, and settled on Bear River.[57] Two Americans, Jared Sheldon and Hiram Taylor, came to California by way of New Mexico and found their ways to Sutter's Fort.[58] John Chamberlain, an amorous Irish blacksmith and deserter from a whaling ship, worked for Sutter and obtained a grant on the Cosumnes River.[59]

Vallejo and Alvarado regarded Sutter's foreign employees as a rogues' gallery filled with men of questionable and downright disreputable character. Sutter needed them all, at least in the beginning, even though he would have cause to regret hiring some of them. His sidearms were not meant to protect him only from Indians. Mountain men and sailors were rough trade. In 1842 Sutter informed one of his neighbors that he intended to "discharge many strangers . . . as very few among them are trustworthy."[60] A few days later three of his French employees, two French Canadians and Allgeier, were leaving him, he said. "One of them, Big Nicholas [Allgeier] wanted to kill me one day, and caused me a great deal of trouble."[61] Sutter bargained for trouble when he took in such "depraved creatures," as Alvarado described them.[62] Tough and accustomed to the casual violence of the fur trade and seafaring life, Custot, Allgeier, Keyser, Smith, and others like them formed Sutter's Praetorian Guard. Their presence at New Helvetia made it unlikely that a force of disgruntled Indian workers or independent Miwoks would eject him from the valley. Too many hard men with weapons in hand stood in the way.

Military force and Sutter's willingness to resort to violence explain in part his success in planting New Helvetia among Nisenans and Miwoks, but there was more to it. Indians who chose to deal with Sutter expected to benefit in several ways, including access to trade goods and protection from Mexicans, mountain men, and other Indian groups. By naming Indian captains and soldiers and giving them emblems of authority, Sutter established a new system of rank and hierarchy that appealed to some Indians.

The creation of an Indian army and allies provided something new in Sutter's life—ritual obedience. G. M. Waseurtz af Sandels, a Swedish traveler known to history as the King's Orphan (a romantic title gained because he was educated at the expense of the Swedish sovereign), visited Sutter in 1843. Sandel's descriptions of New Helvetia are among the best of the time. "The whole establishment had more the appearance of a fort than a farming industry," he wrote.[63] The Swede happened to be present when the chief of one of the valley tribes gave obeisance to Sutter. Hundreds of Indians had come to work and to acknowledge peace between themselves and the proprietor of New Helvetia. All were unarmed except the chief, who carried a bow and arrows. The assembled Indians danced, making "their customary graceful movements in file, in square, in flanges, and in body," Sandels recalled. Then the chief made a long speech and presented the bow and arrows to Sutter, saying: "Take these, and with them penetrate my heart if I or my tribe betray the trust you now put in us" (probably a free translation provided by Sutter).[64] The accuracy of this quotation may be doubted, but the symbolism of the event is unmistakable. Within the bounds of New Helvetia the only Indians permitted to bear arms were Sutter's soldiers. The Indians who violated Sutter's rules were subject to his summary punishments—imprisonment, lashing, even execution.

Nisenan and Miwok Indians were a necessary part of the human mosaic of New Helvetia. In Sutter's grand scheme they provided labor, customers, and security. If some of them rejected Sutter, this state of affairs did not have to be permanent so far as he was concerned. He continually added Indians to his sphere of influence by force, trade, and diplomacy, although there were always dissidents who resisted his authority. From the standpoint of European and American settlers, Sutter's consistent success in controlling the Native Ameri-

can population made new settlements in the Sacramento Valley tenable. Indeed, much of his prestige as a pioneer founder rested on his reputation as an
"Indian tamer," as William Wiggins put it.[65]

The thoughts of Indians were rarely recorded, but the few instances provide
a less flattering memory of Sutter's enterprise. William Joseph, a Nisenan, said
that Sutter paid his workers; but if Indians failed to work at New Helvetia,
Sutter's chiefs "whipped them with a big whip made of cowhide."[66] He did not
recall labor at Sutter's Fort as a "civilizing" enterprise, but rather as a compul-
sory requirement enforced by corporal punishment.

Sutter did not use corporal punishment and military force to satisfy a cruel
streak hidden beneath his otherwise affable personality. For him, the use of the
lash was merely part of the day-to-day routine of maintaining control over his
Indian workers. Nor was he a missionary for "civilization" among the Indians,
as Wiggins and others seemed to think. He certainly was not a missionary for
any religion. Sutter was consistently silent about his religious views, and there
is no reason to believe that he regarded the conversion of Native Americans as a
benefit to themselves or to anyone else. Insofar as he interfered with Miwok
and Nisenan customs, it was merely a matter of asserting his control over them,
not abolishing heathen practices. In any event, missionaries might have interfered with Sutter's substantive goal, which was, after all, to profit from Indian
labor and his operations in New Helvetia. And profit would be a matter of red
and black ink in the account books of fellow merchants on the Pacific Coast.
Indeed, once Sutter provided for New Helvetia's security and labor, most of his
attention was turned to business arrangements with his Mexican, Anglo, and
American counterparts in California and Hawaii. How would the man who
had failed in all of his previous business ventures fare in California?

CHAPTER 7

A Merchant-Adventurer in Mexico

Sutter looked at the Sacramento Valley and beheld a world of possibilities. Had he been less adventurous and less ambitious, he probably would have been content merely to establish a large livestock rancho, like Vallejo or Marsh or any of the hundreds of native-born and naturalized Mexican landowners in California; but Sutter wanted to expand the operations of New Helvetia so that it would be virtually self-contained and self-sustaining. He envisioned a diverse enterprise that included trapping, grazing, agriculture (especially wheat farming), manufacturing, distilling, milling, and retail sales of New Helvetia's products and other trade goods. The empire he planned to build combined the features of the fur posts, the missions, and the grand haciendas of Mexico.[1]

Sutter hoped that his extensive and varied commercial activities would result in a spectacular business success that would wipe away the series of small business failures that preceded his grand California venture. As proprietor of this great landed venture, he would be a great *seigneur,* lord of the manor, Don Juan Sutter. He would engage scores of white employees and hundreds of Indian and Kanaka retainers. Sutter objected to the Vallejos' autocratic rule of the Sonoma region but never saw the irony of simultaneously asserting that his power was well nigh absolute in the Sacramento Valley.[2] Like Sonoma, New Helvetia was based not on democracy but on personal power.

The successful realization of Sutter's plans to create a personal empire required more than ambition and a capacity for hard work, qualities that he possessed in abundance. Sutter needed capital and financial acumen to build New Helvetia, but he had none of the former and precious little of the latter.

Like all of Sutter's previous business undertakings, New Helvetia required credit, and to obtain it he needed the goodwill of his Mexican neighbors and Anglo merchants. Just as Sutter depended on Indian labor, he also required supplies from merchants and ranchers in order to provision his store and stock his rancho. All of these things, of course, he bought on credit that depended on the trust of his creditors. Sutter's brilliant personality was good enough collateral to establish credit but not sufficient to pay his debts.

Don Ygnacio Martínez was one of the first California creditors to become dissatisfied with Sutter. After sending livestock and supplies to New Helvetia, Martínez expected payment as agreed, but first Sutter deducted wages for the two Indians that Martínez detained. Then Sutter complained that the goods received from Martínez were shoddy and deducted more money from his account with the ranchero. Nor did he pay the remaining debt on time or in the manner specified. The original arrangement had been for Sutter to pay four hundred pesos for Martinez's cattle, half in coin and half in goods. He sent Martínez some cloth as partial payment, but Don Ygnacio returned it because the price was too high. Then Sutter sent a draft on his account with Nathan Spear, which was already extended to the limit. Spear repeatedly refused to honor the draft.[3]

Sutter bluntly told Martínez that "it is absolutely impossible for me to pay you unless it is on the terms which I have made, that is to say by a warrant against Don Nathan Spear." Besides, "since you failed in the quality of the animals which you sent," Sutter argued, "there is no reason why you should wish to exact from me the fulfillment of a contract in which you were the first to fail."[4] At the same time he reneged on his contract with Vallejo, which was also to be paid partially in silver. Instead, Sutter again drew on Spear. "Shall he pay a part of it in silver or not?" he asked rhetorically. For Sutter, it was "all the same, but nevertheless I might have acted differently if you had not failed in good faith and loyalty in sending me the articles about which we have already spoken a good deal."[5] He hoped that his differences with Vallejo and Martínez would not sour their personal relations, "for you know well that [friendship] is one thing and [business] is another."[6] Of course, Sutter's refusal to honor the original contract made a large difference in the financial considerations that Martínez and Vallejo received. According to Sutter, a cowhide was worth about "$1.50 cash, and $2.00 in trade."[7] In other words, in cash-poor California, merchants discounted 25 percent for cash, a potential windfall that Martínez and Vallejo foresaw when Sutter originally agreed to pay them in silver.

Running out of patience, in April 1840 Martínez enlisted the aid of General Vallejo. Martínez, a retired captain, hoped that Vallejo would pay him, because the government owed him back pay. "If Senor Sutter should by chance allege that I have failed in the contract because the jack was blind in one eye, the mares . . . and the milk cows wild, and the wheat wormy," the exasperated Martínez explained, "you can tell him that the jack does not lack one eye; that the herd is [legitimate], [the mares all trained,] and the milk cows are accustomed to being milked by white people, not by Indians."[8] Sutter easily sold the wheat from Martínez to the Hudson's Bay Company, so his objections were merely a pretext to avoid paying his just debt, Martínez reasoned. There was no chance that Vallejo would pay Sutter's debt to Martínez, but he forwarded the matter to the comandante at San José, ordering him to hold Sutter to his contract.[9] Sutter finally settled his debt with Martínez (probably at a discount), but their dispute was by no means unusual. The episode demonstrated to the comandante general that Sutter was not to be trusted, a suspicion that subsequent events would confirm in Vallejo's mind.

Unfortunately, none of Sutter's business ledgers survive, so a complete and detailed accounting of his debts, credit, and business practices cannot be reconstructed. The papers of many of his creditors and much of his business correspondence do exist, however, and they provide a means to describe his dealings in a general way. The unhappy but predictable truth was that Sutter paid his debts slowly and at a discount when he paid them at all. Whether this was a tactic that he used with malice aforethought or as an unforeseen result of his overextended finances is an unsettled question. It made little difference to his creditors. One of his common maneuvers was to run up a debt that was to be paid in cowhides, currency, or livestock. When he could not meet his obligation, Sutter then promised to pay with beaver pelts as soon as his trappers returned from the hunt, thus extending the period of credit and perhaps changing the values of the exchange. When the hunters returned, he would send some pelts to his creditor along with the sad report that the hunt had not gone as well as he expected. More negotiations and discounts followed.

Sutter's dealings with Antonio Suñol were typical. Suñol was a Spaniard by birth but had served in the French navy, which he deserted while his ship was in California. Like most other californios, he owned ranchos and sold livestock.[10] Sutter, a devoted Francophile, must have enjoyed corresponding in French with the former sailor. In the fall of 1840 Sutter bought a thousand cattle from Suñol to augment the herd of five hundred that he had acquired from Martínez, Marsh, and others.[11] "I have credited you with $295," Sutter wrote, "I shall pay, in the time agreed upon, in beaver skins." The original terms of his agreement with Suñol are unknown, but beaver pelts were probably not part of the bargain. Having promised to pay in beaver, Sutter requisitioned still more goods. He asked if Suñol would "kindly get a small cargo of corn, beans, peas, etc.," for Robert Ridley, captain of Sutter's launch, who would arrive in a few weeks.[12] When Ridley arrived, he came not with beaver or anything else to pay on Sutter's debt but with a further request for geese and turkeys. "Kindly give him the bill also," Sutter instructed.[13]

Locally made liquor became a part of Sutter's stock in trade. In the fall of 1840 he informed Suñol that he had "begun to make brandy from wild grapes" and hoped to know the results of the endeavor in a short time.[14] Sutter's experiment must have been successful, for by the next summer he was ordering distilling equipment from Suñol.[15] Visitors in 1841 noticed the distillery with interest. Sutter became famous for entertaining his guests with all the food and liquors at his disposal, although Captain William Dane Phelps tried to convince him to abandon the distillery.[16] Captain Phelps was not above taking a nip of brandy himself but implored Sutter to shut down his New Helvetia distillery. "Capt. S. acknowledged [that] my views of the matter were correct," Phelps wrote, "and promised to abolish the use and manufacture of it." He left Sutter's premises hoping "New Helvetia will become the head quarters of Temperance and Morality in this new intemperate and immoral community."[17] Captain Phelps's plea was in vain, for Sutter continued to make brandy—*pisco,* as one of his visitors called it—and often included it with his shipments by the launch.[18] Phelps was not the last well-meaning soul to urge Sutter in the direction of temperance. During the next two decades Sutter's drinking—or at least the deleterious effects of it—would inspire comment from a host of observers.

In January 1841 Sutter was still sending Suñol beaver pelts, but the debt lingered on through the year and was increased when he purchased lumber and other goods from Suñol.[19] In August Sutter agreed to send Indian laborers to Suñol, another common way in which he put black ink in his ledger.[20] In October he sent some of the brandy that he distilled from wild grapes.[21] His debt was still not fully paid. In the spring of 1842 Sutter asked Suñol to accept deer tallow. "Vessels for Lima and Valparaiso are always ready to purchase this article," he explained. "I can send you enough deer tallow to cancel my indebtedness to you," he added hopefully.[22] Suñol agreed to accept tallow, and Sutter's hunters began slaughtering deer.[23]

The original contract for Suñol's cattle has not come to light, but it may have been something like the one that Sutter struck with John Marsh. Sutter wanted to know if the good doctor would accept "⅔ in goods & ⅓ Money or Beaver Skins" and—perhaps most importantly to Sutter—"how many months you could wait for payment."[24] Such arrangements were certainly vague enough to be subject to a variety of interpretations. Once the bargain was struck, Marsh would receive "goods" of unknown value plus some money or an unspecified amount of beaver skins of indeterminate quality. As the case of

Suñol shows, in Sutter's mind a contract was never immutable but was subject to endless renegotiation as to the mode of payment and the maturity of the debt. Yet he usually paid something, along with promises of a brighter future that would enable him to pay in furs, or wheat or brandy or cattle or something from his small manufacturing rooms at the fort. Someday, Sutter said, he would pay off his debts. For most californios the day would not come soon enough. Meanwhile, he built New Helvetia with other people's money.

In Sutter's defense, he was not the only person in California who lived on credit. The whole province did business on promises to pay. Cowhides and bags of tallow were the principal currency in the 1840s. Californios were land and cattle poor. The biggest markets for their goods were in New England and Great Britain, where factories turned hides into shoes, boots, harness, and leather belting that ran the machines of the industrial revolution. Hides (known as California banknotes) were worth $1.50 to $2.50, more or less, depending on the market when a Yankee trading ship hove into view.[25] Terms of credit were generous. Monterey merchant Thomas Larkin said that "12 to 18 months is considered by us good, and we obtain no interest only on Cash lent."[26] Virtually all manufactured goods were obtained in California from shipboard hide and tallow traders.

California rancheros and merchants customarily made purchases with promises to pay a certain number of hides at a future date, as in the case of William Hinckley's note of March 2, 1842: "I promise to deliver to James Watson on his order One Hundred merchantable bullock hides at Yerba Buena San Francisco in all the month of May next."[27] The note itself served as currency that was used in various transactions before the hides were delivered. Because the note was payable months after it was made, it was actually a contract in hide futures, a gamble that the market would go up (if you were the buyer) or down (if you were the seller). The actual value of the note depended partly on the going rate for hides and partly on Hinckley's reputation for reliability and honesty. If hides were going for $1.50, the note was worth no more than $150 when it was redeemed. When the price of cowhides fluctuated, so did the value of the note. If Hinckley was known to be in financial trouble, if Muquelemne raiders had struck his herd, if his cattle were known to be in poor condition, or if he could not deliver the cattle until months later, the note would be worth less. In this case the note passed through three hands and then back through the chain to Watson, who assigned the note to a Monterey merchant who eventually gave it to William A. Leidesdorff, the final holder, who did indeed receive the hides. While the hides were supposed to be delivered in May 1842, payment was not made until after January 1843. In the meantime a lot of business had been done on this paper promise to present a hundred hides to the bearer, while the cows who wore them placidly chewed their cuds somewhere in California. As the cattle grazed, merchants shifted the debt around as part of their many transactions.

Californios practiced capitalism with the hair on, and this was a business world in which someone like Sutter could survive. He made promises without end then discounted them as rapidly and steeply as he could. Unlike californios, however, Sutter had no fund of accumulated trust on which he could draw. The leading californios were a small group—a few hundred families related by blood, marriage, and god-parentage (*compadrazgo*). Californio parents named godparents for their children at birth and other important life events, eventually assigning perhaps a dozen fictive kin to whom the children owed filial affection and responsibility. Thus the elite californios not only knew each other but were often related in some way.[28] When American and British merchants entered the scene, most of them wisely understood that marriage with a californiana paved the way to business connections and (they hoped) riches.[29] Sutter, who always proudly acknowledged his own marriage and his accomplished children in Switzerland, had none of these ties of kinship on which to rely. When he did not pay his debts, matters could not be smoothed over by family intermediaries who might urge patience and stress filial affection and family honor.

The surprising thing is not that Sutter was overextended in California—this was his long-established business practice—but that he seemed to go out of his way to offend his creditors. Perhaps he disliked the close, family-bound, Catholic, conservative, californio society that regarded him as an outsider. Possibly the elitism and presumptions of a few prominent californios offended him and reminded him of the closed, clannish society and inherited wealth that bedeviled him in Switzerland. Maybe Sutter was prejudiced against Mexicans, or perhaps he was simply tone deaf to the cultural melodies of California, a trait that his mediocre command of Spanish exacerbated. Whatever the reasons, he paid little attention to the impact of his brashly worded explanations for his failure to honor financial commitments.

While Sutter struggled to build his empire of debt in the Sacramento Valley, developments on the coast forecast a rocky future for foreigners in California. Not all Mexican Californians saw the arrival of immigrants as positive developments. Some feared that Americans might rebel against Mexican (and californio) authority much as they had done in Texas. In 1840 Governor Alvarado heard that Isaac Graham and the American riflemen and other foreigners who hung around Graham's mountain still were plotting to overthrow the government and perhaps establish a Texas-style republic. In April Alvarado's soldiers rounded up thirty-eight of these drunken boasters and sent them to Mexico for further disposition. The central government disappointed Alvarado by setting most of them free.[30]

Governor Alvarado had little evidence to support his claim that Graham and his friends planned to deprive californios "of the richest of treasures, your lives and country."[31] The governor may have been motivated by the insulting and sneering familiarity of Graham, who believed with some justification that he and his well-armed cronies had put Alvarado in power in the first place. Graham wanted favors from the governor, whom he impertinently called by his middle name, Bautista. "Ho Bautista, come here, I want to speak with you," the governor quoted Graham as saying. "Bautista, here—Bautista there—and Bautista everywhere."[32]

If Alvarado hoped to reestablish a healthy respect for his gubernatorial authority and a revival of formal forms of address, he was not altogether successful. On June 11 the French sloop-of-war *Danaïde*, J. de Rosamel commanding, dropped anchor in Monterey. The *Danaïde* was bound for Honolulu when Rosamel heard rumors of the Graham deportation and the still more inflaming news that two French citizens had been killed by the californios. So Rosamel trimmed his sails and headed for California to make inquiries, perhaps something more. Two days later Captain French Forrest, acting on intelligence similar to Rosamel's, guided the U.S. man-of-war *St. Louis* to an anchorage near the *Danaïde*. Captain Forrest wished to know why American citizens were detained and robbed of their property. Alvarado and his men gave satisfactory answers to both naval officers: no Frenchmen had been killed or detained; the American prisoners were men of low character who had violated Mexican laws. The French and American officers and men of both ships then settled into a pleasant round of social engagements in the California capital. In the fullness of time both vessels departed and continued their respective patrols, ever on the alert for abuses to French and American citizens, property, and national honor.[33]

Californios had made convincing explanations to Rosamel and Forrest; but if Mexican authorities had not rationalized events to the satisfaction of these naval officers, they might have opened fire on the pueblo. Governor Alvarado and the californios well understood that they had no means of defense against a naval bombardment in Monterey or anywhere in California. There would be no help from a Mexican government that was unable to quell insurrections in California, let alone an attack from a ship-of-war.

The Graham incident was a minor affair in the scheme of international relations, but it had lasting repercussions. Once the prisoners reached Mexico, federal authorities recognized that Alvarado had acted highhandedly. Officials even imprisoned Graham's californio guards for a short time. The American and British prisoners were detained for months; but most were released without trial, thanks to the intercession of the British consul. Only Graham and a few others were tried, found not guilty, and sailed back to California at government expense in 1842. The happy outcome of Mexican due process notwithstanding, Graham and the others were more disaffected than ever when they returned to their desultory pursuits.[34]

After the Graham affair, foreigners and Mexicans were increasingly paranoid and suspicious of one another. Californios feared a rebellion by foreigners. Alvarado's actions proved to some Americans that a Texas-style revolution should put an end to Mexican misrule. Thomas Jefferson Farnham, an Illinois lawyer who had traveled widely in the West, happened to be in California when Graham was arrested. Farnham publicized the affray as an outrage against Americans and vilified Mexican Californians as lazy and cruel in his 1844 book *Travels in the Californias and Scenes in the Pacific Ocean*.[35] The Graham affair was proof, according to Farnham, that California should be seized and governed as an independent republic by Anglos such as himself. California historian Hubert Howe Bancroft forty years later characterized Farnham's book as "worthless trash, and . . . a tissue of falsehoods."[36] Still, among Americans it became a foundation text for their conviction that the United States should take California from Mexico.

Sutter, who was no doubt distracted with building his settlement, took no notice of Graham's deportation. Yet in hindsight the implications for Sutter were clear. New Helvetia attracted the kind of frontier rovers and soldiers of fortune that Alvarado, Vallejo, and their compatriots despised and feared. And perhaps worse, representatives of foreign governments (official and otherwise) found their ways to the Sacramento Valley and made their acquaintance with the hard-charging Swiss Mexican. Sutter was becoming a little famous. New Helvetia was becoming an irritant to the Mexicans, and perhaps something more.

Sutter's fiscal irresponsibility did not prevent him from becoming a citizen of Mexico, for Governor Alvarado still regarded him as a useful pawn to check the power of his uncle, Mariano Vallejo. Sutter returned to Monterey in late August 1840 to be naturalized. Swearing that he was a Swiss Catholic (in his youth he had been raised as a Lutheran) and of good character, he became a Mexican citizen. The governor also commissioned him as justice of the peace.[37] Sutter would be eligible to receive a grant of land after one year as a citizen. Governor Alvarado was his ace in the hole in Mexican California. Sutter would hold this card close to his heart (and his wallet) until he received his grant, but time and circumstances would prove that his loyalty to Alvarado was a temporary thing.

The Hudson's Bay Company was Sutter's main competitor in the valley. He had always seen the fur trade as a potential source of income, but the Hudson's Bay Company gave his trappers vigorous competition that he wanted to stop. The brigade that annually campaigned south from the Columbia River to the Sacramento Valley was a large group of trappers, traders, and Indians. "When they pitched their tents," Sutter recalled, "it was like a village."[38] When Alvarado directed him to tell brigade leader Michel Laframboise to move the camp farther from California settlements in the summer of 1840, Sutter took it upon himself to inform Hudson's Bay Company authorities at Fort Vancouver that the company was forbidden to return to California. His order was ill-considered. At best, Sutter's rash action had put Alvarado in a bad position. At worst, he had instigated a controversy with international dimensions. His edict soon got the attention of Sir James Douglas, the chief factor at Fort Vancouver. In January 1841 Douglas appeared in Monterey in order to set matters straight. Douglas and Alvarado soon came to an amicable understanding that allowed the British company to continue hunting in California, much to the chagrin of Captain Sutter. "As long as this company comes to this country," he complained to Antonio Suñol, "beaver hunting will be a failure."[39]

Sutter's futile attempt to monopolize the valley fur trade was ill-considered, because the Hudson's Bay Company was one of his creditors. Perhaps that is why he smoothed things later in the year by giving passports to the company's trappers so that they could visit the coastal settlements, which was exactly what Alvarado meant to stop in the first place. Sergeant José de los Santos Berryessa complained to Mariano Vallejo that these well-armed men might cause trouble in the Sonoma district and should be closely watched.[40]

In 1841 more well-armed strangers began to appear in California. They were Americans. In November the Bartleson-Bidwell party (named for the group's two leaders, John Bartleson and John Bidwell) crossed the Sierra Nevada and stumbled into northern California. These ragged foreigners were the first party of overland immigrants to California. The band consisted of thirty-two men from the Missouri frontier, accompanied by one woman and a child. During the crossing they had a terrible time. Having abandoned their wagons and consumed their animals east of the mountains, they completed the journey on foot in a pitiable condition. Miraculously, they reached the ranch of John Marsh, about fifty miles southwest of New Helvetia. He helped the bedraggled overlanders but expected to be paid for his trouble. Within a few weeks the newcomers had heard that Sutter offered better hospitality than Marsh, and they headed to the fort.[41]

Rumors of Sutter's generosity were not exaggerations. He provided for the destitute travelers, helped them to get passports, employed as many as he could,

Table 1. Overland Immigration to California
before the Gold Rush

1841	34
1842	—
1843	38
1844	53
1845	260
1846	1,500
1847	450
1848	400
Total	2,735

Based on John D. Unruh, Jr., *The Plains Across: The Overland Emigrants and the Trans-Mississippi West, 1840–60* (Urbana: University of Illinois Press, 1979), 119.

and assisted all who wished to obtain land from the government. Because he wanted to attract as many farmers, artisans, and mechanics to his establishment as possible, it was in Sutter's interest to be openhanded to immigrants. But it must also be said that his generosity was a balm to the bruised, calloused, and hungry people who had made the trek to California. The Bartleson-Bidwell immigrants were the first of hundreds of overlanders that Sutter assisted. As the immigration swelled in the 1840s, Sutter's Fort became the lodestone for the wagon trains that formed on the Missouri River and headed to California (see table 1).

During the 1840s Sutter enthusiastically encouraged the impoverished newcomers to come to New Helvetia. "Sometimes my houses were full of emigrants, so much so that I could scarcely find a place to sleep myself," he recalled. His fort and outbuildings were filled "every winter during emigration times with wet, poor, and hungry emigrants, men, women and children." When Sutter learned of overland travelers who needed help in the mountains, he sent relief parties to aid them. "Often I went with my men and cattle to draw them out of the snow." These starved and ragged supplicants regarded Sutter as their savior, and he genuinely felt a humanitarian obligation to them. "Very few had more than their teams when they arrived, and some lost everything," he remembered.[42] In the years between 1841 and the gold rush, Sutter, the confidence man, rose above self-interest and personal ambition while giving succor to strangers in a strange land. In a long and disorderly life, this was his finest moment as a human being. The men and women he helped would always remember him kindly.

By 1841 New Helvetia looked like it was going to amount to something.

Captain Phelps described Sutter's domain in July of that year. While he complained of the swarms of fleas that feasted on him as he slept ("on getting up I found that my body and limbs bore some resemblance to a 'current dumpling' "), he was otherwise favorably impressed. The walls of the fort were rapidly going up. He noted shops on the inside of the fort for Sutter's "artificers such as Carpenters, Blacksmiths, Coopers &c."[43] Sutter had begun curing the chinook salmon that glutted the Sacramento River in their semiannual spawning runs. "In the latter part of the season the surface of the river is nearly covered with dead rotten salmon floating to the sea," Phelps observed. Sutter directed John Sinclair to preserve some of the fresh-caught fish for sale. The Scot salted a quantity of the fish, but they spoiled. He also smoked a lot of them, and Phelps said that they "were equal to the best I ever tasted. Next season they intend preserving a large quantity."[44] Indeed, salt-cured salmon would become one of Sutter's staple products, packed in barrels made at the fort and shipped to ports on the Pacific Coast.[45]

Phelps saw activity and fine prospects everywhere, including extensive fields and pastures. Behind the fort there was a deep gully partially filled with water that Sutter wished to extend to form a canal between the American and Sacramento Rivers. This excavation would enable him to "bring his boats near to his house, [and he] will also have a fine site for mills." (This project never materialized.) Sutter's "coal burners were at work felling trees and chopping off the limbs to make charcoal."[46] These were remarkable accomplishments. In a short span of time Sutter had harnessed the Indian labor supply, tapped the valley's natural resources, and built a mercantile establishment from nothing. The credit that merchants and rancheros extended helped enormously, to be sure, but Sutter's audacity and hard work were the main forces that built New Helvetia. The question was: could he keep it?

CHAPTER 8

Foreign Intrigue

In June 1841 Sutter passed through the fort's gates and rode across the valley toward the coast, accompanied by two armed guards and two vaqueros (charged with driving thirty horses). They rode hard and fast, keeping up the pace by changing mounts along the way. After crossing Altamont Pass, they raced through Robert Livermore's Rancho Las Positas then to Mission San José, where they exchanged their spent horses for fresh ones. They stopped briefly at the missions along *el camino real* as they sped south through the coastal valleys and over the passes to Monterey. It was an important journey for Sutter. He was going to petition the governor for his land grant.[1]

For nearly two years Sutter had appraised the Sacramento Valley, and now he meant to make his request of the governor. The fort and its pastures and fields near the American River were the focal point of New Helvetia in 1841, but Sutter had his eye on another piece of land to the north. He called it Hock Farm. Named for the Hok Nisenan ranchería, the farm was on the west bank of the Feather River a few miles south of present-day Yuba City. The grant he had in mind included these two widely separated pieces of land, a huge parcel even under Mexico's generous land laws. Accordingly, Sutter requested eleven square leagues (more than forty-eight thousand acres) that stretched north from his fort to the Sutter Buttes "to aggrandize his enterprise and to establish twelve families," as the grant said.[2] The grant (more than sixty miles in length) excluded land that was periodically inundated during the winter; but even with these exclusions it was difficult to stretch its boundaries to include Hock Farm and Sutter's Fort without extreme gerrymandering. The grant's language left much room for doubt about the location of Sutter's land.

While specifying the Buttes, Sacramento, and Feather Rivers, the grant failed to mention the American River, the fort, or any physical feature south of the Feather River's mouth. Why, one might reasonably wonder, did Sutter fail to mention the land and improvements in which he had so much invested? To make matter's worse, his surveyor, Jean Jacques Vioget, got the latitudes wrong, an error that would cause Sutter no end of trouble with squatters and the courts a decade later.[3] Sutter claimed that the Vioget map clearly marked the southern boundary of his grant below the American River, but the original map was lost. Consequently the borders of New Helvetia would be a matter of conjecture in years to come. In effect, Sutter and Alvarado created a floating grant. Within the huge extent of the land within Vioget's defective survey, Sutter was entitled to only eleven square leagues—but which leagues? Neither Sutter nor Vioget described the exact location of the lands that Sutter actually claimed under his grant, but for the time being he possessed a huge, un-developed estate. His status as a landed gentleman and a Mexican official gave him a sense of financial and political security that proved to be entirely false, but that realization would come in the future.

To Sutter, the glimmering future appeared brighter than ever. While in Monterey he recruited a half-dozen mechanics for his workshops. "A Negro was amongst them," he recalled, "a good cooper—the first darkey in the valley."[4] Although the cooper was the first African American to live in the interior, he would join a much larger population of color—Indians, Kanakas, and people of mixed racial parentage. When Sutter prepared to return to the valley, he gathered his new men together in David Spence's yard. The motley assemblage led a ship's captain who happened to be there to exclaim: "My God! How can you manage such vagabonds!" "Well enough," was Sutter's response.[5] He might have added that for the time being there was no one else to whom he could turn, so off he rode with his tough new employees.

The late summer and fall of 1841 brought many visitors to New Helvetia, including some who represented foreign governments. The first to arrive was a contingent from the U.S.S. *Vincennes,* which carried the U.S. Navy exploring expedition commanded by Charles Wilkes. While the *Vincennes* lay at anchor in San Francisco Bay, Lieutenant Commander Cadwalader Ringgold led six small boats and fifty men up the Sacramento River to Sutter's Fort, where they found an enthusiastic welcome. The Wilkes report described New Helvetia as a large farming establishment with thousands of livestock and extensive fields under cultivation, although Sutter's crops had suffered because of a severe drought. His Indian laborers had built several adobe structures, including a "line of wall, to protect him . . . more from the present authorities of the land, than from the tribes about him, who are now working in his employ."[6] Captain

Sutter wore "a kind of undress uniform, with his side-arms buckled about him." He entertained Ringgold with large stories about his military service in Europe, his accomplished Swiss family, "whom he expects to join him soon," and an Indian dance.[7]

While the Wilkes expedition was in California rumors circulated (probably retailed by Sutter to Ringgold) that Vallejo was jealous of Sutter's power and influence. "It was thought that had it not been for the force which [Sutter] could bring to oppose any attempt to dislodge him, it would have been tried," Wilkes reported. "In the meantime, Captain Suter [sic] is using all his energies to render himself impregnable."[8]

On September 1 a character as colorful as Sutter himself arrived in the Sacramento Valley.[9] Count Eugène Duflot de Mofras, French attaché of a delegation to Mexico, reconnoitered California so that he could inform his government about the condition of the place and whether it might be nudged into French hands.[10] California, long known to be poorly defended by the Mexican government and populated by restive inhabitants, seemed ripe for the taking. Mofras had little respect for the californios, who regarded him as a rude guest.[11] Sutter was delighted to entertain the expansive visitor, who tickled his Francophilic predisposition.

Mofras was impressed with the defenses of Sutter's Fort and the development of New Helvetia. "New Helvetia houses . . . 30 white men, including Germans, Swiss, Canadian, Americans, Frenchmen, and Englishmen" who were "engaged in cutting wood, operating forges, or in carpentry."[12] Others scoured the valley for beaver. According to Mofras, all of Sutter's white employees lived "with Indian or Californian women and the colony totals no fewer than 200 souls," which implied a large number of mixed-race children. The largest of the structures within the fort "is intended for [Sutter's] family, whom he intends to bring out from Basle, together with some additional Swiss colonists."[13] New Helvetia "was destined to be a settlement of considerable importance, being the point through which trains coming overland from Canada, the Columbia River, and the United States will pass," Mofras predicted.[14] He even claimed that Sutter wanted to "have a few French missionaries reside at his fort to civilize the neighboring Indians," but it is unlikely that Sutter seriously desired French Jesuits to oversee the moral development of New Helvetia.[15] Indeed, there is nothing in Sutter's letters or reminiscences that indicates that he gave any consideration whatever to religious matters personally or for the purpose of colonizing the Sacramento Valley.

Mofras emphasized Sutter's affinity for France and all things French (including the tale about serving in the French military) and went so far as to say that the Swiss "poses as a Frenchman." "In fact," he informed his government,

Sutter "considered himself under the protection of France." Mofras approvingly reported that Sutter engaged French and French-Canadians at his post.[16] The French agent learned that Vallejo was jealous of Sutter and disclosed that if the Mexican officer continued to make trouble Sutter "would hoist the French colors over his fort, leave for Sonoma, and force the issue."[17] Whatever Sutter might do, Mofras was convinced that California would soon change masters— "and the day is not remote," he added.[18] This account sounds as if two like-minded men discussed the future of California over several glasses of Sutter's homemade pisco. They had plenty of opportunities to toast the tricolor inasmuch as the French agent stayed with Sutter off and on for about one month.

Sutter was still emphasizing his French connections when the Oregon contingent of the Wilkes expedition arrived at the fort after an overland trip from the Columbia River. William Dunlop Brackenridge, one of the party, described Sutter as "perfectly military, height about 5 ft. 8 inches, rather stout but well proportioned, hair fair—countenance of a rudy complection [sic]." Brackenridge did not doubt Sutter's well-rehearsed stories of service "for a considerable number of years in the French Army." He noticed the military advantages of the fort, which would "make the place more formidable against any attack from the Spanish population who are not very friendly towards him."[19] Before leaving for San Francisco Bay to link up with the seaborne part of the expedition, Brackenridge noted in his journal that "in a few years there will be nothing in California to compete with him in point of strength, wealth, & influence."[20]

Visitors to New Helvetia consistently remarked on its growing strength and formidability against potential Mexican threats. To californios these developments were ominous. Sutter's Fort not only posed a possible military danger but brought more unpredictable, potentially dangerous frontiersmen for the government to deal with. These possibilities especially nettled Vallejo, but there were other ways in which the Swiss could upset the comandante general.

Sutter's most serious aggravation began with good news for Vallejo—or so he thought. In July 1841, while Sutter entertained Ringgold, Vallejo wrote to his nephew, the governor. "The news I am going to give you is too good for me not to be persuaded that you will share my rejoicing," he said. Peter Kostromitinov (Don Pedro, as Vallejo cosily called him), the Russian-American Company's agent in Yerba Buena, offered to sell Fort Ross with surrounding properties and improvements to Vallejo. General Vallejo in turn wanted the Mexican government to make the purchase. The departure of the Russians and acquisition of Ross would mean that "all my desires will be consummated," Vallejo told his nephew. "You know that we all have our little bit of self-esteem," he added. Vallejo had already settled an extensive territory around

Sonoma at his own expense, and by adding Ross to the Sonoma frontier "you will know that I have secured my greatest triumph."[21]

Vallejo allowed his ego to run far ahead of the political realities. The Mexican government was not willing to purchase property from the Russians—whose settlement within Mexican territory was illegal, after all, from the Mexican perspective. Even the buildings were constructed from materials on Mexican land, it was argued, so the Mexican nation rightfully owned them too. Alvarado feared his uncle's ambitions too much to use his limited influence as governor to convince the central government to secure Vallejo's "greatest triumph." Perhaps it would be best just to let the Russians leave northern California. Then californios acting under Mexican authority could occupy the fort and dispose of the remaining property. What choice would the Russians have in the matter? Where would they find another buyer? The answers to these questions were not long in coming. In the meantime Vallejo offered $9,000 for the Russian livestock.[22]

While trying to work out a deal with Vallejo the Russians also opened negotiations with Sutter. Like Vallejo, he was at first leery of purchasing anything but livestock, so Kostromitinov redoubled his efforts to get Vallejo to buy everything if he could get official approval. Learning of this development, Sutter assumed that Vallejo had outbid him. "The Russians have found purchasers for all their houses and ranchos, and I am not at all pleased," he told Antonio Suñol. Sutter felt that the Russians had double-crossed him. "We can see what the Russian character is like," he snorted. "They used to say very openly that they would prefer to burn all their houses than to sell them to a man belonging to this country, and especially Mr. Vallejo who had insulted the Russian flag etc., etc." Sutter professed astonishment that the Russians would sell to Vallejo for "a few thousand dollars more. . . . Only Russians could act so. I would prefer not to have had any dealings with them."[23] He would soon overcome his high-minded business scruples about dealing with Russians.

On September 1 word reached Sutter that the Russian deal with Vallejo had miscarried, a revelation that Mofras evidently conveyed when he arrived on the same day. "It appears that the Russians cannot come to an agreement with Mr. Vallejo and that they are reopening negotiations with me," Sutter revealed to Suñol. "Now I shall be more exacting."[24] Mofras claimed that he had encouraged the Russians to sell to Sutter, motivated by Sutter's Francophilia and his own hatred of Vallejo.[25]

Sure enough, on September 4 the Russian schooner *Constantine* dropped anchor at Sutter's Sacramento River embarcadero.[26] Alexander Rotchev, governor of Fort Ross, disembarked and offered him all of the property at Ross, the port at Bodega, and outlying ranchos. The bargain included buildings, furnishing, tools, machinery, and livestock but not the land (although Sutter would try to claim that as well). Sutter quickly forgot his anti-Russian prejudices and sailed with Rotchev to San Rafael. There they took horses to Bodega, where they met Kostromitinov, who offered Sutter all the Russian company's California holdings for $30,000 in wheat and other produce payable over a period of four years beginning in 1842.[27] The Russians added this new debt to Sutter's other Russian "current account for various merchandise, provisions and materials," amounting to $3,868.16.[28] "I accepted the offer," Sutter told Bancroft.[29]

After his September meeting with the Russians, Sutter informed Vallejo that he had bought "all the movable and fixed property of the settlement of the Honorable Russian American Company at Ross." Furthermore, he was sending "a party of men by land to that place for the embarking of the above mentioned furniture, &c." Sutter asked Vallejo to allow his men to pass through the Sonoma frontier and "not to put any obstacle in their way."[30]

Russian-American Company officials prepared two sale documents. On December 12 Rotchev executed a bill of sale that ostensibly deeded to Sutter the California lands that the Russians had occupied since 1812, along with the movable property. The document asserted that the Russian-American Company was empowered to sell this land by "the institution and spirit of the laws sanctified by Spain and Mexico," a bald-faced declaration that flew in the face of all official Spanish and Mexican protestations to the contrary.[31] Nor did Rotchev have company authority to make such a deed. There can be little doubt that Sutter prompted Rotchev to draw up this completely bogus document, which was not notarized and not filed with Mexican authorities. Legal or not, the potential value of the document to Sutter was clear enough. In the event of a change of sovereignty in California, he had a plausible claim to yet another extensive estate, even if the Mexican government did not recognize the legality of the land transfer. With a bit of luck Sutter could make his claim good or perhaps sell the unproven claim to a speculator.

On December 13 in Yerba Buena Sutter and Kostromitinov signed the bill of sale for the movable Russian property. The Russians knew their man. "The deed was written in French," Sutter recalled. Even more impressive were the opening words, "with the consent of the Emperor of all the Russias," which Sutter found flattering to himself. Before solemnly signing the document the party had a "grand dinner" aboard the Russian ship *Helena*. "Champagne flowed freely," Sutter fondly remembered many years later. "The Emperor's health was drunk and the health of the new owner of Ross and Bodega." Sutter believed that the toasts invested him as the new proprietor of Ross. "Before the document was signed I was thus the acknowledged owner of all the Russian possessions in California," he thought, no doubt mentally including the real estate that he had "purchased" the day before.[32] The parties signed the contract in the Hudson's Bay Company office in Yerba Buena in the presence of alcalde Francisco Guerrero and other witnesses.

Sutter was impressed with the Russians' evident trust in him. "They required from me no note nor paper of any kind," except the signed bill of sale, of course.[33] Even "before I set out for Yerba Buena the Russians began to abandon their place," proof that they took Sutter at his word.[34] If he said that he would buy, he would buy. If he said that he would pay, he would pay. Sutter's word was good enough to seal the bargain and good enough for the tsar's agents in America. In his mind, the document was a mere legal formality. Among gentlemen such as Sutter and the trusting Russians, a verbal promise, a toast, and a handshake were sufficient. This was the sort of personal business dealing that he most prized, believing that he was good at this kind of intimate negotiation. From another point of view, the Russians had hit upon a formula for business negotiations that always worked with Sutter: with enough liquor and flattery he would agree to anything.

Sutter was already deep in debt and ill prepared to take on a large new financial obligation, but the enticement of buying the fine Ross establishment on credit was too much for him to resist. As Bancroft observed, Sutter "would perhaps have bought anything at any price if it could be obtained on credit," and so it was with Ross.[35] John Bidwell, the earnest immigrant who came penniless to Sutter's Fort in 1841 and became his lifelong friend, attributed this proclivity for taking on new debts to Sutter's "peculiar traits." His "necessities compelled him to take all he could buy, and he paid all he could pay; but he failed to keep up with his payments."[36] This tendency to overextend was a thread that ran through Sutter's entire life.

The Russian contract obligated Sutter to pay $5,000 in produce in 1842 and 1843, double that in 1844, and $10,000 in coin in 1845 (see table 2). Even if he could have kept up with his payments in produce, there was virtually no chance that Sutter could have come up with $10,000 in coin. Where and how in cash-poor California would he get such a sum? But in Sutter's world 1845 was a long time off and only good things would happen in the future.

In the meantime Sutter immediately tried to liquidate some debts by selling the land that he now believed he owned by virtue of the Rotchev deed. He was obligated to Alpheus Basil Thompson, a seagoing merchant from Maine and sometime resident of Yerba Buena and Santa Barbara.[37] Sutter paid Thompson with drafts on Eliab Grimes, the long-suffering Honolulu merchant who was one of his largest creditors; but Grimes refused to honor them.[38] So the day after ceremoniously signing the bill of sale with the Russians, Sutter offered the

Table 2. Sutter's Schedule of Payments to the Russian-American Company

Value of products in dollars/Cash	1841	1842	1843	1844	1845	Total
Cash (dollars)	2,000				10,000	12,000
Wheat @ $2/bushel		3,200	3,200	6,400		12,800
Peas @ $2.50/fanega		250	250	500		1,000
Beans @ $3/fanega		75	75	150		300
Soap @ $14/quintal		700	700	1,400		2,800
Suet @ $2/arroba		400	400	800		1,600
Tallow @ $1.50/arroba		375	375	750		1,500
Total	2,000	5,000	5,000	10,000	10,000	32,000

Based on Clarence J. DuFour, "The Russian Withdrawal from California," *California Historical Society Quarterly* 12 (September 1933): 240–76.
Note: The fanega, quintal, and arroba are Spanish units of measure: 1 fanega equals approximately 1.5 bushels; 1 quintal equals approximately 1 hundred-weight; 1 arroba equals approximately 25 pounds by weight or 4.26 gallons of liquid.

Bodega rancho. "I propose . . . to let you have the half part of this property on reasonable terms." "Some good houses for Gentlemen are there," he enthused. "The port of Bodega will be a great place in a few years. It is no doubt of that, and when I tell you the reasons you will believe me."[39] Thompson did not take the bait.

Sutter's offer to Thompson violated the letter and spirit of his Russian agreement, which stipulated that the buildings at Bodega and two of the adjacent Russian ranches should be maintained as they were until he made the final payment in 1845. This was no great matter to Sutter. Once the Russians sailed over the horizon, he ignored the fine print and made the most of his bargain. In September 1843 he sold the buildings at Bodega and some livestock and produce for $1,600 paid on his account with David Spence. As late as 1859, when his claim embroiled him in a lawsuit, Sutter maintained that he had purchased the former Russian lands.[40]

Sutter's purchase of Ross had to be a bitter development for Vallejo. His hated rival not only snatched from him his great triumph but acquired considerable valuable property. He cooperated with Sutter nonetheless. Sutter's men quickly got about the business of moving the Russian inventory to New Helvetia. Robert Ridley was the first overseer of Sutter's Ross property. In January 1842 he replaced Ridley with John Bidwell, who plunged into the huge task of stripping the Russian settlement.[41] He even dried the apricots and apples from the orchards and made some cider. Sutter's men drove nearly one thousand horses and mules, seventeen hundred cattle, and nine hundred sheep, more or less, to New Helvetia. Farm tools of all description, plows, two windmills, millstones, a tannery, and dairy equipment were all carried away.

Sutter added a cooperage, a cordage machine, forges, smithing tools, and other implements to his manufacturing inventory. Saddles, bridles, and harnesses by the dozen would fill tack rooms in New Helvetia. Carts, wheels, and boats large and small improved his transportation network.[42] Sutter also obtained Russian uniforms, powder, rifles, and artillery, with which he equipped his Indian army and strengthened his fort.[43] After 1841 Sutter's Miwok and Nisenan soldiers wore uniforms that probably had graced the backs of Aleut and Pomo defenders of the Russian-American Company. His men dismantled Fort Ross for its magnificent redwood lumber, doors, and windows, which he intended to use at his own fort. The twenty-ton Russian schooner *Constantine* was part of the bargain too. Sutter renamed it the *Sacramento* and used it to carry goods from Ross to New Helvetia.[44]

The transfer of property took nearly two years, with losses along the way. One hundred cattle drowned while crossing the Sacramento River, although Sutter mitigated this blow by stripping the hides from the carcasses.[45] There were other problems. His men were able to disassemble a lovely greenhouse pavilion but could not reconstruct it because they did not understand Russian carpentry. Although he dearly wanted the magnificent, sixty-foot redwood threshing floor that Russian craftsmen had fabricated, he was unable to dismantle it. Sutter's men somehow carried it to the ocean and floated it, hoping to tow it to New Helvetia behind the *Sacramento*. Sadly, the tow line parted, and the coveted floor broke up on the rocky Pacific Coast.[46] The worst damage, however, was to his already submerged solvency. For Sutter, who was always operating on the margins, the new debt was a crushing, insupportable obligation. It proved impossible for him to meet the terms of the contract.

To secure Sutter's promise to pay, the Russians demanded a mortgage on New Helvetia.[47] If he defaulted, the Russians would receive the property, a disagreeable fact that Kostromitinov made known to Governor Alvarado soon after the contract was signed. The Russian explained that he had sold "Ross with its real estate and furniture" to Sutter and that New Helvetia "with all of its movable and fixed property shall be a *guarantee*."[48] Governor Alvarado, of course, rejected Kostromitinov's assertion about Sutter's purchase of the land, but the Russian's communication was nonetheless troubling. If Sutter failed to make good on his contract, the Russians could move into the Sacramento Valley. Instead of being a minor irritant on the coast (and a convenient source of smuggled goods for Vallejo and his friends), the Russians could establish a mortal threat to Mexican California with a military post in the interior. The possibility that Sutter's undercapitalized enterprise might collapse was very real, and the implications were not lost on Alvarado. Many years later he lamented that in buying Ross "Sutter, the poor adventurer," had "interfered in a matter of so delicate a nature and one that so greatly harmed the interests of the general and Departmental governments."[49] Sutter's precarious financial position put all of Mexican California at risk.

Nevertheless, Sutter was suspicious about the californios' intentions. Rumors floated upriver that José Castro, one of Alvarado's military commanders and a boyhood friend of Vallejo, planned to force Sutter out of New Helvetia. Castro had also commanded the californios who deported Graham, an exploit well known to Sutter. The proprietor of New Helvetia had made himself very unpopular among californios, especially his impatient creditors, but there was no hard evidence that Castro was mustering troops to march on Sutter's Fort. Be that as it may, on November 8 Sutter decided to mount a preemptive strike in the form of an inflammatory letter to Vallejo's brother-in-law, Jacob Leese, who lived just across the plaza from Vallejo. The letter—a mixture of paranoia, threat, insult, and bluster—soon reached Vallejo's desk, just as Sutter had intended. Sutter had heard "Very curious Rapports . . . from below." The "poor wretches don't know what they do," he continued. He had asked the Scottish merchant David Spence to explain to "these ignorant people" the consequences of an attack. "The first french fregate who came here will do me justice"—a remarkable statement for a Mexican citizen to make, but one that probably rang true in Vallejo's ears. "It is too late now to drive me out of the country," Sutter explained. "The first step they do against me . . . I will make a Declaration of Independence and proclaim California a Republique independent from Mexico."[50]

The letter included inflated estimates of Sutter's military strength. "I am strong now," and overland immigrants from Missouri and another band of men from the Columbia River would soon augment his Indian army and white employees. In addition, he could send to the Willamette settlements for sixty or seventy more white men. He threatened to "dispatch [a party] to the mountains and call the hunters and Shawnee and Delaware, with which I am very well acquainted." Once he called on the chaguanosos, the foreign horse thieves whom the californios feared so much, he would send an Indian emissary to Missouri "and raise about 2 or 300 men more. That is my intention, sir, if they let me not alone." Sutter's artillery included ten guns to protect his fort and two field pieces. "I have also about 50 faithful Indians which shot their musquet very quick." If "this rascal of Castro should come here, a very warm and harty welcome is prepared for him." In addition to these treasonous statements Sutter had the effrontery to add a demand that the government pay him for the expense of maintaining his fort! Then "I will be a faithful Mexican."[51] In the meantime he threatened to crush Mexican California between the hammer of the French navy and the anvil of the chaguanosos.

Sutter could neither command the French navy nor control the chagua-nosos, but he believed himself to be in a strong military position because of new additions to the white population at New Helvetia. The Bidwell-Bartleson party had swelled his ranks with well-armed Americans. Bidwell, who knew about the threatening letter to Leese, believed that Sutter sent it only after the frontiersmen arrived because he viewed them "as a great addition to his strength."[52]

In light of the californios' actual experience with American hunters and the French navy, Sutter's threats seemed plausible and frightening. Vallejo decided to forward the letter to the minister of war and marine in Mexico City. He took the trouble to explain that Governor Alvarado had given the Swiss inter-loper land and "an appointment as *representative of the government, deputy justice*" on the Sacramento River. Sutter insultingly named his settlement New Helve-tia, called himself governor of the place, and ruled "arbitrarily and despot-ically." He made "frequent campaigns among the neighboring tribes which he forces to work in his settlement, and sells the children that the campaign reduces to orphanage." And finally, he dared "to make seditious threats, as your excellency will see in the enclosed original letter, unquestionable *corpus delicti,* of which your excellency will make the use that you consider best."[53] The following year Vallejo still had Sutter's threats in mind. "French war ships . . . they say, only wait his sign to take possession of California." Moreover, Vallejo worried that "the small force there is here [in Sonoma is] quite sufficient for ordinary cases, but entirely inadequate in case the Indians of the San Joaquin, joined with those of the Sacramento and the hunters from Missouri, attack me on the one side, and the Satiyomi [Sotoyome Pomo] attack me on the other."[54] With his new holdings at Ross, Sutter had Vallejo outflanked. If he could enlist the Pomos, Vallejo was in real trouble.

Evidently Vallejo's complaints made their way to the Mexican minister of the interior, for Governor Alvarado found himself explaining Sutter's activities to that serene official. Alvarado painted a very different picture of Sutter than the one limned by Vallejo in his letter. The governor complimented Sutter for establishing a peaceful ranch with only eight white men to help him. "His peaceful and kindly character" attracted more than three hundred settlers to New Helvetia, where they were peacefully employed. Sutter's humanitarian nature caused him to establish "a school of elementary education" for young Indians—a ridiculous assertion, unless child labor is counted as an educational experience. Despite Sutter's pacific personality, Alvarado added, he made fre-quent campaigns among the Indians in order to recover stolen livestock. "A great part of the quiet that this department is now enjoying is due to this settlement." Alvarado mentioned nothing about a fort, artillery, Sutter's private army, or his traffic in Indian persons. "If some personal differences on purely private matters have given rise to the sharpness shown by the Commandancy General [Vallejo] toward this person [Sutter]," Alvarado concluded, "I can only assure your Excellency that they lack any legitimate foundation."[55] According to the governor's account, Vallejo's complaints amounted to a mere personality conflict. Alvarado had done no wrong and had accomplished much good in permitting the Swiss émigré to settle in California, or at least so he justified himself to his superiors in Mexico.

Alvarado's explanations were not enough to save him from the paper war that Vallejo carried on against him. As Vallejo kept up a steady barrage of complaining letters to the general government, Alvarado's support of Sutter was only one of many examples of his nephew's incompetence that Vallejo gave to higher authorities. California's civil and military government must be united under one official, Vallejo recommended, and he offered his own resignation as comandante general as proof of his sincerity.[56]

In Mexico City it became clear that something had to be done to establish political order in the frontier province. In January 1842 President Antonio López de Santa Ana appointed Manuel Micheltorena governor, commanding general, and inspector of California. President Santa Ana had already lost Texas; he did not wish to lose California. Micheltorena was an experienced military man who had served with Santa Ana in Texas. It was widely believed that one of Micheltorena's missions was to get rid of Sutter. In May a rumor made the rounds in Honolulu that the Mexican government intended to send five hundred soldiers to California "to put Sutter in order, or root him out," as one American merchant put it.[57] All waited to see what would develop.[58]

By July Micheltorena had gathered some three hundred men for the small army that would accompany him to California. About half were from Mexican prisons. They embarked from Mazatlán on four vessels. After beating against the notorious headwinds off Baja California, they reached San Diego in August. Here the new governor began to acquaint his soldiers with military discipline. Evidently he hoped that the long march from San Diego to Monterey would help whip them into shape. They reached Los Angeles in late September and settled in for a long stay, at once raising the ire of *angelenos* with their pilfering.[59] Governor Micheltorena went out of his way to mollify Alvarado, Vallejo, and other californios; but unfortunately for all concerned, his poorly trained soldiers made up for their lack of pay by foraging on private ranchos. These *cholos,* as the californios sneeringly called them, caused widespread discontent that exacerbated political instability.

While Micheltorena's larcenous soldiers nursed their marching blisters and stole chickens, an international storm was brewing in the Pacific. Commodore

Thomas ap Catesby Jones, commander of the U.S. Pacific Squadron, was in Callao when the British naval commander abruptly sent his vessels to sea with secret orders. Commodore Jones was rightly concerned about French and British designs on California. Gunboat diplomacy was rife in the Pacific Ocean. The French navy had recently occupied the Marquesas and Washington Islands, and Jones heard a rumor that Mexico had ceded California to the British. His suspicions duly aroused, Commodore Jones conferred with the U.S. chargé d'affaires at Lima. They strongly suspected that the United States and Mexico were at war. Without specific orders to meet this contingency, Jones was forced to make a weighty decision on his own authority. He set his lantern jaw and sailed north to thwart the "occupation of California by Great Britain under a secret treaty with Mexico"—or so he supposed.[60]

When Jones sailed into Monterey Bay with three U.S. men-of-war, he completely surprised the *montereños,* who were utterly unprepared to cope with the threat that now confronted them. Alvarado was acting as governor until Micheltorena arrived. He had few troops at his command. The Monterey presidio had little operational artillery and nothing that could outduel the eighty naval cannons that bristled from Jones's gun ports. When Commodore Jones sent a representative to demand surrender, Alvarado denied that he was the governor. Nevertheless, a bloodless capitulation was quickly arranged while a courier madly rode south to inform Governor Micheltorena that his capital had been captured.

Then the level-headed Thomas Larkin began to ask some obvious questions of his conquering countrymen. Who had declared war and when? Why was there no word of the supposed conflict in the Mexican newspapers that he had in his possession? Larkin's queries aside, Jones's officers noted that there was no hint of hostilities in the official and unofficial correspondence that existed in Monterey's government offices.[61]

Within hours of the conquest, Jones reconsidered his position. "Gentlemen," he explained to Alvarado and other Mexican officials, "some information has this moment come to me, which leaves little doubt in my mind that the late difficulties between the United States and Mexico have been amicably adjusted; and anxious to avoid all causes which would have a tendency to excite unfriendly feelings in a state of peace, I propose to restore the Mexican authorities in Monterey," hoping at the same time, no doubt, to avoid being cashiered for his rash action.[62] Jones restored the Mexican flag, apologized to all concerned, sent a friendly letter to Micheltorena, and eventually returned to Washington to face an inquiry. Happily for him, upon his return he was commended for his prompt action.[63]

The invasion, conquest, and restoration of California happened so quickly that Sutter could not have become involved even if he had wanted to. Yet Commodore Jones's ridiculously easy seizure of Monterey confirmed just how vulnerable Mexican California was to the kinds of threats that Sutter made. In mid-October, while Commodore Jones sailed belligerently toward Monterey, Vallejo reminded Micheltorena of the danger that Sutter posed. While complaining to the governor about Sutter's arrogance and presumptive authority, Vallejo insisted that he had enough power to "banish him in case I think it desirable for the national honor." Sutter's banishment, however, was not really his goal, he explained, because he did "not want Sutter and his friends to lose the fortunes that they have invested on the Sacramento."[64]

Vallejo realized that Sutter had the californios over a barrel. If his business failed, all of his creditors would suffer, because the Russians had first claim on New Helvetia and all of Sutter's property. In addition to financial disaster, Sutter's failure would bring a new military menace to California with the Russian occupation of New Helvetia. His bankruptcy would knock down a large part of California's financial house of cards, which was based on promises to pay. In effect Sutter had made his creditors co-investors in his business. Californios had everything to lose if he failed, and they were in a double bind because of the Russian mortgage.

Once Micheltorena arrived, Sutter understood that he needed to make friends with the new governor. He sent Charles W. Flügge to Micheltorena's Los Angeles encampment. Flügge had come to California in 1841. An old Missouri acquaintance of Sutter, Flügge was German born and possessed some legal training. Sutter hoped that the lawyerly Flügge could convince Micheltorena that his client "had no intentions against the Mexican government, but only against the encroachments of the Californians, who were constantly interfering with . . . my business . . . General Vallejo in particular."[65]

Sutter was especially miffed at Vallejo because he required that Sutter's vaqueros drive his Russian cattle from Ross to Sonoma for inspection before they proceeded to the Sacramento Valley. The wary californio wanted to make sure that no animals with his brand were included in Sutter's herd—not an unreasonable suspicion given the accusations against Sutter and his associates. Nevertheless, Vallejo's power over Sutter's operations, limited though it was, galled the lord of New Helvetia. These were the concerns that Flügge placed before the governor, who invited Sutter to visit him in Monterey.[66] When Micheltorena and Sutter finally met, they would have common enemies and much to discuss—but that lay in the future.

Perhaps Flügge's assurances improved the governor's opinion of Sutter, but Micheltorena may have come around on his own. By 1842 it was clear that Sutter was a major force in California. Even men who despised him had to take him seriously. Sir George Simpson, governor-in-chief of the Hudson's Bay Company in North America, derisively regarded Sutter, who owed money to the Honorable Company, as "a man of speculative turn and good address," who "had given to the Hudson's Bay Company . . . particular grounds for taking an interest in his welfare and prosperity."[67] Evidently Simpson had made inquiries about Sutter. "He had successively tried his fortune in St. Louis, among the Shawnee Indians, in the Snake Country, on the Columbia River, at the Sandwich Islands, at Sitka, and at San Francisco, uniformly illustrating the proverb of the rolling stone, but yet generally contriving to leave anxious and inquisitive friends behind him." Sutter was living on a Mexican land grant, wrote Simpson, "about sixty miles long and twelve broad, trapping, farming, trading, bullying the government, and letting out Indians on hire; being in short, in a fairer way of figuring in the world as a territorial potentate than . . . the Duke of Bordeaux."[68]

Simpson's droll contempt could not mask his fears that Sutter's presence fostered "Brother Jonathan's [the United States'] ambitious views," because his fort commanded the practical land routes between California, the Willamette Valley, and Missouri. "If Captain Sutter, or any other adventurer, can gather round him a score of such marksmen as won Texas on the field of San Jacinto," Simpson prophesied, Americans would claim all of the interior and eventually take the port towns as well. Sutter's settlement made it all but inevitable, he believed, that California would fall to the Americans unless Great Britain took preemptive action and occupied the ports beforehand.[69]

In only three years Sutter had caused international incidents in California that threatened to involve France, England, the United States, and Russia in the affairs of Mexico's weak and isolated frontier province. Sutter was like an agent provocateur without portfolio, in the employ of every nation but Mexico. He was a loose and loaded cannon in lotus land, untrammeled, unpredictable, and too dangerous to be fooled with. Vallejo and many other Mexican Californians hated Sutter; but they could do nothing to dislodge him without damaging their own interests.

Somehow Sutter had penetrated the extremely complicated and fluid world of Indian, provincial, national, and international intrigue in California and made it all work for him, at least for the time being. The Swiss expatriate cared nothing about the international problems that he created for the Mexican government. Nuances of Mexican and californio politics were lost on him, and he was heedless of californios' complaints and threats. He believed himself to be absolute master of the Sacramento Valley, an independent force answerable only to himself, and he acted accordingly. Oddly, Sutter's indebtedness secured him as much as his adobe-walled fortress and the Indian army clad in Russian uniforms. If his fortunes crumbled, the wealth of many others would follow him into the dust.

Eventually Sutter's luck would run out, as it always did. New Helvetia, as Mofras and others pointed out, was at a geographic crossroads. It stood at a historical junction, too, at the very fulcrum of forces at work on the Pacific Coast that Sutter could not control. Inchoate in the early 1840s, those forces would soon materialize before his eyes and transform the world.

CHAPTER 9

Domain and Dominion

Sutter's domain stretched far beyond the indeterminate boundaries of his floating grant. The location of New Helvetia made Sutter's Fort the port of entry for overland immigrants who came to California in growing numbers before the Mexican War. Once they arrived, they learned that Sutter's lands extended from the fort to Los Tres Picos (the present-day Sutter Buttes) in the north, embracing tens of thousands of acres perhaps as far east as the Sierra Nevada. In 1842 Sutter could claim virtually any tract within the general limits of his grant. One thing was certain. He was determined to make the most of his nebulous domain.

Sutter laid claim to all he surveyed, but there were limits to what he could do in the Sacramento Valley. The environment encouraged some activities but retarded or entirely prohibited others. Miles of open, parklike oak savanna covered parts of the valley that were high and dry enough to support such growth. But ragged tule flags waved over extensive lowlands, marshes, and sloughs that dominated the low-lying areas of the valley. How could Sutter utilize these very different environments?

When Sutter arrived, the valley was not in a state of undisturbed nature or wilderness as Europeans imagined it to be. The valley was a cultural landscape—an environment that Native peoples had molded to their own purposes for centuries. Miwoks and Nisenans used fire to maximize the production of resources that they most prized—acorns, grass, and game animals. They took special care of the oak trees that produced acorns, their most reliable source of food. California Indians regarded the oak trees as sacred. Controlled fires kept the oak savannas free of the underbrush needed to fuel truly disastrous wild fire that could destroy the acorn-producing trees. Regular fires encouraged the growth of grasses for human food and raw material to make baskets. Abundant grass sustained antelope, elk, and deer, and the open landscape made it easier to hunt them.[1]

Native management practices and goals conflicted with Sutter's purposes. He intended to bring the valley's resources to an international marketplace that stretched from California around the globe. In order to do so, he needed to renovate the Indian cultural landscape to create an extensive wheat and live-stock ranch. When Sutter looked at the mighty oaks on the Sacramento Plain, he saw something very different from the Indians' sacred source of food. He saw commodities: lumber, firewood, charcoal, bark for his tanning vats. The destruction of ancient oaks that formerly supplied food for Miwoks and Nisenans troubled him not at all. A Nisenan story illustrates the incompati-bility of Sutter's and the Indians' ideas about oak trees. Soon after white people arrived in the Sacramento Valley, the story goes, one of the newcomers de-cided to cut down the Creator's oak, the sacred first tree from which all other oaks sprang. The Indians begged him to stop, but he felled the tree and cut it into firewood for the winter. The tree shook the ground with a terrible crash, and the earth still shudders when it remembers the loss. Blood flowed from the stump.[2]

The story of the Creator's oak encapsulates the conflicting Native and Euro-pean views of nature and its proper uses in Sutter's time. Oak trees were not the only source of conflict. His livestock grazed on grass that Indians had relied on for food and raw material. His crops grew on land where Indians once foraged and hunted. Sutter's enterprise limited, and in some cases eliminated, the landscape's potential to support Native peoples according to their customary food-gathering and hunting practices. Happily for Sutter, Indians became more dependent on him to earn a living through wage labor as the develop-ment of New Helvetia proceeded.

As far as Sutter was concerned, this was as it should have been. Like most Euro-Americans of his time, he did not wish to preserve wilderness, much less a Native cultural landscape, but to convert it to profitable uses. To him, grazing cattle and waving wheat fields represented progress, which was a good thing for Sutter and other newcomers. Insofar as these environmental changes meant dispossession and dependency for Miwok and Nisenan people, so much the better, for in Sutter's mind that too represented progress. The settlement dy-namics of New Helvetia gradually transformed independent Indian tribes into dependent people with labor to sell.[3]

Sutter could not eliminate Indian management practices overnight. In the summer of 1843 grassland fires were still a frequent sight in the valley, much to the vexation of white settlers. Sandels, the Swedish visitor, noticed frequent grass fires north of the American River. The conflagrations frightened cattle from their regular pastures into areas where they were "annoyed by the bears," as Sandels put it. He did not say how the fires started, but Sutter's Nisenan neighbors no doubt set them. Electrical storms are rare in the Sacramento Valley, even in the dry summer, so it is unlikely that lightning ignited the dry grass. Fires gave the valley a sere appearance, even near the streams. "Very few flowers presented themselves along the creek," Sandels wrote, "for all had been burnt over by recent fires."[4] He continued his trip upstream to the Feather River, where "the crackling noise of the raging fires on the prairies" was so loud that it disturbed his sleep.[5]

While roaring fires and billowing smoke signified the ongoing conflict between Sutter and Native peoples over environmental management, water placed additional limits on the development of New Helvetia. Sutter's agricultural plans required a reliable water supply. Water for agriculture seemed to be abundant in the valley, but that was an illusion. Like farmers in the humid East and Europe, Sutter relied on summer rains to water his crops. When the rains did not come, he thought that he was a victim of drought, but he misinterpreted his predicament. Summer drought was the natural and ordinary seasonal condition of the valley and much of the rest of California. Rain ordinarily fell only from October to May, the precipitation pattern of the so-called Mediterranean climate. In New Helvetia annual rainfall was less than twenty inches. For reliable cultivation of crops in the Sacramento Valley farmers would have to irrigate, but this was a lesson that Sutter had yet to learn.[6] He and other newcomers would eventually understand that the seasonal runoff from deep snow packs in the Sierra Nevada was the dependable source of water for their summer crops, not the wispy clouds that floated over the valley.

Rivers posed a barrier as well as an opening to New Helvetia. Most of Sutter's commerce was river-borne, linking his embarcadero to San Francisco Bay and the world, but rivers limited overland travel. Even in the dry season, only a few safe fords permitted people and livestock to cross safely. If Vallejo had decided to march overland to attack Sutter, he would not have been able to cross the rivers that guarded the fort on the north and east without raising an alarm. Rivers and extensive marshlands dictated roundabout land routes to New Helvetia. From Sonoma, riders crossed the Coast Range and traversed the valley, crossing the Sacramento River opposite Sutter's embarcadero. Travelers from south of San Francisco Bay crossed the San Joaquin River south of present-day Stockton and then looped north, crossing the Calaveras, Mokelumne, and Cosumnes Rivers. It was nearly impossible for intruders to reach New Helvetia without his Indian allies warning him beforehand. In the 1840s a vast, natural moat surrounded Sutter's Fort.

Every few years severe flooding covered the plains with sheets of water that made travel virtually impossible, except by boat. Water backed up into miles of sloughs that stretched back from the rivers then into tule marshes, spread over lowlands that were ordinarily dry, and finally covered vast sections of the valley. Much of the land west and south of Sutter's Fort was low and susceptible to overflow at these times. Niklaus Allgeier recalled a flood in the 1841 Christmas season when he was living on the Feather River. He took his boat down the Sacramento River to "where [Sacramento] is," turned east, and paddled "straight to the fort," where he landed about thirty feet behind the back wall.[7]

Sutter's grant excluded these periodically overflowed lands, evidently including the future city of Sacramento and much of the land bordering the Sacramento, American, Feather, and Yuba Rivers. Sutter and his antagonists would dispute this matter in court in years to come. For now he had to contend with the water itself, rather than its legal implications. Tule-choked lands were useful pasturage in the late spring and summer when they were relatively dry but not in the wet seasons. In 1842, knowing that when the floods came there was not enough high ground near the fort to rescue his livestock from the tules, Sutter moved virtually all of his horses and cattle to Hock Farm, reserving only enough animals for his operations south of the American River. He maintained a herd of sheep south of the fort. Sutter's wheat fields occupied the relatively high ground between the fort and the American River. A few miles east of the fort, at a place later called Brighton, Sutter cultivated the high land near the American River.[8] Thus the indeterminate watery boundaries of New Helvetia determined the limits of its development.

Like other settlers, Sutter believed that the dry lands were best for crops, the lowlands better suited to grazing. The opposite was true. Once they were drained, the exposed soil of tule marshes was rich in nutrients, but Sutter did not have the means to reclaim this land. No one did in the 1840s. The harnessing of capital, technology, and political power needed to transform the land and water of the valley would be the work of the coming century.[9]

Like much of the Far West, the Sacramento Valley was a land of extreme conditions and seeming contradictions; but in this case extremes existed side by side or followed each other in seasonal succession. Extensive marshlands bordered dry uplands. Fog-bound winters and rainy springs were followed by long, dry summers when the thermometer stood above a hundred degrees. The ever-changing borders between fertile valley soils and overflowing streams, between seasons of unbroken dry heat and seasons of persistent rain and flooding, would prohibit the realization of a dream of development based on landscape models and farming expertise from western Europe and eastern America.

Governing New Helvetia's growing non-Indian population proved to be as tricky as managing the natural world, but at least Sutter could rely on the authority that the governor had conferred on him. He personally governed New Helvetia and inflated the limits of his civil and military authority as far as he stretched the boundaries of his grant. In New Helvetia "I was everything," Sutter fondly reminisced, "patriarch, priest, father, & judge."[10] Indeed, it is difficult to identify any limits on the plenary powers that he conceived for himself. "I had the power of life and death over both Indians and white people," he told Bancroft in 1876.[11] In New Helvetia he presided over funerals for the dead and blessed the marriages of the living, an arrogation of power that outraged Catholic priests when they learned of it. Under Mexican law only priests had the authority to perform marriages between Catholics.[12] Mexican and Catholic officials permitted Protestant ceremonies to be held only in private, to avoid offending the californios' Roman Catholic sensibilities; but Sutter had no more civil authority to marry Protestants than he did Catholics.

Perhaps Sutter merely imagined this complete mastery over the human population of New Helvetia when Bancroft interviewed him in his parlor in his old age. Yet his identification with absolute power over everyone and everything in his New Switzerland unveils an authoritarian aspect of Sutter's personality. He craved respect and complete control over his environment. New Helvetia was an improvement over Old Helvetia because he had an unlimited supply of both—or so he claimed. He was a smiling tyrant who preferred to win white and Indian friends with generosity and guile rather than force, but he never hesitated to use organized military violence to assert personal control over his section of California. The Switzerland of his youth had rejected him for the very qualities that served him well in Mexican California—impetuosity, ambition, social climbing, and reckless business ventures. For Sutter, the perfect world was one in which he was in charge of everything. How could anything go wrong in such a place?

When Sutter looked back, he recalled with pleasure an autocracy of his own devising; but in the 1840s he was wise enough to recognize that his fantasy of absolute power did not completely conform to the real world in which he lived. He could not afford to alienate the people he needed most—the mountain men, overland immigrants, merchant marine deserters, and other free-booting sojourners on the Pacific Rim. "In my intercourse with the mountaineers, trappers, and Americans, I was free and social, shaking hands with them, though I made them treat me with respect," Sutter insisted.[13] He might have added that these independent men, accustomed to an unfettered life in the mountains, were not likely to bow and scrape before Sutter or anyone else.

Sutter's assumption of military courtesy favorably impressed many of the Americans who came to his place. John Bidwell recognized the importance of Sutter's meticulous manners. "He was of fine and commanding presence and courteous as a prince," Bidwell recalled. He also understood that Sutter's princely bearing had a practical aspect: "He had come to the Pacific Coast without means but he had what brought means, a magnificent address. One more polished in his deportment I have never known. Always liberal and affable, no one could be more obliging than he, and especially to strangers," as the hungry immigrants who ate beef at Sutter's table well knew.[14]

Sutter sometimes extended his courtesy to frontiersmen he should have shunned, as Bidwell learned when he had to deal with one of these characters. S. Kinney, a hard case who lived at New Helvetia for a short time, stole 75 of Sutter's mares, and the lord of the manor asked Bidwell to recover them.[15] Bidwell had trepidations about confronting Kinney, who was known to be violent. The faithful Bidwell armed himself, took the animals from Kinney without incident, and returned them to Sutter. But that was not the end of Sutter's dealing with the rustler. When Kinney decided to return to the United States, he offered Sutter a "fine gun" in return for livestock and provisions. "Knowing that the fellow was a rascal, I was rather suspicious," Bidwell recalled. Acting on behalf of Sutter, he asked to try the rifle. Kinney wanted to load the gun, but Bidwell loaded it himself and fired it without incident. Then he took the rifle to the blacksmith, who dismantled it and found that it was cracked inside. "I told Sutter that the gun had been burst and was worthless." The next morning, however, Sutter told Bidwell: "Give Mr. Kinney credit for $100." When Bidwell asked why, Sutter replied, "Well, I have taken the rifle; he said that it was a good gun." Bidwell left the fort immediately, thinking that he would quit Sutter for good.

> I did not know where to go to. Walked perhaps ten miles, revolving in my mind as to how I could get out of California. I had stood by Sutter many times when his life was in danger, and could not understand why he should believe a stranger's word to mine. I returned that night and Sutter begged me to remain.[16]

Bidwell returned to Sutter's service, but this incident taught him a bitter lesson about his employer. As Bidwell said, Sutter was always liberal, affable, and obliging, but the lord of New Helvetia was not able to tell friend from foe or the honest pioneer from a violent criminal. Sutter's inability to discriminate among the motley frontier population would contribute to his ultimate undoing. Bidwell remained a lifelong friend, despite Sutter's self-destructive tendency to believe whatever any charlatan told him.

Sutter's treatment of Mexicans, however, was a different story. He demanded that Mexican Californians show the "deference which they were accustomed to pay their own officers." When Mexican soldiers made official visits to the fort, Sutter made "officers & men" doff their hats.[17] Rough Americans and californios alike noticed these distinctions in social address, which placed one more nettle in the blanket that Sutter required the californios to wear while in New Helvetia.

Sutter imagined that his grant gave him complete control over his lands and that Alvarado's appointment invested him with supreme authority over all those who resided in the surrounding district. The land grant contained several limitations and stipulations, however, that were meant to constrain Sutter and foster the development of a frontier community. The eleven leagues were for Sutter's "personal benefit, *and that of twelve families.*"[18] The patriarch had to find some families—someone besides the fiddle-footed single men who worked for him—to occupy his patrimony, not an easy chore in the early 1840s. The grant further required that he "maintain the native Indians of the different tribes on those places in the free enjoyment of their possessions, without troubling them, and he may only reduce them to civilization through prudent measures and a friendly intercourse; and not cause them hostilities in any way without previously obtaining authority from [the] government."[19] Sutter roundly violated this clause of his grant whenever he chose. The boundaries of New Helvetia contained at least fifteen Indian rancherías whose inhabitants toiled for Sutter and white settlers in his domain.[20]

Every ranchero in California exploited local Indian populations to a greater or lesser degree, so Sutter had little cause to worry that the Mexican government would hold him to the letter of his grant regarding Indians. Still, he wanted at least to give the appearance of meeting the minimum legal requirements of his grant. This may explain why he assumed the authority to officiate at the weddings of the residents of New Helvetia. He needed to settle twelve families, so why not create them by "marrying" the Indians and whites who lived in the vicinity? Sutter began by interfering with Indian marriage customs. "When I went to the valley polygamy obtained among the Indians," he related, "and I determined to stop it."[21] The Nisenans and Miwoks both permitted polygyny, a form of polygamy which permits one man to have two or more wives.[22] Before Sutter's arrival the practice was usually limited to chiefs and other important men. When Miwoks were in the mission, priests compelled the neophytes to abandon polygynous unions; but once Miwoks returned to the valley, they evidently restored this time-honored custom. Sutter claimed that the chiefs had so many wives that "the young men complained they could have none."[23] The patriarch's judgment was probably correct. Indian populations were in decline throughout California, and women died at a higher rate than men. Consequently, the eligible grooms outnumbered the few potential brides, a trend that was exacerbated by polygyny.[24] Sutter's solution was as simple as it was radical. "I took the men and put them all in one row, and the women in another," he recalled.[25] "Then I told the women one after another to come forward and select for a husband the man they wanted." From then on Sutter did not allow the chiefs "more than one or two wives each."[26]

Sutter's marriage decree affected only those rancherías that he controlled. Within those limits, New Helvetia's patriarch may have enabled some Indians to form new families by breaking up polygynous unions; but the marriages also reinforced his power among Indian chiefs and captains because he allowed them to maintain polygyny on a restricted basis. Because Sutter appointed some Indian leaders, Indians now associated the privilege of plural wives with his authority. Monogamous grooms who married Indian women who became available because of Sutter's divorce decree had him to thank for their new wives.[27]

While Sutter always acknowledged his marriage to Anna and claimed that his family would join him in California presently, he maintained other intimate relationships, as was befitting for the great captain of the Sacramento Valley. Perhaps the best known of these arrangements was his long association with Manuiki, one of the two Hawaiian women who accompanied him to California in 1839. She was his favorite consort for several years, although not the only one. Sutter jealously guarded his exclusive access to Manuiki, once clapping an English sailor named William Daylor in the guard house for dallying with her. Eventually Sutter dropped Manuiki and allowed her to marry Kanaka Harry, another Hawaiian who had come with him in 1839. In gratitude, or perhaps as payment for their services, Sutter set aside a garden for them on the American River near the place where he first landed.[28]

According to Heinrich Lienhard, one of the Swiss émigré employees, Sutter also kept Indian women concubines at the fort and was rumored to have fathered several children by them.[29] Sutter's own census of the New Helvetia population in 1848 enumerated ten mixed-blood children but did not identify the fathers.[30] Lienhard noticed that in a room adjoining Sutter's office "a group of Indian women were invariably waiting. According to rumor, they belonged to Sutter's harem." Lienhard "was told" that one of these women was Sutter's favorite, who "was kept there all the time."[31]

Lienhard also claimed that Sutter was a pedophile who kept young Indian girls in a room at the fort. The Swiss employee, who was not one of Sutter's admirers, went so far as to suggest that his boss had raped an Indian child and caused her death.[32] Lienhard is one of the most important and reliable sources on Sutter at New Helvetia. Yet his testimony about Sutter's molestation of girls as young as ten years old is the only accusation concerning these sexual crimes.

The story about Sutter's alleged rape came to Lienhard indirectly, through his friend Charley Burch, who heard it from a Tahitian named John, who happened to be married to the sister of "an influential squaw who lived in Sutter's anteroom," who told the story of the rape to John's wife.[33] We may reasonably suppose that the story passed through several languages and cultural filters by the time it got to Lienhard. There are too many questionable links in this chain of evidence to accept it at face value. Lienhard indiscriminately spread rumors about Sutter's sex life, some of which were well founded and others not. He saw Indian women in Sutter's anteroom, but he relies on others to explain by inference what Sutter did with them in private.

Yet this portrait of Sutter's sex life must be given some credence. Lienhard's claims were in line with Sutter's activities as a labor contractor. As Sutter's blacksmith John Chamberlain said, "it was customary for Capt Sutter to buy and sell Indian boys & girls."[34] Sutter's own letters show that he trafficked in Indian children, although he was apparently uneasy about it and did not say that the trade was sexual in nature.[35] He frequently made war on surrounding tribes and took the orphaned Indian boys to the fort, but he says nothing of orphaned girls.[36] Perhaps the girls in the anteroom were the kin of the boys who were waiting to be sent downriver to other rancheros, and Lienhard's sexual innuendo was mere calumny. Whether or not Sutter sexually abused these hapless victims of warfare, his participation in the trade of Indians of all ages shows him at his ruthless worst.

There is no reason to doubt that Sutter cohabited with Hawaiian and Indian women. Mofras noted in 1841 that "all" the white men of New Helvetia lived with "Indian or Californian women."[37] He may have exaggerated the situation, but he did not make it a point to exclude Sutter from his generalization. Nearly twenty years later a witness in Sutter's land claims case testified that he had purchased land from "Sutter's Indian wife," who held the title by virtue of Sutter's written statement confirming that the land belonged to her and her people.[38] It was customary among mountain men of the time to take an Indian wife, or several, who would consolidate relations with the women's tribes. Often these marriages were temporary arrangements that white traders and trappers abandoned when they left Indian country, but some maintained life-long commitments to their spouses and offspring.[39] Lienhard called Sutter a "typical Don Juan with women," but his several Indian consorts may have had as much to do with frontier diplomacy as with sexual desire.[40] Each carnal connection gave him an association with the woman's ranchería and perhaps a source of intelligence as well.

Yet the motivational power of pure lust should never be discounted when it came to the sexual behavior of white men on the frontier, where new sexual rules prevailed. Indians and whites operated according to different codes of social conduct. Newcomers frequently misunderstood Indian sexuality as a mere lack of moral standards. Indian women were easily available to white men because the newcomers appeared to be powerful and because they were rich by the standards of that time and place.

In 1843 the Swedish traveler Sandels unabashedly bedded two young Indian women near Hock Farm in return for a few shirt buttons.[41] He recalled the incident with a kind of Bohemian tolerance for the young women's aggressiveness (by European standards) as well as his own loose conduct. Sandels was after all far from home, a stranger in the strange land of New Helvetia. He no doubt understood the exchange of buttons for sex to be an act of prostitution, but it is likely that the women thought in terms of reciprocity—an exchange of favors that symbolized an ongoing relationship. This was a common misunderstanding among Indians and Europeans who exchanged gifts and sex. The Indians thought that they were cementing a relationship; the Europeans believed they were purchasing a moment of pleasure that was free of incumbrance.[42]

Indians' ideas about reciprocity may explain some of the things that Lienhard saw at Sutter's Fort. If the women in the anteroom had sex with Sutter, they obligated him to them and their communities through sexual gifts, at least as far as they were concerned. Likewise, "the many young Indian loafers" whose "wives received special consideration from the master of the fort" created serious obligations for Sutter in the minds of the Indian participants if not in his own mind.[43] Sutter "gave to his men women for wives," Sandels reported, which implied reciprocal relationships involving Sutter, his employees, and Native people.[44]

These mixed marriages were neither permanent nor legal under Mexican law, but they were important to the social and economic life of New Helvetians, white and Indian alike. In 1842 John Yates, master of Sutter's schooner *Sacramento,* toured the Sacramento Valley and visited Niklaus Allgeier on the Feather River (the same "Big Nicholas" who once threatened to kill Sutter). There he found the mountain man, who was "capital company where grog and cards were striving," living with an Indian woman who called him "Nicholassee." The local Nisenan Indians "constantly visited the loan [*sic*] settler Nicholas, to inquire if he stood in need of their assistance, and were always ready to give him a helping hand to any extent."[45] Yates attributed Nisenan willingness to Allgeier's kindness, but his kinship obligations were probably important too. Sometimes white husbands explicitly recognized their Indian kin, as when Theodor Cordua, who had a ranch on the Yuba River, introduced an Indian boy to Lienhard as his brother-in-law.[46] Yates noticed that Sutter's blacksmith was "given to gazing on the native females. I learnt that he had been married nineteen times to native women."[47] Following the well-established customs of New Helvetia, Yates had two Indian women who kept him company. Yates must have valued his Indian wives, for he refused to give them up after he married a young English woman, a choice that seriously perturbed his new in-laws.[48]

The intimate relations involving Sutter, Sandels, Yates, Chamberlain, Allgeier, and all the unnamed white men and Indian women shaped the social world of New Helvetia, where Sutter ruled with few constraints. "I, Sutter am the law," Lienhard heard him say.[49] Informal marriages among frontiersmen and Indians were not likely to arouse more than disapproving eyebrows among Mexican officials, but Sutter's matchmaking caused trouble when he solemnized the unions of white couples, especially if one of them was a Catholic. Word eventually reached Catholic priests that Sutter officiated at several such marriages. One of the bridegrooms, Cyrus Alexander, married a New Mexican woman named Rufina Lucero. Sutter had assured the engaged couples that "I ish der law, I cans perform der serremony, und all ish den right," according to Alexander family tradition.[50] All was not right, however, and the priests commanded the errant couples to go to Santa Clara to be legally married in a Catholic ceremony. Three couples who had been joined by the patriarch of New Helvetia (including the Alexanders) complied.

Sutter's illegal weddings irritated Mexican and American officials alike. Governor Alvarado soon learned that Sutter "went to the extreme of performing marriages for persons resident in New Helvetia." Alvarado thought that Sutter was guilty of a serious crime that "the laws punished . . . severely" but did not explain why no attempt was made to discipline him.[51] Some American citizens complained to the U.S. consul, Thomas O. Larkin, about Sutter's marriages. One couple wed at Sutter's Fort decided that they no longer wished to be married and asked Larkin for a divorce, a request that he could not grant under Mexican or U.S. law. He informed Sutter that he could not legally marry people and feared "future trouble from those you have joined as man and wife."[52] The spouses might later claim that the marriage was illegal; or if one of the spouses died, distant relatives might claim the decedent's estate and keep it from the surviving spouse.

The heirship of illegitimate children was a particular concern to Larkin, who became concerned that his own marriage was illegal while looking into

Sutter's activities. He and his wife were not Catholics, so they would not be married by California priests. John Coffin Jones, consul at Honolulu, asserted that he had the legal power to marry U.S. citizens and married Larkin and his wife on board an American ship that was in Monterey. Jones presumably acted under his authority as consul, but Larkin learned that no such authority existed. Consequently, he remarried his wife in a Catholic ceremony, despite religious qualms.[53]

Jones and Sutter probably acted in good faith when they presided over these pseudo-marriages; and despite the misgivings of some of the spouses, the couples no doubt wished to be legally and permanently married by civil officials. The Larkins, Alexanders, and other couples, for example, went to the trouble to have their irregular marriages solemnized in the Catholic Church to make certain that their unions were legal and binding. Surprisingly, very few if any of the men of New Helvetia married californianas, perhaps because Mexican Californians objected to unions with men who were rough and seemingly unprincipled.[54] Consequently, in the early 1840s New Helvetia society resembled the society of the fur trade, with impermanent mixed unions of Indian women with Americans and Europeans predominating.

Despite the illegality of Sutter's marriages, the slow proliferation of couples and families gave an air of permanence and stability to the settlement. In some cases settlers worked for Sutter and lived on his land. Sometimes he sold and leased large parts of his claim to his creditors in order to satisfy old debts. Often Sutter assisted newcomers who wished to establish their own Mexican claims. In later years, he would give the names of these people as evidence that he had satisfied the stipulations of his grant.[55]

In 1843 Sutter began parceling out his holdings in order to shore up his shaky finances. Late in 1842 Theodor Cordua, a German merchant, arrived in California on a trading vessel. At Yerba Buena, Cordua met Sutter's confidant Charles W. Flügge, who had known Sutter in St. Louis and traveled overland from Missouri with the Bidwell-Bartleson party in 1841. By chance, Cordua had known Flügge's uncle in Germany. Flügge advised Cordua to go to Sutter's place and settle in the Sacramento Valley, an idea that appealed to Cordua. He soon learned from other sources that Sutter "had contracted many debts and did not think of repaying them"; but Flügge, Sutter's "Duzbruder" (close friend), convinced Cordua to go to Sutter's Fort.[56] Although Sutter coveted the considerable stock of goods that Cordua had brought with him from the Hawaiian Islands, he had no cash. In return for the merchandise, Sutter agreed to lease Cordua several leagues of land north of the junction of the Yuba and Feather Rivers for a period of nine years. He also gave Cordua a considerable quantity of cattle and horses. Cordua, of course, gained access to the labor of the Indians who lived on this land. They figured that the whole deal was worth $8,000. Eventually Cordua sold the lease to others, who bought the land from Sutter.[57]

Sutter made two land sales in 1843. Like the arrangement with Cordua, these conveyances were probably intended to cover his debts. In August he sold a narrow strip of land bordering the Sacramento River between the mouths of the American and Feather Rivers, approximately three leagues in all, to Eliab Grimes, the Hawaiian merchant. The details of this financial transaction do not survive, but it is known that Sutter had purchased goods on credit from Grimes's Honolulu trading house. In the summer of 1842 some Hawaiian houses had stopped honoring Sutter's drafts.[58] His Hawaiian credit crisis was averted when Hiram Grimes, nephew of Eliab, agreed to honor all of his drafts.[59] The details of this arrangement are not known, but in September Sutter asked another merchant to help him straighten out his business with Hiram Grimes.[60] Evidently Grimes agreed to take payment in cattle, but in November Sutter reported that the price was "so low that I cannot afford to sell at that rate."[61] Consequently, he bartered away the resource that he had in greatest abundance: land. On August 10, 1843, Sutter conveyed a narrow 13-mile-long strip of land to Eliab Grimes and his partner, John Sinclair, the old Hudson's Bay Company man who had represented Sutter in Hawaii.[62]

One month later Sutter conveyed a square mile of land to Niklaus Allgeier, the former Hudson's Bay man who had worked for Sutter since 1840. In 1841 Allgeier lived on Sutter's claim on the east side of the Feather River about thirty-five miles north of the fort. He hunted and trapped for a living, probably under an arrangement with Sutter. Sutter later said that he "did not charge him anything" for the land, so the 1843 conveyance was likely a transaction that covered his financial obligations to Allgeier, although the specific details are lacking.[63]

These land transfers were risky ventures for all concerned. The extent of Sutter's claim was not known, and all of New Helvetia was already mortgaged to the Russians. If Sutter's paper empire collapsed, the Russians might claim prior right to the lands that he had leased and sold. Staying afloat financially was costly for Sutter. In 1843 he bargained away almost one-third of the eleven leagues that his grant allowed him, not including the land that he leased to Cordua for nine years plus an option for nine more. If Sutter was to emerge from his financial finagling as a major landholder, he would have to acquire more property. In the meantime he simply portrayed himself as the owner of a vast estate with limits that no one knew precisely.

In an effort to satisfy the terms of his grant from Alvarado, Sutter settled several families on the lands that he claimed. In 1854 John Bidwell testified in federal court about Sutter's land claim and gave a rough census of the people who lived in New Helvetia in 1841. Makaina, one of Sutter's Hawaiian employees, farmed a plot between the fort and the American River. Three other Kanaka men who lived with their wives "were settled in and about Sutter's settlement between the years 1841 and 1845."[64] James Burchum lived at a place called the Sheep Ranch at a lagoon a few miles south of the fort. Perry McCoon, Henry Bee, John Chamberlain, William Daylor, G. F. Wyman, Pablo Gutiérrez, and dozens of lesser-known characters lived in the vicinity of the fort and Hock Farm. Bidwell testified that many of these men were married but did not bother to say that some of these unions were with Indian spouses. He thought that as many as fifty or sixty non-Indians lived at New Helvetia. Some of these people worked for Sutter on shares and did not acquire land of their own. Others became Mexican citizens and established their own land-grant ranchos.[65]

Whatever the flaws in Sutter's business practices or in his assumptions about the extent of his landholdings, his settlement attracted more than a dozen additional grantees to the Sacramento Valley. William A. Leidesdorff was a West Indian–born African American who captained a vessel that regularly sailed between Honolulu and San Francisco Bay. He became a Mexican citizen and obtained a 35,000-acre grant east of Sutter on the American River.[66] Similarly, Eliab Grimes added 44,000 acres to his New Helvetia holdings by virtue of a Mexican grant in 1844.[67] Within a few years ranchos developed along the courses of the Sacramento, American, Feather, Yuba, and Cosumnes Rivers—all within Sutter's jurisdiction.[68]

Sutter's Fort and his small army made it possible for white settlements to proliferate, no doubt; but his supposed power of life and death did not define his relationship with his new neighbors. Many of them, like Grimes and Leidesdorff on the American River and Thomas Larkin on the Sacramento, were his creditors. Others, like Cordua, were business associates who worked the land according to contractual arrangements with Sutter. Men like Bidwell were employees who worked for wages. And still others were in debt to Sutter and paid him with their labor.[69]

Sutter, of course, set the gold standard for debt in the Sacramento Valley. His attempts to keep his financial canoe afloat fill his correspondence. The Russian-American Company was his major creditor, and Sutter strove mightily to make the required payments when they came due in September of each year. He failed. In 1842 he managed to make a partial payment on the $5,000 that was due in produce. In 1843 he planted more wheat, but nature defeated him. Sandels, his Swedish visitor, noted that drought had taken its toll on New Helvetia's wheat crop, which was "next door to failure."[70] Sutter ordered his

Indian workers to harvest the pathetic yield, but there was not even enough to make a token payment to the Russians, whose unladen ship sailed back to Sitka to report this sorry turn of events to company officials.

Perhaps foreseeing such difficulties, the Russians had included a clause in the bill of sale that required Sutter to pay "all expenses incurred by the ship from Sitka to Port San Francisco," including port fees, "maintenance of the crew and the cost of freight," if the vessel returned to Sitka without the agreed-upon cargo.[71] So Sutter made his excuses and sent the Russian bark back to Sitka. He duly wrote to the port master, Francisco Guerrero, and offered to pay the fee in the only way that he could, with a promise. "I obligate myself to pay the amount—I do not know how much it will be, but it will not be much, for the bark is very small—in the period of three months."[72] Instead of reducing his debt, Sutter was beginning to accrue substantial interest and penalties. It was the same old story of poor business judgment, poorly founded optimism, and bad luck. Never mind that New Helvetia was mortgaged to the Russians: Sutter simply assured his friends that he was easily able to extend the loan.[73] The Russians saw it differently, as did the Mexican government.

Nor was Sutter able to meet all of his financial obligations to Mexican Californians. The situation with Suñol and his brothers-in-law, the Bernals, continued to fester. He had purchased cattle from them and was not able to pay them as agreed. "As I do not want them to think I am acting in bad faith," Sutter agreed to "pay them interest on the delayed payments, as is the custom in all civilized countries." The Bernals already had seized some cattle with Sutter's brand, and rumor had it that they intended to ride to New Helvetia to round up the cattle that they had sold to Sutter. "That would be very difficult as most of them no longer exist" (slaughtered, no doubt, for their hides). "Of my Russian cows," Sutter added, "I would not exchange one for three of another kind." Besides, the Bernals' rumored roundup would result in "nothing but waging useless war and carrying on endless disputes." Sutter was willing to pay Bernal in good horses, however, "and as horses are not so numerous where they are, I think this proposition will please them."[74] Happily, wild grapes were abundant that year, and the Nisenan Indians near Feather River agreed to bring them in so that Sutter could make brandy. Although Sutter promised to pay up his debt by January 1843, he did not. In April 1843 he still owed Juan Bernal $1,546 for 406 cattle.[75]

Suñol and the Bernal brothers continued to make threats about forcibly retrieving their four-legged property. Sutter held them off with promises and bluster. He even agreed to round up two hundred or three hundred young cattle and deliver them to the Bernals as partial payment, and he tried to make up the rest in deer tallow, brandy, a pair of rifles, and, as always, beaver pelts.[76]

Sutter was especially hopeful about the quality of his brandy: "If the brandy suits you, I can pay you everything that I owe with this article"; but the very young brandy proved unsatisfactory.[77] "I think the brandy we are making here will not suit you," he reported six months later, "because it is fresh and made from corn. It always has a bad taste."[78] Corn brandy, perhaps an early attempt to distill whiskey, was a concoction that appealed only to the most bibulous of Sutter's clients.

In one form or another, liquor from Sutter's distilleries was conspicuous in New Helvetia. He had always been a drinker, and alcohol was prominent in the earliest accounts of his business activities on the Santa Fe trail and in California. In his old age Sutter claimed that he strictly controlled the drinking habits of New Helvetians: "I gave them nothing but water to drink the first six or seven years . . . no intoxicating liquor."[79] His letters, however, included frequent references to brandy as part of his trade. Nor do travelers' descriptions depict a world where liquor was hard to come by. Nevertheless, his reminiscences portray Sutter as a reluctant purveyor of spirits to his workers. Indeed, he himself revealed that his workers threatened to leave him if he did not provide liquor on Christmas and the Fourth of July, which he did. On the advice of one of his sailor hands, the lord of New Helvetia discreetly disappeared for a few days while his men binged on holidays.

But this story masked the reality of the liquor trade at New Helvetia. In 1841 Sutter planted a vineyard at Brighton, a sure indication that he planned to make wine and brandy.[80] As was usual in the fur trade, Sutter used liquor in his dealings with Indians. "Send . . . plenty of Grog" to the Indian trappers, Sutter advised Pierson B. Reading, who managed the fur trade for him.[81] The use of liquor was one of the most common and abusive aspects of the Indian trade. Unscrupulous traders brewed god-awful concoctions of adulterated liquor for their Indian clients. There is no evidence that Sutter prepared such poisonous liquors, although he may have laid off on Indian trappers the least palatable distillations, such as the corn brandy that he would not sell to Suñol.

Sutter, of course, was not the only man to use and abuse alcohol in New Helvetia; nor were Indians the only victims. During the first half of the nineteenth century, drinking at all times of the day was so common that one historian called his book on the subject *The Alcoholic Republic*.[82] William Buzzell, the farmer who managed William Leidesdorff's Rancho Río Americano, was one exemplar of American drinking patterns in the Sacramento Valley. He begged his employer for "one gallon of good liquer for my own use, for it is werry hot weather here . . . I like to have my bitters in the morning when I work hard in the hot sun all day[.] [T]he thermometer has stood here for the last week from 100 And 4 to 100 And 6."[83] Nowadays Buzzell's drinking habits would mark him as a desperate alcoholic, but in his own time the farmer's morning tippling was not unusual. Strong drink was one of the few pleasures available to people who wore out their bodies with hard physical labor.

Daily drinking was a common habit, but shrewd observers knew that liquor could be used to take advantage of white men as well as Indians. William Gulnac, once an employee of Sutter's, was such a man. Sutter helped Gulnac to obtain a land grant in the northern San Joaquin Valley. Charles Weber then bought the grant, where he founded Stockton, "for a low price," which "Weber paid Gulnac mostly in Whiskey, for Gulnac had taken badly to drink," Sutter said.[84] Looking back on this transaction thirty years later, he seemed to find fault with both Weber and Gulnac. He would have done well to take a lesson from his former employee's drinking problems, for Gulnac's downfall foreshadowed some of the worst disasters that befell Sutter during the gold rush.

In the early 1840s Sutter's steady drinking marked him as a convivial host rather than a man with a serious health problem that compromised his judgment. Most of his visitors appreciated the rustic libations that he offered. Pisco brandy slaked the thirst of many weary travelers who had drained the last of their whiskey jugs somewhere east of the Sierra Nevada. Under the circumstances, few needy immigrants were inclined to criticize Sutter's drinking habits.

Yet it appears that whatever control Sutter exerted over his alcoholism in the early 1840s began to collapse after 1844. The availability of stronger spirits may have been one of the reasons. In October 1844 Sutter obtained the services of a "first rate Beer brewer and Distiller," a German named William Meart.[85] In the following season Sutter (probably using Meart's expertise) for the first time "made whiskey from barley, which was a great curse and caused more trouble than anything he ever did," according to Bidwell.[86] After 1844 Sutter had new reasons to drink, as his political and economic circumstances became more complicated. His judgment was questionable at best, and now he had to decide on momentous questions while the fate of California and his own destiny hung in the balance. Drunk or sober, he was not up to the task. John Sutter, the lord of New Helvetia, would go wrong at nearly every turn.

CHAPTER 10

Misguided Diplomacy

While Sutter struggled to manage his personal kingdom in the Sacramento Valley, the managers of the rising American empire worked to make matters come out to their liking in California. Commodore Thomas ap Catesby Jones and the Pacific Squadron stayed on station in California after his short-lived and premature conquest of Monterey. Jones and his subordinate officers showed not the slightest embarrassment over the affair; nor were they bashful about asserting their right to protect U.S. interests in Mexican California.

The fatiguing business of projecting American power on the Pacific coast required the officers' constant vigilance over their sailors, a rough lot given to drinking and other lapses of naval discipline and decorum. C. K. Stribling, the commander of the USS *Cyane,* was a determined man who brooked not the slightest transgressions among his crew. Drunken sailors commonly received up to a dozen blows from the cat-o'-nine-tails for their unlawful inebriation under the fish-eyed captain's administration of naval justice.[1] In one case sailors who got drunk on Christmas were charged with mutiny, and Commodore Jones sentenced some of them to one hundred cutting blows from the dreaded cat.[2] Officers no doubt regarded their commander's extreme punishments as a token of his enthusiasm for good order rather than mere severity. The men who stripped to the waist and stood to the mast saw it differently. In short, the *Cyane* had a morale problem that manifested itself in a desertion rate exceeding what would normally be expected because of California's natural attractions.

The *Cyane*'s African American cook, Anderson Norris, was one of those who became fed up with Stribling and shipboard discipline. With two shipmates he bolted and struck out for less punishing employment in the spring of 1843. His two companions were soon apprehended, but for a while Norris eluded detection. He might have done well to head for New Helvetia, where Captain Sutter usually hired newcomers without inquiring too closely about their backgrounds. Instead he headed north into the country that fell under the watchful eyes of the brothers Vallejo. The disaffected cook made it to the Pomo nation near Clear Lake. Norris was one of many black frontiersmen who sought asylum among the Native peoples of North America, but Clear Lake proved to be a false refuge. Salvador Vallejo, brother Mariano's bulldog for Indian intimidation, assaulted the Pomos and heedlessly killed Norris. Some evidence suggests that Salvador murdered Norris to take revenge on Americans for the conquest of Monterey, but this was not definitely proved. The rumors persisted. One of the warrant officers on the *Cyane* said that he "heard for a fact that Norris was murdered by Salvador Vallejo."[3]

U.S. naval authorities were not inclined to overlook Norris's death as the act of a fellow enthusiast for strict discipline. Instead they raised with Governor Micheltorena the general matter of Mexican abuse of U.S. citizens in California. The governor did not point out the irony that Norris had been fleeing from Commander Stribling's lash when killed but addressed the issue in polite and diplomatic terms. Micheltorena promised to investigate and prosecute if circumstances warranted, although nothing ever came of it. Nevertheless, Stribling sent a copy of the governor's letter to John Marsh, to show that he was looking out for Americans in California. Stribling hoped that Americans would obey Mexican laws "and thereby entitle themselves to the protection of their own country, as well as of that in which they reside." Stribling recommended, however, that Americans "should be ready to defend themselves against the lawless decrees and vexatious orders of the subaltern military officers on the frontier." "Otherwise," he continued, "they will be constantly exposed to every kind of annoyance."[4]

By linking his inquiry into the Norris killing and supporting U.S. resistance to the bad behavior of Mexican military officers, Stribling practically guaranteed naval support for an American rebellion, if not with guns then with aggressive naval diplomacy. Stribling did not name the vexing Mexican officers that he had in mind, but the Vallejos were no doubt among the prime examples. Sutter also fit into the category that Stribling described. In 1843 Sutter's past, present, and future allegiances were unfathomable. Who could tell to which nation this Swiss expatriate, Francophile, Mexican officer with Russian creditors would turn in a crisis? Marsh, however, was still an American citizen who had intimated to Commodore Jones that the United States should acquire

California.[5] Marsh corresponded with the powerful U.S. Senator Lewis Cass and wrote letters encouraging American immigration.[6] In a pinch there would be no question about Marsh's national loyalties.

Sutter's loyalties were suspect, but his fort occupied a strategic piece of real estate. Overland immigrants from Oregon and the Missouri frontier all headed for Sutter's Fort, where they received a cordial welcome, supplies, and information about the country. He wanted to attract Swiss and Germans to his settlement, but only a few came. Meanwhile the fort quickly became the center of American settlement and a source of concern for Mexican authorities. Whatever Sutter's political leanings, he had gathered about him a cadre of Americans with little affection for the Mexican government, save a love of the young republic's generous land policy.

The growing community of New Helvetia even attracted the attention of Marsh. Early in 1844 he inquired about settling near Sutter, who was delighted at the prospect. Sutter knew of a good location and promised to "declare to those who want to claim it that it is claimed by you." He encouraged Marsh and gave him advice about how to obtain a land grant. As a further inducement, he assured Marsh that he would "do everything what lays in my power to prevent that we are not troubled on this side of the San Joaquin of Horse-thiefs and also Cattle thiefs and Hide Robers [sic]."[7] Marsh's January enthusiasm for the Sacramento Valley did not survive the coming of spring. He decided to stay where he was, but his inquiry illustrates New Helvetia's growing importance in California.

Late winter brought a visitor to New Helvetia that foreshadowed dramatic developments in years to come. On March 6 Captain John C. Frémont of the U.S. topographical corps and his scout Kit Carson appeared at the gate of Sutter's Fort. They were wearing the Scottish caps that Hudson's Bay Company men customarily wore. Sutter asked if they were company men. Frémont laughed and replied, "I know why you ask"; he identified himself as an American officer.[8] He and Carson were in terrible shape, suffering from malnutrition and exposure. The rest of Frémont's debilitated force was in camp a few miles away. They had come south from the Oregon country, making a perilous winter passage over the Sierra Nevada through mountain passes that ordinarily were not open until summer. Short of food and with failing horses, they descended the American River in search of Sutter's establishment, where they hoped to find relief.

They were not disappointed. Frémont stayed for three weeks and then headed south into the San Joaquin Valley on the first leg of his return journey to the United States. Following his arrival home, with the assistance of his wife,

Jessie, he wrote the account of his harrowing journey to California. It became an instant best-seller that made Frémont a national hero and provided the first trustworthy geographical information about the route to California.

New Helvetia's proprietor entertained Frémont and supplied him with food, saddles, horses, and other provisions "at cost," Sutter said. He accepted Frémont's drafts on the U.S. government, which Sutter eventually sold at a 20 percent discount.[9] Frémont paid $2,910 for livestock and $981 for "Sundries," as he put it.[10] "I should have charged them more," Sutter later declared. "I did myself a great injury." "No one in California would have trusted him a dollar."[11] Even at a 20 percent discount, Sutter probably profited from the transaction. He asked Frémont to write one draft for $600 in favor of Joseph Chiles, a Sacramento Valley settler whom Sutter had known in Missouri, evidently to satisfy an old debt.[12] Sutter sold Frémont 130 horses and mules and about 30 cattle, including 5 milk cows. The horses and mules "were wild and unbroken," Frémont recalled, the cattle "nearly as wild as buffalo."[13] An average price of eighteen dollars a head for wild stock (say twenty dollars for a horse and five dollars for a cow) seems substantially above the market prices reported for stock elsewhere in California at this time.

Sutter's assertion that he was the only merchant in California who would have advanced goods to Frémont was wrong, and he probably knew it. Thomas O. Larkin, the U.S. consul at Monterey, was arguably California's most successful merchant. He would gladly have provisioned Frémont, yet Sutter did not bother to inform Larkin or Governor Micheltorena of the U.S. officer's visit. Still, word of Frémont's presence reached the governor in Monterey by word of mouth. Micheltorena ordered a military detachment to New Helvetia to see what was up. After learning of Frémont's presence from Micheltorena, Larkin wrote Sutter, asking if he could be of help, and placed the letter in the hands of a Mexican officer that the governor had detailed to investigate the matter.[14] While the Mexican troop rode to New Helvetia, Frémont and his men were riding up the San Joaquin on Sutter's horses, eating his provender.[15] Unquestionably, Sutter provided much needed help to the American explorer, but he could have been even more helpful if he had taken the logical step of informing Larkin, who had access to his own substantial stock of goods as well as the ability to request stores from U.S. naval commanders. As usual, Sutter preferred to act independently—and no wonder. Even at a discount, the paper from Frémont must have eased Sutter's straitened finances.

Frémont, who had arrived at Sutter's gate in a starving condition, was grateful for the help; but his opinion of Sutter was mixed. While recuperating near the fort, Frémont accused three men in his expedition of pilfering sugar, Sutter recalled. The details of the case are now unclear, but the theft must have been from one of the denizens of New Helvetia, because the men were tried by Sutter. He found them not guilty, which "Frémont did not like. He said the men should not remain with him."[16] Frémont discharged the men, and one of them, Samuel Neal, worked for Sutter as a blacksmith.[17] At least this is the version of events that Sutter gave.

Frémont told a somewhat different story. He said that he released five men, including Neal, "who had done his duty faithfully, and had been of very great service to me."[18] The other men "were discharged with their own consent."[19] There was no mention of theft or a trial in Frémont's report. It may be that he was reluctant to blacken anyone's name in a public document and that Sutter in his old age mistakenly recalled Neal as one of the sugar thieves. The important point, however, is that Frémont had at least one man on the ground in New Helvetia who would be able to provide intelligence when he returned to California. If Sutter's memory of events was correct, his failure to convict the miscreants may have soured Frémont's opinion of him.

The day after Frémont left Sutter's Fort, Lieutenant Colonel Rafael Téllez, two additional officers, and twenty-five dragoons rode up to the gates. Téllez handed Larkin's letter to Sutter and no doubt made his own inquiries about the Americans. The colonel probably got the same bland explanations that Sutter gave to Larkin: Frémont was in distress, had no choice but to enter Mexican territory, remained only long enough to get supplies, and promptly left.[20] "The visit of this Exploring expedition [sic] I attribute entirely to accident," Sutter assured Larkin.[21]

Larkin sent an excerpt from Sutter's letter to the U.S. secretary of state, who in turn forwarded it to the secretary of war. Larkin emphasized the geographical significance of New Helvetia and its fort. "All parties by land from Oregon or from the United States to California touch at this establishment first," he informed his superiors.[22] New Helvetia was now on the map of the leaders in Washington who were wondering about the future of California.

In April Larkin decided to enlist Sutter as a source of intelligence about U.S. immigrants. "You will oblige me and perhaps my Government, by . . . giving the arrival of every Company, their number, Captains name, time from the United States, distance travelled, accidents, or particulars, circumstances that may have happened on the road, how many women and children, whether from the Origon [country] or the States." The consul also asked for "every information of consequence in which my countrymen are concerned."[23] Sutter obliged Larkin with occasional reports on American newcomers.[24]

Frémont's visit to California was a prelude to a series of events that culminated in the U.S. conquest of California and Mexico's other northern provinces. The pace and drama of these episodes established a virtually operatic narrative that proceeded relentlessly toward the goals of the United States. As the story unfolded, Sutter's role inexorably transformed from a pivotal character to an interesting bit player on the margins of the main action. Between 1844 and 1846 the scenery that Sutter occupied became more significant to the plot than Sutter himself. He initiated this devolution of character by attempting to upstage California's Mexican political leaders. It was a risky and ill-advised piece of stagecraft that might have destroyed him.

Frémont's brief appearance was followed by troubling news about the impending Mexican-U.S. conflict over Texas. In May 1844 the Mexican minister of war told Governor Micheltorena that war was imminent because the United States was about to annex Texas. Micheltorena was told to prepare for the war that would result. The report was premature, but Micheltorena cautiously made preparations. In July the governor moved his headquarters some twenty miles from Monterey to the inland hamlet of San Juan Bautista, which he deemed more defensible or at least safe from bombardment by the U.S. Navy. He ordered the enrollment of all male citizens (including naturalized foreigners) between the ages of sixteen and sixty. The governor also commissioned militia commanders, including Sutter, who received a captaincy, thus making official the honorific title that he had used for years.[25]

Many Americans were delighted at the prospect of a U.S. takeover. "I have got some very good news for you today," Ephraim Fravel enthused to his friend John Marsh in June. Captain William Heath Davis's schooner had arrived from Mexico "with an express Dispach for the generall to keep a bright look out[.] America has declared war with Mexico." Fravel explained that "[t]he genereall is going to retire to Saint Johns [San Juan Bautista] with all his troops[.] The scooner was back expressley on this business with out any other news whatsoever."[26] We may speculate that Fravel, an American by birth, probably was not anxious to enroll in Micheltorena's militia; nor were the other Americans, whose numbers were increasing.

Some who had gone to Oregon intended to continue on to California. "The states turned out backwoods men very well last ye[a]r," Samuel G. McMahan reported to Marsh from Oregon. Some seven hundred had arrived, and many of them intended to take the Klamath River route to California. McMahan thought that he would accompany them. "I am [a] bungler at [this writing]," he apologized, "but what you cant read mayby you caan gess at it. I hope you are harty as you ust to be and that you have plenty of egg corn [acorn] bread which I cann not get her[e] and I hope to help you eat some of it soon."[27]

Sutter understood the implications of these developments. "The oregon Company [will] most certainly arrive in a few days," he wrote Marsh. "What impression will their arrival make at the time with the government?" he asked rhetorically. The "arrival of large party coming from under a government with whom war exists. Will not the Conclusion be reasonable? that hostilities would be directed against them?" he answered.[28] Yet he gladly accepted Micheltorena's commission and organized the New Helvetia militia company. Men who refused to serve in the militia would be required to serve ten years in the regular Mexican army. "Of course we are also good Citizens, and ever ready to *obey* the Mandate of the glorious Mexican Republic," he wryly explained to Marsh.[29] If the United States annexed Texas, Sutter believed that "Mexico in protection of her *bright escutcheon*—is determined [to show] to the world that she [is determined] to preserve *unsullied,* her *National Honour,* and *dignity.*"[30] In August Sutter heard rumors that there would be a new governor, that U.S. troops would soon arrive aboard the USS *Levant,* and other intelligence of dubious authenticity.[31]

When the Oregon men showed up, Captain Sutter respectfully told Consul Larkin about arrivals from the Columbia River, even as he presumably prepared to combat U.S. forces under the Mexican flag and Micheltorena's orders.[32] National and personal loyalties slipped precariously in Sutter's hands. Always he followed the bright star of his own interests, insofar as he understood them. Happily for all concerned, the U.S.-Mexican crisis soon passed, and California briefly returned to a state of relative calm. A storm would follow, however, and the shifty Sutter would be at its center.

At about the same time that these Oregon men arrived, a party of Walla Walla, Cayuse, and Nez Perce Indians from the Oregon country also appeared. Oregon Indians had journeyed to California perhaps as early as 1800 to obtain livestock by trade and theft. Sutter had met some of these people when he stopped at the Whitman mission in 1838, but there is no clear record of Oregon Indians in New Helvetia before August 1844.[33] About thirty-six Indians (twenty men and the rest women and children) showed up at the fort under the leadership of the well-known Walla Walla chief Peopeo Moxmox. The chief's son, Elijah Hedding, was with him. Methodist missionaries had educated Elijah (whom Sutter called "Leicer"), but the young man had not absorbed much in the way of Christian charity or humility. "Their object is to trade for cattle to take to their Country in the spring," Sutter told his neighbor John Marsh.[34] He gave them permission to hunt in his territory but would soon learn that the Oregon Indians liberally interpreted the extent of Sutter's jurisdiction. They would play an important part in the story that was unfolding.

In October 1844 Sutter visited Governor Micheltorena in Monterey. His loyal employee John Bidwell accompanied him, along with an armed escort, servants, and a band of saddle horses to keep the company swiftly moving.

Three land matters that occupied Sutter's mind were probably the main object of his trip. He wanted to obtain a Mexican title to the former Russian lands at Bodega. He also wanted to transfer the southern portion of New Helvetia to his son, John A. Sutter, Jr. Sutter probably linked these two matters, because New Helvetia was mortgaged to the Russians until he fulfilled his contract with them. Perhaps he could avoid Russian foreclosure by making his son the owner of Sutter's Fort. This would not be the last time that Sutter used this ploy.

Mexican authorities never recognized a Russian claim to California land, but Sutter's possession of Bodega and Ross under a Mexican title would not help the Russian cause if they chose to foreclose. Certainly his possession of a second huge land grant would strengthen him, whatever the Russians did. The third land matter concerned the Muquelemne Miwok Indians, long associated with horse stealing in central California. Sutter struck a bargain with them. If they foreswore rustling, he would help them to obtain four leagues of land of their own in the southern Sacramento Valley.[35] In Mexican eyes all of these proposals were questionable at best. Sutter would need some leverage to make headway in Monterey.

En route to Monterey, Sutter encountered the wayfaring Oregon Indians near the San Joaquin River. His conversation with them immediately raised concerns. "They think to pass the Winter on the feather river," he told his overseer Pierson Reading; but Sutter told them to wait at the fort until he returned. "Please do all possible to prevent them" from going to Hock Farm. "I am afraid they will kill me some cattle," he explained.[36] Sutter also noted that one of the leaders of the Oregon Indians, a Cayuse chief, was near death after being mauled by a bear.[37]

After leaving the Oregonians, Sutter stopped at the residence of the British vice consul, James A. Forbes, near San José. Forbes revealed disturbing intelligence about an impending californio revolt. Forbes knew of the plot because he was married to a californiana and "in [on] the secrets of the Californians," Sutter said. Forbes told Sutter that the rebels were plotting to exile Micheltorena and the "Mexican cut-throats" who manned his army. His curiosity thus piqued, Sutter made further inquiries with "other Gentlemen" (possibly Charles Weber and Jean Jacques Vioget, whom he also visited), who "did not know that the General and Myself were friends, and told . . . me the whole plan."[38]

There was more to the plot than Sutter probably knew. Micheltorena had already despaired of holding California for Mexico. The californios were impossible to govern, he thought. The governor had already arrested Alvarado for plotting against him but later released him—a decision that Micheltorena would come to regret. Late in 1843 he sent an emissary to Mexico City to urge the government to cede California to British creditors as the only way to prevent the province from falling to the Americans, whose numbers were increasing daily. Mexico owed British creditors more than fifty million dollars and was incapable of paying off so large a sum, but the Mexican government was not prepared to act favorably on Micheltorena's recommendation. Nor were British creditors inclined to take Mexican land instead of cash. The British government did not want California to fall into American hands; neither did it wish to go to war with Mexico or the United States to prevent it, so nothing was done.[39]

Californios who wished to declare independence from Mexico also looked to the British for assistance. On August 20, 1844, several californios (probably including Alvarado) called on vice consul Forbes and informed him that they intended to get rid of Micheltorena and Mexican rule. If they declared California independent, would England protect it? Forbes was enthusiastic and wrote approvingly about the scheme to his government. The californios promised to "wait quietly" while he learned "the pleasure of Her Majesty's Government."[40] He was still waiting for a reply when he disclosed the californios' plans to Sutter. Why Forbes would tell Sutter anything about such a delicate matter is an open question.

Armed with tantalizing intelligence, Sutter went to Monterey and told the governor what he knew, a betrayal of confidences that seemed not to bother him. "This was the first [Micheltorena] knew of it, and [he] was glad I told him."[41] Surely this was bad news for Mexico. Perhaps it meant that England was making a secret deal with the californios that would prevent Mexico from using California to pay old British debts. To resist this threat, the governor needed as many allies as he could get, so he entertained Sutter accordingly. Micheltorena received Sutter "with greatest Civil and Military honors," the Swiss recalled.[42] After a suitable amount of formal dinners, troop reviews, and flattery, Micheltorena made a deal with Sutter. If he would raise a militia and assist the governor against the rebels, Micheltorena agreed to "secure me, and all the other settlers in the valley, titles to their lands, and pay all the costs of soldiers & everything."[43] Micheltorena provided Sutter with more than promises. "The Governor received me very well and treated me with great Distinction," Sutter reported to Weber, "& I received also a good supplie of Armes and Ammunition for Infantrie and Cavallry which I have now to organize." Unfortunately, "the business, particular the Land affaires, are going very slow on account of Don Manuel Casarin Jimeno," the secretary of state.[44]

While Sutter was in Monterey, the USS *Savannah,* Commodore James Armstrong commanding, sailed into the harbor. Governor Micheltorena and a retinue including Sutter paid a courtesy visit to the man-of-war. One of the ship's officers noted Sutter as "a man of medium, or rather low stature, but with a marked military air. He wore a cap, and plain blue frock coat, a mustache covered his lip. His head was of very singular formation, being flat and wall-shaped behind, and rising high above the crown, with a lofty and expanded forehead. His manners were courteous, but displayed great precision."[45] He told the usual yarns about his service in the Swiss Guard but also informed his listeners about his many leagues of land, hundreds of employees, fort, and private army. He claimed to be experimenting with plantings of tobacco, hemp, and cotton.

After a stay of about two weeks, Sutter left Monterey in early November. Intending to embark on an American merchantman, the *Sterling,* Sutter first called on the *Savannah.* This was no doubt a social visit; but whatever Sutter's purpose, he "was detained on board" for so long that the *Sterling* sailed without him but with his baggage. He hired a small boat to catch the *Sterling* but failed and returned to the *Savannah,* where he spent the night. The next morning Sutter departed on the *Don Quixote* for Yerba Buena, where he caught up with his wayward luggage and met with representatives of the Russian-American Company. There is no record of the meeting with the Russians, but it is safe to assume that Sutter's delinquent mortgage payments on the Ross property were the main topic of conversation. He arranged for Peter Kostromitinov, the company's agent, to visit New Helvetia in November. Then Sutter paid his respects to the Mexican customs officials, boarded his own schooner, and sailed to New Helvetia.[46]

The development of organized opposition to Micheltorena in the following weeks adds importance to the details of Sutter's itinerary. A few days after he had spent the night on the *Savannah,* Commodore Armstrong led a hunting party out to Alisal, where former governor Alvarado was meeting with his confederates. Armstrong told Alvarado that he was suspected of disloyalty and urged him to leave Alisal to be out of Micheltorena's reach. On the road, Alvarado encountered Jesús Pico, who with fifty other hotheads had already stolen a Mexican government horse herd. Now Alvarado, who had promised Forbes to wait for word from London, was in a pickle. A revolt had already broken out, and he was suspected of leading it. Reluctantly he joined and tried to convince his uncle Mariano Vallejo to do likewise. The final californio revolt against centralist Mexican authority was underway.[47]

A confrontation between Micheltorena and the californios was probably unavoidable, but Sutter may have inadvertently added fuel to the fire. Acting purely out of self-interest, hoping to secure and expand his claims on California land, he carried rumors to Monterey that convinced the governor that the californios were about to rebel. Micheltorena had always been suspicious of Alvarado's loyalty and now was certain of his treasonous intentions. Sutter, anxious to ingratiate himself, assured Micheltorena that he would provide indispensable help from New Helvetia, thus giving the governor more confidence in the likelihood of military success. After a couple of weeks with the governor, Sutter spent a night on board the *Savannah*. There is no record of what he told his hosts, but he was not known for his discretion, especially when in his cups. He probably told Commodore Armstrong something about his suspicions about Alvarado and Micheltorena's plans. Armstrong then told Alvarado what he knew. Overtaken by events and already identified with the rebels, Alvarado sided with them, rather than waiting for word from the British about the proposed protectorate. Perhaps these events would have played out in much the same way without Sutter, but it is hard to avoid the conclusion that his rumor-mongering exacerbated an already inflammatory situation. Sutter did not care about that. He sailed back to New Helvetia believing that he had made an alliance with Micheltorena that would serve him well. If hostilities broke out, he was obligated to provide military assistance to the governor. As soon as he was safely back at the fort, he began to prepare for that eventuality.

CHAPTER 11

Misfortunes of War

While the war clouds gathered, Sutter assembled the militia for Micheltorena. But if Sutter hoped that his cordial relationship with the Mexican governor would solve his land problems, he was sadly mistaken. The governor, perhaps because he did not wish to alienate the californios further, followed the advice of Manuel Casarín Jimeno (the californio secretary of state) and turned down Sutter's request to transfer part of New Helvetia to his son and to grant land to the Moquelumnes. Sutter's absentee son was not a citizen of Mexico, so the title could not be transferred to him, Casarín reasoned. As for the Indians, they were not organized in a pueblo, so there was no guarantee that they would cultivate the land as was legally required. The Muquelemnes could remain on the land and cultivate it until such time as they could obtain a grant in the way prescribed by law, Casarín added. Nor would anything be done about Sutter's wish to add Ross and Bodega to his real estate portfolio. Sutter, who was understandably disappointed and annoyed at these developments, claimed that Micheltorena supported his aspirations but did not attempt to explain why the governor failed to influence the secretary of state.[1]

As if Sutter did not have enough to think about, the Oregon Indians once again claimed his attention. He found them at the fort when he returned from Monterey. In his absence they had been busy. In addition to hunting, they had stolen horses from California Indians, who had probably rustled them from Americans and californios in the first place. Ordinarily the recovery of stolen horses was a cause for celebration because, according to the custom of the country, they could be returned to the rightful owners. The Walla Walla, Cayuse, and Nez Perce men, however, argued that the animals now belonged to them, stolen fair and square, as it were. Elijah Hedding, the Methodist son of the Walla Walla chief, was the most obdurate advocate of this interpretation of ownership. Hedding had already caused a lot of trouble by killing one of the Indians in his party near the fort, a murder that was discovered when hogs partially devoured the body. No one, least of all Sutter, attempted to bring young Hedding to justice for his crime. He would have killed another of his companions too, if a white man had not disarmed him. "He was the terror of the old Chiefs," Sutter said.[2]

But Hedding held no terror for Grove Cook, one of Sutter's white employees. Cook was a Kentucky hunter who had made his way to California with the Bidwell–Bartleson party in 1841 and had found work with Sutter. He had a reputation as a vicious Indian hater who killed without provocation.[3] The Kentuckian noticed a mule with his brand among the Oregonians' animals and demanded its return. Hedding told him that he could have the mule if he was brave enough to take it, or words to that effect, and leveled his rifle at Cook. Sutter stepped in and tried to mediate the dispute but was interrupted by the arrival of Peter Kostromitinov, representative of the Russian-American Company, who evidently had come to discuss Sutter's debt.

Sutter left the disputants, the Indian chiefs (presumably including Hedding's father, Peopeo Moxmox) and about fifteen Americans, in his office. Thirty minutes later a shot rang out. Sutter and his Russian guest rushed in to see Hedding dead on the floor. It was a case of self-defense, Cook said, and he had a lot of American witnesses who backed him up. Hedding had called Cook a liar, and that insult apparently escalated the conflict and led to the killing. The Indians left the fort in a hurry, driving the captured horses north to Oregon and raiding livestock herds along the way. This would not be the end of Sutter's trouble from this murderous incident, which probably occurred in mid-November.[4] The aggrieved Indians would report the affair to their Indian and white friends in Oregon, touching off an international controversy the following spring.[5]

Hedding's violent death did not preoccupy Sutter for long. Soon conflict between Micheltorena and the californios erupted in earnest as the governor and the rebels jockeyed for military position near Santa Clara. The mounted rebels under Alvarado and José Castro (including a company of foreigners organized by Charles Weber at San José) outnumbered the Mexican troops by about 220 mounted men to 150 infantrymen. There was much maneuvering and posturing, including a threat by Micheltorena to execute foreigners who sided with the rebels, but no actual fighting. Vallejo diplomatically excused himself from the hostilities by disbanding his militia with the claim that he could not bear the expense. Some of the former militiamen joined the rebels.

Vallejo's move conveniently prevented him from responding to any call to arms from Micheltorena, but he probably would not have ridden to the governor's defense in any case. He later claimed that he was behind the revolt in the first place.[6] By late November it became clear to Micheltorena that he had no hope of defeating Alvarado and Castro, so he sued for peace. On December 1 he signed a treaty acceding to all of the californios' demands—sending the Mexican soldier-convicts back to Mexico within three months' time but allowing Micheltorena to remain as governor. Micheltorena almost immediately began planning to break his solemn word. His treachery would involve Sutter.[7]

While retreating to Monterey with his troops, Micheltorena happened upon John Bidwell, who was on his way to New Helvetia. According to Bidwell, the governor halted and talked with him for about half an hour. "He desired me to beg the Americans to be loyal to Mexico," Bidwell recalled, "and in due time would give them all the lands to which they were entitled. He sent particularly friendly word to Sutter." Musing on the governor's promises, Bidwell rode on to the Mission San José. There he chanced to meet the triumphant rebel leaders Castro and Alvarado, who treated him "like a prince." They too "protested their friendship for the Americans," said Bidwell, "and sent a request to Sutter to support them."[8] Now Sutter had choices to make.

When Bidwell rode into the fort, he brought plenty of interesting intelligence for Sutter to consider. In addition to the news of the bloodless discomfiture of Micheltorena and his meetings with the governor and the rebels, Bidwell probably told Sutter that his land petitions had been denied. Sutter was naturally disappointed that the californio secretary of state had prevailed in this round, and the prospect of Castro and Alvarado gaining the whip hand did not auger well for future success in the land-grant business. Sutter considered his options and cast his lot with the governor. He wrote his assurances to the governor and dispatched them to Monterey with Pablo Gutiérrez, the loyal Mexican who had ridden with Sutter from Missouri. Gutiérrez would soon have cause to regret his fidelity to a lost cause and rash friends.[9]

Sutter's decision embittered the californios; but from his perspective, it was an easy choice. Micheltorena was the lawful governor and had made him promises couched in convincing flattery. The rebels were not reliable friends. Even if they succeeded in deposing Micheltorena, the central government might retaliate. Then what would become of the rebel leaders and Sutter if he sided with them?

While the rest of California celebrated the false peace, Sutter redoubled his military efforts. "I am still in a state of war," he informed William Hartnell on December 13. "Every day drilling is going on." Sutter's letter included his complaints against Hartnell's brother-in-law, Casarín, and a request for help in gaining the secretary of state's reconsideration. "I shall be willing to pay you whatever you ask," he added. The letter contained not-so-veiled threats. Casarín "might be very sorry for his procedure for a time will come and it is quite near when Mr. Jimeno [Casarín] will be glad that I protect him; it is being said that one good turn merits another." Sutter claimed to have "several thousand Indians which have all been notified and are ready for service in a moment," an exaggeration that played to californios' fears.[10] The British-born Hartnell was also Vallejo's cousin by marriage, so out of brotherly affection he forwarded Sutter's letter to the frontier commander.[11] It should also be noted that Hartnell hoped that England might eventually succeed Mexico as California's sovereign.[12]

Hartnell was not Vallejo's only source of intelligence about Sutter. Vallejo's Indian ally Chief Solano and Juan Vaca also reported on Sutter's military preparations. Vallejo decided to set Sutter straight by sending a letter with a swift horseman. For the next few days riders would cross the northern California frontier, carrying express messages between the two men. The treaty had settled everything, Vallejo asserted. The country was at peace, so Sutter did not need to ride to the governor's defense. There had been no rebellion against Micheltorena. All the californios wanted was to be rid of the cholo soldiers. "The movement which took place at Monterey was done at my direction," Vallejo pointedly added, because "it was not good for the people of California that there should remain in their midst more than three hundred criminals." If there was a rebellion against Micheltorena, "I, who hold the first post on the frontier and who hold myself to be a patriot, could never permit my subalterns to take the initiative in a matter which it is my place to direct." He warned Sutter that if anyone attempted "to attack the government in the territory under my command, the authors of such an attempt would not be long at receiving at my hands condign punishment for such unheard of daring."[13] In sum, Vallejo's letter said that the commander of the northern line was behind the events that alarmed Sutter and that he should stay out of it if he knew what was good for him.

Sutter was not inclined to follow Vallejo's suggestions. His response seemed to indicate that he had not understood Vallejo or that he was trying to smoke him out. Sutter was assembling at New Helvetia "foreigners and citizens" who were loyal to the legitimate government "to march under your orders to Monterey to protect General Micheltorena, so that he may not be again obliged to capitulate to the rebels." Sutter also demanded a hundred horses from Vallejo's government herd. He cloaked himself in Mexican patriotism and friendship for Vallejo, although his old nemesis did not see it that way. "Comandante General," Sutter unctuously assured Vallejo, "if you have need of us . . . I will unite my people and march to aid you." He added: "I wish to defend my life and the Mexican Republic, and you, General, the protector of all foreigners and naturalized citizens."[14] Vallejo's reassurances had not convinced Sutter that all was well. "I am satisfied that you are for the legitimate government," he told Vallejo on December 17, "and that perhaps you are ignorant of the plan which Castro and Alvarado have formed; but I, being well informed, can do no less than to march to protect order for the general."[15] With that, Sutter sent some of his men to take horses from Vallejo's herds at Soscol. While they were about it, they threatened to attack Sonoma and bragged about taking Alvarado dead or alive.[16]

Vallejo had done all that he could to dissuade Sutter from taking precipitous action; exasperated, he forwarded Sutter's letters to Alvarado. "According to his plan of campaign and his operations at each moment, I expect that he will first direct himself to this point." The rustling of Vallejo's horses convinced him that he was already under attack, thus implying that his small force would be needed to protect the northern frontier.[17] Once again Vallejo would avoid taking a direct part in the fighting that was to come, and the nettlesome Sutter was the excuse.

Matters were already on a hair trigger, but Sutter had put the whole department in an uproar. Castro wrote, demanding to know his intentions. He also sent a copy with a letter to Micheltorena, blaming the governor for authorizing Sutter's actions and fomenting civil war. Rumors spread among the californios that Sutter had promised to bring Micheltorena the heads of Alvarado and Castro and that he carried manacles for the captured rebels. More than thirty years later Alvarado's bitterness toward Sutter remained sharp. "If this way of acting agrees with the obligations the Swiss think incumbent on persons who receive a favor from another," he wrote in his "Historia de California," "I promise to pray to the Supreme Creator from this day on to free me from the gratitude of my friends and instead of saying *panem nostrum quotidianum da mihi hodie* [Give us this day our daily bread] I will say *Deus meus liberta me de gratitudo helveticorum* [Free me, my Lord, from the gratitude of the Swiss]."[18]

As the governor's troubles mounted, he evidently decided to reward Sutter and the American settlers. On December 22 Micheltorena gave Sutter extraordinary power to grant lands to settlers under a general title from the governor, who was "too much occupied to issue one by one, the separate titles . . . upon them and their families . . . who have obtained an agreeable report from Señor Sutter, up to the present time."[19] Accordingly, Sutter gave some eighteen deeds to immigrants under Micheltorena's authority. In all, he "granted" more than 330,000 acres in the Sacramento Valley under the

Micheltorena general title, but to no avail. U.S. courts later denied the validity of these grants.[20]

Questionable as they proved to be, these conveyances served a very real purpose in December 1844. Without the original documentation, it is impossible to know whether Micheltorena actually made this extraordinary concession, but it is plausible that he did so in order to solidify Sutter's loyalty. From the American perspective, Micheltorena's apparent confidence in Sutter seemed to confer on him real power that was meaningful to land-hungry new arrivals. A good relationship with him might result in a major land grant. Isaac Graham and some others had the additional motive of revenge against Alvarado and Castro, who had put Graham in irons a few years before.[21]

Not everyone was taken in by Sutter's dreamy propositions. Charles Weber, who had sided with Alvarado a few weeks earlier, now believed that Americans should remain neutral. Weber hoped for a U.S. takeover and could foresee only trouble in the course that Sutter was taking.[22] Consequently, the German went to New Helvetia in order to dissuade foreigners from taking part in the rebellion. This was criticism that Sutter would not tolerate. He arrested Weber and imprisoned him in the fort. Some Americans thought Sutter's reaction to Weber's talk was harsh, but the German settler remained imprisoned during the upcoming hostilities.

Hoping for a large reward in land, American immigrants flocked to Sutter's standard and on January 1, 1845, marched "with music and flying colors" to defend Mexican authority in California.[23] By early California standards, Sutter led an impressive force, perhaps the largest military contingent ever to march there. "My force consisted of four hundred men," he reminisced, "100 riflemen under Captain [John] Gantt" (including Isaac Graham and some of his gang), plus "40 soldiers, cavalry who had deserted General Vallejo and joined me—native Californians, & the balance were artillery and infantry," who were probably mostly Indians commanded in German by Ernst Rufus. The Indian contingent included Muquelemne Miwoks under the command of their chief, Second Lieutenant Rufino. Ensign Homobono kept the muster roll. Sutter took his Russian field piece with him. Three drummers (one Indian and two African Americans) and an African American fifer added martial airs to the wintry atmosphere. John Bidwell accompanied Sutter as his secretary, Samuel J. Hensley as commissary, Jasper O'Farrell as quartermaster, and John Sinclair and Dr. John Townsend as aides-de-camp.[24] Ninety Indians were armed with muskets, but not all of them had shoes. Eventually Sutter shod them with rawhide sandals that made the long march easier for them.[25] Mexican Californians looked with horror on an Indian army that included Moquelumnes, who were virtually synonymous with horse thieves in their minds. In his absence, Sutter left Pierson Reading in charge of the fort's garrison and business affairs.

Sutter divided his forces and headed for John Marsh's ranch on the slopes of Mount Diablo. The cavalry rode overland while Sutter and the infantry sailed to Marsh's embarcadero in the *Sacramento*. The Sacramento Valley foreigners marched with Sutter because visions of landed estates danced in their heads, but other foreigners had misgivings. Like Weber, they preferred an American takeover and could not see how supporting Micheltorena furthered that goal. Sutter believed that Marsh was against him, but Marsh joined him to avoid imprisonment in one of the fort's dark bastions.[26] Marsh eventually proved to be a seditious force among the ranks, as did other American recruits. For now, they marched toward San José.

These rough frontier characters proved troublesome almost immediately. At mission San José Sutter was pleased to find that the padres supported the governor, but his militiamen became offensive guests when they tippled too much mission wine. Sutter decided to march sooner than he had planned in order to get his drunken soldiers away from temptation. When he reached the pueblo of San José, ten miles away, he sent word to the alcalde to lock up the grog shops to prevent trouble. "I had some bad customers among my riflemen," he confessed.[27] The bad behavior of Americans and convict-soldiers alike confirmed the fears of californios, who worried over the security of their families and property.

There were other bad omens. Sutter sent Pablo Gutiérrez on another courier mission to the governor in Monterey, but the californios arrested him. Caught red-handed with Sutter's dispatches for Micheltorena, Gutiérrez could only hope for mercy from his captors. They showed none: somewhere near present-day Gilroy the rebels hanged Gutiérrez from a tree.[28] A few days later Sutter's men found his clothes.[29] Sutter did not express grief or regret over the execution of his loyal employee and companion of ten years. Perhaps he was too preoccupied with the details of military command to dwell on the fate of Gutiérrez. Still, the death of his old friend must have reminded Sutter that his support for Micheltorena was a deadly serious matter.

Sutter's force marched on to Monterey, where the californios had besieged Micheltorena. His approach frightened off the rebels, and Micheltorena marched out to greet him with eight hundred of his own soldiers. Now they had a formidable force to pursue the californios. The rebels rode to southern California, where they hoped to find reinforcements. Meanwhile Sutter enjoyed the complimentary cigars (a thousand of them!) that Consul Larkin sent to him.[30]

Castro and Alvarado and their two hundred supporters scoured the country for horses as they went. Every conflict in California was determined in large part by control of the horse herds. Horses gave both forces the ability to move swiftly. Infantry could move only as fast as sandal-shod feet could march, so keeping the military horse herds replenished was essential. The Indian soldiers in Sutter's force were especially useful in carrying out this mission. Stripping the ranchos of horses also brought the California economy to a standstill. Without horses, the hide and tallow trade could not be carried on. Both sides agreed to repay the rancheros for their losses, but that was an uncertain promise. The longer the war went on, the greater would be the losses of rancheros and merchants alike. The depletion of their horse herds was an important reason why the californios feared Sutter and his force of Indian and American militiamen.[31]

American militiamen proved difficult to keep under strict military discipline. They formed a council with elected representatives, finally electing a committee of three consisting of Gantt, a former U.S. army officer; Charles McIntosh, a man of Delaware or Cherokee descent; and William Dickey, an Irishman. Marsh acted as their secretary.[32] These embodiments of frontier democracy and republican virtue gave unwanted advice and undermined Sutter's authority. "They say they will act with me," Sutter explained to his New Helvetia major-domo, "but it is not true, they are just contrary and want to use me only for a tool. . . . Never I thought that certain persons could act so against me."[33]

Micheltorena made Sutter a brevet colonel. The combined force marched southward, following the old mission road up the Salinas River. At the Mission Soledad, Micheltorena addressed his troops, promising "that every one recommended to him by me," Sutter recalled, "should be entitled to a Rancho, after our return from the Campaign."[34] Micheltorena's reinforcement of Sutter's influence and the militia's greed for land propelled the troops up the Salinas Valley and then across the coast range to San Luis Obispo. From there they followed the coast southward, at times a few miles inland and sometimes along the shore. Where the route took them to the beach, Sutter's men had to make a primitive road so the cannon would not sink in the sand. It was rough going for all of the troops, but especially so for the sandal-shod Indians.

Sutter marked Micheltorena's courtesies along the road as signs of confidence. Indeed, he believed that every visit to Micheltorena's tent meant that "he held me on terms of equality with himself."[35] The march was not without difficulties for the commanders. A severe case of piles forced Micheltorena to recline in a buggy rather than riding horseback as befit a military commander. The force rested and provisioned at Santa Barbara, where Sutter's force bivouacked in the mission.

The army moved forward to Rincon, a few miles farther down the road toward Mission San Buenaventura, but Sutter remained in Santa Barbara with a 25-man escort so that he could purchase supplies at the store of Captain John Wilson. Sutter wanted a hundred pairs of pants, shirts, tobacco, and other supplies. He paid with government orders. "In this way I impressed horses, and everything I required," Sutter recalled.[36] He took pride in his success at preventing looting by his soldiers, but in the end there would be little difference between a stolen horse and one that was obtained with a worthless order that the Mexican government did not pay. Trousers were a special problem. By this time some of Sutter's men were in tatters; one was forced to wrap a blanket around his loins to preserve his dignity, if not his military splendor.[37]

Castro's outnumbered force was thirty miles farther south at the Mission San Buenaventura. It seemed only a matter of time before Micheltorena and Sutter would overwhelm the rebel force, but things began to go wrong. Sutter sent a squad of fourteen or fifteen men, mostly Americans, to reconnoiter Castro's position. Somehow Castro's men managed to surprise and capture them; but the Americans refused to give up their weapons, fearing that they would be shot. Castro asked William Streeter, an American dentist and mechanic who sometimes lived in Santa Barbara, to act as translator and reassure the armed captives. Streeter cheerfully pointed out to his compatriots that the californios could kill them with or without their rifles. However, he also assured them that Castro would treat them well and convinced them to turn over the weapons. He told Castro that he should hold the men for a few days, treat them generously, explain the californio cause, assure them that he meant no harm to foreigners (who should stay out of this conflict among Mexicans), and then parole them. This he did, to the benefit of the californio campaign.[38]

After giving Castro their word that they would no longer fight against him, the men, including MacIntosh and Streeter, returned to Micheltorena's camp at Rincon. When they declared that they were honor-bound to abandon hostilities, Sergeant Gantt took it upon himself to address the troops with a motivating speech. Much like the legendary scene at the Alamo, Gantt formed the men into a line and explained that they had promised Micheltorena that they would fight the rebels. He hoped that none would desert the cause, but anyone who wanted to abandon the fight should step out of line. The fourteen parolees and ten more men stepped forward. This was not the edifying response to his oratory that Gantt had wished for, so he re-formed the men and gave an even more impassioned harangue. This time fifty men stepped forward. That was the end of Gantt's speechifying.[39]

One of the Americans, a man named Green, decided that Streeter was to blame for dissension in the ranks and demanded to know who he was. Streeter (a dentist) replied that he was a doctor, drew a Bowie knife from his boot and said that it was his lancet, and then produced a pepperbox pistol and called it his pillbox. Green turned on the parolees and called them all cowards, whereupon McIntosh pulled his knife, gave a war yell, and chased Green to the sanctuary of Micheltorena's tent. From that point on, defections from the ranks continued at a steady pace. According to Streeter, even John Sinclair, Sutter's aide, was fed up with rain and starvation rations. Evidently Sinclair's concern about the propriety of Sutter's imprisonment of Weber had become an additional cause for resentment among defectors. Heading north, Sinclair declared that if Weber was still a prisoner he would "tear down every building in the place."[40]

Sutter evidently remained in Santa Barbara when these stirring scenes unfolded, but his presence probably would not have changed things. Unity among the Americans had crumbled. If Castro meant them no harm, why should they fight him? They would be better off cutting a deal with the californios. By this time the troops were ill clad and ill fed. The Indians lived on the mussels and clams that they dug on the beach, and the rest of the troops were probably scavenging too. The weather had turned rainy; one can imagine the misery of the situation. It is not surprising that the prospect of free land had become less important to some than dry feet and a full belly.

Still, Sutter made the most of his sojourn near Santa Barbara. Before advancing to Buenaventura, where he assumed there would be an engagement, he implored the governor to grant him the surplus, the so-called *sobrante* lands associated with the New Helvetia grant approved by Alvarado. Evidently Sutter wanted the lands that were periodically inundated and that were specifically excluded in the Alvarado grant: "in case I was killed my family would get something."[41] The governor was in a generous mood and acceded to his earnest petition, "for the good conduct and services which the said Sutter has rendered and is rendering at the present time," granting him twenty-two additional square leagues of land.[42]

According to Sutter, Micheltorena had the title drawn up on the spot. But unfortunately for Sutter the original was somehow lost, and in later years he had to rely on a questionable copy in his possession. Ultimately, the U.S. Supreme Court would decide the validity of the so-called sobrante grant, but in the meantime Sutter blithely acted as though his uncertain and irregular claim was as good as gold.[43]

Armed with the certainly that his family would be well provided for in the unhappy event of his honorable death in the service of Mexico, Sutter marched his troops toward Buenaventura in a driving rain. If his version of events is accepted, he daringly attacked at dawn and drove Castro's men (who were recovering from the effects of a fandango the night before) from the mission. Other accounts simply have the californios withdrawing without a shot being fired.[44] Thrilled with this modest military accomplishment, Sutter demanded food and wine from the mission's majordomo, who grudgingly produced it in "great plenty." For the next day Sutter and his army had "plenty to eat and drink." Indians came in from a neighboring mission, made music, and danced for his entertainment. Perhaps less entertaining was their tale that the californios intended to nail Sutter to the large cross in the mission yard, if they could only catch him.[45]

The forces of Micheltorena and Sutter marched toward Los Angeles; but by this time Castro and Alvarado had gained fresh recruits from among the southern Californians, including a goodly contingent of Americans. These men, many of whom had married into californio families, were generally more comfortable with Mexican society than were the new arrivals and Americans who lived near New Helvetia.[46] The prospect of fighting other Americans was not pleasing to the riflemen who accompanied Sutter. Desertions caused a serious problem for the Micheltorena forces. The day before he took Buenaventura, Sutter reported that they had only three hundred men remaining. He worried about the security of New Helvetia and sent Marcelino, Lieutenant Rufino's brother-in-law, to recruit "25 or 30 good Christian Indians near San José" for service at his fort.[47]

On February 20 the opposing armies converged near Cahuenga Pass on a plain called Álamo at the southern edge of the San Fernando Valley. The ensuing engagement—one can scarcely describe it as a battle—would not resemble in the least the fight at the Alamo in Texas. Both sides had artillery. Micheltorena brought two cannons, and Sutter brought a field piece obtained from the Russians. The californios had two big guns in the fight. Both sides thoughtfully positioned their batteries just out of range of the enemy and opened fire. No soldier was injured in this exchange, but two or three horses lost their lives. The Álamo was cut with arroyos, in which Sutter and his riflemen took shelter to avoid becoming unlucky casualties of this ineffective bombardment.

During the cannonading, Americans on the californios' side approached their fellow expatriates under Gantt with the object of convincing them to drop out of the fight. Isaac Graham had already switched sides, and the rest would soon follow. Sutter arrived at this parley only to find Gantt and his men busy balloting. "What are you doing here not obeying orders, why do you not advance?" he demanded.[48] Gantt replied that they were voting on whether or not they should remain with Micheltorena. "This is the time to fight & not to vote," Colonel Sutter manfully declared.[49] He argued that Micheltorena was the friend of American settlers and that the Castro–Alvarado forces would persecute them. William Workman, leader of the Americans who sided with the californios, and perhaps José de Jesús Pico, who according to one source went to the ravine under a flag of truce, said that Micheltorena could not fulfill his promises to the Americans because they were contrary to Mexican law. Furthermore, the californio leaders promised to grant lands to the newly arrived Americans as long as they abided by Mexican law and became citizens. This settled things as far as Gantt and the others were concerned. All of the Americans withdrew, leaving the Mexican troops and Sutter's Indians to decide the issue with the californios.[50]

According to his account, Sutter was on his way back to Micheltorena when about thirty californios captured him. One of his captors saluted and said, "I am glad you are here." "Yes," said Sutter, "but I am not."[51] Thus his Mexican military career ended honorably, if not heroically. Sutter, of course, made himself the hero of his own story, at least insofar as he could under the circumstances. His account of an honorable capture at the hands of superior forces, however, does not coincide with the narratives of other participants. While there is some confusion of facts, all of the californios' reminiscences declare that Sutter surrendered voluntarily. Some say that he made a deal with the californios in advance. Others have him quitting with the Americans. No one claims credit for capturing Sutter. The californios, of course, hated him and may not have wished to grant any degree of honor to their vanquished foe, even in old age. Perhaps in 1845 events unfolded just as Sutter recalled them in 1876; but it may also be true that he abandoned Micheltorena when it became clear that he was backing a losing cause. John Coffin Jones succinctly reported to Larkin that "Suiter & Graham went into Castros camp and gave themselves up."[52]

Whether Sutter surrendered voluntarily or under duress, his troubles were far from over. Californios had many reasons to punish him, perhaps even to execute him. Rumors of his plans to shackle californio leaders and behead Castro and Alvarado inflamed his enemies. Rebels in California were magnanimous in victory, but their rancor toward Sutter was strong. He worried that they would make an example of him as an ungrateful foreigner, just as they had hanged his unfortunate friend Pablo Gutiérrez. Soon after his capture Alvarado arrived, dismounted, and embraced the prisoner "like an old friend," Sutter recalled, not that Alvarado's demeanor allayed his concerns. Alvarado, who was known as a steady drinker, sent for a bottle of *aguardiente* and shared a draft with his captive. Presently Castro rode up. "Castro," Alvarado called, "dismount and salute Captain Sutter."[53] There was more embracing. Then the three unlikely amigos mounted and rode to a nearby adobe, where Sutter was confined under guard.

After Castro and Alvarado returned to the battlefield to settle things with

Micheltorena, curious californios came to look at Sutter, "as if I were a strange animal." For a while he kept his sword, but an officer appeared and took it. Now completely disarmed, Sutter felt vulnerable. He bluffed his captors, claiming that it was improper to deprive a high-ranking officer of his sword and to keep him under a common guard. It worked. They returned his sword and invited him into another room, where they invited him to take another drink, which he did with some relief. In the evening the californios sent Sutter to Los Angeles, where he stayed in the home of Abel Stearns, a well-to-do Massachusetts-born merchant and ranchero who had married into a prominent californio family.[54]

Late that night Stearns knocked on Sutter's door. Fatigued from the events of the day, Sutter was difficult to rouse, but he finally got up to find Stearns with Andrés Pico and James McKinley, who urged him to write a letter advising Micheltorena and Ernst Rufus (commander of Sutter's Indians) to surrender. Although Sutter believed that the governor's situation was hopeless, he did not want to tell Micheltorena to give up, at least not in writing. Claiming that he could not write Spanish and that Rufus could understand nothing but German, Sutter agreed to communicate with Micheltorena in French and with Rufus in German. He claimed to write "in such a manner that he could understand my position & that I was forced to write."[55] Micheltorena capitulated the following day. Why Sutter claimed that he was writing secretly under duress when it was perfectly clear that he was a prisoner of the californios is baffling, especially when the net result was Micheltorena's surrender. Like so many of Sutter's claims, this may have been meant to make him appear in the best light—that is, as a helpless prisoner in the hands of his enemies, rather than as a turncoat.

The articles of capitulation that Micheltorena negotiated with the californios protected Sutter and the other Mexican citizens who fought with him; yet Sutter was undoubtedly nervous about his future while in Los Angeles.[56] He was entirely at the mercy of men he had sworn to fight—men who had many reasons to despise him. To dramatize this point Sutter recalled a dramatic conversation when Bancroft interviewed him in 1876. On the morning of Micheltorena's surrender, Alfred Anselin, a French surgeon who had once worked for Sutter, visited his one-time employer. "I have bad news for you," said the physician. "There is much discussion as to what shall be done with you. . . . Some are for fusillading you, and others for transportation and confiscation of all your property."[57] "I am in your power," replied Sutter. "You can do with me what you want."[58]

While Sutter remained a prisoner, Micheltorena and his cholo soldiers were at liberty until they were transported to Mexico. The general was even allowed to pass through Los Angeles with music and flying colors, an event that depressed Sutter. "This music was like a dead march for me. I was really the greatest sufferer."[59]

Sutter may be forgiven such ruminations while contemplating the prospect of a firing squad, but he was not the greatest sufferer. His Indian soldiers were treated much worse than anyone else. The californios disarmed them and forced them "to carry burdens like pack-animals to San Pedro, provisions to supply the vessels of the Mexican soldiers," with "no pay & scarcely food enough to live on," Sutter complained.[60] Rufino and his Moquelumne soldiers had embarked on this expedition at Sutter's behest, but he did not reveal what promises he had made to them. It is reasonable to suppose that they expected booty in the form of stolen horses. Sutter and Micheltorena may also have promised them the land grant that had been turned down the previous year. At least the Muquelemnes had horses to ride on the journey south. Sutter's other Indian soldiers had to march on foot (sometimes without shoes) more than four hundred miles. Instead of reaping the rewards of victory, they lost everything except their lives. Dismounted, disarmed, and abused, Sutter's Indian soldiers faced a very uncertain future.

Sutter, however, showed his captors Governor Micheltorena's letter, which convinced them that he had merely followed Micheltorena's orders and should not be punished for that. Finally, he promised the new government that he would be loyal to it, just as he "had been faithful to the old."[61] Pío Pico (the new governor), Castro (now comandante general), and Alvarado agreed that he should retain all of his property and offices, including (Sutter claimed) those conferred by Micheltorena.

Why did the new government deal so leniently with Sutter? First, his power and influence in the Sacramento Valley were real. If he were to be removed from the scene, what would the Indians and foreigners there do? If Sutter was executed or deported, what response might come from his supposed foreign supporters, like the French navy? Would the United States use this as a pretext to grab California? There was also the question of Russian interest in New Helvetia. A dead or deposed Sutter could not honor his contract with the Russian-American Company. Would the Russians foreclose and occupy Sutter's Fort? Better to rehabilitate Sutter and put him to work for the new government than to risk the uncertain consequences that might follow his elimination.

A chastened Sutter returned to New Helvetia in March 1845. The journey was difficult. He could only scrounge thirty horses, purchased on credit from a German friend in Los Angeles. Upon reaching the Tejón Pass, Sutter's Indians, "who looked sour" to him, asked to proceed.[62] "They could find roots & grass to live on & would soon be at home."[63] The disgruntled Indians reached New Helvetia several days ahead of Sutter's party, which included one Hawaiian, eight white men (including the loyal Bidwell), and four vaqueros (probably californios). They had scanty provisions, and their horses were about to give out by the time they reached the Merced River. As luck would have it, they spotted four "Indian horse thieves" with about twenty horses stolen from San José.[64] Sutter and his men charged the outnumbered Indians and seized the much-needed animals.

The Stanislaus River was swollen, so they built a makeshift ferry out of brush for the men. The horses had to swim the stream. As they were approaching Miwok country, the so-called horse-thief Indians, perhaps alerted by Rufino and his associates, began to molest the travelers. Sutter's status in Miwok country was no doubt damaged by the ignominious end to the Micheltorena affair. The possibility of exacting revenge on a newly vulnerable Sutter may have been irresistible to the Miwoks. To avoid Indians, the lord of New Helvetia and his attendants pushed on at night, following the North Star. Out of provisions and subsisting on horsemeat, the destitute men reached the Mokelumne River, where they met a relief party sent from the fort by Reading. Refreshed and remounted, Captain Sutter passed through the gates of his fort in late March or early April.[65]

Meanwhile other Americans straggled back to New Helvetia as best they could. Most of them were disillusioned with Sutter's failed schemes. "The 'bugs' [Micheltorena supporters] arrived (as the Indian says), *with their hearts on the ground,* down tumbled all the '*air built castles*' and most dreadful was the crash," John Gantt told his friend John Marsh. Gantt fumed at Sutter and Bidwell, claiming that both hoped to gain salaries from the Mexican government: Sutter for his military rank and Bidwell with a customs house appointment under Micheltorena. Gantt publicly called Bidwell "a liar, sycophant, Parasite puppy & coward and [he] swallowed the whole very patiently," which "gave offense to all the *Bugs,* but how could they help themselves poor devils they have no stings." The so-called bugs thought that the californios were great cowards, although none of the Americans had shown much heroism in the late campaign. Some still held out hope that Micheltorena would return with troops from Mexico. "They intend to flock to his standard," Gantt declared, adding that "the few foreigners at this place[,] to hear them talk[,] you would suppose they ruled the destinies of California." As for Gantt, "I am . . . against the *Bugs* and all '*Air Castle*' *builders* and if the Genl should return I'll be found one to oppose him if he is on the side of Mexico. Now mind what I tell you[.] The first '*Bug*' that gives me the least excuse I intend to wring his *Proboscis.*" As for Sutter's administration of affairs at New Helvetia, Gantt observed, "They want a new & disinterested Alcalde here."[66] Such were the sentiments of one of Sutter's former soldiers.

Californios, however, were content with Sutter's discomfiture and believed that his power had been broken. Vallejo was nearly giddy with happiness. "Justice always shines because it always spreads forth," he enthused. "Sutter lost," he concluded.[67] John Coffin Jones, former American consul in Honolulu and a longtime acquaintance of Sutter, issued a biblical judgment: "He has fallen and I think, like Lucifer, never to rise again."[68]

CHAPTER 12

The Indian Business Again

Sutter found an unsettled New Helvetia when he returned from the ill-fated Micheltorena campaign. The Americans' faith in him was shaken. His Indian allies and workers were restive. Sutter's purse was empty, creditors were unforgiving, and the Russian wolf was at the door. If he did not find some way to satisfy the Russians, Sutter had no future in California. Somehow he had to produce wheat while maximizing every other source of revenue.

One way or another, Indians were at the heart of all Sutter's concerns. He absolutely depended on Indian field hands. Without them he had no hope of cultivating the wheat that the Russian contract required. The Indian population had to be controlled if Sutter and other settlers were to remain in the valley, but the Muquelemnes were now disenchanted with the lord of New Helvetia. He had failed to obtain the land grant that he had promised to the Muquelemnes, and his military adventure with Micheltorena had ended in a humiliating defeat. Leaders like Rufino no longer saw a future in friendly relations with Sutter. Potential trouble with Indians loomed everywhere in the spring of 1845.

If Indians were a problem for Sutter, they were also a large part of the solution. While some Miwoks festered with old and new grievances, most local Miwoks and Nisenans remained substantially loyal to him. Sutter counted on them. These Indian workers and soldiers remained the core of his settlement, and some of them would remain at his side long after his power was but a memory. In the meantime Sutter's loyal Indian soldiers were his fist in the wilderness. The prospect of war with defiant Indians was not an altogether bad thing for him. Indian captives were a valuable commodity in Mexican California, another source of revenue for New Helvetia's strapped proprietor. For the next eighteen months Sutter would balance three concerns: his need for Indian labor, the suppression of livestock raiding, and the usefulness of an Indian slave trade. It was one of the few times when he showed himself to be an effective and ruthless entrepreneur.

Sutter's first order of business was to convince the Indian population that he was not dead after his defeat in southern California. Rumors of his demise had swept through Indian country as unhappy former soldiers drifted back to New Helvetia. "When the report of my dead [sic] came here," he told Thomas Larkin, "on the whole feather River and Sacramento was an awful mourning for me, and all was very sorrowful, as they look upon me now as their father and benefactor and Protector." He claimed that chiefs and headmen came to the fort to assure themselves that Sutter was yet alive. The "Affection and gratitude of the poor Indians was very satisfactory to me," he rhapsodized.[1]

Perhaps, but within weeks of his return Sutter and his soldiers were in the saddle fighting Miwoks down on the San Joaquin River. He marched south to avenge Thomas Lindsey, a rancher who lived in a tule hut near present-day Stockton. Miwoks from the Sierra foothills had driven off Lindsey's cattle, killed him, and burned his body in his grass house. When Sutter showed up, the Indians did not go quietly. While he and his men were scouting the area, Indians shot and killed the man who rode at his side, Juan Vaca, a New Mexican who had come to California in 1841. Many of Sutter's men were wounded in this scrape, although he emerged unscathed.[2]

During the spring Indian raiding seemed to be on the rise. A Miwok named Raphero was one of the prominent leaders. Evidently José Castro, unhappy that Sutter was still in charge of New Helvetia, encouraged Raphero because he wanted to eliminate Sutter once and for all. Sutter learned about Castro's plans, captured Raphero, executed him, and displayed his head above the fort's gate as a warning to Indians who thought that he had lost his power. Heinrich Lienhard saw the gruesome trophy with "long black hair and skull" later that year.[3] The execution of Raphero outraged Rufino and finally drove him to break with Sutter. First the Muquelemne chief killed his own brother-in-law, one of Sutter's Indian soldiers. Then he began to pillage the herds of Sutter and his neighbors, an irritating state of affairs that continued for several months.[4]

Unsettled conditions in Indian country caused talk about Sutter. Perhaps he had lost his magic touch with the Indians. Jean Jacques Vioget, the Swiss sailor and surveyor who had charted Sutter's grant in 1841, told Larkin that the Indians were in a state of rebellion. "I don't know who could have told Capt. Vioget such a storey," Sutter elided in June. "The Indians all are very good friendly and obedient," he told his creditor. "When I arrived here from the

Campagne I had to regulate a few disorders among the tribes; but in General the[y] behaved themselves very well."[5]

The happy picture that Sutter painted for Larkin contrasted sharply with the practical advice that he was giving to Reading up at Hock Farm, which Sutter was developing as his chief farm and eventual residence. The local chiefs should present themselves to Reading, he advised; and if they did not, Reading should go to them. "I see now how it is," he declared frankly; "if they are not Keept strickly under fear, it will be no good."[6] While Sutter wanted to preserve the Indian population as a labor force, he also believed in giving "severe punishment" to those who stole livestock. "All the tribes which show hostility of course you will use Arms against them, that the whole valley respect in future the white Men more and more."[7] Sutter meant to be a stern patriarch among his Indian friends and an implacable foe among his Indian enemies.

Indian bondage helped to reduce Sutter's debts, and his military actions increased the number of Indian captives available for shipment to other rancheros. Sutter, who used every means at his disposal to keep his business going with Antonio Suñol, promised the old ranchero thirty Indian workers in May by way of Marsh's farm. "I shall send you some young Indians," he added, "after our campaign against horse-thieves, which will take place after the wheat harvest."[8] Sutter expected to receive a shipment of dried meat from Suñol for the workers that he sent in May. A few weeks later Marsh reported to Suñol that thirty-one Indians from Sutter had arrived, "as usual, dying of hunger, and I gave them the meat of two calves, for which, if you think right, you can put to my account six dollars."[9] There was money to be made on the Indian business all around. Sutter described the hungry Indians that he sent to Suñol as "among the best we have, and [they] work with a good will." Best of all, they had "never been associated with the Mission Indians and are perfectly guileless." Sutter also sent an Indian boy named Pulé to act as interpreter.[10]

Sutter shipped Indian workers young and old to rancheros and merchants near and far.[11] Few financial details are known about these transactions, but Sutter's account with his neighbor William Leidesdorff shows that the trade in enslaved and free Indians was an important part of his business dealings. Sutter received as much as two dollars a day per Indian for short-term service contracts. Long-term Indian servants went for as much as twenty dollars a month, although eight or nine dollars was more common.[12] Indian wars improved Sutter's balance sheet with many a California creditor. He employed the remorseless Indian killer Grove Cook, who had murdered the Walla Walla Elijah Hedding, to deliver Indian servants to his clients.[13]

Hedding's murder caused a great uproar in Oregon. The returning Indians had complained about the killing to their American missionary friends, including Elijah White, who was also a U.S. Indian subagent for Oregon. White, described by one historian as a "scheming man, swollen with the importance" of his appointment, sent letters to Sutter and Larkin in the custody of mountain man James Clyman, who was headed to California.[14] Clyman arrived in New Helvetia on July 12, 1845. Sutter wrote to Larkin a few days later but said nothing about the Hedding affair, probably because he did not think it was important. He gladly reported that the immigrants had "a descent appearance and some very useful Men among them[.] Some of them will remain here." Better yet, he had received a letter that Lansford W. Hastings was leading a party of one thousand overlanders "direct from the U.S."[15]

Larkin took a much more serious view of the Hedding killing when White's letter fell under his eyes. "This unhappy affair agetates [sic] and embarrasses our relation with too large a portion of the aborigines of this country for a moments safety to us in our weak and defenceless condition," White told Larkin. He hoped that the matter could be adjusted "upon principles of equity and justice" and that Cook could be sent to White in Oregon. "But sir as this may be impracticable I[,] with pleasure and confidence, leave the whole matter in the hands of yourself and Mr. Clyman for adjustment and rectification," White wrote.[16] Clyman added a great many details about the situation in Oregon that White had not committed to paper, including the claim that two thousand Oregon Indians were preparing to go to California. It is unclear whether Sutter informed Larkin about Hedding's murder before White's letter prompted him to do so, although he corresponded frequently with Larkin on business matters and gladly told him about other Oregon visitors. The possible consequences of two thousand angry Indians (this turned out to be an exaggeration) coming to California for retribution were too clear to require comment in Larkin's correspondence, beyond his spare acknowledgment that they "may cause much trouble."[17]

Sutter explained the circumstances as best he could, claiming that Hedding was largely to blame for his own fate: he was "saucy," a horse thief and murderer who probably had it coming. "We believe here that Leicer," as Sutter rendered "Elijah," "was a great Rascal."[18] This explanation was not well calculated to calm the Oregon Indians or to satisfy subagent White, and Larkin knew it.

When Larkin responded to White, he put him off by saying that his letter had not come in an official form. He also claimed not to know the details of the murder or the name of the murderer, although he probably had Sutter's narrative of events in hand by that time. Moreover (and this was true) Larkin had no means or authority to apprehend Cook. California officials were the only ones authorized to deal with the murder, Larkin explained, and so White could expect the California governor to do justice in this case. "As the distance is great between us," Larkin observed, "much time will be required to settle this affair."[19] He was not being altogether frank with White. Sutter named Cook as the murderer, and Larkin had done business with him over the years. Eventually Cook, who was never called to account for his deed, became Larkin's partner in a quicksilver mine.[20]

Larkin continued to be concerned with the Hedding murder in the fall. He hoped to put off the Walla Wallas' return until the following year and enlisted Sutter's help to do it. The consul wanted him to collect cattle to "make up the complement lost by the friends of the Deceased." Sutter was to keep the animals and any other property of the Indians until they arrived. Larkin directed him to write to White in duplicate, with one copy for Larkin and the other to go through Larkin to White. "In your letter you will write only on this subject," Larkin instructed.[21] The American consul wanted to manage this controversy carefully, taking no chances with Sutter.

Sutter did not worry much about the Walla Wallas' return. That, after all, was in the future and could be dealt with when the time came. In the summer of 1845 he was occupied with raising his wheat. The crop had failed the previous two years for lack of water; but this looked like a good year, and Sutter wanted to make sure that he could deliver a full cargo to the Russians. "For make this business sure, it is necessary that I take the Water from the American fork to Water my Wheat fields." Sutter had found the secret to successful agriculture in the Sacramento Valley. The land was rich and capable of producing bountiful crops, but the California weather was uncooperative. It seldom rained from May through October, and promising crops had dried up in the field in 1843 and 1844. Water management was the answer, Sutter now recognized. "Great advantages will come from this business," he promised his creditor Larkin. "I can build on the same Canal a Grist and Saw Mill, and the Ditch will enclose the rincoan [rincón, inside corner or angle], so that no Cattle can passe over and go in the fields." Not only would this new arrangement permit Sutter to satisfy his debt with the Russians, but they would buy all that he could produce. "In one Word the Establishment is here to produce [for] the demands of the Russians."[22]

But as always Sutter needed credit, and there were few in California now who could or would provide him with needed goods. Enemies (formerly friends and business associates) like Charles Flügge and John Marsh "do their best to ruin my Credit"—as though Sutter had not had any part in establishing his poor credit rating among Californians. Some of his neighbors, like Theodor Cordua and John Sinclair, had inveigled his Indian trappers to sell Sutter's furs to them. "Dr. Marsh is the badest of the all. He give the Grog for furs and robed [*sic*] me in this Manner of a large Amount," Sutter complained, "but I shall take Measures about this." What he needed now was four or five thousand dollars' worth of goods from Larkin. Sutter hoped that Larkin would supply all of his needs so that he could pay off his other creditors. He sent William Wiggins and Grove Cook to make arrangements with Larkin, who cautiously advanced Sutter some of what he needed.[23]

It was a grand plan, which showed that Sutter had learned a great deal about the California interior in the six years that he had lived there. The Sacramento Valley received less than twenty inches of rain per year, but its great rivers carried millions of gallons of water past Sutter's fields every summer. While the snow melt from the mighty Sierra Nevada charged through the valley, his fields parched. Conversely, heavy rains frequently caused winter and spring flooding that drowned the countryside and made agriculture and human habitation impossible in the lowlands that made up much of the valley. Sutter was the first to realize that tapping the water of the rivers was the key to successful agriculture in New Helvetia, and he made a start at diverting the river as early as 1841. He would continue ditching until the gold rush diverted labor and redirected his attention to the mines. Billions of dollars have been spent in realizing Sutter's dream of an irrigation empire in the past 150 years, which all began with his plea for shovels and spades from Larkin.[24]

The year 1845 was a bountiful one for Sutter. The wheat harvest was good, and he needed it. Through the fall his Indians harvested, thrashed, winnowed, and bagged wheat for the Russians. Bidwell gave the best description of this process. "Imagine," he reminisced many years later,

three or four hundred wild Indians in a grain field, armed, some with sickles, some with butcher-knives, some with pieces of hoop iron roughly fashioned into shapes like sickles, but many having only their hands to gather up by small handfuls the dry and brittle grain; and as their hands soon would become sore, they resorted to dry willow sticks, which were split to afford a sharper edge with which to sever the straw. But the wildest part was the threshing. The harvest of weeks, sometimes a month, was piled up in the straw in the form of a huge mound in the middle of a high, strong, round corral; then three or four hundred wild horses were turned in to thresh it, the Indians whooping to make them run faster. Suddenly they would dash in before the band at full speed, when the motion became reversed, with the effect of plowing up the trampled straw to the very bottom. In an hour the grain would be thoroughly threshed and the dry straw broken almost into chaff. In this manner I have seen 2,000 bushels threshed in a single hour. Next came the winnowing, which would often taken another month. It could only be done when the wind was blowing, by throwing high into the air shovelfuls of grain, straw, chaff, the lighter materials being wafted to one side, while the grain, comparatively clean, would descend and form a heap by itself.[25]

All through the fall Sutter's men loaded wheat on Russian vessels that docked at his Sacramento River embarcadero.[26] Sutter was still behind in his payments to the Russians, but he had at least demonstrated that he could deliver substantial quantities of wheat when conditions were right. He no doubt hoped that his 1845 payments on the Russian debt presaged full satisfaction on this obligation in the near future.

Meanwhile much of Sutter's time was taken up with the management of his Indian workers. His labor force consisted of a mixed group of Indians who were not always happy to work for him. Sutter was constantly concerned with apprehending runaways and punishing Indians who committed crimes great and small. The Indian Augustin, a formerly reliable man, "deserted with his woman, Chanayuck and Valentin[,] two good boys which he certainly persuaded," and four horses. Sutter was particularly vexed at the loss of the good horses that drove the bark mill, "a bad trick" that compromised New Helvetia's production of tanned leather. He blamed Augustin's flight on Mexicans who had influenced him.[27] Sutter's men soon captured Augustin, who "got now his punishment and Passport," meaning banishment from New Helvetia.[28]

Indians had plenty of reasons to leave New Helvetia without prompting from californios. Sutter did not specify Augustin's punishment, but lashing was a common means for disciplining Indian and white workers alike. The Indian Solinan got twenty-five stripes for stealing a butcher knife, and "everybody had a pleasure to see it," Sutter observed. Solinan "say he is very glad that he got the 25 and that he will steal no more." Perhaps, but Solinan had agreed to accompany an American returning to the United States and was no doubt relieved to be out of range of Sutter's whip.[29]

Rufino's luck ran out in September. Now a captive, the Muquelemne chief appeared before Sutter, who tried him for the murder of his Indian soldier. On September 16 the New Helvetia tribunal found him guilty. The judicial process was probably as perfunctory as John Bidwell's diary entry that recorded it. "Rufino[,] chief of the Moquelumnes, was tried for murder, found guilty, and executed—started D. Martin for lumber."[30] There was no appeal and no clemency, just a quick death, probably by firing squad, and an unceremonious burial in the New Helvetia cemetery, one hundred rods northeast of the fort's walls.

In early November Sutter got word that José Castro and a contingent of

Mexican officials were headed for his fort by way of Sonoma.[31] Castro's intentions were unknown to Sutter, so the comandante general's rumored visit made him apprehensive. On November 11 Sutter's watchful Indians reported that riders had appeared opposite his Sacramento River embarcadero. When Sutter sent Bidwell to inquire, he found Castro, Andrés Castillero (a Mexican official), Victor Prudon (Vallejo's secretary), Jacob Leese (Vallejo's brother-in-law), and a military escort of about fifteen men. They wanted to see Sutter.

After crossing the river on Sutter's ferry, the contingent rode to the fort, where Captain Sutter raised the Mexican flag and ordered a seven-gun salute from his cannons. The formalities over, he invited Castro, Castillero, Leese, and Prudon into the fort. They got down to business. The Mexican government had authorized Castillero to purchase Sutter's Fort "with all its appurtenances" for a hundred thousand dollars. Sutter said he would "think of it" and then withdrew to his office, where he consulted with Bidwell, Reading, Samuel Hensley, and William Loker, four of his most trusted American employees. They thought it was a high price but wondered "what will all the settlers in these valleys do if you abandon us to the Mexicans?" "This determined me," Sutter reminisced to the historian Bancroft many years later. "I was bound they should have protection. But for this I should have accepted the offer." Characteristically, Sutter explained his actions by his high-minded and selfless desire to protect helpless American immigrants from Mexicans.[32]

Sutter informed his visitors that he would not accept their proposition. Castro was no doubt disappointed but made the best of a bad situation by delivering a proclamation to the immigrants. They would be allowed to remain at New Helvetia on a provisional basis. If immigrants desired to go to Sonoma or San Juan Bautista, they could get a passport from Sutter, whose job it was to "inspire them with obedience to the government and confidence in the Commandancy General of the Department." Castro also required Sutter to make regular reports to him concerning the movements of foreigners.[33] Castro's statement, which was translated for the benefit of Americans who did not know Spanish, was meant to be a conciliatory gesture, perhaps one that would convince Americans that Sutter's departure would do them no harm. At the very least, he reminded them that Sutter was a Mexican official with obligations to the government.

The Castro party stayed overnight in New Helvetia, with Castro, Castillero, Prudon, and Leese sleeping in rooms inside the fort and the Mexican soldiers bivouacking in outbuildings outside the fort's walls. The next day Sutter, Bidwell, and three vaqueros accompanied Castro's company as they started their return journey to Monterey by way of the San Joaquin. About one mile south of the fort a "great troop of horsemen, in all about fifty men, mechanics vaqueros & others under the command of Mr Hensley," came running up behind the travelers. Castro asked what the commotion was about. "Only some of my men," Sutter said, "who would have followed us sooner as our escort, had they been able to get their horses up sooner." Hensley and the others thought that Castro had kidnapped Sutter and were riding to the rescue. Sutter laughed it off and rode on with Castro for about twenty miles before returning to the fort.[34]

That evening Sutter was sitting in his room when to his surprise Prudon entered. He urged Sutter to consider Castillero's offer. "But we will do better," Sutter quoted Prudon as saying, "I am authorized by General Castro to offer you for 'New Helvetia' in addition to the one hundred thousand dollars, all the lands and cattle belonging to the Mission San José." This was a tempting offer, but once again Sutter conferred with his American employees and declined.[35]

There has always been some suspicion in regard to Sutter's claims about these princely offers. Bancroft as much as says that Castillero made no such offer, asserting that the story was just a figment of Sutter's self-aggrandizing imagination or alternatively that Sutter had first broached the possibility of selling the fort to Mexico. Indeed, Vallejo wrote to Mexico, saying that it would be worth paying a hundred thousand dollars for the fort in order to assure the security of the country.[36]

During sworn testimony concerning Sutter's New Helvetia land claim in 1853, Prudon supported Sutter's declaration that Castillero was authorized by the Mexican government to offer a hundred thousand dollars to Sutter for "the establishment of New Helvetia" and that Sutter turned down the offer as well as the additional inducement of the Mission San José property. "He would not accept any proposition," Prudon insisted, although he gave no hint as to Sutter's motivations. According to Prudon, Castillero carried instructions from the president of Mexico authorizing him to negotiate the sale with Sutter. Prudon was in a position to know these details, because Castillero had asked him to act as his secretary and to prepare the necessary documents if Sutter agreed to sell New Helvetia.[37]

During the same proceedings Jacob Leese gave a somewhat different version of events. He, too, swore that Castillero's object was the purchase of New Helvetia and that the Mexican carried written instructions to that effect along with a pocketful of blank checks with the president's signature. Leese claimed, however, that the opening bid was sixty thousand dollars, conditioned on Sutter's departure from California. Sutter then asked for eighty thousand dollars, which was evidently too much for Castillero. On the morning of November 12, according to this account, Leese urged Sutter to accept the sixty thousand "on conditions that he would pay him down the money and [allow

Sutter to] remain in the country." Castillero later told Leese that "he did not negotiate with Capt. Sutter, in consequence of his demanding the pay down."[38]

Given the disparate testimony on the matter, what is to be made of this episode and why is it important? First, there is Sutter's insistence that he refused all offers because he wished to protect the immigrants, especially Americans. Second, if the Mexican government was willing to buy out Sutter to get rid of him, it shows how important Mexican officials thought he was in California affairs. They reasoned that much mischief could be avoided by eliminating him. If Sutter, Prudon, and Leese are to be believed, there can be little doubt that Castillero was authorized to buy New Helvetia rather than only the fort, as Sutter claimed. It is also plausible that Sutter's departure from California was to be part of the deal, at least as far as the Mexican president was concerned. In Leese's version of events, Sutter appeared to be willing to sell or at least to talk about selling, but not in Sutter's or Prudon's version. In the end Castillero could not make a deal; there is no disagreement about that.

Taking all of the testimony into account, a hypothetical narrative based on the evidence may be constructed. Castillero arrived in California with presidential instructions and checks to buy New Helvetia and eject Sutter. After consulting with Alvarado, Castro, and Vallejo, he issued a conciliatory statement to immigrants at Sonoma. Castillero added Prudon and Leese to his entourage because both men were on good terms with Sutter and could help in negotiations. Prudon was French and fluent in Spanish; he could help smooth out any linguistic confusion in the negotiations between Castillero and Sutter. Arriving at Sutter's Fort, Castillero got down to business: in return for sixty thousand dollars, Sutter would turn over New Helvetia and leave California. This sum might have allowed Sutter to pay off his debts and break even, but little more. He asked for more money, perhaps eighty or a hundred thousand dollars. Sutter also wanted to remain in California, probably at Hock Farm. We may suppose that this sum and Sutter's conditions exceeded Castillero's discretion and that he sent in Leese to break the impasse. Leese urged Sutter to accept the original offer and perhaps privately told him that Castillero was carrying signed checks. Knowing about the checks, Sutter raised the stakes and asked for a hundred thousand dollars. Castillero could not agree to this price, so he left Sutter's Fort, saying that he would have to consult with his government before agreeing to Sutter's demand. But perhaps there was another way. He sent Prudon to offer a very tempting sweetener in the form of the Mission San José. Sutter would be far less dangerous there, where he could be watched. Sutter, who still wanted enough cash to satisfy his debts, did not accept but hoped that the Mexican government would finally come around.

The truth of the matter may be at variance with this imagined account, but it seems likely that the visit of Castro and Castillero resulted in an open-ended negotiation rather than a foreclosure of any possibilities for a sale. Two days after the Mexican party departed, Sutter told Larkin that he had "[t]he pleasure to have Señores Castro y Castillero etc. here." He mentioned nothing about an offer to buy him out but thought: "No doubt this visit will be to our mutual benefit." Sutter was now "on the most friendly terms with Don José Castro, and with Señor Castillero."[39] Sutter's vague intimations are impossible to interpret with confidence; but six weeks after Castro's visit, Sutter asked Prudon if the government intended to buy his place. "I would like to be certain of that so that I could take the necessary measures," he wrote hopefully. "In case the government decides to make the purchase do you believe it will be possible to obtain a part of the sum on account sufficient to pay a part of my debts?" he asked. "I could give possession of the establishment after the harvest." He added that "the government will do well not to neglect this affair, for next autumn there will be very many emigrants from the United States." Sutter consoled himself with the hope that there would be "many Germans, French, and Swiss among" the new immigrants.[40] These are not the words of a man who refused to sell because he wished to protect American settlers from the Mexican government but rather the wishful thinking of a man who was anxious to sell and rid himself of insupportable debts.

It is also worth noting that Sutter wanted a portion of the purchase to be put on account to pay some of his debts. One of his fears was that no one would honor the Mexican notes for his property. In his reminiscences Sutter quotes Prudon as saying that "the Mexican government were poor pay . . . but such a trifle as this" was no problem. Besides, they would give Sutter "a good sum down, and orders on the custom house for the balance."[41] This probably amounted to Sutter's counteroffer to Castillero: a hundred thousand dollars, part in notes and part on account, plus Mission San José and Sutter's continued residence in California—too much for Castillero to swallow on his own authority.

But there was another sticking point: Sutter's Russian creditors, who held a mortgage on New Helvetia. Larkin explained the difficulty to the U.S. secretary of state in 1846. He stated flatly that the "Mexican Government have proposed to assume [the Russian debt] and other debts, and take Captain Sutter's Establishment." Then Larkin revealed that in 1845 he spoke with an unnamed Russian official, who "was convinced that Captain Sutter was the best and surest debtor and objected to any arrangement that the Mexican Government could make and [also stated that] Captain Sutter would not vacate the place for any sum that could be obtained."[42] The Russian also told Larkin that Sutter was a better credit risk than the Mexican government, a belief that speaks volumes for the rickety fiscal reputation of Mexico.[43]

In late 1845 Sutter was ready to cash out, if he could get the right price. Had California remained in Mexican hands, it is possible that the Mexican government and the californios might have assembled an offer that he could not have refused, but it was not to be. While Sutter met with Castillero and Castro, a few dozen men toiled across the Great Basin toward the Sierra Nevada escarpment. Frémont had returned.

CHAPTER 13

Signs and Portents

Frémont had become a great celebrity in the United States, an explorer hero whose achievements fired the imaginations of westering Americans, expansionists, and armchair pioneers alike. His *Report of the Exploring Expedition to the Rocky Mountains,* written with the assistance of his talented wife, Jessie Benton Frémont, became an instant best-seller.[1] Combining romantic prose descriptions with scientific observations and accurate maps, the report inspired people to go west and gave them enough reliable geographical knowledge to do it. The *Report* was reprinted, translated, and published in Europe, even in Sutter's homeland. Frémont's father-in-law, Thomas Hart Benton, the powerful U.S. senator from Missouri, promoted the explorer's popularity with the public and in the halls of government. The young officer, now promoted to captain and known to the public as the Pathfinder, was an American hero who seemed fitted for the coming contest over the Mexican-American borderlands—confident, brave, young, intelligent, and strong.[2]

The release of Frémont's report coincided with the inauguration of President James K. Polk, the Tennessee Democrat who campaigned for the presidency on a frankly expansionist platform that called for the annexation of the Republic of Texas and the Oregon country, which the United States jointly occupied with Great Britain. Polk hoped to acquire California and New Mexico too, but this was not part of his public campaign. His dreams of a sea-to-sea republic risked war with Mexico and Great Britain, but he hoped to avoid these undesirable outcomes through adroit diplomacy. Just as Frémont was putting the finishing touches on his report and Polk was preparing his inaugural address, however, Congress admitted Texas as a state. War with Mexico seemed inevitable, a possibility that made conflict with England even more unpalatable.

In this bellicose atmosphere, Frémont and Benton, both dedicated to national expansion, lobbied for a new western topographical expedition under Frémont's command. The orders were not long in coming, but they were not as expansive as Benton and Frémont had hoped for. President Polk thought that the young officer was impulsive, and the new secretary of war was not interested in aggravating international tensions. Therefore Frémont was to investigate the headwaters of the Red and Arkansas Rivers "within reasonable distance of Bents Fort," as his instructions read.[3] The details meant little to Frémont as long as he had orders to go west. He set off for the Missouri frontier. Intending to enter Mexican California as soon as possible, Frémont would construe "reasonable distance" to mean about a thousand miles.

There was no shortage of volunteers when Frémont recruited men in St. Louis in late May. Fifty-five hand-picked men signed up. Each was issued a Hawken rifle, two pistols, a knife, and other accouterments. Frémont's corps of discovery was not technically a military expedition, but he assembled a tough, well-armed, intimidating set of frontiersmen. The company, about sixty in all, included mountain men, nine Delaware Indians, and two California Indians (who had joined Frémont's party in 1844) as well as Kit Carson, Bill Williams, and Joseph Walker, who joined later on the march.[4] It is likely that a few of these men had been among the chaquanoso horse thieves who had been pestering californios for decades. They took the well-known trail from Missouri and followed the Arkansas River to Bent's Fort, where Frémont made cursory observations. Then he rode into Mexican territory, crossed the Rocky Mountains into the Great Basin, and kept moving west.

While Frémont was on the trail, President Polk sent John Slidell to Mexico City with secret instructions to buy California and New Mexico, a negotiation that merely insulted and alienated Mexican officials. Polk also made provocative military gestures by stationing the navy in waters off the Texas coast, claiming disputed lands between the Nueces River and Río Grande as part of Texas, and sending a small army to occupy that country. These diplomatic and military initiatives were unknown to Captain Frémont, of course; but when he finally entered California, he fully understood that war with Mexico was probable. He expected to have a part in it.[5]

California was far removed from the intriguing people and events that would determine its future, but rumors and suspicions abounded in 1845. Four-month-old newspapers from New York and New Orleans carried the most recent news on international developments. Stories about a Mexican army preparing to invade California to chastise the californio rebels circulated among foreigners.[6] Letters from the states provided additional intelligence to Americans in California, but the long delay in communication often made them seem oddly irrelevant or plainly wrong by the time they arrived.

One letter seemed prophetic. In July Thomas Jefferson Farnham, the determined American expansionist who had visited California a few years earlier, sat at his Wall Street desk in New York and penned a few lines to John Marsh. He told his old friend that he intended to return to California sometime in 1846. "The strongest desire of my heart," Farnham said, was "that the 'Republic of California' should arise—exist—& shed the blessing of Freedom over that delightful land." But he cautioned Marsh not to move too fast. "The excitement consequent on the admission of Texas into the Union must have time to abate. The winter of '46 will do."[7] Farnham handed the letter to Lansford Hastings and asked him to deliver it.[8]

Hastings was about to depart for California and shared Farnham's hopes for a California republic—dominated by Americans of course. In 1842 he had led a party of Oregonians to New Helvetia, where Sutter provided his usual help and hospitality. Favorably impressed with the country, Hastings became convinced that the Mexican province should become a part of the United States. He departed for the east, promising to promote American emigration. The extent of Sutter's contact with Hastings in 1842 is unclear, but they had some common interests. Both wanted to advance immigration, although Hastings's ideas were not congruent with Sutter's expressed wish for Mexican troops at his fort or its outright purchase by the Mexican government.[9]

Farnham's timetable for the establishment of a California republic by the winter of 1846 was too slow for many foreigners who lived there. In November 1845 Charles Weber, also writing to Marsh, speculated on Castillero's offer to buy New Helvetia and ranted about California's political conditions and the inaction of Americans. "We are without Government & Justice." Lives and property were at risk because criminals went unpunished. "But Doctor!" Weber continued, "What are we foreigners, the Lords of the Country doing all the time? Everybody appears stuck in Lethargy. Is there no Descendant of the great Washington in the Land to rouse the Spirit of Freemann [sic] to claim their rights & establish peace & order? When shall we have public Meetings? I will not say anything more, for my heart is bleeding to see around me a Lot of Man unworthy [of] there noble birthright of Americans."[10] Help was at hand for Weber's bleeding heart.

On December 10, 1845, John Charles Frémont and Kit Carson arrived at Sutter's fort without warning. Bidwell was in charge because Sutter was at the little village of Yerba Buena, soon to be renamed San Francisco. Frémont demanded horses, mules, pack saddles, food, and access to one of Sutter's forges so that his horses could be shod. The Pathfinder was in a hurry. He had divided his party east of the Sierra and crossed over the Truckee River route (now Donner Pass) with Kit Carson and some others. He sent Joseph Walker and the rest of his men to cross the mountains farther south, agreeing to meet them at a predetermined point in the mountains east of the San Joaquin Valley. Forcing a crossing so late in the fall was risky, but Frémont and Carson had beaten the snow and hoped that Walker had been as fortunate as they had been. Early snows in the Sierra Nevada could doom unwary travelers.[11]

Relations between Frémont and Bidwell quickly soured. Bidwell was willing to help but said that he had no mules and that the smithy was temporarily out of coal. Horses could be obtained, however, and the fort's artisans would make pack saddles. Frémont "became reticent," Bidwell remembered, said something "in a low tone to Carson, rose and left without saying good-day, and returned to his camp." Before leaving the fort, Frémont was overheard to say that Bidwell was unwilling to accommodate him. Greatly concerned over this unintended insult to the American officer, Bidwell went to his camp to smooth things over. Frémont then "stated in a very formal manner, that he was an officer in one government and Sutter the officer of another; that difficulties existed between these governments; and hence his inference that I, representing Sutter, was not willing to accommodate him."[12]

Bidwell was shocked at Frémont's attitude. Sutter, after all, had always helped American immigrants and had provisioned Frémont in 1844. Despite this chilly encounter, Bidwell did the best he could. In two days he delivered horses to the Americans' camp and even found some mules for them. While Frémont rode south to find the rest of his men, Frémont's farrier shod the expedition's spare horses in the fort's shop.[13]

Sutter returned to New Helvetia four days after Frémont's departure for the San Joaquin. He was no doubt chagrined to hear Captain Frémont's opinion of him. Perhaps some personal diplomacy with the explorer was in order. Meanwhile, Sutter had to consider his official duty as a Mexican officer. He wrote a letter to Mariano Vallejo, informing him that the American officer and about fifty men intended to spend the winter in California and go to Oregon in the spring.[14] Sutter was not being entirely forthright. He dated the letter December 10 (when he was in Yerba Buena) and indicated that he sent it from New Helvetia. Sutter could not have written the letter before December 17, when he returned to the fort; and he might have waited even longer, because Vallejo did not receive his report until December 30. Sutter also informed Larkin of Frémont's arrival.[15]

The discrepancies in Sutter's letter did not escape Vallejo's notice. On the back he penned a furious note to his secretary, commanding him to inform

Sutter "that it was received after twenty days' delay, and charge him, in the quickest way possible, to send detailed information about the new emigrants; a thing which has always been done in similar circumstances, even in the case of small parties, and which he inopportunely failed to do when it was most necessary, and even urgent."[16]

Sutter's delight in military regalia inadvertently reenforced Frémont's concerns about him. On January 15, 1846, Sutter rode from his fort with William A. Leidesdorff, American vice consul under Larkin, and William Hinckley, captain of the port of San Francisco. Leidesdorff had a grant on the American River, and the three men went up to look over the land that sharecropper William Buzzell worked for one-third of the produce.[17] Noticing that Captain Hinckley wore his Mexican uniform, Sutter decided to wear his Mexican colonel's outfit. Military pomp and circumstance always appealed to him; he was not about to be outranked in his own domain.[18]

The three men unexpectedly ran into an encampment a mile or two from the fort. Failing to find the rest of his men in the southern Sierra Nevada, Frémont had returned to New Helvetia to wait for them. Sutter was puzzled about who these men were until he spotted Kit Carson. "Where is Captain Frémont?" he asked. "There in his tent," Carson replied. "He is fatigued and not yet up." Frémont's desire for sleep evidently meant little to Sutter, who "ordered him called." The tired explorer dutifully emerged from his tent to hear Colonel Sutter's introduction of Leidesdorff and Hinckley and invitation to the fort for a feast later in the day. As they rode off, Frémont watched the Mexican uniforms disappear from sight and kept his thoughts to himself. When he arrived at the fort Sutter fired an artillery salute in his honor.[19] The Pathfinder might well have wondered if the cannon shots were a mere courtesy or a demonstration of military power to his still undermanned company.

Frémont's frank assessment of differences with Sutter and Bidwell, in regard to military commissions in potentially opposing armies, was based on more than mere appearances. Sutter's national loyalties had always been suspect; there were good reasons to believe that he would again side with Mexico in a fight. After his defeat at the hands of Castro and Alvarado, he had spoken too often and too freely about the possibility of Mexican troops returning to punish the rebels.

Just a few days after saluting Frémont with his cannons Sutter forwarded a rumor to John Marsh. Mexico was sending two thousand troops to California, to be spread throughout the province. "Here no doubt I will get a good supply of them," he opined, "and I am very glad of it, as some of the foreigners in the Valley are committing depredations, and I have no force to prevent them from so doing."[20] Since the troops never arrived in California, Sutter's statement was impolitic, to say the least. Marsh was nominally a Mexican citizen but like most

Americans hoped that the United States would soon snatch sovereignty away from Mexico.

Frémont was not the only hopeful American expansionist to come to the fort in late 1845. From across the Sierra, Lansford Hastings and eleven men showed up on Christmas Day.[21] "If they had arrived one day later they would have been cut of[f] by the immense quantity of Snow," Sutter recalled.[22] Like the Pathfinder, Hastings and his companions had been lucky to outrun the snow. For more than a year Sutter had been expecting him to lead a large immigration to California, but Hastings evidently had trouble raising money for the journey. To make money and publicize immigration, Hastings had lectured and published the *Emigrants' Guide to Oregon and California,* a book that would soon become infamous in trail history as the travel atlas of the Donner Party. His book advised overlanders to take a shortcut to California that Hastings had never seen. His *Guide* offered this concise description of that route: "The most direct route, for the California emigrants, would be to leave the Oregon route, about two hundred miles east from Fort Hall; thence bearing west southwest, to the Salt Lake; and thence continuing down to the bay of San Francisco."[23] The pioneers who tried to follow these optimistic but misleading directions would learn to hate Hastings for giving dangerous advice.[24]

Always the promoter, Hastings reported to Sutter and Marsh that there was great excitement about California back in the United States. At least six thousand and perhaps twenty thousand overlanders would cross the deserts and mountains to California in the coming season. "As to the natural, the inevitable result, of this unprecedented emigration to the western World," Hastings wrote rhetorically in his letter to Marsh, "I need not trouble you with my own speculations, for the result must have been, long since, anticipated by yourself."[25] Hastings had not tried the cutoff that he advertised in his *Emigrant's Guide,* but he was certain that it would work.

Enthusiasm about the coming immigration was contagious. Sutter repeated the Hastings assessment of American zeal for relocating to California. There was "a great excitement through the whole of the U. States to emigrate to Oregon and California," he told Marsh. "We could expect several thousand of them here, and a good many of Wealth and Capital, and some rich Marchants [*sic*] from New York, Steamboats will be here in the Month of April, a Printing press, and thousands of other usefull [*sic*] articles."[26] Teams were straining in their harnesses, ships were relentlessly steaming forward, every eye was turning toward California. So said Hastings, and so believed Sutter.

They were not wrong. As historian Bernard DeVoto famously wrote, 1846 was the "year of decision."[27] Overland emigrants departed for California in historic numbers: about fifteen hundred arrived before the end of the year.

More would come by sea. This figure was nowhere near the most conservative estimates by Hastings, but it was five times greater than the total overland emigration from 1841 to 1845. By the standards of Mexican California, this was a veritable flood of foreigners. Something new was happening. Larkin recognized it too. Ever the astute businessman, he noted that most of the several hundred immigrants who had recently arrived had settled near New Helvetia. This had driven the value of land up to "100$ pr sq league." "Yr rancho," he told Sutter's neighbor Hiram Grimes, "will in 3 years, to all appearances have a great Value."[28] Indeed it would—a value far greater than Larkin could foresee, and for reasons that were as yet unimaginable.

California was turning on a pivot in early 1846, and every thoughtful observer recognized it. With events in motion and the center of gravity so clearly shifting toward the United States, why did Sutter tell Marsh that he would welcome Mexican troops who would control unruly foreigners? The Pathfinder was camped in his front yard; thousands of Americans were poised to cross the plains; the U.S. Navy patrolled the coast; a war between the United States and Mexico over Texas was imminent. What part of this scene did Sutter miss?

Certainly Sutter was misinformed about the international situation. He told Marsh that England had sent troops to Oregon and that "War is so good as declared between England and the U. States."[29] This was not true. Despite President Polk's hawkish rhetoric on Oregon, a compromise was in the works that resulted in the establishment of the present boundary in June 1846. British officials did not want to go to war over Oregon and even agreed not to interfere in the U.S. dispute with Mexico.

Sutter, of course, had no way to know the strategies and outcomes of high diplomacy between the United States and Great Britain. In the absence of reliable information he evidently believed that the United States would not be able to fight Mexico and Great Britain effectively, so he bet on Mexico's ability to keep California. Or perhaps he merely hoped that Mexico would hold it long enough for him to sell his property to the government. Mexico would pay him a large sum, take over the Russian debt, occupy the fort with regular troops, and Sutter would retire a rich man—or so might he confidently have imagined.

Sutter's misreading of the international tea leaves was not the only reason to tell Marsh that he welcomed Mexican troops. He always craved respect and vindication. His support for Micheltorena had been Sutter's worst political miscalculation. Men like Weber, Marsh, Gantt, and other Americans had opposed taking sides in the revolt or later realized that it was a mistake and moved on. Sutter's prestige and authority among foreigners had been weakened by his mistake. Rather than admitting his error and rebuilding his reputation with more prudent leadership, he wanted to be justified in his failed alliance with Micheltorena. And he especially enjoyed needling Marsh. Even Larkin noticed the friction between the two men; "yet," he reminded Sutter, "both have the same interest in the all engrosing [*sic*] subject of the Country, viz. Emigration."[30] Sutter's personality, however, required something more than cooperatively working for a common goal. His need for political authority, public respect, and personal power always interfered with his ability to perceive his own best interest, let alone the common good. His ego-driven desires, rather than a realistic willingness to learn from mistakes, colored Sutter's whole life, a trait manifest in his apparent approval of Mexican centralist authority in California.

Not that Sutter was consistent in his political views. He often trimmed his sails according to the company he kept. Even so careful an observer as Larkin thought that he lived "but in expectation of this country belonging to the United States," the consul informed his government.[31] After all, Sutter had told Larkin that if an American man-of-war would not protect the Americans, "*I will do it*. All are protected here and before I suffer an injustice done, to them, I die first."[32] In later years (as has been shown) he was anxious to prove that he had only the interests of Americans at heart, but in 1846 Marsh, Gantt, Frémont, and other Americans in northern California were not convinced of this. Sutter's own actions and words kindled suspicions that if push came to shove he might side with Mexico.

While Sutter vainly waited for Mexican reinforcements, Frémont tired of waiting for the rest of his expedition to appear.[33] On January 19 he and eight of his men took Sutter's launch to Yerba Buena, the first stop on his way to see Larkin in Monterey.[34] Eight days later Frémont arrived in Monterey and presented himself to Larkin, who welcomed him as a guest and began to smooth the way for him. Before Larkin could officially introduce Frémont to Manuel Castro (the Monterey prefect and brother of comandante general José Castro), the prefect inquired about the American officer's presence under Larkin's roof. Frémont assured him that he was there on a peaceful mission, that he was on a scientific expedition seeking the best route to the Pacific, and that he would leave for Oregon after wintering in the San Joaquin Valley. He hoped to obtain provisions in Monterey. This explanation satisfied Castro and other californio authorities for the time being, but they expected Frémont to leave the Mexican settlements as soon as possible. Larkin advanced $1,800 and provided winter clothing and other supplies to Frémont. Thus provisioned, and with the apparent permission of californio authorities, Frémont bought some horses and left Monterey to set up camp near San José.

Despite Frémont's assurances to Castro, his subsequent actions quickly made californios suspicious. Instead of leaving the Mexican settlements, Frémont seemed determined to linger in the vicinity of Monterey. It is hard to know just what he had in mind. Neither Frémont's writings nor Larkin's offer much help. We may assume that he spoke with Larkin about his understanding of President Polk's intentions, insofar as he understood them, but how much he revealed is uncertain. Larkin, who told one of his correspondents that "great plans are meditated to be carried out by certain persons," appears to have been in the dark about the Pathfinder's plans after he left Monterey.[35] Larkin was clearly pleased with all that Frémont had done to promote immigration to California, and he hoped for American annexation if war broke out with Mexico; but every American in California was leaning into that breeze.

At his new encampment Frémont entertained visitors, including John Marsh. Meanwhile the rest of Frémont's party had found their way into the San Joaquin Valley. Tired of waiting for Frémont and low on provisions, they headed north toward Sutter's Fort. On the Calaveras River they chanced to meet William "Le Gros" Fallon, mountain man and sometime employee of Sutter. Fallon told them that Frémont was in the Santa Clara Valley, so Joseph Walker rode his spent horse to meet his leader there. He found him living on Laguna Farm, the abandoned rancho of the Boston sea captain William Fisher. Fresh horses were sent to the Calaveras River, and the party reunited at Laguna. Sixty strong, this command of very tough, well-armed mountain men and Indians began to appear to the californios to be something very different and far more dangerous than a party of topographical engineers pursuing a scientific exploration.

Now serious trouble started to brew. It began with a dispute over horses. Sebastián Peralta visited the Laguna camp and claimed that one of Frémont's horses belonged to him. Frémont dismissed the claim and drove Peralta out of camp. The aggrieved Peralta then complained to the San José alcalde, José Dolores Pacheco, who wrote to Frémont. The Pathfinder was outraged. He claimed that he had brought the horse in question from Missouri. After attempting to obtain this animal under false pretenses, Frémont averred, Peralta was lucky to have escaped from the camp without being horsewhipped. True, he said, his men had acquired four horses from Indians in the San Joaquin Valley, but he would gladly return them if proof of ownership could be shown.[36]

Frémont's high-handed treatment of Peralta and Pacheco is difficult to understand. Trained California horses commonly carried a brand that could be used to determine the animal's provenance, if not absolute ownership. It is hard to believe that a californio would try to claim an unbranded (and thus wild and unvalued) horse from such a hard-looking group of men. If the horse was branded and Frémont was telling the truth, then he had unknowingly purchased in Missouri a mount stolen in California and ridden it home. Perhaps it was a Delaware horse acquired on one of the many chaguanoso raids. Maybe it was one of the animals that Bidwell had provided from Sutter's herds. These are all plausible explanations, but it seems most likely that the horse was one of those that his men had recently acquired in the San Joaquin. For whatever reason, Frémont refused to acknowledge Peralta's claim and sent him away with insults. From the Mexican perspective, Frémont and his men were beginning to look like another set of freebooters. They were just more numerous and better armed than previous marauding bands—and they were riding under American colors.

If californios were proud and easily took offense, so did the arrogant Frémont. When the Peralta incident made the color rise in his cheeks, he needlessly affronted Pacheco. The captain of topographical engineers expected a war with Mexico very shortly. He was not about to bow to California authorities in the meantime. Matters were not helped when one of Frémont's men invited one of the Castro clan's daughters to drink with him. It was time to leave the Santa Clara Valley. Poised to cross into the San Joaquin Valley, Frémont instead turned west and rode toward the hamlet of Santa Cruz on the northern bend of Monterey Bay. Then they rode south along the coast toward Monterey in leisurely fashion. What were these *norteamericanos* up to? They turned east and picked up the Salinas River, camping at William Hartnell's Alisal rancho on March 3.

Exactly what Frémont's plans were during this slow military parade around Monterey Bay was anyone's guess. He later claimed that he was on his way to the Colorado River, but this was not what he had told the californios and was certainly not the most direct route. Even Larkin was baffled by his movements. Whatever the American's aims, californio authorities could not tolerate his threatening marches around the capital. On March 5 José Castro peremptorily ordered him out of California. Who could blame the comandante general for his suspicions? Frémont, of course, chose not to see matters from a Mexican perspective.

Determined to stand up for his personal and national honor, Frémont directed his men to occupy Gavilán Peak. They raised the American flag, cheered, built breastworks, and waited for Castro's next move. General Castro gathered several hundred mounted men, mostly irregular californios, and moved cannons near Gavilán Peak. Frémont observed these preparations and held his position. Being apprised of these developments, Larkin was frantic. He shot off letters to Frémont urging caution and tried to mediate the affair with Castro. On March 9 Frémont reconsidered his position. Perhaps he was not acting in the best interests of his country. Maybe the prospect of a desperate Alamo-like last stand lost its appeal as he watched Castro maneuver his troops and artillery. In any case he now believed that he had made his point with the californios and resolved to abandon his hastily assembled barricade. In the middle of the night, he withdrew and moved away from Castro's forces. The war for California would not start at Gavilán Peak. Instead of fighting, the expedition deliberately withdrew to the interior and headed back toward New Helvetia.

While Frémont postured near the coast, intelligence filtered back to Sutter through various sources. On February 19 he learned that Mexican troops would not be arriving in California. Sutter would have to deal with unruly foreigners on his own. Moreover, the same source told him that the United States would likely take over soon, but this was still mere speculation.[37] As far as anyone knew, Mexico and the United States were still at peace. On March 14 Marsh sent Sutter an express messenger describing Frémont's controversy with Castro and the Pathfinder's expulsion from California.[38] Sutter may be forgiven if at this point he figured that all the talk about a California republic and American annexation was just a flash in the pan. Affairs in Mexican California would likely continue on their erratic course, controlled by local conditions as usual. Sutter did not say this, but his actions imply that this was his state of mind in late winter.

While Frémont provoked the californios, life proceeded apace at New Helvetia. Pierson Reading was in charge of Sutter's trapping party, which was doing well, trapping thirty to fifty beavers and about half that number of otters per month. Indian hunters brought in racoon and elk skins as well, receiving trade goods in return. Marsh complained that one of Sutter's Indians had killed one of the American's cows while hunting beavers near Los Meganos, but this was a minor irritant as far as Sutter was concerned. He advised Reading to punish Indians as he saw fit. Sutter simply denied that his Indians could have been responsible for Marsh's dead cow, a response that surely did not satisfy his testy neighbor.[39]

Sutter took time to inform Governor Pico that he was on top of Indian affairs. "A few days ago one of the principal chiefs of the Indian horse thieves came to this place, surrendering himself and his whole tribe to my authority and promising to aid me against the other thieves who live in the mountains next to his land." Sutter hoped "to end the robberies that are committed daily on the frontiers of the San Joaquin," he added optimistically.[40] He did not precisely identify these Indians, but later developments seem to indicate that they were Muquelemne Miwoks. Sutter's relentless campaigning had no doubt taken a toll on them. With the white population growing near Sutter's Fort, peace with him might have seemed like the most prudent move.

Sutter may have wanted to sell his property, but he continued to improve it.

He spent some time surveying the American River, where he hoped to build a water-powered gristmill, and overseeing the work of men who were digging an irrigation ditch there. He wanted to lay out a town in preparation for the new American immigration that would surely bring an increase in commercial activity. If the thousands predicted by Hastings actually arrived, the fort's trading post would not be adequate for their demands. Besides, merchants would want stores of their own. He reasoned that a prospective town site must be safe from the periodic floods that swept the valley. The lowlands where his embarcadero was located on the Sacramento River were unsatisfactory on this account. Dry lands near the fort were in short supply, so Sutter located his proposed city, Sutterville, about three miles southeastward on a low bluff overlooking the Sacramento River, where there was no danger of flooding. Hastings and Bidwell laid out the town, and both received a share of the lots. George Zins built the first brick house there in 1846, but development of the town was slow.[41]

On March 21 Frémont returned to New Helvetia and camped on the American River across from the fort.[42] He did not stay long. Three days later he began moving up the Sacramento Valley toward Oregon, staying at American ranchos along the way. Sutter was probably glad to see him go. Frémont and his men had unsettled northern California, and this did not help Sutter. Frémont's presence may have caused some Americans who thought a change was at hand to lose respect for Sutter's Mexican authority. Many Americans living in the interior were not of the best character, Sutter complained to Marsh. Some of them went so far as to lay hands on him. Three men who were enraged because he had "defended my property . . . touched me and I was every minute waiting for a merciful knife or a ball." Once the unquestioned patriarch and supreme authority in his domain, Sutter was now subject to being manhandled on his own estate. He described himself as "entirely discouraged." "I am indeed very tired and wearied because a great many foreigners behave very bad. Your property is no more safe like it was 6 months ago, no more obedience to the laws. They march with their feet on the authority," he lamented. To Americans who wanted to establish an independent republic, or who anxiously waited for the United States to act, Sutter's days as ruler of the Sacramento Valley were numbered. His style of autocratic rule did not conform to democratic norms as they were understood by American frontiersmen. "If the [Mexican] government would purchase the establishment and pay in gold and silver I would sell it, pay all my debts, and go somewhere else."[43]

Sutter had a belly full of Lansford Hastings too. Sutter claimed that American settlers wanted to kill him because he had promoted California as "a paradise" and were disappointed when they learned the truth. "I like to be hospitable but I am very glad when Capt. Hastings is gone because he makes me a disagreeable situation," Sutter said vaguely. "I dont like to tell him to leave, particular as it is only a few days longer."[44] Hastings would leave, although, like Frémont, he would be back.

But there was some good news that Sutter was happy to share with Marsh. He had received letters from his family in Switzerland. Much to Sutter's credit, he always acknowledged his family with pride and hoped to bring them to California. His precarious finances had kept him from sending for them, but he wrote to them via a circuitous route that took his letters by way of his Russian connections from California to Alaska to Kamchatka to Siberia to St. Petersburg and so on to Switzerland. Responses came back by the same tedious chain. It took years to complete the circuit of correspondence.[45] Twelve years had passed since Sutter had fled Switzerland; his children were grown nearly to adulthood. "With the greatest of pleasure I see that my oldest Son 20 years and 6 months old [actually he was nineteen] is on his way to California and will be here in about 6 or 7 months," he enthused. All of his children had been well educated, he claimed. John Augustus, Jr., had apprenticed "in one of the first counting houses in Switzerland, he speaks and writes several languages, and no doubt will be an able Clerk." His second son, Emil Victor, was "in a celebrated Agricultural Institut," and Wilhelm Alphonse was "in a Military School or academie as Cadet." His daughter's education was also complete. "It was a great pleasure to read all their letters out [of] which I could judge how the[y] received their education, and [it] was to my greatest satisfaction," he added proudly. Sutter expected that the entire family would follow his eldest son in about two years. The timetable for his son's arrival was too optimistic by about two and a half years. Still, the news gave him a much-needed boost.

In mid-April Frémont was gone and Hastings had told Marsh that he intended to go to the Green River or Fort Bridger, where he could conduct immigrants over his shortcut to California.[46] Sutter took the trouble to inform General Castro that Frémont had departed and further said that the Pathfinder had bought twenty-one horses "from Indian thieves."[47] Sutter had sent a sharp letter to Frémont demanding the return of these horses but had not heard anything more about it. While Frémont had not replied to the letter, he bristled at Sutter's suggestion that his intercourse with the Miwoks was exceptionable. Captain Frémont jealously guarded his reputation; he was fully capable of holding a grudge against anyone who tarnished it, as Sutter would soon learn.[48] Castro no doubt hoped that he had heard the last of these troublesome Americans, whose effrontery had offended the californios' sense of personal dignity and national honor. Wishing would not make it so.

Young John A. Sutter. This idealized portrait of Sutter in his Swiss militia uniform captures his good looks and personal magnetism. In his youth, he brushed his hair forward in the European romantic style that he tried to recapture in his old age. California State Library.

Sutter's Fort, ca. 1846. U.S. naval lieutenant Joseph Warren Revere's drawing depicted Sutter's Indian soldiers drilling in front of the fort. California State Library.

Fort Ross, ca. 1830. Sutter's 1841 purchase of the Russian-American Company's California property at Fort Ross and Bodega nearly bankrupted him. His employees worked for years to dismantle the Russian establishment and move it to New Helvetia. California State Library.

Hock Farm in bloom. Even though Sutter made Hock Farm into a horticultural showcase, there are few illustrations that portray the beauty of the place. This picture at least gives a hint of Hock's lushness and the splendor of Sutter's house before an arsonist destroyed it in 1865. California State Library.

Anna Sutter, 1850. Mrs. Sutter looks rather grim in this photograph, but the trial of sitting through the long exposure required in those days might account for her expression. Still, it is difficult to escape the conclusion that this is a woman who had seen hard times. California State Library.

Sutter, ca. 1850. In this earliest known photograph of Sutter, one catches a glimpse of his powerful good looks: strong jaw, high forehead, piercing light blue eyes. California State Library.

John A. Sutter, Jr. Sutter's namesake lacked the handsome features of his father. After their long separation, father and son fell to quarreling over how to manage Sutter's business affairs. California State Library.

Anna Eliza Sutter. Eliza seems attractive in this picture, but not everyone thought so. Sutter vainly tried to marry her to a man of distinction. Finally, with great pomp and ceremony, she wed an innkeeper and musician at Hock Farm. California State Library.

Emil Victor Sutter. Sutter's middle son staunchly defended his father's reputation. Never a happy man, Victor committed suicide in 1881. California State Library.

Sacramento in 1849. This view shows how rapidly Sacramento had grown from nothing into a bustling commercial center. The sale of city lots at inflated gold-rush prices saved Sutter from financial ruin. A few months after this picture was made winter storms flooded the city, ruining many who had invested in low-lying property. California State Library.

Sutter in uniform, 1853. Sutter loved uniforms, and he loved to be painted and photographed. He planned to make lithographs of this painting by William S. Jewett. Instead the cash-strapped Sutter sold the portrait to the state for $2,500. The legislature purchased oil portraits of governors but seldom paid more than $500. California State Library.

Hok ranchería. The few people shown in this scene would have worked on Hock Farm for Sutter. He depended on Indian labor from 1839 until he left California in 1865. California State Library.

Sutter, ca. 1875. Sutter never tired of his own likeness. Scores of photographers and painters made images of him. Here, late in life, he sweeps his hair forward, as he did in his youth. His eyes are still bright for the camera. California State Library.

Sutter in front of his home, Lititz, Pennsylvania. Sutter was very proud of his last home, claiming that it cost $10,000 to build it. Judging by the young trees, this photograph was probably taken to mark the home's completion in 1870. California State Library.

Sutter's Fort in ruins, ca. 1880s. The fort's central building was all that remained when this photograph was made. Once proposed for the state "lunatic asylum," the building served as a hotel, saloon, and pigsty before the Native Sons of the Golden West purchased the site and gave it to the State of California in 1890. California State Library.

Sutter sculpture. The people of Switzerland and Swiss Americans intended this statue to stand on the grounds of Sutter's Fort Historic Park, but public objections kept it from being mounted on state property. The statue, now on the grounds of Sutter General Hospital, gazes at Sutter's Fort across the street. The symbolic dispossession of Sutter was not what the Swiss donors intended, but it is historically fitting. Photo by author.

Hock Farm Monument. Erected by the Sutter and Yuba Bi-County Federation of Women's Clubs in 1927, this monument is evidently made from the iron shutters of Sutter's farm house. Alternatively, metal may have come from a prefabricated building on the farm where the marriage of Sutter's daughter took place. The bronze plaque is riddled with bullet holes. Refurbishing of the monument was underway in the spring of 2005. Photo by author.

Sutter's Fort, ca. 1940. Well-manicured lawns replaced the once-dusty grounds outside the fort. Palm trees, vine-covered walls, and tile roofs created a lush landscape that was far from the reality of Sutter's Fort in the 1840s. California State Library.

Sutter's Fort interior, ca. 1940. The central building was all that remained of the original fort. Topped with a tile roof instead of tule thatch or shingles, the structure looks more like a restored mission than Sutter's trading post. Gardeners planted trees and a rose garden in incongruous spots. By 1940 the fort had become Sacramento's attic, as local residents contributed artifacts of questionable provenance for display in the fort's exhibit cases. Currently the fort sports more realistic shingle roofs and less luxuriant foliage. Actors portray Sutter and other fort characters for the benefit of schoolchildren. Indians, who substantially outnumbered non-Indians in Sutter's time, are not seen in these reenactments. The interpretation of Indian history and life takes place in the State Indian Museum, a separate building behind the fort. California State Library.

Sutter's grave, ca. 1939. John and Anna Sutter share this grave in Lititz, Pennsylvania. From time to time Californians propose the removal of the Sutters' remains to Sacramento, but the objections of their Pennsylvania descendants have stopped all such schemes. Sutter contentedly lived his last ten years in Lititz and never expressed a desire to be buried in California. California State Library.

CHAPTER 14

American Conquest

If Sutter thought that Frémont's departure heralded a return to the normal routines of New Helvetia, he was mistaken. Two weeks after the Pathfinder left for Oregon, Archibald H. Gillespie and his African American servant Benjamin Harrison stepped off a whale boat at Sutter's embarcadero.[1] Gillespie told Sutter that he was traveling for his health and that he represented the Boston trading house of William Appleton & Co. He also happened to carry personal letters for Captain Frémont and was in a great hurry to see him. Unfortunately, Frémont was far to the north, perhaps already in Oregon. The trail to reach him was long and dangerous; but the ailing merchant was not deterred. Gillespie bought horses and hired four men, including Samuel Neal, whom Frémont had released from the first California expedition, mountain man Peter Lassen, and two others. Neal and Lassen both had ranchos in the upper Sacramento Valley. Gillespie paid the four men the extraordinary sum of two dollars a day "in silver," Sutter reported.[2] The hastily assembled troop left the following morning.

Sutter was suspicious of Gillespie and his true purpose, and rightly so. Gillespie was in truth a lieutenant in the United States Marines, traveling under secret orders from the secretary of the navy, George Bancroft. He did have personal letters for Frémont, and he also carried official letters from the government ordering Commodore John B. Sloat, commander of the Pacific Squadron, to seize San Francisco and other California ports upon hearing of war between Mexico and the United States. Another letter from the secretary of state appointed Larkin a confidential agent with the purposes of hastening the peaceful acquisition of California and checking any other foreign designs on the territory. By the time Lieutenant Gillespie reached New Helvetia he had already delivered the letters to Sloat and Larkin, so the stage was set for the next act in the struggle for California.

Sutter guessed at Gillespie's true mission, as he reported to José Castro; but as usual he was in no hurry and waited two weeks to give this important information to the comandante general. He had seen Gillespie's name on a list of officers, he told Castro. Indeed, Sutter had questioned Gillespie on this point; the lieutenant had replied, "Yes, formerly," but claimed that now he was retired. "He told me that he is traveling for his health and that he has letters for Captain Frémont from his family, but I can not believe this." Sutter recounted for Castro Gillespie's purchase of horses and his hiring of men to pursue Frémont. "From all this it seems that this gentleman has important instructions from his government for Mr. Frémont, and it may be that he is going to return to the [California] frontier."[3]

At the same time Sutter reminded Castro that thousands of American emigrants ("but not ten thousand as they say") were on their way to California. "I recommend to your excellency placing a considerable garrison at this point before the emigrants from the United States enter the country." Whatever happened, Sutter still held out hope that the Mexican government would buy his place and bail him out of debt: "Believing that the government will buy my settlement I shall put everything in the best order." But events were moving much too fast.[4]

Indeed, momentous events were already underway. On April 24 Mexican and American forces clashed along the Rio Grande in Texas, thus providing President Polk with a convincing cause to ask Congress for a declaration of war. Polk's war aims included not only the establishment of the Rio Grande as the international border, but a general invasion of Mexico and the acquisition of California and New Mexico. It would take months for the news of these developments to reach Sloat and Frémont, but in the meantime Polk ordered the Army of the West under General Stephen Watts Kearny to march out of Fort Leavenworth through New Mexico into southern California. At Fort Leavenworth a force of Mormon volunteers joined Kearny's forces and would follow him to California. Commodore Robert Field Stockton was already en route to California waters to reinforce the Pacific Squadron. Still other forces prepared to invade central Mexico by land and sea.

Meanwhile Gillespie, Neal, and company followed Frémont's trail north through the widely spaced American ranchos in the Sacramento Valley. Frémont left trouble in his wake. Acting on the complaints of American ranchers, he assaulted an Indian community that was suspected of planning an attack on the settlements. One participant claimed that more than a hundred Indians were killed, and Carson later said that this affray was "a perfect butchery."[5] Faint reverberations reached Sutter, who told Castro the scant details he knew. "A massacre with Indians on the frontier of [by] some foreign hunters, and Captain Frémont, who aided them, I believe is in the territory of the United States," a geographical error that may have been meant to placate Castro.[6] Frémont believed that his preemptive strike would intimidate the local Indians, but soon he would learn better.

Moving north into Oregon, Frémont camped on Klamath Lake, where he pondered his next move. On the evening of May 8 he caught the sound of horses' hooves. "There emerged from the darkness—into the circle of firelight—two horsemen, riding slowly as though horse and man were fatigued by long traveling." Sam Neal and another man had ridden nearly a hundred miles in two days to find Frémont. Riding the strongest horses, by mutual agreement they had left the rest of the Gillespie party and their fagged mounts somewhere behind. Gillespie had letters, Neal said, and was in danger. Indians had been shadowing them, and it was entirely possible that they were already dead. The next day Frémont hastened back down the trail, covering about forty-five miles of hard riding. Somehow Gillespie, Lassen, and the others had eluded the Indians and rode into Frémont's camp.

That night Frémont read his letters and talked with Gillespie. The letters have been lost, but Frémont later claimed that they, together with Gillespie's verbal communications concerning Polk's maturing plans for California, "absolved me from my duty as an explorer" and left him free to act as he thought best.[7] He decided to return to California. No doubt distracted by thoughts of the impending crisis, Frémont failed to post sentries, an especially strange lapse of security given recent events. The oversight was costly. Klamath Indians attacked the camp and killed three of his men. Frémont delayed his march south to avenge the killings. Hoping to overawe the Indians, he circled the lake, killing Klamaths as he found them. Then he turned his face to California.[8]

Frémont's strikes against California and Oregon Indians did nothing to calm the Indians in that part of the country. Rumors of Indian hostility would be a constant backdrop in the drama that was unfolding in northern California. Frémont's preemptive attacks had added to the Indians' long list of grievances. Ironically, this recklessness made Sutter's skill and reputation among the Indians even more necessary to Frémont in the coming conflict.

While Frémont rode south, Sutter was preoccupied with Indian affairs. There were many signs that Indians were planning to attack the Sacramento Valley settlements. In late May Sutter interrogated a Miwok chief from a Cosumnes River ranchería. The headman had visited the settlements near San José and possessed intelligence that Sutter found disturbing in the extreme. José

Castro (the comandante general, who, Sutter had hoped, would broker the sale of New Helvetia to Mexico) had instead incited a revolt against foreigners among the valley Indians. With Castro's encouragement, Indian raiders were to torch the tinder-dry wheat fields, steal livestock, and harass the settlers. Castro would then fall upon the weakened and demoralized settlers.

Sutter was a special target of Castro's Indian war. Loss of his wheat crop to Indian arsonists would devastate Sutter, who needed the grain to keep his Russian creditors at bay. According to Sutter, Castro went so far as to give the Muquelemne leader Eusebio a rifle with which to kill Sutter and called the chief "hijo and hermano [son and brother]" to symbolize their newfound friendship.[9] So much for Sutter's hope for a profitable real-estate transaction. Perhaps Castro had tired of his demand for an extravagant price for his holdings. Whatever motivated the comandante general, Sutter was now in a bad fix. He faced an Indian revolt; his maturing wheat crop was threatened; there was no hope that Castro would help in a government purchase; he was a marked man. A few weeks earlier Sutter had sent a curt letter to Frémont (with a copy to Castro), chastising the American for his dealings with Indian horse thieves. Now he sent a courier to Frémont's camp to fill him in on Castro's plans.[10]

We have nothing but Sutter's word for the existence of this conspiracy, but the chronology of events seems to support his sincere belief that it was real. On June 1 he prepared to march on the Muquelemnes, but they beat him to the punch. On the night of June 2 Sutter's sentinel gave the alarm that someone was attempting to rustle the horse herd in the adobe corral directly in front of the fort. He and his men went after them, but they escaped into the woods. Sutter then took Reading and several dozen men to strike the Muquelemnes in their own country. The small legion met with near disaster along the way. While crossing the Mokelumne River at night, one of their rafts capsized. Reading and another man nearly drowned and Sutter lost "10 Rifles, and 6 prs. of Pistols, a good supply of Ammunition, and the Clothing of about 24 Men."[11] Now some of his men were without arms and clothes, so they ignominiously huddled on the riverbank while Sutter and the rest of his force went after Eusebio and his Muquelemnes.

After unsuccessfully seeking the Indians all night on the Calaveras River, Sutter sent out a scouting party to hunt for them. On his other campaigns he liked to attack without warning at dawn; that was no doubt what he intended in this case. Since the Muquelemnes were closer than he had suspected, this time he would not have the element of surprise. One of the Indians' dogs came to Sutter's camp, and almost simultaneously a scout galloped in to say that the rest of his companions were already fighting with the Indians. Sutter and his men sprang to their saddles and rode to the skirmish. It was not going well: "Already some of our Men was wounded and unable to fight"; but the reinforcements turned the tide. Soon the Muquelemnes retired to a "large hole like a Cellar in the bank of the Calaveras" and continued to pepper Sutter's men with rifle balls and arrows. In the end he was forced to retreat, "on account of having no more powder and balls." The bedraggled force returned to the fort on June 7. Eusebio was still at large, presumably with Castro's rifle in his hand.[12] Sutter now put a price on Eusebio's head—one hundred dollars in trade goods for the Indian who brought him in "death or a life," as Sutter put it.[13]

The day after Sutter returned from the nearly disastrous scrape on the Calaveras, Captain Francisco Arce and half a dozen soldiers drove a herd of 150 government horses through New Helvetia on their way to Santa Clara to reinforce Castro's cavalry. Captain Arce stopped by the fort before moving on. His appearance in New Helvetia with a government herd inspired a host of rumors that Castro's mounted army would use the horses to drive foreigners out of the valley. Meanwhile Frémont had relocated his camp to the Sutter Buttes, not far from Hock Farm. Several settlers approached Frémont at the Buttes and asked him to lead a raid on Arce's small detachment, but he refused. Ezekial Merritt, a lanky American settler, took matters into his own hands, leading ten American volunteers after Arce. They caught him on the Cosumnes River on June 10. It was a bloodless dawn ambush that took Captain Arce completely by surprise. After returning their arms and mounts, Merritt released the Mexican soldiers and told them that by the time they reached Castro Americans would have captured Sonoma and would be holding Vallejo prisoner. It was not an idle boast.

Events were outpacing the ability of either Sutter or Frémont to control them. In early June Sutter wanted to save his investment and his skin. Frémont was evidently waiting for certain news that the United States and Mexico were at war. He wanted to take a leading role in the military conquest of California without striking the first blow. While he dithered, American settlers were more than ready to act on their own, and they did not understand his reluctance to join them. None of the Americans turned to Sutter as a potential leader when Frémont rebuffed them. Sutter now understood that he was unlikely to have a bright future in Mexican California, at least if Castro had anything to say about it. His friends such as Bidwell and Reading would contend that he had always supported an American takeover, but he had probably said too much about his hope for Mexican troops and the sale of New Helvetia. Frémont apparently believed the news of Castro's plot but remained skeptical about Sutter's allegiance.

Captain Frémont struck camp at the Buttes and resumed his slow parade southward, arriving at the American Fork on June 12. Although the Pathfinder accepted the stolen Mexican herd from Merritt, he declined to lead the Americans on a raid against Sonoma. They went anyhow. As Merritt had foretold, Americans took Sonoma (which was undefended) without firing a shot, raised a makeshift Bear Flag, captured Vallejo with his brother Salvador, his brother-in-law Jacob Leese, and Victor Prudon, and took their prisoners to Frémont, who by this time was encamped at Sutter's embarcadero. The Pathfinder at first did not want to accept the prisoners but finally relented and sent Vallejo and the other captives to Sutter's Fort. This act seemed to galvanize Frémont, who not only took responsibility for the prisoners but took command of the Bear Flag rebels.

Frémont also assumed command of Sutter's Fort. Sutter, who was now an enthusiastic supporter of the American cause (an allegiance no doubt fostered by Castro's plots against him), expected Frémont to accept him as a brother-in-arms against their common enemy. Frémont remained cool toward Sutter, who did not understand his aloofness. After all, even before the revolt Sutter had thrown open the fort's gates to Frémont and his men. Sutter asked Carson why "Frémont seems unfriendly." "Remember the letter," Carson answered, referring to Sutter's critical letter to Frémont concerning the purchase of stolen horses.[14] When Frémont put the prisoners in Sutter's Fort, he bluntly explained his views on Sutter's loyalty. Upon delivering the prisoners, the two men spoke just out of John Bidwell's earshot, "but in a few minutes Sutter came to me greatly agitated, with tears in his eyes, and said that Frémont had told him he was a Mexican, and that if he did not like what he (Frémont) was doing he would set him down across the San Joaquin River and he could go join the Mexicans."[15] Frémont took over the fort, renamed it Fort Sacramento, and placed the expedition's young artist, Edward Kern, in charge. Sutter, who gave up his brevet colonelcy in the Mexican army, remained at the fort as New Helvetia's nominal owner. Stripped of all official military rank, he was practically a supernumerary at Fort Sacramento. With little choice in the matter, Sutter humbly submitted to Frémont's authority, virtually a prisoner in his own house.

With the fort under new management, Sutter's only official role was to keep the Vallejos and the other prisoners under close guard as Frémont ordered. As far as the Pathfinder was concerned, his Swiss-Mexican subordinate never did an adequate job of it. Sutter, believing that he should extend all due courtesy to captured officers and his upper-crust californio prisoners, boarded them "in my best rooms and treated them with every consideration." He invited them to dine at his own table in his private rooms and did not place guards at the door as

Frémont commanded. He took walks with them too and tried to be as lenient a keeper as possible. Sutter even ordered some brandy for the "Gentlemen prisoners which I wanted to treat so well as possible."[16] After all, the captives were "men of property," as he said, and were not likely to escape. None of this escaped Frémont, who insisted that Sutter take stricter measures. "He asked me with harshness, 'Do you not know how to treat prisoners?' 'Captain Frémont,' said I, 'I do; I have been a prisoner myself,'" a reference to his incarceration during the Micheltorena revolt.[17] He told Frémont to take charge of the prisoners himself if he did not like the treatment they were receiving under Sutter's roof.

Frémont then turned over the prisoners to one of Sutter's clerks, William Loker, but he did not like the job and soon departed with the Bear Flag volunteers. Now it was John Bidwell's turn to take charge of the prisoners, but he treated them just as cordially as Sutter did. He even tutored Prudon in English in exchange for Spanish lessons. Soon Bidwell departed, and the prisoners were placed under Lieutenant Kern's supervision. He too treated his charges better than Frémont liked. During the steady change in guards, Sutter continued to visit Vallejo and the others. Frémont finally threatened to incarcerate him if he continued to fraternize with the californios, and Sutter acquiesced, however reluctantly.

Colonel Frémont now turned his attention to establishing control of the northern frontier and holding it against any californio forces that Castro or anyone else might command to march against his motley army. He maneuvered his forces between Sonoma and San Francisco Bay. There was no actual fighting, but by early July the Bear Flag rebels dominated the country on the north side of San Francisco Bay. After celebrating Independence Day at Sonoma, Frémont and his men returned to the American Fork, where they heard the stunning news that Commodore Sloat had raised the Stars and Stripes over Monterey. Once convinced that the United States and Mexico were at war, Sloat issued a statement. "I declare to the inhabitants of California," he proclaimed, that "I come as their best friend—as henceforward California will be a portion of the United States." He went on to declare that "a great increase in the value of real Estate and the products of California" would occur.[18] The commodore helped to foster these happy changes by eliminating all duties on U.S. goods and cutting duties on all foreign goods to one-quarter the current Mexican rate.

News of Sloat's proclamation reached Frémont on the evening of July 10. The Bear Flaggers were "electrified" at the news and the following morning raised the American flag with an artillery salute at the fort.[19] There was so much firing of guns that "nearly all the glass in the fort was broken," Sutter recalled. The tumultuous raising of the Stars and Stripes emboldened him to disobey Frémont by telling the prisoners what the commotion was about. "Now," Sutter grandly recalled telling them, "we are under the protection of this great flag, and will not be henceforth afraid to talk to one another. Frémont is a tyrant."[20] These events may have inspired Frémont to consider a magnanimous policy toward his prisoners. Someone (perhaps Sutter) told Mariano Vallejo that Frémont planned to visit him that day. Frémont did not come, however, so the anxious Vallejo wrote to him: "to calm the restlessness of the gentlemen who share my jail and for my own satisfaction, I wish you would let us know if our imprisonment . . . has ended."[21]

Frémont did not respond as Vallejo had hoped. Perhaps the conclusion of Vallejo's letter—"the state of the nation cannot be worse than the state in which it was before the change"—struck him as insufficiently enthusiastic. In any event, the men remained in custody while the Pathfinder led his men to Monterey at the instruction of Commodore Stockton. He was adamant about the prisoners. "Without regard to any order that you may receive in my absence, you will retain Messrs. Vallejo, Preuxdon [sic], Leese and Carrillo at the fort," Frémont ordered Lieutenant Kern. "Iron and confine any person who shall disobey your orders—shoot any person who shall endanger the safety of the place," he added.[22] As far as Frémont was concerned, the status of the fort, Sutter, and the prisoners had not changed with the change of flag. Still held incommunicado, Vallejo got messages from the outside hidden in corn tortillas that his wife sent him. "We still have no news if we will leave soon and this keeps us anxious," he told her on July 12.[23]

Commodore Stockton finally ordered the parole of the prisoners on August 1. The initial conditions of his parole were strict, threatening him with death if he left the Sonoma district. A few days later the bonds were loosened when naval captain John B. Montgomery, who was in charge of the northern district, asked only for Vallejo's friendship and neutrality in the conflict between the United States and Mexico.[24]

No one needed to worry about a threat from Vallejo. He hated Sutter's jail but welcomed the American takeover. Moreover, his incarceration at Sutter's Fort had broken his health, and he was in no condition to join a revolt. Like so many other valley visitors, Vallejo contracted malaria from the ubiquitous mosquitoes that swarmed in the lowlands.[25]

While Sutter recalled Vallejo's imprisonment as a time of bonding between the two men and Sutter's demonstration of courage and chivalry in the face of Frémont's severity, Vallejo had no fond memories of the experience. "My imprisonment caused a breaking of my spirit and my physique," he told his friend Juan Bandini. The malaria caused temporary blindness "when I was locked up *incomunicado* [*sic*] in Sutter's death-dealing fort." He returned to Sonoma "half dead" and spent the next three months in bed. "I shall always remember my imprisonment because the manner in which I was treated was unjust and because I have almost lost the most precious of the senses."[26] Vallejo's severe illness could not have gone unnoticed by Sutter. The navy sent a physician to the fort to minister to Vallejo, but Sutter mentioned none of it. Vallejo no doubt hoped that his recovered eyes would not catch sight of Sutter again, but within months circumstances would throw them together once more.

While the ailing Vallejo languished in Sutter's Fort, Frémont parleyed with U.S. Navy officers in Monterey. Sloat, who was old and sickly, gave up command of the Pacific Squadron to the vigorous and ambitious Commodore Robert F. Stockton. Frémont rejoined the U.S. military, while his forces were incorporated as volunteers known as the California Battalion. He and the battalion rode to southern California. The conquest was deceptively quick and easy. By the end of August U.S. troops were in control of all the major settlements, and the californio military and political chiefs had fled or gone into hiding. It was a false peace.

While Stockton and Frémont pacified the south in late summer, Sutter threw himself into his new duties as Kern's subordinate. He chafed under his reduced status. He never acknowledged in his reminiscences that Kern was in charge. As far as historical memory was concerned, Sutter continued as the commander of his own fort, but that was far from the truth.[27] At the time he assured Leidesdorff that it was "not very pleasant to have another as Comander in his own house and establishemt [*sic*]."[28] He made the best of a bad situation by befriending Kern.[29]

Some things had not changed. Sutter still held the key to Indian relations in the interior; his Indian soldiers still guarded the fort. He sent Bidwell and a few other men to the Cosumnes River "for horses and to caution the Indians in that direction to give intelligence in case of the approach of any people from below."[30] Eusebio was still free. As Castro's ally, he might cause trouble for American forces as well as for Sutter, but not for long. Sometime in July Eusebio visited Pollo, "a formerly horsethief Chief" that he wanted to recruit for his fight against Sutter.[31] The lord of New Helvetia had gotten to Pollo first with a tempting offer of a hundred dollars in trade goods. "The Chief Pollo already received my Orders and Killed him"; "the head of Eusebio was delivered" to Sutter. Sutter, Eliab Grimes, and Leidesdorff each promised to pay one-quarter of the reward, and a combination of other men picked up the remainder. Pollo's assassination of Eusebio had caused the dead chief's confederates to seek asylum at a rancho in the San Joaquin Valley. "So soon as the war is over," Sutter told Leidesdorff, "I shall get them punished."[32] The fortunes of war, however, would decree a kinder fate for the Muquelemnes.

Sutter's effectiveness among the Indians did not go unnoticed. In August he took an oath of allegiance to the United States and received a commission as lieutenant of volunteers, entitled to the pay and allowances of that rank. Likewise his Indian guard of thirty men enrolled as volunteer privates. This small force and other Indians in Sutter's employ who were "expert in the use of firearms" were sufficient to defend the post for the time being.[33] Sutter was grateful that the U.S. government now took the burden of supporting the private army that he had maintained for seven years.

Sutter's appointment as lieutenant did not improve his position as second fiddle at the fort. When the overland immigrant Edwin Bryant arrived on September 1, he noticed two Indian sentinels marching to and fro in front of the fort's gate, now decorated with Eusebio's long black hair. A white man dressed in buckskin pants and a blue sailor's shirt told Bryant that "the fort now belonged to the United States, and that Captain Sutter, although he was in the fort, had no control over it." Nevertheless, Bryant asked to see Sutter, whose generosity to weary travelers was legendary. "Capt. S. soon came to the gate," he observed, "and saluted us with much gentlemanly courtesy, and friendly cordiality." After confirming that he no longer controlled the fort and therefore had to refuse Bryant and his companions admission, Sutter gladly provided them "with a supply of beef, salt, melons, onions, and tomatoes, for which no compensation would be received."[34] Dispossessed or not, he treated needy visitors with his usual generosity, probably more bountifully than he could afford.

Sutter was still working hard to bring his wheat to harvest so that he could pay the long overdue Russian debt. As the Mexican-American War unfolded in California, he attended to the mundane details of running his agricultural enterprise, a task that was made more difficult by the exigencies of war.[35] For a time his launch was detained, and he had to pay to ship his wheat downriver to the Russians.[36] Still, heady changes were underway, while it seems that Sutter was becoming a little more economical in his business dealings. "It is my rule now," he told merchant sea captain William Heath Davis, "that I buy no more goods when I cannot pay in a short time."[37] Perhaps Sutter realized that the time was not far off when American lawyers and courts would enforce contracts. The days of endless renegotiation of debts and uncertain values would come to an end. Sutter understood that big changes were taking place and knew that he would have to make some adjustments. He looked forward to buying the latest agricultural machines "at cheap prices, then it will be different as [now] I have to pay a good many Indians" with trade goods.[38] Sutter spent much of his time scrambling to find a supply of manta, a coarse cotton shirting woven in Mexico that California Indians preferred above all others. But manta would not be available for months to come, probably because of the dislocations in Mexican trade caused by the war.

The manta scarcity was a serious problem for California ranchers who depended on Indian labor. Indian workers would not accept substitutes. "Them blue shirts you sent[,] the indians will not have them," William Buzzell complained to his absentee landlord William Leidesdorff. "I gave one to an indian this morning and he went to put it on and . . . it tore nearly in tew[.] He took it off and said it was shie[t] that is good for nothing."[39] Sutter and his neighbors struggled through the year to obtain enough manta to satisfy their fussy Indian clients and workers.[40]

No one in California could afford to dispense with Indian labor in 1846; nor could they safely ignore potential threats from Indians. While Sutter celebrated the death of Eusebio, some Indians from Oregon were on their way to New Helvetia.[41] As the sun went down one early September evening the wife and children of William B. Ide were startled to find a troop of mounted Oregon Indians in their cabin yard near present-day Red Bluff. Ide was one of the leaders of the Bear Flag rebels campaigning with Frémont in the south, so his family was alone. Through an interpreter one of the Indians asked if the Ides "belonged to Captain Sutter." Ide's daughter said no: "We belong to our father." The chief, probably Peopeo Moxmox, was determined to kill one of Sutter's men, preferably the murderer of his son Elijah, or at least obtain a compensation in horses and cattle.[42]

The Ides soon learned that the Oregonians meant them no harm, but news of the Indians' return to California spread like a grass fire in the dry season. One thousand Indians were on their way to the Sacramento Valley to take bloody revenge, or so the rumors said, although no one had seen more than the forty or fifty plus women and children. On September 9 couriers reached the fort, spreading the alarm of a huge and implacable Indian force that was moving toward Fort Sacramento.[43] Kern sent a dispatch to naval authorities, who authorized the reinforcement of Fort Sacramento with mounted riflemen. Captain Montgomery direly ordered Kern to hold out "as long as your provisions last."[44]

Montgomery scoured northern California for men to reinforce Kern's garrison and named naval lieutenant Warren Revere to organize this redeployment. Revere went about his job with extraordinary energy. By mid-September it was becoming clear that the Walla Walla threat had been blown out of proportion. Nevertheless, Lieutenant Revere had assembled his troops at Fort Sacramento and was determined to make a reconnaissance in force north of the fort.

After reviewing his mixed force of white volunteers and Indians, Revere was preparing to mount when, much to everyone's surprise, an unarmed Peopeo Moxmox rode up and introduced himself. He had come to see his son's grave, he said, and to take the livestock that Sutter owed him. He also hoped to see justice done for his son. Revere congratulated the Walla Walla chief for his peaceable demeanor and said he would take under advisement his complaint about the murdered Elijah.[45] There would be no justice for Elijah's death, and the issue would not go away as far as the Oregon Indians were concerned.

Lieutenant Revere was convinced of the Walla Wallas' peaceable intentions, but the settlers who had volunteered for an Indian war still had blood in their eyes. Many of them came from the northern region, where Frémont had stirred up the local Indians with his raids, and some of the volunteers still believed that there were hundreds of Oregon Indians lurking in the underbrush. Consequently, Revere marched his force northward past Hock Farm to the Sutter Buttes, but he and his men found no sign of Walla Wallas. The local Konkow Indians were peaceful enough, but some volunteers wanted to attack them anyway. Revere recalled that one of Sutter's employees, the French Canadian François Gendreau, suggested that the volunteers should

> exterminate a ranchería or two. . . . for the purpose of obtaining Indian servants according to

> —the good old rule,
> —the simple plan—
> That they should take who have the power,
> And they should keep who can.[46]

Northern California's good old rule revolted Revere, who demurred and marched his men back to New Helvetia. On the way he found the Oregon Indians encamped at the mouth of the Feather River. "A more unhealthy spot could not have been chosen," he observed.[47] Many of the Indian and white volunteers caught malaria during their visit to the Sacramento Valley. Months later Revere complained that he "had a devil of a shake & so has [sic] all the men who went to the Walla Walla War."[48]

Sutter probably helped to organize New Helvetia's Indian army during the so-called Walla Walla War, although there is no record of his activities then. However, his importance in Indian affairs could not be ignored. In September the American occupation of Mexican California turned for the worse, as californios rebelled against the unnecessarily harsh measures imposed by Lieutenant Gillespie in Los Angeles. Californios were not about to be mistreated in silence; with little hope of success or help from Mexico, they rose up and drove Gillespie from Los Angeles. Their initial success caused the revolt to spread while land and naval forces headed to the southern part of the territory to reestablish control. Stockton and Frémont sent out a call for more volunteers.[49] Lieutenant Revere thought the situation was desperate. "Call in *all* Americans *to Arms,*" he ordered Kern. The californios threatened Americans with "utter extermination."[50] Revere exaggerated the peril, but the message was well calculated to motivate malingering settlers and newly arrived American immigrants who were coming to Fort Sacramento. Edwin Bryant and other immigrants signed up to scour the country for more American volunteers and "as many Indians, as we deem safe to accompany us."[51]

The disaster in the south was an opportunity for Sutter to demonstrate his usefulness and loyalty to the United States. Control of the horse herds was critical to military success, and he knew Indians who were good at stealing horses and willing to fight. Sutter reported that Frémont asked the lieutenant of volunteers to accompany him and quoted Frémont as saying that "Sutter is the only man who can control the Indians."[52] The story is probably apocryphal, but it summed up a reality that was widely understood in 1846. Sutter seriously considered going to aid the California Battalion with the new volunteers. According to George McKinstry, "Capt. S. Has raised 100 Indians 'horse-thieves' that will accompany him if he accepts."[53] Sutter evidently thought better of riding to Frémont's side, but he sent the Indians, including the Walla Wallas, telling them that "if they would go and fight they should be paid."[54] He appointed the French Canadian Gendreau, who was married to an Oregon Indian woman, to lead them and agreed to feed the Indian families at the fort. On November 2 the Oregon Indians rode up to the fort "in full costume, music and yells."[55]

Sutter also sent word of the opportunity to join American forces against the Mexicans to the Muquelemnes, "old horse thieves now reformed," on the Mokelumne and Stanislaus Rivers.[56] They were led by José Jesús and probably included the men who had been with Eusebio. The Americans, Walla Wallas, and Muquelemnes met up in the San Joaquin Valley and headed south to find Frémont.[57] This mixed Indian force joined the California Battalion. The Muquelemnes formed Company H, but the Walla Wallas evidently fought as an independent force. The Oregon Indians distinguished themselves in fighting at Natividad on November 20, but Frémont was vague about the duties of the California Indians, saying only that they camped without fires in advance of the battalion. The Indians' services are perhaps best described by the californios' nickname for them: the "forty thieves."[58]

Sutter did not explain why he decided to remain at Fort Sacramento rather than fall in with the California Battalion. In the fall of 1846 he had plenty to occupy him at New Helvetia, including the Russian-American Company's renewed efforts to collect his long-overdue debt. The war had ruined Sutter's hope that Mexico would buy New Helvetia, but now perhaps the United States would purchase the fort. He reckoned that the government owed him a thousand dollars per month in back rent from the time that Frémont had seized the fort, and he was willing to sell the place to the United States for eighty thousand dollars. These prices seemed reasonable to him because he provided food for the "garrison . . . many familys [of the] Volunteers, and also the Walla-Walla." How much of Sutter's costs the United States would be willing to assume was anyone's guess in 1846; but he added them all to the credit side of his mental ledger, where he kept books on future profits that were piling up. "It is the first time I have done so good a business," he told Antonio Suñol, a long-time creditor, who must have wondered when he would finally be paid.[59]

Sutter decided that he could enlist the help of the Russians to encourage American authorities in the purchase of the fort. Surely they had an interest in improving his impecunious condition. He cheekily asked the Russians to reduce his debt by ten thousand dollars, assuming, it may be supposed, that they would jump at the chance to get anything from their bargain with Sutter, who paid with promises and excuses instead of wheat and silver.[60]

The Russians, who had as yet received only a few thousand dollars in wheat from Sutter, had a better idea.[61] Recognizing that contracts were more likely to be strictly enforced under the United States than under Mexico, they attempted to attach Sutter's property by filing with Washington A. Bartlett, the alcalde at Yerba Buena. Sutter responded by hiring a lawyer, William H. Russell, and threatened to sue "for damages all engaged in this affair."[62] Pressure from Bartlett and the Russians may have prompted Sutter to redouble his farming efforts, for he delivered considerable wheat in 1846 and 1847. By the end of 1847 the Russians reported that Sutter had liquidated one-fourth of the debt. The remainder, approximately $23,000 (including interest on unpaid sums), was still a considerable amount, and the Russians had no intention of forgetting about it.[63]

The war in California ended on January 13, 1847, when harried californio patriots surrendered to Frémont at Cahuenga Pass. The californios fought for their honor but paid heavily with losses to their horse and cattle herds. In the end they had to go back to their homes and families so that they could tend to their business and personal affairs. The extent to which the Indians that Sutter had recruited contributed to the californios' discouragement cannot be quantified, but neither should it be discounted. For decades Indian horse thieves and their American friends had put California rancheros on the defensive. In the largest sense the Mexican–American War determined which nation would possess California. In local terms the war was the most recent phase of the ongoing struggle for control of California's livestock herds.

In February 1847 Frémont disbanded Company H. The Muquelemnes were entitled to $25 per month as volunteers, but they were paid in receipts that could be redeemed in cash once Congress appropriated the money, a matter that remained unsettled until 1858. By that time the Indians had either sold their receipts at a steep discount or received no pay at all. José Jesús remained loyal to Sutter for the time being, but other Miwoks drifted back to the San Joaquin in early 1847 and took up their old pursuit of livestock raiding.[64] The fight for California's horse herds was not over, and Sutter would have a part in it once again.

The Walla Wallas were unhappy too. They had been promised booty for their services, especially livestock. Sutter claimed that they "brought back much spoils, trophies, clothing of the Mexicans that they had killed," but that was not enough. They accused Sutter of deceiving them and threatened to declare war.[65] The Oregon Indians hung around Fort Sacramento for several months, waiting for Sutter and Frémont to pay them. In the meantime Sutter worried whether they would make good on their bellicose threats.

For the time being the war was over, and Sutter could look forward to peace and the restoration of unfettered control over his fort; but there would be important changes too. His police and judicial authority had slipped away. In September 1846 the denizens of New Helvetia had elected a new alcalde, John Sinclair. Soon thereafter George McKinstry was elected sheriff.[66] Sutter's sparring with the Russian-American Company foreshadowed a new world of lawyers, courts, and contracts under U.S. law. Still, in 1847 Sutter's prospects seemed better than ever to him, if not to his creditors.

CHAPTER 15

A Restoration of Sorts

While the Mexican-American War unfolded in the summer of 1846, Lansford W. Hastings busily pioneered a new overland route southwest of Fort Bridger, Wyoming. He aimed to shave a few hundred miles off the California trail by detouring overlanders through the rugged Wasatch wilderness and across the Great Salt Desert. From there the travelers would pick up the Humboldt River and follow it to the Sierra Nevada escarpment and thence to California. He hoped that his road-locating efforts would make up for the lack of geographic specificity in his *Guide* and that grateful immigrants would remember him kindly, perhaps by buying one of his town lots in Sutterville.

Hastings had never seen it, but the route he envisioned as a shortcut was not entirely daft. Such a trail could be inferred from Frémont's map of the Great Basin, although the Pathfinder was too geographically savvy to suggest a route that he had not seen. Hastings was made of bolder stuff; but he soon realized that the new road—Hastings Cutoff as it became known—was more trying than he had imagined. First he guided a group of wagons through Weber Canyon; but finding that passage too challenging, he thought that it would be better to go through the Wasatch Mountains instead. He fixed a note with this advice in a bush at the head of Weber Canyon.

In early August a group of eighty-seven immigrants from Illinois found it there. They were about to become the most famous overland immigrants in American history: the Donner Party. Hastings was occupied guiding another caravan, the scrap of paper advised, but if they sent for him he would show them the new trail. James Reed, one of the party's leaders, ran after Hastings and found him at the Great Salt Lake. Although Hastings refused to accompany Reed all the way back to his companions' encampment, he gave vague directions to the new trail. Reed hurried back to his party, but his errand consumed eighteen days, just one of many delays caused by the Hastings Cutoff. Despite assurances from Hastings, the new route was tortuous. The immigrants literally had to build a road in the winding canyon country. Instead of taking a week, the journey to Salt Lake consumed thirty days. Additional delays were occasioned by the difficulty of crossing the desert. The Donner Party's unaccountably long rests wasted more precious days.[1]

It was too late in the season to waste a minute. By the time the Donner Party reached eastern Nevada, it was weeks behind the other caravans that had marched across the desert. When their perilous position finally dawned on the immigrants, they dispatched William McCutcheon and C. T. Stanton to New Helvetia to beg Captain Sutter to send relief. Things got worse. While they were following the Humboldt River across Nevada, tempers flared, and Reed fought with a popular young teamster for beating his oxen and swearing in front of the women. Reed killed the man with a knife. Even though it seemed to be a matter of self-defense by the standards of that day, angry friends of the deceased wanted to hang Reed then and there. Instead he was banished, and he too rode ahead to Sutter's Fort.

Sutter was true to his reputation. When Stanton and McCutcheon reached the fort in early October, Sutter provided Stanton with a fresh mount, two Indian vaqueros, and seven pack mules laden with provisions. (McCutcheon was ill and could not accompany the relief party.) On October 19 Stanton found the Donner Party on the Truckee River. They were near starvation. Without Sutter's provisions it is possible that they might have died right there. Stanton and the Indians, who might easily have returned to Sutter's Fort, stayed with the stricken immigrants. It would cost them their lives.

Instead of using their regained strength to push steadily onward, the immigrants tarried until snow prevented them from crossing the mountains. The Donner tragedy then played out in all of its mythic pathos: fecklessness and inefficiency led to fatal delays, marooning, starvation, death, cannibalism, and— for some—final deliverance. The tale included heroes too, the selfless Stanton being chief among them. James Reed led relief parties back to the immigrants' winter camp near Donner Lake. In the dead of winter three expeditions from Sutter's Fort crossed the mountains and brought back survivors. Sutter's attempts to save the Donner Party secured his well-deserved name as the immigrants' generous friend. "Often I sent them aid," Sutter recalled in his old age; but he also had a macabre reason for remembering his help to the Donner Party. "They killed and ate first the mules, then the horses, and finally they killed and ate my good Indians."[2]

Two villains stand out in the tragic story, Lansford Hastings and Louis Keseberg, one of the members of the Donner Party who was not rescued until the spring of 1847. Hastings got the blame for directing the Donner Party into the Wasatch Canyon, where so much time was lost. He was an easy mark for blame because of his reckless advertisements for an untried road, but if the Donner Party had been better led they could have made it safely across the mountains before winter. Californians unfairly reviled Keseberg as an enthusiastic cannibal, although he was only one of many to partake of human flesh. Like the others who ate their dead companions, Keseberg was driven to cannibalism by starvation, not epicurean taste. By chance, both men wound up in Sutter's employ in 1847.[3]

If James Reed, who managed to get his family out of the mountains, held Hastings responsible for the Donner tragedy, he did not let it get in the way of his business interests. In the spring he partnered with Hastings to buy a herd of cattle.[4] What was left of the Donner family may have been less forgiving. At the same time that Reed and Hastings dealt in cattle, three scantily dressed barefooted girls wandered among the tents and wagons in the immigrant encampment that had sprung up outside the fort's walls. One of them carried a thin blanket. "We are the children of Mr. and Mrs. George Donner," they said when begging. "And our parents are dead."[5]

While the Donner Party ate boiled leather and huddled against the bitter Sierra cold, a farcical controversy ensued among the American military leaders. General Stephen Watts Kearny arrived in California with 120 men in December. The general and his troops had quickly seized New Mexico and marched on to California with 300 men. En route he met Kit Carson, who was headed east with news of the conquest. After Carson told Kearny that California was already pacified, the general sent more than half of his force back to New Mexico and soldiered on. Much to his surprise, Kearny found California in the midst of a revolt. A force of californio lancers promptly defeated Kearny's exhausted and ill-mounted troops, but Commodore Stockton sent a force to the rescue. One might imagine that Kearny was mortified that his small army had to be rescued by a navy man, and worse humiliation was yet to come. Kearny carried orders from the secretary of war to assume the military governorship of California, but Commodore Stockton had already named himself military governor. Stockton and Frémont had become fast friends, so when the commodore left California he turned over the governorship to Frémont, who refused to defer to Kearny. This was too much for General Kearny, who sparred with Colonel Frémont over the governorship for several months. By March Kearny had won out, but hard feelings continued until he ordered Frémont back to Washington.[6]

California could ill afford the dispute between Kearny and Frémont. If californios were to be conciliated, as Kearny's orders required, the new regime had to take measures to control the Indian livestock raiding that had plagued all Californian ranchers for decades. During the war some raiders had taken the opportunity to attack unprotected herds. After the war the problem became worse. At the end of February Sacramento Valley settlers complained to Lieutenant Kern at Fort Sacramento that they would have to "abandon our farms and leave our property to the Murcy [sic] of the Indians [or] purhaps something worse."[7] Two weeks later Sheriff George McKinstry explained to the military government that a force of the "best men in garrison with carbines and lances" had recently marched north of Sutter's Fort to a "disturbed district." "The soldiers of this Garrison," McKinstry explained, "are Indians instructed in the Science of war by Capt J. A. Sutter for the past seven years and can be employed at one half the expense than white men can and are far preferable for the service." Formerly Sutter's Indian army had protected the valley, but now that "an enlightened nation has raised her Flag Capt Sutter will throw down the walls of his Fort . . . and as an American Citizen look to that Flag for protection."[8] Evidently Sutter fully expected the United States to take over the job of guarding northern California's livestock herds, for in June he discharged all but five of his Indian cavalry.[9]

Complaints about Indian raiders came from all over California to the governor's headquarters at Monterey. It was clear that something had to be done.[10] Wisely, Governor Kearny decided to employ men in the Indian service who knew the situation well. On April 7 he named Sutter to serve as Indian subagent for the Sacramento and San Joaquin Valleys. He ordered Sutter to apprise the Indians of the recent change of government. The Indians had recently caused trouble by "driving off horses & cattle & attacking small parties, at the Ranches & on the Road." Such conduct must cease, the governor declared, and "I am in hopes that by good advice & prudent council which your perfect acquaintance with them will enable you to give, they will be induced from giving further cause for complaint against them." Otherwise Kearny would send an army to punish them. Following long-established federal practice, Kearny intended to win the friendship of the Indians with gifts that he would eventually provide. The cash-strapped Sutter would receive $750 per year for his services.[11] One week later Kearny gave Mariano Vallejo a similar appointment for the district north of San Francisco Bay.[12]

Sutter's reminiscences are silent on his appointment as an American Indian subagent, but he must have been very pleased at the time. Here was a federal appointment and official recognition that he could render a valuable service to the new government. The title of "subagent" was not as prestigious as a military rank, but it was something. Although most people still called him by his honorific rank of captain, Sutter had lost all of his Mexican titles and authority (real and imagined), but this was something new to build on. Sutter promptly thanked Governor Kearny for the appointment, complimented him on the appointment of Vallejo, and reported on the men, horses, and munitions at the fort. Anticipating Kearny's orders, Sutter had ordered neighboring Indian leaders to come to the fort to inform them of the new state of affairs. His Indian soldiers were more dependable for protection against the horse thieves than white men, he informed the governor, and they were indispensable now because the Walla Wallas were still in the neighborhood. Sutter invited Kearny to visit the fort so that he could tell the governor more interesting things about the country.[13]

On June 12 Kearny and Frémont, traveling in separate parties, arrived at New Helvetia. They were on their way east, where Frémont would face a court-martial, although he did not yet know of Kearny's judicial plans for him. The feuding officers even camped at different places. The next day Captain Sutter, now restored to full authority over his fort, received Kearny with the usual military pomp: an eleven-gun salute from his ancient battery and a garrison parade. "A very pleasant Day," Sutter recorded in his diary.[14] Evidently Frémont chose not to visit the fort, or if he did Sutter did not bother to record it. Frémont settled up with the Walla Wallas, giving them "a lot of old broken down government horses, stamped U.S. which were roaming about the fort."[15] A couple of days later Sutter paid Peopeo Moxmox "for his private demands, and [was] presentet [sic] with a good Many things." The Oregon Indians "left contented and started homeward."[16]

The Indians may have seemed content to Sutter, but the Walla Wallas took an entirely different view of things. They had lost one of their men in the fighting, and Elijah Hedding's murder had not been avenged. To add to the poor herd that Frémont had given them, they raided Indian rancherías and American ranches on their way back to Oregon. It is not clear whether Sutter had given them the livestock he owed them from the previous year or tried to mollify them with other presents. As far as the Walla Wallas were concerned, these unsatisfactory developments reflected poorly on Frémont, Sutter, and the United States, which now controlled their destinies in Oregon too. The Walla Wallas complained about bad treatment in California when they returned to their homeland. These bad feelings contributed in some small measure to the Cayuse War that erupted there in 1847. The missionaries Marcus and Narcissa Whitman, with whom Sutter had supped in 1838, were the first victims of this war. Peopeo Moxmox was still complaining about his son's unavenged murder in 1855.[17]

Sutter's growing contentment stemmed in part from his influence with the military government's Indian policy. Acting on the advice of Sutter, Vallejo, and other old California hands, Governor Kearny and his successor, Colonel Richard Barnes Mason, promulgated a series of orders meant to quiet the Indian frontier in California. Recognizing the importance of Indian laborers, the governors' edicts required them to carry written passports, prevented them from "going about in crowds," and authorized regular patrols to enforce these regulations as well as to apprehend horse thieves. Military authorities, noticing that not all Indian laborers worked voluntarily, made some attempts to free Indians who were held in bondage. Sutter and Vallejo were expected to protect Indians from the abuse of their employers, but this was akin to assigning the wisest old foxes to patrol the chicken yard.[18]

In many ways these new regulations meant business as usual for Sutter, Vallejo, and their free and unfree Indian workers. Even though the Indians were afforded nominal legal protection, enforcement remained difficult at best. The subagents were not likely to blow the whistle on themselves or their friends and neighbors. But Sutter did report incidents that threatened the peace of the Sacramento Valley. On July 7 a Sacramento Valley settler reported to Sutter that Robert "Growling" Smith, John Eggar, and Antonio María Armijo, all from Sonoma, had visited a ranchería about sixty miles north of the fort. The Indians received them with hospitality and food.[19] Thirty minutes later the guests fell on their hosts without warning, murdered thirteen of them, and abducted thirty-seven as slaves. Sutter did not immediately report this outrageous assault to higher authorities. He waited five days until he received additional disturbing information. Two Mexicans, Rafael Altamirano and Lázaro Higuera, went to the Yusumne Nisenan ranchería on the Cosumnes River.[20] Altamirano and Higuera cruelly whipped the headman, Shululé, cut up his hat, and stole some horses that Lieutenant Warren Revere had left in the care of these loyal Indians. The humiliated Shululé complained to his patron Sutter, who ordered the arrest of his tormentors. They escaped.[21]

The presence of Nisenans in Miwok country requires some explaining. The rearrangement of Nisenan and Miwok geography was the result of Sutter's management of Indian affairs since 1839.[22] As some Miwok communities moved to New Helvetia in order to work for Sutter, former Miwok land and resources became available to his Nisenan allies. The Yusumne Nisenans moved their ranchería to the Cosumnes River near the present Slough House, probably at Sutter's command. Jared Sheldon had recently established a ranch on the Cosumnes River, and the Yusumnes no doubt worked for him. Shululé recognized that if anything was to be done about the whipping he had received, Sutter would have to do it.

Sutter appealed to Governor Mason, who seemed more concerned with the slavers than with the horse thieves. He ordered the return of the captured Indians and declared that "the safety of the frontier shall not be put at hazard by a few lawless villains." "The perpetrators of the outrage shall be made a public example of," he concluded.[23] California's first newspaper, the *California Star,* reported the incident in graphic detail and supported the apprehension and punishment of the perpetrators.[24]

Governor Mason was serious. In August Smith, Eggar, and Armijo were captured (although nothing more was heard of Altamirano and Higuera).[25] The governor ordered them to be tried at Sutter's Fort for "murder as well as the capturing and carrying off into slavery of several peaceful Indians."[26] He then appointed Sutter and Vallejo as judges and instructed them to impanel a jury of twelve men and to conduct a "full, fair and impartial trial."[27] On August 30 a military launch delivered Smith and Eggar to Sutter's embarcadero. Armijo could not come because he was too ill, possibly from a measles epidemic that was then sweeping the valley. Vallejo arrived on the same day, evidently in preparation for the impending trial. The next day, however, Sutter recorded that "[t]he trial has been postponed until the 18th October next on account of Armijo's illness and great distance to call the witnesses."[28] Vallejo, who probably could not get out of Sutter's Fort fast enough to suit him, departed for Sonoma that evening.

Armijo was not the only Californian to fall seriously ill in that fatal season. A large part of Sutter's Indian labor force sickened, and many died. The Walla Wallas and other Indians had measles when they returned to Oregon too, adding a major grievance that culminated in the Cayuse War. Captain Sutter went so far as to hire a physician, a shadowy character known to history only as Dr. Bates. The good doctor worked hard to cure Sutter's Indians, but with no good effect. Following customary medical practice, Dr. Bates bled his patients, a procedure that probably weakened them further and hastened the deaths of some.[29]

Indians died by the score, making it difficult for Sutter to bring in his wheat. "I am sorry to say that I will loose [*sic*] at least about 3000 fanegas of Wheat in the fields, on account [of] the prevailing decease among the Indians," Sutter told his neighbor William Leidesdorff in September.[30] This was a very large loss for Sutter, amounting to $6,000 that he could have applied to his Russian account, 26 percent of the remaining debt. Sutter needed 200 field hands, but "had hardly from 20 to 25 Indians. . . . The time has past when it could be depended on Indians, we need now cutting and thrashing machines, or it is not possible to raise large crops." The future might be bright with the flashing blades of agricultural machinery, but for the moment Sutter needed Indian labor. He called on all of his old Indian allies, but it was nearly hopeless until the epidemic abated. Even Dr. Bates got sick, although he recovered and returned to his rounds among the Indians. He paid special attention to Sutter's Indian allies—Anashe, Pollo, Homobono, Augustin, and others. But Sutter's demands for labor fostered the spread of the disease, as he called Indians to bring in his threatened wheat crop. When they became too ill to work, he sent them back to their rancherías, with devastating results. On September 28 Sutter sadly recorded that "Shulule a good and useful chief died."[31] Then he sent Augustin to take charge of Shululé's ranchería.

Of course Sutter cannot be blamed for measles or the lack of effective treatments in 1847. In fairness, we should acknowledge that he provided a physician to minister to the Indians, and he sometimes accompanied the doctor on his rounds. But concerned as he was with getting his wheat harvested, Sutter's standard labor recruitment practices facilitated the spread of the epidemic.

Sutter may have contracted measles himself, as he concluded not to go to Sonoma for the Smith, Armijo, and Eggar tribunal "on account of the inflamation [sic] in my eyes," a problem caused by measles in some patients.[32] This is Sutter's first reference to ill health. From that time on, his physical condition seems to have deteriorated. Gone were the days when he would spring to the saddle and dash after horse thieves. In his mid-forties, Sutter was still a young man by today's standards, but many observers noticed that he was using a cane. Alcohol abuse no doubt contributed to his physical decline. Malaria almost certainly had stricken him too; and quite likely his long hard life on the frontier had simply taken its inevitable toll. Whatever the causes, Sutter was noticeably enfeebled.

The trial at Sonoma went on without Sutter. Governor Mason had added Lilburn W. Boggs, formerly governor of Missouri and now alcalde of Sonoma, to the tribunal "in order to provide for cases that might otherwise arise out of differences of opinion between" Sutter and Vallejo."[33] In Sutter's absence, Vallejo and Boggs were in perfect agreement. They reported that a local jury acquitted the accused. According to the presiding judges, Sutter was at least partly responsible for the outcome. "Capt. Sutter did not even take an affidavit against these men until some time in the present month," the judges complained, and it was "very singular and imperfect."[34] Vallejo and Boggs said nothing about the difficulty of convicting the Sonoma men of crimes against Indians by a jury of their peers on their home turf in Sonoma. Vallejo took the trouble to inform the governor that the main causes of conflict in northern California were Indian laziness and alcoholism but offered no suggestions on what to do about whites who murdered and enslaved Indians.[35]

Sutter recovered sufficiently from his illness to make the best of his short-handed harvest and planned for a brighter future. In 1847 he developed two improvement schemes for New Helvetia. He wanted to build a water-powered gristmill on the American River a few miles upstream from the fort, approximately where California State University, Sacramento, now stands. Planning on a typically grandiose scale, he envisioned a large commercial mill with four runs of stones. This project, which would replace his old horse-driven mill, entailed the construction of ditches to power the mill and to irrigate his fields. If all went well, the project would be proof against drought and provide enough capacity to grind his neighbors' grain as well as his own. It was a good idea. The population of American California was sure to grow, and Sutter reasoned that they would eat bread made from Sacramento Valley wheat. He already had competition to think of. His neighbor Jared Sheldon was building a similar mill on the Cosumnes River.[36]

Sutter's second project is far better known to history: a water-powered sawmill on the south fork of the American River about thirty-five air miles from the fort. Sawn lumber was comparatively scarce in California, despite seemingly inexhaustible lumber resources in virgin redwood, pine, and fir forests. There were a few primitive sawpits on the coast, and Peter Lassen had built a small water-powered mill near Santa Cruz in 1841 or 1842 that Isaac Graham acquired. Part of Larkin's stock in trade included redwood lumber from Graham's modest mill and wherever else he could acquire it. In 1844 another entrepreneur imported a small steam engine to run a mill near Bodega Bay, but this venture produced little lumber. A few other small mills grew up near Santa Cruz, but lumber remained scarce in California and in the Pacific Islands, where colonization spurred demand for building materials.[37] Sutter had acquired a cache of finished lumber when he dismantled Fort Ross and Bodega, but that supply was long since exhausted. Tired of buying expensive lumber from Larkin and other merchants, he hoped to float his boards down the American River to New Helvetia and ship some to San Francisco Bay for sale.

In the summer of 1847 Sutter's estimation of the future seemed realistic; his schemes to produce food and building material were intelligent, even prosaic. Had he not amassed a mountain of debt in the past, his plans for the future would have had a can't-fail-Yankee-practicality-stick-to-basics air about them. To complete the mills, however, Sutter needed two things: someone with enough imagination and technical skill to build a mill and a reliable source of labor. In his first American season as proprietor of New Helvetia, he found both.

James Wilson Marshall was an unusual man by all accounts. Born in New Jersey, he combined mechanical knowledge and frontier experience with a moody disposition and eccentric ways. Sutter described him as "a very curious man, [who] quarreled with nearly everybody though I got along with him very well. He was a spiritualist. He dressed in buckskin and wore a serape. I thought him half crazy."[38] Most businesspeople would veer away from such a man, but he was useful to Sutter. Before the war "he made looms, ploughs, spinning wheels & all such work" at the fort. Sutter asked Marshall's advice about mill seats and construction. In the summer of 1847 they looked for appropriate sites, settling on one first identified by Samuel Kyburz in Koloma Nisenan country in the lower reaches of the Sierra pine forest on the banks of the wild American River. However, Sutter still lacked enough reliable workers for such a large-scale project.

The construction of Sutter's gristmill waited on the arrival of a competent and reliable labor force that materialized in his domain from an entirely unexpected source—the Mormon Battalion. This unusual military unit grew from the needs and fears of the American government in the early days of the Mexican-American War and the desperate plight of the Church of Jesus Christ of Latter-Day Saints (or Mormons as they were commonly called). In June 1846 President Polk authorized the formation of the battalion, in part to keep disaffected Mormons from supporting a supposed British plot to take California. Brigham Young and other Mormon leaders were interested in the arrangement because it would provide much needed cash for the impending migration of the Saints beyond the Rocky Mountains. Founded in upstate New York, the beleaguered church had been chased out of Missouri and Illinois. Under the leadership of Young, the main branch of the church was headed westward to an as yet unknown destination, while another band of Saints sailed to San Francisco. Eventually the two groups were supposed to link up, perhaps in California or elsewhere beyond U.S. boundaries.[39]

When the war broke out, thousands of Mormons were gathered in frontier refugee camps near present-day Omaha when Brigham Young decided to act favorably on President Polk's request for Mormon men to join Colonel Kearny's Army of the West, which was headed to New Mexico and California. It was a shrewd decision. The Mormons' prospective refuge was about to become part of the United States, and Young thought it wise to make a demonstration of patriotism. Five hundred men, young and old, untrained and entirely inexperienced in military matters, marched to join the Army of the West but wondered what would become of the destitute families they left behind at Council Bluffs. Nevertheless, the "Army of Israel," as Mormon historians came to call it, followed the Santa Fe Trail to New Mexico then built a wagon road across the southwestern deserts into southern California. Arriving after the fighting was over, the Mormon soldiers never fired a shot but provided much needed reinforcement for the small force of regular and irregular Americans who had conquered California.

In July 1847 the army discharged the Mormon Battalion in Los Angeles. The Mormon volunteers, anxious to restore themselves to the bosom of their families, set out for the Great Basin.[40] While one contingent took the Old Spanish Trail across the southern California desert, the largest group marched north to Sutter's Fort, planning to take the well-known California trail route across the Sierra to the Great Basin. They reached New Helvetia in August. Some tarried only long enough to get supplies before continuing up the emigrant trail. Sutter was glad to see customers with army pay in their pockets. He charged one dollar per hoof to shoe the Mormons' jaded horses. The traveling Saints bought coarse flour at $8.00 per sack and peas for $1.50 a bushel. Other Mormon Battalion veterans, lacking livestock and provisions, decided to work for Sutter, who "was offering pretty fair wages," according to one of them.[41] On August 26 a committee of Mormons went to Sutter asking about prospects for work. They were willing to wait for their pay until the following season, when they would go to Salt Lake. Best of all from Sutter's perspective, they would accept livestock and supplies for their wages.[42]

The Mormons were just the sort of workers that Sutter needed to complete his two big mill projects. "We had carpenters, blacksmiths, wheelwrights, millwrights, farmers, and common laborers," one of them recalled.[43] On August 27, the day after the Mormon committee called on Sutter, he and Marshall made a contract to construct his sawmill that obligated Sutter to supply all of the labor, supplies, and food.[44] Marshall provided the needed expertise and on-site management. They would split the profits. Like most of Sutter's deals, "[i]t cost me a great deal," he recalled.[45] On August 28 Sutter made contracts with as many as sixty Mormons to work on his mills and other projects.[46]

While these Mormons went to work for Sutter, others hurried eastward. On the trail at Truckee Meadows (the site of modern Reno) they met California's most prominent Mormon leader, Samuel Brannan, who was returning after a hurried meeting with Brigham Young. In 1846 Young and his advisors had sent Brannan and a shipload of Saints from New York to San Francisco Bay to scout out Mormon settlement opportunities there. Favorably impressed, Brannan had tried to convince Young to come to northern California with the whole body of Saints; but after seeing the Wasatch region, Young could not be moved. Brannan, soon to become an infamous Mormon excommunicant as well as one of Sutter's most costly business associates, was returning to California to run church affairs and attend to his own business concerns. A few hours later the anxious Mormon veterans met a courier with orders from Young: all men without families should remain in California for a season and make as much money as they could before going on to Salt Lake. There were not enough resources to support them at the newly founded Mormon community. The single men once again dutifully put church discipline and communal needs ahead of personal desires and turned their faces back to Sutter's Fort on September 8.[47]

Sutter had work for them, and lots of it. He engaged perhaps eighty of the Mormons to dig the races for his gristmill and agreed to pay then 12½ cents per cubic yard of earth moved, a bargain that earned each hard-working man about $1.50 per day.[48] As with the other Saints, these Mormons agreed to take their pay in livestock and supplies when they departed the following year.[49] This was a perfect deal for Sutter, who always preferred to trade in kind rather than cash. Impressed with the Saints' productivity, he sent some of them to help Marshall with the sawmill. There they joined Sutter's Indian and white workers, including some other Saints, non-Mormons Peter Wimmer and his wife (who cooked for the men), and the Wimmer children.[50]

The Mormons worked with a will, so much so that a few of them fell ill "on account [of] their working to[o] hard," Sutter recorded.[51] Some of them had the fever and chills characteristic of malaria, while others may have come down with the measles.[52] Sick or well, the Mormons were the most reliable employees that Sutter ever had, as he happily reported to his various correspondents. "The Mormons are the best workers I have," he told his old nemesis Vallejo in October; "without them the mills could not be made." His new workmen fueled Sutter's natural optimism. The sawmill would be completed "in a few weeks . . . the large flour mill we are getting ahead with . . . by the end of the month of December we shall finish up everything."[53] He gave similar reports to Larkin. Mormons worked in his other small factories as cobblers and tanners. "If I would have had Mormons 4 or 5 years past I would have a fortune," he enthused to the merchant, "but so long I am here I has only a few good men, the balance was a bad kind of people." Things were looking up for Sutter, who predicted that when the new mills were running "I will soon be out of my difficultys."[54]

Sutter put great faith in the new mills, especially the sawmill, but there were delays. Despite his assurances to his creditors, his Mormon workers were unable to complete the gristmill by the end of the year. Marshall was a clever man with competent helpers, but he had problems finishing the sawmill project, perhaps because he had never built such a complicated machine before. The races, other waterworks, and superstructure of the mill were essentially complete in mid-January, but the mill had been set too low. The water that coursed through the races was too high, a condition that prevented the waterwheel from turning. Marshall ordered his men to deepen and widen the tail race that carried water out of the mill works. At night the men closed the gates to the forebay to impound water above the mill. In the morning they opened the gates, and the water rushed through and scoured out the race, thus adding hydraulic assistance to the back-breaking pick and shovel work. Marshall then departed for Sutter's Fort for supplies. When he returned a few days later, he "found everything favorable, all the men being at work on the ditch."[55] The next morning, as usual, he inspected the tail race. It was January 24, 1848.

Late January was cold and rainy in the Sacramento Valley. Drenching rains and muddy roads made travel difficult, so the last thing that Sutter expected was to see Marshall on the wet afternoon of January 28. His arrival was all the more puzzling because Sutter had supplied him with everything he wanted for the mill just a few days before. Still, Sutter thought Marshall a "queer" man with peculiar ways, so nothing that the New Jersey millwright did was too surprising.[56] Marshall first met him in his small office near the fort's gate and demanded that they retire to Sutter's rooms in the big house at the center of the compound. The puzzled Sutter complied. Then Marshall asked him if they were alone and told him to lock the doors, a detail that Sutter did not take seriously. The distracted visitor asked for two bowls of water, a redwood stick, twine, and a piece of sheet copper. This was too much even for the forbearing Sutter. "What do you want of these things?" he asked.[57] Marshall, the mechanic, wanted to make some balance scales. "But I have scales enough in the apothecary shop," Sutter replied, and he fetched them. Marshall withdrew a rag from his pocket and opened it on Sutter's table, revealing about two ounces of native gold. At that moment an unsuspecting clerk entered the unlocked room; Marshall snatched the glittering stuff and returned it to his pocket. "Here!" Marshall exclaimed. "Did I not tell you that we had listeners?"[58]

Once the intruder was dismissed, Marshall again displayed his small cache of lustrous metal, "flaky & in grains, the largest piece not quite so large as a pea and from that down to less than a pin-head in size," Sutter recalled. "I believe this is gold," Marshall said, "but the people at the mill laughed and called me crazy."[59] "Well," Sutter opined, "it looks so; we will try it." They tested it with nitric acid, compared it with silver, and, using Sutter's encyclopedia as a guide, applied various tests. "I believe that this is the finest kind of gold," Sutter concluded.[60]

In after years Sutter claimed that the excited Marshall left immediately for the mines and that he himself followed the next morning.[61] Sutter's daily journal, however, shows that Marshall remained until the next morning and that Sutter left for the mill on February 1, camping at the gristmill dam that evening and arriving at the sawmill the following day. Sutter's delay is best explained by his conviction that the mines were probably not extensive and that he should attend to business at hand before going to the mountains for a few days. Marshall made good use of the three days while he waited for Sutter. He ordered the workmen to lay off two quarter sections of land (160 acres each), one above the mill and one below. Marshall intended these parcels to be preemption claims for Sutter and himself. Under federal law bona fide settlers could claim land that they occupied in the public domain. After laying off the quarter sections, the workers built a cabin on each, giving additional proof of Marshall's and Sutter's intentions to occupy their claims.[62]

When Sutter finally arrived, Marshall had prepared a surprise for him. For the past week the Mormon workers had been picking up loose gold while they were at work and in off hours. First skeptical of Marshall's find, they now realized that the stuff appeared to be scattered promiscuously; they had only to look for it. "And now boys," Marshall said, "we have all got a little gold." He proposed that they all scatter some of their flakes so that Sutter could find them. The result, Marshall hoped, would be predictable: "the old gentleman" would become so excited that he would "set out his bottle and treat, for he always carried his bottle with him."[63] Sutter was almost forty-five years old, only seven years older than Marshall, but his peers already thought of him as old. "Just as we finished breakfast," Henry Bigler recalled, "we saw the old gentleman coming hobbling along with his cane, Mr. Marshall on one side and Mr. Wemer [Peter Wimmer] on the other."[64]

The trick that was meant to loosen Sutter's grip on the bottle nearly failed when some of the Wimmer children prematurely picked up much of the gold that the Saints had salted in the tail race. After examining about fifty dollars' worth of gold in one child's hand Captain Sutter jammed his cane into the ground and declared: "By Joe! It is rich!" There was enough gold left for Sutter to find on his own, and, sure enough, he provided a bottle of liquor for his Mormon mill hands *cum* prospectors.[65] Sutter later had the find of that day fashioned into a heavy gold ring "with my family's coat of arms engraved on the outside, and on the inside . . . 'The first gold, discovered in January, 1848.' "[66]

Sutter asked his workers to keep quiet about the discovery for six weeks, the time he reckoned it would take to complete work on his flour mill. He feared that if word got out his mill would never be finished. The workers had little choice in the matter, "for every tool and all the provisions in that part of the country belonged to Capt. Sutter and Mr. Marshall, and they had full control," the Mormon James S. Brown recalled, adding: "we were depending on the completion of the mill for our pay."[67] The Mormons, who had not yet received a penny for their four months of labor, were agreeable. Marshall permitted them to mine in their spare time and promised them mining privileges once their mill work was done.

To protect their interests, Sutter and Marshall called in the Indians and executed a twenty-year lease for the mill site and surrounding country from the Yalisumni Nisenans for about $150 per year in goods. The Yalisumnis were not native to the area but came from downriver. Following his usual practice, Sutter had sent his loyal Indians to work for Marshall. The agreement should have been with the Koloma Nisenans; but under the terms of the indenture the Kolomas were not mentioned in the lease—nor was there any mention of gold. The partners eventually forwarded the lease to Governor Mason in the hope that he would recognize the validity of the agreement, thus giving Sutter and Marshall undisputed control of the Coloma (as it came to be known) gold mine. Sutter no doubt hoped that his post as Indian subagent would smooth the way for these questionable claims with the governor, especially if the preemption claims were disallowed.[68]

Firsthand accounts of Sutter's reaction to the Coloma gold discovery indicate that he was cautiously enthusiastic, although he had no idea of the extent or richness of California's gold deposits. Given his well-established propensity to see a prosperous future and silver linings in every cloud, one might reasonably suppose that Sutter immediately imagined a future for himself as the new Midas; but like all other Californians, he was slow to realize the immense richness and importance of the discovery. After all, this was not the first gold to be found in California. In 1842 a gold find at Placerita Canyon in southern California caused some local excitement, but the strike was insignificant, with no lasting effect. Sutter no doubt believed that the Coloma mines would be similar in richness and scope.

In early 1848 Sutter's goals were relatively modest: finish the mills, put New Helvetia's business affairs on a secure footing, pay off debts, monopolize and develop the gold mine that Marshall had found. Still, he must have regarded the find as a stroke of good luck when he pondered the meaning of this event on the ride back to the fort. How could the discovery of a source of specie be anything but good fortune in chronically cash-short California? Not so, Sutter said just nine years later. "On the way home, instead of feeling happy and contented, I was very unhappy, and could not see that it would benefit me much," he recalled, "and I was perfectly right in thinking so."[69] Gold, he explained to Bancroft in 1876, was not his salvation but his undoing. Even as Marshall showed Sutter those first glittering flakes, "the curse of the thing burst upon my mind. I saw from the beginning how the end would be."[70] Sutter's apocalyptic vision was likely a product of hindsight after his final California failures rather than an immediate flash of intuition. In 1848 he still had choices to make that would influence what the gold rush would mean for him and for his family.

CHAPTER 16

The Gold Rush Cometh

In February 1848 Sutter occupied an incomparably advantageous position for the exploitation of the newly discovered gold diggings. His herds and fields could feed thousands of miners. Sutter's mills, once completed, could help supply some of their needs for lumber and flour. His store was the largest trading house in the interior and was close to the mines. Just as importantly, Sutter was located on a navigable river that connected his enterprise with the port of San Francisco, giving him access to imported goods and international markets. The value of his land was bound to increase immensely. He had access to Indian labor, which he could employ to exploit his mining claim. He could sell or lease Indian workers to other miners, just as he had supplied rancheros with laborers. Sutter's position as federal Indian subagent lent official color to his control over the Indians, if not actual legal authority to exploit them. He had executed a lease with the Indians that, if recognized, gave him and Marshall a legal claim to the Coloma diggings. He was arguably the best-known Californian of his time. Most overland immigrants had passed through New Helvetia upon their arrival, and they would go through there again on the way to and from the mines. Any one of these advantages, if properly managed, might have resulted in a fortune for Sutter. And yet he squandered all of them.

Marshall's crew finished the sawmill as they promised, but word about the gold discovery soon leaked out. Not surprisingly, Sutter could not keep such a delicious secret for long. One week after returning from Coloma, he let the cat out of the bag in a letter to Vallejo, who had asked Sutter to sell him a still. Sutter replied that he needed the apparatus, but he could not resist gloating about his gold mine. His sawmill was finished, and everything was moving forward. "And," he added, "I have made a discovery of a gold mine, which so far as we have examined it, is extraordinarily rich."[1]

Sutter revealed the "secret" to others. Around mid-February he decided to share his knowledge of gold with some of the men at the fort. After dinner he produced a dirty rag containing grains of gold. The incredulous guests began to wonder if it was truly gold and prevailed on the blacksmith to carry out some crude tests that convinced them that it was indeed gold. "Gold, gold, gold, it's gold, boys, it's gold!" one of them cried. "All of us will be rich. Three cheers for the gold!" Evidently this was the agreeable effect that Sutter had hoped the gold would produce. "My secret has been discovered," he said. "Since we expect to be rich, let's celebrate with a bottle of wine."[2] Sutter produced a bottle that was quickly emptied, which, indeed, may have been his goal of the moment.

All of the evidence points to Sutter as the first to reveal the gold discovery, but he blamed others. According to his recollection, about two weeks after he returned from Coloma he sent some wagons to resupply Marshall. Several Indian boys drove the teams, and Sutter sent teamster Jacob Wittmer to supervise them. When the caravan arrived at Coloma, the Wimmer children told Wittmer that they had found gold, but he did not believe them. According to Sutter, Mrs. Wimmer confirmed the boys' story, saying, "Look here, what do you call that?" In Sutter's retelling of the story, Mrs. Wimmer became one of many authors of his tragic undoing. "This woman little knew the consequences to me of this thoughtless wagging of her tongue," he complained.[3]

Wittmer acquired a small hoard of gold, took it back down to the fort, and entered Charles C. Smith's store in one of Sutter's outbuildings. Smith claimed to be related to the Mormon prophet Joseph Smith. His partner in this enterprise was Samuel Brannan, the nominal leader of California Mormons and publisher of the *California Star,* a new weekly newspaper published in San Francisco (as Yerba Buena was now grandly called). Sutter sneeringly called Smith and Brannan's modest operation a "shirt-tail" store that assumed importance only after the gold rush began in earnest. "Women and whiskey helped the thing along," he added cattily; but he also noted that he sometimes purchased things for the Indian trade from Smith and Brannan. Wittmer knew what he wanted with his newfound wealth. He called for a bottle of brandy at the counter, where Smith was tending the meager bar. According to Sutter, the "shirt-tail" store never sold liquor on credit, because "[t]hat was altogether too choice an article to be sold on time."[4] Wittmer laid his dust on the counter, and Sutter recounted the following conversation:

"What is that? You know very well liquor means money," exclaimed brother Smith. "That is money," replied the teamster. "It is gold." "Damn you, do you mean to insult me?" roared Smith. "Go to the fort and ask the captain if you don't believe me." Smith came in hot haste and said, "Your man came to me and said that this is gold. Of course I knew he lied and told him so." "Nevertheless, it is gold" said I, and the secret was out.[5]

The strict accuracy of this conversation, most of which Sutter did not hear in the first place, cannot be vouched for. But it captures a dramatic moment and demonstrates one of Sutter's most charming characteristics: his ability to tell a good story while completely ignoring his own culpability in revealing the "secret." Smith passed on the news to Brannan.

Sutter's recollections revealed a man convinced that gold would cause his ruin; but prospects seemed bright whenever he mentioned gold at the time of discovery, and rightly so. He possessed every advantage. On February 8 he sent Charles Bennett, one of the sawmill workers, to Monterey to assert Sutter's and Marshall's preemption claims before Governor Mason. Bennett, who carried a few ounces of California gold folded in a sheet of paper, proved to be no more tight-lipped than his employer. He was in Benecia, a new town on the north side of Carquinez Strait, when he overheard some men talking about the discovery of a coal mine on the slopes of Mount Diablo. Coal seemed poor stuff to Bennett, who could not resist revealing the discovery of a gold mine, offering as proof dust from his own pocket. He pressed on with his errand to Monterey but left men in his wake who pondered the meaning of the few golden grains they had seen. In San Francisco Bennett met Isaac Humphrey, a man with experience in the Georgia gold mines and Illinois lead mines. They evidently had a meeting of the minds, so Humphrey accompanied Bennett to the governor's office in Monterey, where they asked young Lieutenant William T. Sherman, Mason's secretary of state, for a private interview with Governor Mason.[6]

Once sequestered in the governor's office, Bennett gave Mason a letter from Sutter explaining that he was building a sawmill at Coloma at great expense to himself and for the general benefit of the settlers in that vicinity. He had found gold in the millrace and wanted a preemption to the quarter section that embraced it. Bennett unfolded his paper and displayed the gold on the table. Humphrey, the experienced miner, no doubt vouched that the exhibit was indeed placer gold. Mason called Sherman into his office and asked him to identify the substance on the table. As Sherman fingered the ore, Mason asked:

"Is it gold?" Sherman replied that he had seen native gold in Georgia in 1844, although it was not as coarse as Bennett's sample. Sherman bit one of the larger pieces, "and the metallic lustre was perfect." The lieutenant then asked his clerk to bring an axe and a hatchet from the yard. "I took the largest piece and beat it out flat, and beyond doubt it was metal, and a pure metal." Although Mason and Sherman were convinced that the stuff was gold, neither of them thought it was very important. They knew of the small gold mine in southern California and considered it to be of little value. This new find was doubtless of similar quality and worth.[7]

The governor then turned to the matter of preemption rights and ordered Sherman to draft a letter to Sutter.[8] Mason did not know that the American and Mexican negotiators had concluded the Treaty of Guadalupe Hidalgo just a few days before. That news would not reach California for months. California was still a Mexican province that the United States held by mere conquest, the letter explained, and the federal land laws did not yet apply. Once the United States assumed sovereignty, a preemption claim could be made only after a public survey. Consequently the governor could not guarantee a preemption, although the isolated location of the mill made it unlikely that Sutter would be disturbed by trespassers. Mason's assumption that isolation would protect Sutter's interest in the new gold mine seems naive today. Within months Coloma would become one of the best-known spots on the globe and the destination for thousands of gold seekers from virtually every nation; but this outcome would have seemed mere fantasy to anyone in California in February 1848.

Sutter may have taken some comfort in this letter, for Mason did not dispute Sutter's right to build a mill or to dig for gold. The general practice of the military government was to maintain Mexican laws until further notice, but Mason made no attempt to apply Mexican mineral law in Sutter's case. The mill seat was far beyond the elastic boundaries of Sutter's grant no matter how hard he stretched them, so he had no reasonable claim to it under Mexican law. For the time being, his mill and mine were in legal limbo.

Most accounts of Bennett's trip emphasize that Sutter did not reveal the existence of gold to the governor. According to Sherman's reminiscence, however, Sutter frankly revealed the gold find to the governor and even sent a sample with Bennett expressly to support his claim. Maybe Sutter believed that the find would strengthen his preemption claim.[9] Neither Sutter's letter nor Mason's letter has come to light, so this will remain a matter of conjecture until conclusive evidence is discovered.

Mason's refusal to approve a preemption claim did not entirely close the door. After learning of the governor's decision, Sutter wrote a second letter to

Mason on February 22. This time he enclosed his January 1 lease with the Yalisumnis, which embraced several square miles of land surrounding the mill. The lease permitted Marshall and Sutter to build a sawmill "and other machinery for their purpose," cultivate the land, and so forth. The twenty-year arrangement, Sutter argued, was good for the Indians, who would "learn habits of industry." The lease did not specifically mention gold but claimed there were indications of silver and lead.[10] He may have mentioned lead because for decades the United States leased lead lands to miners. Congress had abandoned this policy in 1847, but Sutter and Marshall were probably unaware of this change in federal law. Hoping his new ploy would secure his claim to Coloma, Sutter placed the letter and lease in the hands of Bennett and sent him to Monterey, perhaps accompanied by the trustworthy George McKinstry.

While Sutter waited for Mason's reply, Marshall and his men got the sawmill running in early March. It still needed some work, but the mill soon began producing boards. Sutter hoped that this would enable him to produce the lumber needed to finish the gristmill downstream. Like many of his other schemes, one part depended on another; if one element failed, the whole plan fell apart. As he waited for Governor Mason's reply, Sutter's plan began to unravel. As long as the gristmill remained unfinished, Sutter sent his wheat to Sheldon's mill on the Cosumnes River. From January through March wagon after wagon left New Helvetia laden with wheat and returned with sacks of flour.[11] Looking forward to the opening of his own mill, Sutter hired the miller away from Sheldon on January 24. This ill-advised move no doubt antagonized Sheldon. In March Sutter was galled to learn that Sheldon was charging him more than other farmers for wheat grinding. Sutter's bad credit justified Sheldon's double standard. "You consider my pay not so good as Mr. Cordua's who get it ground at 50 cents per fanega," Sutter complained, "and you charge me one dollar per fanega." Understandably miffed, he could not fathom why this should be the case. Things had changed. "Everything which I have to dispose of, and which I sell, is all understood Cash price," he told Sheldon, "because it is no more like formerly, trade and Cash price."[12]

Somehow Sutter thought that the evolving money economy should work to his benefit, even though he was the biggest debtor in the country. The opposite was true. He was better off when he could endlessly renegotiate his debts and the schedule for payment. In the days before the gold rush began, he simply failed to grasp that the new economy placed him at a disadvantage. Jared Sheldon understood Sutter's position perfectly. If Sutter wanted credit, he would have to pay for it, and at a steep rate too.

In March Sutter got bad news from Governor Mason.[13] "The United States do not recognize the right of Indians to sell or lease the lands on which they reside . . . to private individuals." Mason, who was still unaware of the Treaty of Guadalupe Hidalgo, reasoned that the federal government would no doubt follow its usual practice and negotiate treaties with the Indians in order to extinguish their rights to the land, which would become "at once part of the public domain."[14] Although the governor did not mention gold, Mason's letter made it plain that Sutter had no greater right to gold-bearing lands than anyone else did. Mason's opinion followed the federal Indian and land laws of the time. But he did not order Sutter to leave lands that could reasonably be assumed to be in Indian country. Under federal law, no one had a legal right to mine on lands that were still in Indian hands; but in reality there was no military or police power in California that could stop it.[15]

Not long after Mason dashed Sutter's hopes for a monopoly on the gold mine at Coloma, it began to dawn on Sutter that his gristmill might never be finished. In March lumber from Coloma began to arrive at the flour mill site, sometimes called Natomas, meaning upstream or east in Nisenan.[16] Unbeknownst to Sutter, Mormons from the sawmill had told their co-religionists at the gristmill about the gold. Moreover, after prospecting for themselves in their spare time, some of them had located new mining sites downstream from Coloma, outside the area of Sutter and Marshall's supposed preemption claim. In early March two steady Mormon hands "[Wilford] Hudson & S[idney]. Will[e]s left for the mountains with the intention to work in a Gold Mine," Sutter recorded.[17] After visiting their friends at Coloma and finding gold flakes there, Hudson and Willes located a rich strike on the south fork of the American River about fifteen miles west of Coloma, a place that became known as Mormon Island. Mormons now began to wash gold in diggings that Sutter and Marshall did not claim for themselves. This placer find proved to be much more abundant and richer than deposits at Coloma.

With Mormons locating their own claims, it became clear that Sutter and Marshall should systematically work their Coloma mine. On April 2 Sutter, Marshall, Isaac Humphrey ("a regular miner"), and Peter Wimmer (one of the non-Mormon sawmill laborers) agreed to mine the Sutter-Marshall claim. Sutter "furnished Indians, teams and provisions to this Company" and sent them to the mountains on the following day. About this time some of Sutter's employees and neighbors began to go up the American fork to see what the gold mines were all about.[18]

The gristmill was still unfinished, and it was increasingly difficult to get hands to work. On April 10 some of the Mormon Battalion veterans began to settle their accounts with Sutter, because they were anxious to return to their families at Salt Lake. When they departed, all hope of finishing the mill went with them.[19] Sutter paid the Mormons entirely in livestock and provisions, rather than partly in cash as he had first promised. Nevertheless, he claimed: "In settling accounts [with the Mormons] I had not a word of difficulty with any of them."[20] Not all Mormon memories of the transaction were as green as Sutter's. "I worked 100 days for the [Sutter and Marshall] firm," complained James Brown, "and never received one farthing for it."[21] Sutter excused himself by saying that his bookkeeper had run off to the mines. Many Mormon Battalion veterans went to mine at Mormon Island. Because snow blocked the Sierra passes, they did not leave for the Great Basin until the end of June.

While some of Sutter's workers deserted so that they could try their hands at mining, a few continued to work on the gristmill. New faces began to appear at New Helvetia. The *Californian* reported the discovery on March 15, and the *California Star* followed suit three days later.[22] When word first leaked out, Californians discounted the news about gold. After all, nothing much had come of a minor gold discovery in southern California a few years before. This new find, if it truly was gold, would doubtless prove to be similarly limited in scope; it was nothing to get excited about—or so it seemed in late winter. That cautious estimate of California's mineral wealth was about to change.

Sam Brannan, Sutter's mercantile competitor and publisher of the *California Star*, would be instrumental in the adjustment of public opinion, but even he required some convincing. Brannan, a shrewd businessman, visited the fort from April 7 to 10, conferring with his partner in the New Helvetia store and listening to Sutter's Mormon Battalion workers.[23] Brannan was not excited by what he saw and returned to San Francisco. In mid-April his nineteen-year-old editor, Edward Kemble, went up to the Coloma mines with Sutter and Reading to see if the rumors of gold were credible. As the first newspaperman at the site of the discovery young Kemble had a chance to make journalistic history. What he saw, however, convinced him that the stories of golden riches in the mountains were humbug. Sutter's workmen unhelpfully told him that he might find gold "anywhere you're a mind to dig for it," but Kemble found none. Reading had scarcely better luck and washed out only a few pennies' worth in an Indian basket. Upon his return to San Francisco Kemble reported that there was gold, but nothing of great importance. He would spend the rest of his life trying to explain why he had missed the opportunity to scoop the world on the beginnings of the greatest gold rush in history. Kemble's failure to recognize the importance of the Coloma strike may be chalked up to the inexperience of youth, but there was another reason for his pessimism about the Coloma mine. "No gold washing was being done—no rocker at work—no sign of the rich placer afterwards developed was manifest anywhere," Kemble recalled more than thirty years later. "Reading (who was something of an expert besides being a cultivated gentleman) and Sutter both held the prospect of extensive diggings in rather cheap estimation, and I (being a boy of nine-teen) took my view of the situation from theirs. I saw nothing—'yet all there *was* (visible) I saw.' "[24]

Kemble did not say so, but it looks like Sutter and Reading were prejudicing the young newspaperman against mining prospects. Sutter had every reason to promote a negative view of the discovery among the California reading public. With no superior legal claim to the Coloma site, he wanted it to remain isolated to reduce competition. Perhaps the "regular miner" Humphrey, who was now working the claim with Marshall, explained the undesirability of revealing the extent of the claim or the means for working it. Such prudence was uncharacteristic of Sutter when left to his own devices.

Sutter gladly told others that the mines were valuable. "We intend to form a company for working the Gold mines which prove to be very rich," he told his neighbor William Leidesdorff, "would you not take a share in it?"[25] As always, Sutter had a different story for every audience. A mining partnership might have enabled him to write off part of his debt with Leidesdorff. Leidesdorff also had the task of collecting the long-overdue Russian-American Company debt. Sutter may have hoped to gain new influence with his creditors through Leidesdorff, but it was not to be. Within a month Leidesdorff died at the age of thirty-eight, but the Russian contract with Sutter remained very much alive.

In mid-April the Willes brothers went to San Francisco and told Brannan about the new find at Mormon Island, which appeared to be richer and more easily worked than the Coloma mines. The possibilities now began to intrigue Brannan. He first appealed to the Mormons' piety. According to Henry Bigler, Brannan asserted that he could somehow "secure the mine as church property and advised for all the Battalion boys to go to work in the mine and pay one-tenth to him and he would turn it over to the church as their tithing, with the understanding" that Brannan would get a share of the Willes claim.[26] The gullible Willes agreed to Brannan's outrageous proposition, and so did many of the Mormon Island miners, although there is some confusion about whether Brannan tithed for the church or merely cut himself in on the deal. By this time Brannan was tiring of leading the Mormon flock in California, and many Mormon faithful had long been complaining about the quality of his leader-ship. Yet Brannan's desire to capitalize on the Mormon discovery and the Mormons' wish to be faithful servants of the church briefly united in the making of one of California's first gold-rush millionaires.

Brannan decided to see for himself what glittering possibilities lay in the unity of God and mammon. On his way to the diggings he cadged a horse from Stephen Cooper. He told Cooper, "I know the biggest speculation in the world, and if there is anything in it, on my return I will let you into the secret," and rode off on the borrowed horse.[27] He passed through Sutter's Fort on May 4 and rode on to Mormon Island. "While there," Azariah Smith reported, "Brannan called a me[e]ting, to see who was willing to pay toll and who was not."[28] Most of the devout miners, including Smith, were willing and ponied up 30 percent of their take: 10 percent each to Hudson and Willes, the discoverers, and 10 percent to Brannan for his unspecified services in securing the mine for the church. Willes alone paid thirty dollars, so Brannan's purse was full of gold when he returned to Sutter's Fort.

Sutter reported: "Mr. Brannan visited the new town where he intend[s] to build a Warehouse & a store."[29] The "new town," scarcely more than a few tents and shanties, had already sprung up spontaneously at Sutter's Sacramento River embarcadero, the most convenient spot to offload goods from San Francisco. This low spot near the mouth of the American River was not Sutter's choice for a permanent town, because it was subject to winter floods. Indeed, all one had to do was look up in the trees to see the flotsam deposited by previous inundations. Knowing this, Sutter had laid out Sutterville on high ground a few miles below. Sutterville had a few small buildings, but there was no way for cargo to be landed there. Already the demands of the first miners forced the use of the old embarcadero and fostered the erection of whatever rude structures were needed to facilitate commerce. Brannan recognized immediately that an inferior natural site that could be used at once was better than a superior place requiring time-consuming and expensive improvements. While Sutter tried to keep up business as usual, Brannan and others planned for the new era that was already upon them.

Having secured a site for his warehouse, Brannan was in a great hurry to return to San Francisco. He rode hard and broke down the horse that he had borrowed from Cooper. He exchanged it for another, ran it into the ground, got another, and finally arrived at Cooper's place. "He told me that he had stood over a man five minutes, and in that time had seen him wash out $8.00," Cooper recalled, "and remarked that there was more gold than all the people in California could take out in fifty years."[30] Brannan pressed on to San Francisco. The hard trip had not diminished his enthusiasm. Benjamin Hawkins, a Mormon Battalion veteran, saw Brannan take his hat off and swing it, shouting in the dusty streets that gold had been found.[31] Brannan, equipped with plenty of gold as proof for the incredulous, convinced the villagers that the golden millennium was at hand. By this time the existence of gold was generally known, but he persuaded them that it was a big thing, maybe the biggest thing in the world. He particularly urged the Saints to be off to the mines. Many of them dutifully obeyed their leader, left their San Francisco occupations, and headed for Mormon Island.[32]

Sutter was entirely unprepared for the rush of would-be miners that followed, small as it was compared to the mighty influx of people who would come in 1849. Towns and ranchos emptied, and their former residents coalesced into a steady parade to the mines. Virtually all of the hopeful men (and a very few women) passed through Sutter's Fort, yet he was not able to sell them much in the way of provisions. The little "shirt-tail" store of Brannan and Smith, however, did a booming business in the small structure outside the fort. Brannan tried to corner whatever goods there were in San Francisco and sent them to his New Helvetia store. Sutter had a three-month head start but did nothing to get a jump on the commerce that was likely to follow when news of gold got out. Why? First, laying in a new stock of goods would have required Sutter to purchase from Larkin, Leidesdorff, and other merchants on credit, and he was already overextended. He said that he had invested twenty-four thousand or twenty-five thousand dollars in his gristmill alone; most of this consisted of goods and supplies bought on credit and promises to pay his workers. Second, if only he could finish his gristmill, he had a reasonable hope of supplying flour to miners as well as to Russians. When the gristmill failed to materialize, Sutter had no fall-back plan.

For two months Sutter struggled to keep his agricultural operations going, but the old familiar patterns were passing away. Life at the fort was changing too. His trusted lieutenants such as Bidwell, McKinstry, and Reading quickly caught onto the new world of gold and went into mining or other ventures. From this point they would work infrequently for their old employer and only on a part-time basis. Newcomers had no interest in working for Sutter, who quickly lost control over the rough mining society that emerged. Drinking and drunkenness were not innovations at New Helvetia. Formerly Sutter had controlled the supply of liquor and claimed that he limited drinking at the fort. In 1848 he lost control of liquor sales as new merchants and sources of supply came to New Helvetia. "A good Many people here pretty well corned," Sutter noted in his journal in February.[33] "Drinking going on briskely," he wrote in March.[34]

Friends and foes alike noticed Sutter's pattern of daily heavy drinking during this period. This apparently more advanced phase of alcoholism may have come on gradually due to a lifetime of drinking or because of the easy availability of strong spirits since he had built a whiskey still in 1845.[35] Heinrich Lienhard, the young Swiss sojourner who idolized his famous countryman when he arrived in 1846, soon learned that his hero had a destructive weakness. Sutter employed the likely young man as an overseer, who went to Sutter's private rooms daily for instructions during the period when the mills were under construction. "Since Sutter was addicted to strong drink, he believed everyone else had the same tastes," Lienhard observed. "Morning after morning, when I went to his room for the daybook, he urged me to sample his whisky, and he never failed to set me an excellent example." The young overseer returned the daybook in the evening. "At this time another drink was forced on me."[36] Sutter's hard drinking was one of the reasons why Lienhard became disenchanted with his employer. The captain was frequently drunk in public and sometimes so incapacitated that he had to be helped to bed.[37]

Alcoholic torpor was not a condition that served Sutter well as the rush for gold grew. Men who were shrewder, more ruthless, and much less scrupulous soon ruled the day. Brannan led the pack, and the fort was soon overrun with them. Sutter's entries in the daily journal tell the story:

May 15: "Mr Hoeppner & Dr Heyermann and a good many others arrived from Sonoma, bound for the Gold Mines."

May 16: "Hardy left for the Gold Mines. A small Launch arrived with a many passengers and some Goods. Mr Brannan, Mr McDonnald, Everhard and others arrived, and a launch close by."

May 17: "Doctor Heyermann, Mr Hoeppner and a many others left for the Mountains." "Cleaned and white washed the Magasin (penitentiery) and rented the whole to C. C. Smith & [Brannan] Co. for a store."

May 18: "Some families arrived from San francisco bound for the Mountains. Getting Goods from the Landing for C. C. Smith & Co."

May 19: "Arrived Messrs Norris, Ward and a great many others, all bound for the Mountains." "Despatched 3 Wagons to the Mountains for Mr Brannan. Getting planks for him from the Landing place."

May 20: "Continually new arrivals from Sonoma, San francisco & Pueblo de San José. Dispatched two Wagons for Mr Brannan to the Mountains."

May 21: "Messrs Brannan & Ward left for the Mountains with Comock." "Continually people arriving from below." "C. C. Smith & Co., moved the store in the large Granary to make Room to Mr Kyburz to establish a Boarding house. A good many people here, a pleasant day."

May 22: "Continually people arriving by water & land, and going up to the Gold regions." "Mr Kyburz left my Services and established a boarding house in the old Baquero house, Olimpio entered in my service as Key Keeper."

May 23: "People arriving from below by Water and by land, bound for the Mountains, a fine day."

May 24: "More and more people comming bound for the Mountains."

May 25: "A number of people continue travelling to the Mountains."[38]

May 25 was Sutter's last entry in the daily journal. This date marks the effective demise of New Helvetia.

"The fort was then a veritable Bazaar," Sutter declared when recalling the earliest days of the gold rush; but it was not his bazaar. In 1848 his only financial hope was to make the gold rush work for him. One of Sutter's most valuable assets was possession of the only trading post within a day of the mines. Instead of capitalizing on his advantage by maintaining control over this strategic enterprise, he rented rooms in the fort to merchants and saloonkeepers. He leased his competitive advantage to his most ruthless and effective competitor, Samuel Brannan, and leased the fort's large central building to Samuel Kyburz, who converted it into a hotel. In return the cash-hungry Sutter received monthly rents, but he lost one of his chances to exert some control over the tumultuous events that followed. A few years later Sutter recollected that "Mr. Brannan was erecting a very large Warehouse, and [he has] done an immense business."[39] He always argued that Brannan took unfair advantage of him, but how? Sutter freely made bad deals with Brannan and others then complained when things did not work out better. Alcoholism partially explains his bad judgment and inattention to business matters, but it does not remove from his shoulders the responsibility for his failings.

Sutter finally realized that he could not continue to operate New Helvetia as usual and hope for the best. On June 1 Lansford Hastings told his friend McKinstry that "Capt. Sutter agrees to go into the go[ld bu]siness as soon as his crops are har[vested] which is perhaps the best course."[40] Sutter did not wait for the harvest and could not. "I began to harvest my wheat, while others was digging and washing Gold, but even the Indians could not be keeped longer at Work."[41] The faithful Olimpio remained with Sutter, and he managed to keep some Indian ferrymen working at the embarcadero by paying them "after deduction for a few bottles of brandy."[42] But Sutter's herds and fields were untended, the gristmill went unfinished, and hides rotted in the tanning vats. The old New Helvetia was utterly finished by June 1848.[43]

Sutter remained at the fort through July and part of August. Perhaps he was relying on the profits from his partnership with Marshall, Humphrey, and Wimmer, although he eventually pulled out of this arrangement, saying that "I was loosing [*sic*] instead [of] making something."[44]

In July Governor Mason, Lieutenant Sherman, and several other officers and soldiers passed through Sutter's Fort on their way to inspect the mines. The gold rush had already caused trouble for the military government. So many soldiers had deserted for the mining districts that there were not enough troops to pursue them.[45] Desertions continued, and Mason eventually did not have enough men to carry on the work of the military government. The governor's retinue arrived at the fort just before the Fourth of July, and Sutter insisted that Mason stay long enough to celebrate the holiday. Sam Kyburz, the fort's new hotelier, put out a holiday dinner for his distinguished guests. Sherman remembered that "after a substantial meal and a reasonable supply of *aguardiente* we began the toasts." Sherman's recollections were a little foggy after the passage of years, but he remembered that Sutter spoke, along with several others. Captain Sutter, Sherman reported in his memoirs, was "tight" on that occasion, a term that he changed to "enthusiastic" in later editions of his book after Sutter complained about it in 1875.[46]

Well refreshed and suitably inspired by the patriotic occasion, the governor and his staff continued to the mines. Mormon Island was the first stop. They noticed that some miners were using a machine commonly called a cradle or a rocker to wash out gold. "With this rude machine four men could earn from forty to one hundred dollars a day," Sherman thought.[47] Brush huts served as stores, boardinghouses, and cabins. The influx of non-Mormon miners had diluted the exclusively Mormon character of the mining settlement, but the Saints were still much in evidence. One of them, identified by Sherman as Mr. Clark, asked Governor Mason: "What business has Sam Brannan to collect the tithes here?" "Brannan has a perfect right to collect the tax," Mason replied, "if you Mormons are fools enough to pay it." Sherman claimed that was the end of Brannan's tithing at Mormon Island. More importantly, the governor went on to say that "this is public land, and the gold is the property of the United States; all of you here are trespassers, but as the Government is benefitted by your getting out the gold, I do not intend to interfere."[48] With this statement the governor gave everyone a license to mine gold without fee or special authority; neither Brannan nor Sutter had any special rights in the matter. Sadly, under

Mason's interpretation the Indians had no special rights that miners ought to respect. The Indians of California would pay a heavy price for Mason's openhandedness.[49]

Mason forged on to Coloma and other placer diggings that independent miners had established nearby. "We spent nearly a week in that region," Sherman recalled, "and were quite bewildered by the fabulous tales of recent discoveries, which at that time were confined to the several forks of the American and Yuba Rivers."[50] Mason's official report, sober and factual, could not mask his amazement. He made particular note of the advantages of employing Indian labor. On Weber Creek just below Coloma, Antonio Suñol, Sutter's longtime creditor, "had about thirty Indians employed, whom they pay in merchandise." Some employers of Indians had truly become rich overnight. A former employee of Sutter amassed $10,000 in profit in one week after paying off his workforce of a hundred Indians. Sutter's neighbor John Sinclair netted $16,000 employing sixty Indians who washed gold in willow baskets. Using fifty Indian workers, Job Francis Dye of Monterey and his partners had gotten 236 pounds of gold in seven weeks. "Large quantities of goods were daily sent forward to the mines, as the Indians, heretofore so poor and degraded have suddenly become the consumers of the luxuries of life." Sam Brannan's Coloma store had taken in some $26,000 by July 10 in payment for goods. Mason estimated that there were four thousand miners "in the gold district, of whom more than half were Indians; and that from $30,000 to $50,000 worth of gold, if not more, was daily obtained."[51]

Sutter's name was not mentioned among the new men of wealth that Mason found in the mines. Yet his friends, neighbors, former employees, competitors, and strangers were piling up fortunes by using the Indian labor force that Sutter had formerly employed. Indian labor and Indian trade put tens of thousands of dollars into other people's pokes every day. Why not Sutter? By all accounts Sutter had more influence among the Indians than anyone else did. Why did he not press this obvious advantage?

The most probable answer is that he thought he was making use of his Indian workers by forging partnerships with others and sending them to the mines. Heinrich Lienhard is a good example. "One August day Sutter spoke to me about going into a partnership with him in the mines, saying I could take all the Indian boys I wanted, and that he would supply all of the food, working equipment, and other necessary things in return for half of all the gold found."[52] Lienhard agreed in part because Sutter now owed him $900 and the partnership was the only way he would get his money. Sutter said he knew of a rich claim downstream from Mormon Island and that an Indian there would identify it. So Lienhard took seven Indians and a wagonload of provisions to the place that Sutter had generally identified. No Indian guide appeared, so Lienhard went on to Mormon Island.

By now Mormon Island was a dangerous community that included many of the rough customers who had plagued Sutter at the fort. They bullied Lienhard, stole from him, and even shanghaied the Indian boy who cooked for him. Lienhard acquired a rocker, and his Indians soon washed out $600 worth of dust. Sutter still owed him $900, but the young Swiss dutifully separated Sutter's share from his pile and sent it off to him.[53] Sutter gave Lienhard the impression that his partnership with the young man was a mark of special respect and gratitude for his loyalty. Lienhard later learned that Sutter made many similar arrangements; in fact, "he gave them to everyone as readily as he did to me."[54]

Not everyone was as successful or honest as Lienhard, who made it a point to learn some of the Indian language. Sutter's other partners "washed all their gravel in pans, were unaccustomed to hard work, and the natives could not understand what they said."[55] Poor judgment in the selection of business partners was a hallmark of Sutter's repeated failures. Once he decided to get into the mining game he was content to let others do the work with his Indians in return for a share of the take, but he failed to go to the mines to oversee his many partnerships. Thus he relied on the word of men he scarcely knew, and he had no way to collect if he disputed their accounting.

By late summer it had become clear to Sutter that he could not sit in the old fort and wait for gold to come rolling in from the mountains. If he was to profit from the gold strike, he had to take personal charge of his own mining and trading operations in the mountains. According to one of Sutter's published reminiscences, his Indian laborers begged him to go to the mines so that they could get gold, but he was reluctant. "At last I consented, got a number of wagons ready, loaded them with provisions and goods of all kinds, employed a clerk, and left with about one hundred Indians and about fifty Sandwich Islanders (Kanakas) which had joined those which I had brought from the islands."[56] A kind regard for the opinions of the Indians, however, was not Sutter's chief motive in going to the mines; nor were their best interests uppermost in his design. He no doubt hoped that his personal direction of Indian miners would make gold dust flow directly into his pockets. Judicious manipulation of the Indian trade would bring the same sort of profits that Brannan enjoyed. Sutter took his Indians, Kanakas, and supplies to a spot about ten miles north of Mormon Island and sent for Lienhard.

Lienhard had not struck it rich as some had but was modestly successful. He had considered abandoning Sutter to join some German miners that he knew but finally rejected their offer out of misplaced loyalty to Sutter. Then a letter from Sutter arrived, asking him to come at once. Sutter was now at a rich placer, "where a man could wash about fifty dollars' worth of gold in one day," just a few miles upriver from Lienhard's claim. Lienhard was skeptical but joined Sutter. The diggings were not as good as Sutter had promised, but Lienhard judged them to be "satisfactory."[57] There he worked among other Sutter partners in mid-September.

A few days after Lienhard settled in at the new camp Sutter showed up, accompanied by two Indians carrying lances. Word had just come from the fort that his son John A. Sutter, Jr., commonly called August, had arrived. Sutter was understandably anxious to meet August after a separation of fourteen years. Before taking his leave, he asked Lienhard to lend him some of his gold, "not because he needed it, but merely to show his son."[58] This request surprised Lienhard because he had already given Sutter his share of the gold that he had found with Sutter's Indians, more than a thousand dollars. Nevertheless, he weighed out more than a thousand dollars of gold and handed it to Sutter, who promised that he would return it whenever Lienhard asked for it. Sutter rode off to make a good impression on his son with Lienhard's gold, which was never again seen by the trusting young Swiss.

CHAPTER 17

Sacramento and Solvency

The appearance on the scene of his long-lost son August marked a new chapter in Sutter's life. In one way it was a hopeful new beginning that presaged the reuniting of the Sutter family. On the practical side there was now someone trustworthy to help Sutter, now that reliable employees like Bidwell and Reading were gone. His failings were major obstacles to even the most faithful and honest servants and sons, however, as August would soon learn. Nor was August an ideal business associate. Earnest and hard-working, he was not quite twenty-two when he embraced his father. He was well educated and possessed some business acumen, but he was green as the short February grass in the Sacramento Valley. August would soon learn that he was among men who believed that gold was for those who could keep it and who had no qualms about taking it from the Sutters.

August had set out from Switzerland with no inkling that gold had been discovered. Although Sutter was expecting his entire family to arrive, they did not have the means; so August went ahead as an advance scout with the duty of seeing to it that the money was sent. In the meantime his mother, sister, and two brothers waited in Burgdorf, "I can assure you not in brilliant circumstances," August later recalled.[1] In Sutter's absence the family had been under the watchful eye of lawyer Martin Birmann, Sutter's brother-in-law and second husband of Anna's sister. They depended on help from the Birmanns and lived in straitened circumstances in a modest house outside Burgdorf. August sailed to New York and then booked passage to California on the *Huntress* in April, four months before the *New York Herald* announced the gold discovery and predicted "for California a Peruvian harvest of the precious metals, as soon as a sufficiency of miners, &c., can be obtained."[2] August probably began hearing about California gold when he was somewhere on the Pacific Coast at a port of call or perhaps from a passing ship, which in those days commonly stopped to exchange mail and news.

One can imagine how young August interpreted the bare facts of Sutter's California life as they filtered into little Burgdorf: owner of many leagues of agricultural land and thousands of horses, cattle, and sheep; famous proprietor of a fort and trading house; commander of a private army; purchaser of the Russian establishment; generous friend of immigrants; founder of New Switzerland. It is likely that the child August idealized the image of his pioneer father in America and cherished the favorable reports of Sutter's exploits that reached Switzerland.

August's illusions about his father came under attack as soon as he debarked in bustling San Francisco on September 14.[3] Whatever dreams he had were quickly replaced by conflicting tales told by Sutter's friends and foes. Some told him that his father was "the richest man on earth and did not know himself his wealth; others in the country told me in confidence that my father on account of his dreadfully loose and careless way of doing every business transaction was on the brink of ruin and that instead of having in his employ good and trustworthy men, he was surrounded by a parcel of rogues and immoral men, which, instead of helping him, only would accelerate and in a short period accomplish his utter moral, physical, and financial ruin." On his first day in California Sutter's creditors presented long overdue bills to August. Others suggested that he take over his father's business affairs, "if I wanted to save something yet for my mother, brothers, for my father himself and for me."[4]

August departed the next day for New Helvetia on his father's schooner *Sacramento,* which was making its regular rounds between San Francisco and the Sacramento Valley. "All these contradictory reports had made a dreadful impression upon my mind." Could his father really be a drunk as he had been informed? Was he rich or on the brink of financial destruction? Once at the fort, all of the alarming things that August had heard in San Francisco were "confirmed but painted to me in stronger and more vivid colors than ever before."[5]

With mounting misgivings about his father, August waited at the fort for Sutter to come down from the mountains. He saw firsthand that Brannan and other traders at the fort appropriated Sutter's livestock and anything else they wanted. Brannan ran up bills in Sutter's name. His father's loose business habits compounded his troubles. "Indians, Negroes, Kanakas, and white men of any nation indiscriminately by applying to my father, easily obtained letters of credit from him to any amount for any stores existing then in or about the fort."

In bygone days Sutter could get debtors to pay him in labor, but no more. Nor did he now have an army or political authority to pursue defaulters and compel payment. As in San Francisco, August found that there was no shortage of people who wanted to tell him the worst about his father. "Everyone told me a different tale, each more or less dreadful accounts, in the same time calumniating one another."[6]

Two of Sutter's most dependable former employees, Samuel Hensley and George McKinstry, not only confirmed what August had already heard but also revealed the unpaid Russian debt. August had met Hensley by chance several months earlier when he passed through Washington, D.C. The two men gave August gloomy news. Sutter owed a large amount, perhaps $20,000, to the Russian-American Company, which would soon foreclose if something were not done immediately. In all, Sutter's debts amounted to about $80,000, McKinstry and Hensley estimated. They urged August to convince his father to sign over all of his California property to him. Such a move was not strictly legal, for the Russians had already instituted legal action to satisfy the debt. Nevertheless, all recognized that California's unsettled political status would stall the Russians at least until Congress established a territorial government for California. Perhaps the questionable transfer would buy enough time to settle Sutter's debts and prevent foreclosure and financial ruin.[7] Within days of his arrival, August (with only scant knowledge of the country and his father's shaky business affairs) was expected to be his father's financial savior. The weight of this new and hitherto unimaginable prospect pressed hard on the young man as he waited for his father to come down from the mountains. How would Sutter react to McKinstry's and Hensley's proposition?

"After a week of terrible excitement and anguish, my father, whom I had not seen for fifteen years, arrived." August's worries about meeting his father vanished at once. Sutter's "affectionate and sincere" greeting, accompanied by mutual tears, quickly made his son forget everything he had heard. The two spoke about August's mother and the other children, with more heartfelt tears. Finally, "we commenced to converse on his present state of affairs." Sutter gave a vintage response filled with optimism and little realism. "He would soothe all my fears, telling me of his plans for the time to come, of his hopes to be soon out of all difficulties." Sutter employed the same kind of happy predictions to calm his son that he had used for decades to hold off his creditors, but his financial peril was too plain to be ignored. McKinstry joined them and proposed the transfer of all of Sutter's property to the son. Sutter's response to McKinstry's drastic plan tells as much about his business failures as does his sunny, alcoholic disposition. "My father, seeing the necessity of it, at once consented to it very readily."[8] Sutter's affable compliance in the transfer of his property without insisting on safeguards for himself should have raised an alarm with young August. It may be supposed that the son was proud that his father reposed so much trust in him. In reality, Sutter was ready to trust almost anyone with his property, especially when he was in his cups—which was often.

On October 14 Sutter signed the papers transferring the property to his son.[9] There were two deeds: the first signed over land and the second conveyed chattels. The first deed included the New Helvetia grant (11 leagues), the so-called *sobrante* grant ostensibly made by Governor Micheltorena (22 leagues), the Fort Ross lands (6 leagues), and 640 acres on the south fork of the American River embracing the property surrounding the sawmill. The deed said that August gave his father $50,000 for the land, but no money changed hands. The second deed conveyed all of Sutter's livestock, saddles, bridles, and all other personal property to August for $15,000, another imaginary exchange of money.

Sutter may have been a drunkard, but he had not forgotten to reassert all of his questionable land claims. Once again he claimed the Russian property, even though the Mexican government had granted some of those lands to other claimants several years earlier. Sutter made a second attempt to gain ownership of the Coloma site, although the legal basis for his claim to 640 acres is unstated. The deed made no mention of Marshall or any other partners, debts, or creditors. On paper August had become the greatest landholder in California if he could fend off the creditors—but how?

That was a problem that Sutter senior was only too willing to leave in the hands of August. After divesting himself of his encumbered property, Sutter rode back to the mountains, where he would make little money and much trouble. When he returned to the American River diggings, he told Lienhard he knew of a place south of the Cosumnes River where a man could wash out $150 in one day. That "sounded like a real bonanza" to Lienhard, so he packed up and followed Sutter's wagons to the new place, soon to be known as Sutter Creek. There was already a crowd of miners, but only Sutter had a tent, which was naturally the center of camp life. Lienhard noticed that Sutter had some new friends. "I was told they were highway robbers and scoundrels, who acquired gold by any method that did not involve honest labor."[10] This was perhaps an exaggeration, but to Lienhard's eye Sutter was traveling in rough company.

The strike proved to be thin pickings. Lienhard was surprised to see so many idle miners hanging about, but soon the attraction of Sutter Creek became clear: many of the prospectors were there to mine Sutter. As Lienhard said, "His friends were all men who tried to divert some of Sutter's reputed wealth into one of their own business ventures."[11] Recognizing that Captain Sutter admired titles, each petitioner introduced himself as a captain, a colonel, a judge, or a governor from somewhere. Knowing that he reveled in flattery, they larded it on. Sutter ate it all up. His son provided him a new opportunity for braggadocio. No one understood the latest scientific developments as well as August, Sutter said. He always kept his visitors' "whiskey bottles, and his own, well-filled." Thus lubricated, Sutter would milk his new friends for praise. "So you have heard about me in the States?" he would ask, priming the flattery pump.[12] Yes, indeed, they had heard all about Sutter, especially his fame as a courteous and generous host. There were toasts and more drinks, and then came a business proposition. Thoroughly besotted, Sutter would readily enter into a new partnership or advance money and supplies to men he had barely met. It was all, as Lienhard witnessed, quite sad.

August had to deal with the consequences of his father's drunken commerce. "With everybody he went in partnership for mining purposes; he furnished provisions, Indians to do the work," August reported, "and always his partners got the sole and whole benefit of it." Rents from the fort amounted to $3,000 per month but "were always drawn upon in advance." Men like Lienhard who entrusted gold to Sutter for safekeeping could not get it back from him. To repay them Sutter would "give them orders on me," August recalled, "to pay them as well and as fast as I could." While August sweated to bring order to his father's affairs, Sutter was "on a general frolic intoxicated."[13] Doubled over with old debts and staggering under the new obligations that his father assumed, August was desperate for a dependable source of revenue.

In late fall the senior Sutter decided to move his camp from Sutter Creek. "The work was going on well for a while, until three or four traveling grog-shops surrounded me," he complained. He claimed that his Indian and Kanaka workmen took the dust to these new establishments "for drinking, gambling, etc., and then the following day they were sick and unable to work, and became deeper and more indebted to me, especially the Kanakas."[14] Sutter's complaints about drunk, disorderly, and indebted workers seem farcical when laid alongside contemporary descriptions of himself. Still, his complaint described yet another of his serious financial problems. Indian and Hawaiian workers quickly learned that Sutter was slow pay, poor pay, or no pay at all, so why should they bring the gold to Sutter when they could exchange it for goods elsewhere? By Sutter's accounting they owed him money because he had supplied them with provisions for a share of their take; hence they were deadbeat debtors. Formerly Indians and Kanakas would have had little choice but to accept Sutter's trade goods on a schedule determined by him. Competition undermined that old system.

Sutter's departure from Sutter Creek was eventful. While his men struck camp, packed mules, and saddled horses, he embroidered fanciful stories about his military adventures. He was more inebriated than usual, having begun a three-day drinking spree. All was in readiness for the departure, but Sutter was too drunk to ride. His disgusted men finally dismounted and unpacked. That night Sutter took on an amorous mood and headed over to the bed of Mary, an Indian who once had been his favorite consort. August had suggested to his father that he should give up his Indian mistresses, so Sutter may have broken off his relationship with Mary in honor of his soon-to-arrive wife and family. In any event Mary was then the wife of an Indian man, and the couple had accompanied Sutter to the mines. Sutter's drunken approach to Mary did not result in a night of lovemaking. When she spurned his advances, Sutter threatened to shoot her. Perry McCoon came to Mary's defense, and Sutter threatened to shoot him too. His threats came to nothing, but caused a great uproar in camp.[15]

After this scandalous affray, Sutter removed to Coloma, where he partnered with Lansford Hastings and two other men in a store. Another pair of mercantile businesses were established there by the time he arrived. The main competition for Sutter and company was Samuel Brannan, whose clerk, R. F. Peckham, reported on the inflated prices that marked the early days of the gold rush, with gold commonly valued at sixteen dollars per ounce. "Crackers and flour, one dollar a pound; six quart tin pans, sixteen dollars a piece; pickels [sic], sixteen dollars a quart; canned meats and sardines sixteen dollars a can or box; whiskey sixteen dollars a bottle and everything in proportion."[16] Beef that had been worth four dollars per carcass a few months before now sold for one dollar a pound in Coloma. The other Coloma store operated under the partnership of Governor Mason, Lieutenant Sherman, Lieutenant Norman Bestor, and Captain William Warner. The governor, having noticed that neither officers nor men could live on government pay and rations, liberally agreed to allow his men some time to work on their own. Under the circumstances, Mason felt it was not amiss to invest $500 in the Coloma store with his subordinate officers "and received his share of the profits, fifteen hundred dollars," his grateful partner Sherman said.[17] This was not a princely sum by gold-rush standards, but Mason invested in one of Larkin's trading expeditions to China and thereby perhaps increased his capital. As for Sutter, he confessed that he withdrew from his Coloma firm in January, "with many sacrifices."[18] From August's perspective, little came out of his father's ventures in mining or commercial enterprises. "Instead of gaining anything in the mines," he complained, "wagon loads of provisions . . . were taken off by him [Sutter] and his agents to his camp," where everyone "robbed and stole what they could; very little gold I ever saw from their labor."[19]

Some problems were beyond Sutter's ability to control. He and Marshall could not find enough men to keep the sawmill running. On December 20, 1848, Sutter sold his interest in the mill to Alden Bayley and John Winters for $6,000, including "the privilege of cutting timber for mill purposes, he (Sutter) claiming no right as a pre-emptor, to the land," according to Winter's affidavit.[20] Marshall also sold them a one-third interest in his half of the mill. This agreement contradicted the language and intent of Sutter's transfer of property to his son in October. He expressly included the sawmill at Coloma when he transferred his holdings to his son. Strict construction of the law aside, this is one of the few Sutter deals that probably made sense, assuming that Bayley and Winters paid as agreed. Like Sutter and Marshall, they could not operate the mill profitably because of the high cost of labor.

Sutter had other reasons to sell the mill and store at Coloma. Friction developed between Indians and whites and between whites who controlled Indian labor and those who did not. In 1848 rancheros who commanded troops of Indian workers made the first fortunes in the mines. Independent miners were jealous of their success. Sutter had been the region's largest employer of Indians, federal Indian agent, and the one to whom Indians might look for protection. Although the details are unknown, he attempted to mediate a dispute between Indians and whites while he was at Coloma. The results were distinctly unsatisfactory for all concerned. The Indians blamed Sutter for bringing white men to obtain "yellow dirt." Indians and whites alike threatened to kill him.[21] It was time for Sutter to leave Coloma; but the snows came, and he had to stay on into January.

While Sutter shivered in Coloma, August contemplated the deep financial problems that his father had created. Almost everyone except Sutter seemed to make money, and anyone who had the nerve could make money out of Sutter. The bills were coming due; creditors were at the door. Without some new source of income, the Sutter family would be broke before the gold rush was fairly underway. What was August to do? Sam Brannan had a helpful suggestion that could save the Sutters from ruin and benefit that keen merchant too. Brannan had already established a warehouse at the embarcadero, where the water was deep enough to accommodate ocean-going vessels. The site was closer than Sutterville to the fort, which was still the chief location for businesses. Capital would be required to improve Sutterville's waterfront with docking facilities before shipments could easily be offloaded there. Sales of Sutterville lots were slow, despite the best efforts of Sutter's agent, Lansford Hastings. Why not, Brannan proposed, lay out a new city in the angle made by the Sacramento and American Rivers that extended from the embarcadero back to the fort?

August at first dithered over Brannan's idea. He asked Lienhard, who was now living at the fort and dunning him for the gold that he had loaned to Sutter. Despite Lienhard's disappointment at August's inability to pay his father's debt, the two young Swiss gentlemen became friends. (Lienhard eventually settled the debt for a flock of sheep.) Lienhard had purchased a Sutterville lot, but he thought the proposal for a new town site was a good idea. As Brannan said, it would cost a lot of money to improve the Sutterville site, while at the embarcadero "lots could be sold without delay at good prices."[22] Besides, August observed, "Squatters already then wanted to intrude upon our rights at the embarcadero and I saw that it was necessary to do something [because] a great many people [wanted] locations for stores, boarding houses, a.s.f."[23]

Having made a decision, August hired Captain William Warner, then on leave from his duties with the U.S. Army, to survey the town in December. Warner laid out Sacramento much as it stands today. Like other cities that were platted in the nineteenth-century American West, the streets formed a regular grid. First Street (later called Front Street) paralleled the Sacramento River, followed by Second through Thirty-first Streets, which marched past the fort. Streets lettered from A to Y ran at right angles to the numbered streets. Each block contained eight lots divided by an interior alley. The civic-minded August gave to the new city twelve public squares of one block each, the alleys and streets, plus a commodious cemetery located on the southern city limits.

The level floodplain meant that few concessions to topography were needed, and few were made. Only the rivers and the lowlands broke up the regular procession of streets and blocks. Even these watery features seemed to cause little concern for Captain Warner and August. Broad boulevards coursed along the borders of both rivers and dared them to flood. A large marshy pond took up about ten blocks at the mouth of the American River, but that was no great matter. They called it Lake Sutter and platted it over with blocks as if they could be floated on the pond's surface. Warner did not accord even this ghostlike recognition to the sloughs that extended into the city limits from both rivers. Competent engineers could easily defeat such ephemeral features; they had no place on the map of Sacramento City, as August called it.[24]

To make certain that his Sacramento venture succeeded, August needed an honest and diligent agent to take charge of the sale of lots. He had made some good business decisions, but by December he understood that he could not handle the hard and violent men who flocked to Sutter's Fort. They had shoved him around and insulted him. He needed someone who was familiar with frontier land sales, who would not be intimidated, and who knew the law. He found all of those qualities in Peter Hardeman Burnett. Born in Tennessee in 1807 and raised on the Missouri frontier, Burnett grew up on dirt floors and knew well the life of hardscrabble pioneer farmers. He met and admired famous western politicians like Sam Houston and David Crockett. Burnett studied law, practiced successfully in Missouri, and in 1843 moved to Oregon, where he helped to organize the territorial government. He headed for the California gold fields when news of the discovery reached Oregon.[25]

After a successful stint in the mines, Burnett arrived at the fort on December 21 and reacquainted himself with some old friends, including Pierson Reading and Sam Hensley, Sutter's partners in a store at the fort. Acting on the advice of Hensley and Reading, August approached Burnett and asked him to be his agent and attorney. "I was to attend to all of his law business of every kind, sell the lots in Sacramento City, and collect the money," Burnett recalled, "and for these services I was to receive one fourth of the gross proceeds arising from the sale of city lots."[26] Burnett's fee was steep; but as he said, "there was a heavy amount of old business to settle up; and, while the labor was certain, the compensation was speculative," because no one knew for sure whether Sacramento or Sutterville would become the leading metropolis of the region. Most historians have been critical of August and suspicious of Burnett, but the lawyer gave his complete attention to all phases of his fiduciary obligation, including paying off Sutter's old debts. In December 1848 few men would have seriously thought such a goal was possible, and fewer still would have diligently labored at it. Burnett set to work immediately.[27]

In early January Burnett sold the first lots near the fort, where most business was still being done. At the time there were only two semipermanent log structures on the embarcadero, a saloon and a cabin. Other embarcadero businesses, like Brannan's, operated out of brush shelters and tents. Toward the end of the month, purchases of lots near the embarcadero picked up. The winter of 1848–49 was relatively dry, so there were no floods or thoughts of floods in the minds of optimistic buyers, who snapped up lots as fast as they could. Whatever drawbacks the site had, in early 1849 it was clear that the embarcadero was the best place to unload goods from San Francisco. Under Burnett's management, lots sold at set prices to discourage speculation. Those near the embarcadero sold for $500, while parcels farther inland went for $250.[28] Burnett frequently went to San Francisco, where he briskly sold Sacramento lots to newcomers who were getting off ships from distant lands.

August began selling off the fort piecemeal. The central building went to one buyer, the shops along the walls to others. The new owners modified the structure to suit their own needs, and the fort became a shambles. The fort had been the symbol of Sutter's military power and stature in Mexican California, but in 1849 it was hardly worth saving. The roof was leaking, and the adobe walls were in need of repair. "Only the scarcity and enormous price of lumber (one dollar pr foot) could induce people to buy it," said August. The inflated gold-rush economy enabled him to get $40,000 for the fort. "What would we have got for it afterwards?"[29]

If Burnett sold all the Sacramento lots, the Sutters would gross hundreds of thousands of dollars even after Burnett took his steep commission. August had saved the family! Not everyone was happy with this turn of events, least of all the elder Sutter, who remained in Coloma while August founded Sacramento. Sutter still favored Sutterville and claimed that his nascent town was a going concern that would have flourished if Brannan and other interested speculators had not convinced his son to start a rival city. Besides, Sutterville was safe from floods. "Had I not been snow-bound at Coloma that winter Sac[ramento] never would have been built."[30]

But Sacramento was turning out to be a money machine for the Sutters. The proceeds from lot sales enabled Burnett to attack the worst of Sutter's overdue debts. Indeed, the Missouri lawyer attended to these old obligations with astonishing determination, promptness, and effectiveness. In January the Russian-American Company's agent, William M. Steuart, demanded that Sutter immediately pay nearly $20,000 or face the consequences. Before paying him, Burnett stalled briefly by demanding proof that Steuart was indeed the Russian agent. "We had quite an earnest discussion," Burnett recalled, but he assured Steuart "that our intentions were to pay the Company as early as possible." To do otherwise, he told August, would invite "long and extensive litigation, and most-probably . . . ultimate financial ruin."[31] His young client agreed. Burnett personally pledged to secure Sutter's debt to the company with good notes, an assurance that convinced Steuart that he could wait a few weeks more.

Burnett was true to his word. On April 13, 1849, Steuart provided the required documentation, and Burnett handed over $19,788 in notes and gold. The Russian debt that had hung over Sutter's head for eight years was gone. Likewise, Burnett paid off other creditors large and small. William French, the Hawaiian merchant who had staked Sutter to a line of credit in 1839, took his payment in Sacramento lots ($3,000). Burnett also liquidated the old debts with the Hudson's Bay Company ($7,000). Newer debts owed to Brannan's store ($15,000) and other merchants vanished as Burnett swiftly paid creditors in notes, lots, and gold. Some Missouri creditors with fifteen-year-old debts showed up too, and he duly paid off these old bills. By April there was only one large old debt that remained to be paid, to Antonio Suñol ($10,000).[32] Sutter was almost entirely debt free and still had most of his land (including three-quarters of the Sacramento city lots), a state of affairs that had been inconceivable just a few months earlier.

The transformation from debtor to creditor did not delight all of Sutter's friends and business associates. Sutter's agent for Sutterville, Lansford Hastings, who was heavily invested in that town site, was disgusted when August laid out Sacramento. He suspected that Sutter was behind the new development. "If a man so disposed had the influence and had a tract of thirty leagues, he would, in all probability, lay off, sell and demolish, and lay out again, until he had traversed the whole tract and runed [*sic*] the whole community," he complained to fellow Sutterville investor George McKinstry. "Some apprehend danger of our town being blown up, but it is the best, the very best site on the river and with a little concert of action on the part of owners and proprietors of lots we may safely bid defiance to all opposition."[33] When the high waters finally came, these old hands knew, Sutterville's residents would smugly watch the people and property of Sacramento float away on the flood. Hastings was tending the store in Coloma, so he was in a good position to work on Sutter while they were snowbound.

Brothers George and John McDougal were also unhappy, but for a different reason. Sutter senior had leased the embarcadero ferry to George, who construed the agreement as an exclusive right to use the entire length of the embarcadero—several thousand feet of prime Sacramento commercial property. He challenged August and Burnett's right to sell the lands that he thought he controlled, but to no avail. When Sutter came down from Coloma in late January, he refused to see his son or Burnett, whom he styled "a hypocrite, a jesuit, a designing swindler," and stayed with the McDougals instead.[34] They took him to San Francisco and "after having made him intoxicated," convinced him to sign away one square mile of land adjoining Sutterville.[35] The agreement was supposed to be a "settlement of the injury" done to George's exclusive right to the embarcadero by the sale of Sacramento lots.[36] The land had been signed over to August, of course, but Sutter agreed to pay McDougal $20,000 if he failed to convince August to convey the land to McDougal. Facing this potential loss, August gave McDougal the land even though Burnett advised against it.

Early in the year Sutterville's proponents seemed to be gathering momentum. McKinstry went into business with Theodor Cordua, another of Sutter's one-time New Helvetia associates, who had a ranch on the Feather River. They bought a brigantine in San Francisco, stocked it with goods, and sailed it to Sutterville, where it would serve as a floating store. McKinstry had made arrangements with "old Capt Sutter" to secure a half mile of waterfront for Cordua, and George McDougal had contracted to build a "w[h]arf 100 Yards long." McKinstry was convinced that Sutterville lots would sell quickly and that Sutterville developers would make "our 'pile' this summer."[37]

By this time August and his father had moved from the fort to Hock Farm, but relations between them remained cool. In April August decided to rid the Sutter family of one source of trouble. He sold his father's still to Vallejo for $400.[38] Good riddance, but it did not stop his father's drinking. Sutter spent most of May at Hock Farm. "The old Gentleman is up there . . . with a party of Dutch men and some new fangled [sic] gold machines, on some new wild-goose chase," one observer reported.[39]

Brisk lot sales did not change Sutter's opinion of Sacramento or his preference for Sutterville. August retained title to all of Sutter's land, but his father did what he could to promote Sutterville investors. His constant support for Sutterville baffled his son. "He must have seen the almost self evident fact that Sacramento City had been the means of paying all his debts," August wrote, "and that there could be made a hundred times more out of it yet, than of Sutterville, where McDougal owned one entire mile, Hastings another half mile and himself a very small portion in proportion to all the other shareholders."[40] Yet Sutter remained faithful to the hamlet that bore his name, perhaps for no other reason than that.

In the spring suffering Sutterville merchants decided to draw business away from Sacramento by selling their goods at cost. They hoped that this desperate tactic would begin a stampede of businesses to Sutterville. By the end of May it was clear that the fire-sale strategy had failed. "They have done themselves more hurt than their enemies could," said Henry Schoolcraft, Sacramento's first magistrate and recorder of deeds. "People went there to buy and found that they either had not the goods or they refused to sell them at the prices stated" in the handbills that McDougal had distributed in Sacramento.[41] McDougal's failure may have been helped by a timely burglary that relieved him of the stock he needed to carry on his business. Some suspected that Brannan was behind the deed, but no one was ever formally accused.[42]

Suttervilleans needed a new method to destroy Sacramento, and they promptly found one. One day when August arrived at the embarcadero "Schoolcraft came running up to me with some other gentlemen . . . in great excitement, telling me that the place was going to be ruined."[43] Hastings, McDougal, McKinstry, and Cordua had offered eighty to two hundred Sutterville lots to key merchants, including Sam Brannan, Hensley, Reading, and other important Sacramento businessmen. Burnett might have quelled the panic among the Sacramentans, but he was in San Francisco. The merchants insisted that August sign over two hundred lots to induce them to stay in Sacramento. "My father heard everything himself, told me he knew McDougall had made such offers to these gentlemen and said: Well, if it is so, you cannot do anything else, you must let have Mr. Brannan the same advantages to induce him to stay."[44] With his father's approval, August signed over five hundred lots to Brannan and the others.[45] This transfer was a substantial loss to the Sutters, but they still retained a large majority of the lots while putting an end to the Sutterville challenge. After June 1849 the threat to Sacramento would be natural rather than commercial.

August was coming to the end of his career as his father's keeper. Like so many other residents of the valley, he came down with malaria and suffered with the intermittent fevers and chills that characterize the disease. His eyes became seriously inflamed too, perhaps a result of the malarial infection. He was so weak that he sometimes fainted and had to be carried to bed. In late May he went up to Hock Farm with his father, Schoolcraft, and Archibald Peachy, a lawyer. August would soon learn why these men were there. "The day after our arrival I was called in my father's room where everything had been prepared; my father told me that, as I was so unwell and there was now not any more necessity of the property being in my name, he wanted me to sign a conveyance transferring back to him all his property" so that he could fire Burnett and appoint Peachy and Schoolcraft in his place. In his weakened condition, August could not resist his father and signed without a murmur. Sutter, Peachy, and Schoolcraft immediately departed for Sacramento, "and I was left alone with my fever."[46]

For several months August was physically debilitated and nearly blind, living a semi-invalid life at Hock Farm; but he performed one more deed to promote his family's welfare. August's father had always insisted that his family would join him in California. There is no reason to doubt Sutter's sincerity, but he did nothing to bring about his family's reunion. Although August was very anxious to send funds to his mother so that she and his siblings could make the journey, Burnett cautioned him against it. All of the proceeds from the Sacramento lots should go to pay off old debts, the lawyer argued. Anything else would look bad to creditors. August agreed and waited as Burnett eliminated the debts. Finally he could wait no longer. In April he arranged for Lienhard to go to Switzerland and return with his mother and family. The journey would cost $12,000, $8,000 for expenses and $4,000 for Lienhard, who insisted on being paid in advance. Bitter experience had taught him not to rely on promises, even though August was still in control of Sutter's property when the agreement was struck. "I have had no reason to doubt your word," Lienhard told August, "yet your father is the man who is actually responsible, and I have lost so much money through promises he failed to keep that I cannot do anything for him without being compensated in advance."[47] August well understood Lienhard's caution, but he did not have $12,000. Since his father offered no assistance, August raised the money "with great difficulties," borrowing part of it by "paying heavy percentage" in interest to William Daylor, Sutter's old Cosumnes River neighbor who had once been a cook at Sutter's Fort.[48] In June almost all of the money was in hand. Lienhard finally agreed to take a Sacramento lot as part of his payment.

In charge of his own affairs once again, Sutter was free to make hash of August's successful management. Sutter was nearly free of debt and owned many leagues of increasingly valuable ranch land, as well as the lion's share of California's most important inland city. He still had a share in Sutterville and what remained of the fort. August and Burnett had been able to liquidate his debts because the gold rush had caused a tectonic shift in California's economy. In short, Sutter's pre-1848 debts were paid off because of inflated gold-rush prices for land. In late 1849 Sacramento and San Francisco lots commanded prices that formerly purchased entire ranchos. Sutter, for example, sold a lot in San Francisco for $8,000 in November, a price that was by no means extraordi-nary.[49] In Mexican California money was scarce; now the apparently inex-haustible hoard of placer gold seemed to solve that problem. Nominally valued at sixteen dollars per ounce, gold in California was worth somewhat less, in part because it was impure to one degree or another. Gold dust was so com-mon that its value fluctuated according to the usual market rules of supply and demand. In December 1848 William Heath Davis said that gold in San Fran-cisco sold at eleven dollars per ounce but was "slow at that—there being some $50,000 in cash in the market for that purpose."[50]

Gold was plentiful, and so was credit—but at usurious interest rates in the red-hot gold-rush economy. There were no banks in the early days, so men like Brannan lent money at 10 percent *per month,* an outrageous rate anywhere; but in gold-rush California the gold supply seemed limitless and new strikes came in every day.[51] The overheated speculative economy drove these interest rates for several years, leading to the ruin of many a careless businessman.[52] The gold rush saved Sutter from ruin in 1849 because he could pay off old and (by gold-rush standards) relatively small debts with plentiful new money that he acquired for land sold at inflated prices. If Sutter contracted new debts, how-ever, he would obligate himself to pay inflated prices and astronomical interest that would come due after the gold-rush boom had subsided. The gold rush giveth, and the gold rush taketh away.

In later years Sutter often repeated the claim that the gold rush had ruined him, thus evading any personal responsibility for the mismanagement of his assets. But, in fact, due to the gold rush and the sale of Sacramento city lots, in the summer of 1849 Sutter seemed safe from business troubles for all time. Cloaked with claims to tens of thousands of acres of land, he lived in a lordly fashion and entertained the endless stream of guests who knocked on his door.

His land claims, including the city of Sacramento, had not yet been confirmed under U.S. law. Some of the claims, like those at Ross and Bodega, were dubious at best. Nevertheless, Sutter used his claims as collateral for loans or sold the land outright while guaranteeing a good title. It was risky business, but to his way of thinking the future would always be his savior. Had not recent events proven that?

Sutter's inattention to detail immediately caused trouble. After reclaiming his property from August, Sutter gave Archibald Peachy power of attorney to sell all of his Sacramento lots.[53] However, Sutter had failed to notify Burnett that he had been relieved. In the confusion that followed, Burnett continued to sell lots under the power of attorney that August had given him. When Burnett learned that he had been fired, he demanded his pay, one-fourth interest in Sacramento, a sum that Sutter paid with title to 765 city lots. Many years later he famously complained that Burnett "made a fortune most too quickly to suit me."[54] He failed to mention that as part of the settlement Burnett agreed to pay Sutter's last old debt from the Mexican era, $10,000 to Antonio Suñol. For the first time in his adult life Sutter was debt free and credit worthy.

There is no question that Burnett did very well with his settlement from Sutter. About one month after he received the lots, two men offered Burnett "$50,000 in gold-dust for one undivided half" of his Sacramento property; "and we want an answer by ten to-morrow morning," they added. After consulting with his wife, Burnett appeared at the appointed time and accepted the offer with the proviso that he retain sole ownership of a few choice lots. The buyers promptly accepted Burnett's counteroffer. Then another man from Sacramento jumped up and pumped the hands of Burnett's new partners, declaring that it was a splendid purchase and that there was a fortune in the property. Burnett kept quiet during this long congratulatory outburst, which implied that the two men had put one over on him. Finally he rose and said, "Gentlemen, I am glad to hear that I am a much richer man than I supposed I was. If these gentlemen can make a fortune out of the undivided half they have purchased, what do you think I can make out of my half, and the fifty thousand dollars to begin with?"[55] Burnett's cool reply subdued the celebration. He had a half interest in Burnett, Ferguson & Company, plus sole ownership of the high-value lots that he had exempted from the sale. And his new partners had paid Burnett $50,000 to make the partnership with him. In late 1849 speculation in Sacramento lots took off. Lots that formerly sold for hundreds now sold for thousands. By 1851 the taxable value of Burnett's interest in Sacramento lands stood at over $340,000, and this figure did not account for the lots that he had sold between 1849 and 1851 or the cash he got from his partners.[56] No wonder August maintained in 1855 that "if Judge Burnett could have been retained for the management of our affairs up to the present date, my father would now be one of the richest men in California."[57]

Sacramento's growth was truly astonishing to all who witnessed it. By July 1849 the population had increased to several thousand. "Although there was not a single brick and but few wooden houses in the city," Burnett observed, "it had become an active business place, teeming with people, who mainly lived and did business in canvas tents and cloth shanties."[58] A shrewd merchant named William Prince set up shop there and reckoned it would cost him $4,000 for a lot and a wooden store. He planned to charge ahead despite the cost because mere rent for such a structure would cost $600 per month. As it was, Prince paid five dollars a day for half of a canvas store plus another four dollars a day in expenses. "The *excess* in gold weighing will nearly pay all this," Prince added with a wink and a nod, "as people use gold more recklessly than Dollars indeed it matters little what price is asked for an article if it is really wanted by the purchasers who come in from the mines."[59] Prince got his lot and store and made money on the deal.

Not everyone made money in Sacramento land and business. All enterprise was highly speculative; one could just as easily lose money as make it. Merchants sent for goods on the east coast that took six months or more to reach California by ship. By then the market might be flooded with the merchandise that had been ordered. Or the articles were no longer in demand because there was something better in the market. Goods that sold quickly at high prices in one season could not be moved at any price the next. Still, careful attention and strict economy resulted in profits for many a California entrepreneur who mined the miners. A good deal of this sort of mining went on in Sacramento, the most important inland entrepôt for the mines and the second largest city in California. Sutter, who owned the majority of city lots even after Brannan, Burnett, and others had taken perhaps one-third, stood to make a fortune out of the urban bonanza that his son had created. But in gold-rush California fortunes came and fortunes went with bewildering speed.

CHAPTER 18

A New State and Its Founder

The year 1849 marked the beginning of a great demographic transformation in California. In 1848 California contained approximately a hundred and fifty thousand Indians and perhaps fourteen thousand non-Indians. About half of the non-Indians were Mexican citizens; the rest were Americans and foreigners.[1] The 1850 U.S. census enumerated over ninety-two thousand white and nonwhite residents, not counting Indians, and this figure was a serious undercount that omitted San Francisco and two other counties.[2] A second census in 1852 found more than a quarter million people in California, including some thirty-one thousand "domesticated Indians." Even that number was regarded as smaller than the actual figure. The true population was no doubt well over a hundred thousand by 1850 and may even have approached that number by the fall of 1849. No one knew for certain, and it would have been impossible to find out. Every ship that sailed into San Francisco debauched scores, even hundreds, of unnamed passengers who struck out to find their fortunes. They formed an undifferentiated mass that broke apart as it washed up on the beach, headed for the mines in streams and rivulets, briefly coalesced in mining camps, dispersed again, and reformed in new camps as circumstances dictated. About twenty-five thousand more arrived by way of the overland trail.[3] Almost all the forty-niners were young men.

The forty-niners were not a community but an impulsive wave of humanity with one object in mind—gaining quick wealth from California's golden treasure. Not everyone succeeded in getting rich, but those who did inspired the rest to keep on trying. Instead of amassing great individual wealth, most placer miners made a daily living from long hours of unremitting toil, often standing hip deep in ice-cold Sierra streams. They dug out gravel and washed it in simple pans, Indian baskets, or the primitive rockers that they grandly called "machines." It was brutal, back-breaking work. According to the most careful student of gold-rush labor and production, in 1849 the average daily wage amounted to sixteen dollars for an ounce of pure gold, if a miner could find someone who would pay that much and weigh it on an honest scale.[4] Miners then had to buy food, shelter, equipment, and clothing at inflated gold-rush prices. The average wage steadily declined until it reached about three dollars per day in 1856 and remained there. The rate of inflation subsided too, but one thing became clear to miners very quickly: great riches did not come except through extraordinary luck. Industrious miners who found a good claim, worked hard, lived frugally, and carefully guarded their earnings could make "a pile" and go home. The size of the pile for an independent miner might amount to a few thousand dollars, more or less. Some became discouraged quickly and returned home at the first opportunity. Others did not have the nerve to go home because they had not made enough money to justify their effort. Still others decided to remain in California because they liked the place. Some forty-niners thrived on the rough society, along with the stimulating sense of great possibilities that filled the air in mining camps. They would ultimately spend their lives moving from one gold rush to the next—California, Nevada, British Columbia, Colorado, Australia, Arizona, Idaho, the Black Hills, the Yukon, or wherever glittering dust in the pan beckoned them.

Amusements for the forty-niners were few. Gambling, drinking, and prostitution topped the list, as one might expect in a population composed predominately of young men. Liquor dealers, cardsharps, and whores from the United States, South America, and Europe arrived in large numbers, along with boatloads of hopeful miners. Some prostitutes worked at their trade aboard ship. The arrival of French harlots was noted in newspapers and acknowledged approvingly by miners.[5] It was, in the minds of some of the young men, a grand adventure far from home and the restraints of church, family, and friends. "Let none wonder that the time was the best ever made," wrote San Francisco's first historians in 1855.[6] They had been lucky enough to survive those boisterous times. Many died in California and on the trail from scurvy, malaria, cholera, violence, exposure, and misadventure. Still others were debilitated by malaria in the Sacramento Valley and foothills or by the effects of alcohol and liaisons with syphilitic prostitutes.

The newcomers who flooded the gold fields in 1849 had opinions about Indians that sharply differed from those of the old-time Californians. Most of the forty-niners feared and hated Indians. Unlike Sutter and the californios, they saw no useful place for Indians as inexpensive laborers. Worse, they regarded the use of Indians in the diggings as something akin to slavery, which was abhorrent not because Indians were abused but because command over Indian labor was unfair competition with free white men. As the white population grew by the thousands every week, such attitudes became ever more prevalent in the mining districts.

The most virulent and potentially violent Indian–haters in 1849 were among the Oregon contingent. Many had been in Oregon during the Cayuse War, which began with the Whitman murders at the Methodist mission. The killing of Narcissa Whitman was especially hateful to them, symbolizing as it did an attack on women and religion. Christian charity toward Indians was not common among the Oregonians who went to California in 1849. The murder of Elijah Hedding, the measles outbreak, and unfair treatment of the Walla Wallas by Sutter and the United States in California were among the myriad causes of the Cayuse War; but these mitigating details were probably unknown to the Oregon men, who would have regarded such attempts at explanation as mere temporizing. They hated Indians and killed them whenever they could.

In April 1849 some Oregonians reached the Coloma vicinity and commenced mining. Evidently some of these men raped local Nisenan women. In retaliation the Nisenans killed five Oregonians at a site later named Murderer's Bar, about ten miles northwest of Coloma. The enraged comrades of the murdered men decided to kill the Indian perpetrators or at least to kill some Indians. They gathered in Coloma, recruited reinforcements, and went out looking for Indians. Samuel Osgood, a portrait painter and journalist for the *New York Tribune,* watched them go. Not suspecting that these men were in deadly earnest, he joked, "Bring me a scalp."[7] The next day one of the Oregon men rode up to Osgood's tent and gave him a scalp. Horrified, he threw the bloody trophy in the millrace where Marshall had discovered gold.

The avengers had killed four Indians. The Indians who survived this assault set fires atop the mountains surrounding Coloma. They threatened one man in particular, John Greenwood, son of mountain man Caleb Greenwood and an Indian woman. Young Greenwood had scalped the victims of the previous day's raid, Indians who probably had nothing to do with the murder of the Oregonians. Osgood reported that Greenwood coolly said that he would now be obliged to shoot them all. "He is what might be termed a hard case to deal with."[8]

Greenwood organized a bunch of Oregonians who were now determined to have their vengeance on whatever Indians they could find. Norman Bestor, army officer and partner of Mason and Sherman in the Coloma store, observed: "Many of these men are so violent that they denounce every one who advances any reason why a wholesale slaughter should not be made, and charge him with taking the part of the Indians against them for an expression of opinion on the subject which happens to differ from their brutal and cowardly mode of procedure. Our lives are threatened also."[9]

In Coloma James Marshall was the chief defender of the Indians. By the spring of 1849 he was widely regarded as an unusual and unpopular man. His spiritualist beliefs and fair treatment of the Indians probably did not improve his reputation. Many of the newcomers believed that Marshall and his Indians knew where every last nugget of gold was and that they refused to divulge the information out of pure cussedness. Sutter's partner was the nearest white man who exemplified all that was supposed to be bad about the Mexican system of Indian relations, forced labor, and monopoly of resources. No one was going to listen to him. As Greenwood organized his killers, Marshall and a few other level-headed men sent an express rider to find Sutter. Perhaps he could avoid a slaughter by convincing the Indians to hand over the guilty men or negotiate some sort of settlement.

While the messenger sped downriver, the Oregonians scoured the countryside, massacred twenty Indians on Weber Creek, took forty prisoners there and forty more from another nearby ranchería, and herded them all into Coloma. Some wanted to kill every one of the captives. More moderate thinkers suggested that the execution of chiefs and alcaldes would suffice. Marshall and others wanted to wait until Sutter arrived. Finally the mob agreed to free most of the prisoners but kept seven Indians who were friendly to Marshall until they heard from Sutter. On April 19 Sutter's response came by way of the express rider. It was not a reprieve for the luckless captives. Sutter explained that there was no use in him coming because the Indians and whites had both threatened him when he had tried to mediate Indian and white disputes the previous winter.

With no guidance from Sutter, the Colomans held a meeting to decide the fate of the seven prisoners. The council was not a model of frontier democracy in action. A few pleaded for a cessation of violence, but the drunken mob insisted that the Indians in custody should die and threatened to kill anyone who interfered. They brought out the prisoners with the intention of holding a sort of trial. The understandably terrified Indians decided not to wait for the verdict of the drunken miners. They broke and ran in a vain effort to escape. The crowd killed two with rifle fire and three with Bowie knives. Two made it to the river, where an Oregonian finished one of them with a Colt revolver. The seventh victim drowned after being stunned by a rock. Someone shot one of Marshall's Indian work hands, making a total of eight deaths.[10] Marshall's courageous but ineffective effort to protect his Indian laborers convinced some miners that he was not to be trusted. Fearful for his own life, the discoverer of gold fled.[11] The Coloma killings marked the beginning of more than a decade of violence against Indians in California. Wholesale slaughter of entire Indian communities and casual murders of individuals were part of the day-to-day violence that characterized the gold-rush era.

There can be no denying the racial hatred that inspired the massacre of Indians at Coloma, but it is important to understand that racism and revenge were not the Oregonians' only motivation. As one defender of the Oregonians involved in this massacre explained, "the old California system was the real cause" of the Oregonians' rage, because it was "a system of inequality—of proprietors and peons." The Oregonians wanted "the system of free labor, and to root out the contract system, or rather the peon system."[12] In the system of rough equality that these men envisioned, Marshall and Sutter represented a privileged class controlling a labor system that had to be destroyed, whatever the human costs might be.

Many of the young men who flooded into California in 1849 held views that were similar to the ideas expressed in extreme fashion at Coloma. Their beliefs about freedom and equality were limited to white men generally and Americans in particular. Still, they fervently desired to establish democratic institutions. One of their most common complaints was that Congress had failed to provide them with a regular territorial government. Ever since the adoption of the 1787 Northwest Ordinance, Congress ordinarily organized western lands into federal territories; the president appointed a governor, territorial secretary, and three judges. In 1836 Congress permitted new territories to elect a legislature. When the total population reached sixty thousand, the territory was eligible for admission to the union as a state, although Congress was under no obligation to admit a new state just because the territory was eligible. In 1848 California had the requisite number of residents to qualify for organization as a territory and soon thereafter enough people to qualify for statehood, but Congress did not act. By 1849 some residents thought that California should skip the territorial stage altogether and immediately become a state, as had happened in the case of Texas. A few even advocated independence for California, although this faction never had great importance. Until Congress acted, a military form of territorial government (lacking an elected legislature) ruled. This did not conform to the earnest expectations of the republican-minded Americans who swarmed to California.

As early as 1847 California's infant newspapers assailed the military government as military despotism and complained about taxation without representation, even though Californians were taxed at a lower rate than citizens of the United States. They objected to military governors' appointments of alcaldes and the principle of following Mexican laws until Congress disposed otherwise. The people of San Francisco and Sacramento soon elected governing councils, but the military government was not bound to recognize them and in the case of San Francisco did not. Until a territorial or state government officially chartered a city government, anyone could question the authority of these irregular civic bodies. Finally, on June 3, 1849, Governor Bennet Riley proposed that a constitutional convention with elected delegates should meet in Monterey. Some republican purists complained about the propriety of the military governor ordering the sovereign people of California to hold an election and form a government, but these dissenters gave way to the general demand to establish a popular representative government, regardless of who had authorized the convention. The governor established voting districts and scheduled the election of delegates for August 1, with the successful candidates to assemble in Monterey on September 1.[13]

Governor Riley's proclamation roughly divided California into ten districts that would each elect several delegates. The Sacramento District, where Sutter resided, was to send four delegates to the convention. Some of Sutter's friends had political aspirations for him. They probably considered his election to this post as a crucial first step toward higher office. Heinrich Lienhard was at the fort with Sutter in mid-June, a few days before he departed for Switzerland to get Sutter's family. One evening the captain introduced two men to Lienhard. The drunken trio was "having a hilarious time together." These gentlemen, whom Lienhard identifies only as a former governor and a former judge, wanted Sutter to run for governor. "No, no gentlemen," Lienhard heard Sutter say, "please don't try to force that high office on me. I don't want it."[14] Nevertheless, they pressed him. Sutter was the best-known man in California, they said, and would undoubtedly be the most popular candidate on the ballot.

Sutter's feigned reluctance to run for office masked his pleasure with his friends' political designs. "Those two gentlemen would not leave me alone," he said when he was alone with Lienhard. "They kept urging me to be candidate for the first governor of California. The people feel they owe me this honor. Yes, Mr. Lienhard, you can see how they feel toward me."[15] To the contrary, Lienhard thought that the men were manipulating Sutter for their own ulterior motives, just as so many others had done.

There is no record of Sutter campaigning to be a delegate, but on August 1 the people of the Sacramento District elected him. The huge district included the Sacramento Valley and adjacent mining areas. Polling was no doubt an informal affair, given the lack of facilities and dispersed population. Voting in the Sacramento District was especially troublesome, and returns were late. The day before the convention was supposed to meet, the *Alta* still could not report the official results for that sprawling region. Sacramento District voters believed that they deserved ten representatives, so they voted for that number without denoting which of them were supernumeraries. The *Alta* advised that such irregularities "will probably throw upon the convention the *onus* of a decision in the case." Despite these uncertainties, the *Alta* reported there was "no doubt of the election of John A. Sutter" and several others.[16] The newspaper's confidence was well founded. Sutter had succeeded in his first political trial, an experience that doubtless reenforced his conviction that the people owed him the honor.

As the convention opening approached, Sutter traveled to Monterey, where he stayed with his old friend David Spence in company with Abel Stearns, a delegate from the south. Sutter was briefly ill with "fever" (probably malaria) when he first arrived, but soon felt well enough to attend the assembly of Californians who met in Colton Hall on September 1.[17] A two-story stone structure with a Greek Revival portico, Colton Hall was unique among the low adobe structures in the town of Monterey. Its lower floor served as a school, and the upstairs was a single large meeting hall where the convention met. The hall was "about sixty feet in length by twenty-five in breadth," wrote the travel writer Bayard Taylor, who attended the convention. "A Railing, running across the middle, divided the members from the spectators. The former were seated at four long tables, the President occupying a rostrum at the further end, over which were suspended two American flags and an extraordinary picture of Washington, evidently the work of a native artist." The place was "exceedingly dignified and intellectual," Taylor thought, "and parliamentary decorum was strictly observed." When the debates became too tedious, members took their ease on a second floor balcony where they could "enjoy the mild September afternoon, whose hues lay so softly on the blue waters of the bay."[18] Although Colton Hall was stately and commodious, there was not a single visible reminder of California's Spanish and Mexican past, except for the few californio delegates.

Lacking a quorum on the first day, the convention could do no business. The southern delegates were delayed because their chartered steamer nearly sank; but Sutter was there, along with his fellow Sacramento delegates Jacob Rink Snyder, W. E. Shannon, and Winfield S. Sherwood.[19] On September 3 Governor Riley sent the election returns to the convention and recommended that additional delegates who had received votes be seated. He left this detail to the delegates, who debated the matter.

Delegate William Gwin, soon to be one of California's first U.S. senators, made his reasons for adding additional members to the convention clear. "It was not for the native Californians we were making this Constitution," he explained, "it was for the great American population, comprising four-fifths of the population of the country."[20] There were only seven californios and a few naturalized Mexican citizens (including Sutter) among the thirty-two delegates, but Gwin wanted to dilute their voice even further by bringing in additional newcomers. Whether because of prejudices like Gwin's or because of more high-minded democratic sentiments, the duly elected convention members agreed to add to their number any candidate who received one hundred votes or more. This raised the total number of attendees to forty-eight. Sacramento's infusion included Lansford W. Hastings, John Bidwell, John S. Fowler, M. M. McCarver, John McDougal, Elisha O. Crosby, W. Blackburn, James Queen, R. M. Jones, W. Lacy, and Charles E. "Philosopher" Pickett, although several of these putative new members did not attend.

The men gathered in Colton Hall were in no way representative of California's population, except that they were extraordinarily young. The mean age was thirty-five, the youngest being twenty-five. Nine men were in their twenties, and twenty-three were in their thirties.[21] By the standards of that time and place, Sutter was an old graybeard. A photograph taken at about that time, or perhaps a little later, shows that his gray-tinged hair had gallantly retreated to make its last stand above a high forehead and distinguished nose. He still cut a figure. Clothes were important to him and hung well on his frame. He wore a silk scarf tied in the romantic fashion. Above all, Sutter looked out at the world with piercing light blue eyes. If clothes and looks said anything, they said that here was a man of substance, a man to be reckoned with. The drunk was nowhere to be seen in this picture; nor was the semi-invalid fellow who navigated unsteadily with the use of a cane.

Sutter identified his profession as farmer, an occupation that would have put him solidly in the majority before 1849 in California or anywhere else for that matter. There were only eleven farmers and ranchers at the convention, compared with fourteen lawyers and nine merchants, the other leading professions represented. Oddly, nobody claimed to be a miner, although there were no doubt some who had at least dabbled in the search for treasure. One debonaire gent from Texas listed his profession as "elegant leisure."[22] Sutter was one of only ten old-timers with ten or more years of residence. What a change! When the Mexican War began, Sutter was still a relative newcomer as a seven-year resident, and he had been a Mexican citizen for only six. Thirty of the delegates had been in California for three years or less; some measured their residency in months. At the convention only twelve members had once claimed Mexican citizenship. Thirty-eight of them had resided in the United States, although at least one of them (Sutter) had not been an American citizen. Seventeen hailed from slave states, while twenty-one came from free states.

The convention quickly got to the main order of business. Should they organize a territorial or a state government? Although there was some debate, the men decided overwhelmingly to draft a state constitution. Sutter voted with the majority on this key issue. On September 4 the convention elected as their president Robert Semple, a lanky six-and-a-half-foot Kentuckian who had lived in California for five years. The delegates then elected Sutter and Mariano Vallejo, a delegate from Sonoma, to escort President Semple to his new paramount chair.[23] It was a moment of high symbolism, the sort of occasion in which Sutter reveled. But what did the selection of Sutter and Vallejo symbolize? The union of Mexican, foreign, and U.S. interests? The old and new California? Californios and immigrants? Or did the two men together symbolize California's discredited *ancien régime,* a dysfunctional collaboration of Mexico and Europe that finally elevated one of their Anglo-American betters (Semple) to a position of authority over them? Symbolism is slippery and can mean different things to different people. We may be certain of one thing: Sutter understood his selection to be a great honor.

The question of slavery arose almost immediately. Because the U.S. Senate was evenly divided, the admission of new states had been exceedingly ticklish since the admission of Missouri in 1820, as politicians and statesmen tried to maintain a balance between slave and free states. The question of what to do about slavery in California and the rest of the Mexican cession would generate one of the great debates in senatorial history. One-third of the convention delegates had resided in the South, so many observers expected that they would attempt to introduce slavery in California. There was significant pro-slavery sentiment in California, especially in the southern part, where former slave-state residents made up a larger proportion of the population. Nevertheless, it was widely recognized that the majority of miners vehemently opposed slavery as a threat to free labor. Consequently, the convention unanimously agreed to outlaw slavery. Sutter, who had lived in a slave state, did not speak out on this issue. He and the others who voted for this provision narrowly conceived of slavery as a southern-style form of African American racial bondage. Captain Sutter and other delegates had impressed into servitude uncounted California Indians, but this vote had nothing to do with Indian rights, which would be addressed in the course of debates over citizenship.

During the discussion of California citizenship and suffrage, several delegates used Sutter as an illustrative example. Who should be accorded the right to vote and hold office? One well-meaning gentleman, noting that there were very few women and families among the forty-niners, proposed that only men who brought their families with them should be accorded political privileges. This silly, unenforceable idea would have disfranchised most of the married Americans in California. The absurdity of the proposal moved Sutter, who had been separated from his family since 1834, to rise and protest. "It would be very hard," the secretary recorded him as saying, "if he should, after his long residence here, be deprived of his right to vote because his family was elsewhere."[24] The proposal failed.

As symbol and exemplar, Sutter served several purposes at the convention, some flattering and some not. When Jacob Rink Snyder demanded that Congress pay for the costs of the convention, he castigated the United States for failing to pay $100,000 in claims that he believed the government owed to Californians. "I can point to a gentleman now present who holds claims against the Government of the United States to the amount of from twelve to fifteen thousand dollars," he said, possibly referring to Sutter's claim for rent for his fort during the war. Snyder argued that all the nations of the world and especially the United States were benefiting from the discovery of gold. "To whom are they indebted for the discovery?" he asked. "To the pioneer veteran, Capt. J. A. Sutter, through whose generosity and benevolence, protection and assistance have been afforded to the travel worn emigrants." Snyder concluded: "I need not say how they have been recompensed for the toils and dangers they encountered in opening the road to the stores of wealth that are now drawn from the inexhaustible placers of California. Neglect, gross neglect has been their reward."[25] In his diatribe against the federal government, Snyder hammered on the themes that Sutter would always emphasize in asserting his place in history: I succored the starving and defenseless immigrants; I am responsible for the discovery of gold that has brought untold riches to the world; I have been grievously wronged by almost everyone and especially by the U.S. government.

The transient nature of the population caused other delegates to support reactionary restrictions on office-holding. Sutter's sometime business associate John McDougal proposed that no one who had not been a U.S. citizen or Mexican California citizen for ten years should be governor. Delegate Shannon, another Sacramentan, spoke against McDougal's plan. "Now the gentleman's friend and my friend (Captain Sutter), if we chose to nominate him as a candidate for [governor], would come directly under this clause, and be rendered ineligible. He has not been a citizen of the United States, I believe, ten years, neither has he been a citizen of California quite ten years."[26] McDougal explained (incorrectly) that Sutter had been a citizen of the United States in Missouri for six years and a California citizen for more than ten years. Sutter did not bother to correct McDougal with the facts. He had never been a U.S. citizen, and his Mexican California citizenship began in 1840. A speech on this matter would have been pointless anyhow. McDougal's amendment was soundly defeated.[27]

While the issue of slavery had been decided, many members wanted to restrict citizenship and suffrage on the basis of race. This was an especially touchy issue because many of the californios were of mixed racial heritage. Many had Indian forebears, and a few had African American ancestry. Allowing them to vote and hold office flew in the face of the prejudices of most American delegates. Indeed, a substantial minority of members wanted to prohibit free blacks from even entering the state, much less enjoying suffrage, but they did not carry the day.

The failure to prohibit African Americans from living in California did not put an end to racially motivated tinkering with the constitution. On September 29 the convention considered an amendment that would limit the right of suffrage to white men and every citizen of the United States and Mexico except Indians, Africans, and descendants of Africans. Mexican Californians were especially threatened and outraged by this amendment, for it looked like an indirect way to disfranchise some of them. Pablo Noriega de la Guerra lectured the assembly on Mexican history and argued that some of the leading men of that republic were Indians. His argument went unheeded. In a spirit of compromise, Henry W. Halleck offered an amendment to the amendment that permitted Indians taxed as owners of real estate to vote. He no doubt intended to mollify californios by admitting rancheros to the polling place, but he inadvertently raised a new fear in the minds of some racially motivated men. J. D. Hoppe, a Missourian with three years' residence in California, argued that the Indians in question were living on ranchos and that there was not a ranchero in California who could not control the votes of "fifty or a hundred buck Indians, and the owner could run these freemen up to the polls, and carry any measure he might desire." Halleck explained that his amendment would admit only property-owning Indians to the polls, but Hoppe continued to speak about the supposed evils of Indian voting. There were ranchos in certain districts, he said, "where the California proprietors could control at least two hundred votes in favor of any particular candidate; and these votes could be purchased for a few dollars, for Indians knew no better."[28]

Hoppe's argument inspired Winfield Sherwood, a lawyer with four months' residence in California, to say that he knew his constituents were opposed to giving Indians the right to vote. If they adopted Halleck's amendment, he asserted, not a man in the mines would vote for the constitution. "Under such a state of things," the argument ran, "his friend Captain Sutter, if so disposed, if he desired to become a politician, and wished office, could, by simply granting a small portion of land to each Indian, control a vote of ten thousand."[29]

Sherwood's claim bordered on hysteria. No one bothered to point out that creating ten thousand Indians freeholders by making donations of land would be a ruinously expensive way to cadge votes. The arguments that Hoppe and Sherwood made were racial, but they were also class-based. The owners of vast land-grant ranchos by virtue of their Mexican citizenship, these delegates implied, enjoyed unfair advantages that could be turned into political capital if Indians were given any chance at suffrage—or so many Americans believed.

Sutter made sure that his recorded vote showed that he was on the side of the angels—white angels at least. He voted in favor of the original, most restrictive amendment, which failed by a vote of sixteen to twenty-six. Then the Halleck amendment came up, permitting propertied Indians to vote. Sutter opposed it, and the amendment failed by one vote. In the end the second vote went for nothing, because the chair ruled that the Halleck amendment was out of order. Still, Sutter's votes show how he thought about this issue. He was opposed to Indians voting in general, so he voted against suffrage for Indians with property.

The result of this debate was to let stand the original language on suffrage in the constitution, which restricted the vote to "every white male citizen of the United States and every white male citizen of Mexico" who elected to become an American citizen under the provisions of the Treaty of Guadalupe Hidalgo.[30] Even without the mean-spirited amendment, California was to be a white man's world. If Sutter ran for governor, he would win or lose fair and square by white men's rules and white men's votes.

One additional important matter bore on the question of slavery: the determination of state boundaries. Here again southerners indirectly resurrected the issue of slavery. Some of them supported the division of the state into northern and southern parts, an idea that favored the interests of rancheros as well as those who hoped to bring slaves to California. If California's boundaries included the southern region as well as the northern mining districts, property owners in the south would bear the expenses of the state government by paying property taxes, while northern miners who owned no land would enjoy the benefits of government without sharing in the expense. This proposal failed too; Sutter voted along with the majority for one large state.

Sutter also disagreed with those imperial Californians who would take all of the Great Basin and present-day Arizona. "I understand that my friend, Captain Sutter, desires to speak on this question," Lansford Hastings announced. "The House, I have no doubt, will be much pleased to hear him." This was one of the few occasions when Sutter addressed the convention: "I speak English so imperfectly that I will only make a single remark." While Sutter wanted to include about two-thirds of present-day Nevada, he was against including any more land than that. "It is impossible for gentlemen who have come by way of Cape Horn, to imagine what a great desert it is, and know how impolitic it would be to the State of California to embrace within its limits such a country." To this reasonable statement Sutter added that a small amount of land on Salt Lake was valuable to the Mormon settlers there, "but there is such an immense space between us and that part of the country, that I consider it of no value whatever to the State of California." Therefore, he supported the committee report that recommended an eastern boundary at 114 degrees of longitude, although he recommended an amendment "to facilitate the trade of the people of San Diego with Sonora and New Mexico, to include that portion, to the confluence of the Gila and Colorado rivers," which he erroneously believed was not included.[31]

Sutter's brief remarks were sensible and reflected the sentiments of the majority. The convention eventually cut down the boundaries so California assumed its current shape; there would be one large, free state on the Pacific Coast, as Sutter wished.

Considering the potentially volatile sectional, ethnic, and racial issues that were vigorously discussed, the convention worked with remarkable goodwill. In scarcely more than a month the delegates hammered out a document that met the basic requirements of California's white population. It was republican in form, with executive, legislative, and judicial branches and principles that were familiar to Americans. But it was a deeply flawed document too. While it spoke of liberty and natural rights, the new constitution restricted the suffrage; and the convention's debates set the stage for even greater legal restrictions on California's Indians. The delegates were an amicable lot, but there were no Madisons among them. As a framework for state government, the constitution proved so inadequate for adapting to changing circumstances that Californians wrote a new one thirty years later.

As the convention drew to a close in the second week of October, the delegates were in a self-congratulatory mood. They decided to give a ball for the citizens of Monterey, who had treated them so hospitably. Forty-four delegates contributed $25 each for food and entertainment. On October 12 Colton Hall was cleared of the tables, chairs, and detritus of the convention. To decorate the place, workers brought in American bunting and fresh young pine trees from the surrounding hills. Hired musicians (two guitarists and two violinists) played dance music. People dressed as best they could, although Bayard Taylor noticed that few men, including himself, had a complete set of ball clothes. "White kids [gloves] could not be had in Monterey for love or money, and as much as $50 was paid by one gentleman for a pair of patent-leather boots." Men dressed in borrowed clothes and castoffs if they could find them. Taylor resorted to wearing outsized trousers borrowed from a naval officer and made to fit with pins. He spoke more approvingly of the sixty or seventy women present. "The dark-eyed daughters of Monterey, Los Angeles and Santa Barbara mingled in pleasing contrast with the fairer bloom of the trans-Nevadian belles." The ladies' finery was also an amalgam of styles that included the "dark, nun-like robe . . . one of pink satin and gauze," followed by a "bodice of scarlet velvet with gold button, . . . then a rich figured brocade, such as one seen on the stately dames of Titian."[32]

Taylor complained about the music, saying that the players only seemed to know three songs and played them imperfectly. Yet he complimented them for playing long and enthusiastically. Taylor was impressed with the californios' dance etiquette, which "was marked by that grave, stately courtesy, which has been handed down since Spanish times." Taylor had an eye for men of distinction. He saw General Riley and other soldiers in uniform with their ribbons and medals. "In one group might be seen Capt. Sutter's soldierly moustache and clear blue eye; in another the erect figure and quiet, dignified bearing of Gen. Vallejo." Dancing continued until midnight, when dinner commenced. "The refreshments consisted of turkey, roast pig, beef, tongue and *patés,* with wines and liquors of various sorts, and coffee."[33] The guests devoured it all and danced on. Some of the ladies left at about two, but others were still dancing when Taylor retired at three.

The next morning found several of the conventioneers indisposed from the effects of the night's entertainment, but Sutter was there. President Semple was sick (whether from the previous evening's gala or from some other cause is uncertain), so the convention was in need of someone to take the head chair. After William Steuart proposed Sutter, he duly took his place, presiding over the few details that remained to be resolved. Following a break for lunch, President Semple returned to his chair in preparation for the formal signing ceremony. All the windows were open, and the salubrious Monterey breezes played among the young pines and banners that still decorated the hall. At a signal, the American colors were run up before the old government buildings. Then an officer at the presidio began to fire a stately cannonade, thirty-one blasts for the thirty-first state-in-waiting.

Taylor witnessed the moment seizing Sutter, who was "the old soldier again. He sprang from his seat, and, waving his hand around his head, as if swinging a sword, exclaimed: 'Gentlemen, this is the happiest day of my life. It makes me glad to hear those cannon: they remind me of the time when I was a soldier. Yes, I am glad to hear them—this is a great day for California!'" Tears streaming down his face, Sutter sat; and three spontaneous cheers erupted from the delegates, who could be heard throughout the town. When the thirty-first gun roared, a delegate yelled, "That's for California!" and more cheers went up from Colton Hall.[34]

It was indeed a great day for California, and it was a great day for Sutter too. The convention designated him to give a brief address to Governor Riley. All the delegates marched down to see the governor. A sergeant-at-arms led the way, followed by Sutter with William Gwin on one arm and M. M. McCarver on the other. Sutter's short speech was worthy of the occasion and certainly bore the hallmarks of the sort of sentiments that he frequently expressed. If Sutter spoke the words, however, someone else had cleaned up the grammar and syntax, for his published address bore none of the distinctive cadences of his characteristic broken English.

Taylor described the occasion. "Captain Sutter . . . drew himself into an erect attitude, raised one hand to his breast as if he were making a report to his commanding officer on the field of battle, and spoke":

> General: I have been appointed by the Delegates, elected by the people of California to form a constitution, to address you in their names and in behalf of the whole people of California, and express the thanks of the convention for the aid and coöperation they have received from you in the discharge of the responsible duty of creating a State Government. And, sir, the Convention, as you will perceive from the official records, duly appreciates the great and important services you have rendered to our common country, and especially to the people of California, and entertains the confident belief that you will receive from the whole of the people of the United States, when you retire from your official duties here, that verdict so grateful to the heart of the patriot: "Well done, thou good and faithful servant."[35]

Riley, visibly moved by Sutter's words, responded in plain and handsome language that this was the proudest day of his life. "Then," Sutter recalled, "he brought out wine, of which he had a good store, and toasts were drank [sic]."[36]

With that, the work of the convention was over. Riley lent army ambulances to transport Sutter and other delegates to San José. As Sutter rumbled over the primitive mountain roads, he had good reasons to feel proud. Years later his satisfaction was still evident. "At this convention we worked very hard."[37] Some people who "had nothing else to do" wanted to "spin it out as long as they could." But others, including Sutter, voted to hold "night sessions & in six weeks we got the thing done." Sutter and his compatriots had done their duty to the new state, Congress willing. He had even voted to serve without pay, although other members outvoted him on that score.[38]

Because Sutter spoke infrequently at the convention, some regarded him as little more than a decoration—"an ornamental appendage to the convention without much force," said Elisha Crosby, one of the Sacramento delegates.[39] But at least he was a well-dressed, grand decoration.[40] Taylor's description of Sutter at the convention gives an idea of the impression that he made on the people who were there. "He is still the hale, blue-eyed, jovial German—short and stout of stature, with broad forehead, head bald to the crown, and altogether a ruddy, good-humored expression of countenance. He is a man of good intellect, excellent common sense and amiable qualities of heart."[41] On the few occasions when Sutter spoke on the record, he displayed just those traits that Taylor described. If he spoke little, at least he was not a pettifogger, like some delegates. His convention votes show that he was caught up in the hypocrisy of race and slavery, as were many millions of other Americans. Still, it would have been a gratifying demonstration of those "amiable qualities of heart" that Taylor admired if Sutter had said something in defense of the Indians, without whom he could not have survived in Mexican California.

Sutter must have impressed more people than Taylor at the convention. He later claimed that some people "wanted to nominate me for governor there at Monterey, but I declined."[42] The convention had given him something to think about when considering his political future. There is no question that Sutter was generally well liked and that Americans were grateful for the help he had given to immigrants in distress. But some delegates cast Sutter as a great landholder, as indeed he was. In an age when great landlords and speculators were regarded with suspicion and scorn, his status as a leading member of California's landed gentry was not a recommendation for popular election.

Once Sutter returned to his home turf, he changed his mind about running for governor, but it was late in the game. The time for campaigning was very short, because the election was to be held on November 13, just one month after the convention completed its work. The electorate was supposed to approve the constitution as well as elect candidates to the offices provided for therein. Sutter had not even bothered to show up for a large public meeting in Sacramento to speak in favor of the new government framework.[43]

Sutter did not throw his hat in the ring until early November, so his campaign was even more truncated than the efforts of his opponents, who included Peter Burnett, Winfield Sherwood, and William Steuart.[44] One observer thought Sutter would poll strongly in Sacramento, but it was "rumored that the worthy captain seeks not the arduous duties of the office, but the distinction merely."[45] Captain Sutter stood out in the crowd in another negative way too. "The old fellow must be immensely rich," forty-niner Franklin Buck wrote three weeks before the election. "At any rate he keeps drunk all the time."[46] Sutter was certainly not the only hard drinker in gold-rush California, but he set a standard that was hard to match even among politicians.

Sutter campaigned for miners' votes in the mountains, but he had too many things against him to win a majority of votes among Americans who were new to California. "Burnett stumped the state and beat me," Sutter frankly declared in his reminiscences.[47] "He was ahead of me several days up in the mountains, otherwise he never would have beaten me."[48] Sutter claimed that he got ten thousand votes in San Francisco alone, although this assertion was very wide of the electoral truth. He won a little over a thousand votes in San Francisco and only about 2,100 votes out of 11,326 votes cast for governor in the whole state, finishing third behind Burnett and Sherwood. In his home district of Sacramento, he polled only 843 of 4,813 votes cast, good enough for third place.[49] Considering his name recognition and the small number of votes cast, Sutter's defeat was a repudiation. Remarkably, Winfield Sherwood, who had only been in California for a few months, got more than double the number of votes that Sutter received in the Sacramento District. Considering Sherwood's convention rant against Sutter's potential to control ten thousand Indian votes, we can imagine the sort of stump speech he gave. Sutter never again ran for political office.

Political defeat was not the only challenge that Sutter faced in late 1849. Some of the men who voted against him were not inclined to respect his property rights either. In late fall miners began to come down from the mountains to winter in Sacramento. They pitched their tents on any open ground that they chose, disregarding the claims of Sutter and property owners who held title from him. As the tent city grew, the problem became serious. Sutter feared the worst. He wrote his friend Governor Riley, who remained in office until Congress approved the new constitution, and asked for protection from "the Squatters who have taken possession of my lands & of many lots in Sacramento City." These men were determined to hold the land even though they did not pretend to have a valid title. "Their number is so great, that in the event of an attempt on my part in connection with others who labor under similar grievances, to protect our rights, the worst consequences are to be expected." Sutter had no doubt that his title to the lands in question would finally be upheld, but in the meantime he wanted a company of soldiers stationed at Sacramento to enforce civil judgments against the squatters. Otherwise, he feared that legal actions "inevitably must lead to bloodshed."[50]

A few months earlier Sutter dreamily believed that "the people" were so far indebted to him for his help in settling the Sacramento Valley that they would elect him governor simply to give him the honor that was due. The people, however, were a fickle and unruly lot who cast a jaundiced eye on Sutter's bloated land claims. Their challenge to his lordly possessions opened a new and calamitous period in his life.

CHAPTER 19

Land Troubles

Americans were astonished at the extent of individual landholdings in California. Californians "never speak of acres, or even miles," Walter Colton observed, "they deal only in leagues." "Capt. Sutter's farm in the valley of the Sacramento," he added, "is sixty miles long," and Sutter counted his livestock by the thousands. It was unimaginable to the average American, who thought of 160 acres as adequate land for a family farm. "Only fancy a farm covering sixty miles in length! Why a man would want a railroad through it for his own private use. Get out of the way, ye landlords of England and patroons of Amsterdam, with your boroughs and dykes, and give place to the Californian with his sixty mile sweep!"[1]

Colton scarcely exaggerated when he spoke of Sutter's sixty-mile farm, for as the crow flew that was about the distance from the Sutter Buttes to Sutterville, the New Helvetia grant's northern and southern limits. In 1849 few people understood that Sutter's grant embraced only the high ground in the great swath of the Sacramento Valley. Even so, to newcomers the extent of his claim seemed preposterous. Certainly it was an insult to republican values. Soon some of the newcomers would begin to question the legal extent of Sutter's grant, and Sacramento would be the focal point of their concerns.

Nature helped the controversy along. Forced out of the diggings by winter rains, miners swarmed into Sacramento in late 1849. This proved to be a problem for the young city and its landlords. Speculators had pushed lot prices to the thousands, far out of the reach of destitute miners. There was no place for them if they could not afford a primitive hotel room or space in a leaky tent. Some men were sick, and there was only one hospital, located near the fort—

Brannan's old store now converted to this new use. The miners put up shelters wherever they could and to hell with the property owners who demanded as much as $12 per day for the privilege of camping on their land. Squatters had come to Sacramento. As far as they were concerned, they had come to stay through the winter, come the devil or high water.[2]

The winter of 1849 proved to be much wetter than the previous year. Thirteen inches of rain fell in December alone, and in early January new storms dumped more water than the ground could absorb or the rivers could carry away. Rain in the mountains worsened the situation by melting the snow pack. On January 8 the American River overflowed into an old channel called Sutter Slough and ran into the low-lying city at the embarcadero. At once some parts of the nascent town were twelve feet under water. Sacramentans floated to safety on their cots or drowned, some going down from the weight of the gold in their pokes. Speculators and squatters alike headed for high ground out near the fort and waited for the water to subside.

The proprietors of Sutterville saw a ray of hope in Sacramento's grim, gray flood days. Perhaps Sacramento merchants would now see the wisdom of removing to their competing town on high ground. It did not happen, and realists like John Bidwell could see the final message written on the wall: "If the high floods which have swept Sacramento City and the river generally, will not turn the attention of people to Sutter[ville], nothing within our reach will do it."[3] As a stakeholder in Sutterville, Bidwell was willing to give land to promote the place, "but no money."[4] Sacramento merchants, however, were willing to invest a lot of money to save their landed investment and improvements. As soon as the weather cleared, they began building levees to keep out future floods. This expenditure amazed Bidwell. He reckoned that "[h]alf the money required to construct a levee around Sacramento city would make several ship canals from the river to the high land at Sutter." Perhaps "[i]f five or six of the most wealthy and influential merchants of Sacramento city could be interested in this matter, and enter into the scheme with all their might, it would succeed," Bidwell thought, "otherwise—Sutter[ville] will go down."[5] And so it did.

While Sacramentans bailed water, scraped mud, and built dykes, Sutter was concerned with a momentous personal matter. On January 21, 1850, his family arrived in San Francisco on board the steamer *Panama*. Heinrich Lienhard found rooms for Mrs. Sutter, their daughter, and their two sons at the Graham House, a large four-story wooden structure that had been shipped in sections from Baltimore. Despite the hotel's imposing appearance, mere cotton blankets partitioned the rooms. By then the Sutters must have been wondering what sort of place California was. A fire had destroyed much of the new city in December, and stormy weather had made San Francisco streets into an almost impassable sea of mud. After housing his charges, Lienhard went up the flooded river aboard a small, rickety steamer to fetch Sutter.[6]

The arrival of Mrs. Sutter was news. The *Alta* predicted a joyous meeting when the Sutters were reunited. "After an absence from 'faderland' of nearly twenty years, which period has been fraught with event in California, we can reasonably imagine the happiness with which the distinguished adventurer will greet familiar forms and faces, endeared by the sacred ties of relationship, to the country he has learned to love so well." Such a long separation "was indeed a blank in one's existence when eked out in the wilderness."[7]

Lienhard found Sutter in Sacramento at the City Hotel, where the captain must have felt right at home. The three-story building was constructed on the frame of the unfinished gristmill, purchased from Sutter and moved to a lot on Front Street in September 1849.[8] He was completing a deal to sell "the big wheatfields northeast of the fort" to some Swiss gentlemen, Lienhard observed.[9] Sutter was understandably eager to be reunited with his family, so he and Lienhard arranged for passage to San Francisco on a steamer leaving the next morning. Sutter was so anxious to be reunited with Anna and his children that he neglected to send for August at Hock Farm, an oversight that exacerbated the bad feelings between father and son. They spent the night in rough and ready style at Sutter's zinc warehouse, a prefabricated metal building that had been shipped to California. The place was infested with rats, no doubt refugees from the recent flood.

The reunion was as warm as the *Alta* had predicted. "Sutter and I went directly to . . . the room occupied by his wife and daughter," Lienhard wrote. "As the door opened, an affectionate greeting took place between the entire family, who were reunited for the first time in seventeen years." Unfortunately, the Sutters were not alone. "A clever speculator was also in the room," Lienhard noted with distaste.[10] The young chaperone was at some pains to get the man to leave the Sutter family to themselves. Speculators, like cloth walls and plentiful gold, were just part of the new world that Swiss family Sutter would have to get used to. But for the present Sutter took pleasure in his reunified family. "I can assure you this has been a most happy meeting," he informed Bidwell. "My family arrived safe by the Steamer Panama, they are all in good health, and this evening we shall be on board the Senator, which leave here to Morrow early for Sacramento City, from there we are bound with the Lawrence to Hock."[11]

The Sutter family was not as content as the patriarch wanted to believe. Based on his experience, August had already formed an entirely realistic view of his father, whose habitual drinking and moronic business decisions were matters of public discussion. August had valiantly struggled to right his father's sinking financial ship, but Sutter inexplicably rejected his son. Swindlers warned August that his father planned to ship him back to Switzerland in chains while at the same time convincing Sutter that his son was a scoundrel who spoke against his father. In a drunken fit at the fort, Sutter told Lienhard that he wished his son had never been born and added, "I would like to kill him." In a flash Sutter redirected his rage at himself. He seized a double-barreled pistol and yelled, "I am going to shoot myself."[12] Lienhard grabbed the pistol and wrestled him to a nearby bed, where Sutter slept it off. Lienhard's revulsion at Sutter's behavior only increased when he discovered that the pistol was not loaded. It is impossible to know if Sutter was serious about killing August or himself—probably not. But the language of their estrangement was elemental and poisonous. Perhaps gathering the whole clan at Hock would reestablish loving family bonds, but there was much to repair.

Sutter had missed almost all of the childhood of his children, who arrived with fully formed personalities and a lifetime of waiting for their father. Anna Eliza was almost twenty-one when she set foot in California. According to Sutter, Eliza's formal education was complete by the time she was nineteen, and he insisted that she was very accomplished.[13] Some men regarded her as unattractive. Thomas Kerr, an Irish workman at Hock Farm, thought her "a very bold Masculine Girl" with a noticeable "wag of her carriage & the nasty shake she gives her elbows when walking." Still, he noted that she superintended the "Tradesmen meals[;] she is decidedly a hard working girl though very small[;] its no silly joke to attend to the mess of from 15 to 20 people 3 times a day."[14] A squatter who camped a couple of miles from Hock Farm observed that Sutter had a daughter, "but I guess I am in no danger of seeing her . . . the old man seems to have some notion of being aristocratic."[15] Sutter told Lienhard that his children could "marry into the finest families of Philadelphia and New York," and he hoped to marry Eliza to someone of significant social standing.[16]

The second son, Emil Victor Sutter, born in 1830, had been educated at an agricultural institute. He was the least appealing of Sutter's three sons. Unattractive, dour, and taciturn, Victor was happiest when working in the garden. He may have been moody because he was hard of hearing and often did not understand conversation.[17] His morose disposition did not improve. As he aged, Victor became more detached, depressed, and defensive. He often wrote letters to newspapers defending his father and the family.

Wilhelm Alphonse, the third son and youngest child, was quite a different case. Handsome and outgoing, Alphonse had inherited his father's genial nature. He was the favored Sutter sibling among Californians who knew him and probably within the family too. Only seventeen when he arrived, Alphonse had been a cadet at a military academy. He inherited his father's love of all things martial and also some of his ego. "I will be made supreme general of the State of California," Alphonse once said. He must have had a musical side as well, for Sutter bought a piano and hired a teacher for him.[18]

Sutter's wife, Anna Dübeld Sutter, is perhaps the most difficult member of the Sutter family to know. She never learned English and left no letters. Photographs show her as a sad-looking, straight-laced, angular woman, with a permanent frown of the sort caused by bad false teeth. One must look very hard to see the attractive nineteen-year-old that Sutter had wooed in Burgdorf. In later years her glowering visage appeared at the door to turn away unwelcome visitors, who expected Sutter to entertain them with wine and brandy as in days of old. If her countenance gave a true picture of inner life, Anna's unhappiness was well earned. Sutter left her with five children in 1834. The youngest son died in 1839. She depended on the charity of her sisters, but that did not save her from a life of toil. Thomas Kerr, the industrious Irishman who worked at Hock Farm, thought she was rude and overbearing, but his Irish eyes saw something else too. "From the appearance of her hands, she must have known what hard work was: she is a fretted looking woman," he concluded.[19] Sutter would give her more reasons to fret in California, and she would not be a stranger to hard work for long.

Descriptions of the Sutter sons suggest that all had inherited some of their father's traits. Interest in business, military affairs, and agriculture marked each of them. Eliza took after her industrious mother. They were all vain, like their father. Despite the family resemblance, in 1850 the Sutters were a family in name only. After sixteen years, August and Eliza were probably the only children who remembered their father in Switzerland. What Anna thought of her husband, their long separation, the many promises broken, or prospects in California no one can know. She quickly established her role as the woman of the house, with Eliza as her domestic apprentice. August claimed that he did not tell his siblings what he had learned about his father's personal and business habits. They would have plenty of opportunities to see for themselves.

Sutter's instability in business matters was obvious to anyone. This persistent trait was well illustrated by the powers of attorney that he granted in rapid succession in 1850. In one five-month period Sutter gave five men the authority to handle his California real estate. In May he replaced Archibald Peachy with Albert Winn, an extensive landholder in Sacramento. Two months later Sutter revoked all other powers of attorney and appointed Jonathan Fowler as his sole representative. But wait; two weeks later he gave Henry Schoolcraft the right to sell his unsold Sacramento lots. That arrangement lasted for a month before Sutter had second thoughts and reinstated Fowler, who held his confidence for five weeks. B. F. Tarr handled Sutter's affairs for eight months.[20] Sutter eventually slowed the pace of his revolving-door arrangements but not the pattern of his relations with his agents and attorneys. He gave them a percentage of land sales, "a large one," but when they made money Sutter was convinced that they were swindling him, as perhaps they were. "Peachy made a fortune out of me in a short time," he complained, and so did others.[21] Whether bewildered by liquor, swindled by designing men, or both, Sutter simply had no ability to judge people. If they seemed sincere and accommodating, had a firm handshake, and liked to drink, that was good enough for him. As one droll newspaperman put it, Sutter's "instinctive humanity has made him powerless in every department of close and calculating economy."[22]

Still, Sutter took some sensible steps to secure his family's financial future. If there was to be a Sutter fortune, land would be its foundation. Congress had yet to act on statehood or the Mexican land grant question in early 1850, but Sutter understood that he would eventually have to support his claims with evidence that he had fulfilled the condition of his grants. The so-called sobrante grant from Micheltorena was especially troublesome because it was not supported with standard documentation. To buttress his claim, he had contacted Micheltorena in Mexico, but "he can no more remember every circumstance, and the boundaries which we have taken in," Sutter complained. Perhaps the general's memory could be refreshed. Therefore Sutter wanted Bidwell to prepare an affidavit in Spanish for Micheltorena's signature. "The date have to be," Sutter explained, "at the same time while we have been at Monterey."[23] Refreshed or not, Micheltorena's memory would prove to be of little use. The governor died in 1852, and Sutter would have to rely on the testimony of others to support the sobrante claim.

True to form, Sutter was piling up debts at ruinous interest rates with no immediate hope of repayment.[24] His business agents made matters worse. Acting under power of attorney, Albert Winn borrowed $5,000 in Sutter's name at 10 percent interest per month and did not bother to inform him about it. The unpaid debt sat silently for years, secretly undermining Sutter's always precarious financial condition.[25] Sutter was headed for ruin even without Winn's perfidy, for he was fully capable of foolishly borrowing money on his own. After all, he had plenty of land that was increasing in value, or so it seemed in 1850. There is some question as to how ignorant Sutter was concerning his mounting debts. In July he transferred Hock Farm (defined as twelve square miles on Feather River) to four of his business associates, who immediately conveyed it to his wife, Anna, a transaction that might afford some protection against foreclosure.[26]

There can be no doubt that Winn and others made pie out of Sutter's domain and ate their fill. Several of these supposed trusted associates refused to give him an accounting of the lots that they sold, a lapse that led to multiple sales. Winn even had an expensive portrait painted and paid for it with Sutter's Sacramento lots. In later years Sutter admitted that he "gave men power of atty to sign deeds and they swindled me on every side."[27]

Sutter always portrayed himself as an unwitting victim of calculating men, but his fondness for liquor was a great aid to those who wanted to fleece him. One Sacramento merchant thought Sutter was "a good meaning pleasant man, but the most sappy headed fool you can conceive of—& excited with wine usually & half the time half drunk—& the Yankees have used him & flattered him, & made him believe that he owns the greater part of Calia."[28] Roland Gelston, another local merchant, well understood that liquor and flattery were powerful tools in any negotiation with Sutter. Gelston was a major Sacramento property owner. Rumor had it that he had not paid a cent for his lots. J. T. Mott, a Sacramentan who purchased several lots from Gelston at $3,000 each, said that Gelston went up to Hock Farm "with some boxes of wine and liquor to make Sutter drunk, as he is known to take an extra glass frequently." Both men "got drunk and had a *high time* of it," and Sutter then signed over the lots to Gelston. Once sober, Sutter remorsefully published a statement saying that the lots had been obtained fraudulently. Whether this is strictly true or not, Sutter's notorious drunken transactions threw "a heavy cloud on the titles of many Saco. Lots, and they are now literally worth nothing & unsalable," Mott complained, although taxes still had to be paid.[29]

Clearly Sutter was neither an entrepreneurial role model nor a good source for business advice; but when he advised August to enter into business with the German lace merchants Julius and Gustavus Wetzlar, August agreed. He suspected that his father wanted to get him away from Hock Farm and the rest of the family. Meanwhile August had come under the influence of a shadowy German physician, known to history only as Doctor Brandes. The good doctor treated August, who came to admire him as his "best friend, a man of education and a superior character," with a "thorough kno[w]ledge of men and the world."[30] Brandes recommended that August form a partnership with the Wetzlars. The brothers told August that they required $30,000 in capital in order to break off their other business arrangements. He went to his father and asked for the money. Sutter was probably flattered that his son would ask him for help. For him a mere $30,000 was but a snap of the fingers, and he agreed to provide the money. August made sure that Brandes was included in the partnership without investing anything, "to watch closely over my own private interests," he hoped. "I saw him as the only physician able to attend to me in my sickness," he explained. "To keep him near me, I should have made any concessions. I thought I should die if he was going to leave me."[31]

Unbeknownst to August at the time, Brandes was dosing him with drugs that impaired his judgment, likely some sort of opiate such as laudanum. Since young Sutter also took to drinking during this period, the combination of drugs and alcohol made a change in him. When Lienhard returned to Hock Farm, he saw "an unfamiliar figure clad in buckskin trousers and a red flannel shirt. He had a brown felt hat on his head, and was wearing a long bowie knife in a leather belt around his waist." He did not seem to recognize Lienhard. After walking slowly from the house down to the river within thirty or so feet of Lienhard, he "looked, first at me, and then off across the river. He seemed to be a stranger."[32]

Impaired and trusting the judgment of his corrupt physician, August had become a younger, uncertain version of his father. Desperate to fit in with California's tough frontier populace, August affected their dress and attitudes. In this state he showed some of the same vulnerabilities as his father. Unsure of himself, he followed the advice of unscrupulous men who promised to serve him but who did not look beyond their own wallets. August forgot his native business instincts and became one of the many supplicants who asked his father for money.

Sutter was happy to oblige. He even offered to help with letters of credit in the amount of $10,000 for New York merchants, although no one would honor them in San Francisco. Nevertheless, Gustavus Wetzlar steamed off to New York to obtain stock, leaving brother Julius in charge of the partnership. Julius gladly provided assurances to August that business was going well. August periodically went to Sacramento to check the books and found that all was in order, although he later understood that the books were cooked.[33]

While August convinced himself that he was in a safe and profitable business relationship with reliable friends, Sacramento squatters took a careful look at Sutter's New Helvetia grant. On March 16, 1850, John Plumbe published in the *Placer Times* an assertion that Sacramento was outside the legitimate Sutter grant.[34] On April 23 Plumbe backed up his statement with a translation of Sutter's New Helvetia grant. The effect of the plain language of Sutter's grant was electrifying. On the one hand, it seemed to make the mouth of the Feather River the southern limit of New Helvetia; on the other, it excluded lands that were periodically inundated. Sutter's claim to Sacramento thus failed on two counts. Either it was not included in the language of the grant in the first place or it was excluded because (as the recent flood demonstrated) Sacramento was regularly overflowed. This line of reasoning convinced squatters that law and right were on their side. If Sutter had no right to the land, then it was public domain. The newly formed Settlers' Association began issuing deeds to Sacramento lots. The property owners who bought from Sutter and his agents who remained convinced that they held valid titles became known as Sutterites. The people of Sacramento began to organize around the question of the validity of Sutter's grant. Both sides were well armed.

Sutter, of course, believed the courts would support him. In 1849 he began publishing advertisements in the local papers: "Notice to Squatters," claiming everything from the Buttes to a point just south of Sutterville.[35] After Plumbe's revelation the tables were turned. "Is Capt. John A. Sutter a squatter or not?" asked the *Sacramento Transcript* on June 4, 1850.[36] Sutterites, not to mention Sutter, regarded this as an absurd question. Had not Sutter built a fort and farmed the land around Sacramento? Did he not have a grant from the Mexican authorities? What serious-minded observer could doubt that the United States would uphold Sutter's claim, however grand it may seem to the squatters?[37]

Sutter still had unwavering confidence in his claim. As if to underscore his status as the preeminent pioneer in the Sacramento Valley, he entertained one and all at Hock Farm. Four steamboats a day passed his place, and many of them stopped so that passengers could visit the famed Captain Sutter. Indeed, he established himself, his family, and his farm as a sort of tourist attraction. On June 2 Sutter hosted a special excursion on the steamboat *Governor Dana* from Sacramento to Hock Farm, where there was a gala reception and dinner for about a hundred people. When the *Dana* rounded into view, Sutter touched off a cannon. The Sutter family came down to the landing, and the passengers gave nine cheers for "the great pioneer of California." As a brass band struck up a tune, the party was led to a long table in front of the house that was "loaded with the delicacies of the season." General Winn, who was still in good odor with Sutter, presided as master of ceremonies. Sutter and his family took the central seats, and Winn offered a toast "To Mrs. Sutter!" Sutter responded for her with a "hearty welcome" to Hock Farm. Dozens of toasts followed: to Sutter, the ladies, Miss Sutter, Sutter's hospitality, the spirit of republicanism, the reunion of the Sutter family, and so on and on. At last the party thanked Sutter for his "princely hospitality," filed back to the boat, and steamed back to Sacramento to the strains of "Yankee Doodle."[38] This was a formal affair that had been planned in advance, but uncounted travelers, friends, strangers, grifters, and the merely curious stopped by Hock Farm on a daily basis. They expected, and received, Captain Sutter's famed hospitality. Whatever else may be said of him, he was a gracious and openhanded host, generous to a fault.

But the portrait of the happy Sutter family thinly veiled disputes that shook the household. In the spring of 1850 Eliza had her eyes open for a suitable mate. They fell on someone near at hand: George David Engler, Alphonse's piano teacher. Lienhard unflatteringly described him as "a small frail man, with a sallow complexion, dark hair, and large eyes for a man of his size."[39] Yet Engler was sociable and popular, played a large repertoire of songs on the piano, and sang to boot. Eliza thought he was wonderful. One day she asked Lienhard to go riding with her. "As soon as we had passed through the gate, Miss Eliza whipped her horse to a brisk gallop; I had to put the spurs to my horse to keep up with her." When she finally reined in her mount, she bluntly asked Lienhard's opinion of Engler: "Is he the man for me?" "I like him very much," she confessed, "but my father will not give his consent to the match. He thinks I should marry a captain or a major—someone with more standing." Flustered, Lienhard was reluctant to give his frank opinion of a man who had not favorably impressed him. When pressed by the infatuated Eliza, he said, "[I]f you like him why don't you marry him?" Finding Lienhard to be an ally, she exclaimed, "That's exactly what I think! Father shouldn't say anything about the fact that he is poor, for he had no money when he married my mother."[40] August did not like Engler either, but Eliza chalked up her brother's attitude to the fact that he had borrowed some money from Engler and did not want to pay it back. Realizing that he was in the murky waters of a family dispute, Lienhard decided not to comment further.

Rumors about Eliza and Engler began to spread. One day while visiting the dilapidated fort, August heard talk that the pair were "extremely friendly" and expected to marry. To August's ears this was scandalous stuff that disgraced the entire Sutter family, so he reported the rumors to the patriarch at Hock Farm. When Sutter learned that the low-born Engler wanted the hand of his daughter, he flew into a rage, fired the piano teacher, and ordered his daughter to break off the relationship. According to Lienhard, Sutter "spoke so harshly to his daughter that she tried to commit suicide by cutting an artery in her wrist with a knife."[41] He even offered her a pistol so that she could end her life more efficiently. Attempts to mollify Sutter were futile, and the now-separated lovers were disconsolate.

Amid the myriad distractions of family, farm, and fortune, Sutter decided he did not have time for public service. In May he resigned as Indian subagent for the Sacramento District. "My old age and the decline of life together with the multiplicity of my private business would render it impossible for me to discharge the duties of the office in such a manner as would be satisfactory to myself or acceptable to the Government," Sutter explained at the ripe age of forty-seven.[42]

Preoccupation with business was doubtless Sutter's primary reasons for resigning, although he did not attend carefully enough to his financial affairs. True to form, he had borrowed $7,511.38 on two notes that were due in July and November. He made only one payment of $1,000 and was in default for the rest. This seemingly small debt would grow exponentially when Sutter's creditor successfully sued and the court ordered him to pay the amount owed plus interest at 10 percent per month. When the judgment was finally made, Sutter owed at least $3,200 in interest alone, a sum that was mounting at a ruinous rate. The court ordered him to mortgage a substantial piece of Sacramento real estate to guarantee payment.[43] Thanks to Governor Burnett, Sutter was clear of debt in 1849. One year later he was again out of cash.

Even if Sutter had the time and inclination to devote to the Indian service, it is difficult to imagine him serving as an effective agent in 1850. He had learned at Coloma the year before that he did not have much influence over Indians or whites in California anymore. The Oregon men had begun a full-fledged war of extermination against California Indians in the mines in 1849. Now that the state government was organized, the legislature set about enacting laws that governed Indian affairs. The best known of those statutes was deceptively styled "A Law for the Government and Protection of the Indians." This law provided for the indenture of adult Indians who were not employed by whites and Indian children who were orphans. In effect the state of California institutionalized the nefarious labor practices of Sutter and other Mexican rancheros. Less well known were "An Act concerning Volunteer or Independent Companies" and "An Act concerning the Organization of the Militia."[44] These laws gave counties broad authority to call out local militia companies and to pay and arm them.

Volunteers were soon in the field fighting Indians for real and imagined depredations against the honest miners while giving full vent to all of their racist presentiments.[45] The results of these wars of extermination, as Governor Burnett called them, were devastating for the Indians. There is no guarantee that Sutter's experienced voice would have had a moderating influence over these volunteer organizations, but his voice was not heard.[46]

While his father juggled finances, August struggled to keep up with the financial shenanigans of partners whose sole aim was to mulct him and his father with the help of Doctor Brandes. August signed notes to raise cash for the new partnership while waiting for Sutter to put in the required $30,000. Sutter, who could not pay his other debts, was unable to give him the money at the appointed time, so August went to his mother for part of it and sold some of the Hock Farm livestock to raise additional funds. (Evidently Sutter was again shifting assets to his family in order to protect himself from creditors.) Sutter gave his son his share in the zinc house at Sacramento. August transferred one-fourth interest in all of his property to the partnership and in return received a one-fourth interest in the firm. "Here again I was made their dupe, as I confess, I do not know how," August wrote later when his head finally cleared.[47]

Somehow August's partners made him and his father responsible for their business failure. "Mr. Wetzlar told me that I had disappointed them and that my father was the only cause of their bad circumstances and precarious situation," August recalled.[48] Blaming Sutter seemed plausible to August in his drug-befogged state. His partners "took pleasure in reporting to me the bad policy and follies of my father, that in a few years my father would have squandered all his property, that then all our family would be left without a dollar to subsist on, and finally it was high time for me to interfere and to save whatever I could from general ruin for my own and the rest of the family's benefit."[49]

August went to Hock Farm with Doctor Brandes, determined to obtain his father's remaining interest in Sacramento plus a square mile of land adjoining Sutterville. Sutter resisted August, but "after a very violent scene with my father," the patriarch signed over the property. August then tried to determine exactly what Sacramento lots he owned, but this proved to be an impossible task. Sutter's multiple attorneys had sold some lots twice or even three times to different buyers. "It appeared to me impossible," August thought, "to sell any lots without running the risk of falling more and more into difficulties and law suits without end." Young Sutter had had enough of gold-rush California. He decided to retire to "some other part of the world, I did not care where, provided I should enjoy good health and not hear any more of these confusions and my unpleasant business altogether."[50]

Ever attentive to August's health and welfare, Brandes had an idea. First, settle with Wetzlar for all of his claims against the unprofitable partnership. That fair gentleman offered to trade him the property owned by the partnership while getting all of the Sutters' interest in the zinc house. Rats or no, the zinc house sat on one of the most valuable embarcadero lots in town. The generous partner also suggested that Brandes be given $10,000 for all of the trouble he had gone to on August's behalf. August agreed, and only then learned that he had received all of the concern's liabilities as well as the property, which was not enough to cover the debts. With more than $14,000 in property taxes coming due, he now owed more than $30,000, which he could not pay because he did not know what lots were available for sale.[51]

August had to act fast because he believed (with the encouragement of Brandes) that he would die if he remained in Sacramento. He told Wetzlar that he was willing to sell the whole of his troublesome property. His faithless partner thought it would be hard to find a buyer for so much property, but he would try. He did not have to search for long. Sam Brannan, who already owned much of Sacramento, "and some gentlemen from San Francisco" were willing to buy if the price was low enough. August was willing to sell everything for $125,000 as long as the buyers took on all title claims that might come against him. Wetzlar and Brandes thought this was a very good arrangement for August and encouraged him to sell. Of course, such a large sum of money could not be obtained at once. August agreed to accept $25,000 on signing a conveyance, a second installment of $25,000 in three months, and a final payment of $75,000 one year from the date of the sale. By this time he was bedridden in a Sacramento hotel and in no condition to haggle over details.[52]

Ever helpful, Wetzlar agreed to have the necessary papers drawn. On the evening of June 20 he told August that all was ready. Seeing that August was unable to get out of bed, Brandes administered one of his drugs, and the prostrate man rose unsteadily. In this enervated condition August accompanied Wetzlar and Brandes by candlelight to a lawyer's office. Brannan and two partners, Samuel C. Bruce and James A. Grahame, were already waiting. To his astonishment, August learned that Wetzlar was Brannan's fourth partner in the purchase. August agreed to appoint Wetzlar as his attorney to collect the future payments from the partners. Wetzlar was evidently a little short of cash at the signing of the conveyance, so August permitted him to pay later. With this transaction the major part of the Sutters' interest in Sacramento vanished. August evidently received $18,750 in cash, with Wetzlar's share deferred, but only a few thousand dollars remained after he paid off Brandes and Wetzlar. It got worse. A few days later Wetzlar told August that his brother in New York had sent bills amounting to $6,000. Temporarily embarrassed for funds, he begged for $2,000 to tide him over. August, who had about $1,400 in gold dust, gave Wetzlar as much as he could spare.[53]

A few days after these transactions, August was taking his leave at Hock Farm. Somehow he became offended by one of the Indians who worked there, so he tried to torch the ranchería.[54] This event may have been one of those that August later denied. "Of a great many things which I am told passed then, I have not the slightest recollection, and . . . [I] denied the facts, even to my brother, until my mother herself tells me now the same thing. I must have been out of my senses."[55] On July 1 August steamed away with Brandes and his powerful medicine kit by his side. He hoped never to see the godforsaken country of California or the hellhole of Sacramento again.

The ugly dispute with his son and the loss of his Sacramento property must have shaken Sutter. It was clear now that if he was to hold onto his claims he needed help. Mounting debts were troublesome too, but he believed that time was on his side. Surely the federal government would confirm his claim, and he would be able to evict the squatters or sell property to them at a fair price. In the meantime he wanted to rid himself of the legal headache of managing his vast real-estate holdings. On the day that August departed, Sutter and his wife executed a deed of trust that authorized Henry E. Robinson, Eugene Gillespie, John Fowler, and John McDougal, prominent Sacramento speculators all, to expel squatters and sell any of his California lands, excluding Hock Farm. The Sutters would get only one-sixth of the proceeds, and the Robinson partnership would receive the rest. In exchange for five-sixths of his property, Sutter received $6,000 in cash. By a separate deed Robinson and friends conveyed all of Hock Farm, defined as twenty-four square miles on the west bank of the Feather River, to Anna. Nothing from Hock Farm could be sold without her written permission.[56]

Sutter was well known for making bad business deals, but this arrangement smacks of desperation. One year earlier he had complained bitterly about Burnett getting one-fourth of the proceeds from the sale of Sacramento lots. Now he readily gave up a majority of his assets in return for the serenity and financial safety that he hoped would come with a strong partnership. The Robinson trust did not protect the Sutters or provide any income. Instead of working on the Sutters' behalf, his new partners quarreled over how best to benefit personally from the arrangement. Nevertheless, the trust remained in effect through most of the 1850s, a complicating factor in Sutter's business. Placing the ownership of Hock Farm in the sole hands of Anna Sutter seemed to protect the family farm from any more bad business deals. The Robinson deed required Anna's permission to sell or encumber Hock Farm with mortgages. But sign she did, many times over, as the voluminous property records of Sutter County show.

Two days after August departed, Sutter received a visitor, Prince Paul Wilhelm of Württemberg, one of the wealthiest men in Europe. Liberal in his political views, the prince had a scientific bent and traveled the world collecting biological specimens and observing indigenous peoples. He was already well known in the American West when he came to see the elephant in California.[57] John Sutter was one part of the elephant that Prince Paul wanted to observe. On July 2 or 3 he met Captain Sutter at a Sacramento restaurant, probably the Hotel de France, which was next door to the City Hotel.

Prince Paul and Sutter hit it off nicely. The lord of New Helvetia still knew how to impress and entertain guests. A friendship developed that the duke later confessed he "kept fresh in my heart through the intervening years." Still, Prince Paul was a shrewd observer. Had Sutter "been a person at all intent on building up a vast fortune, [he] would . . . be the richest man in the world." Sutter's possessions were "a kingdom in extent." He learned that Sutter had disposed of much of his California property for a tiny fraction of its worth. "If that is true one cannot help regretting the lack of vision which could permit the surrender of a prospective fortune, . . . so great that kings and emperors would stand aghast at the enormity of the loss."[58]

Governor Burnett invited Prince Paul to the Fourth of July fete in the little town of Brighton, a few miles east of the old fort near a bend in the American River. On the morning of the celebration the prince got into a carriage with the governor, Lieutenant Governor McDougal, and Sutter. Evidently Burnett and Sutter set aside their personal and business differences in honor of the occasion. Several other carriages with distinguished passengers on board had a retinue of mounted horsemen for an escort. The horses started at a brisk canter and soon were at a dead run, what "seemed like a mad dash for life" to the prince.[59] A collection of carriages, "stagecoaches, omnibuses, and buggies" raced "over the rutty streets of the city and out onto the plain where the oak trees thinned out gradually until at last they disappeared entirely to give way to the open country." Welcome to California, your Highness. The wild procession paused at Sutter's Fort, where "there was an enthusiastic salute to its beloved founder," and then moved on to Brighton, where a large hall called the Pavilion sheltered them from the heat.[60]

The celebration at Brighton was a standard affair. Guests raised wine glasses and offered toasts to California and the republic while a cannon periodically fired noisy salutes. A grand dinner capped the occasion. There were predictable speeches, all forgettable, save one that caught the ear of Prince Paul, by a Mr. Walker. One historian suggests that this was William Walker, who would soon achieve fame as a filibuster known as the "grey-eyed man of destiny." E. J. C. Kewen, however, a young lawyer who would become one of Walker's close filibustering associates, was the only speaker named in the papers. But there were many toasts, and Walker may have spoken in that capacity. In any case Sutter would have more substantial connections with filibusters in the coming years. In the evening they attended a play by "a miserable theatrical company," and the prince accepted Sutter's invitation to visit Hock Farm after a tour of the gold fields and nearby Indian rancherías.[61]

On July 5 Paul departed for the mines by way of the Feather River towns Eliza (named for Sutter's daughter), Marysville, and Yuba City. At Hock Sutter introduced the prince to his family. Sutter took his guest to the Indian community that served his ranch with labor and provided a list of common Nisenan words.

After enjoying Sutter's hospitality and admiring Hock Farm the prince decided to travel to Mount Rainier. "Mr. Sutter fitted out this expedition with the help of a white guide who had been a trader among the Indian tribes of the lower Columbia River. All the combined experience of these two marvelous pioneers was directed to bring together everything that was needful for so long and hazardous an undertaking," the prince gratefully recalled. The party included "a dozen well-armed and seasoned men" and many horses.[62] Captain Sutter did not accompany the prince, but he sent his moody son, Victor. The prince's account of the trek to Mount Rainier has been lost, but the party returned safely to Hock Farm in early fall.

While the royal expedition proceeded northward, political conditions in Sacramento worsened. In late June so-called Sutterite landowners began evicting squatters and demolishing their improvements. The big speculators were in some financial trouble, because property values began to decline as the speculative gold-rush bubble subsided. Sutter's claim to the land seemed increasingly likely to be upheld in the courts, however, whenever they got around to adjudicating Mexican land grants. During this period speculators strove to acquire all of Sutter's Sacramento lands that they could. The Brannan purchase from August was the grossest example of this trend, which made the squatters angrier than ever. As the speculators' house of cards became more precarious, they became more concerned about challenges to the Sutter title from the Settlers' Association that represented the squatters. Even if the courts did not uphold the squatters, their agitation over titles tended to depress land values, which were the foundation of the speculators' paper wealth. In August two banks failed, including one that had acquired a partial interest in the lots that August had sold to Brannan and his friends. A general collapse seemed imminent. Something had to be done about the squatters.[63]

As Sacramento's financial structure tottered, a case involving the eviction of a Sacramento squatter made its way through the courts. When the squatter lost in the City Recorder's Court, the Settlers' Association appealed to the County Court, where Judge E. J. Willis also ruled against the squatter. This was not unexpected, and the association planned on appealing the case to the State Supreme Court. The judge stated that he was uncertain that state law permitted such an appeal, which the squatters took as a declaration that no appeal was possible. California was governing itself as if it were a state but still had no word from Congress on the question of admission, so the judge's confusion about legal procedure was not entirely unwarranted. Judge Willis was himself a speculator, however, and the squatters thought his decision was biased.

Outraged squatters called a public meeting, passed resolutions, and issued a manifesto declaring that they would no longer obey decisions of the courts and town council. Charles Robinson, the leader of the Settlers' Association, declared that they had "deliberately resolved to bear arms, protect their sacred rights, if need be, with their lives."[64] Robinson's rhetoric and the squatters' resolve and potential firepower were matched by the determination of Sacramento authorities and the Sutterites who backed them. Cooler heads did not prevail. When the settlers marched on August 14 to protest an eviction of a squatter, shooting erupted. In this clash and a second armed confrontation the following day, four men were killed and five were wounded, including the sheriff and Mayor Hardin Bigelow. Bigelow's serious injuries forced him to give up his duties as mayor. A few months later he died of cholera while recuperating from his injuries.[65] This brief and bloody fight became known as the squatters' riot, although it could just as easily have been named for the speculators or the Sutterites.

Sutter played no direct role in this affray, although there is no doubt that he sided with the speculators, whose property rights were based on his New Helvetia claim. Speculators like Brannan and Wetzlar may have swindled Sutter in every way they could, but they were staunch defenders of his land claim. If his claim failed in court, the speculators would lose everything. It was not for nothing that the squatters called them Sutterites.

Captain Sutter's social pretensions, notices to squatters, grand partying, love of ceremony, and public hobnobbing with European potentates confirmed the squatters' conviction that Mexican land claims in general and Sutter's in particular were undemocratic and unfair. Despite the bloodshed in August 1850, squatters would continue to occupy land that Sutter claimed. In one guise or another, the men who allied themselves with the squatters of 1850 would fight bitterly for more than a decade against the inclusion of Sacramento in the New Helvetia grant.

While the Settlers' Association and the Sutterites squared off in Sacramento, Sutter and his family were incapacitated by malaria. The symptoms were so severe that the Sutters' physician placed a notice in the *Placer Times* requesting friends to forego visits to Hock Farm. "His generous and hospitable disposition makes all welcome to his mansion, but it is impossible for him to entertain at present, and he earnestly desires a respite."[66] When Prince Paul and Victor returned from Mount Rainier in the fall, they found the Sutters incapacitated. The prince helpfully informed Sutter that he had a "physician's certificate from a German medical school," and Sutter "was so overjoyed that he embraced me. Tears flooded his eyes, so relieved did he feel."[67] Fortunately, Sutter kept on hand a good stock of medical supplies. The royal physician dosed the sick with quinine and other preparations. In two weeks even the worst cases had improved.

Thus Prince Paul was able to repay Captain Sutter for his hospitality. Years later he fondly remembered how their "hearts would throb in unison whenever we would discuss in the long summer evenings the grandeur of our country's history." When the prince finally left Hock Farm, "it was only natural that Herr and Frau Sutter and Victor, the only one of their three sons who was at home just then, and their charming daughter . . . should embrace and kiss me in token of their eternal friendship." As his coach pulled away, Prince Paul looked back at the happy family. "I could see them waving handkerchiefs, the gigantic figure of the kingly Sutter the last to vanish from view."[68]

The "kingly Sutter" and his diminished royal family no doubt put up a good front for Prince Paul, but the prince's perspective was limited. Sutter was once again beset by creditors. Much of Sacramento, his one sure profit-making venture, had been lost to swindlers. Worse, he had lost his eldest son, his namesake and heir. Physical debilitation increasingly marked Sutter. He suffered for months from malarial fevers and chills. By the time the prince rolled down the road, Sutter must have felt very old and tired indeed. The demands of the coming decade would tap heavily into his reserves of energy and psychological resilience.

CHAPTER 20

Hock Farm Homestead

While Sacramentans fought in the streets over the question of the legitimacy of Sutter's title to their town, Congress struggled with the question of California statehood. The Mexican cession forced Congress to deal with the always difficult issue of slavery. California's application for admission as a free state posed a challenge as Congress endeavored to find a compromise on the issue of slavery in the territories acquired in the Mexican cession. The legendary 1850 congressional debates put off a final resolution of the slavery question, but Congress eventually decided in favor of California statehood. On September 9 the admission bill passed the Senate, making California the thirty-first state.[1]

Preliminary word of the Senate debates over statehood had filtered back to California during the summer and fall. Californians were disappointed and a little puzzled that Congress seemed to be unwilling to admit California with all its riches. If Congress failed to act, some proposed, California should set up an independent government. Meanwhile, the putative state government functioned as though it had already been admitted. Headquartered for the time being at San José, the legislature passed laws, raised revenue, created counties, incorporated cites, established courts, named judges, and made a reputation for itself as a fellowship of drunks. While waiting for admission, Governor Burnett administered state government, signed laws, and authorized volunteers to kill Indians in the mining districts. The state government, however, did not deal with the burning question of Mexican land claims. In this matter the legislature deferred to the federal government, because it involved the Treaty of Guadalupe Hidalgo. In other instances where the United States had acquired lands that had once been Spanish and French territory (the Louisiana Purchase and the Floridas), Congress had determined how land claims would be adjudicated. So Californians—Sutterites and squatters alike—impatiently waited for Congress to act on admission and the great land question. On the morning of October 18, 1850, the mail ship *Oregon* steamed into San Francisco Bay with guns blazing and banners unfurled, proclaiming "California is a State." In the spontaneous celebration that followed, Californians forgot about their disgruntlement and separatist sentiments. Surely, Congress would now provide for a swift resolution of the fundamental debate over land titles.[2]

Congressional action on the land claims front was about six months away. The law would be a disappointment to Sutter and other claimants who hoped that Congress would simply validate Mexican land grants as the language of the treaty and the Protocol of Querétaro seemed to promise. Under the Land Claims Act of 1851, however, claimants were required to present evidence to a Land Claims Commission, which would determine the grant's validity. Claimants could appeal the commission's decision to federal district court and from there to the U.S. Supreme Court. The process took years to complete and entailed great expense, especially in legal fees. In the meantime titles remained clouded and property values adversely affected. For Sutter, whose outsized claims constituted his capital and collateral for loans, the drawn-out legal process sat on his back like a huge weight, crushing his financial prospects.[3]

Sutter was not fazed by the presumptive burdens that lay before him. He fully expected that the commission and the courts would confirm his title to New Helvetia (eleven leagues), Micheltorena's sobrante grant (twenty-two leagues), and perhaps something from the Russian claim too. Until then Sutter would settle into the life of a gentleman farmer at Hock Farm, live well, and richly entertain guests. Hock Farm was the heart of Sutter's New Helvetia claim. The lands that were indisputably included in the New Helvetia grant extended from the Sutter Buttes to the mouth of the Feather River and lay between the Sacramento and Feather Rivers. In 1850 the state legislature appropriately named this area Sutter County. The county's grand proprietor reserved twelve square miles for himself (four miles of riverfront extending west for three miles), but the developed part of the farm consisted of about six hundred acres surrounding the house. Lumber for fencing was still in short supply, so Sutter resorted to deep ditches to keep livestock out of his fields. The rest of Hock Farm was given over to livestock grazing—and pesky squatters who disregarded Sutter's Mexican claim.

There was much for visitors to see at Hock Farm besides the pioneer in residence. Sutter busily (and expensively) turned his homestead into a showplace. Before the Mexican-American War Bidwell had overseen the construction of a large adobe two-story home with a central portico in the Greek

Revival style. It had wings on either side and possibly a courtyard. Sutter spent a lot of money finishing the interior and furnishing the rooms in a style that was commensurate with his high standing in gold-rush California. At the rear of the house stood stables and outbuildings. Several acres in front were fenced off as a garden, where rows of vegetables and flowers grew in profusion. Some of this truck gardening was for the Sutter family table, but he sent much of it to friends as a demonstration of the kinds of crops that could be raised in the region. Like other farmers in gold-rush California, Sutter planted wheat and raised cattle to meet the insatiable demands of the mining population, but he also raised imported specimen plants to see how they would do in California. He invested in fruit trees, flowers, and "a choice variety of the grape . . . giving the most encouraging hopes of a successful cultivation of the vine," according to a *Sacramento Transcript* reporter.[4] The newspaperman was not the last observer to notice Sutter's attention to grapes and viticulture. At first Sutter relied on varieties that were already at hand, obtaining most of his vines from the Mission San José.[5] He was not the only man in California raising grapes, but he deserves notice as a pioneer vintner. Time and experience rightly convinced him that wine-making had an important future in California.[6]

In 1850 Sutter had a lot of help running Hock Farm. According to the census, twenty-eight people resided in the main house: Sutter and his immediate family plus laborers, carpenters, blacksmiths, farmers, a clerk, a steward, a cook, a hostler, and a captain for Sutter's sloop. They were a distinctly European group. Including the Sutters, there were eight Swiss (August was still in residence), seven Germans, seven French, one Pole, and one Irishman. Two of the American residents were from New York, and two were from Illinois.[7] In addition, fifty to seventy-five Indians at the Hok ranchería worked for Sutter.[8] There was plenty for them to do. The three carpenters probably put finishing touches on the house, softening the look of raw adobe walls with woodwork and floors. Most of the labor went into agriculture and livestock. The census reported that Sutter owned more than a thousand horses and mules and nearly as many cattle, five hundred sheep, and sixty swine valued at more than $46,000. By contrast, the census-taker noted agricultural production of only two hundred bushels of wheat and fifty bushels of Indian corn.[9]

Produce from Sutter's elaborate gardens went unmentioned in the 1850 census, perhaps because it was not intended for market. Sutter's determination to create a horticultural showplace full of demonstrations and specimens may have made Hock Farm less productive than it might have been. The bulk of his agricultural worth was tied up in livestock. If he had concentrated on making beef and wheat for the market, he would have made more money. But paltry considerations of profit and loss were seldom part of Sutter's calculations. As the *Transcript* reporter stated, "The hardy pioneer who owns this place . . . is laboring to show all who are open to conviction, that the earth will reward the husbandman for his toil, if he deserves aught of her," unless the husbandman's name was Sutter.[10] In the coming years he would struggle to make a living on some of the most productive farmland in California. Ironically, he would fail in the midst of horticultural splendor that he created at great expense but to no profit.

While the family patriarch developed his Sutter County acreage, August was having second thoughts about the deal he had made in Sacramento. He steamed south to Mexico with Doctor Brandes but waved a final good-bye to his cunning physician in Acapulco. Captivated by the small town's charms, August decided to stay for a while. Once Brandes and his supply of drugs were gone, August's head began to clear. As he came to realize that the doctor's medications were the cause not the cure of his ills, young Sutter began to wonder about the business deals that Brandes had urged on him. He also noticed "a young woman, extremely pleasant and amiable and the most elegant in the city of Acapulco," María del Carmen Rivas, daughter of a prominent local family.[11] August was smitten. Later he declared that they were married in late 1850, although no marriage record has been found. Whether the marriage was legal or not, they lived together as man and wife for several years, bearing three children.[12]

August did not find his relationship with María sufficiently distracting to forget about his California worries entirely. The second installment for Sacramento was overdue, and Wetzlar owed him money too. The fretful August arranged for a new friend and business associate, Julius Lecacheux, to collect these debts. Lecacheux and L. Galley were French wine merchants with headquarters in San Francisco who had brought a load of goods to Acapulco. Lecacheux offered August a share in the Mexican branch of the wine business and agreed to accept the $25,000 overdue payment plus $25,000 from the final payment due from the Brannan partnership in July 1852. When the Frenchman arrived in San Francisco with August's power of attorney in hand, Wetzlar ignored him. Alarmed, Lecacheux went to the French consul, who advised him to retain counsel on behalf of August. Then he sent for August to straighten out the matter.

August arrived in January 1851 but had no better luck than his French friend. August's father had given the four buyers an opportunity to claim that they had not received all of the land they had purchased because he had sold a two-thirds interest in the entire river front between Sacramento and Sutterville a few days before August sold the same property to Brannan et al. The partners valued the loss of that portion of the property at $40,000 and insisted on additional deductions before settling with August. After failing to interest lawyers in defending his case, he agreed to a final payment of $40,000 in March. As usual, no actual money changed hands. August received only notes, which were due on July 1, 1851. Before giving the notes, however, the four partners demanded that August sign receipts for the unpaid installments of $25,000 and $75,000. Between March and July he was set upon by creditors who stripped him of most of the money from these transactions before it was even paid to him. After these expenses, August managed to save about $3,500 from the July payment, but he still found himself $3,839 in debt.[13] Now that young Sutter had been completely fleeced, the proposed partnership with Lecacheux vanished. Of all the characters involved in his undoing, August reserved kind words only for Lecacheux, Galley, and their clerk Mr. Lafforgue, whom August reckoned as "loyal and true friends and am sure that even now [1855] their feelings toward me have not undergone any change."[14]

August bears some responsibility for agreeing to such a monumentally disadvantageous arrangement, but partners Wetzlar, Brannan, Bruce, and Grahame and perhaps a dozen culpable attorneys are to blame for this shameful business. As they did with August's father, the Brannan consortium took advantage of someone who was manifestly unable to defend his interests, using every means at their disposal. Legal niceties, moral principles, and common decency did not pose any insuperable barriers. To call these ruthless swindlers capitalists, businessmen, or entrepreneurs who merely played by the rules of the rough and tumble frontier financial game in gold-rush California, as some commentators have done, misses the point. Brannan and his compatriots coolly conned the Sutters out of their land with no intention of paying full value or even of paying the money that they had agreed to pay in the first place. More's the pity that the Sutters were the all too willing victims of their scam.

Evidently August made no direct contact with his father while in California. Indeed Wetzlar told August that his father intended to sue him for funds that he had taken out of Hock Farm resources, evidently a reference to some of the money that August had used to transport the Sutter family to California. So the estrangement persisted and August, newly married and with no means of support, returned to Acapulco in the early summer of 1851. Demoralized and with a pregnant wife to support, August moved his family-in-the-making to Guaymas, Sonora, on the Gulf of California, where his son John A. Sutter III was born. The young Sutter family remained in Sonora for two and a half years. August lost his small remaining capital in Guaymas and decided to hide his "misery, without hardly any means, in the interior of Sonora amongst the Indians. What I with my family have suffered in Sonora I even do not try to bring to paper." August thought it best to pass over this dark period of "incredible sufferings and mental agonies, in which my wife stood faithfully and cheeringly by my side, with silence."[15]

A few details should be added to August's silence. During the period of his residence there, Guaymas was the beachhead for no fewer than three French filibustering expeditions that originated in San Francisco. Having tired of the gold-rush lottery, several Frenchmen, evidently with the approval of the French consul in San Francisco, went to Sonora ostensibly to help Mexicans repel Apache attacks on their settlements. In return the French legions hoped for government land grants of the sort that were approved in Texas and California. There was even some thought that the presence of French irregular forces would forestall future U.S. incursions. Some of the French freebooters moved inland and attempted to establish settlements northwest of Arispé on the Apache frontier. Mexican authorities eventually decided that French forces were no more helpful to their cause than Americans had been. In the fall of 1852 one French leader decided that Sonora should be independent and took Hermosillo. He eventually was forced to leave but was greeted with general applause when he returned to San Francisco. Americans did so admire a conquest, even a short-lived one.[16] And if a crowd of French filibusters could invade Mexico, perhaps Americans could do it too.

Where was August in all of this? By his own words he was "in the interior of Sonora amongst the Indians." There is no direct evidence that Sutter joined any of these filibustering expeditions, but surely he did not march into Apache country with only his wife and baby for company. It is likely that the French expeditions would have been appealing to August. The only friends in San Francisco that he could count on were his former French partners, and it is possible that he met some of the filibusters while in that city during the first half of 1851. The possibility of recouping his California losses with a new Mexican grant (or one from an independent Sonoran Republic) would have been attractive to the young family man. The naming of his son shows that he had an interest in carrying on some sort of Sutter tradition. Perhaps August had more in common with his father than met the eye. Although he was not a soldier by inclination, financial desperation and the impulse to prove himself in a hard world could have motivated him to take up with the filibusters.

Whatever August was doing in Sonora, French adventurers there inspired Americans to follow their example. Foremost among the would-be Anglo-American filibusters was William Walker, perhaps the inspiring speaker who had so impressed Prince Paul when he attended the Fourth of July celebration with Sutter in 1850. Since then Walker had kept in the public eye by noisily editing the *Herald* in San Francisco, where he had been thrown into jail by a humorless judge who was not amused at Walker's journalistic attention to his administration of law. In 1851 Walker established a law practice in Marysville, where one of his colleagues noted that "he often perplexed both court and jury with his subtleties, but seldom convinced either."[17] Walker's interest in Sonora matured as he practiced law on the banks of the Feather River, a few miles north of Hock Farm. In time, tangible connections would materialize among Sutter, Walker, and filibusters.[18]

Meanwhile Sutter improved his gardens with exotic imported specimens. In the spring of 1851 he received "hundreds of fruit and ornamental trees, a large variety of vines and garden seeds" purchased from the Grand Duke of Darmstadt's Garden, the *Sacramento Union* reported. The care of these plants was entrusted to a gardener who had labored for nine years in Queen Victoria's garden. "There can be little doubt about the quick-growing beauty of Hock Farm." The reporter rhapsodized about the calming influence that Hock Farm had on Captain Sutter, who had been so badly bruised by unscrupulous speculators. Sutter claimed a higher purpose for the horticultural work at Hock Farm than mere personal satisfaction or (perish the thought) profit. "He says he is going to have a place to which the democratic exiles of the Old World can come and see all the beauties of agriculture without feeling the trammels of monarchical rule."[19] Thus Sutter portrayed his development of Hock Farm as a public service to the downtrodden, who were yearning to breathe free.

Sutter's high-minded efforts to provide aesthetic pleasure to others were expensive. He paid for plants and vines from the duke's garden with borrowed money, of course. Even though his notes were "not worth 6 cts," according to one Sacramento merchant, speculators continued to loan money to Sutter, who used Hock Farm as collateral.[20] Everyone knew that Sutter could not pay his debts, but his creditors looked to the collateral for eventual satisfaction. When he could not pay as agreed, he refinanced, often borrowing additional money to pay taxes or make further improvements. Between January 1, 1851, and December 30, 1852, Sutter and his wife mortgaged Hock Farm at least six times.[21] Some of the unpaid notes were quietly purchased by speculators, who hoped for the day when they could foreclose. Chief among these forward-thinking investors were Edwards Woodruff and his partner, John Q. Packard.[22]

Eliza Sutter provided a new reason for Sutter to borrow money. She had never forgotten her piano-playing beau. Her unhappiness led Sutter to try to find a new and more suitable match for her. In March 1851 he offered the hand of his daughter to his old friend and confidant John Bidwell. The proposal took Bidwell entirely by surprise. Ever loyal to Sutter but disinterested in Eliza, he wrote a polite but firm letter that put an end to Sutter's hopes for the marriage. "To crown all your acts of attention and esteem you [have] made me an offer—

and I know it must have been from the fullness of an affectionate heart and a sincere desire for my happiness,—of the hand of an only daughter. Capt. Sutter I am not ungrateful, but I often want either means or ability to display my gratitude." Bidwell assured Sutter of his everlasting friendship, but "I cannot persuade myself to marry. I hate the very name of old bachelor, and yet I do not know that I shall ever marry. Let this be a secret between you and me."[23]

Happiness for Eliza would have to come from some other quarter. Some-time after Sutter's attempt to draft Bidwell for a son-in-law, the artist William Shaw came to Hock Farm to paint the family. Sutter loved to have his portrait painted, and Shaw had something of a reputation, having won a medal for his likeness of President Zachary Taylor. Eliza evidently found him attractive, or at least her father thought that there was a spark there. In January 1852 he told a friend that a marriage was in the offing; but for some reason it did not come to pass.[24]

By this time Engler was leading a more prosperous life than he had known as an itinerant piano teacher. He operated a Marysville hotel and brewery, where Tyrolese singers entertained his patrons. The passage of time and Engler's comparative success as a local host may have softened Sutter's stand on the match with his daughter, or maybe he was becoming anxious about marrying her off while she was still in her early twenties. In any case, he agreed to a marriage with Engler. A date was set for March 21, 1852.

Once Sutter had warmed to the idea of his daughter marrying Engler, he spared no expense in staging a lavish wedding at Hock Farm. He invited a few hundred guests and transported some of them from Marysville and Sacramento by special steamers that simultaneously arrived at his landing. Cannons fired continuously, in the old Sutter-style of welcome. Captain Sutter and his lady received their guests in the house and then all proceeded to a prefabricated metal building, said to be "a chapel which the Captain had erected for the benefit of the Indians upon and about his ranch." Everything at Hock Farm had been cleaned and polished, "the buildings ornamented and festooned with flowers and evergreens, and every prominent point surmounted with flags and streamlets." The chapel was "surrounded with about fifty Indians dressed in an array of colors not more brilliant than anomalously blended." When the bridal procession entered the chapel, "a large brass band filled the iron walls of the building with the richest echoes of music melody and welcomed the special votaries of Hymen to the application of the congenial trammels of a life-long bondage." After a civil ceremony by a local judge (which says more about Sutter's religious views than the supposed Indian "chapel"), the wedding party and guests repaired to the Sutter home, where all were "seated at a table which was perfectly overwhelmed with viands and wines. Toasts, speeches, exhilaration and dancing terminated an entertainment which marked the loss of a lovely daughter and the finding of a lovely wife."[25]

And then there was the morning after. A traveler whose steamer briefly stopped at Hock Farm went in to see the captain. He found him "sitting at a table amongst the bottles half and quite empty, wine-glasses and tumblers, showing what once had filled them, and stumps of half-used cigars, the floor covered with all the débris of a supper; the captain scarcely recovered from his indulgences."[26] It had been a great party, but at enormous expense.

Unfortunately the grand celebration did not result in "a life-long bondage," as the *Union* reporter put it. Scarcely more than a year later Engler deserted his young wife and went to Mexico for reasons that went unrecorded. In 1855 Eliza successfully filed for divorce in Sutter County.[27]

Not long before the ill-starred wedding, Sutter confessed (or bragged) to one of his friends that in the past two years he had spent $100,000 making Hock Farm "a civilized place," as he put it. The price of civilization came high in Sutter County. A few months after Eliza's wedding creditors were once again barking at the door. He temporarily solved his problem by executing new mortgages at high rates of interest. By the end of the year all of Hock Farm was papered over with mortgages.[28] In 1852 Sutter just barely managed to retain possession of his homestead and to keep up appearances, which in his case meant living like a landed baron. He was banking on a quick confirmation from the Land Commission and the courts so that he could sell his surplus land at a premium, but he was only able to file his claim before the commission a couple of weeks before the nuptials at Hock Farm. Final resolution of the land question was still years away.[29]

From outward appearances in late 1852 it seemed that Sutter's artful manipulation of mortgages had averted catastrophe. Knowledgeable observers knew that it had been a near thing. In October Sutter and his sons sent specimens of Italian wheat that they had grown from seeds that they had diligently recovered from the straw packing around an imported statue of George Washington to an agricultural exposition in Sacramento. The results were judged to be "magnificent," though limited in extent. The keynote speaker, John F. Morse, gave special attention to the proprietor of Hock, "a man . . . with a head and heart so voluminously generous, as to unfit him for defending himself against the subtle and destructive incursions of human cupidity." In Sutter's heart, Morse elucidated, circulated "sympathies that flow like the clear rivers of Eureka." Rather than grub for gold, Sutter obeyed the poet's summons to till the land. Sadly, "in his secluded devotion to the claims of Agriculture, he at one time almost lost the Homestead remnant of that immense domain which was ceded to him by

Spanish authorities." The impending disaster was averted, and "it is not presumption to predict that the American people will never allow the beautified fields known as Hock Farm to be alienated from this man, so long as he desires such a home."[30] Like many other Americans, Morse praised Sutter for his service to American immigrants during the Mexican era and believed that in his old age (now forty-nine years old!) he should be protected and rewarded for it.

Alas, Morse's sentiments did not predict the future; but for the moment Hock seemed to be safely in Sutter's hands and appeared to be a going concern. With the help of his sons Victor and Alphonse and a generous providence, the Sutter plantation might yet survive. Moreover, Sutter had friends in high places. Former Governor McDougal (a trustee in the Robinson arrangement) named his son for Sutter and christened him at Hock Farm.[31]

The new governor, John Bigler, and some members of the legislature talked about giving Sutter a generalcy in the state militia. Sutter talked endlessly about his imaginary brilliant military career in Europe, and this had become part of his pioneer legend. Late in 1852 a group of Sacramentans formed the "Sutter Light Infantry" and invited the old captain to attend a celebration in his honor.[32] On October 28 the grand parade came off with the sort of martial pomp that Sutter gloried in.[33]

Sutter's youngest son, Alphonse, must have been impressed with the military ceremony too. His father had tried to get him into West Point, but to no avail. Sutter was especially galled that Vallejo had succeeded in getting an appointment for one of his sons. "I believe I have done so much for the Country as Genl. Vallejo," he sniffed.[34] Captain Sutter would have to advance his son's military ambitions in some other way.

The public recognition of Sutter's military persona fueled his ego and made him feel that he was appreciated. Many Americans did appreciate him, as a symbolic representation of their own destiny. Others saw him merely as a worn-out relic of a bygone era who was incapable of effectively managing his affairs. These divergent opinions of Sutter made him an ambiguous hero in the new, go-ahead, Yankee age in gold-rush California.

Sutter's Fort, the architectural symbol of his military life, rapidly deteriorated as Hock Farm grew in splendor on the banks of the Feather River. By 1851 there was not much left of the fort, which once had been the hub of mercantile activity in the Sacramento Valley. Its walls collapsed as pillagers plundered the place for its timber and shingles. William Prince took a stroll to see it. "The mud walls are crumbling & in 2 or 3 years will be pretty much demolished— One family occupy a small part of Sutter's old mansion within the fort— & outside two or three new buildings have been erected for a hospital."[35] The glory days of Sutter's Fort were over. Its condition tugged at the memories of the old California hands who remembered it as an important military establishment and the center of social life and trade in northern California. George McKinstry described the place to the fort's former commander, Edward Kern. "The old Fort is fast going to decay; the last time I was there I rode through, and there was not a living thing to be seen. What a fall is there, my fellow!"[36]

In 1852 Alden Bayley, the owner of the fort's large central building and one-time hotel, offered it and the bake house to the state of California for a "lunatic asylum." Bayley thought that the structure was ideally suited for such a purpose. "The middle story contains nine furnished rooms fit for immediate use, and a very small outlay will adopt the whole to the purpose proposed." "Title perfect," he helpfully added.[37] The economy-minded legislators were not interested in providing for lunatics at Sutter's Fort. The old structure would continue to disintegrate until only the large two-story central building remained. In a few decades the preservation of the fort's remains and reconstruction of that which had been lost would challenge Sacramento's history-minded citizens.[38] But in the 1850s the old fort was simply a white elephant, a useless souvenir of ancient times.

CHAPTER 21

General Sutter and the Filibusters

Sutter's financial horizon was darkening, and the final confirmation of his land grant was not yet in sight. In late 1852, while he lavishly feted wedding guests, esteemed visitors, and casual acquaintances alike, calculating men considered how to relieve him of his real estate. For two years a San Francisco entrepreneur, John T. Steinberger, schemed to obtain Sutter's lands and finally managed to force him into a sale in January 1853. "All time I escaped him, as I did know [him] to well by Renowne," Sutter revealed; "but now I entered in the Trapp by advise of my friends, [and] I am afraid it will turn out a very difficult and serious affaire."[1] The Sutter County Book of Deeds reveals the transaction as a straightforward business deal.[2] In bland legal prose, the deed says that Sutter sold the New Helvetia and sobrante grants to Steinberger for $150,000. Steinberger was to pay Anna $100,000 for Hock Farm; Eliza Engler $5,000 for her interest in the sobrante grant; Victor $15,000 for his sobrante share and his interest in Yuba City lots; Alphonse $20,000 for a tract lying opposite Hock Farm. Sutter would get $10,000.

Sutter portrayed Steinberger as a swindler, but he might have been a creditor who simply wanted his money when it was due. Perhaps he had purchased notes from others who had loaned to Sutter, or maybe he loaned money directly to the strapped captain. It is unlikely, but possible, that Sutter decided to sell out and get rid of all of the trouble of presenting his claims, defending lawsuits, and struggling with debt. His financial affairs are so muddled with refinancing, side deals, and the reassignment of notes that it is impossible to know much more than the outcome of his transactions. Sutter himself probably did not know the full extent of his obligations.

Steinberger immediately took possession of Hock Farm, although the Sutters remained in the house. He proved to be a disagreeable landlord in every way, but he had to pay the purchase money to the Sutters by the March deadline. Steinberger tried to raise cash by cutting the oak timber on Hock Farm, probably to sell to the steamboats on the Feather River. In his haste to raise money, the new proprietor of Hock Farm abused Sutter's French and German retainers as "if they would be Negroes," Sutter said. "He is a most disgusting man in every way and shape; you can think what for an unpleasant time we must have had since his arrival here."[3] Evidently Steinberger had big plans for the farm that distressed the Sutters, but in the end he could not carry them out. The San Francisco schemer could not raise the money that the contract called for, so Sutter told him to clear out.

It took several months for Sutter to arrange new financing for his property. He signed a note for $12,000 at 4 percent interest per month, payable to Charles Polhemus in eight months. Polhemus already held a $24,000 bond that he was bound to pay. Sutter's mountain of debt would be impossible to climb in the time stipulated. Hock Farm did not produce enough income, and he had no means to pay his debts unless his grant was confirmed and he could sell his property. Eight months came and went. Sutter refinanced again, this time with John Packard and Edwards Woodruff, who had already picked up some of his other unredeemed notes.[4]

Sutter remained remarkably cheerful in the face of these difficulties. After confessing to Bidwell in February 1853 that he had made the ill-fated sale to Steinberger, he crowed, "At least I got once the rank of a Major General, how you will have seen in the papers, and I assure you that I feel proud of it."[5] Evidently Sutter had been anticipating his appointment. Five days after Governor Bigler signed Sutter's commission, the new general published the names of his staff in the newspapers.[6] The list included one full colonel and nine lieutenant colonels, quite an entourage. Sutter recommended these commissions to the governor on the basis of friendship and business association. Officers and men were not paid unless they served in one of the Indian "wars." Sutter and his staff had no intention of going to the mountains and sleeping in wet blankets. For them, militia rank represented social position and honor, so Sutter's military patronage was something valuable, which he distributed with care.[7]

Sutter believed that because his commission said he was "Major General of the State of California" he was *the* major general of the state militia. Indeed there was much confusion about the organization of the militia. In effect, there were two state militias.[8] One state law provided for the establishment of "Volunteer or Independent Companies," and another organized the state militia.

The volunteer units were temporary in nature and locally organized, usually in response to an Indian threat in the mining districts. The governor, who was the state's commander-in-chief, commissioned the officers that these volunteer companies elected and distributed arms and pay for them. The permanent state militia was supposed to be composed of all able-bodied men between the ages of eighteen and forty-five, except for men who were exempted because of prior service or disability, or who paid an annual two-dollar commutation fee. The 1852 law under which the legislature appointed Sutter divided California into seven military districts, divisions, and brigades, but there was no explicit relationship between divisions and the districts. The law further said that each division would be commanded by a major general like Sutter. Every division had two brigades, and each county organized companies to fill out the brigades.

It was essentially a paper army. With the exception of an inglorious and ineffective attempt to quell the San Francisco vigilance committee in 1856, the state militia was merely a ceremonial outfit. As one historian explained, the militia "lent color to California's frontier society, gave a good outlet for social expression, and helped introduce the social graces of the more settled societies."[9] Richly uniformed, Sutter paraded with sociable state militia units like Sacramento's Sutter Rifles, while grizzled miners volunteered to burn rancherías and slaughter Indians in the mining districts.

Sutter's misconception that he was second in command only to the governor was due in part to a defect in the law that did not clearly delineate the generals' responsibilities or the chain of command. California adjutant general William Kibbe identified these flaws and urged legislation that would clarify the militia's organizational structure, in conformance with federal law.[10] Accordingly, the legislature reorganized the militia in 1855 and clarified the role of the major generals, much to Sutter's dismay.[11]

Whatever Sutter's relative place in the chain of command in the militia, his duties were purely ceremonial during the 1850s. Among his preening staff were two brothers, Lieutenant Colonels William S. Mesick and R. S. Mesick.[12] William Mesick had recently enjoyed the privilege of exercising Sutter's power of attorney.[13] He also managed Hock Farm.[14] His previous experience included a clerking stint in the Sacramento county recorder's office, where he developed detailed knowledge and deep interest in the Sutters' complicated land transactions.[15] Armed with this information, Mesick somehow became Sutter's agent in September 1852 and was still enjoying his confidence five months later. So it was natural for Sutter to recommend his agent and his agent's brother for field grade commissions.

In February 1853 the Sutter Rifles paid $1,200 at auction for the first ticket

to a Sacramento recital by the renowned singer Kate Hayes and presented it to
Sutter. Always proud of any public recognition, Sutter recalled this event with
special satisfaction. "A deputation of the company came up to Hock Farm and
escorted me to Sacramento," where "the entire company met me." He was
seated in the front in a place of honor, flanked by uniformed officers of the
Sutter Rifles, "amidst the applause of the whole house."[16] The prolonged
cheering prevented Hayes from performing until the conductor struck up the
"Marseillaise" to quiet the crowd. Sutter said nothing about the quality of her
singing or anything else about the event. In his own selective memory, he was
the main act.

The Sutter Rifles were not alone in extending martial honors. The an-
nouncement of Sutter's commission inspired one of San Francisco's militia
companies, the Marion Rifles, to elect him to an honorary life membership.[17]
On the Fourth of July in 1853 the Marion Rifles hosted Sutter, the Sutter
Rifles, and other northern California militia units at a grand military celebration in San Francisco. The colors were presented to Sutter as the honored
guest.[18] Six weeks later A. Andrews, "Late Captain commanding Company A,
Second Ohio Regiment," presented Sutter with a sword, as "an expression of
the esteem which, in common with my fellow-citizens, I entertain for your
personal kindness and self-sacrifice, for the good of the State." Andrews assured General Sutter that he was "honored and esteemed by not only those
who have known you, but wherever your reputation has extended."[19] This was
the sort of military service that Sutter was interested in—little duty and much
honor. The rank, parades, and recognition fed his ego, giving him hope that he
would have enough reputation and influence to overcome any objections to
his land claims.

While Sutter paraded and accepted honors, his financial condition worsened. Even though Steinberger's personal threat was brief, the influence of the
aborted sale of Sutter's California lands was permanent, as he had feared. Sutter
tried to meet his new financial obligations by releasing his workforce to cut
expenses. Only his sons and perhaps fifteen Indians remained at work on Hock
Farm. To make matters worse, epidemic illness struck again, so much of what
had been planted was lost because no one was able to water the garden. Sutter
apologized to James Warren, publisher of the *California Farmer and Journal of
Useful Science,* for his inability to send an exhibit to the agricultural fair in 1853.
"Under the harassing Circumstances in which I am now I could not afford to
keep a Gardener any longer as my property has been attached again." Sutter
told his agent and state militia aide-de-camp, Lieutenant Colonel William
Mesick, that he could not keep him on. "He was vexed about it and have done
against me what he possibly could do." So much for the loyalty of subordinate

officers in the state militia. The long delay in the adjudication of Sutter's land claim forced him to borrow $5,000 just to pay taxes on all the land that he claimed. In the meantime "the Surrounding Squatters [on Sutter's land] have nothing to pay." At this juncture, he decided to get out of farming altogether and rent his land except for the garden, vineyard, and orchard. It was depressing. Sutter thanked Warren for the invitation to the 1853 agricultural fair, "but I am sorry that we cannot be present, as we could not have pleasure nowhere." At this moment Sutter seemed to understand his situation clearly. Things would improve if he received title to his lands; otherwise "I am gone forever."[20]

Warren and other leading farmers sympathized with Sutter and appreciated his pioneering efforts in California agriculture. When they organized the California Agricultural Society in December, they elected him a vice president—another nice honor, and well deserved too, but it would not pay the bills.[21] No wonder that Sutter appreciated the pomp and circumstance of the state militia.

Not everyone who had military ambition in California was interested in mere show and socializing. William Walker, sometime doctor, newspaper editor, and Marysville lawyer, had paid attention to the failed Franco-California filibusters in Sonora. He thought there was a future for him in that sort of thing. In the summer of 1852 he went to Guaymas and was there when the French were being thrown out. He stayed around for a while and, according to one of Sutter's friends, "conceived his plan of obtaining adventurers in California for the conquest of some portion of the sparsely inhabited sections of Spanish America."[22]

Walker cut quite a figure in Guaymas. A contemporary described him: "Below the medium height, and very slim, I should hardly imagine him to weigh over a hundred pounds. His hair light and towy while his almost white eyebrows and lashes concealed a seemingly pupilless, grey, cold eye, and his face was a mass of yellow freckles, the whole expression very heavy." He wore "a huge white fur hat, whose long knap waved with the breeze, . . . with a very ill-made, short-waisted blue coat, with gilt buttons, and a pair of grey, strapless pantaloons."[23] Walker advanced the usual plan to the Mexican authorities: I will protect you from the Apaches in return for a large grant of land near Arispé. After so much trouble with the French (not to mention previous experiences with foreigners in Texas and California), the Sonorans did not find the proposition attractive. Walker sailed back to California to raise an expedition to conquer the reluctant Sonorans for their own good.[24]

Walker, now called Colonel Walker by his men, found about four dozen Californians in San Francisco who were willing to accompany him on his Quixotic quest. In October 1853 he embarked for Mexico. Knowing that he did not have enough men and ordnance to conquer Sonora, he redirected his hired vessel to La Paz, Baja California, where he proclaimed the Republic of Lower California with himself as president. A few dozen puzzled Mexican residents of the tiny pueblo looked on. Then he moved his forces to Cabo San Lucas and thence to Ensenada, near the U.S. border.

Things did not go well. The Mexican army put up some resistance. Walker had not brought enough supplies for his men, so they began to forage among the citizens of the new republic. Baja californios' hostility toward their erstwhile liberators grew by the day. Walker then determined to add Sonora to his new nation, although how he thought this would be possible, given his limited resources, remains a mystery. Walker's proclamations and confused movements pleased U.S. authorities not at all. He had violated U.S. neutrality laws, so the government sent a man-of-war to tell him so. On May 8, 1854, Colonel Walker and his remaining bedraggled force crossed over to American territory near San Diego. They gave their parole of honor to a U.S. Army officer, promising to go to San Francisco to face federal charges.[25]

Walker's invasion was a complete fiasco that accomplished nothing. His small force suffered fifteen killed and eight wounded, with seven more dead from disease.[26] These facts and an impending trial on federal charges did not dismay the patriotic men of San Francisco, who hailed Walker as a conquering warlord. He was tried in October before U.S. district judge Ogden Hoffman. Walker defended himself, claiming that his intentions were peaceful and that he was motivated only by humanitarian feelings for the helpless Mexicans. The jury acquitted him in eight minutes. Colonel Walker was the hero of the hour.[27]

Just as the Walker trial was about to begin, August Sutter steamed into San Francisco Bay with his wife and infant son, John A. Sutter III. His brother Alphonse had sent a letter to August in the wilderness of Sonora, explaining that it was now common knowledge that Brandes and Wetzlar had drugged and duped him into signing away Sacramento for a song. Lawyers (perhaps even Lieutenant Colonel William Mesick) told Alphonse that something might still be done to recover part of his losses from Sacramento. Alphonse wanted a power of attorney from his older brother so that he could pursue these options. "It appeared to me then a light, a star," August later recalled, "had suddenly cleared up to me a night of darkness," so he decided to go to California "to clear up . . . the clouds thrown upon my character, a sacred duty I owe myself, to my family and to everybody else; to defeat this way my enemies and to watch as much as possible over the interest of my poor mother, who stands on the brink of a profound abyss blindfolded and without even dreaming of it."[28] With renewed confidence and resolve, August returned to Hock Farm and the warm embrace of his family, including the patriarch himself.

August must have known the French filibusters in Sonora and perhaps had met them in San Francisco in 1851. Nor could he have missed the trip that the flamboyantly dressed Walker made to Guaymas in 1852 and 1853. August was not willing to commit his Sonora experiences to writing, but one can well imagine Sutter's interest in whatever his son knew about the filibusters, especially with all of the talk about Walker in the air. Sutter made no secret of his admiration for the filibusters and their methods. A few days after August's arrival, Sutter's friend James Warren reported to the readers of *California Farmer and Journal of Useful Science* that he had met Sutter on the aptly named steamboat *Confidence*. Despite the impending loss of Hock Farm (notes were coming due), Sutter was optimistic. "If I am deprived of my home here," he exclaimed, "I am known elsewhere; the name of Sutter is noble—I wear a sword—I can go and win a home any where—the world is wide—I have strength yet—I can still lead on—and the broad field of *Central America* is still open; I can still be a Pioneer."[29] In Sutter's mind, people like Walker carried on a tradition of frontier conquest that he himself exemplified. He was not alone in that belief.

It is doubtful that Sutter seriously thought of joining the filibusters in Latin America, but there is no doubt where his heart was. Even before Walker went to trial, Sutter was aware of some of the filibusters' plans. In July William V. Wells, an associate of Walker's, approached Sutter for a commission in the state militia. General Sutter promptly forwarded his recommendation to California's secretary of state with this frank statement: "The bearer of this Wm. V. Wells Esqr. is going to Central America, and wishes to become a Member of my Staff, which standing will be very useful for him, and knowing Mr. Wells as a Gentleman, I don't hesitate a Moment to recommend him to you for a Commission as Aid-de-Camp of my staff with the rank of Lieut. Colonel, when it is agreeable to the Department."[30] Wells was more than Walker's casual acquaintance. He regarded Colonel Walker as a great hero, accompanied him on his exploits, and wrote a book chronicling his filibustering activities.[31] Sutter obtained a lieutenant colonelcy for his friend and fellow horticulturalist Warren too.[32]

While Sutter promoted filibustering and conquest in Central America, August's steely resolve to reclaim Sacramento and redeem his reputation seeped away. Perhaps the contrast between his father's brave talk and the plain facts of his financial condition was too much to bear. August again fell ill. Sometime after February 1855 he and his wife departed for Acapulco, but they left their son at Hock Farm. John III remained with his grandparents until adulthood. A few years later his two sisters joined him, because August thought that his children could get a better education in California than they could in Mexico. August settled in Acapulco for good, but he had not heard the last of Sacramento.[33]

Not long after returning to Acapulco, August received a visitor, one William Mesick. His father's former agent explained that during his deep researches in the dusty archive of the Sacramento County Recorder he had found what he believed to be vital flaws in the armor of August's enemies. First, August's deed to the Brannan cabal did not contain a specific description of the property to be conveyed. Second, August had not been paid for the property. Mesick made August a proposition: sell the same property to me for a sum of money and I will sue the bastards to establish my title. On July 9 Mesick gave $500 for the Sacramento lots, which this time were carefully enumerated and described in the new deed, and $10,000 for a San Francisco lot and all of August's share of any of his father's California land claims. This was a risky arrangement that depended on a decision of the court to give Mesick clear title to the Sacramento lots and the rest. In the meantime, however, Mesick's claim would put a cloud on property that Brannan and his partners had already sold to innocent third parties. Many of them would pay Mesick for quitclaim deeds to protect their titles from Brannan. There was money in this, whatever the final legal outcome.[34]

Mesick immediately returned to Sacramento and asserted his right to the Sacramento lots. This development caused an uproar. The *Sacramento Union* averred that if August "had been paid once for this property, and then sold it the second time, he must be a man lost to all sense of honor and honesty."[35] Sutter answered this editorial insult a few days later. He declared that Brannan, Wetzlar, and company had roundly swindled his son, who had received only a fraction of the money that the purchasers owed him. Soon, Sutter claimed, his son's full story would become known to all: "It will astonish the world."[36]

Now it was Julius Wetzlar's turn to respond to Sutter's public accusation. Claiming that the facts would show that August had been paid as agreed, he then turned his sarcasm on Sutter. It was "well known that Gen. Sutter is very much in the habit of signing deeds, and other papers and instruments, without knowing what they contain," Wetzlar wrote. Thus it was "not necessary to notice the charge of swindling, which he has signed for somebody."[37]

The public exchange of insults did not settle the matter. For three years Mesick's suits and countersuits went up and down the court system. The state supreme court eventually decided in favor of Mesick and against Brannan, but it was a decision without much force because the court also said that the title of third parties should not be disturbed. Meanwhile Mesick had sold his quitclaim deeds and passed on as much as $51,000 to August.[38] August had finally learned to play the California land game, where wealth was gained from the land not by productive enterprise but by words, lawsuits, and gall.

In May 1855, shortly before August sold his California claims to Mesick, the California Claims Commission confirmed Sutter's claims to New Helvetia and the sobrante lands.[39] It was a Pyrrhic victory. In June Packard and Woodruff foreclosed.[40] They won a $24,000 judgment against Sutter, who conveyed "the undivided twenty one and two thirds one hundredths (21 ⅔ 100ths) equal parts to thirteen sixtieths ¹³⁄₆₀ of the undivided whole of that certain tract," described as the two Mexican grants except Hock Farm and other properties already conveyed, which amounted to about 20 percent of Sutter's confirmed land.[41] On the same day Sutter conveyed 74 percent of his remaining property to a new combination headed by Henry Robinson. His other holdings were held in trust by Lewis Sanders.[42] Most of Sutter's sixty-mile sweep of land was gone. He preserved his home and surrounding acreage, but even this was heavily mortgaged.

The Land Commission decision did not finally establish the legitimacy of Sutter's land claims. A federal statute required the appeal of all the commission's decisions to federal district court, which would consider the case for another eighteen months.[43] Moreover, the "other properties" mentioned in the Packard/Woodruff settlement referred to mortgages amounting to about $40,000 on Sutter's remaining property. These notes were due in 1857. Once again Sutter's landed estate hung in the balance, and the clock was ticking. Even worse for his ego, his sliding financial condition was a matter of indisputable public notice. Friends sold five-dollar tickets for the Sutter Relief Fund. Similar private efforts to aid him continued in the 1860s.[44]

Perhaps hoping that a friendly gesture would stay the hand of his main creditors, Sutter obtained a militia commission for Edwards Woodruff.[45] If he regretted recommending Woodruff or anyone else for a commission, he never said so. The exchange of honors in hope of future favors was not a concept that Sutter originated, although his gestures in this direction were distinctly unsuccessful. There was one commission, however, that he would have good reason to regret. Shortly after obtaining a commission for Lieutenant Colonel Woodruff, Sutter used his influence to elevate his youngest son, Alphonse, to the military status that he craved.[46] Alphonse became a captain in the state militia cavalry.

Whatever Sutter's intentions for his son may have been, Alphonse was not about to parade in California while he watched his father's financial ship sink. William Walker was recruiting California youths for service in Nicaragua. There was a rebellion against landed classes, and the rebels needed help. Walker offered his services. Alphonse wanted to go and was willing to pay for the privilege. Potential rewards seemed appropriately high. Land grants were the payment for service, if the right side won. It was a fine cause: democracy and republicanism against autocracy. Alphonse had the military temperament of his father, plus enthusiasm untempered by experience in actual warfare. To be a leader of men in a military conquest—that was the life, and perhaps a solution to the family's indebtedness. But how could he get the money to raise a company of men to follow him to Walker's side?

Alphonse had four sections of land from his father. Colonel Mesick, Alphonse's fellow officer in the state militia, made him an offer that he could not refuse. Sutter estimated that the land was worth about $40,000. "My Son who is going to Nicaragua . . . has done a very bad business," he lamented. Mesick offered Alphonse $10,000, "of which he got only $2,000 in cash and the balance in Notes without Security, which causes us a great deal of Chagrin."[47] Sutter declared that Alphonse was no longer welcome at Hock Farm.

Alphonse, it seems, was no shrewder at business than his father or his older brother, but no matter. He used his money to raise a company for Walker, who made him aide-de-camp.[48] The winter season aided Alphonse's effectiveness in the recruitment of volunteers for Walker's Nicaragua legion. Cold and rain drove miners down from the mountains. The Argonauts who had failed to make a pile in the previous season lived on the streets of large and small villages that had sprung up in the valley. They were not welcome there. Perhaps hoping to avoid squatter riots of the sort that had plagued Sacramento, California towns passed laws concerning vagrancy. Duly constituted authorities forcefully drove away violators. One volunteer writing under the pseudonym of Samuel Absalom said that anyone who walked behind him in the winter of 1856 would have read "Stockton Mills. Self-Rising Flour!" on the seat of his pants, the "well-known label in California, at that day, of greatest embarrassment."[49] Enlisted volunteers were promised 250 acres of Nicaraguan land and $25 per month for their services. Captains like Alphonse got $100 per month and probably an unspecified chunk of Nicaraguan real estate.[50]

The reality of Nicaragua did not measure up to the promises and dreams that were made in California.[51] Walker (who was now a major general) had been there since the early summer of 1855. Ostensibly fighting on the side of the liberals in favor of a democratic constitution that had fallen into disfavor with the current conservative-minded president of Nicaragua, General Walker and his allies for a time gained the upper hand. He made inexplicable mistakes too, such as interfering with the steamship business of tycoon Cornelius Vanderbilt. Eventually Walker managed to win the presidency of Nicaragua in a highly questionable plebiscite. If Walker was successful, favored officers like Alphonse could expect large rewards. Until then the new government paid its troops with scrip that was worth less than 10 percent of face value.

By the time Captain Sutter arrived it seemed likely that the conservative president of Costa Rica would intervene against the liberals and Walker in Nicaragua. Walker immediately found a use for the young officer. In order to placate the Costa Rican president, Walker sent Captain Sutter, one of Walker's Nicaraguan officers, and a third man to Costa Rica to disavow any hostile intentions in Central America. As diplomatic missions go, this one was less than successful. Walker's Nicaraguan representative joined the Costa Rican army, which eventually intervened against Walker in the Nicaraguan civil war. Alphonse and the other diplomat were summarily thrown out of Costa Rica.[52]

General Sutter eventually forgave his son's rash decision to join Walker. Perhaps he recognized something of himself in Alphonse's love of military life and adventure. Sutter avidly followed the copious news coverage of Walker's exploits, hoping no doubt for some account of his son. Even if he still believed his son's actions to be ill advised, he could do little now but hope for the best. Perhaps Alphonse would win a new landed estate for the Sutter family. While August campaigned in Nicaragua, Sutter and his middle son, Victor, tended to Hock Farm and tried to make ends meet.[53]

Sutter's financial management was not helped by his well-known addiction to drink. His friend Bidwell, a lifelong temperance man, worried about him and arranged for Sarah Pellet, a celebrated temperance lecturer, to visit Hock Farm. It did no good. "I told her, that she could not convert me," Sutter explained to Ed Kern, "as I have so many acquaintences in the City, that I could not do otherwise, and particularly when I am with the Citizen Soldiery and on great Diner Parties." He went on to explain that parties at his place were nearly a daily thing. "Last Monday a Party of Actors was here. . . . Some Gentlemen from Sacramento the following day, yesterday a party from Marysville."[54] Poor Sutter; after describing the disease, he could not stomach the cure. Let the good times roll on, said the genial, overgenerous host of Hock Farm. Surely all would be well when his lands were finally confirmed. Liquor clouded his judgment and dulled his senses as he waited for the courts' final word.

With Sutter's finances on a razor's edge, he had to use every slight advantage to make Hock Farm pay. Now that he was forced to release his white work-men—and with his youngest son in Nicaragua—he turned to the only source of labor available to him: Indians. Indians had worked on Hock Farm from the very beginning. The Hok ranchería was just a mile or so above the Sutter manse on the banks of the Feather River, but its population had shrunk to scarcely more than a dozen survivors of the disease and violence that crushed

Indian society during the gold rush. The Yukulme Nisenans formerly lived about three miles south of Hock Farm, but the remnants of that community had moved to Hok, making altogether thirty-five men, women, and children there. In olden times the lord of New Helvetia paid Indians with trade goods or in his privately minted tin money; but times had changed. In 1856 Indians well understood the value of gold and currency. They left Sutter's farm to work for money in Marysville. "Nothing as the Dollars could bring them to work," he complained.[55]

As Sutter saw it, the problem was that he no longer had the power to compel Indians to work for him. To rectify the situation, he asked the federal superintendent of Indian affairs, Thomas Henley, to give him "control *only of the* Hock and Yukulmey Indians" so that he could "make them work and pay them a reasonable Compensation, in food and Clothing." Henley appointed Sutter as special agent to the Indians and threatened to remove them to a reservation if they did not obey him. Faced with the prospect of removal, the Indians agreed to work for Sutter in return for cast-off clothing and food.[56] Ironically, the Indians had adjusted to California's new cash economy, but Sutter could survive only by returning to the system of coerced labor and trade goods. The retention of Indian labor proved to be merely a stopgap that would not save him from financial ruin and dispossession.

While his father cobbled together a workforce with the help of the federal government, Alphonse faced the rigors of civil war in Nicaragua. There is little specific information about Captain Sutter's service with Walker, although it may be supposed that as Walker's aide-de-camp he was near the general's side as fighting progressed. There was more than enough combat to satisfy the martial heart of young Sutter. The war was bitterly fought, and both sides killed prisoners when it suited their purposes.[57] Yellow fever and cholera added to the horrors of war. As Walker's fortunes declined, he and his army of about one thousand were besieged. Starvation compounded their misery. With no hope of success and starvation or slaughter the only alternatives, Walker finally surrendered in May 1857. The U.S. Navy guaranteed the safety of Walker and his men as they left Central America. Walker chalked up another spectacular filibustering failure. Anxious to return to Central America for more glory, he went to the eastern United States to recruit a third army.

Alphonse Sutter would not be one of Walker's new recruits. By July 1857 he was back in the bosom of his family at Hock Farm and, according to Sutter, "swore that he never in his life would go filibustering again."[58] Hard experience had changed Alphonse, who never fully recovered from the eighteen months he spent in Nicaragua. He came home with tuberculosis or possibly yellow fever or perhaps both. For the time being he was content to recuperate at Hock Farm.[59]

In 1860 Walker finally managed to get back to Central America with a force of filibusters. He did not last long. He surrendered to a British naval officer, who turned him over to Honduran authorities. A firing squad put an end to Walker's filibustering and buried him in the sand.[60]

The filibusters associated California pioneers like Sutter with their own exploits and blamed the Latino victims of their aggression for their failures.[61] General Sutter gladly connected himself with the filibusters and helped them when he could. Filibusters and pioneers alike, if distinctions must be made, draped their enterprise in virtue and sanctified American blood while vilifying their enemies. The difference between California and Nicaragua was the difference between victory and defeat. This was the kind of thinking that made Sutter a pioneer hero while at the same time he was castigated for taking too large a share of the spoils of his own filibustering acquisitions in the Sacramento Valley. The *filibusteros* of the 1850s were latter-day reflections of the myth of Sutter's California conquest. Unfortunately for them, luck and circumstances were not on their side. Sutter's luck, such as it was, had run out too.

CHAPTER 22

The Final Fall

Despite uncertainty about his land title and pressing debts, Sutter carried on his program of improvements at Hock Farm as best he could, "because it is of no use of loosing [sic] the courage," he explained to his old friend Bidwell.[1] Sutter was convinced that the future lay in developing the viticultural possibilities of northern California. In March 1856 he had twelve acres of well-tended vineyards with more than seventeen thousand vines. He planned to have as much as sixty acres in grapes in a couple of years, if things went well. Indeed, he believed that when all of his land issues were settled, he could pay his debts and still retain about four thousand acres free and clear. As always, the future looked bright to Sutter, but the journalist who recorded Sutter's hopes was not as optimistic about the general's chances. "It appears to be a settled thing to cheat and defraud him of his property, he being looked upon as game, for every one to aim at."[2]

For now Sutter concentrated on his vineyard. In July he reported that he had twenty-six thousand vines, which represented a large new investment of energy and borrowed money. He had lost faith in wheat and barley production. "My principal business shall be the cultivation of the grape vine," he told the *California Farmer*. He also intended to plant thousands of fruit trees and to convert his grain fields into meadows to make hay, "which will remunerate me well enough."[3] This was a bold vision at a time when most of the Sacramento Valley's farmers devoted their arable land to the cultivation of grain. Sutter was not alone in recognizing the future importance of viticulture in California. Vintners in Sonoma County and southern California were also producing credible wines.[4] Experience in wine-making increased Sutter's certainty that viticulture had a bright future and that he was in on the ground floor of an important agricultural development.

Victor, Sutter's horticulturally inclined son, supervised the vineyard to good effect. Indian workers planted the vines in precisely spaced rows and trained each vine to a redwood stake so that it formed a rough pyramid, each plant giving shade to the next. The bearing vines produced about four hundred and seventy-five gallons of wine in 1857. The California State Agricultural Society awarded the Sutter vineyard "a framed Diploma & $30.—of which I am very proud," he told Bidwell.[5]

As 1857 began it seemed that things were looking up for Sutter. On January 14 the federal district court confirmed both of his grants, but his joy did not last long. Two weeks later the U.S. attorney filed an appeal and took the case to the U.S. Supreme Court.[6] Sutter was in for another round of litigation with an uncertain outcome. His trustee, Lewis Sanders, hit upon a plan to raise money in Sacramento. He argued that Sutter's one-time attorney had illegally sold certain portions of the city and that Sutter retained the title to those lots. Therefore Sanders advertised that he would sell quitclaim deeds at public auction. This plan outraged Sacramentans who thought they had clear title to their lots, many of whom had already purchased quitclaim deeds from Mesick to cover August's supposed claim. The sale was stopped by court injunction; but between the claims of the Sutters and their agents, there seemed to be no end to litigation and title disputes over Sacramento property.[7]

A few months later Sutter's wobbly financial situation began to fall apart. In the spring Edward Taylor, one of his many creditors, finally ran out of patience and obtained a judgment against him. This time there seemed to be no hope of saving Hock Farm. On May 1 the county sheriff sold all of Sutter's property at public auction. The highest bidders turned out to be Packard and Woodruff, who also held notes against Sutter for large sums. A legal provision that gave him six months to redeem his land before it was finally conveyed to the buyers provided the only glimmer of hope.[8] Sutter perhaps put some faith in his long-standing relationship with Colonel Woodruff, while the purchasers did not seem to be in any hurry to evict the Sutters. After all, the Supreme Court had not yet spoken on the matter of his claims. His cooperation might be needed before a final confirmation was handed down.

Nor should one discount the possibility that Packard and Woodruff were genuinely sympathetic to Sutter's plight. It somehow did not seem right that he had been dispossessed entirely of his grand sixty-mile sweep of California land. The friendly editorial voice of the *California Farmer* spoke up for the old pioneer:

Has the State of California no heart? Have the people of California forgotten their early benefactor? Have they no gratitude? Where are the hundreds and thousands that were fed, clothed and cared for, in the early days of California? Where are those who made their pilgrimage to Sutter's Fort, as the first object of their attainment when they landed on the banks of the Sacramento?—if these are all silenced by death, where are those men who have been made rich by the possessions they have acquired through the liberality of our early and generous pioneer?[9]

The *Daily Alta* echoed these sentiments. It was "a pity, it was a shame, a disgrace, that those who have enriched themselves through his means (and some of them by means not the most honorable) should not at least have seen that the old man, in his declining years, should have a home of his own."[10] One and all recognized that Sutter was responsible for his financial pickle, but it seemed somehow unjust that the first pioneer of the Sacramento Valley was now to be homeless. Not so long ago the destitute Sutter had been the prince of the valley, and pioneers who depended on him then still held him in a fond regard that misty memory improved as his status declined. Calls for public recognition and relief for him were heard for the next several years.

The general sympathy for Sutter may have motivated Packard and Woodruff to reach an accommodation that allowed him to retain 600 acres of his estate, including his home, barns, vineyards, and orchards. They were careful, however, to make Sutter liable for taxes on his remaining land, and he still owed them a substantial sum of money.[11] In October Sutter reported this agreeable development to the *California Farmer:* "I am very happy to tell you that Hock Farm has been redeemed, and I can now sit under my own vine and fig tree again."[12] He did not explain that, as usual, his vine and tree were mortgaged right down to the roots. Nevertheless, for the time being Sutter at least retained the heart of Hock Farm and a roof over his head. When this news reached the State Fair, "a shout of joy went up . . . and in a very short space of time a beautiful wreath of Evergreen and Roses was placed around the portrait that graced the exhibition hall, over which was inscribed—'Our noble Pioneer.' "[13]

Some of Sutter's old friends scrambled to help him out of his financial troubles. Pierson Reading gave his share of Yuba City lots to Mrs. Sutter. "My wife is under the greatest Obligations to you for your Kindness to her," Sutter wrote.[14] After he redeemed Hock Farm, John Bidwell and other friends sent him livestock to help him get back on his feet. Sutter asked Bidwell to make a bill of sale for the animals to his sons. "It is necessary to do so to safe them from being attached," he explained.[15]

Sutter continued to wait on the Supreme Court for a decision that would confirm his title to the New Helvetia and sobrante grants. Others waited with him, especially those who were anxious about their titles to Sacramento. Those who held land under deeds that derived from Sutter's claim wanted a final confirmation that would validate their titles beyond dispute. Others (the so-called squatters) claimed ownership based on preemption, however, and they wanted Sutter's claims to fail so that their claims would be valid.

Deciding to enlist Sutter in their cause, the squatters sent a delegation to Hock Farm. The delegation included B. B. Redding (ex-mayor of Sacramento), Samuel M. McCullough, and one other man. Improbably, their meeting with Sutter resulted in some success. McCullough came away from the meeting with the conviction that Sutter was on their side. Sutter told them that "his agents heretofore [e]mployed by him has sought a confirmation of land outside of [the grant] boundaries so as to include the City of Sacramento and according to the true intent and meaning of the grant itself does not include the City of Sacramento."[16] He then gave Redding his power of attorney to represent this claim in Washington.

Redding had no influence on the Supreme Court's decision, but Sutter's inconsistency once again served to unsettle land titles in Sacramento by undermining the security of titles held under his name. What he hoped to accomplish by giving the Redding committee this version of events is impossible to know. Maybe he told the truth. Perhaps he was in his cups and merely wished to humor his guests. Whatever the case, McCullough was elated. "There can be no doubt of success," he said. "I here state as soon as it is ascertained beyond a doubt that the Sutter Title does not cover this Place property will take a rise at least twenty-five per cent." He added that "improvements of all description will be made."[17] McCullough would soon discover that his faith in Sutter's assurances was misplaced.

The Supreme Court did not decide the Sutter case until December 1858, and it was not publicly announced for several months. The court confirmed the original eleven-league grant that Alvarado had made in 1841 but denied Micheltorena's twenty-two league grant, arguing that he had already been deposed by the insurgents who replaced him when he approved the grant. Moreover, even if Micheltorena had retained the governorship, the grant did not conform to Mexican law and well-established procedures.

Years later Sutter claimed that it was this decision that ruined him. "I gave deeds when I made sales of the *sobrante* lands, warrantee deeds, which I had to make good from my other lands & so all went."[18] Sutter was already ruined, of course. Creditors had stripped him of virtually all the lands that he held under the Alvarado grant, and now he was struggling to retain his heavily mortgaged

600-acre remnant of Hock Farm. Even if he had retained the whole Alvarado grant, how could he make good the sale of twenty-two leagues from the eleven that were legally his? To make matters worse, Sutter had sold even more than the thirty-three leagues that he thought he owned. Some of the hapless owners of deeds to sobrante lands would have to shift for themselves.

News of the Supreme Court decision came as a shock to Sacramento. First reports reached the city in March 1859, stating that the Alvarado grant was confirmed and the Micheltorena grant had been remanded to federal district court for further consideration, "merely delaying the final confirmation."[19] Two weeks later the *Sacramento Union* corrected this misapprehension by publishing the Supreme Court decree that unequivocally repudiated Sutter's Micheltorena claim.[20] There was good news for Sacramentans who owned land under Sutter titles. The court had declared the southern boundary of the grant to be four miles south of Sutter's Fort, so as to include Sacramento and Sutterville. The squatters' claims were dead. The justices recognized that the northern boundary was just south of the Sutter Buttes, but they remanded the case to the federal district court to superintend a survey that would determine exactly which lands belonged within the grant. Thus the court obligated Judge Ogden Hoffman to come up with a gerrymandered map of Sutter's holdings that, if possible, included all of the property that Sutter had sold under the Alvarado grant. No wonder that Judge Hoffman "felt more difficulty and embarrassment in arriving at a conclusion in this case than in any other it has been my duty to decide."[21] Four more years would pass before he approved the final survey.

Many irregularities made Sutter's claim difficult. The original papers and maps were lost, so the Land Claims Commission and courts had to rely on copies of documents in Sutter's possession as well as testimony from witnesses. The maps that he produced were confusing, because they marked boundaries according to erroneous latitudes. His surveyor, Jean Jacques Vioget, claimed that faulty instruments caused this discrepancy. The maps were also of such a general nature that they did not disclose precisely which lands within the vast province of New Helvetia were included in the grant.

After Judge Hoffman appointed A. W. Von Schmidt to survey the final boundaries, Sutter produced yet another map that seemed to mark out his boundaries with some precision. This new representation showed that Vioget had marked off two square leagues south of the American River embracing Sutter's Fort, other improvements, and the sites of Sacramento and Sutterville. Nine leagues on the Feather River included Hock Farm and some land east of the river. Von Schmidt surveyed the land and drew his map accordingly. Judge Hoffman, however, rejected Von Schmidt's survey and ordered another. Sutter's newly produced map had never been introduced into evidence, the judge ruled, and the Supreme Court had insisted on using the maps that had been presented in lower court decisions. So Von Schmidt returned to the field and drew a new map that differed in detail but still delineated the grant as having sections on the American and Feather Rivers, with a very narrow connecting strip on the east bank of the Sacramento River. In 1865 the U.S. Supreme Court rejected this map and ordered Judge Hoffman to accept Von Schmidt's first plat.[22]

While Von Schmidt ran his lines, Sutter needed a source of income so that he could pay his debts and save his Feather River homestead. Perhaps he could salvage something from his deal with the Russians for Ross and Bodega. In 1843 Sutter had sold his claim to the property to Stephen Smith, who had also obtained a Mexican grant, which was confirmed in 1859. Although the Mexican grant covered only a part of the Bodega ranch, Smith's heirs claimed that land too. Sutter asserted that he still held an interest in this land, and in May 1859 he sold it to William Muldrow and others, who began surveying and selling deeds to settlers that Smith's heirs regarded as squatters. The Smith claimants went to court for an injunction against Sutter and his associates, but sales continued until the Sutter claim finally was determined to be invalid. Sutter got some needed cash from the entrepreneurs, who used his claim to milk more money out of Sonoma County farmers.[23] This was a dangerous business. Curtis Tyler, the administrator for the Smith estate, hired several dozen San Francisco goons to remove the settlers forcibly. Violence was averted only by the timely intervention of the sheriff.[24]

Sutter's involvement in the Bodega controversy got some notice in Sacramento after a defense of his Russian claim was published there.[25] The *Union* editor erroneously claimed that Sutter had never fully paid his Russian creditors and dismissed the Sutter claim as unsupported by historical facts.[26] A short time later Victor defended his father and was especially angry about the editor's assertion that Sutter had not paid the Russians.[27] Sutter's middle son increasingly took the role of chief defender of the family honor. With August permanently living in Mexico, Victor was the *de facto* eldest son. He, too, joined a state militia unit, the Marysville Rifles, and was elected second lieutenant.[28] As his father's fortunes waned, Victor was forced to leave Hock Farm to take an instructorship at the Oroville Industrial School.[29] Eventually he became a notary public in San Francisco, perhaps having noticed from his father's business affairs that there was always plenty of work along those lines.[30]

Sutter struggled to make a living from Hock Farm, but it was increasingly difficult. In the spring of 1860 he leased the garden to a Mr. Levinson, who ran it as a "genteel retreat" for the harried citizens of the bustling city of Marysville.

Visitors were impressed with "the rarest shrubberies, . . . beautiful and delicate flowers, . . . the perfume of exotics, . . . avenues of fruit trees," which they appreciated in "luxurious wonderment." They also partook of Sutter's "delicious" wine at the "old 'Hock Farm House.' " Levinson was especially attentive to the wants of Marysville ladies, who disapproved of "public drinking bars—and . . . has also good enough sense to know that well cultivated ladies and gentlemen like to indulge in the sociability of a quiet ice, or a private draft of wine." The *Marysville Daily Appeal* predicted that Hock Farm would be "*the* place of resort during the coming season of coloric [heat]."[31]

Sutter maintained his residence at Hock Farm and ran the agricultural operations as well as he could. His chronic lack of funds hampered his ability to hire farm hands. In 1860 only ten Indians lived in all of Sutter County; they probably worked for him under the agreement that he had made with Superintendent Henley.[32] The 1860 census shows that the patriarch's household had shrunk considerably. The retinue of European retainers who had lived there ten years earlier was gone.[33] Alphonse had married a Swiss woman from Berne and no longer lived with his parents.[34] His residence at this time is uncertain, but he may have moved to Anaheim to manage a vineyard. Victor was still there, as was Eliza, who had remarried the previous December.[35] Her new husband, Xavier Victor Link, was not listed as a resident. He was a physician with a practice in Marysville who kept a residence there. August's children John III and Eliza (aged eight and five) added the vibrancy of childhood to their grandparents' lives. August's third child had not yet come to live with her grandparents. Two farmhands and a female domestic servant rounded out the household, but the Sutters would not be able to keep them for much longer. Victor left, and then the hired hands and household servant. Eliza and Doctor Link resettled in Acapulco with August, who was doing well in his business there. Gone, too, were the thousands of livestock that once grazed on Sutter's miles of open pasture land. By 1860 he had only two horses, two mules, half a dozen milk cows, and two other cattle. He reported that he had $2,000 worth of orchard products and 875 gallons of wine on the premises.[36]

Sutter keenly felt the loss of Victor and Eliza. Without his son, the burden of managing day-to-day farm operations fell to him. Eliza had doubtless helped her mother with the hard work of nineteenth-century farm house management, but she had been helpful in other ways too. Sutter deeded his livestock and agricultural productions to her, no doubt to save them from attachment.[37] In May 1859 Sutter mortgaged Hock Farm to Frederick F. Low, a Marysville banker with political aspirations. Low loaned him $13,482 at the rate of 10 percent per year, payable on the first day of October, with any unpaid interest added to the principal, which was due in five years.[38] Sutter gained needed operating capital, but once more at a heavy cost and with uncertain means to pay.

Around 1862 the Sutter household added a new member, August's third child, María del Carmen. The circumstances are unclear. Apparently August's wife had left him and gone to San Francisco with their child. Eventually she deposited María del Carmen with the girl's grandparents at Hock Farm. The additional burden of a five-year-old could not have been a welcome development in the already hard-pressed Sutter household, although August probably provided some money for his children's care.[39]

By October 1862 Sutter's financial condition made him an object of pity. "He and his infirm wife are alone on the Hock Farm," the *Marysville Daily Appeal* reported, "he performing daily labor in the field while the old lady cooks and performs the kitchen work." John III was his only help, "and the poor boy had his right arm terribly crushed some three weeks ago; but the limb has been saved." At age fifty-nine the general needed "comforts which are out of his reach," the *Appeal* reported, "and which the people of California ought to be proud to bestow."[40] The Society of California Pioneers helped the old man with charity from the Sutter Pioneer Testimonial Fund.[41]

Sutter retained the rank of major general in the state militia, but this honor, too, was on a downward trajectory. At first he believed—and continued to assert to the end of his life—that only the governor outranked him, although he knew that he was one of several major generals who commanded divisions. "I did like better my former position as Major Genl. of California, in which position I have considered myself as the Lieutenant of the Commander in Chief, or second in command," he complained to Governor J. Neely Johnson.[42] Sutter had considered asking the legislature to give him this exalted designation but thought better of it. Instead he wondered if the governor would make it so. It did not happen.

When the Civil War began in 1861, it was clear that the California state militia would have to rise to a higher level of efficiency. Mere parade generals were not needed. Still, Sutter was game. General Sutter, ailing and nearly overwhelmed by work on Hock Farm, promised to "be very actif for the organization of my Division." "It appears that his Excellency the Governor [John G. Downey], is not very actif as Commander in Chief," he impolitically added.[43] Nevertheless, Governor Downey reappointed Sutter for an additional four-year term.[44] Two days later Sutter reported that his "infirmities" would not permit him to attend the muster of one of the brigades that served under him.[45] This was not a promising display of the energy that he had promised. Sutter's infirm condition may have caused the governor to reconsider the wisdom of renewing his commission, because he asked the adjutant general if Sutter's term of appointment was up. Indeed it was.[46] Within days there was a new major general for the Fifth Division, and Sutter was a mere supernumerary.[47] General Sutter's military career was over.

Soon after Sutter lost his command, events in Europe turned in his favor. For twenty-eight years the Swiss courts had withheld Anna Sutter's share of her mother's estate, now amounting to more than more than twenty-five thousand Swiss francs. Sutter's old friend Martin Birmann had looked after the litigation in this matter, and in 1862 Sutter's creditors were finally satisfied. Legal expenses and settlement of his debts no doubt ate into the bequest; but according to Birmann, Anna obtained her inheritance in 1862.[48] Birmann does not reveal what Anna did with her new assets, but it would have been most unwise to transfer them to California and place them at the disposition of Sutter and his creditors. It seems likely that she retained sole control over her newfound wealth, whether keeping it in Switzerland or moving it to the United States.

There was tragedy in the Sutter family too. Sutter's son Alphonse came to the defense of the Union soon after Fort Sumpter fell. Still suffering from the disease that he had contracted in Nicaragua, Alphonse took it upon himself to organize a company of cavalry in Sutter County.[49] He enlisted sixty-seven men for his company; but he was in no condition for the job, and another man replaced him as company commander.[50] Alphonse went to Anaheim, where he managed a vineyard, and then returned briefly to Hock Farm in 1862, suffering from tuberculosis. Finally he moved to Nevada City, where he died on August 12, 1863, leaving his wife and infant son to mourn him.[51] There can be no doubt about the grief that Sutter and his wife bore for their youngest child, the one with the sunny disposition. No surviving letters from Sutter mention Alphonse at the time of his death, but he fondly remembered his son in later years. He thought that Alphonse had inherited his military spirit from him. Alphonse, "a soldier born and bred, died as a Captain of the Cavalry," he told an old friend in 1880.[52] Although his son's illness prevented him from fighting, Sutter asserted, Alphonse had very thoroughly trained his men who "warred against the rebels."[53] There was no need to mention Alphonse's career with Walker or his final years as a consumptive. For the grieving father, Alphonse's brief service to the Union in Sutter County was enough to shroud his casket with the flag, if only in memory.

Sutter's penury continued to inspire compassion among Californians. When he sent figs to the Pacific Fruit Market in 1864, the *California Farmer* reported their availability as an opportunity to help Sutter. Californians could buy boxes of "luscious figs, grown, dried, and packed at 'Hock Farm,' and this was done, principally, by the personal labor and toil of the venerable old pioneer himself, assisted by the companion of his joys and sorrows, both now on in years." The editor chastised the people of California and the nation for allowing the man who had helped so many in the early days to work so hard in his golden years. If the state legislature would not provide for Sutter, then all who cared about him should go to the Pacific Fruit Market to purchase Hock Farm figs and pay liberally for them. "Give a noble price, five, ten, twenty or an hundred dollars for a box of figs from the Hock Farm," the editor urged. The price "will be cheap, and bring back a heavenly blessing, for God repays the deed of noble hearts seven fold. Remember the figs of Hock Farm, and remember the pioneer."[54]

In April 1864 the state legislature, perhaps hoping for a heavenly blessing, responded to the many calls for public aid for General Sutter. "An Act to Appropriate Money for the Relief of General John A. Sutter and His Heirs" provided $15,000 to be distributed in monthly payments of $250 for five years.[55] Frederick F. Low, now California's governor, gladly signed the bill. Whatever sympathy for Sutter he felt was augmented by self-interest. Sutter now had a steady income that could be used to make mortgage payments to Low. The legislature's subsequent extensions gave Sutter an additional five years of relief payments totaling $30,000.[56] He gladly accepted the money but did not construe it as relief. "The $3,000 a year," he proudly told historian Bancroft, "was not a gift of the state to me, nor would I receive it as such." Instead, it was "a return of the taxes which I had paid on the *Sobrante* land grant, which land I did not get."[57] Perhaps the amount more or less matched Sutter's tax bill on his unconfirmed land, but the statutes that provided money to him spoke only of relief, not of tax refunds. Sutter much preferred to think that ideas about justice and equity motivated legislators, rather than pity. Whatever the lawmakers' intent, it was clear that Sutter thought the state owed him something for taxes, past services, aid to the immigrants, the gold discovery, and sundry other contributions that he had made to the welfare of the state and its people.

With regular monthly relief payments in hand, income from farm productions, lease payments from Levinson, and perhaps some help from Anna's estate, August, and his other children, Sutter managed to keep Hock Farm.[58] A few Indians continued to work for Sutter, who was still a special Indian agent, an unpaid position but one that gave him some semblance of official authority over the Indians. He provided them with rudimentary medical care and dosed them with such medicines as he had on hand. Sutter sent chronic and severe cases, especially advanced syphilitics, to Dr. A. S. Long in Yuba City, requesting him to bill the Office of Indian Affairs. His letters to Long do not evince much sympathy for the people in his charge. "If you give him Medicine," he wrote of one Indian patient, "please do not make them complicated, but so simple as possible, as I have not much time to spare to attend to them."[59] "If you can do something for him please do," he wrote when he sent a man with severe venereal disease to Long, "if you cannot then he have to get along so good as he can."[60] When treatment was successful in alleviating the suffering of an Indian worker, Sutter agreeably reported that he was "better now, and at work."[61] Labor was the best indication of health in the general's eyes. Sutter's concern for his workers may have extended beyond self-interest, but one looks in vain for compassionate expressions in the letters describing smallpox, cancer, venereal sores, blindness, and severe rheumatism among the surviving Hock Farm Indians.[62]

Despite Sutter's dependency on his state pension, he always resented any hint that he was no longer in control of Hock Farm. Levinson's operation of the grounds as a public retreat provided needed income, but Victor Sutter bristled when the *Alta* regretfully reported that Hock Farm was leased "as a place of public resort." "There is probably not a person who knows him," the editor continued, "but will sincerely regret to learn that the public at large are to roam at will through the grounds rendered so attractive by his taste and labor, and that in the dwelling where he reared his children and dispensed his hospitality so freely, strangers congregate, and eat, drink, and make merry at their own expense."[63] Victor hastened to set the record straight as to who was the master of Hock Farm. The general was still in residence, and the recent revelers were merely the " 'Marysville Liederkranz,' a vocal society, and its friends holding a picnic." The lessee of Hock Farm had a right to hold picnics there, Victor averred, had done so before, and would no doubt do so again, "which is nothing strange at all."[64] With that declaration of the normalcy of such doings, Victor saved Sutter family honor and retired from the field.

Life at Hock Farm was normal, after a fashion. Sutter still lived there with his wife and grandchildren. He continued to produce fruit and wine for market. Guests (now Levinson's paying customers) came and went. But this was a long way from the halcyon days when Sutter was lord of all he surveyed. He still retained a fragment of his California demesne, but only as a state pensioner, debtor, mortgagee, and family farmer.

It is difficult to gauge how much longer Sutter could have retained Hock Farm under these circumstances—perhaps until his death. But that was not to be his fate. In June 1865 a nameless discharged soldier drifted to Hock Farm and stayed for a few days. It would have been characteristic of Sutter to take him in because he had been a soldier. Or perhaps the man agreed to work in exchange for board. Whatever the case, Sutter caught the man stealing from him. He ordered the thief tied up and may have had him whipped. For a brief moment Sutter must have believed that he had it in his power to punish wrongdoers who poached in his domain, but those days were long gone. Sutter's peremptory corporal punishment turned out to be a bad decision. After the soldier was released, he set fire to Sutter's home and an adjacent barley field that was ripe with grain. The Sutters got out of the house, but they lost virtually everything that he had collected since coming to California. A large library in four languages, "pictures, busts, curiosities, and everything he has been accumulating the last forty years, excepting a medal or two and his family portraits" all went up in flames. When asked about the value of the loss, Sutter struggled to hold back his tears. "It cannot be estimated in dollars and cents." His personal items, keepsakes, and priceless historical documents were irreplaceable, but the *Appeal* reported worse news. "There was no insurance on the buildings."[65]

Without funds or credit to rebuild, Sutter was finished in California. He still had title to the six hundred acres of Hock Farm; but there was little hope of satisfying the mortgage to Governor Low, let alone finding means to rebuild the old manse. He could have remained in California as a dispossessed pensioner, a broken relic of a bygone age. His state pension would have allowed him a decent living, but that was not an attractive future to the old pioneer.

The material symbols of Sutter's remarkable California passage were in ashes, but his most valuable asset was intact: his brilliant personality. At sixty-three, Sutter was still a vivacious conversationalist. He was famous. Some people thought he was a hero. He certainly looked the part in his fine clothes. Sutter knew many powerful and well-placed politicians, famous in their own right, who had left their marks on American history. Could he enlist his fame and these men to make one more attempt to gain from the public treasury the riches he had lost in California? Perhaps he could parlay his fame and reputation into something yet, not as a pioneer in a new land but as a hero claiming compensation from Congress for his contributions to the country. In October he gave Victor sole power of attorney to manage his remaining interests in California.[66] Then he left the Golden State forever. To make his last stand, Sutter strode into the largest arena he could find, the Capitol in Washington, D.C. To the very end, General Sutter would put up a good fight.

Chapter 23

A Hero among the Moravians

The day after Sutter gave his son authority to manage his California affairs, Governor Low sat down to write a letter of introduction to the U.S. Congress for his old friend. "The bearer of this, Major-Gen. Sutter, was one of the early pioneers of this coast, and by his industry, bravery and indomitable energy, did more to subdue the savage tribes and encourage settlement than any other man." Sutter hardly needed an introduction: "his name and fame were world wide," the governor reminded Congress, "as the cause of the discovery of gold in this state." His "kindness and generosity to the early emigrants" were "proverbial." Although he was once the owner of huge Mexican land grants, "delays and expenses incident to the legal adjudication of these titles have stripped him of all his property, leaving him in his old age comparatively penniless." Happily, the California state legislature had recently provided him with an annual annuity of $3,000 for five years. Now Sutter planned to ask Congress "for some recognition with compensation," and the governor earnestly commended his claims to that august body.[1]

In a few words Governor Low ably presented the legend of John Sutter. Brave pioneer, savior of innocent immigrants, gold-discoverer, victim of Congress's slow and unjust confirmation procedure, Sutter had become a pauper dependent on well-deserved public assistance. The national government should be honored to provide even more compensation to the old hero, for he richly deserved it in return for the services he had rendered to the United States. This was the story that Sutter told and retold in hopes of gaining something from the public treasury.

Like most legends, Sutter's contained a good deal of truth. There is no

A HERO AMONG THE MORAVIANS   323

denying that he helped the immigrants or that he was responsible for the early settlement of the Sacramento Valley. His agency in the discovery of gold is indisputable, although cynics might reasonably argue that, after all, *someone* was bound to find gold in California. Nevertheless, Columbus-like, Sutter gets the credit for his part in the inadvertent discovery. The Sutter legend, however, omitted awkward facts from the historical record and completely absolved him of any personal responsibility for his financial travail. As always, he excused himself while blaming others for his troubles. Cynical congressmen might ask, why should Congress single out Sutter for relief? Plenty of Californians found it difficult to adjust to new conditions and lost their land, including a host of Mexican landowners who might justly get some credit for settling California. These obvious questions did not trouble Sutter. He was his own Homer, singing a heroic song that portrayed him as Ulysses.

Sutter, his wife, and his grandchildren arrived in Washington in December 1865. He wasted no time in placing his case before Congress. On January 15, 1866, his petition begged for compensation based on his service to immigrants and the American cause.[2] The sobrante claim was valid, according to Sutter, and he asserted that he had purchased Ross and Bodega from the Russians, land and all, although he did not press his claim to the Sonoma County property. The Mexican government had offered him $100,000 for New Helvetia, Sutter claimed, but he had refused this generous offer, because "the American citizens and other immigrants would have lost all protection which petitioner's then considerable power and position vouchsafed to them." Without mentioning Frémont or the Bear Flag rebels, Sutter "upon request" raised the Stars and Stripes over his fort. New Helvetia was in a flourishing state until the gold discovery that ruined him. Squatters blanketed his lands while rustlers stole his livestock, but worse predators circled his rich pasturelands. While he waited for the courts to confirm his land grants "a certain class of men . . . interposed every possible obstacle to a final adjustment of" his claims while the state imposed taxes on his land that squatters had appropriated.[3]

Thus Sutter was swamped by debt, he informed Congress, even as the fruits of his lordly empire were withheld from him. Only a small fragment of Hock Farm remained in his hands, and it was heavily mortgaged. "Without any vain boast," Sutter told Congress in the long-winded formal phrasing of his petition that he had "been the agent in developing . . . the mineral and agricultural wealth of California; and that his grants from Mexico establish an equity against the United States; that his second [sobrante] grant has been unjustly rejected, . . . ; that he has been, and is, thus deprived of . . . his property by American citizens, . . . under color of [U.S. preemption] laws designed to promote the settlement of the public domain"; that while these things led to his "complete ruin they have greatly increased the national wealth and that of many thousands of individuals to whom his door was ever open in their hour of need, . . . without fee or award save in the action." Sutter had no practical recourse to the courts in California, where a floating population and powerful interests made "laws for his destruction [rather] than his protection," and where "no suits can be maintained without money."[4] In all, Sutter reckoned that he had lost half a million dollars and asked Congress to pass a law giving him "general and special relief" in the form of an as yet unspecified amount of money.[5]

The petition further developed the Sutter legend. Against all odds and at great expense he had promoted U.S. immigration, supported the American cause, discovered gold, promoted California agriculture, and enriched the nation, only to be swindled by designing men who were aided by the laws and inefficiency of the federal government. Now the state had seen fit to provide Sutter with a much-deserved pension and the federal government should do the same. The legal decision of the U.S. Supreme Court was unjust, based on a technicality that Congress should set right by awarding Sutter a sum of money. This is what he called "simple justice."[6]

Congress did not jump at the opportunity to reward Sutter with $100,000, as he first requested, or the more modest $50,000 that calmer minds in the California delegation suggested. Sutter's petition lingered in the congressional committee system for years as he lobbied for his cause in the halls of government.

While Congress considered his case, Sutter enjoyed life in Washington and the other eastern cities that he visited. And why not? For the first time he had a steady income and no pressing debts, except the mortgage on Hock Farm. He and Anna no longer had to labor in the fields. They lived and dined in hotels, so Anna had no heavy domestic responsibilities. Sutter had many friends in Washington, including some of the great names of the Civil War, such as Sherman, Halleck, and Ulysses S. Grant. His old friend Bidwell was serving a term in Congress when Sutter arrived, and he no doubt opened many doors for the old Californian.

Sutter was famous in his own right and was an entertaining bon vivant and raconteur. Even in old age he was a striking figure, as the *New York Times* described:

> His head was massive; his face was high-colored and double-chinned; a snowy white mustache and short side whiskers stood in strong contrast upon his flaming complexion. His eyes were keen and dark; his nose was straight and the mouth was firm. He generally wore a dark blue

coat with brass buttons, a buff vest, and gray pantaloons. His hat was an old-fashioned yellow plush, broad-brimmed and low-crowned.[7]

Well-dressed as always, the distinguished-looking Sutter was an ornament in Washington society. At least he thought so. "I am always in the best society," he told his sister-in-law. His comings and goings were noted in the newspapers, even in New York. Of course, he was at the Capitol every day when Congress was in session so that he could lobby the members.[8]

Sutter attended pleasurable social events too. In the spring of 1868 his old friend Bidwell married Annie Kennedy, who came from a prominent Washington family. General Grant and General Sherman were also there. Traveling in company like this, Sutter had every reason to believe that Congress would ultimately give him the relief he sought. True, the Senate was momentarily preoccupied with the impeachment of Andrew Johnson, he wrote his sister-in-law; but as soon as that disagreeable business was completed, Congress would take up his case. "I have much support from influential persons, as well as senators and members of Congress and the press." Furthermore, "high-ranking ladies will use their influence." General Sutter could still charm women.[9]

There were indications that Sutter had reformed some of his bad habits. He claimed that he did not go to saloons: "that would be ordinary," and he was not about to do anything that made him seem common.[10] "Besides that we save as much as we can, we drink rarely wine, because the wine is very expensive here," he wrote. "[W]e only need from time to time some Xeres (Sherry)," and that only for medicinal purposes. All in all, if Sutter's letters to his sister-in-law are to be believed, the alcoholic wastrel had become thrifty and temperate in his old age. "And so one remains healthy and wholesome, at nine o'clock we go to bed, [we] don't go to any theater, and wake up at five o'clock to read and write." He and Anna (they called each other Mama and Papa) settled into the familiar rhythms of old age.[11]

Sutter's residence in Washington enabled him to lobby for his son's appointment as U.S. representative in Acapulco. August's business was doing well, and he also worked as cashier and bookkeeper for the Pacific Mail Steamship Company. During the tumultuous last days of the French occupation of Mexico under Emperor Maximilian, August sided with the Liberals, a decision that did not go unnoticed by the French and their Mexican allies. August's Liberal sympathies led to his arrest in May 1866, but the pleas of the U.S. consul and intervention by the commander of an American warship effected his release. In October Maximilianists opened August's mail and learned that he was transmitting messages about the shipment of arms from San Francisco to Benito Juárez, president of the Liberal government. August fled Acapulco, to return early in 1867 once the French had been deposed.[12] Young Sutter was on the side of the angels in this dispute, but his actions are reminiscent of his father's meddling in Mexican California and the filibustering of the previous decade.

Surely August's doings do not exemplify the neutrality in the internal affairs of a host nation that might be expected of a U.S. agent. Nevertheless, in July 1868 the State Department appointed him U.S. commercial agent. Letters from his father, Bidwell, and other California luminaries recommended August for appointment as U.S. consul. Sutter personally took the matter to the secretary of state (whose office was across the street from the Sutters' rooms) and received assurances that his son was well qualified and likely to get a position as soon as it could be arranged.[13] In July 1870 President Grant signed August's consular commission, and a few months later President Benito Juárez officially approved.[14] August's official position and strong business situation made him an important person in Acapulco.

While August engineered his advancement in Mexico, his parents continued to live the gypsy life in hotel rooms. City living had its charms, but Sutter did not want to live in a Washington hotel forever. Washington was expensive, and he looked forward to living someplace where the pace of life was slower and the cost of living more reasonable. The Sutters' hotel bill ran $125 per month. The food was all right, he wrote, but the same could be had for much less in Pennsylvania, where his grandchildren were attending school. The rural villages of Pennsylvania attracted him greatly. Less expensive than Washington and New York, the larger towns had many of the conveniences of the city while retaining the agreeable rhythms of the agricultural world. Better yet, many Pennsylvania towns had been founded by Germans and had an orderly, well-kept appearance that appealed to Sutter. In some of them German was the residents' first language. Such a place would be fitting for the Sutters' final home.

Sutter's search for a suitable school for his grandchildren gave him an opportunity to reconnoiter in the Quaker state.[15] First he enrolled them in a school in Bethlehem, but for some reason this proved unsatisfactory. In 1867 Sutter located two schools in Lititz, John Beck's School for John III and Linden Hall for Anna Eliza and María del Carmen. August, who was now prospering in Acapulco, paid the bill for his children's education. (Sutter bragged that August's rancho was "almost as big as Switzerland.")[16] Lititz also had a natural spring with healing waters that eased Sutter's rheumatic bones. The Lititz Spring Hotel and tavern on Main Street provided comfortable lodgings when the Sutters visited. The town was on the line of the Reading Railroad, so the hundred-mile journey to Washington was convenient.[17]

The history of Lititz made it an unlikely place for Sutter to feel at home. The original regulations of the town, founded in 1756 by German members of the Moravian Church who intended the place to be a model of religious and social rectitude, discouraged all but the most devoted co-religionists from settling. According to these rules, there was to be no "light-minded, disorderly and needless conversation, no changing of professions, no giving a night's lodging to any person or no undertaking a journey, either far or near, without permission."[18] The rules required parents to administer corporal punishment to unruly children; playing in the streets was not permitted.

Such draconian restrictions could not last forever. In 1763 the town permitted the construction of the Zum Anchor Inn for the entertainment of strangers. Eventually this establishment became the Lititz Spring Hotel that hosted the Sutters. The Moravian Church strove mightily to maintain Lititz as a Moravian town until 1856. By then the rush of modernity, the railroad, and democratic ideals had made it impossible to enforce the old rules of behavior, so the town was thrown open to non-Moravian residents. In the 1860s Lititz was a bustling agricultural trading town with good rail connections that served the surrounding thrifty farmers. Still, it retained its distinctive ethnic character. The sound of German was often heard in the streets. All in all, finding Lititz an agreeable place, the Sutters began to think about establishing a permanent residence there.

While the Sutters had a decent income from his state pension and Anna's inheritance, and perhaps a bit more from the rent of mortgaged Hock Farm and other California assets, building a home in Lititz would be easier without the burden of the mortgage payments. It was finally time to sell out. In 1868 August and Eliza, both living in Acapulco, sold their share of Hock Farm to John Gelzhauser, who had purchased 400 acres from Emil and Alphonse in 1857.[19] In 1869 Sutter, his wife, and all their children sold their remaining interest in Hock Farm to Governor Low for $5,000.[20] Sutter was finally out of the California real-estate business.

Sutter's share of the proceeds from Hock Farm was small, less than $1,000. Anna may have had some savings remaining from her inheritance; but evidently this was not enough to buy a home in Lititz, at least not the sort of place they wanted. Their eldest son came to the rescue. In 1871 the now prosperous August sent his mother funds to build a substantial home opposite the Lititz Spring Hotel, just down the street from Linden Hall school.[21] August was always concerned about his mother's welfare, and he also wanted a fine home for his children. The home was in Anna's name, a wise precaution considering Sutter's history of borrowing on property. Confined to bed with rheumatism in the neighboring hotel, Sutter himself drew the plans for the house, and Anna supervised the construction. The place was impressive, as it should have been, because according to Sutter it cost $10,000. He described it as "a very beautiful large house with every modern comfort and a beautiful garden."[22] The furnishings alone cost $3,000. Sutter also bragged about the wonderful stove that circulated hot water in the house, the first of its kind in Lititz.

Sutter was justly proud of his new home. It was a robust, two-story brick house with decorative stone lintels over the regularly spaced windows and front door. The roof was made of slate, with dual ceramic pots sprouting from chimneys at either end of the roof. Green shutters, apparently made of iron for fire protection, flanked the windows. The interior was commodious, with parlors and the kitchen downstairs and bedrooms and Sutter's library upstairs. Twelve-foot ceilings and eight-foot doors enhanced the impression of spaciousness.[23] Sutter had his photograph taken in front of it, a gray-haired man in a wide-brimmed hat resting on his cane. From this formidable domestic fortress he periodically sallied forth to do battle with the forces in Congress that resisted giving him the "simple justice" that he demanded.

Sutter's infirmities forced him to be a home body in Lititz, but he was not reclusive. On warm days he sat in his garden behind the house. Otherwise he read the eight newspapers to which he subscribed and studied in his library. Despite his claims to a temperate life, Sutter kept a wine cellar stocked with California vintages with which to entertain his visitors. The town's residents remembered him as "the most interesting conversationalist that Lititz ever had."[24] Who would doubt it? He walked regularly as his health permitted, although never very far. Though enfeebled, Sutter still impressed all who met him. A Sutter family tradition recalls him walking with a friend when they encountered a tramp who courteously tipped his forlorn hat and greeted General Sutter by his military title. "Sutter responded in a like manner, adding 'sir' to his return greeting, much to the astonishment of his friend, who wanted to know the reason for so much attention to a tramp. 'If we haven't got respect for other people, they'll have none for us,' the old gentleman explained to his companion."[25] Manners were everything to Sutter, who all his days politely saluted aristocrat and vagabond alike, as long as they gave him due regard.

Soon after Sutter moved into his new house, he subscribed to the newspapers. Charles Buch delivered them, but the teenager found that his new customer was more demanding than the rest. Sutter would not allow the papers merely to be thrown in the yard or on the porch. Instead he insisted that they be brought to the front door and that the bell be sounded so that the papers could be handed directly to him or Anna. Sutter struck up a friendship with his paperboy and quizzed him about Lititz and its customs. The garrulous old man probably took the opportunity to tell the boy about the exciting days in California. The paperboy was deeply impressed by Sutter, who called him Karl and tipped him a quarter on every holiday. Karl noticed that the general's main interest was to scour the papers for any scrap of news about California. Sutter's courtly manners and exciting history made a lasting impression. In 1929 a local paper reported that whenever the aged Karl visited his boyhood home in Lititz, he went to "the grave of the white haired old man who bought his newspapers back in the 70's and appeared a hero to his boyish imagination."[26]

Sutter was always concerned about his claim in Washington, but when he was at home his grandchildren demanded much of his attention. By the time the Sutters moved into their new home Juan (as they familiarly called John III) was nineteen; Anna Eliza and María Carmen were fifteen and fourteen, respectively. Juan was clearly the apple of his namesake's eye. He studied chemistry at school, and Sutter thought that he would send him to West Point. He had already talked to Generals Grant and Sherman about getting an appointment to the military academy for Juan, but his military dream did not materialize.[27]

Anna Eliza was becoming an attractive young lady with fine musical skills. August purchased her one of the "finest and most magnificent" pianos from New York.[28] Eliza had a great passion for the piano; her practicing in the parlor filled the whole house with music. In Lititz she performed with the local philharmonic society. María was a less talented player, but she was "zu flüchtig" (flighty), Sutter explained.[29] Not much is known about María besides her feckless ways. She probably suffered in comparison with her older siblings, but there is no evidence that she was ill treated. August regularly sent his children ten dollars "Taschengeld" (pocket money).[30]

Whatever talents the grandchildren had, they added life and warmth to the Sutter home. Sutter always spoke about them with love and pride. They provided him with a taste of the family life that he had missed with his own children during their long separation. Anna may have felt differently. One of her great-grandchildren recalled that she thought children should be seen and not heard. She had raised four children alone, and the burden of looking after three more in her old age was an imposition. Still, August took care of the financial needs of his children; and the elder Sutters always needed the extra cash.

Anna's contentment is difficult to gauge, but there are reasons to believe that she liked Lititz. She never learned to speak English, so the prevalence of German-speaking Pennsylvanians must have reminded her of her Swiss home. She had a maid from the town who spoke "Pennsylvania Dutch, which one had to get used to," Sutter explained. The townspeople's vernacular German struck the Sutters as ignorant, especially because they always used the informal "du" (you) form of address, rather than the formal "Sie." The maid called not only Anna "du" but even General Sutter, the pastor, and everyone else. "They don't know any better," the habitually polite Sutter told his sister-in-law.[31] Still, this was a small thing for Anna to endure in return for the luxury of easy communication with most of the people with whom she dealt. She kept to the house most of the time, but she had a keen interest in botany and birds. Consequently, she accompanied school field trips under the direction of a beloved local schoolteacher.[32]

The California pension added materially to the comfort of Sutter's home life. The first pension bill provided $250 per month for five years. In 1870 the legislature extended the payments for two years.[33] When the legislature again considered extending the pension in late 1871, Sutter wrote, begging for relief. "I will have to live only a few years longer, as I am subject to inflammatory rheumatism and have to suffer very severely every year." "Everybody who knows my history knows that I have no other resources to depend on," he added. He was confined to his bed for months at a time, he explained, and then could move about only with the aid of crutches. Swindlers had taken his land from him, and "the Supreme Court, under the administration of poor [President] Buchanan," rejected the sobrante claim "in the most unjust manner. It was the influence of money which defeated me." Again he insisted that he had paid $30,000 in taxes to the state and that this money should be returned to him. Sutter had been laboring for six years to convince Congress that he had been wronged. If he failed during the next session, he would give up his claim. "About the gold discovery, it is not worth while to say more about it than that it occurred through the instrumentality of my having ordered and furnished the means to build a saw mill. Marshall is very jealous about having the credit that he found the first gold in the mill-race," Sutter gratuitously added.[34]

Not all of the California legislators supported Sutter's claim on the state treasury. Some remembered his financial fecklessness and alcoholism all too well. Senator Patrick Munday claimed that there was scarcely an old pioneer from the 1840s who could not claim to have assisted the immigrants. The state had already paid the old man $20,000, "$250 a month to debauch on," Munday proclaimed, but even this sum would not be enough to pay Sutter's liquor bills in Washington. "Go to Missouri," Munday contended, and you would find "just such stories against Sutter as he is now telling against others of robbing and swindling him." Senator Campbell P. Berry lectured on Sutter's "debauchery and consequent imbecility," which allowed "the same piece of land to be sold over and over again by designing persons into whose hands he fell." Berry claimed that he knew of families living in poverty "whose fortunes were blasted by these transactions." As far as he was concerned, Sutter was a swindler as well as a victim. Others chimed in, adding that Sutter should have put out his money at interest rather than spending $1,000 a night for liquor and cigars for his friends. Why, another asked, should Sutter be rewarded? Why not provide a pension for Marshall? Indeed, why should anyone get the "people's money" except for eminent services to the state?[35]

Finally Sutter's defenders came to the rescue. Criticism of him was unseemly at this late date, when the old gentleman might be on his deathbed for all they knew. His generosity was well known. He had helped the immigrants in their hour of need, and no hungry person was ever turned away from his door. How could the legislature spurn Sutter now? For the last time the legislators voted to extend his pension for two more years.[36] The state's payments to Sutter totaled $27,000, which he claimed the state owned him for taxes paid on the sobrante land. Sutter proudly said that the money "was not a gift of the state to me, nor would I receive it as such."[37]

Nevertheless, Victor applied to the legislature for additional relief for his father. The Senate approved it, "but before it passed the assembly I declined it," Sutter claimed.[38] The legislature did provide an appropriation for an old pioneer in 1874, however, in "An Act to Appropriate Money for the Relief of James W. Marshall."[39] Perhaps the legislature's generosity could be stretched only far enough to provide for one esteemed pioneer at a time.

Sutter's pension and other small sources of income gave the Sutters a life of relative ease in Lititz, although no amount of money could alleviate the suffering that he endured from the rheumatic ailments that periodically bedeviled him. The commodious home, servant, and grandchildren must have lent him some comfort when his joints stiffened and made it impossible for him to go out. Some of the Sutter's grandparenting responsibilities eased as the children left the nest. Juan was the first to leave the home on Main Street, but he did not go to West Point as Sutter had hoped. Instead, he got a job as clerk at a Baltimore hotel. He was successful, Sutter said, especially in organizing balls that the young women greatly appreciated. The job did not pay much, so Juan returned to his grandparents' fireside in the summer of 1871. Then he went to New York to take a position with the firm of Ellis and Curtis, wine merchants, probably with the recommendation of his grandfather. "Both [Ellis and Curtis] are my friends," Sutter wrote. He had nominated them for California state militia commissions, Ellis was "battalion commander, the last captain of artillery," and both had returned from the Civil War as brigadier generals.[40] The generals treated Juan like a "young gentleman," and he was "very satisfied with his position."[41] Sutter may not have been able to get him into West Point, but his assiduous cultivation of influence in the state militia finally paid off, yea even to the third generation.

Sutter assured August that his son was doing very well in New York, but Juan's satisfaction with his new position was short-lived. In 1872 he complained to his father that his pay was inadequate and wondered about going to Acapulco to be with his father, his aunt, and his youngest sister, who had gone there in 1871 (perhaps earlier). August encouraged Juan to "acquire through good behaviour the love & esteem of your employers and other friends." It would be a mistake for him to go to Mexico. "People here lose all energy and become very slow and indolent; in every respect."[42] Juan began to beg his father for funds to invest in business ventures, including a questionable life-insurance scheme that August regarded as a mere scam. Juan wanted to make money and wanted to make it fast. With partners he went into the liquor business and asked his father to invest several thousand dollars in the firm. August wanted first to see the contract that Juan and his partners signed. "Be cautious and do not trust everybody who makes fair promises," August advised from hard-won experience.[43]

Evidently there was a shady side to Juan's liquor business. "What I do not comprehend," August innocently asked, "is how you are authorized to use for your sparkling wines, names & labels which do not belong to you by right. Can you not be prosecuted for using them? You had better find out."[44] Juan's answers must have satisfied August, because he took some of the bogus labeled wines on approval. But when he gave some of the stuff to local wine connoisseurs, the results were not good. "They were at once pronounced to be 'Sparkling California'—they will not pass as Champagne."[45] He advised his son to send no more counterfeit wine to Acapulco.

María del Carmen stayed with her father for several years. He complained about the expense of keeping the sixteen-year-old in Acapulco, including the cost of a new piano so that she could keep up her lessons. August worried that there was no good society for her in the Mexican port, but Mary (as he called her) was an adventurous spirit who loved horseback riding in the country.[46] She liked Acapulco, but in 1874 August wanted to send her back to Lititz to be with her grandparents. If she stayed in Acapulco much longer, she would "not know at all how to move amongst people."[47] Eventually Mary went to live in New York with Juan, but this was not satisfactory. Even though August sent his son $40 per month to provide for Mary, Juan paid little attention to her. "She not only needs feeding and *cooping up* in a *small den* or a *cage,*" August chided, "but must have at least some society and some suitable reading material."[48]

Mary soon improved her social situation by marrying and moving to Woonsocket, Rhode Island.[49] Juan married at about the same time (1877 or 1878), and so did Eliza, who ran off with Howard Hull, a Lititz boy who lived a few doors up the street. For the first time in their married life the Sutters lived together without children or grandchildren in the house, but not for long. Eliza's husband could not support her and the children who soon came along.

They moved into the Sutter house until they could get on their feet, much to the irritation of Anna, who thought her great-grandchildren were spoiled and noisy. This was a serious burden on the Sutters, because the California pension payments had ended in 1875. Sutter finally asked them to move.[50]

While the youngest generation of Sutters sorted their marital arrangements, another Californian came east to marry. Hubert Howe Bancroft, bookseller, bibliophile, and historian, was in the midst of compiling his huge library and archival collections for a history of California and the West. While collecting documents and interviewing California pioneers, Bancroft met and eventually married a young woman in New Haven. The happy couple made their honeymoon a working vacation by arranging interviews with easterners who had been prominent in California history. In New York Bancroft took dictations from John C. Frémont and his wife, Jessie. Then it was off to Washington, where he met Supreme Court Justice Stephen J. Field and other Californians, as well as explorer-scientist John Wesley Powell and fellow-historian George Bancroft.[51]

Bancroft wanted to interview Sutter but had made no advance preparations to meet him. He did not even know where Sutter lived. After making inquiries, the historian and his new wife rode the train to Lititz and took a room in the hotel across the street from Sutter's house. Local residents told Bancroft that the old man was ill and unable to receive visitors. The barber who shaved Sutter every day might be able to gain an audience for Bancroft, but the assiduous researcher declined the intercession of that august personage. The next day he went to the Sutters' door unannounced.

Bancroft's manner of presenting himself was not a model of grace, courtesy, or good oral historical practice. He knocked loudly. No answer. He tried again. Nothing. Again. Then "the door was slowly, silently opened a little way, and the head of an old woman appeared at the aperture." "Is this Mrs. Sutter?" Bancroft asked. The woman, who was indeed Mrs. Sutter, said nothing. She was almost totally deaf, and Bancroft knew it. "May I speak with you a moment in the hall?" Anna did not move or acknowledge Bancroft's query. "I must gain admission," the historian thought; "retreat now might be fatal." He moved forward and firmly pushed his way into the house.[52]

Once inside, Bancroft more fully appraised Anna. She was "a tall, thin, intelligent Swiss, plainly dressed," with a "shawl thrown over her shoulders." He presented his card and insisted on seeing Sutter, even though he understood that the old man was ill, perhaps dying. Anna disappeared, and Bancroft waited, fearing that he had come too late "and that all of history that house contained was in the fevered brain of a dying man."[53]

But soon, to Bancroft's "great astonishment and delight, the door opened, and the general himself entered at a brisk pace." Sutter appeared well and younger than Bancroft had supposed. Even in advanced age, Sutter could still impress. "His step was still firm, his bearing soldierly, and in his younger days he must have been a man of much endurance, with a remarkably fine physique." Bancroft described the Sutter who was so familiar to old Californians: "broad full face, fairly intellectual forehead, with white hair, bald on the top of the head, white side whiskers, mustache, and imperial; a deep, clear, earnest eye met yours truthfully." It was easy for the historian to imagine the Sutter of old. "He received me courteously, and listened with deep attention to my plan for a history of the Pacific States as I laid it before him, perceiving at once the difference between my work and that of local historians and newspaper reporters, by whom all the latter part of his life he had been besieged."[54]

Sutter briefly recounted the catalog of grievances that explained how swindlers had laid him low. "The past is past," Bancroft grandly said, and then he boldly rang up the sale. "One thing yet remains for you to do, which is to see your wonderful experiences properly placed on record for the benefit of posterity. You fill an important niche in the history of the western coast. Of certain events you are the embodiment—the living, walking history of a certain time and locality. Often in my labors I have encountered your name, your deeds; and let me say that I have never yet heard the former mentioned but in kindness, nor the latter except in praise." On hearing these generous words, Sutter wept and "signified his willingness to relate to me all he knew." Sutter had just risen from his sick bed, and it was likely that he would be down again in a few days, but he would devote all of his failing energy to Bancroft's project. For five ten-hour days Sutter talked as Bancroft took forty pages of dictation a day. The scribe's new bride sat "sometimes sewing, always lending an attentive ear, with occasional questions addressed to the general."[55]

The story was well rehearsed and came easily to Sutter's lips and to Bancroft's pen. When it was done, Bancroft bound Sutter's "Reminiscences" and placed it on the shelf with other dictations that he and his staff of researchers had taken from California pioneers. Sutter's story and those of Alvarado, Vallejo, Bidwell, and many others were the foundation stones for Bancroft's monumental *History of California,* published in the 1880s. Needless to say, Sutter's story was a major part of 1840s and the gold rush. Historians have ever since relied on these sources for the history of early California. Bancroft needed Sutter's testimony, but Sutter likely hoped that Bancroft's work would help him to secure the relief from Congress that he sought. Little did he know the deliberate pace at which historians work. Sutter was also alive to Bancroft's plea to place his story at the disposal of posterity. Sutter believed that he was a great man who had accomplished great things. He wanted full credit. A historian like Bancroft could provide him with the rich, heroic legacy that Sutter believed he had earned.

Had Sutter lived to read Bancroft's account, he would have been disappointed. Bancroft was sharply critical. With multiple sources at his disposal, the historian noticed that Sutter's version of events was not always reliable or truthful. Bancroft's summary judgment of Sutter was devastating. No other pioneer had "received so much praise from so many sources," Bancroft wrote; "few have deserved so little." Sutter was a mere adventurer "entitled to no admiration or sympathy." His recklessness and lack of business capacity were the causes of the loss of his property. Insofar as Sutter had helped Americans, he did so out of self-interest. Bancroft recognized Sutter's "wonderful personal magnetism and power of making friends," but "of principle, honor, of respect for the rights of others, we find but slight trace in him."[56] There was much truth in Bancroft's harsh appraisal. One gets the feeling that when he returned to his San Francisco library he discovered that Sutter had lied to him. As had happened so often before, Sutter made a glorious first impression; but when Bancroft learned that he had been misled, the historian turned on his genial Lititz host. When his book went to press, Bancroft made certain that he got even. *The History of California* would not be the golden repository for the legend that Sutter had contrived.

Sutter was always attentive to his reputation. Any slight was likely to bring forth a rebuke from him or from his son Victor, who burnished the family escutcheon in California. When General Sherman published his memoirs in 1875, he included a sketch of California in the late 1840s, when he was the aide of Colonel Mason. He described the Fourth of July celebration at Sutter's Fort in 1848 and said that Sutter was "tight." Sutter's drinking and alcoholism were notorious, but he bristled when he saw Sherman's reminiscence of himself in print. When Sutter challenged Sherman's version of events, Sherman wrote a gracious and effusive apology. He also instructed his publishers to change the word "tight" to "enthusiastic" in future editions. In those days Sherman and his fellow officers "looked up to you as veterans and models," he told the old man. He did not use the word "tight" in its common offensive sense, "but rather as General Jackson said to an officer, 'that one who has fought as he had done might get tight when he pleased.' "[57] Nevertheless, Sherman gladly changed the word in his book in order to avoid causing pain to Sutter. The apology was printed in California papers, but that was not enough to satisfy Victor, who fumed that "Sherman is a d[amned] g[oa]t."[58]

Sutter was still complaining about Sherman when Bancroft visited him. "I was no more tight than he was. Men cannot drink liquor without feeling it and it is not for an army officer to partake of hospitality such as I freely gave, drink as they usually drink, and then in a flippant remark accuse their host of drunk-enness." He called Sherman's apology "some lame excuses."[59] Sutter's sen-sitivity about his alcoholism may have caused him to discount the role of liquor at Sutter's Fort in his statement to Bancroft. He claimed that he gave his men "nothing but water to drink the first six or seven years."[60] Then, perhaps remembering that the existence of his still was well known, he added that he did not have a distillery until just before Frémont arrived.

Perhaps Sutter worried too much about his reputation for hard drinking. Among the California pioneers his reputation for generosity and hospitality far outweighed memories of his tippling habits. His Swiss compatriots remem-bered him fondly too. During the 1876 Philadelphia Centennial Exposition, Sutter represented the Swiss nation. He was the embodiment of Swiss energy, the Swiss consul said, and famous the world over.[61] In 1877 Sutter felt well enough to attend a meeting of the Associated Pioneers of the Territorial Days of California in Long Branch, New Jersey. The Pioneers elected him president and brought him to the podium amid rousing cheers. Choked with emotion, Sutter could not address the assembly.[62] He loved nothing so much as to be loved by all, and in this company he was.

Sutter hoped that support from groups such as the Associated Pioneers would help to get his relief bill through Congress. In 1876 his friends in the California congressional delegation put forward a new bill on Sutter's behalf. This one summarized his old complaints about losing the sobrante grant and provided $50,000 to satisfy all of his claims against the U.S. government.[63] The committee on private land claims approved the bill and submitted it to the House for consideration. There it languished. Sutter was sufficiently optimistic that he went to Washington to lend his personal powers of persuasion to the cause.

Sutter was there in March 1878 when the Associated Pioneers met in New York. The members presented him with a cane made of California gold and rosewood in honor of his seventy-fifth birthday. Their tribute recognized that Sutter's life had "the divine precept of 'charity.' " Sutter's response was gracious and humble, if a little morbid. He thanked his fellow Pioneers for their recog-nition of his services. "We are hastening onward to our final resting place," he added, "but the romance of our history as California Pioneers . . . will tend for ages to come to stimulate the energy of our posterity."[64]

Sutter loved to attend the meetings of the Associated Pioneers at the Sturte-vant House in New York City. Health would not always permit him to go. In 1879 illness and a depressed mood overtook Sutter, who telegraphed his re-grets to the Associated Pioneers:

Sick in heart and body, in vain appealing to Congress to do me justice and to return to me only a part of what was taken from me, and with little hope of success this session, unless you my friends by your influence will aid my cause, I could not feel cheerful as your guest at the table tonight, and I did not want to mar your pleasure by my presence. Remember old times without me.[65]

In January 1880 Sutter was strong enough to attend the Associated Pioneers meeting in New York. He fully enjoyed the public acclaim that the organization lavished on him, but family matters occupied him too. To Sutter's great delight his grandson Juan and family arrived, including a toddler, John A. Sutter IV, Sutter's great-grandson.[66] A lavish banquet added to the festivities.

The 1880 meeting was Sutter's last hurrah in front of the Californians who loved him. Ailing and increasingly frail, he carried on his fight in Congress whenever he could. Fifty thousand dollars would certainly ease the financial pinch that the loss of his state pension had caused. He was never in danger of being thrown into the street—his children and friends would never have allowed that to happen—but the nice house on Main Street in Lititz sheltered an elderly couple with no money to spare.

Some money came to Sutter from an unexpected source. Smith Rudd, a Michigan collector of pioneer autographs and documents, sent him a few dollars in exchange for a holograph letter from the old pioneer. Sutter obliged but accepted the small sum as a loan, which he would repay "so soon as I succeed to get my very just & discret [sic] claim against the Government allowed and settled in Congress in the next session."[67] For fourteen winters he had been coming to Washington seeking relief, Sutter explained to Rudd. Even though the California delegation and many other congressmen supported him there was always some obstacle that prevented final passage. But this time, Sutter felt certain, he would prevail.

Rudd declined Sutter's offer of repayment and periodically enclosed five-dollar bills in his letters to the old man, insisting that they be accepted as gifts. Sutter effusively thanked Rudd and told him how things were going in Congress. In acknowledging Rudd's 1879 Christmas gift, he explained that he would be leaving for Washington in mid-January: "that is when I am well enough. I shall make my stay in Washington so short as possible."[68]

The Associated Pioneers had responded to Sutter's plea to get behind the relief bill, and his friends in Congress renewed their effort to push it through in 1880. Once again Sutter made the pilgrimage to Washington, but only for brief stays. During one of these trips he fell ill with a kidney ailment that so alarmed Colonel Frank A. Schaeffer, a longtime friend from the California militia, that he stayed in Sutter's room and nursed him for four nights. "I am now so far restored that I can be dragged to the Capitol at the arm of a friend, in order to exert my entire personal influence to get my claim acknowledged," Sutter told Cincinnati's *Deutsche Pioneer*.[69]

Progress on Sutter's bill in Congress was hopeful. This time the Senate passed the bill and the House demurred. Still, he believed that the bill would finally pass. Once again Congress disappointed Sutter. Senator Daniel W. Vorhees of Indiana became interested in his case and tried to attach the relief measure to an appropriations bill, but his tactic failed. Time was running out, because it was an election year; there was pressure for Congress to conclude its business so that the members could attend their party conventions. On June 16 Congress adjourned without having acted on Sutter's bill.

Sutter's kidney ailment kept him in his room in the Mades Hotel during the last few days of the congressional session. Word of Congress's inaction devastated the sickly old man. He began writing a melancholy letter to Anna but collapsed before he could finish it. The faithful Colonel Schaeffer cared for him in his final hours. He was sitting by the bed when Sutter forcefully grabbed his hand. In a few moments he was gone.[70] It was June 18, 1880, the thirty-ninth anniversary of his New Helvetia grant from Governor Alvarado.

Sutter's death made news throughout the United States. Whatever his flaws, he was the symbol of a bygone frontier era. Those who remembered him marked his passing with reverence. His Washington friends came to the Mades Hotel as soon as they heard of his death. Bidwell was in California; but his wife, Annie, was visiting her mother and went there the next morning. Sutter lay in a parlor with a sheet over him, waiting for a coffin. The loyal Colonel Schaeffer kept to his post and attended to the details of mortuary arrangements. When a barber came to shave Sutter's face for the last time, Mrs. Bidwell departed to permit this final grooming to occur in privacy. She arranged for a handsome floral offering in the form of an anchor and returned in the afternoon. She had tried to round up Pierson Reading's wife (another Washington society lady who was visiting her mother) and children to go to the Mades, but to no avail.

At three a delegation of Californians held a memorial service over Sutter's coffined body. They had obtained California wild flowers from a U.S. government greenhouse. The men laid the "flowers about the face and hands, as tenderly as a woman could have done," Annie told her husband.[71] She was deeply moved by the simple service of these pioneers. "There was no king, general or statesman before whose remains my very soul would have so bowed in reverence," as before those of Sutter, "whom, under God, I felt you and I owed our destiny." When the ceremony was done, she followed the cortege that carried Sutter to the depot, whence the train took his body to Lititz and his grieving widow. "All say that he died of a broken heart. That is the pitiful side, and causes hearts to weep as well as eyes," Annie concluded.[72]

The eulogies for Sutter had only begun. His body lay in state in his Lititz home from Sunday to Thursday. An open rosewood casket displayed Sutter in civilian clothes, wearing his medals. He especially treasured the medal from the Associated Pioneers, who had made him their president. Hundreds of people visited Sutter's bier, including prominent Californians, old forty-niners, and people who just wanted to have a look at the famous pioneer. The California contingent raised a Bear Flag to half staff on the town square. At two in the afternoon, six of Sutter's Lititz friends hoisted his casket and solemnly marched down the street to the Moravian church's small stone mortuary. California pioneers followed the casket. John C. Frémont was the most prominent among them. Then came two hundred townspeople. Sutter would have preferred trumpets; but it was the custom in Lititz for a trombone ensemble to play funeral music, and so it was with Sutter. During a brief service in the church Sutter's remains lay in a stone mortuary nearby. Afterward he was carried to the graveyard behind the church.

General Horatio Gates Gibson and Frémont delivered the graveside eulogies, which were clotted with the legend that Sutter had assiduously constructed. He was the great pioneer who had carved an empire out of the wilderness, the generous benefactor of those who followed him. His nation had forgotten him and left him destitute. Now it was left for his fellow pioneers to remember him with gratitude. Gates concluded with some verse:

> Old Pioneer! Thy name we still
> In all our hearts enshrine,
> God's golden crown thy portion be,
> Dear friend of auld lang syne.[73]

Frémont recalled coming down from the mountains with his starving men thirty-six years before. "He received us with an open-hearted hospitality which made us his life-long, grateful friends." This was no time to disturb the reveries of mourners with uncomfortable facts about Frémont's differences with Sutter in olden times, but an opportunity to remind everyone of how the nation had neglected one of its outstanding pioneers. Congress, Frémont concluded, "abruptly terminated General Sutter's life" when it failed to approve the relief that he so richly deserved.[74] As far as Frémont was concerned, a callous nation had killed a heroic figure. To emphasize the pain that Congress had inflicted on Sutter, Frémont misquoted a line from Shakespeare to finish his eulogy:

> He is no friend
> Who on the rock of this rough world
> Would stretch him longer.[75]

Then the crowd dispersed, with the Californians heading for the depot to catch their train. They left behind a large display with an inscription in violets: "California Pioneers. We Loved Him."[76]

Settlement of Old Debts

Anna Sutter wept in the house on Main Street. She read her husband's letters over and over, but nothing could assuage her grief.[1] Son Victor and granddaughter Eliza were there to help but seemed unsympathetic to her desolation. Mrs. Bidwell told her that she was welcome to live with the Bidwells in California, but she wanted to stay in her house as long as she lived, "where she felt her husband was with her."[2] She wished only to die so that she could join "Papa."[3] Try as she might, Annie Bidwell could not learn the true state of Anna's finances. Victor and Eliza assured her that money from the children was her only income. As far as Annie was concerned, the odd-acting Victor was deranged and Eliza was unreliable. "No sum of money [for Anna] must be so placed as to come under the control of her family."[4] She was afraid that Victor as the estate administrator would "sell the home to get cash to carry out his silly ideas."[5]

Victor stayed with his mother, but he did not have much work to do on his father's estate. Sutter was finally in the black when he died. He had $219 in a Washington bank, three $500 U.S. savings bonds, and miscellaneous coupons and drafts worth $75.[6] All went to Anna. Annie Bidwell need not have worried about Victor selling the house. Anna owned it and would not permit a sale. Her death on January 19, 1881, put an end to her grief.[7]

At the time of her death, Anna possessed the residue of Sutter's estate, the house and contents valued altogether at $6,870. The Sutter's last real estate deal had not done well. The appraiser valued the house that Sutter said cost $10,000 at just half that amount.[8] She left her silver, jewelry, and clothes to her daughter Eliza. Sutter's desk and books went to Alphonse's son, a touching final remembrance of her deceased youngest child. Granddaughter Eliza got all the other furniture. Everything else was divided among August, Victor, and Eliza, share and share alike. They sold the house, which the new owners eventually converted into a hardware store.[9] The survivors' shares did not amount to much, perhaps $2,000 each.

Before his father died, Victor had invested in copper and iron mines. "So far it only cost money," Sutter wrote, but soon Victor hoped to earn $1,000 per month. "That would be beautiful," his father said.[10] Victor acted strangely after his mother's death. He secretively went to Washington one week later to pursue his father's old claim, advising his niece not to reveal "anything as to my whereabouts or moves."[11] Six months later Victor traveled to Ostend, Belgium, where he intended to dispose of his mining interests. On July 3 he checked into the Hotel Bellevue, where the clerks thought he was out of his mind. They found him dead the next morning with a half-empty bottle of laudanum on the night stand and nine francs in his pocket. He was buried at public expense.[12]

August prospered in Acapulco, at least for a while. He started a second family with his young wife and continued as U.S. consul until he retired to his plantation on the Sabana River in 1887. Then things went bad. He had taken an unreliable business partner who stole so much that August feared he might be ruined. He contemplated suicide, but thoughts of his young family kept him from it. For a while he hoped for relief from the Mexican and U.S. governments, which never came. His wife finally sold her jewels to restore the family's solvency. He died in 1897 at the age of seventy-two.[13]

Little is known about Eliza's later life. She was still residing in Acapulco with her husband Victor Link in the 1870s and probably stayed there. August's correspondence suggests that he did not get along with Dr. Link.[14] Eliza's son was living in Acapulco when his cousin, the newly widowed Anna Eliza Sutter Hull, arrived in 1885. Eventually they married.[15]

Sutter's Fort deteriorated until nothing remained but the large central building, which was ignominiously used as a stable, chicken house, and pigsty. The adobe structure sat awkwardly athwart Sacramento's uncompleted street grid. In 1888 the city planned to demolish the building in order to finish the roads. The plan aroused the patriotic sentiments of the Native Sons of the Golden West, who purchased the site and turned it over to the state. Reconstruction of the fort began in 1891. Today Sutter's Fort State Historic Park sits in the middle of Sacramento as a reminder of its builder.[16] Over the years Californians occasionally have proposed the reinterment of the Sutters at the park, but the objections of family members have prevented it. For the foreseeable future, Sutter's grave will remain where he evidently intended it to be, in Lititz.

In 1980 new owners restored the exterior of the Sutters' Lititz home and converted the interior to office space. The building was listed in the National Register of Historic Places, but the offices were vacant in 2003. The name of the old Lititz Springs Hotel across the street was changed to the General Sutter Inn. The town has now become a tourist destination, with Sutter's home and grave among the attractions of the standard walking tour. Sutter is still fondly remembered as the most famous person ever to live in Lititz.[17]

The Associated Pioneers' expressions of love for Sutter were widely felt among Californians, but they were by no means universally shared. Those who suffered financial losses because of the Sutters' real-estate and financial shenanigans can hardly be expected to remember him fondly. Indians did not mourn his passing. Mexican reminiscences are universally critical of Sutter. John Laufkotter, Sutter's jaded friend from Missouri, made something of a hobby out of debunking the Sutter legend. He moved to Sacramento during the gold rush and subscribed to the squatters' point of view that Sutter's grant was bogus. In 1867 Laufkotter published *John A. Sutter and His Grants,* an account that accused Sutter of many misdeeds in Missouri, New Mexico, and California.[18] In the 1880s Laufkotter published no fewer than seven articles and letters devoted to the destruction of Sutter's image in Sacramento newspapers.[19] He exposed many of Sutter's lies about military experience in Europe and his background in Missouri and Santa Fe, but his hatred for the man led him to question almost everything that Sutter said. "Sutter has humbugged the greatest statesmen and Generals, down to the common person, which never has been done before by any foreigner."[20]

The voices of Sutter's numerous friends drowned out those of detractors like Laufkotter. Soon after Sutter's death the Associated Pioneers published *A Nation's Benefactor,* a collection of tributes and an appeal to Congress to act on his request for relief.[21] Memorialists compared Sutter to Christ, Napoleon Bonaparte, and the heroic characters of William Shakespeare and Sir Walter Scott. He had selflessly fed the hungry, clothed the naked, built an empire, discovered gold, and lost everything because of unscrupulous men and the callous disregard of the federal government. His greatest benefaction was that he helped *them* in their hour of need. To their credit they never forgot it. Sutter did not fight with the French Army at Grenoble as he once claimed, but in his old age he led a group of old men who swore undying fealty to him. Whatever Sutter's sins, they forgave him. Fifty thousand dollars was small recompense for the man who had discovered gold and revolutionized the world economy, they said. The money should now go his widow and children, the pioneers argued, but Congress did not act favorably on the Sutter relief bill.

In the throes of grief over the loss of their great chieftain, the Associated Pioneers may be forgiven for their exaggerated claims, but they were by no means the only ones to sanctify Sutter's memory. No one in California was more respected than John Bidwell; nor was anyone more intimately acquainted with Sutter, warts and all. Bidwell wrote: "No pioneer ever did so much for this State as Sutter. More, I verily believe no pioneer ever did so much for the United States, and that few men in modern times have done so much for the world at large, as General Sutter." No one had risked more than Sutter. "Dangers on every side. Obstacles almost innumerable confronted him. But ever trying, persevering, struggling, never discouraged, the fruit of all his labors emerged in the discovery of gold at his saw mill . . . which made our country rich, benefitted all countries, and ushered in an era of prosperity such as the world has never seen."[22]

Bidwell believed that the building of the mill at Coloma was the culmination of the essentially American spirit of industry and determination that motivated Sutter. "Would any man but Sutter have the nerve to build a mill in such a place and at such a time and with such a prospect?" Bidwell asked.[23] Marshall found the first flakes of gold, but "Sutter was the discoverer." The great find led to other mineral discoveries in Australia, in Nevada, and throughout North America. California gold helped the United States to emerge "Phoenix-like, from the fires of the great rebellion—It was the beginning of an era of progress and prosperity that have been felt in every land—an era that promises to extend, with its countless blessings, into the indefinite future." Sutter was "the direct agent of the great discovery that has so signally blessed the world."[24]

One might think that Laufkotter and Bidwell described two different men, but they were one and the same. Sutter's contradictions defined him. He was a feckless dreamer, ambitious visionary, drunken fool, genial host, liar, ministering angel, and devoted husband who abandoned his family. Sutter was a con man who became the victim of California swindlers. Kind to immigrants, he enslaved Native peoples when it suited his purpose and ruthlessly killed any who objected. Sutter was greatly admired in his time because his admirers believed that the conquest of Indian country and the addition of foreign lands to the United States were admirable. Insofar as people thought Sutter deserved credit as an Indian "tamer," it was because he had converted what they regarded as a threat into an asset of conquest. With nothing but a glib story and a shaky line of credit Sutter grabbed all of California that he could and built his short-lived empire. He was an exemplar of the filibustering spirit of his age, the embodiment of Lieutenant Revere's little verse:

—the good old rule,
—the simple plan—
That they should take who have the power,
And they should keep who can.[25]

Sutter's aims and his ways and means are not widely admired today, yet his importance cannot be denied. His settlement in the valley complicated Mexican California's political landscape and made him a primary concern of californio officials. In 1839 Sutter came with nothing. In a few years nothing could be done without taking him into account. He created a settlement where foreigners with no loyalty to Mexico gathered in his fort's long shadow. Sutter's Fort outflanked the californios and made Mexican California indefensible. Without it there would have been no American insurgency in 1846, and Frémont's role would have been very different. Naval forces would no doubt have succeeded in taking California, but it would have been a much more difficult conquest.

As Bidwell said, Sutter deserves credit as the agent of the gold discovery, although it is difficult to imagine gold remaining undiscovered for much longer. He repeatedly blamed the gold rush for ruining him, but it did not. Sutter ruined Sutter. If anything, gold made it possible for him to avoid bankruptcy in 1849. True, sharpers gouged him on every side, but he helped them do it with his needy ego, drunkenness, and inattention to details. Squatters bedeviled him, but he still could have developed Hock Farm into a profit-making enterprise, instead of using tens of thousands of borrowed dollars to create a demonstration showplace. He squandered every grand opportunity and blamed others for his fall.

Sutter was a man of large ability whose flaws prevented him from gaining great wealth, but he did manage to achieve something that he thought was just as important—fame. He did not exaggerate when he said that his name was known around the globe. Who would have predicted that in Burgdorf in 1834? He invented a European military reputation, but by 1849 he did not need it to impress anyone with his credentials as one of the great lords of the North American frontier. Public enthusiasm for Sutter's violent conquest of the Indians and his part in acquiring Mexican California for the United States was genuine and unalloyed. In this field of endeavor he was regarded as a resounding success—the chief reason for the military honors that the state of California heaped upon him.

Time has passed, and attitudes have changed. Many now condemn Sutter's acts and denounce attempts to extend additional public recognition to him.[26]

In the twenty-first century it is important to understand that the national triumphs of the nineteenth century caused dreadful human suffering, that benefits to some meant costs to others. Sutter and California are not unique in this regard; they are prime examples of the troubling and ambiguous history of western North America. Nowadays condemnation of Sutter and his contemporaries for their grievous faults is a logical result of incorporating the stories of Native Americans, Latinos, and all others in American history, as we must do. Yet a troubling issue remains. Most Americans enjoy the benefits brought by frontier conquests even as they condemn them. This is not Sutter's contradiction but our own. Until it is resolved, we will live uneasily with the past and with the memory of John A. Sutter.

Abbreviations

AGLR	Adjutant General, Letters Received, May 2, 1852, to April 30, 1864, CSA.
AMRC	Alice M. Reading Collection, BL.
AW	*Arizona and the West.*
BL	Bancroft Library.
C-A, vol.:doc.	Archives of California, BL.
CDFP	Clarence DuFour Papers, BL.
CFJUS	*California Farmer and Journal of Useful Science.*
CHSQ	*California Historical Society Quarterly,* now published as *California History.*
CLC	*California Land Claims,* vol. 25, *John A. Sutter* (1863) bound volume, CSL-LL.
CMWP	Charles Maria Weber Papers, BL.
CSA	California State Archives, Sacramento.
CSL-CR	California Room, California State Library, Sacramento.
CSL-LL	Law Library, California State Library, Sacramento.
CvS	*Tyler Curtis, administrator,* v. *John A. Sutter, William Muldrow, et al.,* 1859–61. County Records, Sonoma County, District Court (Old Series), nos. 914–17, CSA.
D-J	Decker-Jewett Papers, CSL-CR.
FOEP	Foreign Office and Executive Papers, Series 402, HSA.
FSP	Fort Sacramento Papers, HL.
GAMP	George A. McKinstry Papers, BL.
GMC	George McKinstry Collection, CSL-CR.
HDFP	Henry Delano Fitch Papers, BL.
HL	Henry E. Huntington Library, San Marino, California.
HM	Huntington Manuscripts, HL.
HSA	Hawaii State Archives, Honolulu.
JASC	John A. Sutter Collection, CSL-CR.
JASC JR	John A. Sutter, Jr., Collection, CSL-CR.
JASP	John A. Sutter Papers, BL.
JBP	John Bidwell Papers, CSL-CR.
JCCH-D	Jackson County Deeds, Clerk, Court House, Independence, Missouri.

JCRC   Jackson County Records Center, Independence, Missouri.
JLLWP   J. L. L. Warren Papers, Box 4, BL.
JMC   John Marsh Collection, CSL-CR.
LCHS   Lancaster County Historical Society, Lancaster, Pennsylvania.
LCHS-IF   Information File, LCHS.
LHS   Lititz Historical Society, Lititz, Pennsylvania.
M182   Letters Sent by the Governors and Secretary of State of California, 1847–1848.
                National Archives, Records of the United States Army Continental Commands,
                1821–1920. RG 393, Microfilm Publication M182.
M210   Records of the Tenth Military Department, 1846–1851. National Archives
                Microfilm Publication M210.
M234:reel no.   Office of Indian Affairs, Letters Received, 1849–1880, California
                Superintendency. RG 75, National Archives Microfilm M234.
MHS   Missouri Historical Society, St. Louis, Missouri.
MVSP   Mott/von Schmidt Family Papers, BL.
PHR   *Pacific Historical Review.*
PM   Pioneer Manuscripts, CSL-CR.
PRC   Pierson Reading Collection, CSL-CR.
RM   Smith Rudd Manuscripts, Lilly Library, Indiana University, Bloomington.
SacCo-D   Deeds, Sacramento County, Office of the Recorder, Sacramento.
SAMC   Sacramento Archives and Museum Collection Center, Sacramento.
SAMC-J   Judgements, Sacramento County, Sacramento Archives and Museum Collection
                Center, Sacramento.
SAMC-M   Mortgages, Sacramento County, Sacramento Archives and Museum Collection
                Center, Sacramento.
SAMC-POA   Powers of Attorney, Sacramento County, Sacramento Archives and Museum
                Collection Center, Sacramento.
SCQ   *Southern California Quarterly.*
SGM   Sutter Grant Maps, CSL-CR.
S/LP   Sutter/Link Family Papers, BL.
StCCHS   St. Charles County Historical Society, St. Charles, Missouri.
SuC-D   Deeds, Sutter County, Office of the County Clerk, Yuba City, California.
SuC-M   Mortgages, Sutter County, Office of the County Clerk, Yuba City, California.
T135   Records of the U.S. General Accounting Office, Selected Records of the
                General Accounting Office Relating to the Frémont Expeditions and the
                California Battalion, 1842–1890. National Archives, RG 217, Microfilm
                Publication T135.
VD, vol:no   *Vallejo documentos para la historia de California*, BL.
WF-DJ   William French, Daily Journal, March 24, 1838–January 24, 1839, HSA.
WF-L   William French, Ledger, April 6, 1838–April 12, 1840, HSA.
WFP   Weber Family Papers, BL.
WHDC-L   William Heath Davis Collection, Letterbook, BL.
WLP   William Leidesdorff Papers, HL.
WRPC   William Robert Prince Collection, BL.

Notes

CHAPTER 1

1. White, *"It's Your Misfortune and None of My Own,"* 5–59.
2. Calloway, *One Vast Winter Count,* 267–426 and passim.
3. Hurtado, *Indian Survival on the California Frontier,* 14–54.
4. Calloway, *One Vast Winter Count,* 267–426.
5. Wishart, *The Fur Trade and the American West, 1807–1840.*
6. Van Kirk, *Many Tender Ties;* Brown, *Strangers in Blood;* Anderson, *Kinsmen of Another Kind;* Thorne, *The Many Hands of My Relations.*
7. Ronda, *Lewis and Clark among the Indians,* 256–59; White, *The Middle Ground;* Hurtado, "When Strangers Met," 122–42; Brooks, *Captives and Cousins.*
8. Unless otherwise cited, this account of Sutter's early life is based on Zollinger, "John Augustus Sutter's European Background," 28–46; and Zollinger, *Sutter,* 3–16.
9. Sulloway, *Born to Rebel,* informs my suppositions about the development of Sutter's personality.
10. Anna's given name was Annette, but she was known as Anna in California. I have consistently called her Anna to avoid confusion.
11. Watt, *The Making of Modern Marriage,* 193.
12. Dillon, *Fool's Gold,* 24.
13. Ibid., 23.
14. Zollinger, *Sutter,* 13.

CHAPTER 2

1. Rosenwaike, *Population History of New York City,* 16, 33, 39–40.
2. Dodd, "Astor, John Jacob," 65–66; Ronda, *Astoria and Empire,* 1–2 and passim.
3. Rosenwaike, *Population History of New York City,* 43–44.
4. Sutter, "Reminiscences," 2, BL.
5. Duden, *Report on a Journey to the Western States of North America and a Stay of Several Years along the Missouri.*
6. Sutter, "Reminiscences," 2.

7. See Laufkotter, *John A. Sutter and His Grants,* reprinted in Owens, *John A. Sutter, Sr., and His Grants, by John A. Laufkotter.* All citations are from the original text. The first half of Laufkotter's booklet consists of his account of Sutter in Missouri and New Mexico. When checked against other sources Laufkotter appears to be reliable when he is narrating events for which he has personal knowledge. The second half of his booklet is based on surmise and hearsay and is unreliable. In time Laufkotter became disillusioned with Sutter, and in his old age the German carried his grudge against his former friend to the editorial pages of Sacramento newspapers. See, for example, J. A. Laufkotter, "The Sacramento Pioneer Comes Back as the Old Hunter and Trapper," *Sacramento Bee,* November 19, 1884, transcript, and J. A. Laufkotter, "Was Sutter Overestimated?" *Sacramento Bee,* March 28, 1885, transcript, both in Kretschmer, "The Historical Chronology of a Missouri Pioneer Family," MHS. Nevertheless, Laufkotter's account of the years 1834 through 1837 is one of a very few eyewitness sources on Sutter during that time.

8. "A List of Moneys Collected by the Collector of St. Charles County, 1835, Collector's Statement of Moneys," StCCHS.

9. Foley and Rice, *The First Chouteaus.*

10. "An Aggregate Statement of the Resident and Nonresident Tax Lists, August 25, 1834," Miscellaneous Records, 1830s, StCCHS.

11. Hyslop, *Bound for Santa Fe,* 255–74 and passim.

12. Laufkotter, *John A. Sutter and His Grants,* 6.

13. Ibid., 6.

14. Ibid., 7.

15. Ibid.

16. Ibid.

17. "A List of Moneys Collected, 1835," StCCHS.

18. Laufkotter, *John A. Sutter and His Grants,* 7.

19. Thorne, *The Many Hands of My Relations,* 160–76 and passim.

20. Zollinger, *Sutter,* 24.

21. Sutter, "Reminiscences," 2–3.

22. Ibid., 3.

23. Lawrence, "Horse Thieves on the Spanish Trail," 22–25, 55; Lawrence, "Mexican Trade between Santa Fé and Los Angeles, 1830–1848," 27–39.

24. Hurtado, *Indian Survival,* 32–47.

25. Lawrence, "Horse Thieves," 33–35; Lawrence, "Mexican Trade," 28–31; Weber, *Taos Trappers,* 109, 145–53; Bancroft, *History of California,* 3:172, 358–62, 395–96, 4:76–77, 113.

26. Lawrence, "Horse Thieves," 24.

27. Quoted in ibid., 22; Bancroft, *History,* 4:77, n. 72. I include the Delawares in the definition because they lived on the same reservation and often traveled together with the Shawnees.

28. Flores, *Horizontal Yellow,* 105–109, 115–19; Brooks, *Captives and Cousins,* 174–80, 242–44; Ruby and Brown, *Indian Slavery in the Pacific Northwest,* 26–27, 224, 226–67, 231–32, 253–54, 258, 263, 270, and passim; Hamalainen, "The Rise and Fall of Plains Indian Horse Cultures," 833–62.

29. "St. Charles County Tax Collector, Statement of Moneys, November 1835, State of Missouri, County of St. Charles," StCCHS.

30. Laufkotter, *John A. Sutter and His Grants,* 7.

31. Ibid.

32. Ibid., 8.

33. Hyslop, *Bound for Santa Fe,* 1–229 and passim.

34. Laufkotter, *John A. Sutter and His Grants,* 9.

35. Ibid., 10.

36. Ibid., 13.

37. This gentleman may have been Governor Manuel Armijo. The note was eventually sold for $500.

38. Laufkotter, *John A. Sutter and His Grants*, 10.

39. Nunis, "A Mysterious Chapter in the Life of John A. Sutter as Told by B. D. Wilson," 321–27.

40. Ibid., 322–23.

41. McCoy quoted in Staab, "Sutter in Westport, Part 1," 49.

42. JCCH-D, E:294–95.

43. JCCH-D, E:226–27, 294–95.

44. Staab, "Sutter in Westport," 53–54.

45. Weslager, *The Delaware Indians*, 380–82.

46. Laufkotter, *John A. Sutter and His Grants*, 14.

47. Ibid., 15.

48. Staab, "Sutter in Westport," 55–60.

49. JCCH-D, E:220–21, 280, 281, 282.

50. Lawrence, "Horse Thieves," 23.

CHAPTER 3

1. JCRC, Case No. 440.

2. Staab, "Sutter in Westport: Part 2," 99–100.

3. Sutter, "Reminiscences," 2–3, BL.

4. Weber, *Taos Trappers*, 134–55, 181.

5. Harris, "Memories of Old Westport," 465–75.

6. Nunis, "A Mysterious Chapter," 324.

7. McCoy quoted in Staab, "Sutter in Westport," 99–100.

8. Chittenden, *The American Fur Trade of the Far West*, 1:309–62.

9. Drury, *First White Women over the Rockies*, 2:58.

10. Ibid., 2:73.

11. Ibid., 2:21–60.

12. Ibid., 2:59.

13. Drury, *The Diaries and Letters of Henry Spalding and Asa Bowen Smith*, 52.

14. Drury, *First White Women over the Rockies*, 1:84–85.

15. Ibid., 2:72, n. 3.

16. Goetzman and Goetzman, *The West of the Imagination*, 58–59; Drury, *First White Women over the Rockies*, 2:73.

17. Sutter, "Reminiscences," 4.

18. Drury, *First White Women over the Rockies*, 2:75.

19. Ibid., 2:80.

20. Ibid., 2:108.

21. Drury, *The Diaries and Letters of Henry Spalding and Asa Bowen Smith*, 60–61.

22. Ibid., 61, n. 32.

23. Wishart, *The Fur Trade of the American West*, 62–63.

24. Drury, *First White Women over the Rockies*, 2:88–89.

25. Hurtado, "When Strangers Met," 130–33.

26. Drury, *First White Women over the Rockies*, 2:101.

27. Wishart, *The Fur Trade of the American West*, 190–200.

28. Ibid., 205–15 and passim.

29. Sutter, "Reminiscences," 10.

30. Brooks, *Captives and Cousins;* Ruby and Brown, *Indian Slavery in the Pacific Northwest.*

31. Sutter, "Reminiscences," 4.

32. Simpson quoted in Mackie, *Trading beyond the Mountains,* 64.

33. Galbraith, "A Note on the British Fur Trade in California," 253–60; Hurtado, *Indian Survival,* 41–42.

34. Hurtado, *Indian Survival,* 47.

35. Drury, *First White Women over the Rockies,* 2:108–10; Sutter, "Reminiscences," 5.

36. Drury, *First White Women over the Rockies,* 2:113–14; Sutter, "Reminiscences," 5.

37. Drury, *First White Women over the Rockies,* 2:116.

38. Ibid., n. 44.

39. Sutter, "Reminiscences," 6–8.

40. Ibid., 8–9.

41. Rich, *The Fort Vancouver Letters of John McLoughlin,* 1:256.

42. Sutter, "Reminiscences," 9.

43. There is some question about the number of men who accompanied Sutter on the *Columbia.* In his reminiscences he claimed that he took only the Indian and Wetler to Hawaii. Dillon, *Fool's Gold,* 66, says that he took eight men. In "General Sutter's Diary," 4, Sutter wrote that he had five white men but does not indicate whether they came with him or he picked up some of them in Hawaii and California.

CHAPTER 4

1. "Passengers," *Sandwich Island Gazette and Journal of Commerce* (Honolulu), December 15, 1838, 3.

2. WF-DJ, 437.

3. WF-L, 439, 457, 458, 473, 477, 495, 511, 514.

4. Nunis, *The California Diary of Faxon Dean Atherton, 1836–1839,* 116.

5. Ibid., 119.

6. Breault, *John A. Sutter in Hawaii and California, 1838–1839,* 26–50.

7. Daws, *The Shoal of Time,* 1–105.

8. Lamar, "From Bondage to Contract," 306, 309–10.

9. Daws, *Shoal of Time,* 61–105.

10. Zollinger, *Sutter,* 46, quotes Sutter on this offer, but I have not discovered his source.

11. Sutter, "Reminiscences," 20.

12. Breault, *John A. Sutter in Hawaii,* 41–42, writes that the contract was for nine Kanakas, including an Alii man. The Alii man may not have been included with the Kanaka count, however—thus the apparent discrepancy.

13. Sutter, "Reminiscences," 20.

14. WF-DJ, 428; "Arrived," *Sandwich Island Gazette* (Honolulu), February 16, 1839, 3.

15. WF-L, 251, 276, 296, 304.

16. WF-L, 338.

17. Sutter, "Reminiscences," 11–12.

18. The matter was far more complicated than Bingham made it out to be. Gray was traveling with several Flathead and Nez Perce men who had a herd of horses that they intended to take to Missouri to trade for cattle. Gray and his party made it to the Green River rendezvous, where experienced mountain men tried to convince him that it would be foolish to take so many horses through Sioux country with so few men. Gray did not heed this good advice and set out anyway. The Sioux killed his Flathead and Nez Perce escort and wounded Gray, who escaped along with two other white men. When the mountain men heard of this disaster, they blamed Gray for his pigheaded determination to push through Sioux country and said that they would make him pay for the death

of their Indian friends. The trappers made threatening gestures when they saw Gray at the 1838 rendezvous, but nothing came of it. Sutter to the Editors, *Sandwich Island Gazette* (Honolulu), April 7, 1839, 2.

19. Daws, *Shoal of Time,* 88–90.

20. Ibid., 95.

21. Ibid., 96.

22. "The Columns of Our Gazette," *Sandwich Island Gazette* (Honolulu), April 7, 1839, 2.

23. Sutter to the Editors, *Sandwich Island Gazette* (Honolulu), April 7, 1839, 2.

24. Daws, *Shoal of Time,* 102–103.

25. Sutter, "Reminiscences," 12–13.

26. Owens, "Introduction," in *The Wreck of the Sv. Nikolai,* 25–31.

27. Black, *Russians in Alaska, 1732–1867,* 127–28.

28. Ibid., 209–19.

29. Gibson, *Imperial Russia in Frontier America,* 112–15.

30. DuFour, "The Russian Withdrawal from California," 240–76.

31. Zollinger, *Sutter,* 45, 53–55; Dillon, *Fool's Gold,* 72, 75–76.

CHAPTER 5

1. Sutter said that he landed on July 1 in "Reminiscences," 13. He recalled the date as July 2 in Sutter, "General Sutter's Diary," 4.

2. Bancroft, *History of California,* 3:708–709.

3. Ibid., 3:708–11. On redwood distribution, see Bakker, *An Island Called California,* 93–97; on wasteful logging practices in 1849, see Taylor, *California Life Illustrated,* 35–36.

4. Sutter, "Reminiscences," 14; Sutter, "General Sutter's Diary," 4.

5. Here I deviate from Sutter's recollection in his "Reminiscences," 15, which has him arriving in Monterey on July 5. Instead, I rely on Juan Bautista Alvarado's five-volume manuscript "Historia de California," 4:207, BL. Parts of the "Historia" are translated in CDFP.

6. Bancroft, *History of California,* 5:730–31.

7. Hague and Langum, *Thomas O. Larkin,* 37–55, 103.

8. Miller, *Juan Alvarado,* 67.

9. Harlow, *California Conquered,* 4, 95; Weber, *The Mexican Frontier, 1821–1846,* 13, 204.

10. Miller, *Juan Alvarado,* 67.

11. Weber, *Mexican Frontier,* 255–59.

12. Ibid.; Miller, *Juan Alvarado,* 61.

13. Alvarado "Historia de California," 4:208–209.

14. Sutter, "General Sutter's Diary," 4.

15. James Douglas to the governor of the Hudson's Bay Company, October 14, 1839, quoted in Rich, *The Fort Vancouver Letters of John McLoughlin,* 2:217–20.

16. Sutter, "General Sutter's Diary," 4.

17. French, "Ledger," 358, HSA.

18. Sutter, "Reminiscences," 21.

19. Rosenus, *General M. G. Vallejo and the Advent of the Americans,* 14, 64.

20. Davis, *Seventy-five Years in California,* 105.

21. Rosenus, *General M. G. Vallejo,* 52.

22. Sutter, "Reminiscences," 22.

23. Ibid., 25.

24. Ibid., 23.

25. Rosenus, *General M. G. Vallejo,* 27–28.

26. Sutter, "Reminiscences," 24.

27. Ibid.

28. For brief biographies of Spear and Hinckley, see Bancroft, *History of California,* 3:785–86, 5:730.

29. Sutter, "General Sutter's Diary," 4; Sutter, "Reminiscences," 19–20, claims that he purchased the *Isabella.*

30. Sutter, "Reminiscences," 27.

31. For the life of Davis, see Davis, *Seventy-five Years in California,* ix–xi. In 1876 Sutter ("Reminiscences," 27) recalled August 2 as the date that he sailed from Yerba Buena. In 1889 Davis (*Seventy-five Years in California,* 15) set the date as August 9.

32. Sutter, "Reminiscences," 28.

33. Davis recollected that it took eight days for the entire journey, but Sutter and Davis were trying to recall events that occurred respectively thirty-seven and fifty years earlier: Sutter, "Reminiscences," 28; Davis, *Seventy-five Years in California,* 15.

34. Sutter, "Reminiscences," 29.

35. Bakker, *An Island Called California,* 123–33.

36. Davis, *Seventy-five Years in California,* 15.

37. Ibid., 16.

38. Sutter, "Reminiscences," 30.

39. "The Launch of a Tug Boat," *Sacramento Union,* September 29, 1862, 1; Bennyhoff, *Ethnogeography of the Plains Miwok,* 65–66; Phillips, *Indians and Intruders in Central California, 1769–1849,* 118.

40. Sutter, "Reminiscences," 31.

41. "The Launch of a Tug Boat," 1.

42. Bennyhoff, *Ethnogeography of the Plains Miwok,* 31, 72; Phillips, *Indians and Intruders,* 118.

43. Sutter, "Reminiscences," 32.

44. Davis, *Seventy-five Years,* 15–16.

45. Sutter, "Diary," 5.

46. Sutter, "Reminiscences," 36.

47. Davis, *Seventy-five Years in California,* 16.

48. Sutter, "Reminiscences," 37.

49. Sutter to Ygnacio Martínez, August 14, 1839, JASC.

50. Sutter, "Reminiscences," 37–38; Wiggins, "Reminiscences," 3–4, BL.

51. Sutter to Ygnacio Martínez, September 25, 1839, JASC.

52. Sutter to Ygnacio Martínez, October 9, 1839, JASC.

53. Sutter to Ygnacio Martínez, October 28, 1839, JASC.

54. Laufkotter, *John A. Sutter and His Grants,* 15.

CHAPTER 6

1. Lyman, *John Marsh, Pioneer,* 3–180.

2. Ibid., 189–213.

3. Ibid., 216.

4. George McKinstry, November 1846, [Population Enumeration of the Sacramento Valley], GAMP, 12–13; Sutter, "Estimate of Indian Population," December 20, 1847, GAMP, 14–15.

5. Levy, "Eastern Miwok," 398–413; Bennyhoff, *Ethnogeography of the Plains Miwok,* 164, map 2.

6. Wilson and Towne, "Nisenan," 387–97. See also Heizer and Elsasser, *The Natural World of California Indians,* 37–45, 64–67, 71–73.

7. Wilson and Towne, "Nisenan," 396; Bennyhoff, *Ethnogeography of the Plains Miwok,* 70–72.

8. Hurtado, *Indian Survival,* 32–54.

9. Brooks, *The Southwest Expedition of Jedediah S. Smith,* 136–66. For Mexican accounts of Smith's visit, see Weber, *The Californios versus Jedediah Smith, 1826–1827.*

10. Hurtado, *Indian Survival,* 42–47. Bennyhoff, *Ethnogeography of the Plains Miwok,* 24–32; Phillips, *Indians and Intruders,* 112.

11. Governor José Figueroa to the Minister of War and Navy, April 12, 1833, in Cook, "Expeditions to the Interior of California," 188.

12. José Figueroa, "Order and Decree concerning Robbers of Horses and Other Livestock," November 18, 1833, in Cook, "Expeditions to the Interior of California," 188; Governor Juan Alvarado, July 4, 1840, in Cook, "Expeditions to the Interior of California," 192.

13. José Berreyessa, July 15, 1830, in Cook, "Expeditions to the Interior of California," 187; Carter, *"Dear Old Kit,"* 47–48. Berreyessa said that "Indians" burned the houses but did not make clear if he meant the Indian auxiliaries or the Ochejamnes.

14. Bennyhoff, *Ethnogeography of the Plains Miwok,* 70–72; Phillips, *Indians and Intruders,* 118.

15. Cook, "The Epidemic of 1830–1833 in California and Oregon," 303–25. John Work's firsthand account of the epidemic is found in Maloney, *Fur Brigade to the Bonaventure.*

16. Bennyhoff, *Ethnogeography of the Plains Miwok,* 70–72; Phillips, *Indians and Intruders,* 118.

17. Sutter, "Reminiscences," 36.

18. Wilbur, *A Pioneer at Sutter's Fort, 1846–1850,* 7, 68.

19. Bennyhoff, *Ethnogeography of the Plains Miwok,* 70–72; Phillips, *Indians and Intruders,* 118.

20. "The Launch of a Tug Boat," *Sacramento Union,* September 29, 1862, 1.

21. On Maximo, see "An Aged Indian Chief," *Sacramento Union,* May 25, 1885, 4.

22. Phillips, *Indians and Intruders,* 118–19.

23. Sutter, "Reminiscences," 39.

24. Ibid., 40.

25. Ibid.

26. Bancroft, *History of California,* 4:227.

27. Sutter, "Reminiscences," 38.

28. The reconstructed fort that stands today is somewhat smaller than these dimensions, which are taken from Bryant, *What I Saw in California,* 267. There is disagreement on the fort's dimensions. Lewis, *Sutter's Fort,* 110, describes it as "an irregularly shaped area measuring approximately 425 by 170 feet"; Dillon, *Fool's Gold,* 102, says that it was 320 feet on the north and south sides and 140 and 160 feet long on the east and west sides respectively.

29. Sutter, "Reminiscences," 38.

30. Wiggins, "Reminiscences" (unpaged manuscript). For a brief biography of Wiggins, see Bancroft, *History of California,* 5:774.

31. Wiggins, "Reminiscences."

32. Ibid.

33. Sutter, "General Sutter's Diary," 7. Sutter gave this account in 1856. Twenty years later he claimed that he killed only six Indians in this affray: Sutter, "Reminiscences," 40.

34. Sutter, "Diary," 7.

35. Sutter to José de Jesús Vallejo, October 15, 1840, VD 8:279.

36. Ibid.

37. Sutter, "Reminiscences," 45.

38. Sutter to José de Jesús Vallejo, October 15, 1840.

39. On the Vallejos' relations with the Indians, see Rosenus, *General M. G. Vallejo,* 11–12, 52–53; Phillips, *Indians and Intruders,* 79–81; Forbes, *Native Americans of California and Nevada,* 41–42.

40. Sutter, "Reminiscences," 41–42.

41. Ibid.; Wilbur, *A Pioneer at Sutter's Fort,* 68.

42. Sutter, "Reminiscences," 42.

43. Ibid., 75.

44. Ibid., 77.

45. Ibid., 36–37.

46. "The Alcalde to the Prefect," March 18, 1841, in Cook, "Expeditions to the Interior of California," 193; Salvio Pacheco to the Justice of the Peace, August 19, 1842, in Cook, "Expeditions to the Interior of California," 193; Mariano Vallejo to Sutter, July 26, 1843, VD 11:432, trans. CDFP.

47. Sutter sometimes tried to make livestock recovery part of a larger deal with his creditors. See John A. Sutter to Antonio Suñol, October 7, 1840, Sutter Letters, BL.

48. John A. Sutter to Antonio Suñol, August 10, 1841, and John A. Sutter to Antonio Suñol, June 14, 1845, JASC.

49. Wiggins, "Reminiscences."

50. Sutter, "Reminiscences," 23.

51. Alvarado, "Historia de California," 4:207–19, BL.

52. Ibid.; Bancroft, *History of California,* 2:773.

53. Alvarado, "Historia de California," 4:207–19.

54. Bancroft, *History of California,* 2:691 and 4:700. According to Bancroft, Keyser may not have arrived until 1841. Sutter, "Reminiscences," 60, recalled that Allgeier came to California in 1842, but this is an error.

55. Bancroft, *History of California,* 5:721.

56. Ibid., 5:723.

57. Ibid., 5:719.

58. Ibid., 5:718, 744.

59. Ibid., 2:756.

60. Sutter to Antonio Suñol, May 10, 1842, JASC.

61. Sutter to Antonio Suñol, May 14, 1842, JASC.

62. Alvarado, "Historia de California," 4:207–19.

63. Sandels, *A Sojourn in California by the King's Orphan,* 57.

64. Ibid., 72–73.

65. Wiggins, "Reminiscences." See also Yates, "Sketch of a Journey in the Year 1842," BL; John Bidwell in Quaife, *Echoes of the Past about California,* 81–83.

66. William Joseph quoted in Uldall and Shipley, *Nisenan Texts and Dictionary,* 67.

CHAPTER 7

1. On the development of the hacienda system in Mexico, see Chevalier, *Land and Society in Colonial Mexico.*

2. Sutter, "Reminiscences," 23.

3. Martínez to Mariano Guadalupe Vallejo, May 30, 1840, JASC.

4. Sutter to Ygnacio Martínez, December 10, 1839, JASC.

5. Sutter to Mariano Guadalupe Vallejo, December [?], 1839, JASC.

6. Sutter to Martínez, December 10, 1839, JASC.

7. Sutter, "Reminiscences," 35.

8. Martínez to Mariano Guadalupe Vallejo, May 30, 1840, JASC. Bracketed portions are from Clarence DuFour's translation of the same document in CDFP. The minor differences in translation have to do with colloquial terms concerning horses and other livestock.

9. Marginal comment, Martínez to Mariano Guadalupe Vallejo, May 30, 1840, JASC.

10. Bancroft, *History of California,* 5:738.

11. Sutter, "General Sutter's Diary," 7.

12. Sutter to Antonio Suñol, October 7, 1840, JASC.

13. Sutter to Antonio Suñol, October 20, 1840, JASC.

14. Sutter to Suñol, October 7, 1840, JASC.

15. Sutter to Antonio Suñol, August 10, 1841, JASC; Sutter to Antonio Suñol, August 16, 1841, JASC.

16. Wilkes, *Narrative of the United States Exploring Expedition during the Years 1838, 1839, 1840, 1841, 1842,* 5:191.

17. Phelps, *Alta California, 1840–1842,* 202, 278–79.

18. Pisco is a kind of brandy named for the town in Peru where it was brewed. Wilkes, *Narrative,* 5:191.

19. Sutter to Antonio Suñol, April 24, 1841, JASC.

20. Sutter to Antonio Suñol, August 16, 1841, JASC.

21. Sutter to Antonio Suñol, October 19, 1841, JASC.

22. Sutter to Antonio Suñol, May 14, 1842, JASC.

23. Sutter to Antonio Suñol, June 13, 1842, JASC.

24. Sutter to John Marsh, June 18, 1840, JMC.

25. Underhill, *From Cowhides to Golden Fleece,* 19.

26. Larkin quoted in Hague and Langum, *Thomas O. Larkin,* 58. On operations of the hide and tallow trade, see 57–59.

27. William [Sturgis] Hinckley, "Promissory Note in Favor of James Watson," March 2, 1842, WLP.

28. Griswold del Castillo, *La Familia,* 42; Griswold del Castillo, *The Los Angeles Barrio, 1850–1890,* 97–98; Miranda, "Gente de Razón Marriage Patterns in Spanish and Mexican California," 1–21.

29. Hurtado, *Intimate Frontiers,* 30–37.

30. Bancroft, *History of California,* 4:2–41; Robinson, *Life in California during a Residence of Several Years in That Territory,* 180–82.

31. Alvarado quoted in Robinson, *Life in California,* 181.

32. Ibid., 184.

33. Bancroft, *History of California,* 4:35–36; Robinson, *Life in California,* 183.

34. Bancroft, *History of California,* 4:29–32.

35. Farnham, *Travels in the Californias.*

36. Bancroft, *History of California,* 3:734.

37. Ibid., 4:136–37 and n. 28. Sutter later claimed that he was naturalized in 1841 when he received his land grant ("Reminiscences," 50).

38. Sutter, "Reminiscences," 64.

39. Sutter to Antonio Suñol, May 1, 1842, JASC.

40. Santos Berreyessa to Mariano Vallejo, December 21, 1841, typed translation, CDFP.

41. Quaife, *Echoes of the Past,* 13–74.

42. Sutter, "Reminiscences," 72.

43. Phelps, *Alta California, 1840–1842,* 197.

44. Ibid., 200.

45. In 1846 Sutter was offering salmon at $20 per barrel. John A. Sutter to William A. Leidesdorff, March 31, 1846, April 17, 1846, May 11, 1846, WLP.

46. Phelps, *Alta California, 1840–1842,* 201.

CHAPTER 8

1. Sutter, "Reminiscences," 49–50.

2. *A Faithful Translation of the Papers Respecting the Grant Made by Governor Alvarado to John A. Sutter.* A league equals about 2.6 miles. For a discussion of Mexican units of land measurement, see Uzes, *Chaining the Land,* 291–306.

3. Bancroft, *History of California,* 4:230–31, 5:764, outlines the problems with the Sutter claim. Complete details are available in *CLC.*

4. Sutter, "Reminiscences," 50.

5. Sutter quotes an unnamed captain and his own reply in ibid., 51.

6. Wilkes, *Narrative,* 5:190. See also Stanton, *The Great United States Exploring Expedition,* 260, 264, 265.

7. Wilkes, *Narrative,.* 5:189–92 (quotation on 192).

8. Ibid., 5:192.

9. Sutter to Antonio Suñol, September 1, 1841, JASC.

10. Willys, "French Imperialists in California," 116–29.

11. Bancroft, *History of California,* 4:251–52.

12. Mofras, *Duflot de Mofras' Travels on the Pacific Coast,* 1:245.

13. Ibid., 1:247.

14. Ibid., 1:248.

15. Ibid., 1:249.

16. Ibid., 2:249.

17. Ibid., 1:248.

18. Ibid., 1:242.

19. Brackenridge, "Journal of William Dunlop Brackenridge," 331.

20. Ibid., 332.

21. Mariano Vallejo to Juan Bautista Alvarado, July 27, 1841, VD 10:227, CDFP.

22. DuFour, "The Russian Withdrawal from California," 240–76. Vallejo evidently encouraged his brother-in-law Jacob Leese to make a private deal with the Russians, but it also fell through.

23. Sutter to Antonio Suñol, August 10, 1841, JASC.

24. Sutter to Antonio Suñol, September 1, 1841, JASC.

25. Mofras, *Travels on the Pacific Coast,* 2:249.

26. Sutter, "General Sutter's Diary," 8, gives this date. Mofras claimed that the date was September 8 (*Travels on the Pacific Coast,* 2:249).

27. The transaction was reported in French piasters, Mexican pesos, and American dollars. The amount reported was always the same (30,000), regardless of the currency. In Mexican California the three currencies were roughly equivalent. For the sake of clarity and consistency, I use dollars.

28. There is a discrepancy concerning the amount that Sutter owed to the Russians in addition to the $30,000. He reported (and other historians have accepted) that he paid $2,000 in cash, which covered the cost of a schooner that he acquired from the Russians when he bought Ross. But the inventory of Russian properties included in the $30,000 purchase clearly includes the schooner. In December 1841 Sutter made a $400 payment on his $3,868.16 account, thus reducing the amount to $3,468.16. Here I rely on "Inventory and Bill of Sale Transferring Possession of Russia's California Properties to John Sutter, December 20, 1841," in Dmytryshyn, Crownhart-Vaughan, and Vaughan, *To Siberia and Russian America,* 431–42. Cf. Sutter, "Reminiscences," 55–56; DuFour, "John A. Sutter," 87; Dillon, *Fool's Gold,* 116.

29. Sutter, "Reminiscences," 56.

30. Sutter to Mariano Vallejo, September 19, 1841, VD 10:282, CDFP.

31. DuFour, "The Russian Withdrawal from California," 269–70.

32. Sutter, "Reminiscences," 57.

33. Ibid., 59.

34. Ibid., 57.

35. Bancroft, *History of California,* 4:179.

36. Quaife, *Echoes of the Past,* 80.

37. Bancroft, *History of California,* 5:746.

38. Ibid., 3:767.

39. John A. Sutter to Alpheus Basil Thompson, December 14, 1841, HM 48987.

40. Bill of sale, John A. Sutter to Stephen Smith, September 10, 1843, CvS; *Tyler Curtis, administrator, v. John A. Sutter, William Muldrow, et al.,* CSA.

41. Bidwell, "California, 1841–8," 84–85, BL.

42. "Inventory and Bill of Sale Transferring Possession of Russia's California Properties to John Sutter, December 20, 1841," in Dmytryshyn, Crownhart-Vaughan, and Vaughan, *To Siberia and Russian America,* 431–42.

43. Sutter mentions uniforms, muskets, ammunition, and artillery that he acquired from the Russians, but these items are not included in the inventory. He may have purchased his military supplies in a separate deal. Sutter, "Reminiscences," 59, 77–78.

44. Bancroft, *History of California,* 4:233; DuFour, "The Russian Withdrawal from California," 257–60, includes a detailed inventory that was made for Vallejo.

45. Sutter, "General Sutter's Diary," 9.

46. Bidwell, "California, 1841–8," 85; Bancroft, *History of California,* 4:233.

47. "Deed to Russian Properties," quoted in DuFour, "The Russian Withdrawal from California," 271.

48. Peter Kostromitinov to Juan Bautista Alvarado, December 19, 1841, quoted in DuFour, "The Russian Withdrawal from California," 272–73 (emphasis in original).

49. Alvarado, "Historia de California," 4:234.

50. Sutter to Jacob Leese, November 8, 1841, VD 10:332, CDFP.

51. Ibid.

52. Bidwell, "California, 1841–8," 84.

53. Mariano Vallejo to the Minister of War and Marine, December 11, 1841, CDFP (emphasis in original).

54. Mariano Vallejo to Manuel Micheltorena, October 15, 1842, VD 11:273, trans., CDFP, Box 2. DuFour translated "cazaderos" as "scouts," but "hunters" better reflects Vallejo's meaning, which probably included mountain men as well as chaguanosos.

55. Alvarado to the Minister of the Interior, January 11, 1842, CDFP.

56. Bancroft, *History of California,* 4:198–205.

57. Stephen Reynolds to Thomas O. Larkin, May 23, 1842, in Hammond, *Larkin Papers,* 1:222.

58. Bancroft, *History of California,* 4:198–205; and Miller, *Juan Alvarado,* 92.

59. Miller, *Juan Alvarado,* 92–93.

60. Thomas ap Catesby Jones to A. P. Upshur, September 13, 1842, in Bauer, *The New American State Papers,* 96–97; Harlow, *California Conquered,* 4–5.

61. Harlow, *California Conquered,* 6–7.

62. Thomas ap Catesby Jones to Juan Bautista Alvarado and M. Silva, October 21, 1842, in Bauer, *The New American State Papers,* 100.

63. Harlow, *California Conquered,* 9–10.

64. Mariano Vallejo to Manuel Micheltorena, October 15, 1842, VD 11:273, trans., CDFP.

65. Sutter, "Reminiscences," 81; Bancroft, *History of California,* 3:741–42, 4:380.

66. Sutter, "Reminiscences," 84.

67. Simpson, *Narrative of a Journey round the World,* 1:325.

68. Ibid., 1:326.

69. Ibid., 1:327.

CHAPTER 9

1. White, "John Sutter and the Natural World," 93–110; Heizer and Elsasser, *The Natural World of the California Indians,* 82–113; Dasmann, *The Destruction of California,* 43–74.

2. Simpson, *Ooti,* 45–46 and passim.

3. Hurtado, *Indian Survival,* 55–56.

4. Sandels, *A Sojourn in California by the King's Orphan,* 61.

5. Ibid., 68.

6. Bakker, *An Island Called California,* 63–64; Pisani, *From Family Farm to Agribusiness,* 54–58.

7. *CLC,* 335.

8. Ibid., 338.

9. Bakker, *An Island Called California,* 138; Pisani, *From Family Farm to Agribusiness,* 54–77 and passim; Kelley, *Battling the Inland Sea,* 25–108 and passim.

10. Sutter, "Reminiscences," 46.

11. Ibid., 50.

12. Neri, "Gonzales Rubio and California Catholicism, 1846–1850," 441–57; Hurtado, *Intimate Frontiers,* 40–41.

13. Sutter, "Reminiscences," 78.

14. Bidwell, "California, 1841–8," 114.

15. Little is known about Kinney. See Bancroft, *History of California,* 4:701.

16. John Bidwell, Dictation, BL.

17. Sutter, "Reminiscences," 78.

18. *Titulo* and translation, *CLC,* 74, 80 (emphasis added).

19. *CLC,* 74–80.

20. "Map of the Sacramento, Feather, and Yuba Rivers," SGM. The map bears a notation indicating that Sutter swears on February 20, 1858, that it is more accurate than other maps that were presented.

21. Sutter, "Reminiscences," 46.

22. Kroeber, *Handbook of the Indians of California,* 402; Bean and Blackburn, *Native Californians,* 106–108.

23. Sutter, "Reminiscences," 46.

24. High Indian female mortality is well documented in California. See Hurtado, *Indian Survival,* 65–68 and passim.

25. Sutter, "Reminiscences," 46.

26. Ibid., 47.

27. Hurtado, *Indian Survival,* 62–63.

28. Identifying Hawaiians from the record is difficult because of variant spellings. Sutter names Kanaka Harry and Makaena, probably Manuiki, as living on the south side of the American River, (Sutter to John Bidwell, May 6, 1854, PM). "The Agreement between John A. Sutter and William Muldrow, December 14, 1849," SAMC-POA, identified Muawickiu (perhaps Kanaka Harry or some other Hawaiian). See Wilbur, *Pioneer at Sutter's Fort,* 76, n. 18.

29. Wilbur, *Pioneer at Sutter's Fort,* 75–76. See also Engstrand, "John Sutter," 81–82.

30. "Statistics of the District East of San Joaquin and Sacramento Rivers," January 8, 1848, GAMP, 28–29.

31. Wilbur, *Pioneer at Sutter's Fort.* 75.

32. Ibid., 75–76.

33. Ibid., 76.

34. Chamberlain, "Memoirs of California since 1840," BL.

35. Sutter to William Leidesdorff, May 11, 1846, WLP.

36. Sutter, "Reminiscences," 42; Sutter to Antonio Suñol, May 19, 1845, JASC.

37. Mofras, *Travels on the Pacific Coast,* 1:247.

38. "Deposition of J. M. Sanford, December 21, 1860," *CLC,* 660.

39. There is considerable literature on this phenomenon. See, for example, Swagerty, "Marriage and Settlement Patterns of the Rocky Mountain Trappers and Traders," 159–80; Brown, *Strangers in*

Blood, 73–74, 111–30, 199–230, and passim; Van Kirk, *Many Tender Ties,* 28–52, 231–42, and passim; Hurtado, "When Strangers Met," 130–33.

40. Wilbur, *Pioneer at Sutter's Fort,* 76.

41. Sandels, *Sojourn in California,* 66.

42. Hurtado, "When Strangers Met," 122–42.

43. Wilbur, *Pioneer at Sutter's Fort,* 76.

44. Sandels, *Sojourn in California,* 73.

45. Yates, "Sketch of a Journey in the Year 1842," BL.

46. Wilbur, *Pioneer at Sutter's Fort,* 53.

47. Yates, "Sketch of a Journey."

48. Wilbur, *Pioneer at Sutter's Fort,* 61–62.

49. Ibid., 77.

50. Alexander, *The Life and Times of Cyrus Alexander,* 70.

51. Alvarado, "Historia de California," 4:221, CDFP.

52. Thomas Larkin to Sutter, January 20, 1846, in Hammond, *Larkin Papers,* 4:168–69. See also Larkin to W. A. Leidesdorff, January 20, 1846, in ibid., 4:170–71.

53. Hague and Langum, *Thomas O. Larkin,* 37–41.

54. Hurtado, *Intimate Frontiers,* 38–44.

55. Sutter to John Bidwell, May 6, 1854, PM; John A. Sutter to John Bidwell, May 7, 1854, JBP.

56. Gudde, "The Memoirs of Theodor Cordua," 283.

57. Ibid., 284, 299. Cordua claimed that his lease covered five leagues of Sutter's land (*CLC,* 602–603).

58. Sutter to Antonio Suñol, July 24, 1842, JASC.

59. Sutter to Henry D. Fitch, July 15, 1842, JASC.

60. Sutter to James McKinley, September 5, 1842, HDFP.

61. Sutter to Henry Delano Fitch, November 3, 1842, HDFP.

62. John A. Sutter to Eliab Grimes and John Sinclair, SuC-D, D:308; Bancroft, *History of California,* 5:721.

63. Sutter, "Reminiscences," 60. See also Allgeier's testimony and exhibits, *CLC,* 335–45; Bancroft, *History of California,* 2:691.

64. *CLC,* 47.

65. Ibid., 46–53.

66. Taylor, *In Search of the Racial Frontier,* 46–47.

67. Bancroft, *History of California,* 3:767.

68. Thompson and West, *History of Sacramento County, California,* 181–85; Beck and Haase, *Historical Atlas of California,* map 26, 28, 29.

69. Sutter to Antonio Suñol, October 7, 1842, JASC.

70. Sandels, *Sojourn in California,* 59.

71. Dmytryshyn, Crownhart-Vaughan, and Vaughan, *To Siberia and Russian America,* 440.

72. John A. Sutter to Francisco Guerrero, November 8, 1843, JASC.

73. Sandels, *Sojourn in California,* 61.

74. Sutter to Antonio Suñol, July 24, 1842, JASC.

75. Antonio Suñol to Sutter, April [?] 1843, JASC.

76. Sutter to Antonio Suñol, July 24, 1842, September 8, 1842, October 7, 1842, November 20, 1842, December 14, 1842, JASC.

77. Sutter to Antonio Suñol, December 14, 1842, JASC.

78. Sutter to Antonio Suñol, June 13, 1843, JASC.

79. Sutter, "Reminiscences," 51.

80. *CLC,* 514.

81. Sutter to Pierson B. Reading, May 11, 1845, PRC.

82. Rorabaugh, *The Alcoholic Republic.*

83. Willard Buzzell to William Leidesdorff, July 28, 1845, WLP, Box 1:57.

84. Sutter, "Reminiscences," 70–71. Sutter's accusation seems to be supported in Weber's correspondence. See William Gulnac to Charles Weber, June 22, July 10, and July 29, 1845, WFP.

85. Sutter to Pierson B. Reading, October 30, 1844, AMRC.

86. "Letter from John Bidwell," *Themis,* December 21, 1889, 4.

CHAPTER 10

1. Meyers, *Journal of a Cruise to California,* 11, 18–19, 24, 27.

2. Ibid., 22.

3. Quotation from ibid., 26, 65; Bancroft, *History of California,* 4:362–63.

4. C. K. Stribling to John Marsh, June 19, 1843, JMC.

5. Marsh became a Mexican citizen in 1844 (Bancroft, *History of California,* 4:348, 730).

6. Marsh, "Letter of Dr. John Marsh to Hon. Lewis Cass," 315–22.

7. Sutter to John Marsh, January 4, 1844, JASC.

8. Sutter, "Reminiscences," 130.

9. Ibid., 131.

10. Jackson and Spence, *Expeditions of John Charles Frémont,* 1:382.

11. Sutter, "Reminiscences," 131.

12. Jackson and Spence, *Expeditions of John Charles Frémont,* 1:387. On Chiles, see Sutter to Thomas Larkin, January 26, 1842, in Hammond, *Larkin Papers,* 1:159.

13. Jackson and Spence, *Expeditions of John Charles Frémont,* 1:387, 657.

14. Sutter to Larkin, March 28, 1844, in Hammond, *Larkin Papers,* 2:85.

15. Ibid., 2:94.

16. Sutter, "Reminiscences," 131.

17. Ibid., 132.

18. Jackson and Spence, *Expeditions of John Charles Frémont,* 1:656.

19. Ibid., 1:657.

20. Sutter, "General Sutter's Diary," 10; Hammond, *Larkin Papers,* 2:94.

21. Sutter to Thomas Larkin, March 28, 1844, in Hammond, *Larkin Papers,* 2:85.

22. Thomas Larkin to Secretary of State, April 12, 1844, in Hammond, *Larkin Papers,* 2:93.

23. Thomas Larkin to Sutter, April 29, 1844, in Hammond, *Larkin Papers,* 2:111.

24. Sutter to Thomas Larkin, July 17, 1844, in Hammond, *Larkin Papers,* 2:169.

25. Bancroft, *History of California,* 4:406–408, Sutter to John Marsh, July 16, 1844, JASC.

26. Ephraim Fravel to John Marsh, June 21, 1844, JMC.

27. Samuel G. McMahan to John Marsh, June 16, 1844, JMC.

28. Sutter to John Marsh, July 6, 1844, JASC.

29. Sutter to John Marsh, July 16, 1844, JASC (emphasis in original).

30. Sutter to John Marsh, July 26, 1844, JASC (emphasis in original).

31. Sutter to John Marsh, August 6, 1844, JASC.

32. Sutter to Larkin, July 17, 1844; Sutter to Thomas Larkin, August 7, 1844, both in Hammond, *Larkin Papers,* 2:169, 185–86.

33. Heizer, "Walla Walla Indian Expeditions to the Sacramento Valley," 1.

34. Sutter to John Marsh, August 28, 1844, JASC; Sutter to Thomas Larkin, July 21, 1845, in Hammond, *Larkin Papers,* 3:278–80.

35. Sutter, "Reminiscences," 82–84; "Mokelumne Espediente," Spanish Archives, Translations, vol. 7, 39–40, CSA; John A. Sutter to William Hartnell, December 13, 1844, JASC.

36. Sutter to Pierson B. Reading, October 20, 1844, AMRC.

37. Sutter to Thomas Larkin, July 21, 1845, in Hammond, *Larkin Papers,* 3:278–80.

38. Sutter, "General Sutter's Diary," 12.

39. Jackson, "The British and the California Dream," 259–63.

40. Jackson, "Two Pro-British Plots in Alta California," 107–109 (Forbes quoted at 109).

41. Sutter, "Reminiscences," 85.

42. Sutter, "General Sutter's Diary," 11.

43. Sutter, "Reminiscences," 86.

44. Sutter to Charles Weber, October 30, 1844, WFP.

45. Wood, *Wandering Sketches of People and Things in South America, Polynesia, California, and Other Places Visited,* 227.

46. Sutter to Antonio Suñol, November 9, 1844, JASC; Sutter, "Reminiscences," 87.

47. Cf. Wood, *Wandering Sketches,* 254; Bancroft, *History of California,* 4:459; Miller, *Juan Alvarado,* 102.

CHAPTER 11

1. John A. Sutter to William Hartnell, December 13, 1844, JASC; "Mokelumne Espediente," Spanish Archives, Translations, vol. 7, 39–40, CSA.

2. Sutter to Thomas Larkin, July 21, 1845, in Hammond, *Larkin Papers,* 3:278–80.

3. Bancroft, *History of California,* 2:764.

4. The record of this event is vague as to the precise date of the killing. Some claim that it happened in the spring, but the timing of subsequent events in Oregon and California makes this seem unlikely. In late November 1844 Sutter told Charles Weber that he might be forced go to war with the Walla Wallas, although he does not say why. It seems reasonable that Sutter is reacting to the murder of Hedding. Sutter to Charles M. Weber, November 26, 1844, WFP.

5. Sutter to Larkin, July 21, 1845, in Hammond, *Larkin Papers,* 3:278–80.

6. Mariano Vallejo to Sutter, December 13, 1844, JASC.

7. Bancroft, *History of California,* 4:466–70.

8. Quaife, *Echoes of the Past,* 101.

9. Ibid., 2.

10. Sutter to William Hartnell, December 13, 1844, JASC.

11. VD 34:81.

12. Dakin, *The Lives of William Hartnell,* 260–66; Weber, *Mexican Frontier,* 270.

13. Vallejo to Sutter, December 13, 1844, JASC.

14. Sutter to Mariano Vallejo, December 15, 1844, JASC.

15. Sutter to Mariano Vallejo, December 17, 1844, JASC.

16. Bancroft, *History of California,* 4:481–82.

17. Vallejo to Alvarado, December 23, 1844, JASC.

18. Alvarado, "Historia de California," 4:228–48.

19. Spanish Archives, Translations, vol. 7, 40, CSA.

20. "Memorandum of Grants made under the General Title, Dec 22 1844," PM, John Bidwell; Sutter, "Reminiscences," 86. Legal problems with these grants stemmed from the irregularity of departing from standard Mexican procedures and from the doubtful documentation that Sutter presented to the courts. Claiming that the original document had been lost, he submitted a copy that he had made in 1845, which only made matters seem more suspicious. It was no wonder that the courts struck down these dubious grants. Spanish Archives, Translations, vol. 7, 40, CSA.

21. Francisco Rico recalled that Graham met up with Sutter near Monterey, but it seems clear that Graham was in New Helvetia before Sutter marched. Rico, "Suggestions for the History of Alta California," CDFP.

22. Weber's sentiments are broadly hinted in Charles Weber to John Marsh, March 22, 1845, CMWP.

23. Sutter, "Reminiscences," 88–89.

24. Sutter, n.d., roster, JASP; Bancroft, *History of California,* 4:485–86. Bancroft reckoned that Sutter had only about 220 men with him.

25. Sutter, "Reminiscences," 89; Sutter to Pierson B. Reading, January 15, 1845, PRC.

26. Sutter, "Reminiscences," 89.

27. Ibid., 91–92; Sutter to [Charles] Flügge, January 12, 1845, JASC.

28. Quaife, *Echoes from the Past,* 102.

29. Sutter to Reading, January 15, 1845, PRC.

30. Ibid.

31. Ibid.

32. Ibid.; Bancroft, *History of California,* 2:780–81, 3:752, 4:724.

33. Sutter to Reading, January 15, 1845, PRC.

34. Sutter to James M. Hudspeth, February 27, 1852, WLP.

35. Sutter, "Reminiscences," 94.

36. Ibid., 96–97.

37. Streeter, "Recollections of Historical Events in California, 1843–1878," 4–5, CDFP.

38. Ibid., 1–2.

39. Ibid., 3–4.

40. Ibid., 4–5.

41. Sutter, "Reminiscences," 116–17.

42. *CLC,* 1:81.

43. Ibid., 1:250.

44. Cf. Sutter, "Reminiscences," 98–100; Bancroft, *History of California,* 4:501–502.

45. Sutter, "Reminiscences," 101–102.

46. Bancroft, *History of California,* 4:494.

47. Sutter to Pierson B. Reading, February 15, 1845, PRC.

48. Sutter, "Reminiscences," 105.

49. Ibid., 106.

50. There are conflicting accounts of the defection of Americans. See de la Torre, "Reminiscences" (no pagination); Pico, "Events Which Happened in California," 3; Osio, "History of California, 1815–1848," 2; Gonzales, "Memoirs" (no pagination); Castro, "Account of Events in Alta California" (no pagination); Botello, "Annals of Southern California, 1833–1847," 2; Streeter, "Recollections," 5–6, all in CDFP.

51. Sutter, "Reminiscences," 108.

52. John Coffin Jones to Thomas Larkin, February 24 [25], 1845, in Hammond, *Larkin Papers,* 3:48.

53. Sutter, "Reminiscences," 108.

54. Cleland, *The Cattle on a Thousand Hills,* 184–85 and passim.

55. Sutter, "Reminiscences," 113.

56. The substance of the treaty is found in Bancroft, *History of California,* 4:509–10.

57. Anselin quoted in Sutter, "Reminiscences," 114; Bancroft, *History of California,* 2:698.

58. Sutter, "Reminiscences," 115.

59. Ibid.

60. Ibid., 116.

61. Sutter to the Governor, February 26, 1845, CDFP.

62. Sutter, "Reminiscences," 125.

63. Ibid., 126.

64. Ibid., 127.

65. The date is uncertain. Sutter claimed April 11 in "General Sutter's Diary," 14. Bancroft offers April 1 in *History of California,* 4:516. John Gantt seems to indicate that Sutter was back in New Helvetia by March 11: Gantt to John Marsh, March 11, 1845, JMC.

66. Gantt to Marsh, March 11, 1845, JMC (emphasis in original).

67. Mariano Vallejo to his brother, March 8, 1845, VD 119.

68. John Coffin Jones to Thomas Larkin, February 24 [25], 1845, in Hammond, *Larkin Papers,* 3:49.

CHAPTER 12

1. Sutter to Thomas Larkin, July 21, 1845, in Hammond, *Larkin Papers,* 3:252.

2. Sutter, "Reminiscences," 69–70; Bancroft, *History of California,* 4:714, 5:753.

3. Wilbur, *Pioneer at Sutter's Fort,* 3.

4. Zollinger, *Sutter,* 158.

5. Sutter to Thomas Larkin, July 21, 1845, in Hammond, *Larkin Papers,* 3:252.

6. Sutter to Pierson B. Reading, May 8, 1845, PRC.

7. Sutter to Pierson B. Reading, May 11, 1845, PRC.

8. Sutter to Antonio Suñol, May 19, 1845, JASC.

9. John Marsh to Antonio Suñol, June 16, 1845, JMC.

10. Sutter to Antonio Suñol, June 14, 1845, JASC.

11. Sutter to Henry Delano Fitch, April 17, 1846, HDFP; Sutter to William Leidesdorff, May 11, 1846, Ms. 129, WLP; Sutter to John Marsh, May 17, 1845, JMC.

12. Account of W. A. Leidesdorff, August 1, 1844, to January 27, 1846, WLP. For a more detailed analysis of the Leidesdorff account, see Hurtado, *Indian Survival,* 59–61.

13. "An Old Letter," *Sonoma Democrat,* February 12, 1876, 1, is a letter by Sutter dated April 21, 1845. The editor of the *Democrat* did not reveal to whom the letter was addressed, but it may have been Larkin or Leidesdorff.

14. Quotation from Josephy, *The Nez Perce Indians and the Opening of the Northwest,* 220.

15. Sutter to Thomas Larkin, July 15, 1845, printed in Camp, "James Clyman, His Diaries and Reminiscences (Continued)," 124.

16. Elijah White to Thomas Larkin, May 16, 1845, in Hammond, *Larkin Papers,* 3:187.

17. Thomas Larkin to James E. Forbes, August 1, 1845, in Hammond, *Larkin Papers,* 3:297.

18. Sutter to Thomas Larkin, July 21, 1845, in Hammond, *Larkin Papers,* 3:278–80.

19. Thomas Larkin to Elijah White, July 31, 1845, in Hammond, *Larkin Papers,* 3:286–88.

20. Bancroft, *History of California,* 2:764; Hague and Langum, *Thomas O. Larkin,* 191.

21. Thomas Larkin to Sutter, November 1, 1845, WLP, Ms. 74.

22. Sutter to Thomas Larkin, July 22, 1845, in Hammond, *Larkin Papers,* 3:281–83.

23. Thomas Larkin to Sutter, July 22, 1845, in Hammond, *Larkin Papers,* 3:281–84; Sutter to Thomas Larkin, November 5, 1845, in Hammond, *Larkin Papers,* 4:89; Sutter to Thomas Larkin, March 2, 1846, in Hammond, *Larkin Papers,* 4:218.

24. Kelley, *Battling the Inland Sea.*

25. Quaife, *Echoes of the Past,* 82–83.

26. Sutter, et al., *New Helvetia Diary,* 1, 9, 10, 11, 13, 15.

27. Sutter to Pierson B. Reading, May 10, 1845, JASC.

28. Sutter to John Marsh, May 17, 1845, JMC.

29. Sutter to Pierson B. Reading, May 11, 1845, JASC.

30. Sutter et al., *New Helvetia Diary,* 2.

31. Ibid., 10; Sutter to Thomas Larkin, November 5, 1845, in Hammond, *Larkin Papers,* 4:89–91.

32. Sutter et al., *New Helvetia Diary,* 12; Sutter, "Reminiscences," 133–36.

33. Castro, "Proclamation," November 11, 1845, CDFP.

34. Sutter, "Reminiscences," 136–37.

35. Ibid., 137–38.

36. Bancroft, *History of California,* 4:612–14.

37. Prudon quoted in *CLC,* 27–28.

38. *CLC,* 58–60.

39. Sutter to Thomas Larkin, November 14, 1845, in Hammond, *Larkin Papers,* 4:99.

40. Sutter to Victor Prudon, January 1, 1846, JASC.

41. Sutter, "Reminiscences," 138.

42. Larkin, "Description of California," April 20, 1846, in Hammond, *Larkin Papers,* 4:333.

43. Bancroft, *History of California,* 4:188, n. 62, states that a bargain for the purchase of the mortgage on New Helvetia was struck between Russian-American Company and Mexican negotiators but that war broke out before the deal could be consummated.

CHAPTER 13

1. Frémont, *Report of the Exploring Expedition to the Rocky Mountains in the Year 1842, and to Oregon and North California in the Years 1843–44.*

2. Chaffin, *Pathfinder,* 240–49.

3. J. J. Abert to Frémont, February 12, 1845, in Jackson and Spence, *Expeditions of John Charles Frémont,* 1:396.

4. "Roster of the 1845–47 Expedition," in Jackson and Spence, *Expeditions of John Charles Frémont,* 2:487–88.

5. Chaffin, *Pathfinder,* 252–61, 272–74.

6. Charles M. Weber to John Marsh, July 20, 1845, and Weber to Marsh, November 25, 1845, CMWP.

7. Thomas J. Farnham to John Marsh, July 6, 1845, JMC.

8. Lansford Hastings to John Marsh, March 26, 1846, JMC; Bagley, *Scoundrel's Tale,* 83.

9. Spence, "Introduction," in Hastings, *Emigrant's Guide to Oregon and California,* v–ix; Andrews, "The Ambitions of Lansford W. Hastings," 473–91; Bagley, *Scoundrel's Tale,* 75–104. Bagley outlines a circumstantial and inconclusive case for a "plot" to conquer California involving Farnham, Hastings, Samuel Brannan, the Mormon Church, and important politicos of the time.

10. Charles Weber to John Marsh, November 25, 1845, CMWP.

11. Sutter et al., *New Helvetia Diary,* 14, 16; Bidwell, "Fremont in the Conquest of California," 518.

12. Bidwell, "Frémont in the Conquest of California," 518.

13. Sutter et al., *New Helvetia Diary,* 17.

14. Sutter to Mariano Vallejo, December 10, 1845, JASC.

15. Sutter to Thomas Larkin, December 22, 1845, in Hammond, *Larkin Papers,* 4:127.

16. Sutter to Vallejo, December 10, 1845, JASC.

17. "Agreement of Willard Buzzell to Work Leidesdorff's Farm," April 12, 1845, WLP.

18. Sutter, "Reminiscences," 138–39.

19. Sutter et al., *New Helvetia Diary,* 23; quotation from Sutter, "Reminiscences," 139–40.

20. Sutter to John Marsh, January 31, 1846, JMC.

21. Sutter et al., *New Helvetia Diary,* 19.

22. Sutter, "General Sutter's Diary," 15.

23. Hastings, *Emigrant's Guide,* 137.

24. John A. Sutter to William Hartnell, December 13, 1844, JASC; Spence, "Introduction," v–ix; Andrews, "The Ambitions of Lansford W. Hastings," 473–91.

25. Hastings to Marsh, March 26, 1846, JMC.

26. Sutter to Marsh, January 31, 1846, JMC.

27. DeVoto, *The Year of Decision, 1846.*

28. Thomas Larkin to Hiram Grimes, January 13, 1846, in Hammond, *Larkin Papers,* 4:162.

29. Sutter to Marsh, January 31, 1846, JMC.

30. Thomas Larkin to Sutter, November 12, 1845, in Hammond, *Larkin Papers,* 4:98.

31. Larkin, "Description of California," in Hammond, *Larkin Papers,* 4:333.

32. Sutter to Thomas Larkin, November 5, 1845, in Hammond, *Larkin Papers,* 4:90 (emphasis in original).

33. Except where otherwise noted, the account of Frémont's movements near Monterey is based on Chaffin, *Pathfinder,* 282–88; and Harlow, *California Conquered,* 62–73.

34. Sutter et al., *New Helvetia Diary,* 23.

35. Thomas Larkin to Abel Stearns, March 19, 1846, in Hammond, *Larkin Papers,* 4:260.

36. John C. Frémont to José Dolores Pacheco, February 21, 1846, in Jackson and Spence, *Expeditions of John Charles Frémont,* 2:67–68.

37. Sutter et al., *New Helvetia Diary,* 28.

38. Ibid., 31; Sutter, "General Sutter's Diary," 16.

39. "New Helvetia Account Book, 1845–1846," Sutter to Pierson B. Reading, January 12, 1846, January 29, 1846, February 8, 1846, February 20, 1846, all in PRC; Sutter to John Marsh, January 31, 1846, JMC.

40. Sutter to Pío Pico, March 2, 1846, CDFP.

41. Sutter et al., *New Helvetia Diary,* 24–30; Sutter, "Reminiscences," 180.

42. Sutter et al., *New Helvetia Diary,* 31.

43. Sutter to John Marsh, April 3, 1846, JMC.

44. Ibid.

45. Sutter, "Reminiscences," 74.

46. Hastings to Marsh, March 23, 1846, JMC; Sutter to Antonio Suñol, April 17, 1846, JASC.

47. Sutter to José Castro n.d. [May 12, 1846], CDFP. Sutter refers to a letter that he sent to Castro in April that has not come to light.

48. Sutter, "Reminiscences," 144.

CHAPTER 14

1. Except as otherwise noted, the essential story of Frémont, Gillespie, the Bear Flag Revolt, and the California Battalion is based on Chaffin, *Pathfinder,* 289–381; and Harlow, *California Conquered,* 74–218.

2. Sutter did not mention Lassen by name but seems to indicate that he was hired at the fort. Lassen may have been added to Gillespie's party at his ranch in the northern Sacramento Valley. Sutter to José Castro, [May 12, 1846,] CDFP.

3. Ibid.

4. Ibid.

5. Quaife, *Kit Carson's Autobiography,* 95.

6. Sutter to Castro, [May 12, 1846,] CDFP.

7. Jackson and Spence, *Expeditions of John Charles Frémont,* 2:110.

8. Frémont, *Memoirs of My Life,* 506.

9. Sutter, "General Sutter's Diary," 16–17; Sutter to William Leidesdorff, June 1, 1846, WLP; quotation in Sutter to William Leidesdorff, July 22, 1846, WLP.

10. Frémont, *Memoirs of My Life,* 502.

11. Sutter, "Diary," 16–17.

12. Quotation from ibid., 17; Sutter et al., *New Helvetia Diary,* 41.

13. Sutter to Leidesdorff, July 22, 1846, WLP.

14. Sutter, "Reminiscences," 147.

15. Bidwell, "Frémont in the Conquest of California," 520.

16. Sutter to William Leidesdorff, June 28, 1846, WLP.

17. Sutter, "Reminiscences," 149.

18. John B. Sloat, "To the People of California," FSP.

19. Frémont to Thomas Hart Benton, July 25, 1846, in Jackson and Spence, *Expeditions of John Charles Frémont,* 2:184.

20. Sutter, "Reminiscences," 151.

21. Vallejo to Frémont, [July 11, 1846,] in Jackson and Spence, *Expeditions of John Charles Frémont,* 2:171–72.

22. Frémont to Edward Kern, July 12, 1846, in Jackson and Spence, *Expeditions of John Charles Frémont,* 2:173.

23. Mariano Vallejo to Francisca Vallejo, July 12, 1846, PM, S–Z.

24. Rosenus, *General M. G. Vallejo,* 166.

25. Ibid., 155.

26. Mariano Vallejo to Juan Bandini, March 28, 1847, CDFP.

27. Sutter never mentioned Kern in his "Reminiscences."

28. Sutter to William Leidesdorff, August 14, 1846, WLP.

29. Hine, *In the Shadow of Frémont,* 33–34.

30. Sutter et al., *New Helvetia Diary,* 43.

31. Sutter to William Leidesdorff, July 22, 1846, WLP.

32. Sutter to William Leidesdorff, August 4, 1846, JASP.

33. Quotation in Jonathan Misroon to Edward Kern, August 8, 1846, FSP. See also Misroon to Kern, August 16, 1846, FSP.

34. Bryant, *What I Saw in California,* 246–47.

35. Sutter to William Leidesdorff, August 18, 1846, WLP.

36. Sutter to William Leidesdorff, October 8, 1846, WLP.

37. Sutter to William Heath Davis, August 14, 1846, uncatalogued new acquisition, CSL-CR.

38. Sutter to William Leidesdorff, August 6, 1846, WLP.

39. William Buzzell to William Leidesdorff, February 3, 1846, WLP.

40. For examples, see Pierson B. Reading to William Leidesdorff, March 17, 1846; Sutter to William Leidesdorff, July 1, 1846; and September 11, 1846, all in WLP.

41. Several visitors mentioned a scalp, or perhaps a withered head, above the fort's gate, but none gave the original owner's name. It may be that Sutter routinely mounted the heads of his Indian adversaries. See, for example, Revere, *Naval Duty in California,* 126.

42. Sarah Ide quoted in Hussey and Ames, "California Preparations to Meet the Walla Walla Invasion, 1846," 9.

43. Bryant, *What I Saw in California,* 273–74.

44. John Montgomery to Edward Kern, September 10, 1846, FSP.

45. Revere, *Naval Duty in California,* 126–27.

46. Ibid., 130–31.

47. Ibid., 131.

48. Warren Revere to Edward Kern, October 17, 1846, FSP.

49. John Montgomery to Edward Kern, October 15, 1846, FSP.

50. Revere to Kern, October 17, 1846, FSP (emphasis in original).

51. A proposal signed by Edwin Bryant et al., October 28, 1846, FSP.

52. Sutter, "Reminiscences," 153.

53. George McKinstry to Pierson B. Reading, November 2, 1846, PRC.

54. Sutter, "Reminiscences," 153.

55. McKinstry to Reading, November 2, 1846, PRC.

56. Sutter, "Reminiscences," 154.

57. Bryant, *What I Saw in California,* 359.

58. "Muster Roll of Company H," February 8, 1847, T135.

59. Sutter to Antonio Suñol, November 12, 1846, JASC.

60. Dillon, *Fool's Gold,* 255.

61. For an approximate accounting of Sutter's payments, see Bancroft, *History of California,* 4:187–89. See also E. V. Sutter, "The Russo-Sutter Title Again," *Sacramento Union,* July 9, 1860, 1.

62. Sutter to Washington A. Bartlett, December 9, 1846, JASC.

63. Sutter to Washington A. Bartlett, November 10, 1846, JASC; Sutter to Bartlett, December 9, 1846, JASC.

64. *California Star,* April 10, 1847, 4.

65. Sutter, "Reminiscences," 156.

66. Bancroft, *History of California,* 4:725, 5:675.

CHAPTER 15

1. I follow the Donner Party story as told in King, *Winter of Entrapment.* Relevant documents are found in Morgan, *Overland in 1846.*

2. Sutter, "Reminiscences," 157.

3. Sutter et al., *New Helvetia Diary,* 46, 69–71.

4. John C. Buchanan to James F. Reed, May 2, 1847, PM, A–H.

5. McGlashan, *History of the Donner Party,* 204.

6. Chaffin, *Pathfinder,* 367–77.

7. Daniel Sill et al. to the commander of U.S. forces at New Helvetia, February 28, 1847, FSP.

8. George McKinstry to J. B. Hale, March 13, 1847, M210.

9. Sutter et al., *New Helvetia Diary,* 53.

10. Hurtado, *Indian Survival,* 86–92.

11. Stephen Watts Kearny to Sutter, April 7, 1847, M182.

12. Stephen Watts Kearny to Mariano Vallejo, April 14, 1847, M182.

13. Sutter to Stephen Watts Kearny, May 27, 1847, C-A, 63:175.

14. Sutter et al., *New Helvetia Diary,* 50.

15. Quotation from Sutter, "Reminiscences," 156; Sutter et al., *New Helvetia Diary,* 51.

16. Sutter et al., *New Helvetia Diary,* 51.

17. Ibid.; Edward Kern to his commander, March 30, 1847, FSP; Miller, *Prophetic Worlds,* 104, 113.

18. Hurtado, *Indian Survival,* 91–93.

19. The informant's arrival on July 7 is reported in Sutter et al., *New Helvetia Diary,* 57. Details of the assault are in Sutter to Richard Barnes Mason, July 12, 1847, in U.S. President, *Message from the President,* 351.

20. There is some confusion about the identity of these Indians. The Cosumnes River was traditional Miwok country, and the Yusumne Nisenans lived to the north on Weber Creek. By 1847 Sutter had driven the Miwoks to the south and replaced the Cosumnes with his dependable Nisenan friends and allies. Cf. Phillips, *Indians and Intruders,* 145; Bennyhoff, *Ethnogeography of the Plains Miwok,* 96.

21. Sutter to Mason, July 12, 1847, in U.S. President, *Message from the President,* 351.

22. Bennyhoff, *Ethnogeography of the Plains Miwok,* 32–36, 97–107.

23. Richard Barnes Mason to Sutter, July 21, 1847, M182.

24. "The Indians Again," *California Star,* July 24, 1847, 2.

25. Captain Joseph Folsom to Mason, August 15, 1847, C-A 63:90.

26. "Proclamation of Governor Richard B. Mason," August 19, 1847, M182.

27. Mason to Vallejo and Sutter, August 19, 1847, M182.

28. Sutter et al., *New Helvetia Diary,* 73–74. On measles, see Heizer, "Walla Walla Indian Expeditions," 4.

29. Sutter et al., *New Helvetia Diary,* 58–101.

30. Sutter to William Leidesdorff, September 10, 1847, WLP.

31. Sutter et al., *New Helvetia Diary,* 81.

32. Ibid., 87.

33. Henry W. Halleck to Mariano Vallejo, September 10, 1847, M182. On Boggs, see Bancroft, *History of California,* 2:722.

34. Lilburn Boggs and Mariano Vallejo to Mason, October 30, 1847, C-A 63:124–26.

35. Mariano Vallejo to Richard Mason, October 30, 1847, C-A 63:94–97.

36. Sutter, "Reminiscences," 161; Sutter, "The Discovery of Gold in California," 194.

37. Cox, *Mills and Markets,* 21–23.

38. Sutter, "Reminiscences," 110.

39. Bigler and Bagley, *Army of Israel,* 17–29; Owens, *Gold Rush Saints,* 32–34.

40. Owens, *Gold Rush Saints,* 61–62.

41. Gudde, *Bigler's Chronicle of the West,* 70.

42. Owens, *Gold Rush Saints,* 98.

43. James S. Brown, quoted in ibid., 98.

44. Sutter et al., *New Helvetia Diary,* 72. The connection between the Mormons' arrival at the fort and the signing of the sawmill partnership was first pointed out in Owens, *Gold Rush Saints,* 93, n. 2.

45. Sutter, "Reminiscences," 160.

46. Sutter et al., *New Helvetia Diary,* 73.

47. Bigler, *The Gold Discovery Journal of Azariah Smith,* 102–103; and Gudde, *Bigler's Chronicle,* 78–79.

48. Bigler and Bagley, *Army of Israel,* 409.

49. James S. Brown, quoted in Owens, *Gold Rush Saints,* 98.

50. Owens, *Gold Rush Saints,* 91–124.

51. Sutter et al., *New Helvetia Diary,* 82.

52. Azariah Smith, for example, reported the classic malaria symptoms of fever and chills: Bigler, *Gold Discovery Journal of Azariah Smith,* 105. See also Owens, *Gold Rush Saints,* 87–88.

53. Sutter to Mariano G. Vallejo, October 21, 1847, JASC.

54. Sutter to Thomas Larkin, October 29, 1847, in Hammond, *Larkin Papers,* 7:46–47.

55. Marshall quoted in Owens, *Gold Rush Saints,* 108.

56. Sutter, "Reminiscences," 164. Sutter's accounts of his meeting were well practiced; in later years he may have improved the story by emphasizing the stormy weather for dramatic effect. Sutter et al., *New Helvetia Diary,* 113, indicates that the weather was blustery with intermittent rain but that the rain held off from the time of Marshall's departure. Cf. Sutter, "Reminiscences," 164; Sutter, "Discovery of Gold," 194.

57. Sutter, "Reminiscences," 165.

58. Ibid., 166.

59. Ibid.

60. Ibid., 167.

61. Cf. Sutter et al., *New Helvetia Diary,* 113; Sutter, "Reminiscences," 167–68; Sutter, "Discovery of Gold," 195. Sutter's "General Sutter's Diary," 21, first published in 1851 and evidently based on his journal, accurately states that he went to the mill on February 1.

62. Owens, *Gold Rush Saints,* 111–13.

63. Marshall quoted in ibid., 114.

64. Bigler quoted in ibid.

65. Bigler, *Gold Discovery Journal of Azariah Smith,* 109–10.

66. Sutter, "Discovery of Gold," 196.

67. Brown quoted in Owens, *Gold Rush Saints,* 112–13.

68. Sutter to Richard Mason, February 22, 1848, with enclosure [lease with Yalisumnis dated January 1, 1848], GMC; Owens, *Gold Rush Saints,* 114. See also Hurtado, *Indian Survival,* 102–103.

69. Sutter, "Discovery of Gold," 196.

70. Sutter, "Reminiscences," 168.

CHAPTER 16

1. Sutter to Mariano Vallejo, February 10, 1848, JASC.

2. Wilbur, *Pioneer at Sutter's Fort,* 117.

3. Sutter, "Reminiscences," 171.

4. Ibid., 172.

5. Ibid., 173.

6. Bancroft, *History of California,* 43–44; Owens, *Gold Rush Saints,* 114; Sherman, *Memoirs,* 1:40.

7. Sherman, *Memoirs,* 1:40–41.

8. This letter has not come to light. Sherman recalled writing it for the governor twenty-seven years later.

9. Federal laws regarding mining on the public domain were in a muddle. Until 1847 the government leased lands for mining base metals such as lead; but this proved unsatisfactory, and Congress provided for the sale of lands with base metals. Presumably federal leases were still available for precious metals in early 1848, but neither Sutter nor Mason seemed to know anything about mineral land law. Ellison, "The Mineral Land Question in California, 1848–1866," 71.

10. Sutter to Richard Mason, February 22, 1848, GMC.

11. Sutter et al., *New Helvetia Diary,* 105–25.

12. Sutter to Jared Sheldon, March 24, 1848, PM.

13. "Received [by the launch] letter of Mr McKinstry," in Sutter et al., *New Helvetia Diary,* 123.

14. Richard Mason to Sutter, March 5, 1848, M182.

15. Hurtado, "Clouded Legacy," 90–117.

16. Sutter et al., *New Helvetia Diary,* 122–24.

17. Ibid., 121.

18. Sutter quoted in "General Sutter's Diary," 21; Sutter et al., *New Helvetia Diary,* 127.

19. Sutter et al., *New Helvetia Diary,* 128–29.

20. Sutter, "Reminiscences," 162.

21. Brown quoted in Owens, *Gold Rush Saints,* 123; Gudde, *Bigler's Chronicle,* 107; Bigler, *Gold Discovery Journal of Azariah Smith,* 113 (Bigler claims that Sutter paid in livestock but offers only Sutter's statement as proof); Sutter, "Discovery of Gold," 196–97.

22. Bagley, *Scoundrel's Tale,* 258.

23. Sutter et al., *New Helvetia Diary,* 128–29; Bagley, *Scoundrel's Tale,* 262.

24. E. C. Kemble to Mr. Hittell, October 6, 188[?],PM, I–R.

25. Sutter to William Leidesdorff, March 15, 1848, WLP.

26. Gudde, *Bigler's Chronicle,* 108.

27. Brannan quoted in Cooper's recollection, in Bagley, *Scoundrel's Tale,* 265.

28. Bigler, *Gold Discovery Journal of Azariah Smith,* 115–16.

29. Sutter et al., *New Helvetia Diary,* 134.

30. Cooper quoted in Bagley, *Scoundrel's Tale,* 266.

31. Hawkins quoted in Bagley, *Scoundrel's Tale,* 266.

32. Owens, *Gold Rush Saints,* 132.

33. Sutter et al., *New Helvetia Diary,* 114.

34. Ibid., 122.

35. "Letter from John Bidwell," *Sacramento Themis,* December 21, 1889, 4.

36. Wilbur, *Pioneer at Sutter's Fort,* 67–68.

37. Ibid., 74–75.

38. Sutter et al., *New Helvetia Diary,* 136–38.

39. Sutter, "General Sutter's Diary," 23.

40. Lansford Hastings to George McKinstry, June 1, 1848, GMC.

41. Sutter, "Diary," 21.

42. Ibid., 23.

43. Sutter, "Discovery of Gold," 197–98.

44. Sutter, "Diary," 21.

45. James A. Hardie to William T. Sherman, May 28, 1848, M210.

46. George McKinstry, "Early Days of California: The Fourth of July Celebration at Sutter's Fort in 1848—General Sherman's 'Memoirs,'" *San Francisco Daily Alta,* September 30, 1875, 6; Sherman, *Memoirs,* 49.

47. Sherman, *Memoirs,* 52.

48. Ibid., 53.

49. Hurtado, "Clouded Legacy," 90–117.

50. Sherman, *Memoirs,* 54.

51. Richard Mason to R. Jones, August 17, 1848, in U.S. President, *Message of the President,* 56–64.

52. Wilbur, *Pioneer at Sutter's Fort,* 129.

53. Ibid., 130–34.

54. Ibid., 144.

55. Ibid.

56. Sutter, "Discovery of Gold," 197.

57. Wilbur, *Pioneer at Sutter's Fort,* 139, 143–45 (quotation at 144).

58. Ibid., 145.

CHAPTER 17

1. Sutter, *The Sutter Family,* 90.

2. *Herald* quoted in Watson, "Herald of the Gold Rush," 298.

3. Ottley, "Biography of John A. Sutter, Jr.," 9–10.

4. Sutter, *Sutter Family,* 81–82.

5. Ibid., 83.

6. Ibid., 84.

7. Ibid., 85–86.

8. Ibid., 87.

9. According to August's reckoning, the papers were drawn and signed in late September or early October. The documents are dated October 14, 1848, SacCo-D, A:1–4.

10. Wilbur, *Pioneer at Sutter's Fort,* 147.

11. Ibid., 148.

12. Ibid., 149.

13. Sutter, *Sutter Family,* 89.

14. Sutter, "Discovery of Gold," 197–98.

15. Wilbur, *Pioneer at Sutter's Fort,* 153–56.

16. Bagley, *Scoundrel's Tale,* 272.

17. Sherman, *Memoirs,* 1:64.

18. Sutter, "Discovery of Gold," 198.

19. Sutter, *Sutter Family,* 89.

20. Parsons, *The Life and Adventures of James W. Marshall,* 130.

21. Gay, *James W. Marshall,* 259.

22. Wilbur, *Pioneer at Sutter's Fort,* 162.

23. Sutter, *Sutter Family,* 91; "a.s.f." means "and so forth."

24. The original plat of plan of Sacramento is reproduced in Reps, *The Forgotten Frontier,* 62; Owens, "Begun by Gold," 332–33.

25. Burnett, *Recollections of an Old Pioneer,* 1–96.

26. Ibid., 287.

27. Franklin, "A Forgotten Chapter in California History," 319–24.

28. See, for example, John A. Sutter, Jr., to Pierre B. Cornwall, January 4, 1849, SacCo-D, A:4.

29. Sutter, *Sutter Family,* 92.

30. Sutter, "Reminiscences," 181.

31. Peter Burnett to John A. Sutter, Jr., January 18, 1894, JASC JR, Box 315.

32. I derive these figures from Burnett to Sutter, January 18, 1894, JASC JR, and Sutter, *Sutter Family,* 94–95. The two sources do not agree in all cases, and I give Burnett the benefit of the doubt because he had recourse to his records while Sutter Jr. wrote from memory.

33. Lansford Hastings to George McKinstry, December 20, 1848, GMC.

34. Sutter, *Sutter Family,* 94.

35. Ibid., 96.

36. "Agreement with John McDougal Concerning Lease of Sutter's Ferry," March 6, 1849, JASC.

37. George McKinstry to John Bidwell, March 20, 1849, PM, Bidwell.

38. John A. Sutter, Jr., to Mariano Vallejo, April 23, 1849, JASC.

39. Henry A. Schoolcraft to Pierson B. Reading, May 24, 1849, PM, Schoolcraft.

40. Sutter, *Sutter Family,* 99.

41. Schoolcraft to Reading, May 24, 1849, PM, Schoolcraft.

42. Eifler, *Gold Rush Capitalists,* 52.

43. Sutter, *Sutter Family,* 98. It is difficult to establish the chronology of these events, but late May seems most likely.

44. Ibid., 99.

45. The actual number of lots transferred to Brannan is difficult to determine. Schoolcraft to Reading, May 24, 1849 (PM, Schoolcraft), says, "Branon [*sic*] has made [Burnett] a deed of about 1/4 of his 502 lots," but he does not say why. Schoolcraft's cryptic statement raises the question of Burnett's role in this deal. Eifler, *Gold Rush Capitalists,* 53, estimates that August signed over five hundred lots that amounted to about 80 percent of all Sacramento lots, but this cannot be. There were roughly seven hundred and fifty blocks between A, Y, Front, and 31st Streets with eight lots per block or approximately six thousand lots. By this crude reckoning, Brannan received about 8 percent of the city lots.

46. Sutter, *Sutter Family,* 100.

47. Wilbur, *Pioneer at Sutter's Fort,* 193.

48. Sutter, *Sutter Family,* 97.

49. Sutter to Archibald Peachy and Fredrick Billings, November 28, 1849, WLP.

50. William Heath Davis to David Carter, December 6, 1848, WHDC-L, 1:113–15.

51. For example, see *Suel Foster* v. *John A. Sutter,* SAMC-J, A:103.

52. Eifler, *Gold Rush Capitalists,* 59; Schweikert and Doti, "From Hard Money to Branch Banking," 209–32.

53. SAMC-POA, A:440–42. This power of attorney was dated July 27, but Sutter's agents evidently began selling lots in late May.

54. Sutter, "Reminiscences," 179.

55. Burnett, *Recollections*, 341.

56. Franklin, "Forgotten Chapter," 323.

57. Sutter, *Sutter Family*, 94.

58. Burnett, *Recollections*, 334.

59. William Prince to Charlotte Prince, November 27, 1849, WRPC (emphasis in original).

CHAPTER 18

1. For Mexican and foreigner population figures, see Bancroft, *History of California*, 5:643. On the Indian population, see Cook, *The Population of the California Indians, 1769–1970*, 43, 44, 59, 65.

2. DeBow, *Statistical View of the United States*, 200–201.

3. Unruh, *The Plains Across*, 120.

4. Paul, *California Gold*, 349.

5. Hurtado, *Intimate Frontiers*, 75–113.

6. Soulé, Gihon, and Nisbet, *Annals of San Francisco*, 666.

7. Gay, *James W. Marshall*, 256.

8. Osgood quoted in ibid., 257.

9. Bestor quoted in ibid.

10. Gay, *James W. Marshall*, 259–60; Dunbar, *The Romance of the Age*, 118.

11. For Marshall's account, see Dunbar, *Romance of the Age*, 118; see also Parsons, *The Life and Adventures of James W. Marshall*, 75–85; Gay, *James W. Marshall*, 255–62; Rawls, "Gold Diggers," 38–39.

12. William M. Case quoted in Gay, *James W. Marshall*, 262.

13. Harlow, *California Conquered*, 325–30; Grivas, *Military Governments in California*, 187–98, 211; Eifler, *Gold Rush Capitalists*, 14.

14. Wilbur, *Pioneer at Sutter's Fort*, 206.

15. Ibid.

16. *Alta California*, August 31, 1849, 2.

17. Sutter, "Reminiscences," 190. The namesake of Colton Hall was Walter Colton, a chaplain aboard the U.S. frigate *Congress*. He founded the state's first newspaper, the *Californian*, and edited it with Robert Semple.

18. Taylor, *El Dorado*, 1:149.

19. Browne, *Report of the Debates of the Convention of California on the Formation of the State Constitution*, 7.

20. Gwin, quoted in ibid., 11.

21. Demographic data are drawn from Browne, *Report of the Debates*, 478–79.

22. Ibid., 478.

23. Ibid., 18.

24. Ibid., 75.

25. Ibid., 97.

26. Ibid., 157.

27. Ibid., 158.

28. Ibid., 306.

29. Ibid.

30. "Constitution of the State of California," in ibid., iv.

31. Hastings and Sutter quoted in Browne, *Report of the Debates*, 187.

32. Taylor, *El Dorado*, 1:160.

33. Ibid., 1:161.

34. Ibid., 1:164.

35. Ibid., 1:165. Sutter's speech also appears in Browne, *Report of the Debates*, 476.

36. Sutter, "Reminiscences," 192.

37. Ibid., 191.

38. Browne, *Report of the Debates,* 291.

39. Barker, *Memoirs of Elisha Oscar Crosby,* 39.

40. Zollinger, *Sutter,* 284; Dillon, *Fool's Gold,* 316–19.

41. Taylor, *El Dorado,* 1:158.

42. Sutter, "Reminiscences," 192.

43. "Sacramento City, Oct. 31, 1849," *Alta California,* November 8, 1849, 2.

44. "The Election—Results," *Alta California,* November 15, 1849, 2.

45. "Editorial Correspondence, Sacramento City, Nov. 12," *Alta California,* November 15, 1849, 2.

46. Buck, *A Yankee Trader in the Gold Rush,* 52.

47. Sutter, "Reminiscences," 192.

48. Ibid., 193.

49. "Election Returns," *Alta California,* November 22, 1849, 2.

50. Sutter to Bennet Riley, December 11, 1849, JASP.

CHAPTER 19

1. Colton, *Three Years in California,* 24.

2. The Sacramento squatters' riot has captured the attention of several historians—most notably, Royce, "The Squatter Riot of '50 in Sacramento," 225–46; and Pisani, "Squatter Law in California," 277–310; Eifler, *Gold Rush Capitalists,* 81–161 and passim.

3. John Bidwell to George McKinstry, February 16, 1850, GMC.

4. John Bidwell to George McKinstry, February 25, 1850, GMC.

5. John Bidwell to George McKinstry, June 25, 1850, GMC.

6. Wilbur, *Pioneer at Sutter's Fort,* 211–14.

7. "Local Matters," *California Alta,* January 24, 1850, 2.

8. Culver, *The Sacramento City Directory,* 72.

9. Wilbur, *Pioneer at Sutter's Fort,* 215.

10. Ibid., 216.

11. Sutter to John Bidwell, February 1, 1850, PM, Bidwell.

12. Wilbur, *Pioneer at Sutter's Fort,* 207.

13. Sutter to John Marsh, April 3, 1846, JMC.

14. Kerr, "An Irishman in the Gold Rush," 172.

15. Washington, "Noblet Herbert to Mrs. John Augustine Washington," 300–301.

16. Wilbur, *Pioneer at Sutter's Fort,* 245.

17. Ibid., 251.

18. Ibid., 218–19, 244.

19. Kerr, "An Irishman in the Gold Rush," 172.

20. SAMC-POA, A:23–24, 34, 113–14, 153–54, 222–24, 507.

21. Sutter, "Reminiscences," 179.

22. "Captain John A. Sutter," *Sacramento Daily Union,* April 18, 1851, 3.

23. Sutter to Bidwell, February 1, 1850, PM, Bidwell.

24. *Suel Foster* v. *John A. Sutter,* SAMC-J, A:103.

25. Sutter, "Reminiscences," 183.

26. Indenture between John A. Sutter et al. and John Q. Packard and Edwards Woodruff, April 4, 1854, D–J.

27. Sutter, "Reminiscences," 182.

28. William Robert Prince to Charlotte Prince, August 18, 1850, WRPC.

29. J. T. Mott, n.d., MVSP.

30. Sutter, *Sutter Family,* 103.

31. Ibid., 104.

32. Wilbur, *Pioneer at Sutter's Fort,* 226.

33. Schläfli, "Five Letters of Gustav Friederich Schäfli," 21–58.

34. Plumbe quoted in *A Faithful Translation,* x.

35. *Sacramento Placer Times,* August 11, 1849, 2.

36. "A Squatter," *Sacramento Transcript,* June 4, 1850, 3.

37. G. E. F., "Communicated," *Sacramento Placer Times,* June 7, 1850, 4.

38. "The Excursion," *Sacramento Transcript,* June 4, 1850, 2.

39. Wilbur, *Pioneer at Sutter's Fort,* 244.

40. Ibid., 245.

41. Ibid., 246.

42. Sutter to the Secretary of the Interior, May 23, 1850, M234:32.

43. *Suel Foster* v. *John A. Sutter,* SAMC-J, A:103.

44. Chapters 54 and 77, State of California, *Statutes of California,* 1850, pp. 145–48, 190–96.

45. Thomas B. Eastland to Peter Burnett, May 15, 1850, and Thomas J. Green to Peter Burnett, May 16, 1850, in *California State Senate Journals* (1851), 767–68.

46. Hurtado, *Indian Survival,* 132–35.

47. Sutter, *Sutter Family,* 107.

48. Ibid.

49. Ibid., 108.

50. Ibid., 109.

51. Ibid., 110, n. 71.

52. Ibid., 112.

53. Ibid., 114.

54. Ibid., 37.

55. Ibid., 109.

56. These deeds are printed in *CLC,* 956–60.

57. Hussey, *Early Sacramento,* 7–32, 41.

58. Ibid., 41–42.

59. Ibid., 45.

60. Ibid., 46.

61. "Fourth of July," *Sacramento Transcript,* July 4, 1850, 3; A. Dusty Brick, "The Celebration at Brighton," *Sacramento Transcript,* July 6, 1850, 2; Joseph Clarence Tucker, *To the Golden Goal, and Other Sketches* (San Francisco: William Doxey, 1895), 203; Wells, *Walker's Expedition to Nicaragua,* 21, called Walker the "grey-eyed man of destiny."

62. Hussey, *Early Sacramento,* 69.

63. Eifler, *Gold Rush Capitalists,* 138–48.

64. Ibid., 149.

65. Ibid., 155.

66. The *San Francisco Alta,* August 6, 1850, 2, reprinted the *Placer Times* notice.

67. Hussey, *Early Sacramento,* 72.

68. Ibid., 73.

CHAPTER 20

1. Ellison, *A Self-Governing Dominion,* 98.

2. Ibid., 98–101.

3. Griswold del Castillo, *The Treaty of Guadalupe Hidalgo,* 72–77, 181–82, 189–90; Robinson, *Land in California,* 91–109.

4. "Hock Farm—Agriculture," *Sacramento Transcript,* May 25, 1850, 2.

5. John A. Sutter to James L. L. F. Warren, August 18, 1852, JLLWP.

6. Sutter to James L. L. F. Warren, October 9, 1853, and September 22, 1856, JLLWP.

7. Federal Manuscript Census, 1850, Population, Sutter County, California, CSL-CR.

8. [McKinstry], November 1846 [Population Enumeration of the Sacramento Valley], GAMP; 1852 California Special Census, Schedule I, Sutter County, CSL-CR.

9. Federal Manuscript Census, 1850, Agricultural Productions, Sutter County, CSL-CR.

10. "Hock Farm—Agriculture," *Sacramento Transcript,* May 25, 1850, 2.

11. Howard Joseph Sutter Hull to Allan R. Ottley, February 21, 1941, JASC JR.

12. Albert L. Hurtado, "Introduction," in Sutter, *Sutter Family,* xviii–xix. Allan Ottley, the editor of this book, decided that August's marriage to María was valid despite the fact that diligent searches in California and Mexico did not turn up any documentary proof. Several decades later August left María for a younger woman whom he married without legal difficulty, an unlikely series of events in a Catholic country. No divorce record has come to light, but there is a record of the "second" marriage.

13. Sutter, *Sutter Family,* 114–29.

14. Ibid., 116.

15. Ibid., 128.

16. Officer, *Hispanic Arizona, 1536–1856,* 270, 277, 304; O. Scroggs, *Filibusters and Financiers,* 18–30; Hittell, *History of California,* 3:727–55.

17. Field, *Personal Reminiscences of Early Days in California,* 79.

18. Scroggs, *Filibusters and Financiers,* 15–17, 31.

19. "Captain John A. Sutter," *Sacramento Union,* April 19, 1851, 3.

20. William Robert Prince to Charlotte Prince, March 24, 1851, WRPC.

21. SuC-M, A: 270–72, 275–77, 295–99, 303–306, 307–309, 311–13.

22. SuC-M, A:270–72.

23. Bidwell to Sutter, April 2, 1851, in Gillis and Magliari, *John Bidwell and California,* 114.

24. Sutter to Richard M. Kern, January 10, 1852, HM 20647.

25. "The Wedding," *Sacramento Union,* March 23, 1852, 2.

26. Huntley, *California,* 139–40.

27. Dawson and Ramey, "The Romances of Eliza Sutter," 13–14.

28. SuC-M, A:270–72, 275–77, 295–99, 303–306, 307–309, 311–13.

29. Hoffman, *Reports of Land Cases Determined in the United States District Court for the Northern District of California,* "Appendix," 13.

30. "Address on Agriculture Delivered at the American Theater, Sacramento, October 7, 1852," *Sacramento Union,* October 8, 1852, 2.

31. Sutter to James L. L. F. Warren, July 1, 1852, JLLWP.

32. "Festivities in Honor of Capt. Sutter," *San Francisco Alta,* October 5, 1852.

33. Dillon, *Fool's Gold,* 333–34.

34. Sutter to Richard M. Kern, January 10, 1852, HM 20647.

35. William Robert Prince to Charlotte Prince, March 29, 1851, WRPC.

36. George McKinstry to Edward M. Kern, December 23, 1851, FSP.

37. A. S. Bayley to Mr. Ralston (State Senate), April 29, 1852, Legislative Papers, LP:2042, CSA.

38. "Sutter's Fort State Historic Park," pamphlet distributed to visitors at the fort in 2003; "Some Unwritten History," *Themis,* November 30, 1889, 2.

CHAPTER 21

1. Sutter to John Bidwell, February 24, 1853, JBP.

2. SuC-D, C:250.

3. Sutter to Bidwell, February 24, 1853, JBP.

4. John A. and Anna Sutter to John Packard and Edwards Woodruff, Indenture, April 4, 1854, D-J.

5. Sutter to Bidwell, February 23, 1853, JBP.

6. For Sutter's commission see S/LP; *Sacramento Union,* February 25, 1853, 2.

7. Sutter was elected to his rank by the state legislature and commissioned by the governor, chapter 76, "An Act concerning the Organization of Militia," in State of California, *Statutes of California, 1850.*

8. Cf. chapter 54, "An Act concerning Volunteer or Independent Companies," and chapter 76, "An Act concerning the Organization of Militia," in State of California, *Statutes of California, 1850.*

9. Dayton, " 'Polished Boot and Bran New Suit,' " 321–27.

10. Kibbe, "Quartermaster and Adjutant General's Annual Report for 1853," Governors' Papers, 1:36, CSA.

11. Chapter 116, "An Act concerning the Organization of the Militia," in State of California, *Statutes of California, 1855.*

12. "Sutter and Staff," *Sacramento Union,* February 25, 1853, 2.

13. SAMC-POA, B:211–12.

14. W. S. Mesick for John Sutter to J. L. L. Warren, July 26, 1852, JLLWP.

15. Ottley, "Biography," 43.

16. Sutter, "Reminiscences," 204.

17. "Minutes, Constitution and Bylaws of the Marion Rifles," February 17, 1853, CSL-CR.

18. Dayton, " 'Polished Boot and Bran New Suit,' " 321–27.

19. "A Historical Relic," *Sacramento Union,* January 24, 1894, 2.

20. Sutter to James Warren, October 9, 1853, JLLWP.

21. "California Agricultural Society," *California Farmer and Journal of Useful Science,* January 5, 1854, 2.

22. Wells, *Walker's Expedition to Nicaragua,* 23.

23. T. Robinson Warren, quoted in Scroggs, *Filibusters and Financiers,* 32.

24. Wells, *Walker's Expedition,* 23–24; Scroggs, *Filibusters and Financiers,* 31–33.

25. Scroggs, *Filibusters and Financiers,* 34–48.

26. Wells, *Walker's Expedition,* 38–39.

27. "Trial of William Walker for Filibustering," *San Francisco Daily Alta,* October 19, 1854, 2; "Trial of William Walker for Filibustering," *San Francisco Daily Alta,* October 20, 1854, 2.

28. Sutter, *Sutter Family,* 128–29.

29. "Gen. J. A. Sutter," *California Farmer and Journal of Useful Science,* October 26, 1854, 134 (emphasis in original).

30. Sutter to J. W. Denver, July 6, 1854, JASP.

31. Wells, *Walker's Expedition.*

32. Sutter to James L. L. F. Warren, November 10, 1854, JLLWP.

33. Ottley, "Biography," 43.

34. Ibid., 43. SuC-D, F:24–25 has a copy of the deed for the San Francisco lot and other Sutter grants that Ottley apparently did not see.

35. *Sacramento Union,* October 1, 1856, 2.

36. *Sacramento Union,* October 6, 1856, 2.

37. *Sacramento Union,* October 7, 1856, 2.

38. Brannan et al. claimed that August never received this money, but they were interested in showing that Mesick was a swindler. August made no complaints against Mesick, and he was not shy about accusing others when he was wronged. Ottley, "Biography," 44–48, assumes that August did not receive this money.

39. Hoffman, *Reports of Land Cases,* "Appendix," 13.

40. *Woodruff and Packard* v. *John A. Sutter and Anna Sutter,* SAMC-J, A: 284.

41. SuC-D, D:321–23.

42. SuC-D, D:250–52; quotation from Colton, *Three Years in California,* 24.

43. Robinson, *Land in California,* 103.

44. Account Book for the Sutter Relief Fund, 1850, JASC; Dillon, *Fool's Gold,* 341.

45. Sutter to William Kibbe, September 7, 1855, AGLR.

46. Sutter to William Kibbe, October 12, 1855, AGLR.

47. Sutter to O. C. Pratt, December 29, 1855, JASP.

48. "More Recruits for Nicaragua," *San Francisco Herald,* January 5, 1856, 2.

49. Absalom [Deadrick], "The Experience of Samuel Absalom, Filibuster," 653.

50. Wells, *Walker's Expedition,* 104–105.

51. Unless otherwise noted, the account of Walker in Nicaragua is based on Scroggs, *Filibusters and Financiers.*

52. Ibid., 162–63.

53. "Visit to Hock Farm," *San Francisco Fireman's Journal and Military Gazette,* March 8, 1856, 1.

54. Sutter to Edward Kern, November 23, 1855, HM 20663.

55. Sutter to Thomas Henley, February 9, 1856, M234:35. See also John A. Sutter to John Bidwell, February 13, 1855, PM, Bidwell. For a detailed analysis of the Hok Indians, Sutter, and the Indian Office, see Hurtado, "Indians in Town and Country," 31–51.

56. Sutter to Thomas Henley, December 1, 1856, M234:235 (emphasis in original).

57. For an excellent firsthand account of the war by another junior officer from California, see Jamison, *With Walker in Nicaragua,* 70–162. Alphonse is mentioned on 124.

58. Sutter to Jasper O'Farrell, July 27, 1857, JASP.

59. Accounts of Alphonse's life are sparse, but sources in Nevada County seem to agree that he died of a disease contracted in Nicaragua. Tom Arden to Harry C. Peterson, April 17, 1940, Biographical Letter File, William Alphonse Sutter, CSL-CR; *Sacramento Union,* August 15, 1863, 2; *Grass Valley National,* August 18, 1863, 3; *Sacramento Union,* March 31, 1886, 4.

60. Scroggs, *Filibusters and Financiers,* 390–91.

61. Ibid., 392–93.

CHAPTER 22

1. Sutter to John Bidwell, February 13, 1855, PM, Bidwell.

2. "Visit to Hock Farm," *San Francisco Fireman's Journal and Military Gazette,* March 8, 1856, 1.

3. *California Farmer and Journal of Useful Science,* July 25, 1856, 1.

4. Gates, *California Ranchos and Farms, 1846–1862,* 41–74.

5. Sutter to John Bidwell, October 20, 1857, PM, Bidwell; "Transactions of the California State Agricultural Society," 167.

6. *CLC,* 266–67.

7. "Trustee Sale of Sutter Title," *Sacramento Union,* January 21, 1857, 2; "Sacramento, February 16th, 1857," *Sacramento Union,* February 17, 1857, 2; "That Sale," *Sacramento Union,* February 21, 1857, 2.

8. "Mark Garr, Sheriff of Sutter County, to John Q. Packard and Edwards Woodruff," November 26, 1857, D–J.

9. "The Pioneer Gen. Sutter," *California Farmer and Journal of Useful Science,* June 5, 1857, 164.

10. "His Homestead Gone," *San Francisco Daily Alta,* May 5, 1857, 2.

11. John A. Sutter et al. to John G. Packard and Edwards Woodruff, SuC-D, E: 202–207.

12. Sutter quoted in "Hock Farm Redeemed," *California Farmer and Journal of Useful Science,* October 9, 1857, 100.

13. "Hock Farm Redeemed," *California Farmer,* October 9, 1857, 100.

14. Sutter to P. B. Reading, May 2, 1857, PM, Sutter.

15. Sutter to John Bidwell, October 20, 1857, PM, Bidwell. See also Sutter to John Bidwell, October 21, 1857, PM, Bidwell.

16. Samuel McCullough to Caroline B. Pennoyer, January 31, 1858, McCullough Papers, HL.

17. Ibid.

18. Sutter, "Reminiscences," 178.

19. "The Sutter Grant Confirmed," *Sacramento Union,* March 15, 1859, 2.

20. *Sacramento Union,* April 1, 1859, 7.

21. *CLC,* 786.

22. Ibid., 767–87, 964–73; "The Sutter Survey," *Sacramento Union,* April 13, 1865, 1.

23. Sutter to Stephen Smith, September 10, 1843, and the response of Sutter and William Muldrow's lawyers to Curtis Tyler, n.d., CvS.

24. "Settler Excitement," *Sonoma County Journal,* June 3, 1859, 2.

25. *History and Examination of the Russian Lands.*

26. "The Russo–Sutter Title," *Sacramento Union,* June 25, 1860, 4.

27. "The Russo–Sutter Title Again," *Sacramento Union,* July 9, 1860, 1.

28. [Chamberlain,] *History of Yuba County, California,* 63.

29. "The Son of an Old Pioneer," *Oroville Weekly Union,* November 7, 1863, 2.

30. "Court Details," *San Francisco Daily Examiner,* January 9, 1868, 3.

31. "Hock Farm," *Marysville Daily Appeal,* April 23, 1860, 2 (emphasis in original).

32. Kennedy, *Population of the United States in 1860,* 26–27; Sutter to Dear Old Friend, May 31, 1880, S/LP.

33. Federal Manuscript Census, 1860, Sutter County, Population, 813.

34. Sutter to Dear Old Friend, May 31, 1880, S/LP.

35. Dawson and Ramey, "The Romances of Eliza Sutter," 2–16.

36. Federal Manuscript Census, 1860, Sutter County, Agricultural Productions, 21.

37. Sutter to Anna Eliza Engler, June 25, 1859, and September 28, 1859, SuC-D, F:191, 210.

38. Sutter et al. to Frederick Low, May 24, 1859, SuC-M, B:122–23.

39. Ottley, "Biography," 67, n. 217.

40. *Marysville Daily Appeal,* October 5, 1862, 2.

41. Dillon, *Fool's Gold,* 341.

42. Sutter to J. Neely Johnson, August 22, 1857, JASC.

43. Sutter to William Kibbe, June 7, 1861, JASC.

44. Commission for John A. Sutter, PM, Sutter.

45. Sutter to William Kibbe, December 17, 1861, JASC.

46. William Kibbe to John Downey, December 20, 1861, AGLR.

47. Kibbe to Lorenzo Hubbard, December 24, 1861, AGLR; Kibbe to H. W. Theall, January 6, 1862, AGLR. It is unclear whether Sutter's commission was actually delivered to him. If he was reappointed, he was a general without a command.

48. Birmann, *General Joh-Aug-Suter,* 5.

49. "Sutter County Organizes Cavalry," *Marysville Daily Appeal,* May 8, 1861, 2.

50. Sutter to Kibbe, June 7, 1861, JASC; Sutter to Dear Old Friend, May 31, 1880, S/LP.

51. "Colonel Sutter," *Grass Valley National,* August 18, 1863, 3.

52. Sutter to Dear Old Friend, May 31, 1880, S/LP.

53. "Died," *Sacramento Union,* August 15, 1863, 2; Tom Arden to Harry C. Peterson, April 6, 1940, April 9, 1940, April 17, 1940, Biographical Letter File, William Alphonse Sutter, CSL-CR.

54. "Gen. John A. Sutter," *California Farmer and Journal of Useful Science,* January 8, 1864, 172.

55. State of California, *California Statutes,* 1863–64, chapter 474, 532–33.

56. J. N. Bowman, "California Documents," CSA.

57. Sutter, "Reminiscences," 204.

58. August sent regular payments to his father for the care of his children in the 1870s and probably did so in the 1860s too. "John A. Sutter, Jr., Consul in Acapulco, His Account Current with Genl. John A. Sutter in Lititz," two framed pages on display, LHL.

59. Sutter to A. S. Long, February 5, 1863, M234:42.

60. Sutter to A. S. Long, March 22, 1863, M234:42.

61. Sutter to Long, February 5, 1863, M234:42.

62. See Sutter to A. S. Long, July 25, 1862, October 15, 1862, January 22, 1863, February 5, 1863, March 22, 1863, M234:42.

63. *San Francisco Daily Alta,* June 2, 1864, 1.

64. *San Francisco Daily Alta,* June 3, 1863, 1.

65. "General Sutter's Residence Destroyed," *Marysville Daily Appeal,* June 22, 1865, 3.

66. John Sutter and Anna Sutter, October 3, 1865, October 5, 1865, SAMC-POA, D:519–20.

CHAPTER 23

1. Frederick F. Low to the Senate and House of Representatives of the United States, October 6, 1865, JASC.

2. U.S. House of Representatives, Committee on Claims, *Petition of John A. Sutter,* 1–10.

3. Ibid., 5.

4. Ibid., 6.

5. Ibid., 7.

6. Sutter, "Reminiscences," 201.

7. *Times* quoted in Ottley, *John A. Sutter's Last Days,* 7.

8. Sutter, "Vier Briefe," 62–64 (quotation on 62).

9. Ibid., 60.

10. Ibid., 62.

11. Ibid., 66.

12. Phillip M. Hamer to Allan R. Ottley, August 27, 1941, JASC JR.

13. Sutter, "Vier Briefe," 62.

14. Ottley, "Biography," 60.

15. Sutter to Weyand (no first name), October 14, 1867, PM, Sutter.

16. Sutter, "Vier Briefe," 63.

17. "Local Man Knew Sutter," "Grave of General John A. Sutter," "West Again Seeks Body of Gen'l John A. Sutter," Sutter newspaper clippings, LCHS-IF.

18. Quoted from General Sutter Inn information flyer, Lititz, Pennsylvania.

19. SuC-D, E:250, J:77–78.

20. SuC-D, H:592.

21. H. M. Eberly, n.d., Sutter Files, LHS.

22. Sutter to Dear Old Friend, May 18, 1880, S/LP.

23. Sutter, "Vier Briefe," 66–67; "John Sutter House in National Register," Sutter newspaper clippings, LCHS-IF.

24. Landis, "The Life and Work of Gen. John A. Sutter," 292.

25. Sutter newspaper clippings, LCHS-IF.

26. "Local Man Knew Sutter," Sutter newspaper clippings, LCHS-IF.

27. Sutter, "Vier Briefe," 61.

28. Ibid., 67.

29. Ibid., 65.

30. Ibid., 64–65.

31. Ibid., 69.

32. "The General's Wife," typescript, Sutter Files, LHS.

33. "An Act to Appropriate Money for the Relief of General John A. Sutter," in State of California, *California Statutes,* 1869–70, chapter 1011, 762.

34. J. A. Sutter to Thomas B. Shannon, December 18, 1871, in "The Pioneer Pension Bills," *Sacramento Union,* January 18, 1872, 3.

35. "The Pioneer Pension Bills," *Sacramento Union,* January 18, 1872, 3.

36. "An Act to Appropriate Money for the Relief of General John A. Sutter," in State of California, *California Statutes,* 1871–72, chapter 24, 33–34.

37. Sutter, "Reminiscences," 204.

38. Ibid., 205.

39. State of California, *California Statutes,* 1873–74, chapter 354, 517.

40. Sutter, "Vier Briefe," 68; John Bigler to Secretary of State, September 6, 1855, AGLR.

41. Sutter, "Vier Briefe," 68.

42. John A. Sutter, Jr., to son, January 4, 1873, S/LP.

43. John A. Sutter, Jr., to son, November 7, 1873, S/LP.

44. John A. Sutter, Jr., to son, May 29, 1874, S/LP.

45. John A. Sutter, Jr., to son, August 19, 1874, S/LP.

46. John A. Sutter, Jr., to son, January 4, 1873, December 10, 1873, February 19, 1874, May 29, 1874, S/LP.

47. John A. Sutter, Jr., to son, March 29, 1874, S/LP.

48. John A. Sutter, Jr., to son, September 29, 1876, S/LP (emphasis in original).

49. "Sutter," *Sacramento Union,* July 5, 1880, 2; Sutter, *Sutter Family,* 133.

50. Howard Joseph Sutter Hull to Allan R. Ottley, February 21, 1941, JASC JR; Ottley, *John A. Sutter's Last Days,* 34, 36.

51. Bancroft, *Literary Industries,* 460–61.

52. Ibid., 462–63.

53. Ibid., 463.

54. Ibid., 464.

55. Ibid., 464–65.

56. Bancroft, *History of California,* 5:739.

57. William Tecumseh Sherman to Sutter, quoted in "Early Days in California," *San Francisco Daily Alta,* September 30, 1875, 6.

58. Emil Victor Sutter to George McKinstry, October 25, 1875, GMC.

59. Sutter, "Reminiscences," 197–98.

60. Ibid., 51.

61. Bigler, "General Johann August Sutter und Seine Beziehungen zu Burgdorf," 20.

62. Dillon, *Fool's Gold,* 348.

63. U.S. House of Representatives, Committee on Private Land-Claims, *A Bill for the Relief of John A. Sutter,* 1–2.

64. "General Sutter Caned," *San Jose Pioneer,* March 23, 1878, 2.

65. Sutter to Francis D. Clarke, January 20, 1879, JASC, Box 312.

66. Sutter, "Vier Briefe," 71.

67. Sutter to Smith Rudd, October 30, 1879, RM.

68. Sutter to Smith Rudd, December 26, 1879, RM.

69. Quoted in Zollinger, *Sutter,* 337.

70. Ottley, *John A. Sutter's Last Days,* 26.

71. Ibid., 22.

72. Ibid., 23.

73. Ibid., 43.

74. Ibid., 44.

75. Ibid., 45. The line should read, "He hates him / that would upon the rack of this tough world / Stretch him out longer."

76. "Sutter," *Sacramento Union,* July 5, 1880, 2.

EPILOGUE

1. E. V. Sutter to Smith Rudd, August 10, 1880, RM.

2. Ottley, *John A. Sutter's Last Days,* 36.

3. E. V. Sutter to Rudd, August 10, 1880, RM.

4. Ottley, *John A. Sutter's Last Days,* 36.

5. Ibid., 37.

6. John A. Sutter, Intestate Records, LCHS.

7. Will Book D:574, LCHS.

8. Anna Sutter, Intestate Records, LCHS.

9. "John Sutter House in National Register," news clipping, LCHS-IF.

10. Sutter, "Vier Briefe," 72.

11. E. V. Sutter to Annie [Eliza] Hull, January 25, 1881, S/LP.

12. "Suicide of E. V. Sutter," *Sacramento Union,* February 23, 1883, 3.

13. Ottley, "Biography," 71–72.

14. August Sutter to John A. Sutter III, May 29, 1874, S/LP.

15. Sutter, *The Sutter Family,* 133.

16. Lewis, *Sutter's Fort,* 201–204.

17. "John Sutter House in National Register," news clipping, LCHS-IF.

18. Laufkotter, *John A. Sutter and His Grants;* reprint, Owens, *John A. Sutter, Sr. and His Grants, by John A. Laufkotter.*

19. "Laufkotter's Last Shot," *Sacramento Bee,* clipping, December 12, 1884, 2; "A Plain, Unvarnished Tale," *Sacramento Bee,* October 23, 1884, 2; "The Sacramento Pioneer Comes Back as the Old Hunter and Trapper," *Sacramento Bee,* November 19, 1884, typescript, Kratschner File, MHS; "Was Sutter Overestimated," *Sacramento Bee,* March 28, 1885, typescript, Kratschner File, MHS; " 'Colonel' Obrist, Exploits of a Monumental Swindler of Early Days," *Sacramento Union,* July 21, 1889, 3; "Mr. Laufkotter Touches Up the So-Called Historians," *Sacramento Union,* July 28, 1889, 3; " 'Unwritten History,' Told by a Citizen Who Knew John A. Sutter," *Sacramento Union,* June 2, 1889, 3.

20. "Was Sutter Overestimated," *Sacramento Bee,* March 28, 1885, Kratschner File, MHS.

21. Associated Pioneers of the Territorial Days of California, *A Nation's Benefactor.*

22. John Bidwell to W. F. Swasey, March 12, 1881, in Grabhorn, *Pioneers of the Sacramento,* 26.

23. Ibid., 28.

24. Ibid., 29.

25. Revere, *Naval Duty,* 130–31.

26. Jason Probst, "Sutter über alles," *Sacramento News and Review,* May 6, 2004, 19.

Bibliography

MANUSCRIPTS

Bancroft Library, University of California, Berkeley
Alvarado, Juan Bautista. Historia de California. Translation in CDFP.
Archives of California.
Bidwell, John
Dictation, 1891. California, 1841–8: An Immigrant's Recollections of a Trip across the Plains and of Men and Events in Early Days.
Papers.
Botello, Narciso. Annals of Southern California, 1833–1847. Translation in CDFP.
Castro, Manuel. Account of Events in Alta California. Translation in CDFP.
Chamberlain, John. Memoirs of California since 1840.
Davis, William Heath. Collection. Letter Books.
DuFour, Clarence. Papers.
Fitch, Henry Delano. Papers.
Gonzales, Mauricio. Memoirs. Translation in CDFP.
McKinstry, George A. Papers.
Mott/von Schmidt Family. Papers.
Osio, Antonio María. History of California, 1815–1848. Translation in CDFP.
Pico, José de Jesús. Events Which Happened in California. Translation in CDFP.
Pioneer Recollections.
Powers, Stephen. Sketches of California Pioneers. John A. Sutter.
Prince, William Robert. Collection.
Reading, Alice M. Collection.
Reading, Pierson B. Collection.
Rico, Francisco. Suggestions for the History of Alta California. Translation in CDFP.
Streeter, William. Recollections of Historical Events in California, 1843–1878.
Sutter, John A.
Papers.
Reminiscences.

Sutter, John A., Jr. Letter.

Sutter Letters.

Sutter/Link Family Papers.

Torre, Francisco de la. Reminiscences. Translation in CDFP.

Vallejo, Mariano Guadalupe

 Documentos para la historia de California.

 Historical and Personal Memoirs Relating to Alta California.

Warren, J. L. L. Papers.

Weber, Charles Maria. Papers.

Weber Family Papers.

Wiggins, William L. Reminiscences.

Woodruff, Edwards. Pioneer Recollections.

Yates, John. Sketch of a Journey in the Year 1842 from Sacramento California through the Valley by John Yates of Yatestown.

California State Archives, Sacramento

 Adjutant General

  Letters Received, May 2, 1852, to April 30, 1864.

  Letters Sent, 1852–1864.

 Bowman, J. N.

  Bowman's Guide to Land Grants.

  California Documents.

 Governors' Papers.

 Legislative Papers.

 Secretary of State. Commissions. Military Papers Record Group. Adjutant General.

 Spanish Archives.

 Tyler Curtis, administrator v. *John A. Sutter, William Muldrow, et al.* 1859–61. County Records.

  Sonoma County, District Court (Old Series), nos. 914–17.

California State Library, Sacramento

 California Room

  Bidwell, John. Papers.

  Biographical Letter File.

  California Special Census, 1852.

  Decker-Jewett Papers.

  Federal Manuscript Census, 1850

   Agricultural Productions.

   Population.

  Federal Manuscript Census, 1860

   Agricultural Productions.

   Population.

  Fort Sutter Papers.

  Marsh, John. Collection.

  McKinstry, George. Collection.

  Miscellaneous. Box 23.

  New Acquisitions.

  Pioneer Manuscripts.

  Reading, Pierson B. Collection.

  Royce, Charles C. Scrapbook.

  Sutter Grant Maps.

  Sutter, John Augustus. Collection.

  Sutter, John A., Jr. Collection.

Law Library
   U.S. Supreme Court. California Land Claims, vol. 25, John A. Sutter.
Hawaii State Archives, Honolulu
   Foreign Office and Executive Papers, Series 402.
   French, William. Manuscript Collection 312
      Daily Journal, March 24, 1838–January 24, 1839.
      Ledger, April 6, 1838–April 12, 1840.
Henry E. Huntington Library, San Marino, California
   Fort Sacramento Papers.
   Huntington Manuscripts. 48987, 20647, 20663, 43207.
   Leidesdorff, William. Papers.
   McCullough, Samuel. Papers.
   Stearns, Abel. Papers.
   Thompson and West Papers. Wilson, Benjamin D. Private History of John A. Sutter.
Jackson County Court House, Clerk, Independence, Missouri
   Deeds. Book E.
Jackson County Records Center, Independence, Missouri
   Jackson County Court Records. Case No. 440.
Lancaster County Historical Society, Lancaster, Pennsylvania
   Information File. Sutter newspaper clippings.
   Intestate Records.
   Wills. Book D.
Lilly Library, Indiana University, Bloomington
   Rudd, Smith. Manuscripts.
Lititz Historical Society, Lititz, Pennsylvania
   Sutter Files.
Missouri Historical Society, St. Louis
   Kretschmer, M. A. The Historical Chronology of a Missouri Pioneer Family: Laufkotter,
      Kretschmer, Frederitzi, 1833–1999.
   Naturalization Papers.
   Sappington, John. Account Book.
   Sublette Papers.
National Archives, Washington, D.C.
   Letters Sent by the Governors and Secretary of State of California, 1847–1848. National Ar-
      chives, Records of the United States Army Continental Commands, 1821–1920. RG 393,
      Microfilm Publication M182.
   Office of Indian Affairs. Letters Received, 1849–1890, California Superintendency. RG 75,
      National Archives Microfilm M234.
   Records of the General U.S. General Accounting Office. Selected Records of the General
      Accounting Office Relating to the Frémont Expeditions and the California Battalion, 1842–
      1890. National Archives, RG 217, Microfilm Publication T135.
   Records of the Tenth Military Department, 1846–1851. Records of the United States Army
      Continental Commands, 1821–1920. RG 393, Microfilm Publication M210.
Sacramento Archives and Museum Collection Center
   Sacramento County Judgments. Books A–B.
   Sacramento County Mortgages. Book J.
   Sacramento County Powers of Attorney. Books A–E.
   Sacramento Pioneer Association.
Sacramento County. Sacramento. Office of the Recorder
   Deeds. Book A.

St. Charles County Historical Society. St. Charles, Missouri
    An Aggregate Statement of the Resident and Nonresident Tax Lists, August 25, 1834. Mis-
        cellaneous Records, 1830s.
    County Tax Collector. Statement of Monies, November 1835.
    District Court Records.
    A List of Moneys Collected by the Collector of St. Charles County, 1835. Collector's Statement
        of Moneys.
Sutter County. Office of the Clerk. Yuba City, California
    Deeds. Books A–I.
    Mortgages, Books A–B.

NEWSPAPERS

California Farmer and Journal of Useful Science (San Francisco)
California Star (San Francisco)
Daily Alta (San Francisco)
Grass Valley National
Marysville Daily Appeal
Monterey Californian
New York Daily Tribune
Oroville Weekly Union
Sacramento Age
Sacramento Bee
Sacramento Daily Transcript
Sacramento Daily Union
Sacramento Democratic State Journal
Sacramento News and Review
Sacramento Placer Times
Sacramento Themis
Sacramento Union
Sandwich Island Gazette
San Francisco Call
San Francisco Daily Examiner
San Francisco Fireman's Journal and Military Gazette
San Francisco Herald
San Jose Pioneer
Sonoma County Journal (Santa Rosa, California)
Sonoma Democrat (Santa Rosa, California)

PUBLISHED PRIMARY SOURCES

Absalom, Samuel [David Deadrick]. "The Experience of Samuel Absalom, Filibuster." *Atlantic
    Monthly* 4, no. 25 (1859): 653–65.
——. "The Experience of Samuel Absalom, Filibuster." *Atlantic Monthly* 5, no. 27 (1860): 38–60.
Alexander, Charles. *The Life and Times of Cyrus Alexander.* Edited by George Shochat. Los Angeles:
    Dawson's Bookshop, 1967.
Associated Pioneers of the Territorial Days of California. *A Nation's Benefactor.* New York: Associ-
    ated Pioneers of the Territorial Days of California, 1880.
Bagley, Will, ed. *Scoundrel's Tale: The Samuel Brannan Papers.* Vol. 3 of *Kingdom in the West: The*

Mormons and the American Frontier, edited by Will Bagley. Spokane, Wash.: Arthur H. Clark Company, 1999.

Bancroft, Hubert Howe. *Literary Industries.* San Francisco: History Company, 1890.

Barker, Charles Albro, ed. *Memoirs of Elisha Oscar Crosby: Reminiscences of California and Guatemala from 1849 to 1864.* San Marino, Calif.: Huntington Library, 1945.

Bauer, K. Jack, ed. *The New American State Papers, Naval Affairs.* Vol. 2. Wilmington, Del.: Scholarly Resources, 1981.

Bidwell, John. "Frémont in the Conquest of California." *Century Magazine* 41 (February 1891): 518–25.

——. "Life in California before the Gold Discovery." *Century Magazine* 41, no. 2 (1890): 163–83.

Bigler, David L., ed. *The Gold Discovery Journal of Azariah Smith.* Salt Lake City: University of Utah Press, 1990.

Bigler, David, and Will Bagley, eds. *Army of Israel: Mormon Battalion Narratives.* Vol. 4 of *Kingdom in the West: The Mormons and the American Frontier,* edited by Will Bagley. Spokane, Wash.: Arthur H. Clark Company, 2000.

Bigler, R. "General Johann August Sutter und Seine Beziehungen zu Burgdorf." In *Das Burgdorfer Jahrbuch,* 7–20. Burgdorf: Langlois & Cie, 1934.

Brackenridge, William Dunlop. "Journal of William Dunlop Brackenridge." *CHSQ* 24 (December 1945): 326–36.

Brooks, George R., ed. *The Southwest Expedition of Jedediah S. Smith: His Personal Account of the Journey to California, 1826–1827.* Glendale, Calif.: Arthur H. Clark, 1977.

Browne, J. Ross. *Report of the Debates of the Convention of California on the Formation of the State Constitution, in September and October, 1849.* Washington, D.C.: John T. Towers, 1850.

Bryant, Edwin. *What I Saw in California.* 1848. Reprint, Lincoln: University of Nebraska Press, 1985.

Buck, Franklin A. *A Yankee Trader in the Gold Rush: The Letters of Franklin A. Buck.* Compiled by Katherine A. White. Boston: Houghton Mifflin Company, 1930.

Burnett, Peter H. *Recollections of an Old Pioneer.* 1880. Reprint, New York: Da Capo Press, 1969.

California, State of. *Senate Journals.* 1851, 1859.

——. *Statutes of California.* 1850, 1855, 1863–64, 1869–70, 1871–72, 1873–74.

Camp, Charles L. "James Clyman, His Diaries and Reminiscences (Continued)." *CHSQ* 5 (March 1926): 44–84, 109–85.

——. "Kit Carson in California." *CHSQ* 1 (October 1922): 111–51.

——. "Sutter Writes of the Gold Discovery." *CHSQ* 11 (March 1932): 42–43.

Carter, Harvey Lewis, ed. *"Dear Old Kit": The Historical Christopher Carson, with a New Edition of the Carson Memoirs.* Norman: University of Oklahoma Press, 1968.

Cleland, Robert G. "Bandini's Account of William Walker's Invasion of Lower California." *Huntington Library Quarterly* 7 (February 1944)): 153–66.

Colton, Walter. *Three Years in California.* Edited by Marguerite Eyer Wilbur. Stanford: Stanford University Press, 1949.

Colvocoresses, George. *Four Years in a Government Exploring Expedition.* New York: Lamport, 1852.

Cook, Sherburne F., ed. "Expeditions to the Interior of California: Central Valley, 1820–1840." *University of California Anthropological Records* 20, no. 5 (1962): 151–214.

Cordes, Frederick C. "Letters of A. Rotchev, Last Commandant at Fort Ross and the Resume of the Report of the Russian-American Company for the Year 1850–1851." *CHSQ* 39 (June 1960): 97–115.

Dana, James D. "Notes on Upper California." *American Journal of Science and Arts* 7 (May 1849): 246–64.

Davis, William Heath. *Seventy-five Years in California: Recollections and Remarks by One Who . . . Was a*

Resident from 1838 until the End of a Long Life in 1909. Edited by Harold A. Small. San Francisco: John Howell Books, 1967.

Dmytryshyn, Basil, E. A. P. Crownhart-Vaughan, and Thomas Vaughan, eds. and trans. *To Siberia and Russian America: Three Centuries of Russian Eastward Expansion*. Vol. 3: *The Russian American Colonies: A Documentary Record*. Portland: Oregon Historical Society Press, 1989.

"Documentary—The Fremont Episode." *CHSQ* 6 (June, September, December 1927): 77–90, 265–80, 364–74.

Douglas, James. "A Voyage from the Columbia to California in 1840." *CHSQ* 8 (June 1929): 96–115.

Drury, Clifford Merrill, ed. *The Diaries and Letters of Henry H. Spalding and Asa Bowen Smith Relating to the Nez Perce Mission, 1838–1842*. Glendale, Calif.: Arthur H. Clark Company, 1958.

——, ed. *First White Women over the Rockies: Diaries, Letters, and Biographical Sketches of the Six Women of the Oregon Mission Who Made the Overland Journey in 1836 and 1838*. 2 vols. Glendale, Calif.: Arthur H. Clark Company, 1963.

Duden, Gottfried. *Report on a Journey to the Western States of North America and a Stay of Several Years along the Missouri (during the Years 1824, '25, '26, and 1827)*. Edited by James W. Goodrich, translated by Elsa Nagel, George H. Kellner, Adolph Schroeder, and W. M. Senner. Columbia: State Historical Society of Missouri and University of Missouri Press, 1980.

Ellison, William Henry, ed. "Memoirs of Hon. William M. Gwin." *CHSQ* 19 (March 1940): 1–26.

——, ed. "Recollections of Historical Events in California, 1843–1878: William A. Streeter." *CHSQ* 18 (June 1939): 157–72.

A Faithful Translation of the Papers Respecting the Grant Made by Governor Alvarado to John A. Sutter. Translated by William E. P. Hartnell. Sacramento: Sacramento Book Collectors Club, 1942.

Farnham, Thomas Jefferson. *Travels in the Californias, and Scenes in the Pacific Ocean*. New York: Saxton & Miles, 1844.

Field, Stephen J. *Personal Reminiscences of Early Days in California*. 1893. Reprint, New York: Da Capo Press, 1968.

Frémont, John C. *Memoirs of My Life, with a Sketch of the Life of Senator Benton by Jessie Benton Frémont*. Chicago: Bedford, Clarke & Company, 1887.

——. *Report of the Exploring Expedition to the Rocky Mountains in the Year 1842, and to Oregon and North California in the Years 1843–44*. Philadelphia: C. Sherman, 1844.

Gates, Paul W. *California Ranchos and Farms, 1846–1862, Including the Letters of John Quincy Adams Warren of 1861, Being Largely Devoted to Livestock, Wheat Farming, Fruit Raising, and the Wine Industry*. Madison: State Historical Society of Wisconsin, 1967.

Gillis, Michael J., and Michael F. Magliari, eds. *John Bidwell and California: The Life and Writings of a Pioneer, 1841–1900*. Spokane, Wash.: Arthur H. Clark, 2003.

Grabhorn, Jane, ed. *Pioneers of the Sacramento: A Group of Letters by and about Johann Augustus Sutter, James W. Marshall, and John Bidwell*. San Francisco: Book Club of California, 1953.

Gudde, Erwin G., ed. *Bigler's Chronicle of the West: The Conquest of California, Discovery of Gold, and Mormon Settlement as Reflected in Henry William Bigler's Diaries*. Berkeley: University of California Press, 1962.

——, ed. "The Memoirs of Theodor Cordua." *CHSQ* 12 (December 1933): 279–311.

Hammond, George P., ed. *The Larkin Papers*. 11 vols. Berkeley: University of California Press, 1951–68.

Harris, Nellie McCoy. "Memories of Old Westport." *Annals of Kansas City* vol. 1, no. 4 (1921): 465–75.

Hastings, Lansford W. *Emigrant's Guide to Oregon and California*. 1845. Reprint, New York: Da Capo Press, 1969.

Hoffman, Ogden. *Reports of Land Cases Determined in the United States District Court for the Northern District of California*. 1862. Reprint, n.p.: Yosemite Collections, 1975.

Huntley, Sir Henry. *California: Its Gold and Its Inhabitants.* London: Thomas Cautley Newby, 1856.

Hussey, John A. ed. *Early Sacramento: Glimpses of John Augustus Sutter, Hok Farm and Neighboring Indian Tribes from the Journals of Prince Paul H. R. H. Duke Paul Wilhelm of Württemberg.* Sacramento: Sacramento Book Collectors Club, 1973.

Jackson, Donald, and Mary Lee Spence, eds. *Expeditions of John Charles Frémont.* 3 vols. Urbana: University of Illinois Press, 1970.

Jamison, James Carson. *With Walker in Nicaragua, or Reminiscences of an Officer of the American Phalanx.* Columbia, Mo.: E. W. Stephens Publishing Co., 1909.

Kerr, Thomas. "An Irishman in the Gold Rush: The Journal of Thomas Kerr." *CHSQ* 8 (June 1929): 167–82.

Kibbe, William C. *Annual Report of the Quartermaster and Adjutant General.* 1856. California State Assembly. Document No. 6.

Laufkotter, J. A. *John A. Sutter and His Grants.* Sacramento: Russell & Winterburn, Book & Job Printers, 1867.

Marsh, John. "Letter of Dr. John Marsh to Hon. Lewis Cass." *CHSQ* 22 (December 1943): 315–22.

Marshall, James. "The Discovery of Gold in California." *Hutchings' California Magazine* 2, no. 5 (1857): 199–203.

Mathes, Valerie Sherer. "The Death of John Sutter as Seen through the Letters of Annie and John Bidwell." *Pacific Historian* 26, no. 3 (1982): 40–52.

Meyers, W. H., ed. *Journal of a Cruise to California and the Sandwich Islands in the United States Sloop of War Cyane.* Edited by John Haskell Kemball. San Francisco: Book Club of California 1955.

Mofras, Eugène Duflot de. *Duflot de Mofras' Travels on the Pacific Coast.* Translated by Marguerite Eyer Wilbur. 2 vols. Santa Ana, Calif.: Fine Arts Press, 1937.

Montgomery, C. E. "The Lost Journals of a Pioneer." *Overland Monthly* 7, no. 37 (1886): 75–90.

Morgan, Dale, ed. *Overland in 1846: Diaries and Letters of the California Oregon Trail.* 2 vols. 1963. Reprint, Lincoln: University of Nebraska Press, 1993.

Nugget Editions Club. *French Letters: Captain John Augustus Sutter to Jean Jacques Vioget, 1842–1843.* Sacramento: Nugget Press, 1942.

Nunis, Doyce B., ed. *The California Diary of Faxon Dean Atherton, 1836–1839.* San Francisco: California Historical Society, 1964.

——, ed. "A Mysterious Chapter in the Life of John A. Sutter as Told by B. D. Wilson." *CHSQ* 38 (December 1959): 321–27.

Ottley, Allan R., ed. *John A. Sutter's Last Days: The Bidwell Letters.* Sacramento: Sacramento Book Collectors Club, 1986.

——, ed. *A Sutter Letter, May 4, 1848.* Sacramento: Sacramento Book Collectors Club, 1989.

Owens, Kenneth N., ed. *Gold Rush Saints: California Mormons and the Great Rush for Riches.* Vol. 7 of *Kingdom in the West: The Mormons and the American Frontier,* edited by Will Bagley. Spokane, Wash.: Arthur H. Clark Company, 2004.

——, ed. *John A. Sutter, Sr., and His Grants, by John A. Laufkotter.* 2nd ed. Sacramento: Sacramento Book Collectors Club, 2004.

——, ed. *The Wreck of the Sv. Nikolai: Two Narratives of the First Russian Expedition to the Oregon Country, 1808–1810.* Translated by Alton S. Donnelly. Portland: Press of the Oregon Historical Society, 1985.

Paul, Rodman W., ed. *The California Gold Discovery: Sources, Documents, Accounts, and Memoirs Relative to the Discovery of Gold at Sutter's Mill.* Georgetown, Calif.: Talisman Press, 1966.

Phelps, William Dane. *Alta California, 1840–1842: The Journal and Observations of William Dane Phelps, Master of the Ship Alert.* Edited by Briton Cooper Busch. 1871. Reprint, Glendale, Calif.: Arthur H. Clark, 1983.

Quaife, Milo Milton, ed. *Echoes of the Past about California, by General John Bidwell, and In Camp and Cabin, by Rev. John Steele.* Chicago: Lakeside Press, 1928.

——, ed. *Kit Carson's Autobiography.* 1935. Reprint, Lincoln: University of Nebraska Press, 1966.

Revere, Joseph Warren. *Naval Duty in California.* Oakland, Calif.: Biobooks, 1947.

Rich, E. E., ed. *The Fort Vancouver Letters of John McLoughlin.* 3 vols. London: Champlain Society for the Hudson's Bay Record Society, 1941–44.

Robinson, Alfred. *Life in California during a Residence of Several Years in That Territory.* 1846. Reprint, New York: Da Capo Press, 1969.

Sandels, G. M. Waseurtz af. *A Sojourn in California by the King's Orphan: The Travels and Sketches of G. M. Waseurtz af Sandels, a Swedish Gentleman Who Visited California in 1842–1843.* Edited by Helen Putnam Van Sicklen. San Francisco: Book Club of California, 1945.

Schläfli, Friederich. "Five Letters of Gustav Friederich Schäfli to His Mother and Sister, 1850–1854, June 5, 1850." In *Das Burgdorfer Jahrbuch, 1935,* 21–58. Burgdorf: Langlois & Cie, 1934.

Sherman, W. T. *Memoirs of General William T. Sherman.* 2 vols. 1875. Reprint (2 vols. in 1), Bloomington: Indiana University Press, 1957.

Simpson, Sir George. *Narrative of a Journey round the World during the Years 1841 and 1842.* 2 vols. London: Henry Colburn, Publisher, 1847.

Sutter, Anna. "Declaration of Anna Sutter." *Sutter County Historical Society News Bulletin* 9, no. 4 (1870): 1–2.

Sutter, John A. *The Diary of Johann August Sutter.* San Francisco: Grabhorn Press, 1932.

——. "The Discovery of Gold in California." *Hutchings' California Magazine* 2 (November 1857): 194–98.

——. "General Sutter's Diary." In *John Sutter and a Wider West,* edited by Kenneth N. Owens, 1–25. Lincoln: University of Nebraska Press, 1994.

——. "A Letter from General Sutter." *Century Magazine* 41, no. 3 (1891): 470.

——. *Memorial of John A. Sutter to the Senate and House of Representatives of the United States in Congress Assembled.* Washington, D.C.: Washington Sentinel, 1876.

——. "Vier Briefe des Generals Johann August Sutter aus den Jahren 1868–1880." In *Das Burgdorfer Jahrbuch 1935,* 59–74. Burgdorf: Langlois & Cie, 1934.

Sutter, John A., John Bidwell, and William F. Swasey. *New Helvetia Diary: A Record of Events Kept by John A. Sutter and His Clerks at New Helvetia, California, from September 9, 1845, to May 25, 1848.* San Francisco: Grabhorn Press, 1939.

Sutter, John A., Jr. *The Sutter Family and the Origins of Gold-Rush Sacramento.* Edited by Allan R. Ottley. Originally published as *Statement Regarding Early California Experiences.* Sacramento: Sacramento Book Collectors Club, 1943. Reprint with an introduction by Albert L. Hurtado, Norman: University of Oklahoma Press, 2002.

Taylor, Bayard. *El Dorado, or Adventures in the Path of Empire.* 1850. Reprint (2 vols. in 1), Glorieta, N.Mex.: Rio Grande Press, 1967.

Taylor, William. *California Life Illustrated.* Rev. ed. London: Jackson, Walford & Hodder, 1867.

"Transactions of the California State Agricultural Society." In *Appendix to the Journals of the Senate of the Tenth Session of the Legislature of the State of California,* 167. Sacramento: John O'Meara, State Printer for California, 1859.

Uldall, Hans Jørgen, and William Shipley. *Nisenan Texts and Dictionary.* University of California Publications in Linguistics, vol. 46. Berkeley: University of California Press, 1966.

U.S. House of Representatives. Committee on Claims. 1866. *Petition of John A. Sutter.* 39th Cong., 1st sess., H. Mis. Doc. 38. Serial 1239.

——. Committee on the Library. 1892. *Gen. John A. Sutter.* 52nd Cong., 1st sess., H. Report No. 1255. Serial 3045.

——. Committee on Private Land-Claims. 1876. *A Bill for the Relief of John A. Sutter.* 44th Cong., 1st sess., H. Report No. 718. Serial 1712.

U.S. President. *Message from the President . . . Communicating Information Called for by . . . the Senate . . . Relating to California and New Mexico.* 31st Cong., 1st sess., 1849. Sen. Ex. Doc. 18. Serial 557.

——. *Message of the President . . . to the Two Houses of Congress. . . at the Commencement of the Second Session.* 30th Cong., 2nd sess., 1848. Sen. Ex. Doc. 1. Serial 537.

Upham, Samuel C. *Notes of a Voyage to California via Cape Horn, Together with Scenes in El Dorado, in the Years 1849–'50.* Philadelphia: Samuel C. Upham, 1878.

Vallejo, Mariano G. "Documentary—Bear Flag Movement." *CHSQ* 1 (January 1923): 293–96.

Walker, William. *The War in Nicaragua.* Mobile and New York: S. H. Goetzel & Co., 1860.

Warren, T. Robinson. *Dust and Foam; or, Three Continents and Two Oceans.* New York: Charles Scribner, 1859.

Washington, John A. "Noblet Herbert to Mrs. John Augustine Washington." *CHSQ* 29 (December 1950): 297–307.

Weber, David J., ed. *The Californios versus Jedediah Smith, 1826–1827.* Spokane, Wash.: Arthur H. Clark, 1990.

Wells, William V. *Walker's Expedition to Nicaragua: A History of the Central American War; and the Sonora and Kinney Expeditions, Including All the Recent Diplomatic Correspondence.* New York: Stringer & Townsend, 1856.

Wilbur, Marguerite Eyer, trans. and ed. *A Pioneer at Sutter's Fort, 1846–1850: The Adventures of Heinrich Lienhard.* Los Angeles: Califia Society, 1941.

Wilkes, Charles. *Narrative of the United States Exploring Expedition during the Years 1838, 1839, 1840, 1841, 1842.* 5 vols. Philadelphia: C. Sherman, 1845.

Wood, William Maxwell. *Wandering Sketches of People and Things in South America, Polynesia, California, and Other Places Visited.* Philadelphia: Carey & Hart, 1849.

Woodward, Arthur, ed. *The Republic of Lower California, 1853–1854, in the Words of Its State Papers, Eyewitnesses, and Contemporary Reporters.* Los Angeles: Dawson's Book Shop, 1966.

Wyman, Walker. "California Emigrant Letters." *CHSQ* 24 (March 1945): 17–46.

SECONDARY SOURCES

Anderson, Gary Clayton. *Kinsmen of Another Kind: Dakota-White Relations in the Upper Mississippi Valley, 1650–1862.* Lincoln: University of Nebraska Press, 1984.

Andrews, Thomas F. "The Ambitions of Lansford W. Hastings: A Study in Western Myth-Making." *PHR* 39 (November 1970): 473–91.

Baggelmann, Ted, and Willard Thompson. "John Sutter's Journey, 1834–1839." *Golden Notes* 33, no. 3 (Fall 1987)) (unpaged).

Bakken, Gordon M. "The Development of Landlord and Tenant Law in Frontier California, 1850–1865." *Pacific Historian* 21 (Winter 1978): 374–84.

——. "The Development of the Law of Tort in Frontier California, 1850–1890." *SCQ* 60 (Winter 1978): 405–20.

Bakker, Elna. *An Island Called California: An Ecological Introduction to Its Natural Communities.* Berkeley: University of California Press, 1971.

Bancroft, Hubert Howe. *History of California.* 7 vols. San Francisco: History Company, 1886–90.

Barker, Charles A. "Elisha Oscar Crosby—A California Lawyer in the Eighteen-Fifties." *CHSQ* 27 (June 1948): 133–40.

Bean Lowell, John, and Thomas C. Blackburn, eds. *Native Californians: A Theoretical Retrospective.* Socorro, N.Mex.: Ballena Press, 1976.

Beck, Warren A., and Ynez D. Haase, comps. *Historical Atlas of California.* Norman: University of Oklahoma Press, 1974.

Bennyhoff, James A. *Ethnogeography of the Plains Miwok.* Davis, Calif.: Center for Archaeological Research at Davis, 1977.

Birmann, Martin. *General Joh-Aug-Suter.* Basel: Gute Schriften, 1933.

Black, Lydia T. *Russians in Alaska, 1732–1867.* Fairbanks: University of Alaska Press, 2004.

Blake, Anson S. "The Hudson's Bay Company in San Francisco." *CHSQ* 28 (September 1949): 243–58.

Breault, William J., S.J. *John A. Sutter in Hawaii and California, 1838–1839*. Rancho Cordova, Calif.: Landmark Enterprises, 1998.

Brooks, James F. *Captives and Cousins: Slavery, Kinship, and Community in the Southwest Borderlands*. Chapel Hill: University of North Carolina Press, 2002.

Brown, Jennifer S. H. *Strangers in Blood: Fur Trade Company Families in Indian Country*. Vancouver: University of British Columbia Press, 1980.

California Department of Parks and Recreation. "Sutter's Fort State Historic Park." N.p., n.d.

California Territorial Quarterly 60 (Winter 2004). Special Issue on Sutter's Fort.

Calloway, Colin G. *One Vast Winter Count: The Native American West before Lewis and Clark*. Lincoln: University of Nebraska Press, 2003.

Cendrars, Blaise. *Sutter's Gold*. Translated by Henry Logan Stuart. London: William Heinemann Ltd, 1926.

Chaffin, Tom. *Pathfinder: John Charles Frémont and the Course of American Empire*. New York: Hill and Wang, 2002.

[Chamberlain, W. H.] *History of Yuba County, California*. Oakland, Calif.: Thompson & West, 1879.

Chevalier, François. *Land and Society in Colonial Mexico: The Great Hacienda*. Edited by Lesley Byrd Simpson. Translated by Alvin Eustis. Berkeley: University of California Press, 1963.

Chittenden, Hiram Martin. *The American Fur Trade of the Far West*. 3 vols. 1902. Reprint (3 vols. in 2), Stanford: Academic Reprints, 1954.

C. K. McClatchy High School, Students. *Park Grants of John A. Sutter, Junior*. Sacramento: Nugget Press, 1948.

Cleland, Robert Glass. *The Cattle on a Thousand Hills: Southern California, 1850–1880*. 2nd ed. San Marino, Calif.: Huntington Library, 1964.

Conmy, Peter T. "General John A. Sutter and the Indians." *Grizzly Bear* (March 1939): 3.

——. "General John A. Sutter and the Mormons." *Grizzly Bear* (April 1939): 3, 7.

——. "General Sutter and the Admission of California to the Union." *Grizzly Bear* (September 1939): 4.

——. "General Sutter and the Bear Flag Revolt." *Grizzly Bear* (July 1939): 4.

——. "General Sutter and the Beginnings of Sacramento." *Grizzly Bear* (January 1939): 3.

——. "General Sutter's Claims and the Courts." *Grizzly Bear* (August 1939): 4.

——. "Sacramento and Sutter's Fort." *Grizzly Bear* (February 1939): 3.

Cook, Sherburne F. "The Epidemic of 1830–1833 in California and Oregon." *University of California Publications in American Archaeology and Ethnology* 43, no. 3 (1955): 303–25.

——. *The Population of the California Indians, 1769–1970*. Berkeley: University of California Press, 1976.

Cox, Thomas R. *Mills and Markets: A History of the Pacific Coast Lumber Industry to 1900*. Seattle: University of Washington Press, 1974.

Culver, J. Horace. *The Sacramento City Directory*. Sacramento: Transcript Press, 1851.

Dakin, Suanna Bryant. *The Lives of William Hartnell*. Stanford, Calif.: Stanford University Press, 1949.

Dana, Julian. *Sutter of California*. New York: Press of the Pioneers, 1934.

Dart, Dennis M. "Sacramento Squatter Riot of August 14, 1850." *Pacific Historian* 24, no. 2 (1980): 159–67.

Dasmann, Raymond F. *The Destruction of California*. New York: Collier, 1966.

Daws, Gavan. *The Shoal of Time: A History of the Hawaiian Islands*. Honolulu: University of Hawaii Press, 1968.

Dawson, William, and Earl Ramey. "The Romances of Eliza Sutter." *Sutter County Historical Society News Bulletin* 11 (January 1972): 2–16.

Dayton, Dello G. "'Polished Boot and Bran New Suit': The California Militia in Community Affairs." *CHSQ* 37 (December 1958): 321–27.

DeBow, J. B. D. *Statistical View of the United States . . . : A Compendium of the Seventh Census.* Washington, D.C.: A. O. P. Nicholson, Public Printer, 1854.

DeVoto, Bernard. *The Year of Decision, 1846.* New York: Houghton-Mifflin, 1943.

Dillon, Richard. *Fool's Gold: The Decline and Fall of Captain John Sutter of California.* New York: Coward-McCann, 1967.

Dodd, Gordon B. "Astor, John Jacob." In *The New Encyclopedia of the American West,* edited by Howard R. Lamar, 65–66. New Haven: Yale University Press, 1998.

Drury, C. M. *Marcus and Narcissa Whitman and the Opening of Old Oregon.* Glendale, Calif.: Arthur H. Clark Company, 1973.

DuFour, Clarence J. "John A. Sutter: His Career in California before the American Conquest." Ph.D. diss., University of California Berkeley, 1927.

——. "The Russian Withdrawal from California." *CHSQ* 12 (September 1933): 240–76.

Dunbar, Edward E. *The Romance of the Age; or the Discovery of Gold in California.* New York: D. Appleton & Company, 1867.

Eifler, Mark A. *Gold Rush Capitalists: Greed and Growth in Sacramento.* Albuquerque: University of New Mexico Press, 2002.

Ellison, Joseph. "The Mineral Land Question in California, 1848–1866." In *The Public Lands: Studies in the History of the Public Domain,* edited by Vernon Carstensen, 71–92. Madison: University of Wisconsin Press, 1968.

Ellison, William Henry. *A Self-Governing Dominion: California, 1849–1860.* Berkeley: University of California Press, 1950.

Engstrand, Iris H. W. "John Sutter: A Biographical Examination." In *John Sutter and a Wider West,* edited by Kenneth N. Owens, 76–92. Lincoln: University of Nebraska Press, 1994.

Fenega, Franklin. "Artifacts from Excavation of Sutter's Sawmill." *CHSQ* 26 (June 1947): 160–62.

Field, Alston G. "Attorney-General Black and the California Land Claims." *PHR* 4 (1935): 235–45.

Flores, Dan. *Horizontal Yellow: Nature and History in the Near Southwest.* Albuquerque: University of New Mexico Press, 1999.

Foley, William E. *The Genesis of Missouri: From Wilderness Outpost to Statehood.* Columbia: University of Missouri Press, 1989.

Foley, William E., and C. David Rice. *The First Chouteaus: River Barons of Early St. Louis.* Urbana: University of Illinois Press, 1983.

Forbes, Jack D. *Native Americans of California and Nevada: A Handbook.* Healdsburg, Calif.: Nature-graph, 1969.

Franklin, William E. "A Forgotten Chapter in California History: Peter H. Burnett and John A. Sutter's Fortune." *CHSQ* 41 (1962): 319–24.

Galbraith, John S. "A Note on the British Fur Trade in California." *PHR* 24 (August 1955): 253–60.

Gay, Theresa. *James W. Marshall, the Discoverer of California Gold: A Biography.* Georgetown, Calif.: Talisman Press, 1967.

Gibson, James R. *Imperial Russia in Frontier America: The Changing Geography of Supply of Russian America, 1784–1867.* New York: Oxford University Press, 1976.

Giffin, Helen S. "Into the Valley of Death: The Crabb Filibustering Expedition into Sonora, Mexico, 1857." *Pacific Historian* 19, no. 2 (1975): 363–76.

Goetzman, William H., and William N. Goetzman. *The West of the Imagination.* New York: Norton, 1986.

Gray, W. H. *A History of Oregon.* Portland, Ore.: Harris & Holman, 1870.

Griswold del Castillo, Richard. *La Familia: Chicano Families in the Urban Southwest, 1848 to the Present.* Notre Dame: University of Notre Dame Press, 1984.

——. *The Los Angeles Barrio, 1850–1890: A Social History*. Berkeley: University of California Press, 1979.

——. *The Treaty of Guadalupe Hidalgo: A Legacy of Conflict*. Norman: University of Oklahoma Press, 1990.

Grivas, Theodore. *Military Governments in California, 1846–1850, with a Chapter on Their Prior Use in Louisiana, Florida and New Mexico*. Glendale, Calif.: Arthur H. Clark Company, 1963.

Gudde, Erwin G. , comp. *California Gold Camps: A Geographical and Historical Dictionary of Camps, Towns, and Localities Where Gold Was Found and Mined; Wayside Stations and Trading Centers*. Edited by Elizabeth Gudde. Berkeley: University of California Press, 1975.

——, comp. *California Place Names: The Origin and Etymology of Current Geographical Names*. 3rd ed. Berkeley: University of California Press, 1969.

——, ed. *Neu-Helvetien: Lebenserinnerungen des Generals John August Sutter*. Leipzig: Huber & Co., 1934.

——. "The Source of the Sutter Myth." *CHSQ* 9 (December 1930): 398–99.

——. *Sutter's Own Story: The Life and Times of John Augustus Sutter and the History of New Helvetia in the Sacramento Valley*. New York: G. P. Putnam's Sons, 1936.

Hafen, Leroy, ed. *The Mountain Men and the Fur Trade of the Far West: Biographical Sketches*. . . . 10 vols. Glendale, Calif.: Arthur H. Clark, 1965–72.

Hague, Harlan, and David J. Langum. *Thomas O. Larkin: A Life of Patriotism and Profit in Old California*. Norman: University of Oklahoma Press, 1990.

Hamalainen, Pekka. "The Rise and Fall of Plains Indian Horse Cultures." *Journal of American History* 90 (December 2003): 833–62.

Harlow, Neal. *California Conquered: War and Peace on the Pacific, 1846–1850*. Berkeley: University of California Press, 1982.

Hassig, E. O. "The Russian Settlement at Ross." *CHSQ* 12 (September 1933): 191–209.

Hawgood, John A. "John Augustus Sutter: A Reappraisal." *Arizona and the West* 4 (Winter 1962): 345–56.

Heizer, Robert F. "Walla Walla Indian Expeditions to the Sacramento Valley." *CHSQ* 21 (March 1942): 1–7.

Heizer, Robert F., and Albert B. Elsasser. *The Natural World of the California Indians*. Berkeley: University of California Press, 1980.

Hewett, Janet, ed. *The Roster of Union Soldiers, 1861–1865*. Wilmington, N.C.: Broadfoot Publishing Company, 1997.

Hine, Robert V. *In the Shadow of Frémont: Edward Kern and the Art of Exploration, 1845–1860*. 2nd ed. Norman: University of Oklahoma Press, 1982.

History and Examination of the Russian Lands, Lying and along the Pacific Coast, between Cape Mendocino on the North and Cape Reyes, or Drake, on the South and Inland from the Sea Shore Three Spanish Leagues. Sacramento: H. S. Crocker, 1960.

Hittell, Theodore. *History of California*. 4 vols. San Francisco: Pacific Press, 1885–97.

Hurtado, Albert L. "Clouded Legacy: California Indians and the Gold Rush." In *Riches for All: the California Gold Rush and the World,* edited by Kenneth N. Owens, 90–117. Lincoln: University of Nebraska Press, 2002.

——. "Indians in Town and Country: The Nisenans Changing Economy and Society as Shown in John A. Sutter's Correspondence." *American Indian Culture and Research Journal* 12, no. 2 (1988): 31–51.

——. *Indian Survival on the California Frontier*. New Haven: Yale University Press, 1988.

——. *Intimate Frontiers: Sex, Gender, and Culture in Old California*. Albuquerque: University of New Mexico Press, 1999.

——. "When Strangers Met: Sex and Gender on Three Frontiers." In *Writing the Range: Race, Class, and Culture in the Women's West,* edited by Elizabeth Jameson and Susan Armitage, 122–42. Norman: University of Oklahoma Press, 1997.

Hussey, John Adam, and George Walcott Ames, Jr. "California Preparations to Meet the Walla Walla Invasion, 1846." *CHSQ* 21 (December 1942): 9–21.

Hutchinson, Joseph. "California Cereals." *Overland Monthly* 2, no. 7 (1883): 8–16.

Hyslop, Stephen G. *Bound for Santa Fe: The Road to New Mexico and the American Conquest, 1806–1848.* Norman: University of Oklahoma Press, 2002.

Jackson, Sheldon G. "The British and the California Dream: Rumors, Myths and Legends." *SCQ* 57 (Fall 1975): 259–63.

——. "Two Pro-British Plots in Alta California." *SCQ* 55 (Summer 1973): 105–40.

Josephy, Alvin M. *The Nez Perce Indians and the Opening of the Northwest.* New Haven: Yale University Press, 1965.

Kelley, Robert. *Battling the Inland Sea: American Political Culture, Public Policy, and the Sacramento Valley, 1850–1986.* Berkeley: University of California Press, 1989.

Kennedy, Joseph C. G., comp. *Population of the United States in 1860.* Washington, D.C.: Government Printing Office, 1864.

King, Joseph A. *Winter of Entrapment: A New Look at the Donner Party.* 3rd ed. Lafayette, Calif.: K&K Publications, 1998.

Kroeber, Alfred L. *Handbook of the Indians of California.* 1925. Reprint, Berkeley: California Book Company, 1953.

Kunzel, Heinrich. *Das Fort Neu Helvetien.* Darmstadt: C. W. Leske, 1848.

Lamar, Howard. "From Bondage to Contract: Ethnic Labor in the American West, 1600–1890." In *The Countryside in the Age of Transformation: Essays in the Social History of Rural America,* edited by Steven Hahn and Jonathan Prude, 293–324. Chapel Hill: University of North Carolina Press, 1985.

——, ed. *The New Encyclopedia of the American West.* New Haven: Yale University Press, 1998.

——. "Wilderness Entrepreneur." In *John Sutter and a Wider West,* edited by Kenneth N. Owens, 26–50. Lincoln: University of Nebraska Press, 1994.

Landis, Jacob. "The Life and Work of Gen. John A. Sutter." *Papers Read before the Lancaster Historical Society* 17, no. 10 (1913): 279–300.

Laney, Honora. "History of the Hock Farm from 1842 to 1856." *Sutter County Historical Society News Bulletin* 1, no. 6 (1956): 2–9.

Lawrence, Eleanor. "Horse Thieves on the Spanish Trail." *Touring Topics* 23 (January 1931): 22–55.

——. "Mexican Trade between Santa Fé and Los Angeles, 1830–1848." *CHSQ* 10 (March 1931): 27–39.

Lee, Fred L. "Hard Times for John Sutter in Westport, Missouri." *Kansas City Genealogist* 39, no. 2 (1998): 75–76.

Levy, Richard. "Eastern Miwok." In *Handbook of North American Indians,* vol. 8, *California,* edited by Robert F. Heizer, 398–413. Washington, D.C.: Smithsonian Institution, 1978.

Lewis, Oscar. *Sutter's Fort: Gateway to the Gold Fields.* Englewood Cliffs, N.J.: Prentice-Hall, 1966.

Limerick, Patricia Nelson. "John Sutter: Prototype for Failure." In *John Sutter and a Wider West,* edited by Kenneth N. Owens, 111–26. Lincoln: University of Nebraska Press, 1994.

Lyman, George D. *John Marsh, Pioneer: The Life Story of a Trail-Blazer on Six Frontiers.* New York: Charles Scribner's Sons, 1931.

Mackie, Richard Somerset. *Trading beyond the Mountains: The British Fur Trade on the Pacific, 1793–1843.* Vancouver: University of British Columbia Press, 1997.

Maloney, Alice Bay, ed. *Fur Brigade to the Bonaventure: John Work's California Expedition, 1832–1833.* San Francisco: California Historical Society, 1945.

McGlashan, C. F. *History of the Donner Party: A Tragedy of the Sierra.* Rev. ed. Edited by George H. Hinkle and Bliss McGlashan Hinkle. Stanford: Stanford University Press, 1947.

McGrew, William K. "The Rats of Sacramento." *Overland Monthly* 36, no. 213 (1900): 235–40.

McKitrick, Myrtle M. "Salvador Vallejo." *CHSQ* 29 (December 1950): 309–31.

Miller, Christopher L. *Prophetic Worlds: Indians and Whites on the Columbia Plateau.* New Brunswick, N.J.: Rutgers University Press, 1985.

Miller, Robert Ryal. *Juan Alvarado, Governor of California.* Albuquerque: University of New Mexico Press, 1998.

Miranda, Gloria E. "Gente de Razón Marriage Patterns in Spanish and Mexican California: A Case Study of Santa Barbara and Los Angeles." *SCQ* 63 (Spring 1981): 1–21.

Neasham, Aubrey. "Sutter's Sawmill." *CHSQ* 26 (June 1947): 109–33.

Neri, Michael C. "Gonzales Rubio and California Catholicism, 1846–1850." *SCQ* 58 (Winter 1976): 441–57.

Officer, James E. *Hispanic Arizona, 1536–1856.* Tucson: University of Arizona Press, 1987.

Ottley, Allan R. "Biography of John A. Sutter, Jr." In *The Sutter Family and the Origins of Gold-Rush Sacramento,* edited by Allan R. Ottley, 3–77. Originally published as *Statement Regarding Early California Experiences.* Sacramento, Sacramento Book Collectors Club, 1943. Reprint with an introduction by Albert L. Hurtado. Norman: University of Oklahoma Press, 2002.

——. "The Founder of Sacramento." *Sacramento County Historical Society Golden Notes* 9, no. 4 (1963): 6–25.

Owens, Kenneth N. "Begun by Gold: Sacramento and the Gold Rush Legacy after 150 Years." In *Riches for All: The California Gold Rush and the World,* edited by Kenneth N. Owens, 328–54. Lincoln: University of Nebraska Press, 2002.

——, ed. *John Sutter and a Wider West.* Lincoln: University of Nebraska Press, 1994.

Parsons, George F. *The Life and Adventures of James W. Marshall, the Discoverer of Gold in California.* Edited by Ezra Dane. San Francisco: George Fields, 1935.

Paul, Rodman W. *California Gold: The Beginning of Mining in the Far West.* Cambridge, Mass.: Harvard University Press, 1947.

Phillips, George Harwood. *Indians and Intruders in Central California, 1769–1849.* Norman: University of Oklahoma Press, 1993.

Pioneers of the Sacramento: A Group of Letters by and about Johann Augustus Sutter, James W. Marshall, and John Bidwell. San Francisco: Book Club of California, 1953.

Pisani, Donald J. *From Family Farm to Agribusiness: The Irrigation Crusade in California and the West, 1850–1931.* Berkeley: University of California Press, 1984.

——. "'I Am Resolved Not to Interfere, But Permit All to Work Freely': The Gold Rush and American Resource Law." *California History* 77, no. 4 (1998–99): 123–48.

——. "Squatter Law in California, 1850–1856." *Western Historical Quarterly* 25 (Autumn 1994): 277–310.

Rawls, James. "Gold Diggers: Indian Miners in the California Gold Rush." *California Historical Quarterly* 55 (Spring 1976): 28–45.

Reps, John W. *The Forgotten Frontier: Urban Planning in the American West before 1890.* Columbia: University of Missouri Press, 1981.

Rice, William B. "Last Days of Gen. John A. Sutter." *Out West* 17 (October 1902): 441–45.

Robinson, W. W. *Land in California: The Story of Mission Lands, Ranchos, Squatters, Mining Claims, Railroad Grants, Land Scrip, Homesteads.* Berkeley: University of California Press, 1948.

Ronda, James P. *Astoria and Empire.* Lincoln: University of Nebraska Press, 1990.

——. *Lewis and Clark among the Indians.* Lincoln: University of Nebraska Press, 1984.

Rorabaugh, W. J. *The Alcoholic Republic: An American Tradition.* New York: Oxford University Press, 1979.

Rosenus, Alan. *General M. G. Vallejo and the Advent of the Americans.* Albuquerque: University of New Mexico Press, 1995.

Rosenwaike, Ira. *Population History of New York City.* Syracuse, N.Y.: Syracuse University Press, 1972.

Royce, Josiah. "The Squatter Riot of '50 in Sacramento: Its Causes and Its Significance." *Overland Monthly* 6, no. 33 (September 1885): 225–46.

Ruby, Robert H., and John A. Brown. *Indian Slavery in the Pacific Northwest.* Spokane: Arthur H. Clark Company, 1993.

Schoonover, T. J. *The Life and Times of Gen'l John A. Sutter.* Sacramento: D. Johnston and Co., 1895.

——. *The Life and Times of Gen. John A. Sutter.* Rev. ed. Sacramento: Bullock-Carpenter Printing Co., 1907.

Schwartz, Harvey. "Fort Ross, California: Imperial Russian Outpost on America's Western Frontier, 1812–1841." *Journal of the West* 18 (1979): 35–48.

Schweikert, Larry, and Lynne Pierson Doti. "From Hard Money to Branch Banking: California Banking in the Gold-Rush Economy." In *A Golden State: Mining and Economic Development in Gold Rush California,* edited by James Rawls and Richard J. Orsi, 209–32. Berkeley: University of California Press, 1999.

Scroggs, William O. *Filibusters and Financiers: The Story of William Walker and His Associates.* New York: Macmillan, 1916.

Shatto, Marian L. "General Sutter." *Susquehanna Monthly Magazine* 12 (December 1980): 22–27.

Simpson, Richard. *Ooti: A Maidu Legacy.* Millbrae, Calif.: Celestial Arts, 1977.

Smith, Gene A. *Thomas ap Catesby Jones: Commodore of Manifest Destiny.* Annapolis, Md.: Naval Institute Press, 2000.

Soulé, Frank, John H. Gihon, and James Nisbet. *Annals of San Francisco.* New York: D. Appleton, 1855.

Spence, Mary Nance. "Introduction." In *Emigrant's Guide to Oregon and California,* by Lansford W. Hastings (1845), v–ix. Reprint, New York: Da Capo Press, 1969.

Staab, Rodney. "Sutter in Westport: Prelude for a Pioneer, Part 1." *Overland Journal* 21 (Summer 2003): 42–67.

——. "Sutter in Westport: Prelude for a Pioneer, Part 2." *Overland Journal* 21 (Fall 2003): 94–102.

Stanton, William. *The Great United States Exploring Expedition.* Berkeley: University of California Press, 1975.

Sulloway, Frank. *Born to Rebel: Birth Order, Family Dynamics and Creative Lives.* New York: Vintage Books, 1996.

Swagerty, William R. "Marriage and Settlement Patterns of the Rocky Mountain Trappers and Traders." *Western Historical Quarterly* 11 (April 1980): 159–80.

Taylor, Quintard. *In Search of the Racial Frontier: African Americans in the American West, 1528–1990.* New York: Norton, 1998.

Tays, George. "Mariano Guadalupe Vallejo and Sonoma: A Biography and a History." *CHSQ* 17 (March, June, and September 1938): 50–73, 141–67, 219–42.

Thompson, Thomas H., and Albert Augustus West. *History of Sacramento County, California, with Illustrations Descriptive of Its Scenery.* Oakland, Calif.: Thompson and West, 1880.

Thorne, Tanis. *The Many Hands of My Relations: French and Indians on the Lower Missouri.* Columbia: University of Missouri Press, 1996.

Tikhmenev, P. A. *A History of the Russian-American Company.* Edited and translated by Richard A. Pierce and Alton S. Donnelly. Seattle: University of Washington Press, 1978.

Underhill, Reuben L. *From Cowhides to Golden Fleece: A Narrative of California, 1832–1858, Based upon Unpublished Correspondence of Thomas Oliver Larkin, Trader, Developer, Promoter, and Only American Consul.* Stanford: Stanford University Press, 1939.

Unruh, John D., Jr. *The Plains Across: The Overland Emigrants and the Trans-Mississippi West, 1840–60.* Urbana: University of Illinois Press, 1979.

Uzes, Francois D. *Chaining the Land: A History of Surveying in California.* Sacramento: Landmark Enterprises, 1977.

Van Kirk, Sylvia. *Many Tender Ties: Women in Fur Trade Society 1670–1870.* Norman: University of Oklahoma Press, 1980.

Watson, Douglas S. "Herald of the Gold Rush—Sam Brannan." *CHSQ* 10 (September 1931): 298–301.

Watt, Jeffrey R. *The Making of Modern Marriage: Matrimonial Control and the Rise of Sentiment in Neuchâtel, 1550–1800.* Ithaca, N.Y.: Cornell University Press, 1992.

Weber, David J. *The Mexican Frontier, 1821–1846: The American Southwest under Mexico.* Albuquerque: University of New Mexico Press, 1982.

——. *Taos Trappers: The Fur Trade in the Far Southwest, 1540–1846.* Norman: University of Oklahoma Press, 1971.

Weslager, C. A. *The Delaware Indians: A History.* New Brunswick, N.J.: Rutgers University Press, 1972.

Wheeler, Mayo Elizabeth. "John A. Sutter, a California Pioneer: An Historical Sketch and Collection of Documents." Master's thesis, University of California, Berkeley, 1925.

White, Richard. *"It's Your Misfortune and None of My Own": A History of the American West.* Norman: University of Oklahoma Press, 1991.

——. "John Sutter and the Natural World." In *John Sutter and a Wider West,* edited by Kenneth N. Owens, 93–110. Lincoln: University of Nebraska Press, 1994.

——. *The Middle Ground: Indians, Empires, and Republics in the Great Lakes Region, 1650–1815.* Cambridge: Cambridge University Press, 1991.

Wilbur, Marguerite Eyer. *John Sutter, Rascal and Adventurer.* New York: Liveright Publishing, 1949.

Willys, Rufus Kaye. "French Imperialists in California." *CHSQ* 8 (June 1929): 116–29.

Wilson, Norman L., and Arlean H. Towne, "Nisenan." In *Handbook of North American Indians,* vol. 8, *California,* edited by Robert F. Heizer, 387–97. Washington, D.C.: Smithsonian Institution, 1978.

Wishart, David J. *The Fur Trade of the American West, 1807–1840: A Geographical Synthesis.* Lincoln: University of Nebraska Press, 1979.

Zollinger, James P. "John Augustus Sutter's European Background." *CHSQ* 35 (March 1935): 28–46.

——. *Sutter: The Man and His Empire.* New York: Oxford University Press, 1939.

Index